Lecture Notes in Computer Science 4081

Commenced Publication in 1973
Founding and Former Series Editors:
Gerhard Goos, Juris Hartmanis, and Jan van Leeuwen

T0180658

A Min Tjoa   Juan Trujillo (Eds.)

Data Warehousing and Knowledge Discovery

8th International Conference, DaWaK 2006
Krakow, Poland, September 4-8, 2006
Proceedings

 Springer

Volume Editors

A Min Tjoa
Vienna University of Technology
Institute for Software Technology and Interactive Systems
Favoritenstrasse 9-11/188, 1040 Vienna, Austria
E-mail: amin@ifs.tuwien.ac.at

Juan Trujillo
University of Alicante, Department of Language and Information Systems
Apto. correos 99, 03690 Alicante, Spain
E-mail: jtrujillo@dlsi.ua.es

Library of Congress Control Number: 2006931061

CR Subject Classification (1998): H.2, H.3, H.4, C.2, H.5, I.2, J.1

LNCS Sublibrary: SL 3 – Information Systems and Application, incl. Internet/Web and HCI

ISSN   0302-9743
ISBN-10   3-540-37736-0 Springer Berlin Heidelberg New York
ISBN-13   978-3-540-37736-8 Springer Berlin Heidelberg New York

Springer is a part of Springer Science+Business Media

springer.com

© Springer-Verlag Berlin Heidelberg 2006
Printed in Germany

Typesetting: Camera-ready by author, data conversion by Scientific Publishing Services, Chennai, India
Printed on acid-free paper   SPIN: 11823728   06/3142   5 4 3 2 1 0

Preface

For more than a decade, data warehousing together with knowledge discovery technology have made up the key technology for the decision-making process in companies. Since 1999, due to the relevant role of these technologies in academia and industry, the Data Warehousing and Knowledge Discovery (DaWaK) conference series has become an international forum for both practitioners and researchers to share their findings, publish their relevant results and debate in depth research issues and experiences on data warehousing and knowledge discovery systems and applications.

The 8th International Conference on Data Warehousing and Knowledge Discovery (DaWaK 2006) continued the series of successful conferences dedicated to these topics. In this edition, DaWaK aimed at providing the right and logical balance between data warehousing and knowledge discovery. In data warehousing the papers cover different research problems, such as advanced techniques in OLAP visualization and multidimensional modelling, innovation of ETL processes and integration problems, materialized view optimization, very large data warehouse processing, data warehouses and data mining applications integration, data warehousing for real-life applications, e.g., medical applications and spatial applications. In data mining and knowledge discovery, papers are focused on a variety of topics from data streams analysis and mining, ontology-based mining techniques, mining frequent item sets, clustering, association and classification, patterns and so on. These proceedings contain the technical papers which were selected for presentation at the conference.

We received 198 abstracts, and finally received 146 papers from 36 countries. The Program Committee selected 53 papers, making an acceptance rate of 36.3 % of submitted papers.

We would like to express our gratitude to all Program Committee members and external reviewers who reviewed the papers very profoundly and in a timely manner. Due to the high number of submissions and the high quality of the submitted papers, the reviewing, voting and discussion process was an extraordinary challenging task. Special thanks must be given to Tho Manh Nguyen for all his support in the organization of the PC tasks of DaWaK 2006. We would also like to thank to all the authors who submitted their papers to DaWaK 2006 as their contributions formed the basis of this year's excellent technical program.

Many thank go to Ms. Gabriela Wagner for providing a great deal of assistance for administering the DaWaK management issues as well as to Mr. Raimund Angleitner-Flotzinger for the conference management software.

September 2006   A Min Tjoa

Program Committee

Conference Program Chairpersons

A Min Tjoa, Vienna University of Technology, Austria
Juan C. Trujillo, University of Alicante, Spain

Program Committee Members

Alberto Abello, Universitat Politecnica de Catalunya, Spain
Eugene Agichtein , Microsoft Research , USA
Paulo Azevedo, Universidade do Minho, Portugal
Jose Luis Balcazar, Politechnic University of Catalunya, Spain
Elena Baralis, Politecnico di Torino, Italy
Bettina Berendt, Humboldt University Berlin, Germany
Petr Berka, University of Economics, Prague, Czech Republic
Jorge Bernardino, Polytechnic Institute of Coimbra, Portugal
Elisa Bertino, Purdue University, USA
Sourav S Bhowmick , Nanyang Technological University, Singapore
Francesco Bonchi, ISTI - C.N.R., Italy
Henrik Boström, Stockholm University and Royal Institute of Technology, Sweden
Jean-Francois Boulicaut, INSA Lyon, France
Mokrane Bouzeghoub, University of Versailles, France
Stephane Bressan (SoC), National University of Singapore, Singapore
Peter Brezeny, University of Vienna, Austria
Robert Bruckner, Microsoft, USA
Luca Cabibbo, Università Roma Tre, Italy
Tru Hoang Cao, Ho Chi Minh City University of Technology, Vietnam
F. Amilcar Cardoso, Universidade de Coimbra, Portugal
Barbara Catania, DISI - University of Genoa, Italy
Jesús Cerquides, University of Barcelona, Spain
Chan Chee-Yong, National University of Singapore, Singapore
Arbee L.P. Chen, National Chengchi University, Taiwan, R.O.C.
Rada Chirkova, NC State University, USA
Sunil Choenni, University of Twente and Dutch Ministry of Justice, The Netherlands
Ezeife Christie, University of Windsor, Canada
Frans Coenen, The University of Liverpool, UK
Graham Cormode, Bell Labs, USA
Bruno Crémilleux, Université de Caen, France
Honghua Dai, Deakin University, Australia
Agnieszka Dardzinska, Bialystok Technical University, Poland

Jörg Kindermann, Fraunhofer Institute for Autonomous Intelligent Systems AIS, Germany
Arno Knobbe, Universiteit Utrecht, The Netherlands
Igor Kononenko, University of Ljubljana, Slovenia
Stefan Kramer , Technische Universität München, Germany
Michihiro Kuramochi, Google Inc., USA
Christine Largeron, EURISE Université Jean Monnet Saint-Etienne, France
Pedro Larrañaga, University of the Basque Country, Spain
Jens Lechtenbörger, University of Münster, Germany
Yue-Shi Lee, Ming Chuan University, Taiwan, R.O.C
Guanling Lee, National Dong Hwa University, Taiwan, R.O.C
Jinyan Li, Institute for Infocomm Research, Singapore
Xuemin Lin, UNSW, Australia
Beate List, Vienna University of Technology, Austria
Xiaohui Liu, Brunel University, UK
Donato Malerba, Università degli Studi di Bari, Italy
Nikos Mamoulis, University of Hong Kong, Hong Kong
Giuseppe Manco, ICAR-CNR, National Research Council, Italy
Sebban Marc, EURISE, University of Saint-Etienne, France
Michael May, Fraunhofer Institut für Autonome Intelligente Systeme, Germany
Rosa Meo, University of Torino, Italy
Mukesh Mohania, I.B.M. India Research Lab, India
Eduardo F. Morales, ITESM - Campus Cuernavaca, Mexico
Shinichi Morishita, University of Tokyo, Japan
Tadeusz Morzy, Poznan University of Technology, Poland
Alexandros Nanopoulos, Aristotle University of Thessaloniki, Greece
Wee Keong Ng , Nanyang Technological University, Singapore
Tho Manh Nguyen, Vienna University of Technology, Austria
Richard Nock, Université Antilles-Guyane, France
Andreas Nürnberger, University of Magdeburg, Germany
Arlindo L. Oliveira, IST/INESC-ID, Portugal
Georgios Paliouras, NCSR "Demokritos", Greece
Themis Palpanas, IBM T.J. Watson Research Center, USA
Torben Bach Pedersen, Aalborg University, Denmark
Dino Pedreschi, University of Pisa, Italy
Jian Pei, Simon Fraser University, Canada
Jaakko Tapani Peltonen, Helsinki University of Technology, Finland
Clara Pizzuti, ICAR-CNR , Italy
Lubomir Popelinsky, Masaryk University in Brno, Czech Republic
David Powers, The Flinders University of South Australia, Australia
Jan Ramon, Katholieke Universiteit Leuven, Belgium
Zbigniew Ras, University of North Carolina,USA
Mirek Riedewald, Cornell University, USA
Christophe Rigotti, LIRIS Lyon France and ISTI Pisa, Italy
Gilbert Ritschard , University of Geneva, Switzerland

Stefano Rizzi, University of Bologna, Italy
John Roddick, Flinders University, Australia
Henryk Rybinski, Warsaw University of Technology, Poland
Domenico Sacc à, Universita Della Calabria, Italy
Yucel Saygin, Sabanci University, Turkey
Monica Scannapieco, University of Rome, Italy
Josef Schiefer, Vienna University of Technology, Austria
Markus Schneider, University of Florida, USA
Michael Schrefl, University Linz, Austria
Timos Sellis, National Technical University of Athens, Greece
Giovanni Semeraro, University of Bari, Italy
Manuel Serrano, University of Castilla - La Mancha, Spain
Alkis Simitsis, National Technical University of Athens, Greece
Dan Simovici, University of Massachusetts at Boston, USA
Andrzej Skowron, Warsaw University Banacha 2, Poland
Carlos Soares, University of Porto, Portugal
Il-Yeol Song, Drexel University, Philadelphia, USA
Nicolas Spyratos, Universite Paris Sud, France
Jerzy Stefanowski, Poznan University of Technology, Poland
Olga Stepankova, Czech Technical University, Czech Republic
Reinhard Stolle, BMW Car IT, Germany
Jan Struyf, Katholieke Universiteit Leuven, Belgium
Gerd Stumme, University of Kassel, Germany
Domenico Talia, University of Calabria, Italy
Ah-Hwee Tan, Nanyang Technological University, Singapore
David Taniar, Monash University, Australia
Evimaria Terzi, University of Helsinki, Finland
Dimitri Theodoratos, New Jersey's Science & Technology University, USA
Riccardo Torlone, Roma Tre University, Italy
Jaideep Vaidya, Rutgers University, USA
Panos Vassiliadis, University of Ioannina, Greece
Wei Wang, University of North Carolina, USA
Marek Wojciechowski, Poznan University of Technology, Poland
Wolfram Wöß, Johannes Kepler University Linz, Autria
Mohammed J. Zaki, Rensselaer Polytechnic Institute, USA
Carlo Zaniolo, University of California, USA
Shichao Zhang, Sydney University of Technology, Australia
Djamel A. Zighed, University Lumière Lyon 2, France

External Reviewers

Helena Ahonen-Myka   Ayca Azgin Hintoglu
Periklis Andritsos   Yijian Bai
Annalisa Appice   Spiridon Bakiras

S. Berger
Smriti Bhagat
Validmir Braverman
Yi Cai
Huiping Cao
Michelangelo Ceci
Raymond Chi-Wing Wong
Carmela Comito
Alfredo Cuzzocrea
Ibrahim Elsayed
Nuno Escudeiro
Daan Fierens
Gianluigi Folino
Elisa Fromont
Pedro Gabriel Ferreira
Arnaud Giacometti
Paulo Gomes
Andrea Gualtieri
Yanping Guo
Shuguo Han
Xuan Hong Dang
Ming Hua
Po-Wen Huang
Ali Inan
Laura Irina Rusu
Robert Jäschke
Tao Jiang
Xing Jiang
Antonio Jimeno
Hyun Jin Moon
Dimitrios Katsaros
Matjaž Kukar
Anne Laurent
Thorsten Liebig
Yi Luo
Maggie Man Ki Lau
Patrick Marcel
Elio Masciari
Massimiliano Mazzeo
Enza Messina
Pauli Miettinen
Fianny Mingfei Jiang
Pirjo Moen
Ailing Ni

George Papastefanatos
Julien Prados
Wenny Rahayu
R. Rajugan
Bernardete Ribeiro
François Rioult
Marko Robnik Šikonja
Luka Šajn
Jorge Sá-Silva
Christoph Schmitz
Jouni Seppänen
Cristina Sirangelo
Charalambos Spathis
Giandomenico Spezzano
Konrad Stark
Matthias Studer
Andrea Tagarelli
Rafik Taouil
Hetal Thakkar
Quan Thanh Tho
Christian Thomsen
Ivan Titov
Mihalis Tsoukalos
Nguyen Tuan Anh
Antonio Varlaro
Rifeng Wang
Karl Wiggisser
Alexander Woehrer
Adam Woznica
Robert Wrembel
Xiaoying Wu
Wugang Xu
Xuepeng Yin
Jia-Qing Ying
Xiaofang You
Hwanjo Yu
Yidong Yuan
Dingrong Yuan
Xinghuo Zeng
Ying Zhang
Jilian Zhang
Bin Zhou
Xin Zhou
Xiaofeng Zhu

Table of Contents

Cubes Processing

Data Warehouse Applications

Mining Techniques (1)

Mining Techniques (2)

Frequent Itemsets

Mining Data Streams

Ontology-Based Mining

Clustering

Advanced Mining Techniques

Association Rules

Miscellaneous Applications

Classification

ETLDiff: A Semi-automatic Framework for Regression Test of ETL Software

Christian Thomsen and Torben Bach Pedersen

Department of Computer Science, Aalborg University
{chr, tbp}@cs.aau.dk

Abstract. Modern software development methods such as Extreme Programming (XP) favor the use of frequently repeated tests, so-called regression tests, to catch new errors when software is updated or tuned, by checking that the software still produces the right results for a reference input. Regression testing is also very valuable for Extract–Transform–Load (ETL) software, as ETL software tends to be very complex and error-prone. However, regression testing of ETL software is currently cumbersome and requires large manual efforts. In this paper, we describe a novel, easy–to–use, and efficient semi–automatic test framework for regression test of ETL software. By automatically analyzing the schema, the tool detects how tables are related, and uses this knowledge, along with optional user specifications, to determine exactly what data warehouse (DW) data should be identical across test ETL runs, leaving out change-prone values such as surrogate keys. The framework also provides tools for quickly detecting and displaying differences between the current ETL results and the reference results. In summary, manual work for test setup is reduced to a minimum, while still ensuring an efficient testing procedure.

1 Introduction

When software is changed, new errors may easily be introduced. To find introduced errors or new behaviors, modern software development methods like Extreme Programming (XP) [1] favor so-called regression tests which are repeated for every change. After a change in the software, the tests can be used again and the actual results can be compared to the expected results.

A unit-testing tool like JUnit [7] is well-suited to use as a framework for such tests. In JUnit, the programmer can specify assertions that should be true at a specific point. If an assertion does not hold, the programmer will be informed about the failed assertion. In a framework like JUnit it is also very easy to re-run tests and automatically have the actual results compared to the expected results.

As is well-known in the data warehouse (DW) community, Extract–Transform–Load (ETL) software is both complex and error prone. For example, it is estimated that 80% of the development time for a DW project is spent on ETL development [9]. Further, ETL software may often be changed to increase performance, to handle changed or added data sources, and/or to use new software products. For these reasons, regression testing is essential to use. However, to the best of our knowledge, no prior work has dealt with regression testing for ETL software.

A Min Tjoa and J. Trujillo (Eds.): DaWaK 2006, LNCS 4081, pp. 1–12, 2006.

As a use case consider an enterprise with an ETL application that has been used for some time but that does not scale well enough to handle the data anymore. The enterprise's IT department therefore establishes a developer team to tune the ETL. The team tries out many different ideas to select the best options. Thus many different test versions of the ETL application are being produced and tested. For each of these versions, it is of course essential that it produces the same results in the DW as the old solution. To test for this criterion, the team does regression testing such that each new test version is being run and the results of the load are compared to the *reference results* produced by the old ETL application.

A general framework like JUnit is not suited for regression testing of the entire ETL process. Normally, JUnit and similar tools are used for small, well-defined parts or functions in the code. Further, it is more or less explicitly assumed that there is functional behavior, i.e., no side-effects, such that a function returns the same result each time it is given the same arguments. On the contrary, what should be tested for ETL software is the result of the entire ETL run or, in other words, the obtained side effects, not just individual function values. Although it is possible to test for side effects in JUnit, it is very difficult to specify the test cases since the database state, as argued in [2], should be regarded as a part of the input and output space. But even when the data is fixed in the input sources for the ETL, some things may change. For example, the order of fetched data rows may vary in the relational model. Additionally, attributes obtained from *sequences* may have different values in different runs. However, actual values for surrogate keys assigned values from sequences are not interesting, whereas it indeed is interesting how rows are "connected" with respect to primary key/foreign key pairs. More concretely, it is not interesting if an ID attribute A has been assigned the value 1 or the value 25 from a sequence. What is important, is that any other attribute that is supposed to reference A has the correct value. Further, the results to compare from an ETL run have a highly complex structure as data in several tables has to be compared. This makes it very hard to specify the test manually in JUnit.

In this paper, we present *ETLDiff* which is a semi-automatic framework for regression testing ETL software. This framework will, based on information obtained from the schema, suggest what data to compare between ETL runs. Optionally the user may also specify joins, tables, and columns to include/ignore in the comparison. ETLDiff can then generate the so-called *reference results*, an off-line copy of the DW content. Whenever the ETL software has been changed, the reference results can be compared with the current results, called the *test results*, and any differences will be pointed out. In the use case described above, the tuning team can thus use ETLDiff as a labor-saving regression testing tool.

Consider the example in Figure 1 which will be used as a running example in the rest of the paper. The schema is for a DW based on source data taken from TPC-H [15].

Here we have a fact table, *LineItem*, and four dimension tables, *Date*, *Part*, *Supplier*, *Customer*, and an outrigger, *Nation*. The fact table has a degenerate dimension (*OrderKey*) and one measure. ETLDiff can automatically detect the six joins to perform and which columns to disregard in the comparison. ETLDiff will here make a join for each foreign key and then disregard the actual values of the columns involved in the joins.

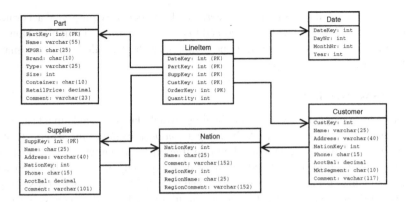

Fig. 1. An example schema

To use the framework the user only has to specify A1) how to start the ETL software and A2) how to connect to the data warehouse, as shown in Figure 2. Apart from this, the framework can do the rest. Thus, the user can start to do regression testing in 5 minutes. Setting this up manually would require much more time. For each schema, the user would have to go through the following tasks: M1) write an SQL expression that joins the relevant tables and selects the columns to compare, M2) verify that the query is correct and includes everything needed in comparisons, M3) execute the query and write the result to a file, M4) write an application that can compare results and point out differences. Further, the user would have to go through the following tasks for each ETL version: M5) Run the new ETL software, M6) run the query from M1 again, M7) start the application from M4 to compare the results from M6 to the file from M3. Even though much of this could be automated, it would take even more work to set this up. Thus, to set up regression testing manually takes days instead of minutes.

```
etlcmd='loaddw -f -x'
dbuser='tiger'
dbdriver='org.postgresql.Driver'
dburl='jdbc:postgresql://localhost/tpch'
```

Fig. 2. Example configuration file for ETLDiff

The rest of this paper is structured as follows. Section 2 describes the design and implementation of the ETLDiff framework. A performance study is presented in Section 3. Section 4 presents related work. Section 5 concludes and points to future work.

2   The Test Framework

In this section we present, how ETLDiff is designed and implemented. There are two basic parts of ETLDiff. A *test designer* and a *test executer*.

A test consists of all rows in the considered tables which are equi-joined accordingly to foreign keys. Thus the fact table is joined to each of the dimension tables. However, only some of the columns are used in the comparison. In the following it is explained how to select the data to compare.

2.1 Process Overview

ETLDiff's test designer makes a proposal about which data to include in a test. It does so by exploring the DW schema and building a *database model* of the schema (task 1). This model is used to build the so-called *join tree* (task 2a) which defines how to join the DW tables used in the test. When this is done, special care has to be taken when handling so-called *bridge tables* (task 2b). Since ETLDiff uses the tool RELAXML [11] to export DW data to offline XML files, certain files that define this process have to be generated as the last part of proposing a test (task 3). When executing a test, ETLDiff exports test results to a file (task 4). This file, with the newest content from the DW, is then compared to a file holding the reference results and differences are pointed out (task 5). In the following subsections, these tasks are explained.

2.2 Task 1: Exploring the DW Schema and Building a Database Model

To find the data to compare, ETLDiff builds a *database model* of the database schema. A database model represents tables and their columns, including foreign key relationships. The model is simply built based on metadata obtained through JDBC. By default, all tables and all their columns are included in the model. However, the user may specify a table name or just a prefix or suffix of names not to include. The user may also specify foreign keys that should be added to the model even though they are not declared in the database schema or may conversely specify specific foreign keys declared in the schema that should not be included in the model. For the DW example from Section 1, the built model would be similar to the schema shown in Figure 1 unless the user specified something else, e.g., to ignore the foreign key between *LineItem* and *Date*.

Next, ETLDiff has to find the columns to compare. In a DW, it is good practice to use surrogate keys not carrying any operational meaning [9,10]. As previously argued, it is not important whether a surrogate key has the value 1 or the value 25 as long as attributes supposed to reference it have the correct value. For that reason, ETLDiff uses a heuristic where all foreign keys and the referenced keys in the model are left out from the data comparison unless the user has specified that they should be included. In the example from Section 1, this would mean that *OrderKey*, *PartKey*, *SuppKey*, *CustKey*, and *NationKey* would not be included in the comparison. The rest of the columns in the example would be used in the comparison. Also columns the user has explicitly chosen not to include will be disregarded. For example, it could be specified that *RegionKey* should not be compared in the running example.

2.3 Task 2a: Building a Join Tree

Consider again the running example. Since both *Supplier* and *Customer* reference the *Nation* outrigger, an instance of *Nation* should be joined to *Customer* and another instance of *Nation* should be joined to *Supplier*.

In more general terms, there must be an equi-join with an instance of a table for each foreign key referencing the table in the database model. This means the database model is converted into a tree, here called a *join tree*. Note that the database model already can be seen as a directed graph where the nodes are the tables and the edges are the foreign keys between tables.

In the join tree, nodes represent table instances and edges represent foreign keys (technically, the edges are marked with the names of the key columns). For a star schema, the root of the tree represents the fact table and the nodes at level 1 represent the dimension tables. Outriggers are represented at level 2 as children of the nodes representing the referencing dimension tables. For a snowflake schema, the join tree will have a level for each level in the dimension hierarchy. The join tree for the running example is shown in Figure 3 (not showing the marks on the edges).

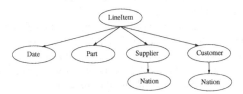

Fig. 3. A join tree for the running example

To convert the database model into a join tree, we use Algorithm 1., BuildJoinTree, which is explained in the following. To avoid infinite recursion when AddTreeNodesDF is called, we require that the database model does not contain any cycles, i.e., we require that the database model when viewed as graph is a directed acyclic graph (DAG). This is checked in l 1–2 of the algorithm. Note that this requirement holds for both star and snow-flake schemas.

In l 3 the array $visited$ is initialized. In l 4, the algorithm tries to guess the fact table unless the user explicitly has specified the fact table. To do this, the algorithm considers nodes in the database model with in-degree 0. Such nodes usually represent fact tables. However, they may also represent the special case of *bridge tables* [9,10] which will be explained later. To find the fact table, the algorithm looks among the found nodes for the node with maximal out-degree. If there are more such nodes, the first of them is chosen, and the user is warned about the ambiguity. Another heuristic would be to consider the number of rows in the represented tables. The one with the largest number of rows is more likely to be the fact table. We let f denote the node in the database model that represents the fact table. In the join tree, the root is representing the fact table (l 5). The recursive algorithm AddTreeNodesDF (not shown) visits nodes in a depth-first order in the database model from the node representing the fact table (l 7–8). When a node representing table t in the database model is visited from node n, a new node representing t is added in the join tree as a child of the latest added node representing n. This will also set $visited[t]$ to true. Note that AddTreeNodesDF *will* visit an adjacent node even though that node has been visited before. This for example happens for *Nation* in the running example.

Algorithm 1. BuildJoinTree

1: **if** database model has cycles **then**
2:      raise an error
3: set $visited[t]$ = false for each node t in the database model
4: $f \leftarrow GuessFactTable()$
5: $root \leftarrow TreeNode(f)$
6: $visited[f] \leftarrow$ true
7: **for** each node t adjacent to f in the database model **do**
8:      $AddTreeNodesDF(root, t)$
9: // Find bridge tables and what is reachable from them
10: **while** changed **do**
11:     $changed \leftarrow$ false
12:     **for** each table node t in the database model where $visited[t]$ = false **do**
13:         $oldVisited \leftarrow visited$
14:         **for** each node s adjacent to t in the database model **do**
15:             **if** $oldVisited[s]$ **then**
16:                 // Before this part, t had not been visited, but s which is referenced
17:                 // by t had, so t should be included as if there were an edge (s, t)
18:                 **for** each join tree node x representing table s **do**
19:                     Remove edge (t, s) from database model // Don't come back to s
20:                     $AddTreeNodesDF(x, t)$ // Modifies $visited$
21:                     Add edge (t, s) to database model again
22:                 $changed \leftarrow$ true

For the running example, the nodes in the database model are visited in the order *LineItem, Date, Part, Supplier, Nation, Customer, Nation*. Only the already explained part of the algorithm is needed for that. For some database models this part is, however, not enough, as explained next.

2.4 Task 2b: Handling Bridge Tables

In the depth-first search only those nodes reachable from f will be found. In fact we are only interested in finding the nodes that are connected to f when we ignore the direction of edges. Other nodes that are unvisited after the algorithm terminates represent tables that hold data that is not related to the data in the fact table. However, nodes may be connected to f when we ignore directions of edges but not when directions are taken into consideration. Imagine that the example DW should be able to represent that a supplier is located in many nations. To do this we would use a bridge table [9,10] as shown in Figure 4. A bridge table and nodes reachable from the bridge table should also be visited when the join tree is being built. Before terminating, the algorithm therefore has to look for unvisited nodes that have an edge to a visited node (l 12 and 14–15). If such an edge is found, it is "turned around" temporarily such that the depth-first visit will go to the unvisited, but connected node. To do this, the edge is removed from the database model (l 19), and a call to AddTreeNodesDF is then made (l 20) as if the edge had the opposite direction. Since the edge is removed from the model, this call will

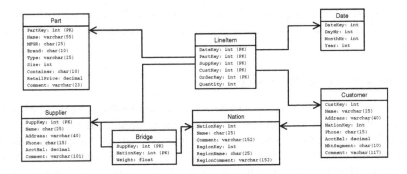

Fig. 4. The example schema extended with a bridge table between Supplier and Nation

not come back to the already visited node. After the call, the edge is recreated (1 21). Before the edge is turned around, it is necessary to make a copy of the *visited* array. The reason is that the algorithm otherwise could risk to find an unvisited node u where the visited node v and the unvisited node w are adjacent to u. The edge (u, v) could then be turned around and the depth-first visit could visit u and w, before (u, v) was recreated. But when w (which is adjacent to u) then was considered, it would be visited and the edge (u, w) would be turned around and too many nodes would be added. This situation does not occur when an unmodified copy (*oldVisited*) of *visited* is used.

2.5 Task 3: Generating Data-Defining Files

ETLDiff uses RELAXML [11] for writing XML files. Proposing a test thus includes generating a so-called *concept* which defines what data RELAXML should export and a so-called *structure definition* which defines the structure of the XML. A concept can inherit from other concepts.

When the join tree has been built, the data-defining concept can be built. In RELA-XML a table can only be used once in a single concept. However, it might be necessary to include data from a table several times as explained above. When this is the case, ETLDiff can exploit RELAXML's concept inheritance. A simple concept is made for each node in the join tree. The concept simply selects all data in the table represented by the node. An enclosing concept that inherits (i.e., "uses the data") from all these simple concepts is then defined. The results of the different concepts are joined as dictated by the join tree. The enclosing concept will also disregard the columns that should not be considered, e.g, dummy keys. In the running example, the final data corresponds to all the columns except those participating in foreign key pairs. The raw data is computed by the DBMS.

After the concepts have been created, a structure definition is created. ETLDiff uses sorting and *grouping* such that similar XML elements are coalesced to make the resulting XML smaller (see [11]). If a supplier for example supplies many parts, it is enough to list the information about supplier once and then below that list the information about the different parts. Without grouping, the information on the supplier would be repeated for each different part it supplies. The use of grouping and sorting means that the order of the XML is known such that it is easy and efficient to compare the two XML documents.

2.6   Task 4: Exporting DW Data to Files

The concepts and the structure definition are then used by RELAXML when it generates the files holding the reference results and the test results. Baed on the concept, RELAXML generates SQL to extract data from the DW and based on the structure definition, this data is written to an XML file. Since the data sets potentially can be very large, it is possible to specify that the output should be compressed using gzip while it is written.

2.7   Task 5: Comparing Data

When comparing data, there should be two data sets to consider. The desired result of an ETL run (the *reference results*) and the current result (the *test results*). ETLDiff thus performs two tasks when running a test: 1) Export data from the DW, and 2) compare the test results to the reference results and point out any differences found. ETLDiff can output information about differences to the console or to tables in a window as shown in Figure 5. The window has two tabs. In the first tab there is a table showing all the rows missing in the test results and in the second tab there is a table showing all the extra rows in the test results.

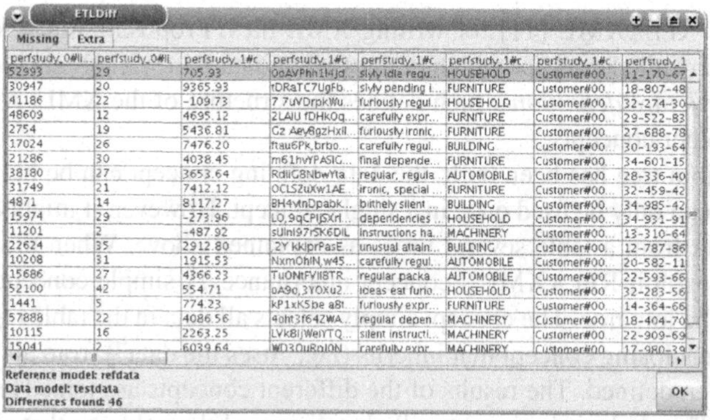

Fig. 5. Window presenting differences between test results and reference results

When comparing test results to reference results, two data sets are read from two XML files. These XML files are read using SAX [14]. Each of the SAX parsers is running as a separate thread. Each thread reads XML and regenerates rows as they were in the join result that was written to XML. In this way it is possible to compare the files part by part with a very small main-memory usage. Only two rows from each of the join results have to be in memory at a given time (each thread may, however, cache a number of rows). So for most use cases, the size of the data in main-memory is measured in kilobytes. Since sorting is used before the XML is written, it is easy to compare data from the XML files row by row.

3 Performance Results

A prototype[1] of ETLDiff has been implemented in Java 5.0. Further, RELAXML has been ported to Java 5.0, given new functionality, and performance-improved in a way that has speeded up the XML writing significantly. In this section, we present a performance study of the implemented prototype. The test machine is a 2.6 GHz Pentium 4 with 1GB RAM running openSuse 10.0, PostgreSQL 8.1, and Java 1.5.0 SE.

In the performance study, the DW from the running example has been used. ETL-Diff has automatically proposed the test (this took 1.5 seconds). The data used originates from TPC-H's dbgen tool. Data sets with different sizes (10MB, 25MB, 50MB, 75MB, 100MB) have been loaded and a data set (which either could be test results or reference results) has been generated by ETLDiff. The resulting running times are plotted in Figure 6(a). The shown numbers indicate the total amount of time spent, including the time used by the DBMS to compute the join result. Notice that the data sets generated by ETLDiff contain redundancy and thus are much bigger than the raw data (10MB in the DW results in 129MB XML before compression and 10MB after compression).

Further, the created test results have been compared to identical reference results. This is the worst case for equally sized data sets since it requires all data to be compared. The running times for the comparisons are plotted in Figure 6(b).

As is seen from the graphs, ETLDiff scales linearly in the size of the data, both when generating and comparing results. When generating, 19.7 seconds are used for each MB of base data and when comparing 9.5 seconds are used. This is efficient enough to be used for regression tests. In typical uses, one would have a data set for testing that is relatively small (i.e., often less than 100MB). The purpose of ETLDiff is to do regression testing to find newly introduced errors, not to do performance testing where

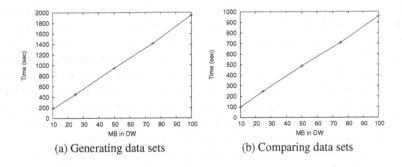

(a) Generating data sets   (b) Comparing data sets

Fig. 6. Running times

---
[1] The source is publicly available from `relaxml.com/etldiff/`.

much larger data sets are used. When regression testing, it is typically the case, that a single test case should be relatively fast to execute or that many test cases can be executed during a night. Thus, a test case should be small enough to be easy to work with but represent all special and normal cases that the ETL software should be able to handle.

4   Related Work

As previously mentioned, we believe that this work is the first framework for regression testing ETL tools. Daou et al. [4] describe regression testing of Oracle applications written in PL/SQL. The test cases to re-run are supposed to be automatically found by the described solution. The method used may, however, omit test cases that could reveal bugs [16]. In a recent paper [16], Willmor and Embury propose two new methods for regression test selection. The regression test selection solutions [4,16] are closer to traditional combined unit and regression testing where there exist many manually specified tests that cover different parts of the code. In the present paper, the result of the entire ETL run is being tested, but in a way that ignores values in surrogate keys that can change between different runs without this indicates an error. Further, the test is designed automatically.

JUnit [7] is the de-facto standard for unit testing and has inspired many other unit-testing tools. In JUnit, it is assumed that the individual test cases are independent. Christensen et al. [3] argue why this should not hold for software that stores data in a database. They also propose a unit-test framework that allows and exploits structural dependencies to reduce coding efforts and execution times. The work is taking side-effects into consideration (such that a test can depend on the side-effect of another) but is still considering the individual functions of the tested program, not the entire result as the present paper does. The main difference is that the solution in the present paper automatically designs the test and is specialized for DWs.

DbUnit [6] is an interesting test framework extending JUnit for database applications. DbUnit can put the database in a known start state before any test run. Further, DbUnit can export database data to XML and import data from XML into the database. With respect to that, DbUnit has some similarities with RELAXML [11] used to write ETLDiff's XML. DbUnit can also compare if two tables or XML data sets are identical, also if specific columns are ignored. In that, it is related to the core functionality of ETLDiff. However, ETLDiff is automatic whereas DbUnit due to its unit test purposes requires some programming. Like in JUnit, the programmer has to program the test case and define the pass criterion for the test. This involves inheriting from a predefined class and defining the test methods. When using ETLDiff, the test case is automatically inferred. Another difference is that ETLDiff automatically will perform correct joins – also when disregarding the join columns in the value comparisons. Columns to ignore must be specified in DbUnit whereas in ETLDiff they are found automatically. A key feature of ETLDiff is that it uses the DW semantic to automate the tests.

One paper [8] considers the problem of discovering dimensional DW schemas (fact tables, measures, dimensions with hierarchies) in non-DW schemas. This is somewhat related to our problem of building a join tree, but as we can assume a DW schema and do not want to find hierarchies or measures, but only join connections, the algorithm in the present paper is much more efficient. Addtionally, the solution in [8] does not handle bridge tables.

Industrial ETL tools like Informatica Powercenter, IBM Datastage, and Microsoft SQL Server Integration Services (SSIS), SSIS offer nice facilities for debugging ETL flows and allow ETL developers to use the testing facilities in Visual Studio, but have no specific support for ETL regression testing, and do not generate the test automatically, as we do.

In the implementation of ETLDiff, the data to compare is written to XML files in a way that allows for memory-efficient and fast processing. This means that when ETL-Diff is comparing data sets, it actually compares data read from XML documents. Much work has been done in this area, see [5,13] for surveys. Since the XML structure allows for a fast and memory-efficient comparison, ETLDiff uses its own comparison algorithm to be more efficient than general purpose tools.

5   Conclusion

Motivated by the complexity of ETL software, this paper considered how to do regression testing of ETL software. It was proposed to consider the result of the entire ETL run and not just the different functions of the ETL software. The semi-automatic framework ETLDiff proposed in the paper can explore a data warehouse schema and detect how tables are connected. Based on this, it proposes how to join tables and what data to consider when comparing *test results* from a new ETL run to the *reference results*. It only takes 5 minutes to start using ETLDiff. The user only has to specify how to start the ETL and how to connect to the DW before he can start using ETLDiff. To setup such regression testing manually is a cumbersome task to code and requires a lot of time.

Performance studies of ETLDiff showed a good performance, both when extracting data to compare from the DW and when performing the actual comparison between the data in the DW and the so-called reference results. In typical uses, less than 100MB data will be used for testing purposes, and this can be handled in less than an hour on a typical desktop PC.

There are many interesting directions for future work. The structure definitions could be optimized with respect to group by such that the resulting XML gets as small as possible. The framework could also be extended to cover other test types, for example audit tests where the source data sets and the loaded DW data set are compared.

Acknowledgements

This work was supported by the European Internet Accessibility Observatory (EIAO) project, funded by the European Commission under Contract no. 004526.

References

1. K. Beck. *"Extreme Programming Explained: Embrace Change"*, Addison-Wesley Professional, 1999
2. D. Chays, S. Dan, P. Frankl, F.I. Vokolos, and E.J. Weyuker: "A Framework for Testing Database Applications". In *Proceedings of ISSTA'00*, pp. 147–157
3. C.A. Christensen, S. Gundersborg, K. de Linde, and K. Torp: "A Unit-Test Framework for Database Applications", TR-15, www.cs.aau.dk/DBTR
4. B. Daou, R.A. Haraty, and N. Mansour, "Regression Testing of Database Applications". In *Proceedings of SAC 2001*, pp. 285–290
5. G. Cobéna, T. Abdessalem, and Y. Hinnach: "A comparative study for XML change detection", TR, April, 2002, ftp://ftp.inria.fr/INRIA/Projects/verso/VersoReport-221.pdf last accessed Jun. 9, 2006
6. dbunit.sourceforge.net, last accessed Jun. 9, 2006
7. junit.org, last accessed Jun. 9, 2006
8. M. R. Jensen, T. Holmgren, and T. B. Pedersen, "Discovering Multidimensional Structure in Relational Data". In *Proceedings of DaWaK'04*, pp. 138–148, 2004.
9. R. Kimball, L. Reeves, M. Ross, and W. Thornthwaite: *"The Data Warehouse Lifecycle Toolkit"*, Wiley, 1998
10. R. Kimball and M. Ross: *"The Data Warehouse Toolkit"*, 2nd Edition, Wiley, 2002
11. S.U. Knudsen, T.B. Pedersen, C. Thomsen, and K. Torp: "RELAXML: Bidirectional Transfer between Relational and XML Data". In *Proceedings of IDEAS'05*, pp. 151–162
12. Microsoft Corporation. SQL Server Integration Services. www.microsoft.com/sql/technologies/integration/default.mspx, last accessed June 9, 2006.
13. L. Peters: "Change Detection in XML Trees: a Survey", 3rd Twente Student Conference on IT, 2005, referaat.ewi.utwente.nl/documents/2005_03_B-DATA_AND_APPLICATION_INTEGRATION/
14. www.saxproject.org, last accessed Jun. 9, 2006
15. tpc.org/tpch/, last accessed Jun. 9, 2006
16. D. Willmor and S. Embury: "A safe regression test selection technique for database-driven applications". In *Proceedings of ICSM'05*, pp. 421–430

Applying Transformations to Model Driven Data Warehouses

Jose-Norberto Mazón, Jesús Pardillo, and Juan Trujillo

Dept. of Software and Computing Systems
University of Alicante, Spain
{jnmazon, jesuspv, jtrujillo}@dlsi.ua.es

Abstract. In the past few years, several conceptual approaches have been proposed for the specification of the main multidimensional (MD) properties of the data warehouse (DW) repository. However, these approaches often fail in providing mechanisms to univocally and automatically derive a logical representation of the MD conceptual model. To overcome this limitation, we present an approach to align the MD modeling of the DW repository with the Model Driven Architecture (MDA) by formally defining a set of Query/View/Transformation (QVT) transformation rules which allow us to obtain a logical representation of the MD conceptual model in an automatic way. Finally, we show how to implement our approach in an MDA-compliant commercial tool.

1   Introduction

Data warehouse (DW) systems provide companies with many years of historical information for the success of the decision-making process. Nowadays, it is widely accepted that the basis for designing the DW repository is the multidimensional (MD) modeling [1,2]. Various approaches for the conceptual design of the DW repository have been proposed in the last few years [3,4,5,6]. These proposals are twofold, on the one hand they try to represent the main MD properties at the conceptual level by abstracting away details of the target database platform where the DW will be implemented. On the other hand, they also define how to derive a logical representation tailored to a specific database technology (relational or multidimensional). However, these approaches are lacking in formal mechanisms to univocally and automatically obtain the logical representation of the conceptual model, and they only provide some informal guidelines to manually undertake this task, thus increasing the development time and cost to obtain the final implementation of the DW repository.

In order to overcome this limitation, in a previous work [7], we have described a model driven framework for the development of DWs, based on the Model Driven Architecure (MDA) standard [8]. In this paper, we present how to apply the Query/View/Transformation (QVT) language [9] to the MD modeling of the DW repository within our MDA framework. Therefore, we focus on (i) defining the main MDA artifacts for the MD modeling of the DW repository, (ii) formally establishing a set of QVT transformation rules to automatically obtain

A Min Tjoa and J. Trujillo (Eds.): DaWaK 2006, LNCS 4081, pp. 13–22, 2006.

a logical representation tailored to a multidimensional database technology, and (iii) applying the defined QVT transformation rules by using an MDA-compliant tool (Borland Together Architect [10]), thus obtaining the final implementation of the DW repository for a specific multidimensional tool (Oracle Express [11]).

The remainder of this paper is structured as follows. A brief overview of MDA and QVT is given in section 2. Section 3 presents the related work. Section 4 describes our MDA approach for MD modeling of DWs. An example is provided in section 5 to show how to apply MDA and QVT transformation rules by using a commercial tool. Finally, section 6 points out our conclusions and future works.

2   Overview of MDA and QVT

Model Driven Architecture (MDA) is an Object Management Group (OMG) standard [8] that addresses the complete life cycle of designing, deploying, integrating, and managing applications by using models in software development. MDA separates the specification of system functionality from the specification of the implementation of that functionality on a specific technology platform. Thus, MDA encourages specifying a Platform Independent Model (PIM) which contains no specific information of the platform or the technology that is used to realize it. Then, this PIM can be transformed into a Platform Specific Model (PSM) in order to include information about the specific technology that is used in the realization of it on a specific platform. In fact, several PSMs can be derived from one PIM according to different platforms. Later, each PSM is transformed into code to be executed on each platform.

PIMs and PSMs can be specified by using any modeling language, but typically MOF-compliant languages, as the Unified Modeling Language (UML) [12], are used since they are standard modeling languages for general purpose and, at the same time, they can be extended to define specialized languages for certain domains (i.e. metamodel extensibility or profiles).

Nowadays, the most crucial issue in MDA is the transformation between a PIM and a PSM [8]. Thus, OMG defines QVT [9], an approach for expressing these MDA transformations. This is a standard for defining transformation rules between MOF-compliant models. This standard defines a hybrid specification for transformations. On the one hand, there is a declarative part, which provides mechanisms to define transformations as a set of relations (or transformation rules) that must hold between the model elements of a set of candidate models (i.e. source and target models). On the other hand, QVT also defines an imperative part which provides operational mappings between models. Within the declarative part, there is a relations language which supports the specification of relationships that must hold between MOF models. A set of these relations defines a transformation between models. A relation contains:

- **Two or more domains:** each domain is a set of elements of a source or a target model. The kind of relation between domains must be specified: checkonly (C), i.e. it is only checked if the relation holds or not; and enforced (E), i.e. the target model can be modified to satisfy the relation.

- **When clause:** it specifies the conditions that must be satisfied to carry out the relation (i.e. precondition).
- **Where clause:** it specifies the conditions that must be satisfied by all model elements participating in the relation (i.e. postcondition).

Using QVT has several advantages: (i) it is a standard language, (ii) transformations are formally established and automatically performed, and (iii) transformations can be easily integrated in an MDA approach.

3   Related Work

MDA has been successfully applied to several application domains, such as web services [13] and applications [14], development of user interfaces [15], multi-agent systems [16], and so on. However, to the best of our knowledge, there is only one proposal that uses MDA for DW development, the Model Driven Data Warehousing (MDDW) [17]. This approach is based on the Common Warehouse Metamodel (CWM) [18], which is a metamodel definition for interchanging DW specifications between different platforms and tools. Basically, CWM provides a set of metamodels that are comprehensive enough to model an entire DW including data sources, ETL processes, DW repository, and so on. These metamodels are intended to be generic, external representations of shared metadata. The proposed MDDW is based on modeling a complete DW by using elements from various CWM packages. However according to [19], CWM metamodels are (i) too generic to represent all peculiarities of MD modeling in a conceptual model (i.e. PIM), and (ii) too complex to be handled by both final users and designers. Therefore, we deeply believe that it is more reliable to design a PIM by using an enriched conceptual modeling approach easy to be handled (e.g. [6]), and then transform this PIM into a CWM-compliant PSM in order to assure the interchange of DW metadata between different platforms and tools.

4   MDA for Multidimensional Modeling

In this section, the MD modeling of the DW repository is aligned with MDA. We show how to define (i) the main MDA artifacts (i.e. models) for MD modeling, and (ii) a set of QVT transformation rules between these models. In Fig. 1, we show a symbolic diagram of our approach: from the PIM (MD conceptual model), several PSMs (logical representations) can be obtained by applying several QVT transformations. Fig. 1 also represents that each PSM is related to one specific technology: relational or multidimensional. While every relational tool supports all relational elements (as tables, primary keys, and so on), there is no standard to represent elements in multidimensional databases and proprietary data structures are normally used in each tool. Thereby, different transformations must be defined in order to obtain the required PSM according to a specific tool (e.g. Oracle Express, Hyperion Essbase, and so on).

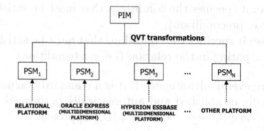

Fig. 1. Overview of our MDA approach for MD modeling of DW repository

The main advantage of our approach is that every PSM (logical representation) of the DW is automatically generated (by applying the corresponding QVT transformations) once the PIM (conceptual model) is designed[1]. Therefore the productivity is improved and development time and cost decrease. Furthermore, since transformations represent repeatable design decisions, once a transformation is developed, we can use it in every PIM to generate different PSMs for several projects. Therefore, we can include MD modeling best practices in MDA transformations and reuse them in every project to assure high quality DWs. Finally, if a new database technology or tool arises, we do not have to change the PIM. Since it is platform-independent, it is still valid, and only the transformations have to be updated in order to obtain the right PSM.

4.1 PIM for Multidimensional Modeling

A PIM describes the system hiding the necessary details related to a particular platform. This point of view corresponds with a conceptual level. The major aim at this level is to represent the main MD properties without taking into account any specific technology detail, so the specification of the DW repository is independent from the platform in which it will be implemented. This PIM for the MD modeling of the DW repository is developed following our UML profile presented in [6]. This profile contains the necessary stereotypes in order to carry out the conceptual MD modeling successfully (see Fig. 2).

Our profile is formally defined and uses the Object Constraint Language (OCL) [21] for expressing well-formed rules of the new defined elements, thereby avoiding an arbitrary use of the profile. We refer reader to [6] for a further explanation of this profile and its corresponding OCL constraints.

4.2 PSM for Multidimensional Modeling

A PSM represents the model of the same system specified by the PIM but it also specifies how that system makes use of the chosen platform or technology.

---

[1] How the PIM is constructed is out of the scope of this paper, but we refer reader to [20] for a detailed explanation.

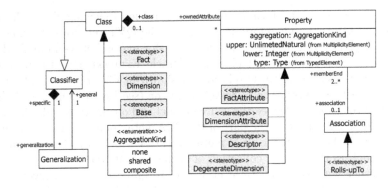

Fig. 2. UML profile for MD modeling

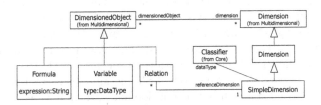

Fig. 3. Metamodel for Oracle Express

In MD modeling, platform specific means that the PSM is specially designed for a kind of a specific database technology, namely relational technology (relational database to store MD data) or multidimensional technology (structures the data directly in MD structures). Since, in a previous work, we have focused on a relational database technology [7], in this paper we focus on a multidimensional technology, in particular, Oracle Express [11].

In our approach, each PSM is modeled by using the *Resource layer* from CWM [18], since it is a standard to represent the structure of data. CWM metamodels can all be used as source or target for MDA transformations, since they are MOF-compliant [18]. Specifically, in this paper we use the *Multidimensional metamodel*, since it contains common data structures that represent every MD property. However, multidimensional databases are not as standardized as relational ones, since the former generally defines proprietary data structures. Therefore, this *Multidimensional metamodel* only defines commonly used data structures in order to be enough generic to support a vendor specific extension. In this paper, we use the part of the *Multidimensional metamodel* shown in Fig. 3 that corresponds to an Oracle Express extension defined in Volume 2, Extensions, of the CWM Specification [22].

4.3 QVT Transformations for MD Modeling

Developing formal transformations, which can be automatically performed, between models (e.g. between PIM and PSM) is one of the strong points of MDA

[23]. In this section, transformation rules are defined following the declarative approach of QVT [9]. Therefore, according to the QVT relations language, we have developed every relation to obtain a transformation between our PIM and a PSM for a multidimensional platform (Oracle Express). Due to space constraints, only a subset of these relations is shown in Fig. 4-5, and only one of them is described: `Dimension2SimpleDimension` (see Fig. 4). On the left hand side of this relation we can see the source model and on the right side the target model. The source model is the part of the PIM metamodel (see Fig. 2) that has to match with the part of the PSM metamodel (see Fig. 3) which represents the target model. In this case, a collection of elements that represents a *Dimension* class together with the root *Base* class (i.e. terminal dimension level) of our UML profile for MD modeling, matches with a *SimpleDimension* class from the CWM multidimensional package. This element must have the same name that the *Dimension* class of the source model and its type is obtained from a simple function that turns a UML data type into an Oracle Express type (`UML2OEType`).

`Dimension2SimpleDimension` relation determines the transformation in the following way: it is checked (C arrow) that the pattern on the left side (source model) exists in the PIM, then the transformation enforces (E arrow) that a new *SimpleDimension* class, according to the PSM metamodel, is created with its corresponding name and type. Once this relation holds, the following relations must be carried out (according to the *where* clause): `DimensionAttribute2Variable`, `Base2SimpleDimension`, and `Fact2SimpleDimension`.

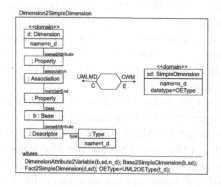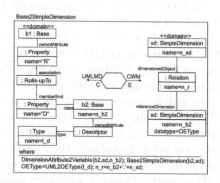

Fig. 4. QVT relations for *Dimension* and *Base* classes

5   Case Study

In this section, we provide an example to describe how to apply the defined QVT transformations by using an MDA-compliant tool (Borland Together Architect [10]), thus obtaining the final implementation of the DW repository for a specific multidimensional tool (Oracle Express [11]).

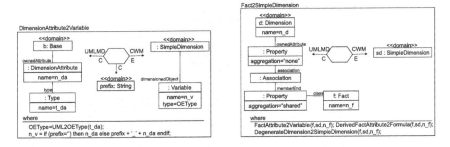

Fig. 5. QVT relations for *DimensionAttribute* and *Fact* classes

Together Architect [10] is a tool designed by Borland to support developers in the design of software applications by using several MDA features. One of the most valuable features of Borland Together Architect is the QVT language in order to implement transformations between models. In fact, this tool only implements the imperative part of the latest QVT specification [9]. Therefore, we have developed the corresponding imperative transformation rules of the declarative ones described in section 4.3, since it is easier to define declarative transformations first (they are clearer and more understandable) instead of developing imperative transformations from scratch.

We have implemented a case study about a hotel. We focus on the *Booking* fact (customers that book a room). This fact (represented as ▦) contains several measures (fact attributes stereotyped with **FA**) to be analyzed (*Price*, *Quantity*, *Discount*, and *Total*). Furthermore, we specify a number of invoice (*invoiceN*) as a degenerate dimension (**DD**). On the other hand, we also consider the following dimensions ( ) as contexts to analyze measures: *Customer*, *Check_in_date* (i.e. the date when the customer checks in), *Check_out_date* (i.e. the date when the customer checks out), and *Room*. We focus on the *Customer* dimension, with the following bases (**B**) or hierarchy levels: *Customer_data*, *City*, and *Country*. Each of these levels can have a descriptor (**D**) or dimension attributes (**DA**).

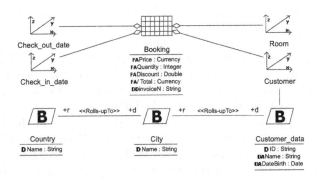

Fig. 6. PIM for hotel case study

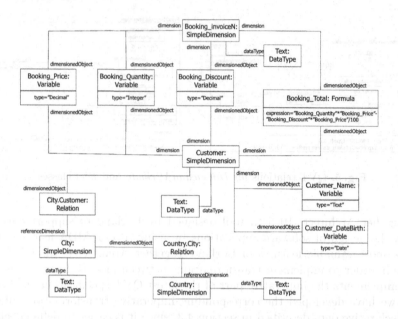

Fig. 7. PSM for hotel case study

From the defined PIM (see Fig. 6), we can use Borland Together Architect to apply the developed transformation rules in order to obtain the corresponding PSM for Oracle Express. In Fig. 8 we show an implementation of the `Dimension2SimpleDimension` transformation rule in Borland Together Architect. After applying every QVT transformation rule to the defined PIM (see Fig. 6), the resulting PSM is shown in Fig. 7, and the final implementation in Oracle Express is shown in Fig. 9.

6   Conclusion and Future Work

In this paper, we have presented an MDA approach for the MD modeling of DWs. We have focused on defining a PIM for MD modeling, a PSM according to a multidimensional database technology by using CWM, and a set of QVT transformation rules in order to derive the PSM from the PIM. An example of applying our approach has been given in order to show every of the developed QVT transformation rules. This example has been developed in an MDA-compliant tool: Borland Together Architect.

According to our MDA framework for the development of the DW [7], we plan to develop transformations for each part of a DW system (ETL processes, data mining, and so on) by using other CWM metamodels. Moreover, we plan to enrich the presented transformations by adding metrics in order to be able to obtain the highest quality PSM.

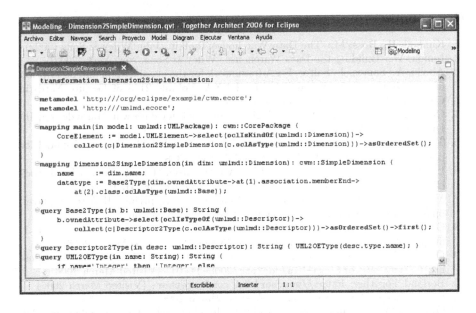

Fig. 8. `Dimension2SimpleDimension` implemented in Borland Together Architect

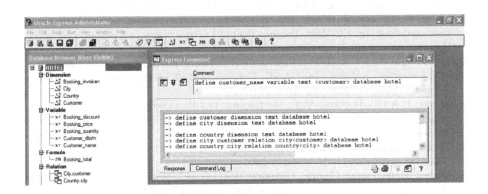

Fig. 9. Oracle Express implementation for our case study

Acknowledgements

This work has been partially supported by the METASIGN (TIN2004-00779) and the DSDM (TIN2005-25866-E) projects from the Spanish Ministry of Education and Science, by the DADASMECA project (GV05/220) from the Valencia Ministry of Enterprise, University and Science (Spain), and by the DADS (PBC-05-012-2) project from the Castilla-La Mancha Ministry of Education and Science (Spain). Jose-Norberto Mazón is funded by the Spanish Ministry of Education and Science under a FPU grant (AP2005-1360).

References

1. Kimball, R., Ross, M.: The Data Warehouse Toolkit. John Wiley & Sons (2002)
2. Inmon, W.: Building the Data Warehouse. Wiley & Sons, New York (2002)
3. Abelló, A., Samos, J., Saltor, F.: A framework for the classification and description of multidimensional data models. In: DEXA. Volume 2113 of Lecture Notes in Computer Science., Springer (2001) 668–677
4. Golfarelli, M., Rizzi, S.: Methodological framework for data warehouse design. In: DOLAP, ACM (1998) 3–9
5. Tryfona, N., Busborg, F., Christiansen, J.G.B.: starER: A conceptual model for data warehouse design. In: DOLAP, ACM (1999) 3–8
6. Luján-Mora, S., Trujillo, J., Song, I.Y.: A UML profile for multidimensional modeling in data warehouses. Data & Knowledge Engineering (**In Press**)
7. Mazón, J.N., Trujillo, J., Serrano, M., Piattini, M.: Applying MDA to the development of data warehouses. In: DOLAP, ACM (2005) 57–66
8. Object Management Group: MDA Guide 1.0.1. http://www.omg.org/cgi-bin/doc?omg/03-06-01. (Visited March 2006)
9. Object Management Group: MOF 2.0 Query/Views/Transformations. http://www.omg.org/cgi-bin/doc?ptc/2005-11-01. (Visited March 2006)
10. Borland Together: http://www.borland.com/together. (Visited March 2006)
11. Oracle: http://www.oracle.com. (Visited March 2006)
12. Object Management Group: Unified Modeling Language Specification 2.0. http://www.omg.org/cgi-bin/doc?formal/05-07-04. (Visited March 2006)
13. Bézivin, J., Hammoudi, S., Lopes, D., Jouault, F.: Applying MDA approach for web service platform. In: EDOC, IEEE Computer Society (2004) 58–70
14. Meliá, S., Gómez, J., Koch, N.: Improving web design methods with architecture modeling. In: EC-Web. Volume 3590 of Lecture Notes in Computer Science., Springer (2005) 53–64
15. Vanderdonckt, J.: A MDA-compliant environment for developing user interfaces of information systems. In: CAiSE. Volume 3520 of Lecture Notes in Computer Science., Springer (2005) 16–31
16. Maria, B.A.D., da Silva, V.T., de Lucena, C.J.P.: Developing multi-agent systems based on MDA. In: CAiSE Short Paper Proceedings. Volume 161 of CEUR Workshop Proceedings., CEUR-WS.org (2005)
17. Poole, J.: Model Driven Data Warehousing (MDDW). http://www.cwmforum.org/POOLEIntegrate2003.pdf. (March 2006)
18. Object Management Group: Common Warehouse Metamodel (CWM) Specification 1.1. http://www.omg.org/cgi-bin/doc?formal/03-03-02. (March 2006)
19. Medina, E., Trujillo, J.: A standard for representing multidimensional properties: The Common Warehouse Metamodel (CWM). In: ADBIS. Volume 2435 of Lecture Notes in Computer Science., Springer (2002) 232–247
20. Mazón, J.N., Trujillo, J., Serrano, M., Piattini, M.: Designing data warehouses: from business requirement analysis to multidimensional modeling. In: REBNITA, University of New South Wales Press (2005) 44–53
21. Object Management Group: Object Constraint Language (OCL) Specification 2.0. http://www.omg.org/cgi-bin/doc?ptc/03-10-14. (Visited March 2006)
22. Object Management Group: Common Warehouse Metamodel (CWM) Specification 1.1. Volume 2. Extensions. http://www.omg.org/cgi-bin/doc?ad/2001-02-02. (Visited March 2006)
23. Kleppe, A., Warmer, J., Bast, W.: MDA Explained. The Practice and Promise of The Model Driven Architecture. Addison Wesley (2003)

Bulk Loading a Linear Hash File

Davood Rafiei and Cheng Hu

University of Alberta
{drafiei, chenghu}@cs.ualberta.ca

Abstract. We study the problem of bulk loading a linear hash file; the problem is that a *good* hash function is able to distribute records into random locations in the file; however, performing a random disk access for each record can be costly and this cost increases with the size of the file. We propose a bulk loading algorithm that can avoid random disk accesses by reducing multiple accesses to the same location into a single access and reordering the accesses such that the pages are accessed sequentially. Our analysis shows that our algorithm is near-optimal with a cost roughly equal to the cost of sorting the dataset, thus the algorithm can scale up to very large datasets. Our experiments show that our method can improve upon the Berkeley DB load utility, in terms of running time, by two orders of magnitude and the improvements scale up well with the size of the dataset.

1 Introduction

There are many scenarios in which data must be loaded into a database in large volumes at once. This is the case, for instance, when building and maintaining a data warehouse, replicating an existing data, building a mirror Internet site or importing data to a new DBMS. There has been work on bulk loading tree-based indexes (e.g. quadtree [6], R-tree [3] and UB-Tree [4]), loading into an object-oriented database (e.g. [15,2]) and resuming a long-duration load [10]. However, we are not aware of a bulk loading algorithm for a linear hash file. This may seem unnecessary, in particular, if both sequential and random disk accesses are charged a constant time; but given that a random access costs a seek time and half of a rotational delay more, a general rule of thumb is that one can get 500 times more bandwidth by going to a sequential access [5]. This seems to be consistent with our experimental findings.

There are a few complications with loading a linear hash file which need to be resolved. First, the file is dynamic and both the hash functions and the record locations change as more data is loaded. Second, the final structure of a hash file depends on factors such as data distribution, the split policy and the arrival order of the records. Third, without estimating a target hash layout, it is difficult to order the input based on the ordering of the buckets in the hash file.

Overview of Linear Hashing: Linear hashing is a dynamic hashing scheme that gracefully accommodates insertions and deletions by allowing the size of

A Min Tjoa and J. Trujillo (Eds.): DaWaK 2006, LNCS 4081, pp. 23–32, 2006.

the hash file to grow and shrink [11]. Given a hash file with initially N_0 buckets and a hash function $h()$ that maps each key to a number, $h_0(key) = h(key) \bmod N_0$ is called a base hash function and $h_i(key) = h(key) \bmod 2^i N_0$ for $i > 0$ are called split functions where N_0 is typically chosen to be 1. Buckets are split when there is an overflow. Linear hashing does not necessarily split a bucket that overflows, but always performs splits in a deterministic linear order. Thus the records mapped to an overfilled bucket may be stored in an overflow bucket that is linked to the primary area bucket.

Loading a Linear Hash: Consider loading a linear hash file with $N_0 = 1$. the hash file initially has a single bucket and grows in generations to 2, 4, ..., 2^n buckets. In the 0th generation, the hash file grows from a single bucket to two buckets. Every record of the old bucket with its least significant bit (referred to here as bit 0) set is moved to the new bucket. In the ith generation, the hash has 2^i buckets and grows into 2^{i+1} buckets in a linear order. For each record key, the ith bit of its hash value is examined and it is decided if the record must be moved to a newly-created bucket.

Paper Organization: Section 2 presents our bulk loading algorithm. In Section 3, we compare and contrast our methods to caching, which can be seen as an alternative to bulk loading. Section 4 presents and analyzes our experimental results. Finally, Section 5 reviews the related work and Section 6 concludes the paper and discusses possible extensions and future work.

2   Bulk Loading

Based on our analysis [13], the cost of loading can be reduced if we can reduce or eliminate random page accesses and record movements.

2.1   Straightforward Solutions and Problems

To avoid random disk accesses in loading a hash file, a general solution is to sort the records based on the addresses they are hashed to before loading. Unlike static hashing where each record is mapped to a fixed location, the address of a record in a linear hash file is not fixed and it changes as more records are inserted or deleted. Sorting the records based on the hash values is not also an option since there is not a single hash function.

An alternative is to estimate the number of generations a hash file is expected to go through, say r, and sort the records based on the function $h(key) \bmod 2^r$ of their key values. This solution can avoid random disk accesses if the hash file (after all the data is loaded) is in a state right at the beginning or the end of a generation, i.e. bucket 0 is the next bucket to split. Otherwise r, the number of bits used for sorting, is not a natural number. Clearly one can solve the problem using $\lceil r \rceil$ bits for addressing, for the cost of an underutilized hash file. But this can almost double the space that is really needed.

The design of a linear hash file (as discussed in the previous section) forces the records within each bucket to have a few least significant bits of their hash values the same. For instance, in the ith generation, the hash values of the records in each bucket must all have their i least significant bits the same. It is clear that there is not a unique final layout that satisfies this constraint. The final layout, for instance, can vary with the order in which the records are inserted.

2.2   Input Ordering and Load Optimality

There are many different ways of ordering a given set of input records, and each ordering may result into a different hash file configuration. To reduce the number of possible hash layouts that we need to search for, we define some equivalent classes of layouts.

Definition 1. *Let $R(b)$ denote the set of records that are stored in either the primary bucket b or an overflow bucket linked to primary bucket b. Two linear hash layouts l_1 and l_2 are equivalent if (1) for every primary-area bucket b_1 in l_1, there is a primary-area bucket b_2 in l_2 such that $R(b_1) = R(b_2)$, and (2) for every primary-area bucket b_2 in l_2, there is a primary-area bucket b_1 in l_1 such that $R(b_1) = R(b_2)$.*

For the purpose of loading, two different configurations may be treated the same if both have the same space overheads and I/O costs. On the other hand, the construction costs of two equivalent layouts can be quite different. We develop a notion of optimality which to some degree characterizes these costs.

Definition 2. *Suppose a target hash file is fixed and has N primary-area buckets. An* optimal ordering *of the records is the one such that loading records in that order into the hash file involves no bucket splits nor record movements and no bucket is fetched after it is written.*

This notion of optimality does not provide us with an actual load algorithm but makes it clear that before a bucket is written, all records that belong to the bucket must be somehow grouped together. Furthermore, to avoid bucket splits and record movements, the final layout must be predicted before the data is actually loaded. Our bulk loading algorithm is presented next.

2.3   Our Algorithm

Suppose a final hash layout is fixed and it satisfies the user's expectation, for instance, in terms of the average number of I/Os per probe. Thus, we know the number of buckets in the hash file (the details of our estimation is discussed elsewhere [13]). For each record, r least significant bits of its hash value gives the address of the bucket where the record must be stored. As is shown in Alg. 1., before the split point is reached, $r = \lceil log_2 N \rceil$ bits. At the split point, the number of bits used for addressing is reduced by one. Since the input is sorted based on b least significant bits of the hash values in a reversed order, all records with the same $r_1, r_2 \leq b$ least significant bits are also grouped together. Hence the correctness of the algorithm follows. Furthermore, the input ordering satisfies our optimality criteria; after sorting, the algorithm does not perform any bucket splits or record movements and no bucket is fetched after it is written.

Algorithm 1. Bulk Loading a hash file

Estimate the number of primary buckets in the hash file and denote it with N;

$r_1 = \lfloor log_2 N \rfloor$; $r_2 = \lceil log_2 N \rceil$
Sort the records on $b \in [r_2, mb]$ least significant bits of their hash values in a reversed order, where mb is the maximum length of a hash value in bits;

Let $p = N - 2^{r_1}$ denote the next bucket that will split
$r = r_2$; $b = 0$; {current bucket that is being filled}
while there are more records **do**
    Get the next record R with the hash value H_R;
    Let h be the r least significant bits of H_R;
    Reverse the order of the bits in h;
    if $h > b$ {the record belongs to the next bucket} **then**
        Write bucket b to the hash file; $b++$;
        if $b \geq p$ {has reached the split point} **then**
            $r = r_1$;
        end if
    end if
    if bucket b is not full **then**
        Insert R into bucket b;
    else
        Write bucket b to the hash file if it is not written;
        Insert R into an overflow bucket;
    end if
end while

Lemma 1. *The total cost of Alg. 1. in terms of the number of I/Os is roughly the cost of sorting the input plus the cost of sequentially writing it.*

Proof See [13].

3   Caching vs. Data Partitioning

Caching the buckets of a hash file can reduce the number of I/Os and may be an alternative to bulk loading, if it can be done effectively. The effectiveness of caching mainly depends on the replacement policy that is chosen and the size of the available memory. When the memory size is limited, a "good" caching scheme must predict the probe sequence of the records and keep the buckets that are expected to be accessed in near future in memory. However, unless the data is ordered to match the ordering of the buckets in the hash file, the probe sequence is expected to be random and every bucket has pretty much the same chance of being probed. Therefore, it is not clear if any replacement policy alone can improve the performance of the loading. If we assume the unit of transfer between the disk and memory is a bucket, reducing the size of a bucket can reduce unused data transfers, thus improving the cache performance at load time (e.g. [1]). However, using a small bucket size can also increase the average access time for searches [9].

An alternative which turns out to be more promising (see Section 4.1) is to use the available memory for data reordering such that the probes to the same or adjacent buckets are grouped together. As in caching, the data is scanned once but partitioned into smaller chunks and each partition is buffered. Sorting each partition in the buffer reorders the records so that the records in the same partition which belong to the same or adjacent buckets are grouped together.

For testing and comparison, both caching and partitioning can be integrated into Berkeley DB which supports linear hashing through its so-called extended linear hash [14]. The database does use caching to boost its performance. When a hash file is built from scratch, all buckets are kept in memory as long as there is room. The size of the cache can be controlled manually. Berkeley DB provides a utility, called *db_load*, for loading but the utility does not do bulk loading. Our partition-based approach can be implemented within *db_load* (as shown in Alg. 2.) by allocating a buffer for data reordering. Alg. 2. is not a replacement for Alg. 1. but it is good for incremental updates, after an initial loading and when the hash file is not empty.

Algorithm 2. Modified *db_load* with data partitioning

Initialize the memory buffer
while there are more records **do**
    Read a record R from the dataset and add it to the buffer
    if the buffer is full **then**
        Sort the records in the buffer based on their reversed hash values
        Insert all the records in the buffer into the hash table
        Clear the buffer
    end if
end while

Obviously, the size of the buffer can directly affect the loading performance. The larger the buffer, the more records will be grouped according to their positions in the hash table. If we assume the size of the available memory is limited, then the space must be somehow divided between a cache and a sort buffer. Our experiments in the next section shows that a sort buffer is more effective than a cache of the same size.

4   Experiments

We conducted experiments comparing our bulk loading to both the loading in Berkeley DB and our implementation of a naive loading. Our experiments were conducted on a set of URLs, extracted from a set of crawled pages in the Internet Archive [7]. Attached to each URL was a 64-bit unique fingerprint which was produced using Rabin's fingerprinting scheme [12]. We used as our keys the ascii character encoding of each fingerprint; this gave us a 16-bytes key for each record. Unless stated otherwise, we used a random 100-bytes charter string for data values. We also tried using URLs as our keys but the result was pretty much the same and were not reported. All our experiments were conducted on a Pentium 4 machine running Red Hat 9, with a speed of 3.0GHz, a memory of 2GB, and a striped array of three 7200 RPM IDE disks. We used the version 4.2.52 of Berkeley DB, the latest at the time of running our experiments.

For our experiments with Alg. 1., we set $b = mb$, except for the experiments reported at the end of Section 4.1; this made the sorting independent of the layout estimation and had a few advantages: (1) external sorting could be used, (2) the data read by our layout estimation could be piped to sorting, avoiding an additional scan of the data. There was not also much improvement in running time when the number of bits used for sorting was less. For instance, external sorting 180 million 130-byte records based on 16 bits took 85 minutes whereas a sort based on 64 bits took 87 minutes. Our timings reported for Alg. 1. include the times for both sorting and layout estimation. For sorting, the Linux sort command was used.

4.1   Performance Comparison to Loading in Berkeley DB

As a baseline comparison, we used the native *db_load* utility in Berkeley DB and compared its performance to that of our bulk loading. *db_load* had a few parameters that could be set at load time including the fill factor (h_ffactor) and the number of records (h_nelem). In particular, when h_nelem was set, *db_load* did a layout estimation and built the entire empty hash table in advance. We played with these parameters, trying to find the best possible settings. In our experiments, however, we did not notice any performance improvements over default settings, except in those cases where the input followed a specific ordering as discussed at the end of this Section. Otherwise, the performance even deteriorated when the parameters were explicitly set. Therefore, unless stated otherwise, we used the default settings of the *db_load* utility.

Scalability with the size of the dataset. To test the scalability of our algorithms and to compare caching (in Berkeley DB) with our partitioning, we varied the size of the dataset from 1 million to 20 million records and measured the running time for Alg. 1., Alg. 2. and the native *db_load*. The size of the sort buffer in Alg. 2 was set to 300MB (our next experiment shows how the buffer size can affect the load performance). If we included the 1MB I/O cache which was automatically allocated by Berkeley DB, the total memory allocated to Alg. 2 was 301MB. To make a fair comparison, we also set the I/O cache of the native *db_load* utility to 301MB. All other parameters were set to their default values in Berkeley DB.

The result of the experiment is shown in Fig. 1-a. When the dataset is small (less than 5 million records), all three methods perform very well and their performances are comparable. This is because both the I/O cache of the native *db_load* and the sort buffer of Alg. 2 are large enough to hold a major fraction of data. When the dataset size is 5 million records (i.e. 590MB), half of the input data cannot fit in the sort buffer of Alg. 2 or the I/O cache of the native *db_load* utility, and Alg. 2 improves upon the native *db_load* by a factor of 1.5. When the dataset contains more than 10 million records, our experiment shows that Alg. 2 outperforms the native *db_load* utility by at least a factor of 3. The performance of our bulk loading algorithm is better than the other two approaches. It takes only 10 minutes and 23 seconds to load the dataset with 20 million records while native *db_load* utility in Berkeley DB requires 1682 minutes and 1 seconds.

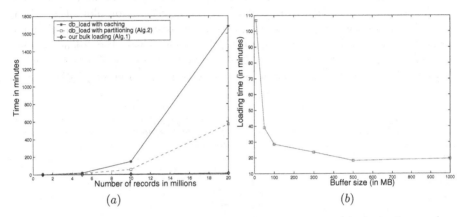

Fig. 1. Running time varying (a) the number of records, (b) the buffer size

Buffer size. As discussed in the previous section, when the dataset cannot be fully loaded into memory, the sort buffer is always more effective than an I/O cache of the same size. In another experiment to measure the effect of the sort buffer size on the performance, we fixed the size of the dataset to 10 million records and varied the sort buffer size in Alg. 2 from 100MB to 1GB. Each record contained a 16-bytes key and a 50-bytes data field. The default I/O cache size of *db_load* was 1MB. The result in Fig. 1-b shows that allocating a modest size buffer for sorting (in this case less than 50MB) sharply reduces the running time. Clearly allocating more buffer helps but we don't see a significant drop in running time. This is a good indication that our partitioning can be integrated into other applications with only a small buffer overhead.

Sorting data in advance. In an attempt to measure the effect of input ordering alone (without a layout estimation), we sorted the records based on i least significant bits of their hash values with i varied from 0 to 32, where 32 was the length of a hash value in bits. As is shown in Fig. 2-a for 10 million records of our URL dataset, the loading time was the worst when data was not sorted or the sorting was done on the whole hash value. Increasing i from 0 toward 32 reduced the running time until i reached a point (here called an optimal point) after which the running time started going up. The optimal point was not fixed; it varied with both the size of the dataset and the distribution of the hash values. However, if we reversed the bit positions before sorting, increasing i from

0 toward 32 reduced the running time until i reached its optimal point after which the running time almost stayed the same[1]. Clearly sorting improves the performance when data is sorted either on the reversed hash values or on the original order but using an optimal number of bits.

We could not do our layout estimation in Berkeley DB but could pass the number of records and let Berkeley DB do the estimation. In another experiment we sorted the data and also passed the number of records as a parameter to the load utility. Fig. 2-b shows the loading time for the same 10 million record dataset when the number of records is passed as a parameter and the number of bits used for sorting, i, is varied from 1 to 32. A layout estimation alone (i.e. when $i = 0$) did not improve the loading time; this was consistent with our experiments reported earlier in this section. Comparing the two graphs in Fig. 2 leads to the conclusion that the best performance is obtained when sorting is combined with a layout estimation (here the layout estimation is done in Berkeley DB).

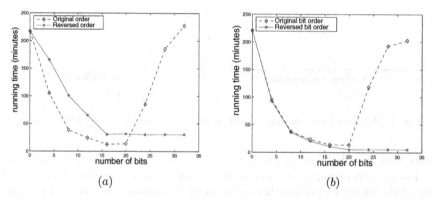

(a) (b)

Fig. 2. Loading sorted data using *db_load* (a) without the number of records set, (b) with the number of records set

4.2   Performance Comparison to Naive Loading

We could not run Berkeley DB for datasets larger than 20 million records as it was either hanging up or taking too long [2]. Therefore we decided to implement our own loading, here called *naive loading*, which as in Berkeley DB inserted one record at a time but did not have the Berkeley DB overheads due to the implementation of ACID properties. To compare the performance of this naive loading to that of our bulk loading (Alg. 1.), we varied the size of the dataset from 1 million to 50 million records and measured the loading time. We couldn't run the naive loading for larger datasets; it was taking already more than 55 hours to run it with 50 million records. The full result of the comparison could not be

---

[1] Increasing i may slightly increase the time for sorting, but this increase (as discussed at the beginning of this section) is negligible.

[2] For instance, loading 20 million records took over 26 hours (see Fig. 1-a).

presented due to space limitations, but loading 10 million records, for instance, using our bulk loading algorithm took 3 minutes and 16 seconds whereas it took 129 minutes and 55 seconds to load the same dataset using the naive algorithm. For 50 million records, using our bulk loading algorithm took 27 minutes and 4 seconds whereas naive algorithm needed 3333 minutes and 18 seconds. Generally speaking, our bulk loading algorithm outperforms the naive loading by two orders of magnitude, and its performance even gets better for larger datasets.

5   Related Work

Closely related to our bulk loading is the incremental data organization of Jagadish et al. [8] which delays the insertions into a hash file. They collect the records in piles and merge them with the main hash only after enough records are collected. Data in each pile is organized as a hash index and each bucket of the index has a block in memory. This idea of lazy insert is similar to our Alg. 2.. A difference is that we use sorting, thus the records that are mapped to the same location in the hash file are all adjacent. This may provide a slight benefit at the load time. Our Alg. 1. is different and should be more efficient. The entire data is sorted in advance using external sorting which is both fast and scalable to large datasets; it is also shown that the total cost of the algorithm is roughly equal to the cost of sorting. On a dataset with 20 million records, Alg. 1. is 50 times faster than our partition-based algorithm (Alg. 2.) which is comparable to a lazy insertion of Jagadish et al. [8].

To the best of our knowledge, hash indexes are not currently supported in DB2, Sybase and Informix; this may change as these databases provide more support for text and other non-traditional data. Hash indexes are supported in Microsoft SQL Server, Oracle (in the form of hash clusters), PostgreSQL and Berkeley DB (as discussed earlier), but we are not aware of any bulk loading algorithm for these indexes.

6   Conclusions

Hash-based indexes are quite attractive for searching large data collections, because of their low cost complexity, however the initial time for loading is a major factor in the adoption of a hash-based index in the first place. Our work, motivated by our attempt to load a snapshot of the Web into a linear hash file, presents a few algorithms for efficiently loading a large dataset into a linear hash file. Our analysis of these algorithms and our experiments show that our algorithms are near-optimal, can scale up for large datasets and can reduce the loading time by two orders of magnitude.

Acknowledgments

The authors would like to thank Margo Seltzer and Keith Bostic for answering many of our questions about Berkeley DB and comments on our earlier draft and Paul Larson for the discussions. This work is supported by Natural Sciences and Engineering Research Council of Canada.

References

1. Ailamaki, A., DeWitt, D.J., Hill, M.D., Skounakis, M.: Weaving relations for cache performance. In: Proceedings of the VLDB Conference, Rome, Italy (2001) 169–180
2. Amer-Yahia, S., Cluet, S.: A declarative approach to optimize bulk loading into databases. ACM Transactions on Database Systems $29(2)$ (2004) 233–281
3. Böhm, C., Kriegel, H.: Efficient bulk loading of large high-dimensional indexes. In: International Conference on Data Warehousing and Knowledge Discovery. (1999) 251–260
4. Fenk, R., Kawakami, A., Markl, V., Bayer, R., Osaki, S.: Bulk loading a data warehouse built upon a ub-tree. In: Proceedings of of IDEAS Conference, Yokohoma, Japan (2000) 179–187
5. Gray, J.: A conversation with Jim Gray. ACM Queue $1(4)$ (2003)
6. Hjaltason, G.R., Samet, H., Sussmann, Y.J.:   Speeding up bulk-loading of quadtrees. In: Proceedings of the International ACM Workshop on Advances in Geographic Information Systems, Las Vegas (1997) 50–53
7. Internet Archive: (http://www.archive.org)
8. Jagadish, H.V., Narayan, P.P.S., Seshadri, S., Sudarshan, S., Kanneganti, R.: Incremental organization for data recording and warehousing. In: Proc. of the VLDB Conference, Athens (1997) 16–25
9. Knuth, D.: The Art of Computer Programming: Vol III, Sorting and Searching. Volume 3rd ed. Addison Wesley (1998)
10. Labio, W., Wiener, J.L., Garcia-Molina, H., Gorelik, V.: Efficient resumption of interrupted warehouse loads. In: Proc. of the SIGMOD Conference, Dallas (2000) 46–57
11. Larson, P.: Dynamic hash tables. Communications of the ACM $31(4)$ (1988) 446–457
12. Rabin, M.O.: Fingerprinting by random polynomials. Technical Report TR-15-81, Department of Computer Science, Harvard University (1981)
13. Rafiei, D., Hu, C.: Bulk loading a linear hash file: extended version. (under preparation)
14. Seltzer, M., Yigit, O.: A new hashing package for unix. In: USENIX, Dallas (1991) 173–184
15. Wiener, J.L., Naughton, J.F.: OODB bulk loading revisited: The partitioned-list approach. In: Proceedings of the VLDB Conference, Zurich, Switzerland (1995) 30–41

Dynamic View Selection for OLAP

Michael Lawrence and Andrew Rau-Chaplin

Faculty of Computer Science
Dalhousie University
Halifax, NS, Canada
B3H 1W5
{michaell, arc}@cs.dal.ca
www.cgmLab.org

Abstract. Due to the increasing size of data warehouses it is often infeasible to materialize all possible aggregate views for Online Analytical
Processing. View selection, the task of selecting a subset of views to materialize based on knowledge of the incoming queries and updates, is an
important and challenging problem. In this paper we explore *Dynamic
View Selection* in which the distribution of queries changes over time,
and a subset of a materialized view set is updated to better serve the
incoming queries.

1 Introduction

In a data warehousing environment, users interactively pose queries whose answers are used to support data-driven decision making. Such queries usually
make heavy use of aggregation, which may be realized using the GROUP-BY clause
in SQL. Since aggregate queries are so common and their results are typically
very expensive to compute, aggregate views of the data are often pre-computed
and stored in OLAP systems in order to speed up future query processing.
From the perspective of efficient query answering, ideally all views would be
pre-computed and made available for answering aggregate queries, however re-
alistically storage and computational constraints limit the number of views that
are usefully pre-materialized.

The problem of choosing a set of views for materialization is known as the
View Selection Problem. In the view selection problem one wishes to select a set
of views for materialization which minimizes one or more objectives, possibly
subject to one or more constraints. Many variants of the view selection problem
have been studied including minimizing the query cost of a materialized view
set subject to a storage size constraint [1,2,3,4], minimizing a linear combination
of query cost and maintenance cost of a materialized view set [5,6,7,8,9], and
minimizing query cost under a maintenance cost constraint [3,10,11,12,13]. Note
however that in most of these cases the problem considered is *static* in that:
1) Query frequencies are assumed to be static (i.e., not changing over time),
and 2) It is assumed that the pool of materialized views is to be selected and
computed from scratch rather than making use of a running OLAP system's

A Min Tjoa and J. Trujillo (Eds.): DaWaK 2006, LNCS 4081, pp. 33–44, 2006.

pool of previously materialized views. While the static view selection problem is important, it captures only the start-up phase of a OLAP system and does not address what is arguably in practice the more important dynamic question: how, given a running OLAP system with an existing pool of materialized views and a new vector of query frequencies, should we identify views that should be added to our materialized pool and views that should be removed in order to best minimize query times subject to a storage size constraint?

The need for dynamic view management was forcefully made by Kotidis et al. in their DynaMat system [14]. As they observe, "This static selection of views [...] contradicts the dynamic nature of decision support analysis." There are a number of ways to approach the dynamic view selection problem, which we review in Section 2.2. In this paper we explore an alternative approach to *Dynamic View Selection*. We consider an OLAP system with two phases of operation: *Startup* and *Online*. In the Startup Phase an initial set of views must be selected based on some estimated query probabilities. This is the classical (static) view selection problem. In the Online Phase an "in use" OLAP system is considered, for which a set of views M has already been selected and materialized. Since over time the relative importance of each type of aggregate query may change due to the changing demands of its users, the system may elect to select a new set of views, M', which better serves the incoming queries. However, view materialization is computationally expensive and the time window in which new views can be materialized may prohibit selection of an entirely new view set. Thus the problem becomes selecting a new view set M' by discarding some views from M, and adding new ones to be materialized. We refer to the problem of incrementally updating a view set as the *Online View Selection Problem* (see Section 2). We believe that the online view selection problem is an important addition to the static variant, as OLAP systems in practice are restarted from scratch only infrequently and must be able to tune their performance to changing conditions on-the-fly.

Our approach to online view selection is to adapt methods that have proven to be effective for the static variant. In this paper we develop online adaptations of the greedy heuristic, BPUS, introduced by Harinarayan et al. [1] and three randomized techniques (iterative improvement, simulated annealing and two-phase optimization) initially proposed for static view selection by Kalnis et al. [3] (see Sections 3 and 4). Our challenge is two-fold. For the static phase, the randomized methods must be adapted so as to take into account maintenance cost in addition to the space constraint and for the online phase all of the methods must be adapted to take into account the existing pool of previously materialized views.

2   Problem Definition and Related Work

2.1   Static View Selection

A typical data warehouse stores its information according to a star schema having a central fact table with d feature attributes (dimensions), and some number of measure attributes. Queries to the data warehouse request aggregated measures from the perspective of some subset of the dimensions in the fact and dimension tables, which can be specified using the GROUP-BY clause in SQL. The aggregated table from which a query's results are collected is called a *view*, and is identified by the dimensions selected. Harinarayan et al. introduced the data cube lattice in [1] expressing the relationship between views as a partial order. There is a path from a view v_1 to a view v_2 in the lattice if queries on v_2 can be answered also using v_1 (although likely at a higher cost). The total number of views in the lattice is exponential in the number of dimensions.

The view selection problem can be formally defined as follows. For each view v in the lattice L, we have some estimate of the number of records r_v in v, and the frequency of queries f_v on v. As in most previous studies, we adopt the linear cost model presented in [1], where the cost of answering a query on a view v is r_v. The cost $q(v, M)$ of answering aggregate queries on view v using a materialized view set M is equal to the number of records in the smallest view in M which is an ancestor of v in the data cube lattice. The overall query time using M is a weighted sum of these terms

$$Q(M) = \sum_v f_v q(v, M),$$

and the size $S(M)$ of M is simply the sum of the sizes of each of the views in M. The update or maintenance cost $u(v, M)$ of a materialized view v in M is modeled based on a maintenance cost which is assigned to every edge (v_1, v_2) in the lattice. This represents the cost of maintaining v_2 using updates from v_1, and the maintenance cost $u(v, M)$ is the smallest maintenance cost over all paths from materialized ancestors of v_1 to v_2. Each node v also has an update frequency g_v, and the total update cost for a set of materialized views M is

$$U(M) = \sum_{v \in M} g_v u(v, M).$$

Note that while $Q(M)$ decreases when new views are added, $U(M)$ does not always increase, as the additional cost of maintaining a materialized view v might be outweighed by the benefit that v has in propagating smaller batches of updates to its children. Our goal for the static phase is as follows: to select a M which has the minimum $Q(M) + U(M)$ subject to the constraint $S(M) < S_{max}$ for some maximum size S_{max}.

Numerous solutions have been proposed to the (static) view selection problem on data cubes. The first is a greedy algorithm presented by Harinarayan et al. [1], which is proven to find a solution within 63% of optimal. In [5] the same heuristic was extended to minimize sum of query and update cost. Shukla et al. give a heuristic minimizing query cost in [2] which is asymptotically faster than that of [1], but achieves the same solution only under certain conditions. In [6] a greedy algorithm for minimizing the sum of query and update cost is given, their update cost modeling is more accurate, however when choosing a view v to select they only consider the update cost of v and not its impact on the entire view set. Gupta gives the first solution to the view selection problem minimizing query cost under an update cost constraint in [13], followed by two algorithms of Liang et al. in [10], and genetic algorithm approaches in [12,11] In [15] Agrawal et al. present a tool and algorithms for selecting a set of views based on a cost metric involving query cost, update cost, index construction and other factors. Nadeau and Teorey give a greedy algorithm minimizing query cost under a space constraint which is polynomial in the number of dimensions [4], but does not perform as well as other greedy heuristics. Kalnis et al. use randomized algorithms to search the solution space of view sets in [3], minimizing query cost and constrained by space or update cost.

2.2   Online View Selection

For the online phase we consider a data warehousing system which has a fixed-sized time window to materialize new views which are not currently materialized, but are perhaps more beneficial to the changing query patterns of the users. However because of the space constraint, a number of views may have to be discarded as well. Based on the size of the available time window for computing new views, the database administrator calculates how much of the materialized view set can be replaced. We do not consider update costs in online view selection because updates themselves are counter to the purpose of online view selection. Online view selection is an act which is typically performed at regular maintenance intervals, based on an observed or expected change in query probabilities. During these intervals, updates are applied to the views and so we do not expect updates to be applied between intervals, hence update cost is not our concern in online view selection. Hence we can define the online view selection problem as follows: Given a materialized view set M and new query frequencies $\mathbf{f}'$, find a M' which minimizes $Q(M')$ with respect to the new query frequencies, and such that

$$\sum_{v \in M \cap M'} r_v \geq (1 - h) \cdot S_{max},$$

for some h which represents a percentage of M (in terms of size) for which the system has enough resources to materialize new views for. Our dynamic view selection involves an initial startup phase consisting of a static selection of views M_1, and multiple online phases where M_1 is updated to M_2, M_2 to M_3 and so on. The decision of when to select an M_{i+1} by updating M_i can be made in many ways, for example during a pre-allocated maintenance window, when average query time degrades past an unacceptable level, or based on measuring the difference between the current query distribution and the distribution at the last online phase.

Our formulation of dynamic view selection is different from that of other studies [9,8,14]. In [9,8], Theodoratos et al. consider what they call dynamic or incremental data warehouse design. In the static phase, they are given a fixed set of queries Q, and views must be selected from multiquery AND/OR-DAGs which answer the queries with minimum cost. In the online phase, additional queries are added to the set Q, and new materialized views are added so that the new queries can be answered. In practice there may not be extra space available for materializing new views, and some previously materialized views must be discarded based on the fact that some queries are no longer of interest. In the dynamic view selection considered here, our materialized view set M is able to answer any possible aggregate query, and its size never increases beyond S_{max} over time. It may be the case that additional space is available for materialized views over time, which can easily be handled by our implementation of the algorithms.

In [14], Kotidis and Roussopoulos approach dynamic view selection by caching fragments of views. A view fragment is a portion of a whole view which results from a range selection on its dimensions. Their approach is fundamentally different from ours in that it can only choose to store aggregate data which has been requested from the user, where as pre-materializing a set of views is more flexible in that any aggregate data which can be produced is considered for storage. Also, their approach is in reaction to user's queries, where as a materialized view set approach aims to prepare the system for future queries. We believe ours to be a more valuable approach to dynamic view selection for the following reasons:

1. As argued in [16], the ad-hoc nature of OLAP queries reduces the chance that stored fragments will be able to fully answer future queries. Storing whole views guarantees that any queries on the same or more highly aggregated views can be answered.
2. Knowledge giving an expectation of future query loads (e.g. daily reports) may be available, allowing advance preparations to be made by choosing an appropriate pre-materialized view set.
3. Multiple unrelated and popular aggregate queries may have a common ancestor which can answer all of them at a slightly higher cost. In DynaMat, this ancestor will never be considered for storage unless it is queried, where as a good approach to view selection will store this ancestor instead of the individual aggregates below it, resulting in significant space savings which can be put to better use.

3   Randomized Algorithms for Dynamic View Selection

In order to apply randomized search to a problem, transitions between feasible solutions are required. Each search process moves stochastically through the graph of feasible solutions called the search space, which can be pictured as a topographical space where elevation represents objective value and locality represents connectivity of the solutions through the transitions defined. Since we are minimizing, the "lower" solutions in this space are the ones we desire. The effectiveness of a randomized search strategy depends on the shape of the search space and in what manner the search moves through it.

For the static phase we define two transitions, based on those in [3]:

1. Add a random view which is not in the current solution and randomly remove selected views as necessary to satisfy the space constraint.
2. Remove a randomly selected view.

The second transition is different from that of [3], which, after removing a view fills the rest of the available space with views. This is because our algorithms minimize both query and maintenance cost, as opposed to just maintenance cost. Under these conditions it is no longer safe to assume that the optimal view set is a "full" one, and the randomized algorithms must adapt to the tradeoff between query and maintenance cost. We similarly modify Kalnis et al.'s method of generating a random solution, by repeatedly adding views to an initially empty view set until the addition of some view v causes a decrease in overall cost, and removing v. This method gave us better results in terms of generating solutions nearer to the favourable ones than another technique of generating random solutions, which was to randomly pick a size S_0 from a uniform distribution on $[0, S_{max}]$, and creating a view set no larger than S_0 by adding as many random views as possible.

The three randomized search algorithms considered here are iterative improvement (II), simulated annealing (SA) and two-phase optimization (2PO), as described in [3].

- II makes a number of transitions, only accepting ones which lead to a better solution. When a number of unsuccessful transitions from a state are made (local minimum), II starts again from a random initial state. The search terminates after some maximum time or number of local minima.

- SA is an analogy to the process of cooling a physical system It works like II, except that uphill transitions may be accepted with some probability that is proportional to a "temperature" which decreases with time. The algorithm halts when the temperature reaches a fixed "freezing point", returning the best solution found during the process.

- 2PO combines II with SA. II is first applied to find a good local minimum, from which SA is applied with a small initial temperature to do a more thorough search of the surrounding area.

II tends to work well if the problem has structure so that good solutions are near each other in the search space. SA is more robust than II in that it can overcome the problem that good solutions may be near each other in search space, but separated by a small number of relatively worse solutions. 2PO attempts to combine the best of both II, which proceeds in a more direct manner towards a solution, and SA, which is able to more thoroughly explore an area.

We modify the transitions for online view selection as follows: If, while removing views to satisfy the space constraint, transition 1 violates the online constraint, then we add the previously removed view back to the solution, and continue only removing views in $M' - M$ from M' until the space constraint is satisfied. If transition 2 violates the online constraint, the removed view is re-added and a randomly selected view in $M' - M$ is removed instead.

4   Greedy Algorithm for Dynamic View Selection

For the static phase, the BPUS heuristic [1] begins with an initially empty view set, and greedily adds views which maximize a benefit heuristic. If the currently selected view set is M, then the benefit per unit space of adding an unselected view v is defined as

$$\frac{(Q(M) + U(M)) - (Q(M \cup \{v\}) + U(M \cup \{v\}))}{r_v},$$

i.e., the reduction in overall cost achieved by adding v, scaled by size. The BPUS algorithm adds the view v with maximum benefit per unit space until either there is no more space for materialized views, or v has negative benefit (when $U(M \cup \{v\}) - U(M) > Q(M) - Q(M \cup \{v\})$). To apply BPUS to online view selection, the same heuristic is "reversed", and the objective cost only considers query time of the materialized view set. When deciding which views to remove from M, we choose the view v which minimizes

$$\frac{Q(M - \{v\}) - Q(M)}{r_v},$$

the increase in average overall cost scaled to the size of v. Once a set of views totalling no more than $h \cdot S_{max}$ in size has been removed from M, we apply the BPUS heuristic (without update cost) to greedily select which views to replace them with, arriving at our solution M'.

5   Experimental Results

In our evaluation we use a variety of synthetic data sets which we can control the properties of in terms of size, dimensionality, skew, etc. In particular we focus on two classes of data sets: 1) *uniform*, where the cardinality of all dimensions are equal, representing data cube lattices with highly uniform view sizes, and 2) *2pow*, where the cardinality of the i-th dimension is 2^i, representing data cube lattices with highly skewed view sizes. In all cases the number of rows in the data sets was set to 1 billion and S_{max} was set to be 10 times this number of rows. We use two different types of query distributions: 1) *uniform random*, where query probabilities are assigned from a uniform random distribution, and 2) *hot regions* [17], where 90% of the queries are distributed amongst a set of views (the "hot region") selected from the bottom 1/3 of the lattice and containing 10% of the total views. The remaining 10% of the queries are distributed uniformly amongst the other views. We believe this to be a realistic but very challenging scenario, due to the underlying semantics of the dimensions of the data warehouse in which some combinations of dimensions may not provide useful information, while others do, hence there may be a large number of views which are simply not interesting at all.

We apply the randomized algorithms to view selection similarly as in [3], although our parameter selection is slightly different due to the different nature of the problem which now involves update costs. The selected parameters are shown in Table 1. Readers are referred to [3] for a description of the meaning of these parameters.

Table 1. Selected parameters for the randomized algorithms applied to both the static and online phases of dynamic view selection

	Static	Online
$cycles_{II}$	$50 \cdot 2^{d-10}$	$40 \cdot h \cdot 2^{3(d-10)/4}$
$min.d_{II}$	$7d$	$3d$
$cycles_{SA}$	$2^d/20$	$h/30\% \cdot 2^d/20$
T_{SA}	10^7	10^3
Δt_{SA}	0.9	0.8
$cycles_{2PO}$	$cycles_{II}/4$	$cycles_{II}/2$
$min.d_{2PO}$	$min.d_{II}$	$2d$
T_{2PO}	10^5	10^2
Δt_{2PO}	0.9	0.64

5.1 The Startup Phase: Static View Selection

In static view selection we are primarily concerned with 1) Quality: the solution values achieved by the randomized algorithms vs. that of BPUS, and 2) Efficiency: the amount of time it takes to converge on a solution. To maintain consistency with the literature [3] and since randomized algorithms are being considered as an alternative to BPUS, we express their solution quality as a factor of the solution quality of BPUS, called the *scaled solution* value.

Figure 1 shows the running time of BPUS, and the time to convergence for all randomized algorithms as the number of dimensions is varied. As the plot shows, the randomized algorithms converge much faster than the BPUS heuristic for both uniform and highly skewed data, especially in larger dimensions.

Now we aim to establish scalability of the randomized techniques in terms of solution quality. Figure 2 shows the scaled cost of the solutions found by the randomized algorithms as the number of dimensions is increased. As the figure shows, the randomized algorithms perform competitively against the BPUS heuristic, with their solutions falling typically within a few percent of it and being especially close with uniform data. Surprisingly, there are classes of problem instances where some of the randomized algorithms outperform the heuristic by as much as 15%. These problem instances are ones for which the update cost is sufficiently prohibitive that the better solutions are ones which contain a small number of views. BPUS finds a maximal solution with respect to size, in that no more views can be added without increasing the overall cost. As a result the randomized algorithms are able to find solutions with a much better update cost, at the expense of a slightly higher query cost.

Although the results from Figure 2 may suggest the randomized algorithms are more favourable for static view selection, we note that this performance is only observed for such problem instances where the query and update cost are relatively balanced. When query cost is the dominant factor, BPUS significantly

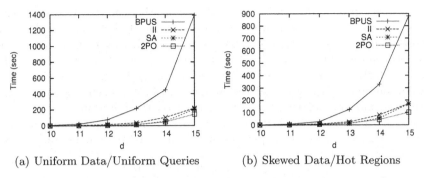

Fig. 1. Running time vs dimensionality for static view selection with 10^9 rows and $S_{max} = 10^{10}$. The mean of 20 independent trials is shown.

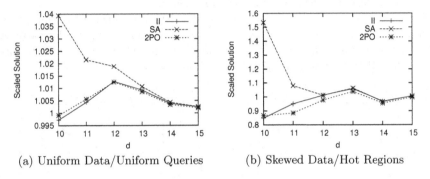

Fig. 2. Scaled solution vs d for static view selection with 10^9 rows and $S_{max} = 10^{10}$. The mean of 20 independent trials is shown.

outperforms the randomized algorithms. This is because, when update cost is not optimized as in [3], the randomized transitions can be designed knowing that the optimal view set will be a "full" one. However with the addition of update cost as an objective, the transitions must guide the randomized algorithms to the region of search space having view sets of the best size, as well as to a good choice of views in sets of that size. This adds another dimension of difficulty to the problem. The poor performance of the randomized algorithms when query cost is dominant is an indication that the randomized transitions have difficulty in guiding the search towards more full view sets. It is suggested that the randomized transitions of [3] be used if update cost is not expected to be prohibitive.

5.2   The Online Phase: Online View Selection

In the following tests each algorithm begins with the same initial view set M, which is selected using BPUS. $d = 12$ dimensions are used, with the parameters of the randomized algorithms summarized in Table 1. Unless otherwise indicated, $h = 30\%$ was chosen for the tests. For the uniform query distribution, the drift in query probabilities for a single iteration was achieved by scaling each view's probability by a random factor chosen uniformly between 0 and 1, and re-normalizing them so that they sum to 1. Using this query drift model the area between distribution curves on an iteration is generally in the range of 0.9 to 1.0 (with the maximum possible difference being 2). For the hot region query distribution, query drift was achieved by selecting both a beginning and ending hot region, and interpolating between the two over the iterations.

For performance on a single iteration, we are concerned with the improvement in query time. We measure the percent improvement of an online iteration from M to M' as

$$Imp(M, M') = 100\frac{Q(M) - Q(M')}{Q(M)}.$$

Note that the percent improvement not only depends on algorithm performance but also the amount that query distribution shifts.

First we examine the scalability of the algorithms in terms of running time. Figure 3 shows the results as we increase the dimensionality of the data sets. As in the case of static view selection, the randomized techniques are significantly faster than BPUS, especially with higher dimensions.

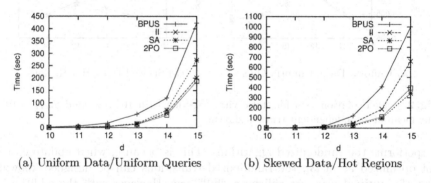

(a) Uniform Data/Uniform Queries   (b) Skewed Data/Hot Regions

Fig. 3. Running time vs. dimensionality for online view selection with 10^9 rows, $S_{max} = 10^{10}$ and $h = 30\%$. The mean of 20 independent trials is shown.

One question which is pertinent to online view selection is how much can we improve the current materialized view set given that we only have time to replace $h\%$ of it, or how much of the view set must be replaced to achieve a given improvement in query time. Figure 4 shows the relative improvement in query time as h is increased. The relative improvement is the percent improvement $Imp(M, M')$ achieved relative to the percent improvement $Imp(M, M^{new})$ which can be achieved if an entirely new set of views M^{new} were selected with BPUS. 0% means that $Q(M') = Q(M)$ (no improvement), 100% means $Q(M') = Q(M^{new})$, and $< 0\%$ means that $Q(M') > Q(M)$ (negative improvement). From the figure we can see that the online version of BPUS is a very strong performer for both uniform and skewed data, able to make 95% of the improvement of a newly chosen view set by replacing as little as 30% of it. A

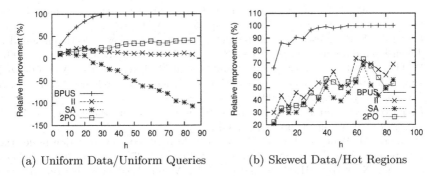

(a) Uniform Data/Uniform Queries   (b) Skewed Data/Hot Regions

Fig. 4. Percent improvement (relative to that of a newly selected view set) as h is increased. A 12-dimensional data cube is used. The mean of 20 independent trials is shown.

larger improvement with smaller h is possible for the hot regions instance, since replacing the views in the hot region is sufficient for considerable improvement.

6   Conclusions and Future Work

In this paper we have described a new approach to dynamic view selection which recognizes that in practice OLAP systems are restarted from scratch only infrequently and must be able to tune their performance to changing conditions on-the-fly. We have described a greedy and three randomized methods for dynamic view selection and implemented and evaluated them in the context of a large-scale OLAP system. Overall, in terms of solution quality, our BPUS-online adaptation appears to outperform the three randomized methods studied. However, as the number of dimensions grows the computational cost of BPUS-online may become impractically large and in this case the randomized methods presented here offer an attractive alternative. One important area of future work is to consider how best the dynamic view selection method proposed here can be combined with established caching and batch query optimization approaches.

References

1. V. Harinarayan, A. Rajaraman, and J. D. Ullman, "Implementing data cubes efficiently," in *proc. SIGMOD '96*, pp. 205–216, ACM, 1996.
2. A. Shukla, P. Deshpande, and J. F. Naughton, "Materialized view selection for multidimensional datasets," in *proc. VLDB '98*, pp. 488–499, Morgan Kaufmann, 1998.
3. P. Kalnis, N. Mamoulis, and D. Papadias, "View selection using randomized search," *Data Knowl. Eng.*, vol. 42, no. 1, pp. 89–111, 2002.
4. T. P. Nadeau and T. J. Teorey, "Achieving scalability in OLAP materialized view selection," in *proc. DOLAP '02*, pp. 28–34, ACM, 2002.
5. H. Gupta and I. S. Mumick, "Selection of views to materialize in a data warehouse," *Data Knowl. Eng.*, vol. 17, pp. 24–43, Jan. 2005.

6. H. Uchiyama, K. Runapongsa, and T. J. Teorey, "A progressive view materialization algorithm," in *proc. DOLAP '99*, pp. 36–41, ACM, 1999.
7. E. Baralis, S. Paraboschi, and E. Teniente, "Materialized views selection in a multi-dimensional database," in *proc. VLDB '97*, pp. 156–165, Morgan Kaufmann, 1997.
8. D. Theodoratos, T. Dalamagas, A. Simitsis, and M. Stavropoulos, "A randomized approach for the incremental design of an evolving data warehouse," in *proc. ER '01*, pp. 325–338, Springer, 2001.
9. D. Theodoratos and T. Sellis, "Incremental design of a data warehouse," *J. Intell. Inf. Syst.*, vol. 15, no. 1, pp. 7–27, 2000.
10. W. Liang, H. Wang, and M. E. Orlowska, "Materialized view selection under the maintenance time constraint," *Data Knowl. Eng.*, vol. 37, no. 2, pp. 203–216, 2001.
11. J. X. Yu, X. Yao, C.-H. Choi, and G. Gou, "Materialized view selection as constrained evolutionary optimization," in *IEEE Trans. on Syst., Man and Cybernetics, Part C*, vol. 33, pp. 458–467, IEEE, Nov. 2003.
12. M. Lee and J. Hammer, "Speeding up materialized view selection in data warehouses using a randomized algorithm," *J. Coop. Info. Syst.*, vol. 10, no. 3, pp. 327–353, 2001.
13. H. Gupta and I. S. Mumick, "Selection of views to materialize under a maintenance cost constraint," in *proc. ICDT '99*, pp. 453–470, Springer, 1999.
14. Y. Kotidis and N. Roussopoulos, "A case for dynamic view management," *J. Trans. Database Syst.*, vol. 26, no. 4, pp. 388–423, 2001.
15. S. Agrawal, S. Chaudhuri, and V. R. Narasayya, "Automated selection of materialized views and indexes in sql databases," in *proc. VLDB '00*, pp. 496–505, Morgan Kaufmann, 2000.
16. T. Loukopoulos, P. Kalnis, I. Ahmad, and D. Papadias, "Active caching of on-line-analytical-processing queries in www proxies," in *proc. ICPP '01*, pp. 419–426, IEEE, 2001.
17. P. Kalnis, W. S. Ng, B. C. Ooi, D. Papadias, and K.-L. Tan, "An adaptive peer-to-peer network for distributed caching of olap results," in *proc. SIGMOD '02*, pp. 25–36, ACM, 2002.

Preview: Optimizing View Materialization Cost in Spatial Data Warehouses [*]

Songmei Yu, Vijayalakshmi Atluri, and Nabil Adam

MSIS Department and CIMIC
Rutgers University, NJ, USA
{songmei, atluri, adam}@cimic.rutgers.edu

Abstract. One of the major challenges facing a data warehouse is to improve the query response time while keeping the maintenance cost to a minimum. Recent solutions to tackle this problem suggest to selectively materialize certain views and compute the remaining views on-the-fly, so that the cost is optimized. Unfortunately, in case of a spatial data warehouse, both the view materialization cost and the on-the-fly computation cost are often extremely high. This is due to the fact that spatial data are larger in size and spatial operations are more complex and expensive than the traditional relational operations. In this paper, we propose a new notion, called preview, for which both the materialization and on-the-fly costs are significantly smaller than those of the traditional views. Essentially, to achieve these cost savings, a preview pre-processes the non-spatial part of the query, and maintains pointers to the spatial data. In addition, it exploits the hierarchical relationships among the different views by maintaining a universal composite lattice, and mapping each view onto it. We optimally decompose a spatial query into three components, the preview part, the materialized view part and the on-the-fly computation part, so that the total cost is minimized. We demonstrate the cost savings with realistic query scenarios.

1 Introduction

One of the major challenges facing a data warehouse is to improve the query response time while keeping the maintenance cost to a minimum. Recently, selectively materializing certain views over source relations has become the philosophy in designing a data warehouse. While materialized views incur the space cost and view maintenance cost, views that are not materialized incur on-the-fly computation cost. One has to balance both these costs in order to materialize the optimal views that incur minimum cost. This problem is exasperated when we consider a *spatial data warehouse* (SDW). This is because, spatial data are typically large in size (e.g., point, line, region, raster and vector images), and the operations on spatial data are more expensive (e.g., region merge, spatial overlay and spatial range selection). As a result, often, both on-the-fly computation cost and the view materialization cost are prohibitively expensive.

---

[*] The work is supported in part by the New Jersey Meadowlands Commission under the project Meadowlands Environmental Research Institute.

A Min Tjoa and J. Trujillo (Eds.): DaWaK 2006, LNCS 4081, pp. 45–54, 2006.
© Springer-Verlag Berlin Heidelberg 2006

In this paper, we take a novel approach to resolve this issue. In particular, we introduce an intermediary view, called *preview*, for which both the materialization and on-the-fly costs are significantly smaller than those of the traditional views. Essentially, the idea of a preview is to pre-process the non-spatial part of the query and materialize this part based on certain cost conditions, but leave the spatial part for the on-the-fly and maintain pointers to the spatial data on which the spatial operation should be performed. In addition, a preview exploits the hierarchical relationships among different views. Obviously, storing previews in a data warehouse introduces overhead because it requires additional storage and process efforts to maintain the data sets during updates. However, we demonstrate that, the performance gain achieved through preview more than offsets this storage and maintenance overhead. Our ultimate goal is to optimize the total cost of a spatial data warehouse, which is the sum of the space cost of materialized views, the online computation cost of queries if not materialized, and the online computation and space cost of previews, if any.

This rest of the paper is organized as follows. We present the motivating example in Section 1. We present some preliminaries in Section 2. We introduce the Universal Composite Lattice in section 3. We define preview in Section 4. We discuss the related work in Section 5. We conclude our work in Section 6.

1.1   Motivating Example

In this section, we present an example that demonstrates that, for certain spatial queries, our approach to maintaining previews results in lower cost than optimally choosing a combination of on-the-fly and view materialization. Assume the spatial data warehouse comprising of a set of maps with their alphanumeric counterparts such as the area, the population amount and the temperature degree, as well as three basic metadata: location, time, and resolution. Assume that these maps specify different subjects of interest such as weather, precipitation, vegetation, population, soil, oil, or administrative region.

Now consider the following query that shows interests on a specific region: find the administrative boundary change of NJ area over last 10 years at 1m resolution level, and shows the vegetation patterns and population distributions within the same area, time frame and resolution level, and finally overlay the population maps and vegetation maps to deduce any relationships between them. The relation to store these data is called Map. An SQL-like query to specify this is as follows: select boundary(M.admin_map), M.vegetation_map, M.population_map, overlay(M.vegetation_map, M.populationa_map) from Map where Map.resolution = 1m AND Map.location = NJ AND 1994 < Map.year < 2005. For the purposes of execution, this query p can be visualized as having four parts, q_1, q_2, q_3 and q_4:

1. q_1: a spatial selection that retrieves boundaries of NJ administrative maps for last ten years on 1 m resolution.
2. q_2: a spatial selection that retrieves vegetation maps in NJ area for last ten years on 1m resolution.

3. q_3: a spatial selection that retrieves population maps in NJ area for last ten years on 1m resolution.
4. q_4 : a spatial join that overlays the results of q_2 and q_3 . Hence q_2 and q_3 are intermediate views for q_4.

The on-the-fly computation cost for each operation (q_1, q_2, q_3, q_4) is 4, 2, 2, 10 (s/image), and the space costs for admin_map boundary, vegetation_map and population_map are 5.0, 7.2, 6.0 (MB) respectively. Given a query q, we assume $S(q)$ denotes the space cost, $C(q)$ denotes the on-the-fly computation cost, and $T(q) = S(q) + C(q)$ denotes the total cost. For the sake of this example, we assume $S(q)$ is measured in Mega Bytes, and $C(q)$ in seconds. When computing $T(q)$, we assume 1MB translates into 1 cost unit and 1sec translates into 1 cost unit. Now let us consider the cost of the above query in the following four cases:

1. The entire query p is materialized. In other words, we materialize the result of q_1 and q_4. $T(p) = S(q_1) + S(q_4) = 5.0 \times 10 + (7.2 + 6.0) \times 10 = 50 + 132 = 182$.
2. The entire query p is computed on-the-fly. $T(p) = C(q_1) + C(q_2) + C(q_3) + C(q_4) = (4 \times 10) + (2 \times 10) + (2 \times 10) + (10 \times 10) = 40 + 20 + 20 + 100 = 180$.
3. Materialize q_1 and perform on-the-fly computation of q_4. Then $T(p) = S(q_1) + C(q_4) = 50 + (20 + 20 + 100) = 190$.
4. Materialize q_4 and perform on-the-fly computation of q_1. Then $T(p) = S(q_4) + C(q_1) = 132 + 40 = 172$.

Obviously one can choose the one among the alternatives that provides the highest cost savings. Now let us examine how using previews can reduce the view materialization cost. Let us assume we store the preview of q_1 and materialize q_4. Specifically, for q_1, we materialize the non-spatial part because its cost is below our pre-set threshold, therefore we store the metadata(NJ, 1995-2004, 1m) and pointers to the New Jersey administrative maps from year 1995 to 2004 and leave the spatial operation textitoverlay on-the-fly. Compared to materializing 10 years boundaries of administrative maps, the space and maintenance cost of storing preview is much cheaper than storing the spatial view itself. Compared to perform on-the-fly computation of retrieving 10 years boundaries of administrative maps, the query response time will be reduced by adding pointers. In another word, we reduce some on-the-fly computation cost of q_1 by paying price of storing its preview, so that the overall cost is optimized. For q_4, we still materialize it due to the very expensive *overlay* operation. The total cost of building a preview is the space cost of storing the preview the on-the-fly computation cost starting from the preview. In this real example, the space of using one row to store the preview is 0.01MB and the online boundary retrieval takes 2 second for each map. We use $PC(q)$ to denote the preview cost of query q, therefore:

1. $PC(q_1) = S(q_1) + C(q_1) = (0.01 \times 10) + (2 \times 10) = 0.1 + 20 = 20.1$
2. $S(q_4) = 132$
3. $T(p) = PC(q_1) + S(q_4) = 20.1 + 132 = 152.1$

Compared to the costs of previous methods, the total cost of query p is further optimized by constructing previews of q_1. In the next sections, we will present the definition of preview, and how we select appropriate set of queries for preview to optimize the total cost of an SDW.

2   Spatial Queries

In this section, we briefly present several important concepts. First, we define the basic algebra expression that is needed for constructing a *spatial query*. We then define an *atomic spatial query*, which serves as the smallest cost unit by decomposing a spatial query. We finally introduce a process denoted as *spatial projection*, which will be used to generate a preview.

The *hybrid algebra*, including hybrid relations R, hybrid operators *op* and hybrid operands X, constitutes the basis for defining a spatial query in a spatial data warehouse. Within an SDW, a base relation is a *hybrid relation* that includes attributes and tuples from both alphanumeric relations and spatial relations. For spatial relations, we adopt the definitions from the standard specifications of Open Geospatial Consortium (OGC). The spatial data types supported by this standard are from Geometry Object Model (GOM), where the geometry class serves as the base class with sub-classes for *Point, Curve (line)* and *Surface (Polygon)*, as well as a parallel class of *geometry collection* designed to handle geometries of a collection of points, lines and polygons. Conceptually, spatial entities are stored as relations with geometry valued attributes as columns, and their instances as rows. The hybrid operators *op* combine a complete set of relational operators *rop* ($\sigma, \pi, \cup, -, \times$), comparison operators *cop* ($=, <, \leq, \geq, >$, $\neq$), aggregate operators *aop* (distributive functions, algebraic functions, holistic functions) and spatial operators *sop* defined by OGC (Spatial Basic Operators, Spatial Topological Operators, Spatial Analysis Operators), or $op \in (rop \cup cop \cup aop \cup sop)$. A *hybrid algebra operand* is a distinct attribute of a hybrid relation, which could be either spatial operand or non-spatial operand. Now we define a spatial query based on the hybrid algebra.

Definition 1 *Spatial Query. A spatial query is a hybrid algebra expression F, which is defined as: (i) a single formula f, can be either unary $(op(X_1))$, binary $(op(X_1, X_2))$, or n-nary $(op(X_1, \ldots, X_n))$, where op is a hybrid algebra operator and each X_i is a hybrid operand, (ii) if F_1 is a hybrid algebra expression, then $F = op(X_1, \ldots, X_m, F_1)$ is a hybrid algebra expression, and (iii) if F_1 and F_2 are two hybrid algebra expressions, then $F_1 \wedge F_2$, $F_1 \vee F_2$, $\neg F_1$ and (F_1) are hybrid algebra expressions.*

In our motivating example, the spatial query is to retrieve the boundaries of administrative maps and overlaid results of vegetation maps and population maps under certain conditions from the hybrid relation Map. Each spatial query is composed of one or more atomic spatial queries, or $p = \{q_1, \ldots, q_n\}$, which is defined as follows:

Definition 2 *Atomic Spatial Query. Given a spatial query p, an atomic spatial query q is a component query within p, which is a hybrid algebra expression aF such that it contains only a single spatial operator sop.*

An atomic spatial query essentially is nothing but an atomic formula that serves as the smallest unit for the spatial operation cost measurement purpose. In addition, an atomic spatial query q can be composed of two parts, the spatial part and the non-spatial part. The spatial part includes a single well-defined spatial operator, and the non-spatial part could include the traditional selection-projection-join operations, comparison operations and aggregate operations. For each q, if we want to construct a preview for it, we need to perform spatial projection defined as follows:

Definition 3 *Spatial Projection. Let q be an atomic spatial query. The spatial projection of q, denoted as q^s, has only spatial operators.*

Essentially, a spatial projection of an atomic spatial query is computed by simply removing all non-spatial operations as well as all the operands associated with these operators. It comprises of only one spatial operation since by definition, the preview contains one spatial operation to begin with.

3   The Universal Composite Lattice

In this section, we define the Universal Composite Lattice (UCL), which captures the hierarchical relationships among all the possible queries in a given spatial data warehouse. UCL is essentially constructed by composing all its dimension hierarchies together. We first introduce a single dimension hierarchy.

3.1   The Single Dimension Hierarchy

For any given data warehouse, each attribute or dimension may vary from more general to more specific; the relationships thus mapped are called the dimension hierarchies or attribute concept hierarchies. Now we formally define the single dimension hierarchy, following the lines in [1].

Definition 4 *Single Dimension Hierarchy. Given an attribute d, we say there exists an edge from node h_i to node h_j, $h_i \rightarrow h_j$, in the dimension hierarchy H of d, if h_i is a more general concept than h_j, denoted as $h_i > h_j$.*

Here h_i and h_j are two nodes in the dimension hierarchy of d. Generally an attribute could have as many nodes as the user specified to capture the relationships among the different levels of the generalization of the dimension. The resultant dimension hierarchy may be a partial order. In figure 1, we present this single dimension hierarchy for each metadata. The concept hierarchy provides a basic framework for the query dependency relationship. Given two nodes h_i and h_j in H, we say there exists a dependency relationship between h_i and h_j if there exists $h_i \rightarrow h_j$. The dependency relationship indicates that the query represented at node h_i can be built by that represented at h_j. In other words, if one materializes the view at h_j, the query at h_i can be answered by simply generalizing the view at h_j. For example, we could generate a map of a country by combining maps of each state in that country, hence we say the query on the country depends on the query on the states. In this way, we can use the lower level query result to answer higher level queries instead of computing from scratch, which has been demonstrated to be an efficient query optimization technique [1].

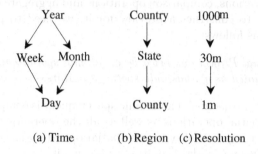

(a) Time   (b) Region   (c) Resolution

Fig. 1. The single dimension hierarchy

3.2   The Universal Composite Lattice

The Universal Composite Lattice (UCL) is built by integrating all the dimension concept hierarchies from a set of attribute domains $D = \{d_1, \ldots, d_k\}$. Therefore, we can use the UCL to represent the hierarchical relationships for all the queries in this data warehouse, and any input query can be mapped into this composite lattice and be evaluated based on its sub-queries. Suppose N_i be the set of nodes in the dimension hierarchy of d_i. Assuming a spatial data warehouse comprises of dimensions $D = \{d_1, \ldots, d_k\}$ of the spatial measures, then the UCL could at most have $(N_1 \times \ldots \times N_k)$ nodes. We define a universal composite lattice as follows.

Definition 5 *Universal Composite Lattice. Let $D = \{d_1, \ldots, d_k\}$ be the set of dimensions in SDW. Each node u in UCL is of the form $u = (n_1, \ldots, n_k)$ such that $n_1 \in N_1$ or null , $n_2 \in N_2$ or null, ..., $n_k \in N_k$ or null. There exists an edge $u_i \rightarrow u_j$, iff every $n_{ik} > n_{jk}$.*

Essentially, a universal composite lattice (UCL) is a directed graph that describes the query dependency relationships for a given spatial data warehouse. Every node in UCL is comprised of at least one node from the each dimension hierarchy or a null. The edge in UCL, as in the single dimension hierarchy represents that the higher level view represented by that node can be constructed from lower level views. Figure 2 shows the UCL constructed by combining the three dimension hierarchies of in figure 1. For the sake of simplicity, we have used the total order for the Time dimension. Generally, for any data warehouse, one can construct such a lattice to indicate the dependency relationships among different queries. The big advantage of this lattice is that every atomic spatial query can be mapped to some node on UCL. We call such mapping process *UCL instantiation*. We will introduce our notion of previews and how UCL instantiation help us to exploit the existing views when computing certain queries on-the-fly.

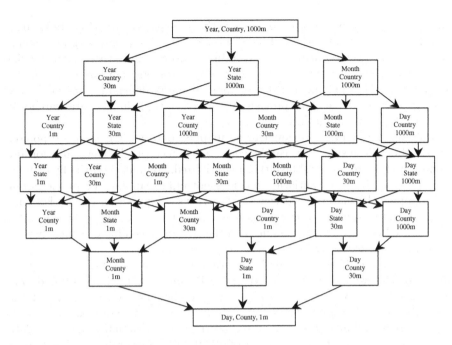

Fig. 2. A sample universal composite lattice

4   The Preview

Essentially, the preview of an atomic query comprises of the view of the prepro-
cessed non-spatial part of the query, and the information necessary to compute
the spatial part on-the-fly. As such it maintains pointers to the spatial objects
on which the spatial operation should be performed. In addition, a preview also
exploits the dependency relationships among different previews. A preview is
formally defined as follows:

Definition 6 *Preview. Let q be an atomic spatial query. The preview of q, denoted as pre(q), is a 4-tuple $\langle M, sop, O, V \rangle$, where: (1) M is non-spatial parts
of q, (2) sop is the spatial operator, (3) O is a set of pointers to spatial objects,
and (4) V is a set of pointers to all the sub-views that q depends on.*

By constructing a preview, we need to first do spatial projection of an atomic
spatial query by separating spatial and non-spatial parts. Then we decide if
we need to materialize non-spatial operations of q based on some pre-set cost
threshold r to get M. Or, if the cost is greater than r, we materialize it otherwise
we leave it on the fly. We also keep O, the set of pointers to the spatial objects.
Then we extract spatial operator sop, which will be computed on the fly when
q is executed. Finally we construct the pointer set V which points to all views
or previews at the lower dependent level by instantiating the given UCL.

   For example, in the motivating example, we perform the traditional selection
and projection on q_1 and store $\langle((1995\text{-}2004), \text{ New Jersey, 1m}), (\text{boundary}),$

(ptr1-ptr10)⟩ as its preview $pre(q_1)$, where the non-spatial part $M = \langle$1995-2004, New Jersey, 1m ⟩ is materialized by SPJ operations, the pointers $(ptr_1 - ptr_{10})$ to maps are projected out based on certain conditions. Since there is one spatial operator involved, we put *boundary* in the operator position for the on-the-fly computation. V could include one or more pointers depending on how many sub-views are available. This preview is stored as a tuple in the data warehouse for further query evaluations.

Now we show how a preview can be mapped onto a UCL, and the pointer set pointing to the sub-views can be constructed accordingly. Generally, for any atomic spatial query, it will be either materialized, computed on-the-fly or built for a preview. UCL instantiation includes not only mapping the previews but also mapping the materialized views or the views computed on-the-fly. For simplicity, we only show mapping a preview onto UCL, and other mappings of a materialized view or a view computed on-the-fly can be conducted similarly with straightforward extensions.

As we introduced before, an SDW comprises of a dimension set $(d_1, \ldots, d_k)$ with dimension hierarchies set $(N_1, \ldots, N_k)$ for each dimension. Each specific node $u = (n_1, \ldots, n_k)(n_i \in N_i, i = 1, \ldots, k)$ has corresponding actual values stored in the base tables of the data warehouse, which is denoted as VL_i. For example, Year is one hierarchy in dimension Time, and its corresponding actual value in the data warehouse is a complete set or subset of (1980-2005). Generally, we denote $u = VL_i(i = 1, \ldots, k)$ iff VL_i is the set of actual values associated to u. For example, in the figure 2, ⟨Year, State, resolution ⟩ = ⟨(1995-2004), New Jersey, 1m ⟩. Given a UCL, a simple linear search algorithm can map a preview of an atomic spatial query q, denoted as $pre(q)$, onto a given UCL (omitted due to space limit).

This algorithm basically performs linear search from the lowest level node to the highest level node in the UCL, and see if the M of a $pre(q)$ includes the actual hierarchy values of certain node. If we find this match, we add a pointer from that node to the $pre(q)$. Therefore we map a preview to an actual node in the UCL. In addition to the previews, we assume the materialized views and views that computed on-the-fly are also mapped onto the UCL, which instantiate the UCL for a spatial data warehouse. Hence if there are any materialized views or previews mapped there, we add a pointer from $pre(q_1)$ to those lower level views, or sub-views. Basically, $V = (t_1, \ldots, t_n)$ where $(t_i, i \in (1, n))$ is a pointer to one sub-view of $pre(q_1)$.

5   Related Work

A lot of work has been done in the area of optimizing cost of a data warehouse. Most of their work deal with selective materialization to reduce the total cost. In the initial research done on the view selection problem, Harinarayan et al. in [2] present algorithms for the view-selection problem in data cubes under a disk-space constraint. Gupta et al. extend their work to include indexes in [3]. Stefanovic et al. in [4] introduce the spatial data warehouse concept and object based selective materialization techniques for construction of spatial data cubes.

Karlo et al. [5] show that the variation of the view-selection problem where the goal is to optimize the query cost is inapproximable for general partial orders. Furthermore, Chirkova et al. in [6,7] show that the number of views involved in an optimal solution for the view-selection problem may be exponential in the size of the database schema, when the query optimizer has good estimates of the sizes of the views. Besides the theoretical research, there has been a substantial amount of effort on developing heuristics for the view-selection problem that may work well in practice. Kalnis et al. in [8] show that randomized search methods provide near-optimal solutions and can easily be adapted to various versions of the problem, including existence of size and time constraints. Recently, certain works have been done on how to materialize views for some specific systems or to answer queries more efficiently. Specifically, Karenos et al in [9] propose view materialization techniques to deal with mobile computing services, Liu et al in [10] compare two view materialization approaches for medical data to improve query efficiency, Theodoratos et al [11,12,13] build a search space for view selections to deal with evolving data warehousing systems, and Wu et al in [14] work on Web data to rewrite queries using materialized views.

However, all of their methods fall into two categories, i.e. either materialize a view or compute it on the fly. Our work presented in this paper differs from the above works in that given the specialty of spatial operations involved in a query, we design a third technique, *preview*, between view materialization and on-the-fly computation, which delivers a provably good solution with cost minimization for a spatial query and eventually a whole spatial data warehouse.

6 Conclusions

A spatial data warehouse integrates alphanumeric data and spatial data from multiple distributed information sources. Compared to traditional cases, a spatial data warehouse has a distinguished feature in that both the view materialization cost and the on-the-fly cost are extremely high, which is due to the fact that spatial data are larger in size and spatial operations are more expensive to process. Therefore, the traditional way of selectively materializing certain views while computing others on the fly does not solve the problem of spatial views.

In this paper we have dealt with the issue of minimizing the total cost of a spatial data warehouse while at the same time improve the query response time by considering their inter-dependent relationships. We first use a motivation example in realistic query scenarios to demonstrate the cost savings of building a preview. We then formally define preview, for which both the materialization and on-the-fly costs are significantly reduced. Specifically, a preview pre-processes the non-spatial part of the query, leaves the spatial operation on the fly, and maintains pointers to the spatial data. In addition, we show that a preview exploits the hierarchical relationships among the different views by maintaining a Universal Composite Lattice built on dimension hierarchies, and mapping each view onto it. We optimally decompose a spatial query into three components, the preview part, the materialized view part and the on-the-fly part, so that the total cost is minimized.

References

1. Han, J., Kamber, M. In: Data Mining: Concepts and Techniques. 1 edn. Morgan Kaufman Publishers (2001)
2. Harinarayan, V., Rajaraman, A., Ullman, J.: Implementing data cubes efficiently. In: Proc. of SIGMOD. Lecture Notes in Computer Science, Springer (1996) 205–216
3. Gupta, H., Mumick, I.: Selection of views to materialize in a data warehouse. Transactions of Knowledge and Data Engineering (TKDE) **17** (2005) 24–43
4. Stefanovic, N., Jan, J., Koperski, K.: Object-based selective materialization for efficient implementation of spatial data cubes. IEEE Transactions on Knowledge and Data Engineering(TKDE) **12** (2000) 938–958
5. Karlo, H., Mihail, M.: On the complexity of the view-selection problem. In: Proc. of Principles of Databases. Lecture Notes in Computer Science, Springer (1999)
6. Chirkova, R.: The view selection problem has an exponential bound for conjunctive queries and views. In: Proc. of ACM Symposium on Principles of Database Systems. (2002)
7. Chirkova, R., Halevy, A., Suciu, D.: A formal perspective on the view selection problem. In: Proc. of Internaltional Conference on Very Large Database Systems. (2001)
8. Kalnis, P., Mamoulis, N., Papadias, D.: View selection using randomized search. Data and Knowledge Engineering(DKE) **42** (2002)
9. Karenos, K., Samaras, G., Chrysanthis, P., Pitoura, E.: Mobile agent-based services for view materialization. ACM SIGMOBILE Mobile Computing and Communications Review **8** (2004)
10. Liu, Z., Chrysanthis, P., Tsui, F.: A comparison of two view materialization approaches for disease surveillance system. In: Proc. of SAC. Lecture Notes in Computer Science, Springer (2004)
11. Theodoratos, D., Ligoudistianos, S., Sellis, T.: View selection for designing the global data warehouse. Data and Knowledge Engineering (DKE) **39** (2001)
12. Theodoratos, D., Sellis, T.: Dynamic data warehouse design. In: Proc. of Data Warehousing and Knowledge Discovery. Lecture Notes in Computer Science, Springer (1999)
13. Theodoratos, D., Xu, W.: Constructing search spaces for materialized view selection. In: Proc. of the 7th ACM International Workshop on Data Warehousing and OLAP. Lecture Notes in Computer Science, Springer (2004)
14. Wu, W., Ozsoyoglu, Z.: Rewriting xpath queries using materialized views. In: Proc. of the Intl. Conference on Very Large Database Systems. Lecture Notes in Computer Science, Springer (2005)

Preprocessing for Fast Refreshing Materialized Views in DB2

Wugang Xu[1], Calisto Zuzarte[2], Dimitri Theodoratos[1], and Wenbin Ma[2]

[1] New Jersey Institute of Technology
wx2@njit.edu, dth@cs.njit.edu
[2] IBM Canada Ltd.
calisto, wenbinm@ca.ibm.com

Abstract. Materialized views (MVs) are used in databases and data warehouses to greatly improve query performance. In this context, a great challenge is to exploit commonalities among the views and to employ multi-query optimization techniques in order to derive an efficient global evaluation plan for refreshing the MVs concurrently. $IBM\ DB2^{®}\ Universal\ Database^{TM}$ (DB2 UDB) provides two query matching techniques, query stacking and query sharing, to exploit commonalities among the MVs, and to construct an efficient global evaluation plan. When the number of MVs is large, memory and time restrictions prevent us from using both query matching techniques in constructing efficient global plans. We suggest an approach that applies the query stacking and query sharing techniques in different steps. The query stacking technique is applied first, and the outcome is exploited to define groups of MVs. The number of MVs in each group is restricted. This allows the query sharing technique to be applied only within groups in a second step. Finally, the query stacking technique is used again to determine an efficient global evaluation plan. An experimental evaluation shows that the execution time of the plan generated by our approach is very close to that of the plan generated using both query matching techniques without restriction. This result is valid no matter how big the database is.

1 Introduction

The advent of data warehouses and of large databases for decision support has triggered interesting research in the database community. With decision support data warehouses getting larger and decision support queries getting more complex, the traditional query optimization techniques which compute answers from the base tables can not meet the stringent response time requirements. The most frequent solution used for this problem is to store a number of materialized views (MVs). Query answers are computed using these materialized views instead of using the base tables exclusively. Materialized views are manually or automatically selected based on the underlying schema and database statistics so that the frequent and long running queries can benefit from them. These queries are rewritten using the materialized views prior to their execution. Experience with the TPC-D benchmark and several customer applications has shown that MVs can often improve the response time of decision support queries by orders of magnitude [9]. This performance advantage is so big that TPC-D [1] had ceased to be an effective performance discriminator after the introduction of the systematic use of MVs [9].

A Min Tjoa and J. Trujillo (Eds.): DaWaK 2006, LNCS 4081, pp. 55–64, 2006.

Although this technique brings a great performance improvement, it also brings some new problems. The first one is the selection of a set of views to materialize in order to minimize the execution time of the frequent queries while satisfying a number of constraints. This is a typical data warehouse design problem. In fact, different versions of this problem have been addressed up to now. One can consider different optimization goals (e.g. minimizing the combination of the query evaluation and view maintenance cost) and different constraints (e.g. MV maintenance cost restrictions, MV space restrictions etc.). A general framework for addressing those problems is suggested in [7]. Nevertheless, polynomial time solutions are not expected for this type of problem. A heuristic algorithm to select both MVs and indexes in a unified way has been suggested in [10]. This algorithm has been implemented in the IBM DB2 design advisor [10].

The second problem is how to rewrite a query using a set of views. A good review of this issue is provided in [3]. Deciding whether a query can be answered using MVs is an NP-hard problem even for simple classes of queries. However, exact algorithms for special cases and heuristic approaches allow us to cope with this problem. A novel algorithm that rewrites a user query using one or more of the available MVs is presented in [9]. This algorithm exploits the graph representation for queries and views (*Query Graph Model - QGM*) used internally in DB2. It can deal with complex queries and views (e.g. queries involving grouping and aggregation and nesting) and has been implemented in the IBM DB2 design advisor.

The third problem is related to the maintenance of the MVs [5]. The MVs often have to be refreshed immediately after a bulk update of the underlying base tables, or periodically by the administrator, to synchronize the data. Depending on the requirements of the applications, it may not be necessary to have the data absolutely synchronized. The MVs can be refreshed incrementally or recomputed from scratch. In this paper we focus on the latter approach for simplicity. When one or more base tables are modified, several MVs may be affected. The technique of multi-query optimization [6] can be used to detect common subexpressions [8] among the definitions of the MVs and to rewrite the views using these common subexpressions. Using this technique one can avoid computing complex expressions more than once.

An algorithm for refreshing multiple MVs in IBM DB2 is suggested in [4]. This algorithm exploits a graph representation for multiple queries (called *global QGM*) constructed using two query matching techniques: query stacking and query sharing. Query stacking detects subsumption relationships between query or view definitions, while query sharing artificially creates common subexpressions which can be exploited by two or more queries or MVs. Oracle 10g also provides an algorithm for refreshing a set of MVs based on the dependencies among MVs [2]. This algorithm considers refreshing one MV using another one which has already been refreshed. This method is similar to the query stacking technique used in DB2. However, it does not consider using common subsumers for optimizing the refresh process (a technique that corresponds to query sharing used in DB2). This means they may miss the optimal evaluation plan.

When there are only few MVs to be refreshed, we can apply the method proposed in [4] to refresh all MVs together. This method considers both query stacking and query sharing techniques, and a globally optimized refresh plan is generated. However when the number of MVs gets larger, a number of problems prevent us from applying this method.

The first problem relates to the generation of a global plan. When there are many MVs to be refreshed, too much memory is required for constructing a global QGM using both query sharing and query stacking techniques. Further, it may take a lot of time to find an optimal global plan from the global QGM. The second problem relates to the execution of the refresh plan. There are several system issues here. The process of refreshing MVs usually takes a long time, since during this period, MVs are locked. User queries which use some MVs either have to wait for all MVs to be refreshed, or routed to the base tables. Either solution will increase the execution time. Another system issue relates to the limited size of the statement heap which is used to compile a given database statement. When a statement is too complex and involves a very large number of referenced base tables or MVs considered for matching, there may not be enough memory to compile and optimize the statement. One more system issue relates to transaction control. When many MVs are refreshed at the same time (with a single statement), usually a large transaction log is required. This is not always feasible. Further if something goes wrong during the refreshing, the whole process has to start over.

To deal with the problems above, we propose the following approach. When too many MVs need to be refreshed and the construction of a global QGM based on query stacking and query sharing together is not feasible, we partition the MV set into smaller groups based on query stacking alone. Then, we apply query sharing to each group independently. Consequently, we separate the execution plan into smaller ones, each involving fewer MVs. Intuitively, by partitioning MVs into smaller groups, we apply query sharing only within groups and query stacking between groups such that MVs from the lower groups are potentially exploited by the groups above. An implementation and experimental evaluation of our approach shows that our method has comparable performance to the approach that uses a globally optimized evaluation plan while at the same time avoiding the aforementioned problems.

In the next section, we present the QGM model and the two query matching techniques. Section 3 introduces our MV partition strategy. Section 4 presents our experimental setting and results. We conclude and suggest future work in Section 5.

2   Query Graph Model and Query Matching

In this section, we introduce the concept of QGM model which is used in DB2 to graphically represent queries. We first introduce the QGM model for a single query. Then we extend it to a global QGM model for multiple queries. This extension requires the concept of query matching using both query stacking and query sharing techniques.

2.1   Query Graph Model

The QGM model is the internal graph representation for queries in the DB2 database management system. It is used in all steps of query optimization in DB2: parsing and semantic checking, query rewriting transformation and plan optimization. Here, we show with an example how queries are represented in the QGM model. A query in the QGM model is represented by a set of boxes (called *Query Table Boxes – QTBs*) and arcs between them. A QTB represents a view or a base table. Typical QTBs are *select* QTBs and *group-by* QTBs. Other kinds of QTBs include the *union* and the *outer-join* QTBs.

Below, we give a query with *select* and *group-by* operations in SQL. Figure 1 shows a simplified QGM representation for this query.

```
select c.c3, d.d3, sum(f.f3) as sum
from c, d, fact f
where c.c1 =f.f1 and d.d1 = f.f2 and
      c.c2 = 'Mon' and d.d2 > 10
group by c.c3,d.d3
having sum > 100
```

2.2   Query Matching

To refresh multiple MVs concurrently, a global QGM for all of the MVs is generated using the definitions tied together loosely at the top. All QTBs are grouped into different levels with the base tables belonging to the bottom level. Then, from bottom to top, each QTB is compared with another QTB to examine whether one can be rewritten using the other. If this is the case, we say that the latter QTB *subsumes* the former QTB. The latter QTB is called the *subsumer* QTB while the former is called the *subsumee* QTB. A rewriting of the subsumee QTB using the subsumer QTB may also be generated at the time of matching, and this aditional work is called *compensation*. The comparison continues with the parent QTBs of both the sumsumer and subsumee QTBs. This process continues until no more matches can be made.

If the top QTB of one MV subsumes some QTB of another MV, then the former MV subsumes the latter MV. This kind of matching is called *query stacking* because it ultimately determines that one MV can be rewritten using the other and the subsumee MV can be "stacked" on the subsumer MV.

In some cases, it is possible that we may not find a strict subsumption relationship between two MVs even if they are quite close to having one. For instance, a difference in the projected attributes of two otherwise equivalent MVs will make the matching fail. The matching technique of DB2 is extended in [4] to deal with this case. In some cases when there is no subsumption relationship between two MVs, an artificially built common subexpression (called *common subsumer*) can be constructed such that both

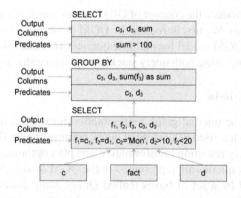

Fig. 1. QGM graph for query Q_1

MVs can be rewritten using this common subsumer. Because this common subsumer is "shared" by both MVs, this matching technique is called *query sharing*. With query sharing, matching techniques can be applied to a wider class of MVs.

In Figure 2, we show examples of query matching techniques. In Figure 2(a), we show the matching using query stacking only. In this example, we have three queries m_0, m_1, m_2. For each query pair, we match their QTBs from bottom to top until the top QTB of the subsumer query is reached. Since there is a successful matching of the top QTB of query m_1 with some QTB of query m_2, there is a subsumption relationship from m_1 to m_2 (m_1 subsumes m_2). This is not the case with queries m_0 and m_1. The matching process defines a query *subsumption DAG* shown in Figure 2(a). In this DAG, each node is a query. Since query m_1 subsumes query m_2, we draw a directed line from m_1 to m_2. In Figure 2(a), we show the subsumption DAG for queries m_0, m_1 and m_2. There is one subsumption edge from m_1 to m_2 while query m_0 is a disconnected component. This subsumption DAG can be used to optimize the concurrent execution of the three queries. For example, we can compute the results of m_0 and m_1 from base tables. Then, we can compute query m_2 using m_1 based on the rewriting of m_2 using m_1, instead of computing it using exclusively base tables. Query m_2 is "stacked" on m_1 since it has to be computed after m_1.

In this example, we also observe that although m_2 can be rewritten using m_1, we cannot rewrite m_0 using m_2 or vise versa. We cannot even find a successful match of the bottom QTBs of m_0 and m_2 based on query stacking. This is quite common in practice. When we try to answer m_0 and m_2 together, and we cannot find a subsumption relationship between them, we can try to create a new query, say t_1, which can be used to answer both queries m_0 and m_2. This newly constructed query is called *common subsumer* of the two queries m_0 and m_2 because it is constructed in a way so that both queries m_0 and m_2 can be rewritten using it. Although the common subsumer is not a user query to be answered, we can find its answer and then use it to compute the answers of both queries m_0 and m_2. As a "common part" between m_0 and m_2, t_1 is computed only once, and therefore, its computation might bring some benefit in the concurrent execution of m_0 and m_2. In the example of Figure 2(b), there is no subsumption edge between m_0 and m_2. However, after adding a common subsumer t_1 of m_0 and m_2, we have two subsumption edges: one from t_1 to m_0 and one from t_1 to m_2.

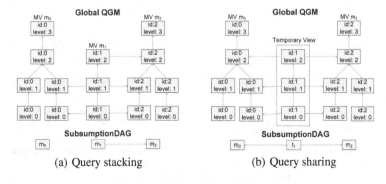

(a) Query stacking   (b) Query sharing

Fig. 2. Query matching

The subsumption relationship graph is a DAG because there is no cycle in it. In most cases, if one MV subsumes another one, the latter one cannot subsume the former one. Nevertheless in some cases, two or more MVs may subsume each other, thus generating a subsumption cycle. The DB2 matching techniques will ignore one subsumption relationship randomly, when this happens, to break any cycles. This will guarantee the result subsumption graph to be a real DAG. In drawing a subsumption DAG, if $m_1 \rightarrow m_2$, and $m_2 \rightarrow m_3$, we don't show in the DAG the transitive subsumption edge $m_1 \rightarrow m_3$. However, this subsumption relationship can be directly derived from the DAG, and it is of the same importance as the other subsumption relationships in optimizing the computation of the queries.

3   Group Partition Strategy

If there are too many MVs to be refreshed then, as we described above, we may not be able to construct the global QGM using both query stacking and query sharing techniques. Our goal is to partition the given MV set into groups that are small enough so that both query matching techniques can be applied, and we do not face the problems mentioned in the introduction. Our approach first creates a subsumption DAG using query stacking only which is a much less memory and time consuming process. This subsumption DAG is used for generating an optimal global evaluation plan. The different levels of this plan determine groups of materialized views on which query sharing is applied.

3.1   Building an Optimal Plan Using Query Stacking

Given a set of MVs to be refreshed, we construct a global QGM using only query stacking and then create a subsumption DAG as described in Section 2.2. Then, we have the query optimizer choose an optimal plan for computing each MV using either exclusively base relations or using other MVs in addition to base tables as appropriate. The compensations stored in the global QGM of a MV using other MVs are used to support this task. The optimizer decides whether using a MV to compute another MV

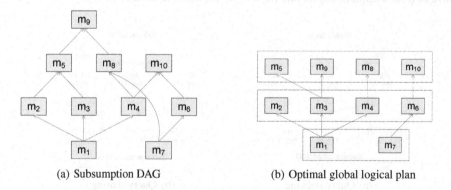

(a) Subsumption DAG   (b) Optimal global logical plan

Fig. 3. Query stacking based refreshing

is beneficial when compared to computing it from the base relations. These optimal "local" plans define an optimal global plan for refreshing all the queries. Figure 3(a) shows an example of a subsumption DAG for ten MVs. Transitive edges are ignored for clarity of presentation. Figure 3(b) shows an optimal global evaluation plan.

Groups are defined by the views in the optimal plan. If one group is still too big for the query sharing technique to be applied, we can divide it into suitable subgroups heuristically based on some common objects and operations within the group or possibly randomly.

3.2 Adding also Query Sharing

By considering the query stacking technique only, we may miss some commonalities between queries which can be beneficial to the refreshing process. Therefore, we enable both query matching techniques within each group to capture most of those commonalities. We outline this process below.

1. We apply query stacking and query sharing techniques to the MVs of each group. Even though no subsumption edges will be added between MVs in the group, some common subsumers may be identified and new subsumption edges will be added from those common subsumers to MVs in the group.
2. We apply the query stacking technique to the common subsumers of one group and the MVs of lower groups. Lower groups are those that comprise MVs from lower levels of the optimal global plan. This step might add some new subsumption edges from MVs to common subsumers in the subsumption DAG.
3. Using a common subsumer induces additional view materialization cost. However, if this cost is lower than the gain we obtained in computing the MVs that use this common subsumer, it is beneficial to materialize this common subsumer. We call such a common subsumer candidate common subsumer. The use of a candidate common subsumer may prevent the use of other candidate common subsumers. We heuristically retain those candidate common subsumers such that no one of them prevents the use of the others and together yield the highest benefit. This process is applied from the bottom level to the top level in the subsumption DAG.
4. We have the optimizer create a new optimal global plan using the retained candidate common subsumers. Compared to the optimal global plan constructed using only query stacking, this optimal global plan contains also some new MVs, in the form of the retained candidate common subsumers.

During the refreshing of the MVs, a common subsumer is first materialized when it is used for refreshing another MV and it is discarded when the last MV that uses it has been refreshed.

In Figure 4, we show the construction of an optimal global plan taking also query sharing into account. Figure 4(a) shows the subsumption DAG of Figure 4(b) along with some common subsumers. Dotted directed edges indicate subsumption edges involving common subsumers. Among the candidate common subsumers, some of them are retained in the optimal global plan. Such an optimal global plan is shown in Figure 4(b). This optimal global plan will have a better performance than the one of Figure 3(b).

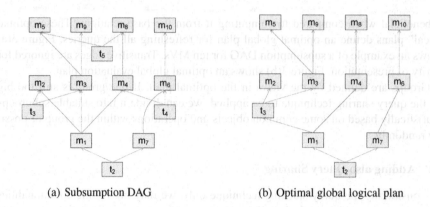

(a) Subsumption DAG   (b) Optimal global logical plan

Fig. 4. Query sharing based refreshing

4   Performance Test

For the experimental evaluation we consider a database with a star schema. We also consider a number of MVs to be refreshed (16 in our test). We keep the number of MVs small enough so that, in finding an optimal global evaluation plan, both the query stacking and query sharing techniques can be applied without restrictions. The performance comparison test is not feasible when we have too many MVs. The goal is to compare the performance of different approaches. We compare the performance of four kinds of MV refreshing approaches for different sizes of databases. These approaches are as follows:

1. *Naive Refreshing(NR):* Refresh each MV one by one by computing its new state using the base tables referrenced in the MV definition exclusively. This approach disallows any multi-query optimization technique or other already refreshed MV exploitation.
2. *Stacking-Based Refreshing(STR):* Refresh each MV one by one in the topological order induced by the optimal global plan constructed using the query stacking technique only. (for example, the optimal global plan of Figure 3(b)) in our example. This approach disallows query sharing. With this approach some MVs are refreshed using the base relations exclusively. Some other MVs are refreshed using other MVs if they have a rewriting using those MVs that are in lower groups in the optimal global plan.
3. *Group-Sharing-Based Refreshing(SHR):* Refresh each MV in the topological order induced by the optimal global evaluation plan constructed using query stacking first and then query sharing only within groups (for example, the optimal global plan of Figure 4(b)).
4. *Unrestricted-Sharing-Based Refreshing(USR):* Refresh all MVs based on an optimal global plan constructed using, without restrictions, both query matching techniques.

Our test schema consists of one fact table and three dimension tables. Each dimension table has 10,000 tuples, while the number of tuples of the fact table varies from 100,000 to 10,000,000. We refresh the set of MVs with each one of the four refreshing approaches mentioned above, and we measure the overall refreshing time. We run our performance test on a machine with the following configuration.

$Model$	OS	$Memory$	$CPUs$	$rPerf$	$Database$
P640-B80	AIX 5.2 ML06	8 GB	4	3.59	DB2 V91

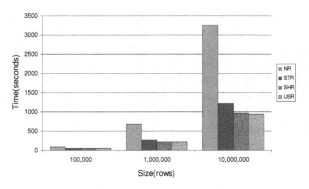

Fig. 5. Performance test result for different refreshing method

Figure 5 shows our experimental results. The unrestricted-sharing-based approach always has the best performance since it allows unrestricted application of both query stacking and query sharing techniques. The group-sharing-based approach has the second best performance because, even though it exploits both query matching techniques, they are considered separately in different steps and query sharing is restricted only within groups. The stacking-based approach is the next in performance because it cannot take advantage of the query sharing technique. Finally, far behind in performance is the naive approach which does not profit of any query matching technique. As we can see in Figure 5 the group-sharing based approach is very close to the unrestricted sharing approach. This remark is valid for all database sizes and the difference in those two approaches remains insignificant. In contrast, the difference between the naive and the pure stacked approach compared to other two grows significantly as the size of the database increases. In a real data warehouse, it is often the case that MVs have indexes defined on them. The group-sharing-based refresh may outdo the unrestricted approach if there is occasion to exploit the indexes of MVs when used by the refreshing of the higher group MVs.

5   Conclusion and Future Work

We have addressed the problem of refreshing concurrently multiple MVs. In this context, two query matching techniques, query stacking and query sharing, are used in DB2 to exploit commonalities among the MVs, and to construct an efficient global evaluation plan. When the number of MVs is large, memory and time restrictions prevent us from using both query matching techniques in constructing efficient global plans. We have suggested an approach that applies the two techniques in different steps. The query stacking technique is applied first, and the generated subsumption DAG is used to define groups of MVs. The number of MVs in each group is smaller than the total number of MVs. This will allow the query sharing technique to be applied only within groups in a second step. Finally, the query stacking technique is used again to determine an efficient global evaluation plan. An experimental evaluation shows that the execution time of the optimal global plan generated by our approach is very close to that of the optimal global plan generated using, without restriction, both query matching techniques. This result is valid no matter how big the database is.

Our approach can be further fine-tuned to deal with the case where the groups of MVs turn out to be too small. In this case, merging smaller groups into bigger ones may further enhance the potential for applying the query sharing technique. Although we assume complete repopulation of all MVs in our approach for simplicity, we can actually apply our approach to incremental refreshing of MVs. In a typical data warehouse application, there usually exist indexes on MVs. Our approach can be extended to adapt to this scenario. Actually, because the existence of indexes increases the complexity of the global QGM, our approach may achieve better performance.

References

1. *TPC (Transaction Processing Performance Council) Web Site: http://www.tpc.org.*
2. Nathan Folkert, Abhinav Gupta, Andrew Witkowski, Sankar Subramanian, Srikanth Bellamkonda, Shrikanth Shankar, Tolga Bozkaya, and Lei Sheng. Optimizing Refresh of a Set of Materialized Views. In *Proceedings of the 31st International Conference on Very Large Data Bases, Trondheim, Norway, August 30 - September 2, 2005*, pages 1043–1054, 2005.
3. Alon Y. Halevy. Answering Queries Using Views: A survey. *VLDB J.*, 10(4):270–294, 2001.
4. Wolfgang Lehner, Roberta Cochrane, Hamid Pirahesh, and Markos Zaharioudakis. fAST Refresh Using Mass Query Optimization. In *Proceedings of the 17th International Conference on Data Engineering, April 2-6, 2001, Heidelberg, Germany*, pages 391–398, 2001.
5. Wolfgang Lehner, Richard Sidle, Hamid Pirahesh, and Roberta Cochrane. Maintenance of automatic summary tables. In *Proceedings of the 2000 ACM SIGMOD International Conference on Management of Data, May 16-18, 2000, Dallas, Texas, USA.*, pages 512–513, 2000.
6. Timos K. Sellis. Multiple-Query Optimization. *ACM Trans. Database Syst.*, 13(1):23–52, 1988.
7. Dimitri Theodoratos and Mokrane Bouzeghoub. A General Framework for the View Selection Problem for Data Warehouse Design and Evolution. In *DOLAP 2000, ACM Seventh International Workshop on Data Warehousing and OLAP, Washington, DC, USA, November 10, 2000, Proceedings*,
   pages 1–8, 2000.
8. Dimitri Theodoratos and Wugang Xu. Constructing Search Spaces for Materialized View Selection. In *DOLAP 2004, ACM Seventh International Workshop on Data Warehousing and OLAP, Washington, DC, USA, November 12-13, 2004, Proceedings*, pages 112–121, 2004.
9. Markos Zaharioudakis, Roberta Cochrane, George Lapis, Hamid Pirahesh, and Monica Urata. Answering complex sql queries using automatic summary tables. In *Proceedings of the 2000 ACM SIGMOD International Conference on Management of Data, May 16-18, 2000, Dallas, Texas, USA.*, pages 105–116, 2000.
10. Daniel C. Zilio, Calisto Zuzarte, Sam Lightstone, Wenbin Ma, Guy M. Lohman, Roberta Cochrane, Hamid Pirahesh, Latha S. Colby, Jarek Gryz, Eric Alton, Dongming Liang, and Gary Valentin. Recommending Materialized Views and Indexes with IBM DB2 Design Advisor. In *1st International Conference on Autonomic Computing (ICAC 2004), 17-19 May 2004, New York, NY, USA*, pages 180–188, 2004.

Trademarks

A Multiversion-Based Multidimensional Model

Franck Ravat, Olivier Teste, and Gilles Zurfluh

IRIT (UMR 5505)
118, Route de Narbonne
F-31062 Toulouse cedex 04 (France)
{ravat, teste, zurfluh}@irit.fr

Abstract. This paper addresses the problem of how to specify changes in multidimensional databases. These changes may be motivated by evolutions of user requirements as well as changes of operational sources. The multiversion-based multidimensional model we provide supports both data and structure changes. The approach consists in storing star versions according to relevant structure changes whereas data changes are recorded through dimension instances and fact instances in a star version. The model is able to integrate mapping functions to populate multiversion-based multidimensional databases.

1 Introduction

On-Line Analytical Processing (OLAP) has emerged to support multidimensional data analysis by providing manipulations through aggregations of data drawn from various transactional databases. This approach is often based on a Multidimensional DataBase (MDB). A MDB schema [1] is composed of a fact (subject of analysis) and dimensions (axes of analysis). A fact contains indicators or measures. A measure is the data item of interest. As mentioned in [2], fact data reflect the dynamic aspect whereas dimension data represent more static information. However, sources (transactional databases) may evolve and these changes have an impact on structures and contents of the MDB built on them. In the same way, user requirement evolutions may induce schema changes; *eg.* to create a new dimension or a new "dimension member" [3], to add a new measure,... Changes occur on dimensions as well as facts.

This paper addresses the problem of how to specify changes in a MDB. The changes may be related to contents as well as schema structures. Our work is not limited to represent the mapping data into the most recent version of the schema. We intend to keep trace of changes of multidimensional structures.

1.1 Related Works and Discussion

As mentioned in [3, 4], the approaches to manage changes in a MDB can be classified into two categories.

The first one, also called "updating model" in [1], provides a pragmatic way of handling changes of schema and data. The approaches in this first category support only the most recent MDB version of the schema and its instances. However, working with the latest version of a MDB hides the existence of changes [3]. This category regroups the following works [5, 6, 7].

A Min Tjoa and J. Trujillo (Eds.): DaWaK 2006, LNCS 4081, pp. 65 – 74, 2006.
© Springer-Verlag Berlin Heidelberg 2006

In the approaches from the second category called "tracking history approaches", changes to a MDB schema are time-stamped in order to create temporal versions. [3] provides an approach for tracking history and comparing data mapped into versions. Their conceptual model builds a multiversion fact table and structural change operators. The proposed mechanism uses one central fact table for storing all permanent time-stamped versions of data. As a consequence, the set of schema changes is limited, and only changes to dimension structure and "dimension instance structure" named hierarchy are supported [4]. The authors detail the related works of "tracking history approaches" and they focus on a model supporting multiversions; *e.g.* each version represents a MDB state at a time period and it is composed of a schema version and its instances [8]. Their approach is not based on a formal representation of versions and their model supports one single subject of analysis. The provided model also does not integrate extracting functions allowing the population of data warehouse version from time-variant transactional sources.

1.2   Paper Contributions and Paper Outline

We intend to represent multidimensional data in a temporally consistent mode of presentation. Our model has the following features.

- The paper deals with the management of constellation changes. A constellation extends star schemata [1]. A constellation regroups several facts and dimensions. Our model supports complex dimensions, which are organised through one or several hierarchies. A constellation may integrate versions, which represents structural changes.
- Our model must support overlapping versions of MDB parts. Each version representing a subject of analysis (fact) and its axes of analysis (dimensions) is time stamped.
- Our model must integrate mapping functions to populate versions.

The remainder of the paper is organized as follows. Section 2 formally defines our conceptual multiversion model dedicated to MDB. Section 3 presents the mapping functions. Section 4 focuses on the prototype implementation.

2   Multidimensional Database Modelling

The conceptual model we define supports temporal changes using multi-versions. The temporal model is based on discrete and linear temporal model. An instant is a time point on the time line whereas an interval represents the time between two instants. We consider in the model valid-time and transaction-time [9]. The valid-time represents time when the information is valid in the real world whereas transaction-time represents time when the information is recording in the MDB. Note that they are various transaction-times at source level and MDB level. At the MDB level, each extraction provides a transaction time point.

2.1 Constellation and Star Version

The model is a conceptual model near user point of views. A MDB is modelled through a constellation, which is composed of star versions modelling schema changes. Each star version is a snapshot of one fact and its dimensions at an extraction time point.

Definition. A *constellation* C is defined by a set of star versions $\{VS_1,..., VS_U\}$.

Definition. A *star version* $\forall i \in [1..u]$, VS_i is defined by $(VF, \{VD_1,..., VD_V\}, T)$

- VF is a fact version,
- $\forall k \in [1..v]$, VD_k is a dimension version, which is associated to the fact version,
- $T = [T_{Start}, T_{End}]$ is a temporal interval during the star schema version is valid.

Example. The following figure depicts an example of constellation evolutions. At T1 the constellation is composed of two star versions ($VS_{1.1}$ and $VS_{2.1}$). Between times T_1 and T_3, the constellation have one new dimension version noted $VD_{2.1}$, which is associated to a new fact version, noted $VF_{1.2}$. A new dimension version, noted $VD_{3.2}$ is deduced from $VD_{3.1}$. According to the model we provided, this constellation is defined by a set of four star versions $\{VS_{1.1}, VS_{2.1}, VS_{1.2}, VS_{2.2}\}$.

- $VS_{1.1} = (VF_{1.1}, \{VD_{1.1}, VD_{3.1}\}, [T_1,T_3])$
- $VS_{2.1} = (VF_{2.1}, \{VD_{3.1}, VD_{4.1}\}, [T_1,T_3])$
- $VS_{1.2} = (VF_{1.2}, \{VD_{1.1}, VD_{2.1}, VD_{3.2}\}, [T_3,T_{Now}])$
- $VS_{2.2} = (VF_{2.1}, \{VD_{3.2}, VD_{4.1}\}, [T_3,T_{Now}])$

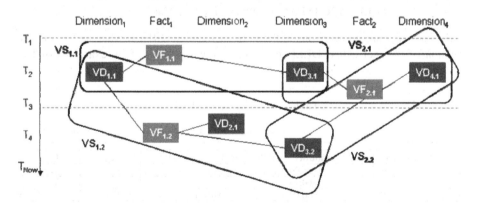

Fig. 1. Example of constellation changes

Note that the model is a multiversion based model because several star versions can be used at a same instant. If source data changes do not require structural change, the current star version is refreshed; *e.g.* new dimension instances and/or fact instances are calculated [10]. If source data changes require structural changes (for example, a hierarchy may be transformed according to new source data), a new star version is defined.

2.2 Star Version Components

Each star version is composed of one fact version and several dimension versions. Each fact version is composed of measures. Each dimension version is composed of properties, which are organised according to one or several hierarchies.

Definition. A *fact version* VF is defined by $(N^{VF}, Int^{VF}, Ext^{VF}, Map^{VF})$

- N^{VF} is the fact name
- $Int^{VF} = \{f_1(m_1),..., f_p(m_p)\}$ is the fact intention, which is defined by a set of measures (or indicators) associated to aggregate functions,
- $Ext^{VF} = \{i^{VF}_1,..., i^{VF}_x\}$ is the fact extension, which is composed of instances. Each fact instance is defined by $\forall k \in [1..x]$, $i^{VF}_k = [m_1:v_1,..., m_p:v_p, id^{VD_1}:id_1,..., id^{VD_v}:id_v, T_{Start}:vt, T_{End}:vt']$ where $m_1:v_1,..., m_p:v_p$ are the measure values, $id^{VD_1}:id_1,..., id^{VD_v}:id_v$ are the linked dimension identifiers and $T_{Start}:vt$, $T_{End}:vt'$ are transaction-time values,
- Map^{VF} is a mapping function, which populates the fact version.

All fact versions having the same fact name (N^{VF}) depict one fact; *eg*. Each fact version represents a state occurring during its lifetime cycle.

Example. The case study is taken from commercial domain. Let us consider the following fact versions:

- $VF_{1.1} = (ORDER, \{SUM(Quantity)\}, Ext^{VF11}, Map^{VF11})$
- $VF_{1.2} = (ORDER, \{SUM(Quantity), SUM(Amount)\}, Ext^{VF12}, Map^{VF12})$
- $VF_{2.1} = (DELIVER, \{SUM(Quantity)\}, Ext^{VF21}, Map^{VF21})$

$VF_{1.1}$ and $VF_{1.2}$ are two versions of the same fact named ORDER whereas $VF_{2.1}$ is one version of the fact called DELIVER. The following tables show examples of fact instances.

Table 1. Fact instances of Ext^{VF12}

measures		linked dimension identifiers			transaction-time values	
SUM(Quantity)	**SUM(Amount)**	**IDP**	**IDT**	**IDC**	T_{Start}	T_{End}
200	1500.00	p_1	2006/01/01	c_1	T_1	T_2
250	1800.00	p_1	2006/01/01	c_1	T_2	T_{now}
150	900.00	p_2	2006/01/01	c_1	T_1	T_{now}

Remarks. $\forall i \in [1..u]$, $VS_i = (VF^i, \{VD^i_1,..., VD^i_v\}, [T_{Start}^i, T_{End}^i])$, $\forall k \in [1..x]$, $i^{VF}_k \in Ext^{VFi}$, then $T_{Start}^i \leq T_{Start}^{VFi}_k \wedge T_{End}^{VFi}_k \leq T_{End}^i \wedge T_{Start}^{VFi}_k \leq T_{End}^{VFi}_k$. In the same way, the transaction time of fact versions or dimension versions may be calculated.

Note that a new fact version is defined when new measures are created or old measures are removed. In the previous example, one new measure, noted SUM(Amount), is created between $VF_{1.1}$ and $VF_{1.2}$ versions.

Definition. A *dimension version* VD is defined by $(N^{VD}, Int^{VD}, Ext^{VD}, Map^{VD})$

- N^{VD} is the dimension name,
- $Int^{VD} = (A^{VD}, H^{VD})$ is the dimension intention composed of attributes, $A^{VD} = \{a_1,..., a_q\} \cup \{id^{VD}, All\}$, which are organised through hierarchies, $H^{VD} = \{H^{VD}_1,..., H^{VD}_w\}$,
- $Ext^{VD} = \{i^{VD}_1,..., i^{VD}_Y\}$ is the dimension extension, which is composed of instances. Each dimension instance is defined by $\forall k \in [1..Y]$, $i^{VD}_k = [a_1:v_1,..., a_q:v_q, T_{Start}:vt, T_{End}:vt']$ where $a_1:v_1,..., a_q:v_q$ are dimension attribute values and $T_{Start}:vt, T_{End}:vt'$ are transaction-time values,
- Map^{VD} is a mapping function defining. It defines the ETL process, which populates the dimension (see section 3 for more details).

Definition. A *hierarchy* H^{VD}_i is defined by $(N^{VD}_i, P^{VD}_i, WA^{VD}_i)$

- N^{VD}_i is the hierarchy name,
- $P^{VD}_i = <p_1,...,p_s>$ is an ordered set of dimension attributes, called parameters, $\forall k \in [1..s]$, $p_k \in A^{VD}$, $p_1 = id^{VD}$ is the *root parameter*, $p_s = All$ is the *extremity parameter*,
- $WA^{VD}_i : P^{VD}_i \rightarrow 2^{A^{VD}}$ is a function associating each parameter to a set of *weak attributes*, which add information to the parameter.

A dimension is depicted by several dimension versions having the same name. Note that a new dimension version is defined when its structure changes; *eg.* when dimension attributes are creating or deleting, hierarchies are adding, deleting or modifying [11].

Example. The facts named ORDER and DELIVER can be analysed according to products. We define two versions of the dimension, named PRODUCT:

- $VD_{3.1}$ = (PRODUCT, ({IDP, Category_Name, Sector_Name, All}, {H^{VD31}_1}) Ext^{VD31}, Map^{VD31}),
- $VD_{3.2}$ = (PRODUCT, ({IDP, Product_Desc, Brand_Desc, Category_Name, Sector_Name, All}, {H^{VD32}_1, H^{VD32}_2}), Ext^{VD32}, Map^{VD32}).

These two dimension versions are composed of three hierarchies, which are defined as follows.

- H^{VD31}_1 = (HSector, <IDP, Category_Name, Sector_Name, All>, { })
- H^{VD32}_1 = (HSector, <IDP, Category_Name, Sector_Name, All>, {(IDP, Product_Desc)})
- H^{VD32}_2 = (HBrand, <IDP, Brand_Desc, All>, {(IDP, Product_Desc)})

The following tables show examples of dimension instances. In Ext^{VD31}, we find two products, denoted p_1 and p_2; two dimension instances represent p_1 because its category name changed at t_2.

Table 2. Dimension instances of Ext^{VD31}

IDP	Category_Name	Sector_Name	All	T_{Start}	T_{End}
p_1	Tv	video	all	T_1	T_2
p_1	Television	video	all	T_2	T_3
p_2	Dvd	video	all	T_1	T_3

Table 3. Dimension instances of Ext^{VD32}

IDP	Product_Desc	Category_Name	Sector_Name	Brand_Desc	All	T_{Start}	T_{End}
p_1	14PF7846	television	video	Philips	all	T_3	T_4
p_1	Flat TV 14PF7846	television	video	Philips	all	T_3	T_{now}
p_2	DVP3010	dvd	video	Philips	all	T_3	T_{now}

Transaction-time is an interval associated to the fact instances and dimension instances. Note that the valid time is modelled by temporal dimension in the MDB.

3   Mapping Function

The approach we present is based on decisional systems, which are composed of three levels: (1) operational data sources, (2) data warehouse and (3) multiversion-based multidimensional data marts, noted MDB. In this context, the data warehouse aims to store relevant decisional data and it supports historical data [12]. Usually a data warehouse is implemented in relational database management systems.

This paper focuses on MDB level, which is modeled through constellations. A constellation is composed of fact versions and dimension versions. These versions are populated from data warehouse tables. The mapping functions of these versions (MAP) model the data extraction. We use the relational algebra for defining the extraction process of relational data warehouse data.

Example. The next figure depicts a relational data warehouse schema. This schema is used for populating star versions.

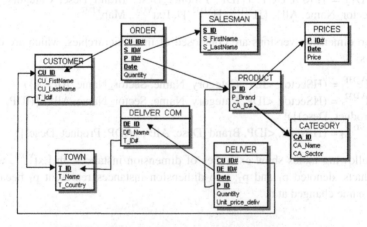

Fig. 2. Example of relational data warehouse schema

From this data warehouse, figure Fig. 3 depicts a constellation schema at T_3 time. This constellation is composed of two star versions

- $VS_{1.2} = (VF_{1.2}, \{VD_{1.1}, VD_{2.1}, VD_{3.2}\}, [T_3, T_{Now}])$, and
- $VS_{2.2} = (VF_{2.1}, \{VD_{3.2}, VD_{4.1}\}, [T_3, T_{Now}])$.

Each star version regroups one fact version and its linked dimension versions. The textual definitions of these versions are:

- $VF_{1.2} = (ORDER, \{SUM(Quantity), SUM(Amount)\}, Ext^{VF12}, Map^{VF12})$,
- $VF_{2.1} = (DELIVER, \{SUM(Quantity)\}, Ext^{VF21}, Map^{VF21})$,
- $VD_{1.1} = (TIME, (\{IDD, Month\_Name, Month\_Number, Year, All\}, \{H^{VD11}_1\}), Ext^{VD11}, Map^{VD11})$,
- $VD_{2.1} = (CUSTOMER, (\{IDC, Firstname, Lastname, City, Country, All\}, \{H^{VD21}_1\}), Ext^{VD21}, Map^{VD21})$,
- $VD_{3.2} = (PRODUCT, (\{IDP, Product\_Desc, Brand\_Desc, Category\_Name, Sector\_Name, All\}, \{H^{VD32}_1, H^{VD32}_2\}), Ext^{VD32}, Map^{VD32})$,
- $VD_{4.1} = (COMPAGNY, (\{IDCP, CName, CCountry All\}, \{H^{VD41}_1\}), Ext^{VD41}, Map^{VD41})$.

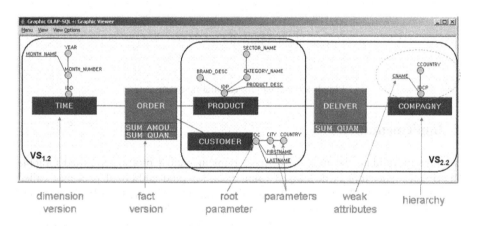

Fig. 3. Graphical representation of a constellation

The extensions of the fact version and its dimension versions of $VS_{1.2}$ are populated from the following map functions.

- $Map^{VD32} = \pi(\bowtie(PRODUCT; CATEGORY; CA\_ID=CA\_ID); \{P\_ID$ AS IDP, CA_NAME AS Category_Name, CA_SECTOR AS Sector_Name, P_BRAND AS Brand_Desc\})
- $Map^{VD11} = \pi(ORDER; \{Date$ AS IDC, **TO_CHAR**(Date, 'mm') AS Month_Number\}, **TO_CHAR**(Date, 'month') AS Month_Name, **TO_CHAR**(Date, 'yyyy') AS Year\})
- $Map^{VD21} = \pi(\bowtie(CUSTOMER; TOWN; T\_ID= T\_ID); \{CU\_ID$ AS IDC, CU_FirstName AS Firstname, CU_LastName AS Lastname, T_Name AS City, T_Country AS Country\})

- Map^{VF12} = **SUM**($\bowtie$($\bowtie$($\bowtie$(ORDER; PRODUCT; P_ID=P_ID); PRICES; P_ID=P_ID); PRODUCT;   P_ID=P_ID);   ORDER.P_ID,   ORDER.Date,   ORDER.CU_ID; ORDER.Quantity **AS** Quantity, PRICES.Price×ORDER.Quantity **AS** Amount)

As illustrating in the following figure, some instances can be calculated from data warehouse data, but others instances may be "derived" from instances of MDB (note that MDB components such as facts and dimensions are viewed as relations). MAP$_1$ and MAP$_4$ are mapping functions defining instances (i_{v1} and i_{v4}) from data warehouse data whereas MAP$_2$ and MAP$_3$ are mapping functions defining instances (i_{v2} and i_{v3}) from instances of the MDB. This mechanism may be interesting for limiting the extraction process; *e.g.* i_{v1} is calculated from data warehouse data, but i_{v2}, which is an alternative instance at the same time instant, is calculated from i_{v1}.

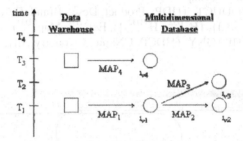

Fig. 4. Mechanism for calculating extensions

4   Implementation

In order to validate the model, we have implemented a prototype, called Graphic OLAPSQL. This tool is developed using Java 1.5 (and additional packages called JavaCC and Oracle JDBC) over Oracle10g Application Server. In [13] we presented the prototype and associated languages and interfaces. The MDB schema is displayed as a graph where nodes represent facts and dimensions while links represent the associations between facts and dimensions (see Fig. 3). These notations are based on notations introduced by [14].

We are extending this prototype for managing versions. Users can display a constellation at one time instant. If several versions (deriving versions) are defined at this time instant, the user chooses its working version, which is displayed. Users express their queries by manipulating the graphical representation of the choosing constellation. The query result is represented through a dimensional-table.

The management of multiversion MDB is based on a metabase. Its schema is represented as follows. A constellation is composed of several star schemata. Each star schema is composed of one fact version and several dimension versions. A dimension version regroups hierarchies which organize attributes of the dimension. A fact version is composed of measures. A same fact version (or dimension version) may be integrated in different star schema. Each fact version (or dimension version) is

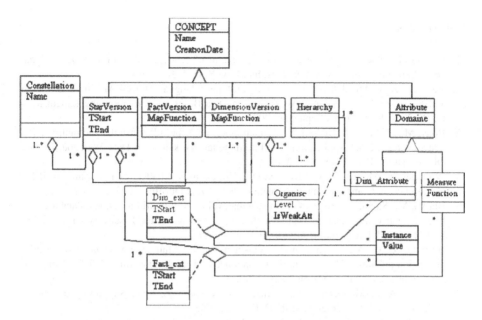

Fig. 5. Metaschema for managing multiversion-based MDB

characterized by a mapping function, its extension (classes Dim_ext or Fact_ext) and its intention.

5   Concluding Remarks

In this paper, we provide solutions for managing data changes of a MDB. The multidimensional model intends to manage several subjects of analysis studied through several axes of analysis. The solution we present is a constellation based on several facts related to dimensions composed of multi-hierarchies.

For supporting changes, a constellation is defined as a set of star versions. A star version is associated to a temporal interval and it is composed of dimension versions (one version per dimension which is composed of a schema and its instances) associated to a fact version (defined by a schema and its instances). A fact version or a dimension version is defined through a mapping function. This function is formalised with a relational algebraic expression on relational data warehouse data to populate the versions. In order to validate our specifications, we are implementing a prototype supporting a multiversion-based constellation.

Our future works consist in specifying a logical model of a multiversion constellation in a relational context [4]. This R-OLAP model must limit data redundancies in order to accelerate OLAP analysis. Moreover, we intend to specify and to implement a query language [15]. In our context, this language must allow the querying of the current star version, or a set of star versions or a specific version. In this paper the mapping functions are based on a single relational data warehouse. We plan to integrate more complex process such as ETL processes [16].

References

1. Kimball, R.: The Data Warehouse Toolkit: Practical Techniques for Building Dimensional Data Warehouses. John Wiley & Sons, Inc, New York, USA, 1996.
2. Vaisman, A.A., Mendelzon, A.O.: A temporal query language for OLAP: Implementation and a case study. 8th Biennial Workshop on Data Bases and Programming Languages - DBPL 2001, Rome, Italy, September 2001.
3. Body, M., Miquel, M., Bédard, Y., Tchounikine, A.: A multidimensional and multiversion structure for OLAP Applications. 5th International Workshop on Data Warehousing and OLAP - DOLAP'02, USA, Nov. 2002.
4. Wrembel, R., Morzy, T.: Multiversion Data Warehouses: Challenges and Solutions. IEEE Conference on Computational Cybernetics - ICCC'05, Mauritius, 2005.
5. Blaska, M., Sapia, C., Hoflin, G.: On schema evolution in multidimensional databases. 1st International Conference on Data Warehousing and Knowledge Discovery - DaWaK'99, pp 153-164, Florence (Italy), August 30–Sept. 1, 1999.
6. Hurtado, C.A., Mendelzon, A.O., Vaisman, A.A.: Maintaining Data cubes under dimension updates. 15th International Conference on Data Engineering - ICDE'99, pp 346-355, Sydney (Australia), March 23-26, 1999.
7. Vaisman, A.A., Mendelzon, A.O., Ruaro, W., Cymerman, S.G.: Supporting dimension updates in an OLAP Server. CAISE'02, Canada, 2002.
8. Bebel, B., Eder, J., Koncilia, C., Morzy, T., Wrembel, R.: Creation and Management of Versions in Multiversion Data Warehouse. ACM Symposium on Applied Computing, pp. 717-723, Nicosia (Cyprus), March 14-17, 2004.
9. Bertino, E., Ferrari, E., Guerrini, G.: A formal temporal object-oriented data model. 5th International Conference on Extending Database Technology - EDBT'96, pp342-356, Avignon (France), March 25-29, 1996.
10. Eder J., Koncilia C., Mitsche D., « Automatic Detection of Structural Changes in Data Warehouses", 5th International Conference on Data Warehousing and Knowledge Discovery – DAWAK'03, LNCS 2737, pp. 119-128, Czech Republic, 2003.
11. Eder, J., Koncilia, C.: Cahnges of Dimension Data in Temporal Data Warehouses. 3rd Int. Conf. on Data Warehousing and Knowledge Discovery – DAWAK'01,LNCS 2114, Munich (Germany), 2001.
12. Ravat, F., Teste, O., Zurfluh, G.: Towards the Data Warehouse Design. 8th Int. Conf. On Information Knowledge Managment- CIKM'99, Kansas City (USA), 1999.
13. Ravat, F., Teste, O. et Zurfluh, G.: Constraint-Based Multi-Dimensional Databases Chapter XI of "Database Modeling for Industrial Data Management", Zongmin Ma, IDEA Group (ed.), pp.323-368.
14. Golfarelli, M., Maio, D., Rizzi, S.: Conceptual design of data warehouses from E/R schemes. 31st Hawaii International Conference on System Sciences, 1998.
15. Morzy, T., Wrembel, R.: On Querying Versions of Multiversion Data Warehouse. 7th International Workshop on Data Warehousing and OLAP - DOLAP'04, pp.92-101, Washington DC (USA), Nov. 12-13 2004.
16. Simitsis, A., Vassiliadis, P., Terrovitis, M., Skiadopoulos, S.: Graph-Based Modeling of ETL Activities with Multi-level Transformations and Updates. 7th International Conference on Data Warehousing and Knowledge Discovery – DaWak'05, LNCS 3589, pp43-52, 2005.

Towards Multidimensional Requirement Design

Estella Annoni, Franck Ravat, Olivier Teste, and Gilles Zurfluh

IRIT-SIG Institute (UMR 5505, University of Paul Sabatier
118 Route de Narbonne, F-31062 TOULOUSE CEDEX 9
{annoni, ravat, teste, zurfluh}@irit.fr

Abstract. Data warehouses (DW) main objective is to facilitating decision-making. Thus their development has to take into account DW project actor requirements. While much recent research has been focused on the design of multidimensional conceptual models, only few works were done to develop models and tools to analyze them. Despite specificities (OLAP, historicization, ...) of these requirements, most of the previous works used an E/R or UML schemas which do not allow designers to represent these specific principles. A main property of DW is that they are derived from existing data sources. Therefore, Extraction-Transformation-Loading (ETL) processes from these sources to the DW are very useful to define a reliable DW.

In this paper, we fill this gap by showing how to systematically derive a conceptual schema of actors requirements using a rule-based mechanism. We provide a conceptual model which tries to be close to user vision of data by extending an object-oriented multidimensional model. Hence, in the early step of DW engineering, designers can formalize actors requirements about information and ETL processes at the same time to make easier understandability, confrontation and validation by all DW actors.

1   Introduction

Building a data warehouse (DW) that satisfies tactical requirements with respect to existing data sources is a very challenging and complex task since it affects DW integration in companies. In addition to tactical requirements in traditional information systems, data warehouse development takes as input requirements existing source databases called system requirements. Moreover, we distinguish strategic and tactical requirements from tactical requirements. The strategic requirements correspond to key performance indicators which make it possible to take decisions about high-level objectives; they are expressed by DW business group. On the other hand, tactical requirements represent functional objectives expressed by end-users group. These two latter requirements are complementary of each other. Therefore, we split DW requirements into three groups as in [1] to analyze separately each one according to their specificities. Hence, the design must distinguish between tactical and strategic requirements and can easily design and handle all DW inputs (tactical, strategic, system).

Previous works of DW design methods implies that the requirements are specified by a classic E/R model. However, Kimball in [2] argues that this model cannot be used as the basis for a company data warehouse. Other works use object-oriented modelling because of the popularity of the UML model which results in reusing of models, tools

A Min Tjoa and J. Trujillo (Eds.): DaWaK 2006, LNCS 4081, pp. 75–84, 2006.

and so forth. But this model has the same drawback as argues Kimball for the E/R model, which is the lack of ability for DBMS to navigate for DW project. Moreover, these works do not exploit one of the great advantages of the object-oriented model which is the definition of the operations.

In this paper, we focus on tactical and strategic requirement analysis step of our method [3] in order to model a data warehouse system in precise, complete and user-friendly manner. We provide a model to represent tactical and strategic requirements close to decision-makers' vision. This model represents both information and processes related to these information. In DW development, they are defined before the design of the multidimensional conceptual schema.

In the following sections, we present progressively our running example. The remainder of this paper is organized as follows. Section 2 discusses related work. Section 3 presents our tactical requirement analysis. Section 4 describes our strategic requirement analysis. Finally, Section 5 points out the conclusion and future work.

2   Related Work

The DW requirement specificities imply proposition of several design methods different from those of traditional information systems. (IS). However, as [1] argue DW requirement analysis process has not been supported by a formal requirement analysis method. These authors define the three groups of actors, but they do not provide any model to represent DW requirement specificities of these three levels.

Most of the previous propositions of DW design implies that this step is already done. Main works do not use specific methods for this step as [4], [5], [6]. The authors of [4] consider this issue by collecting and filtering the tactical requirements using a natural-pseudo language. This expression is interesting because it is close to the natural language but it requires DW designer to handle informal and ambiguous tactical requirements. Likewise the authors of [7], they only take into account information in conceptual schema and processes associated are not analyzed. Moreover, [5] and [6] use UML diagrams resulting in tactical requirement analysis process but they do not specify explicitly how to analyze DW requirements and integrate their specificities. All these works do not distinguish between tactical and strategic requirements and thus do not handle their specificities.

Besides, some approaches of requirements gathering has been provided. [2] considers that the main task is the choice of the business process. According to his experience, the author describes a modelling of the project from the functional requirements. Thus, he considers only tactical requirements. The approach presented in [8] shares similarities with ours, e.g the distinction between tactical and strategic requirements, but it does not define requirement about ETL processes.

3   Tactical Requirement Analysis

3.1   Collection of Tactical Requirements

In order to avoid managing tactical requirements in an informal and ambiguous way, we recommend to use a sample of representative analyses used by decision-makers shown in table 1. These analyses are presented by multidimensional tables. With this tabular representation, the fact of decision-making process is analyzed according to some points of view related to the company. The fact with its measures can be analyzed according to dimensions with several granularity levels. Requirements are represented as a point in a multidimensional space. This representation is close to decision makers' vision of data.

Table 1. Cost evolutions of Acts during the three last years

Acts.		Time.Year		
Cost		2003	2004	2005
Nature.Family	Nature.Sub_family			
Nurse	Bandage	1 147,43	3 445,14	4 624,12
	Vaccine	3 601,85	5 319,81	7 420,95
Surgical	Aesthetic	115 999,26	69 059,42	173 170,09
	Dental	8 958,61	111 429,62	63 769,32

In addition, users may not have a tabular representation. Hence, we collect their requirements by a natural-pseudo language. With this representation, one can define the facts, dimensions with their measures and parameters respectively. Constraints and restrictions on these elements can also be added using a query as follows:

ANALYZE ACTS

WHEN Costs >500

ACCORDING TO Nature.Family, Nature.Sub_family, Medical_Crew

FOR Time.Year IN (2003, 2004, 2005)

Transforming from a query written in a natural pseudo-language to a tabular representation is easy and involves only user data. The query template's major disadvantage is that it is not user-friendly because restrictions on the elements must be expressed in predicates. Basically, we favor tabular representation in the remainder of this paper. Consider a simple example of a medical company that delivers medical acts and wants to analyze the cost of these actsas presented in table 1.

During the analysis, from multidimensional tables we collect also the requirements related to ETL processes such as historicization, archiving, calculation, consolidation and refreshment. In fact, we consider the only functionality which concerns users (i.e reporting) because the other functionalities (i.e loading and storage) concern source systems. In spite of this, these five processes are the most used through reporting manipulations. In addition, many other interests in DW development were argued [9] and [10]. We use a Decisional Dictionary that we define as an extension of the classic data dictionary with columns dedicated to ETL processes. From row headers and column headers, designers formulate the inputs of the decisional dictionary. To fill line by line the other columns (e.g field type, field constraints and calculation, consolidation, historicization, archiving, and refreshment rules), designers must use cell values. Thus, from the multidimensional table 1, we obtain the Decisional Dictionary sketched in figure 1.

This dictionary provides a general view of tactical requirements about information and processes on these information. But, this view is not close to user vision of data. We will provide a model which is better adapted to decision-maker's vision of data in following sections.

Field Name	Field Description	Field Type	Field Constraints	Calculation Rules	Consolidation Rules	Historicizati on Rules	Archiving Rules	Refreshment Rules
Cost	Cost of medical act realized by date	Double		Volume of an act * unit_price of an act per medical act	Function = sum, average, min, max, stddev, var, count	Duration =3 years	Duration = 10 years Function =sum	Frequency= week Mode =merge
Act_code	Code of medical act	Text	Not null			Duration= 3 years	Duration= 10 years Function= sum	Frequency= year Mode =merge
Sub_family	Sub family of medical act	Text				Duration =3 years	Duration = 10 years Function =sum	Frequency= year Mode =merge
Family	Family of medical act	Text				Duration =3 years	Duration = 10 years Function =sum	Frequency= year Mode =merge
Date_day	Date of medical act	Date	Not null			Duration =3 years	Duration = 10 years Function =sum	Frequency= year Mode =merge
Month	Month of medical act	Date				Duration =3 years	Duration = 10 years Function =sum	Frequency= year Mode =merge
Quarter	Quarter of medical act	Date				Duration =3 years	Duration = 10 years Function =sum	Frequency= year Mode =merge
Semester	Semester of medical act	Date				Duration =3 years	Duration = 10 years Function =sum	Frequency= year Mode =merge
Year	Year of medical act	Date				Duration =3 years	Duration = 10 years Function =sum	Frequency= year Mode =merge

Fig. 1. Decisional Dictionary of tactical requirements

3.2 Formalization of Tactical Requirements

From a sample of representative decision-making analyses and the Decisional Dictionary, the DW designer can formalize the multidimensional tactical requirements with our model called Decisional Diagram. In order to guide this task, we provide specific transformation rules from tactical requirements to our model. We intend to achieve a proposal model with the following properties:

- It is close to the way of thinking of data analyzers,
- It represents information and operations related to these information in early steps of DW design,
- It handles separately information and processes in the same model.

Our model is inspired from the object-oriented multidimensional model of [11] which verifies the principles of the star schema [2]. Facts and dimensions are represented by a class of a stereotype. It takes into account ETL processes. To define these processes, we need to associate a behavior to an attribute.

For this same problem, [12] represents attributes as first class modelling elements. But, the authors argue that: "an attribute class can contain neither attributes nor methods". Thereby, it is possible to associate two attribute classes but it is impossible to associate methods to an attribute as we expect. Hence, we propose to add the stereotype "attribute" to the methods only applied on attributes but not applied on all the fact-class or dimension-class. To define precisely on what attribute the method is applied, the attribute is its first parameter. Our method has UML advantages and it offers models and tools for DW problems presented in the following paragraphs.

The ETL processes are defined at class or attribute levels. For each ETL process, we associate a concept called "informativity concept" which is mentioned at attribute level. Informativity concepts are placed with data visibility. We model informativity concepts and the processes associated as follows:

- h : historicize(p, d, c): historicization process at a period p for a duration d with a constraint c ,
- a: archive(p, d, c, fct): archiving process at a period p with a duration d, a constraint c and an aggregate function fct,
- * : refresh(f, m): refreshment process with a frequency f and a refresh mode m,
- c : calculate($\{v_i\}^+$): calculation with parameters v_i,
- s : consolidate(l): consolidation with the level l of consolidation chosen from [13]'s four levels to get meaningful aggregations.

To transform an expression of tactical requirements into a Decisional Diagram, we describe a three rule-based mechanism. It is composed of some structuring rules, well-formedness rules and merge rules :

- the structuring rules enable designers to organize the project environment into one or several Decisional Diagrams. They also make it possible to model facts and dimensions with their measures and parameters respectively into fact and dimension-classes. Some rules help to define the above-mentioned processes from the Decisional Dictionary,
- the well-formedness rules check whether the schema resulting from the analysis of tactical requirements is well-formed. They make it possible to control schema consistency,
- the merge rules indicate how to merge several Decisional Diagrams according to project environment from object names . They take into account fact and dimension-classes in common.

The complete rule-based mechanism is defined in the technical report [14]. Below, we present its application to the table 1 of our running example. We start by applying structuring rules, more precisely on the environment that lies in all multidimensional tables of tactical requirements.

- Rule EI1: the project environment about tactical requirements is composed of one Decisional Diagram because we have one multidimensional table.

Thus, for each multidimensional table we apply first the structuring rules related to facts and its measures, then we apply dimensions and parameters ones. When we apply structuring rules of facts and measures, we find out:

- Rule SI1: the fact "Acts" is transformed into the fact-class "Acts",
- Rule SI2: the measure "Cost" of fact "Acts" is transformed into the attribute "Cost" of fact-class "Acts",
- Rule SI3: the measure "Cost" is calculated, historicized, refreshed, archived, consolidate because it is calculated from the volume of acts and the unit_price per act, historicized every year for three years, refreshed every week according to the merge operation and archived every year for ten years. Therefore, we add the property of informativity "c/h/*/a/s" to the attribute "Cost" of the fact-class "Acts",

– Rule SP1: the ETL processes of facts and measures are defined from the properties of informativity associated to each attribute. Thus, we define the operations from the columns with the same names in Decisional Dictionary. If the constraints are the same for all the attributes of a fact-class per process, the operation is defined at class level. Otherwise, we define an operation per attribute which has its own constraints. In our running example, all the operations of fact-class "Acts" are at class level, except Calculate operation which is specific to the measure "Cost". Therefore, we define the followings :

- • the operation Calculate(Cost, Volume, Unit_price)<<attribute>> means the attribute "Cost" is calculated with the parameters Volume and unit_price. The computation is done by the end-user group. The operation is at attribute level,
- • the operation Historicize(year, 3, NULL) means the attribute of fact-class "Acts" is historicized for the three previous years (because in the table 3 years is analyzed p=year and d=3) without constraints (c=NULL),
- • the operation Refresh(week, merge) means the attribute of fact-class "Acts" is refreshed every week (f=week) according to the merge operation (m=merge),
- • the operation Archive(year, 10 , NULL, sum) means the attribute of fact-class "Acts" is archived for ten years (p=year and d=3) by summing (fct=sum) without constraints (c=NULL),
- • the operation Consolidate(1) means all the aggregate functions can be applied on the attribute of fact-class "Acts" (l=1).

When we apply structuring rules of dimensions and parameters, we find out:

– Rule AI1: the dimensions "Nature" and "Time" are transformed into dimension-class "Nature" and "Time" respectively,
– Rule AI2: the parameters of dimension "Nature" attributes ("Family" and "Sub_family") are transformed into attributes of dimension-class "Nature". The attributes of "Time" dimension-class are the classic "Year, "Semester", "Quarter", "Month" and "Day_Date",
– Rule AI3: the properties of informativity h/*/a are associated to attributes of dimension-classes "Time" and "Nature" because they are historicized every year for three years, refreshed every year according to the merge operation, archived every year for ten years after historicization with sum aggregate function,
– Rule AP1: the ETL processes of dimensions and parameters are defined according to the same criteria as that of the ETL processes of facts and measures. The operations of dimension-classes "Time" and "Nature" are the same because the constraints related to each process per dimension are the same. Moreover, the operations are at class level because the constraints are the same for each parameter per dimension and process. Hence, we define the following operations :

- • the operation Historicize (year, 3, NULL) means the attributes are historicized for the three previous years without constraint,
- • the operation Archive (year, 10 , NULL, sum) means the attribute of fact-class "Acts" is archived for ten years by summing without constraint,
- • the operation Refresh(year, merge) means the attribute of dimension-classes "Time" and "Nature" are refreshed every year.

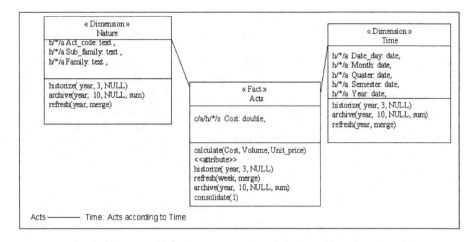

Fig. 2. Decisional Diagram of tactical requirements

We get to the Decisional Diagram as represented in figure 2. This simple diagram is well-formed according to formedness rules. We have only one Decisional Diagram for tactical requirements, therefore we do not need to apply the merge rules.

4   Strategic Requirement Analysis

4.1   Collection of Strategic Requirements

Decision-makers need a synthesis view of the data and their requirement are related to key indicators of enterprise-wide management as shown in table 2. In the context of our contract with I-D6 company which is specialized in decision-making, we notice that strategic indicators composed tables which have only one dimension e.g Time dimension. The indicators are also present in other multidimensional tables expressing tactical requirements. Hence, we consider these tables that we called strategic tables in order to define the kernel of indicators of the future DW. Then, we collect strategic requirements as tactical requirements.

4.2   Formalization of Strategic Requirements

As the strategic requirements are represented through measures which are only depending on the "Time" dimension important to handle these tables with the structuring rules

Table 2. KPIs multidimensional table

	Time.Month	
	January	February
Cost	235025	355186
Day cost	7568	9135
Average cost per act	752	882

EI2. This rule declare any table as a not suitable table when it is not organized by a dimension in column and eventually a dimension in row and when its cells do not match the fact measures.

Hence, DW designers transform the tables by taking into account that each indicator is not a "secondary measure". We called "secondary measures" the measures which can be calculated from other measures called "main measures". In Decisional Diagrams of strategic requirements, the secondary measures are not formalized in order to insure the consistency of the diagrams and to assess the diagrams of the three types requirements. To formalize strategic requirements, the DW designers also define a Decisional Dictionary. The kernel of Decisional Diagrams can be defined from the multidimensional tables of their requirements and the Decisional Dictionary.

In our running example, we must transform the multidimensional table 2 into a multidimensional table with a dimension "Time" and a fact "Acts". At the beginning, this fact contains three measures. But among these measures, two of them can be calculated from the other. The measure "Day cost" and "Average cost per act" can be calculated from the measure "Cost". Therefore, the multidimensional table is structured with "Time" dimension columns where the fact "Acts" has one measure "Cost". The Decisional Dictionary of strategic requirements contains the same rows of "Time" dimension and Acts fact as Decisional Dictionary of tactical requirements. The kernel of Decisional Diagram is composed of the Decisional Diagram represented in figure 3.

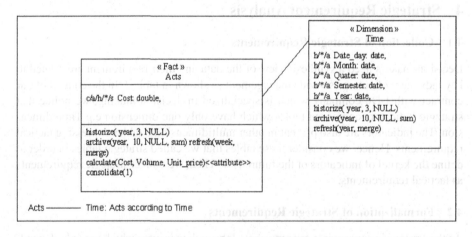

Fig. 3. Decisional Diagram of strategic requirements

In our running example, we have only a strategic table. Thus, we get to the Decisional Diagrams. From the tactical Decisional Diagram and the strategic Decisional Diagram, designer must merge the fact-classes, dimension-classes and attributes present in the two diagrams by using merge rules (presented below). Designers apply these rules with kernel Decisional Diagram as a reference in order to keep its multidimensional objects. The merge rules are :

- FUS1: merge dimension and fact-classes by adding attributes and ETL operations. It makes it possible to gather Decisional Diagrams with the same facts which have common dimension-classes,
- FDS1: merge dimension-classes by adding attributes and ETL operations to define a constellation. It makes it possible to gather Decisional Diagrams with different facts which have common dimension-classes.

Then, after the confrontation of tactical and strategic requirements, designers can assess result of the first confrontation with the result of system requirement analysis. Before the design of the conceptual schema, designers can evaluate whether strategic and tactical requirements can be satisfy since the first iteration of requirement analysis step. If there is inadequacy, this iteration of our DW design method is closed and a new iteration begins in order to enclose the three types of requirements together.

5 Conclusion

This paper presents our model called Decisional Diagram for tactical requirement analysis process. We provide a method to derive a Decisional Diagram form tactical requirements and strategic requirements. The method uses a three rule-based mechanism which is composed of structuring, well-formedness and merge rules. These rules enable data warehouse (DW) designers to get to a Decisional Diagram with respect to tactical and strategic requirements about information and ETL processes.

Our proposal introduces a model between (tactical, strategic) requirements and the conceptual schema to tackle all DW requirements in the early steps of data warehouse design. It has the advantage of enabling DW designers to define ETL operation interfaces. Defining historicization, archiving, calculation, consolidation and refreshment processes during the early step of the DW design may contribute in reducing the important rate of ETL cost and time in a DW project.

As [9], [10] and [12] argue , few researches have been done to develop models and tools for ETL process. Therefore, in the near future we intend to enhance the understandability and user-friendliness of data mappings. These mappings will be useful as a document in DW project validation by its actors at conceptual and logical abstraction levels. Moreover, we are working on the definition of hierarchies during requirements analysis.

References

1. Bruckner, R., List, B., Schiefer, J.: Developping requirements for data warehouse systems with use cases, AMCIS (1999)
2. Kimball, R.: The data warehouse toolkit: practical techniques for building dimensional data warehouses. John Wiley & Sons, Inc., New York, NY, USA (1996)
3. Annoni, E., Ravat, F., Teste, O., Zurfluh, G.: Les systèmes d'informations décisionnels : une approche d'analyse et de conception à base de patrons. revue RSTI srie ISI, Méthodes Avancées de Développement des SI **10**(6) (2005)

4. Golfarelli, M., Rizzi, S.: Methodological framework for data warehouse design. In: DOLAP '98, ACM First International Workshop on Data Warehousing and OLAP, November 7, 1998, Bethesda, Maryland, USA, Proceedings, ACM (1998) 3–9

5. Luján-Mora, S., Trujillo, J.: A comprehensive method for data warehouse design. In: DMDW. (2003)

6. Abelló, A., Samos, J., Saltor, F.: Yam2 (yet another multidimensional model): An extension of uml. In Nascimento, M.A., Özsu, M.T., Zaïane, O.R., eds.: IDEAS, IEEE Computer Society (2002) 172–181

7. Bonifati, A., Cattaneo, F., Ceri, S., Fuggetta, A., Paraboschi, S.: Designing data marts for data warehouses. ACM Trans. Softw. Eng. Methodol. **10**(4) (2001) 452–483

8. Giorgini, P., Rizzi, S., Garzetti, M.: Goal-oriented requirement analysis for data warehouse design. In Song, I.Y., Trujillo, J., eds.: DOLAP, ACM (2005) 47–56

9. Vassiliadis, P., Simitsis, A., Skiadopoulos, S.: Conceptual modeling for etl processes. In Theodoratos, D., ed.: DOLAP, ACM (2002) 14–21

10. Bouzeghoub, M., Fabret, F., Matulovic-Broqué, M.: Modeling the data warehouse refreshment process as a workflow application. In Gatziu, S., Jeusfeld, M.A., Staudt, M., Vassiliou, Y., eds.: DMDW. Volume 19 of CEUR Workshop Proceedings., CEUR-WS.org (1999) 6

11. Luján-Mora, S., Trujillo, J., Song, I.Y.: Extending the uml for multidimensional modeling. In Jézéquel, J.M., Hußmann, H., Cook, S., eds.: UML. Volume 2460 of Lecture Notes in Computer Science., Springer (2002) 290–304

12. Luján-Mora, S., Vassiliadis, P., Trujillo, J.: Data mapping diagrams for data warehouse design with uml. In Atzeni, P., Chu, W.W., Lu, H., Zhou, S., Ling, T.W., eds.: ER. Volume 3288 of Lecture Notes in Computer Science., Springer (2004) 191–204

13. Pedersen, T.B., Jensen, C.S.: Multidimensional data modeling for complex data. In: ICDE, IEEE Computer Society (1999) 336–345

14. Annoni, E.: ebipad : Outil de developpement des systemes d'information decisionnels. Technical Report IRIT/RR-2006-12-FR (2006)

Multidimensional Design by Examples

Oscar Romero and Alberto Abelló

Universitat Politècnica de Catalunya, Jordi Girona 1-3, E-08034 Barcelona, Spain

Abstract. In this paper we present a method to validate user multidimensional requirements expressed in terms of SQL queries. Furthermore, our approach automatically generates and proposes the set of multidimensional schemas satisfying the user requirements, from the organizational operational schemas. If no multidimensional schema is generated for a query, we can state that requirement is not multidimensional.

Keywords: Multidimensional Design, Design by Examples, DW.

1 Introduction

In this paper we present a method to validate user multidimensional requirements expressed in terms of SQL queries over the organizational operational sources. In our approach, the input query is decomposed to infer relevant implicit and explicit potential multidimensional knowledge contained and accordingly, it automatically proposes the set of multidimensional schemas satisfying those requirements. Thus, facts, dimensions and dimension hierarchies are identified, giving support to the data warehouse design process. Conversely, if our process has not been able to generate any multidimensional schema, we would be able to state that the input query is not multidimensional.

Our main contribution is the automatization of identifying the multidimensional concepts in the operational sources with regard to the end-user requirements. Demand-driven design approaches ([12]) focus on determining the user requirements to later map them onto data sources. This process is typically carried out by the DW expert and it is hardly automatized. Therefore, it is up to the expert criterion to properly point out the multidimensional concepts giving rise to the multidimensional schema. Conversely, in our approach we automatically generate and propose a set of multidimensional schemas validating the input requirements, giving support to the DW expert along the design process.

Notice we propose a method within a supply/demand-driven framework. Our method starts analyzing the requirements stated by the user (in terms of SQL queries), as typically performed in demand-driven approaches. However, it analyzes the operational relational data sources in parallel, as typically performed in supply-driven approaches, to extract additional knowledge needed to validate the user requirements as multidimensional.

We start with section 2 presenting the related work in the literature; section 3 presents the foundations our method is based on whereas section 4 introduces our approach. For the sake of a better comprehension, section 5 presents a practical application of our method and finally, section 6 concludes the paper.

A Min Tjoa and J. Trujillo (Eds.): DaWaK 2006, LNCS 4081, pp. 85–94, 2006.
© Springer-Verlag Berlin Heidelberg 2006

2   Related Work

As presented in [12], the DW design process can be developed within a supply-driven or a demand-driven approach. Several methodologies following both paradigms have been presented in the literature. On one hand, demand-driven approaches ([12], [5]) focus on determining the user multidimensional requirements (as typically performed in other information systems) to later map them onto data sources. As far as we know, none of them automatize the process. On the other hand, supply-driven approaches ([11], [3], [7], [6] and [2] among others) start thoroughly analyzing the data sources to determine the multidimensional concepts in a reengineering process. In that case, the approach presented in [6] is the only one partially automatizing the process.

As mentioned, our approach combines a demand/supply-driven approach as suggested in [10]. Other works have already combined both approaches, like [5] and [4]. Main difference with our approach is that the first one does not fully automatize the process whereas the second one does not focus on modeling multidimensionality.

3   Framework

In this section we present the criteria our work is based on. That is, those used to validate the input query as a valid multidimensional requirement:

[C1] Relational modeling of multidimensionality: Multidimensionality is based on the fact/dimension dichotomy. Hence, we consider a **Dimension** to contain a hierarchy of **Levels** representing different granularities (or levels of detail) to study data, and a **Level** to contain **Descriptors**. On the other hand, a **Fact** contains **Cells** which contain **Measures**. Like in [11], we consider a **Fact** can contain not just one but several different materialized levels of granularity of data. Therefore, one **Cell** represents those individual **cells** of the same granularity that show data regarding the same **Fact** (i.e. a **Cell** is a "Class" and **cells** are its instances). Specifically, a **Cell** of data is related (in the relational model, by means of FK's) to one **Level** for each of its associated **Dimension** of analysis. Finally, one **Fact** and several **Dimensions** to analyze it give rise to a **Star**, to be implemented in the relational model through an "star" or an "snow-flake" schemas as presented in [8].

[C2] The cube-query template: The standard SQL'92 template query to retrieve a **Cell** of data from the RDBMS was first presented in [8]:

```
SELECT l_1.ID, ..., l_n.ID, [ F( )c.Measure_1[ ) ], ...
FROM Cell c, Level_1 l_1, ..., Level_n l_n
WHERE c.key_1=l_1.ID AND ... AND c.key_n=l_n.ID [ AND l_j.attr Op. K ]
[ GROUP BY l_1.ID, ..., l_n.ID ]
[ ORDER BY l_1.ID, ..., l_n.ID ]
```

The FROM clause contains the "Cell table" and the "Level tables". These tables are properly linked in the WHERE clause, where we can also find logic clauses restricting an specific **Level** attribute (i.e. a **Descriptor**) to a constant $\mathcal{K}$ by means of a comparison operator. The GROUP BY clause shows the identifiers of the **Levels** at which we want to aggregate data. Those columns in the grouping must also be in the SELECT clause in order to identify the values in the result. Finally, the ORDER BY clause is intended to sort the output of the query.

[C3] The Base integrity constraint: Dimensions of analysis should be orthogonal. Despite it could be possible to find **Dimensions** determining others in a multidimensional schema, it must be avoided among **Dimensions** arranging the multidimensional space in a cube-query, in order to guarantee **cells** are fully functionally determined by **Dimensions** ([1]). Therefore, we call a **Base** to those minimal set of **Levels** identifying unequivocally a **Cell**, similar to the "primary key" concept in the relational model.

[C4] The correct data summarization integrity constraint: Data summarization performed in multidimensionality must be correct, and we warrant this by means of the three necessary conditions (intuitively also sufficient) introduced in [9]: (1) **Disjointness** (*Sets of cells at an specific Level to be aggregated must be disjoint*); (2) **Completeness** (*Every cell at a certain Level must be aggregated in a parent Level*) and (3) **Compatibility** (**Dimension**, *kind of measure aggregated and the aggregation function must be compatible*). Compatibility must be satisfied since certain functions are incompatible with some **Dimensions** and kind of measures. For instance, we can not aggregate `Stock` over `Time` **Dimension** by means of sum, as some repeated values would be counted. However, this last condition can not be automatically checked unless additional information would be provided, since it is not available neither in the requirements nor in the source schemas.

Multidimensionality pays attention to two main aspects; placement of data in a multidimensional space and summarizability of data. Therefore, if we can verify that the SQL query given follows the cube-query template; it does not cause summarizability problems and data retrieved is unequivocally identified in the space, we would be able to assure it undoubtedly makes multidimensional sense. Moreover, since it is well-known how to model multidimensionality in the relational model, we can look for this pattern over the operational schemas to identify the multidimensional concepts. Additionally, we introduce other optional criteria to validate the query, to be used depending on the DW expert:

[C5] Selections: Multidimensional selections must be carried out by means of logic clauses in the WHERE clause (i.e. *field* comparison operator *constant*). However, we could allow to select data joining two relations through, at least, two different conceptual relationships between them and therefore, not navigating but selecting data equally retrieved by those joins.

[C6] Degenerate dimensions: Multidimensionality is typically modeled forcing **Cells** to be related, by means of FK's, to its analysis **Dimensions** (see [C1]). However, in a non-multidimensional relational schema this may not happen, and we could have a table attribute representing a **Dimension** not pointing to any table (for instance, dates or control numbers). In the multidimensional model, these rather unusual **Dimensions** were introduced in [8], and they are known as "degenerate dimensions".

4   Our Method

Our approach aims to automatically validate a syntactically correct SQL query representing user multidimensional requirements, as a valid (syntactically and semantically) cube-query. An SQL query is a valid cube-query if we are able to generate a non-empty set of multidimensional schemas validating that query. Otherwise, the input query would not represent multidimensional requirements. Multidimensional schemas proposed will be inferred from those implicit restrictions, presented in previous section, an SQL query needs to guarantee to make multidimensional sense; playing the operational databases schemas a key role. This process is divided into two main phases: first one creates what we call the *multidimensional graph*; a graph concisely storing relevant multidimensional information about the query, that will facilitate the query validation along the second phase. Such graph is composed of *nodes*, representing tables involved in the query and *edges*, relating nodes (i.e. tables) joined in the query. Our aim is to label each node as a **Cell** (factual data) or a **Level** (dimensional data). A correct labeling of all the nodes gives rise to a multidimensional schema fitting the input query. Along this section, due to lack of space, we introduce a detailed algorithm in pseudo code to implement our method, followed by a brief explanation of each one of its steps. For the sake of readability, comprehension of the algorithm took priority over its performance:

1. **For each** table **in** the FROM clause **do**
   (a) **Create** a node and **Initialize** node properties;
2. **For each** attribute **in** the GROUP BY clause **do**
   (a) $node = get\_node(attribute)$;
   (b) **if** ($!defined\_as\_part\_of\_a\_CK(attribute)$) **then Label** $node$ as Level;
   (c) **else if** ($!degenerate$ dimensions allowed) **then**
       i. $FK = get\_FK(attribute)$; $node\_dest = node$; $attributes\_FK = attribute$;
       ii. **while** $chain\_of\_FKs\_follows(FK)$ **and** $FK\_in\_WHERE\_clause(FK)$ **do**
           A. $FK = get\_next\_chained\_FK(FK)$; $node\_dest = get\_node(get\_table(FK))$;
              $attributes\_FK = get\_attributes(FK)$;
       iii. /* We must also check #attributes selected matches #attributes at the end of the chain. */
       iv. **if** ($FK == $ **NULL and** $\#attrs(attribute) == \#attrs(attributes\_FK)$) **then**
           A. **Label** $node\_dest$ as Level;
3. **For each** attribute **in** the SELECT clause **not in** the GROUP BY clause **do**
   (a) $node = get\_node(attribute)$; **Label** node as Cell with Measures selected;
4. **For each** comparison **in** the WHERE clause **do**
   (a) $node = get\_node(attribute)$;
   (b) **if** ($!defined\_as\_part\_of\_a\_CK(attribute)$) **then Label** node as Level;
   (c) **else if** ($!degenerate$ dimensions allowed) **then**
       i. $attribute = get\_attribute(comparison)$; $FK = get\_FK(attribute)$; $node\_dest = get\_node(attribute)$; $attributes\_FK = attribute$;
       ii. **while** $chain\_of\_FKs\_follows(FK)$ **and** $FK\_in\_WHERE\_clause(FK)$ **do**
           A. $FK = get\_next\_chained\_FK(FK)$; $node\_dest = get\_node(get\_table(FK))$;
              $attributes\_FK = get\_attributes(FK)$;
       iii. **if** ($FK == $ **NULL and** $\#attributes(attribute) == \#attributes(attributes\_FK)$) **then**
           A. **Label** $node\_dest$ as Level;
5. **For each** join **in** the WHERE clause **do**
   (a) /* Notice a conceptual relationship between tables may be modeled by several joins in the WHERE */
   (b) $set\_of\_joins = look\_for\_related\_joins(join)$;
   (c) $multiplicity = get\_multiplicity(set\_of\_joins)$; relationships fitting = {};
   (d) **For each** relationship **in** $get\_allowed\_relationships(multiplicity)$ **do**
       i. **if** ($!contradiction\_with\_graph(relationship)$) **then**
           A. relationships fitting = relationships fitting + {relationship};
   (e) **if** ($!sizeof(relationshipsfitting)$) **then** return $notify\_fail$("Tables relationship not allowed");
   (f) **Create** an edge($get\_join\_attributes(set\_of\_joins)$); **Label** edge to relationships fitting;
   (g) **if** ($unequivocal\_knowledge\_inferred(relationships\_fitting)$) **then** propagate knowledge;

Table 1. Valid multidimensional relationships in a relational schema

Multiplicity	L - L	C - C	L - C	C - L
1 - 1	✓	✓	✓	✓
1 o- 1	✓	✓	×	✓
N - 1	✓	✓	×	✓
N o- 1	✓	✓	×	✓
N o-o 1	✓	✓	×	×
N -o 1	✓	✓	×	×
1 o-o 1	✓	✓	×	×

The algorithm starts analyzing each query clause according to [C2]:

Step 1: Each table in the FROM clause is represented as a node in the multi-dimensional graph. Along the whole process we aim to label them and, if in a certain moment, an already labeled node is demanded to be labeled with a different tag, the process ends and raises the contradiction stated.

Step 2: The GROUP BY clause must fully functionally determine data (see [C3]). Thus, fields on it represent dimensional data. However, we can not label them directly as **Levels** since, because of [C1], **Cells** are related to **Levels** by FK's and dimensional data selected could be that in the **Cell** table. Hence, we label it as a **Level** if that field is not defined as FK or it is but we are able to follow a FK's chain defined in the schema that is also present in the WHERE. Then, the table where the FK's chain ends plays a **Level** role. If [C6] is assumed, we can not rely on FK's to point out **Levels**.

Step 3: Those aggregated attributes in the SELECT not present in the GROUP BY surely play a **Measure** role. Hence, each node is labeled as a **Cell** with selected **Measures**. If the input query does not contain a GROUP BY clause, we are not forced to aggregate **Measures** by means of aggregation functions in the SELECT, and this step would not be able to point them out.

Step 4: Since a multidimensional **Selection** must be carried out over dimensional data, this step labels nodes as **Levels** with the same criteria regarding FK's presented in step 2.

Step 5: Previous steps are aimed to create and label nodes whereas this step creates and labels edges. For each join between tables in the WHERE clause, we first infer the relationship multiplicity with regard to the definition of the join attributes in the schema (i.e. as FK's, CK's or Not Null). According to the multiplicity, we look for those allowed multidimensional relationships depicted in table 1, not contradicting previous knowledge in the graph. If we find any, we create an edge representing that join and label it with those allowed relationships. Finally, if we are just considering one possible relationship, or we can infer unequivocal knowledge (i.e. despite having some different alternatives, we can assure that origin/destination/both node(s) must be a **Cell** or a **Level**), we update the graph labeling the nodes accordingly. If we update one such node, we must propagate in cascade new knowledge inferred to those edges and nodes directly related to those updated.

Next, we need to validate the graph as a whole. However, notice the graph construction may have not labeled all the nodes. By means of backtracking, we first look for all those non-contradictory labeling alternatives, to be validated each one as follows:

6. **If** !*connected*(*graph*) **then** return *notify_fail*("Aggregation problems because of cartesian product.");
7. **For each** subgraph of **Levels** in the multidimensional graph **do**
   (a) **if** *contains_cycles*(*subgraph*) **then**
       i. /* Alternative paths must be semantically equivalent and hence raising the same multiplicity. */
       ii. **if** *contradiction_about_paths_multiplicities*(*subgraph*) **then** return *notify_fail*("Cycles can not be used to select data.");
       iii. **else** ask user for semantical validation;
   (b) **if** *exists_two_Levels_related_same_Cell*(*subgraph*) **then** return *notify_fail*("Non-orthogonal Analysis Levels");
   (c) **For each** relationship in *get_1_to_N_Level_Level_relationships*(*subgraph*) **do**
       i. **if** *left_related_to_a_Cell_with_Measures*(*relationship*) **then** return *notify_fail*("Aggregation Problems.");
8. **For each** Cell pair in the multidimensional graph **do**
   (a) **For each** 1_1_*correspondence*(*Cellpair*) **do** **Create** context edge between Cell pair;
   (b) **For each** 1_N_*correspondence*(*Cellpair*) **do** **Create** directed context edge between Cell pair;
   (c) **If** *exists_other_correspondence*(*Cellpair*) **then** return *notify_fail*("Invalid correspondence between Cells.");
9. **if** *contains_cycles*(*Cells path*) **then**
   (a) **if** *contradiction_about_paths_multiplicities*(*Cells path*) **then** return *notify_fail*("Cycles can not be used to select data.");
   (b) **else** ask user for semantical validation; **Create** context nodes(Cells path);
10. **For each** element in *get_1_to_N_context_edges_and_nodes*(*Cells path*) **do**
    (a) **If** *CM_at_left*(*element*) **then** return *notify_fail*("Aggregation problems among Measures.");
11. **If** *exists_two_1_to_N_alternative_branches*(*Cells path*) **then** return *notify_fail*("Aggregation problems among Cells.");

Step 6: The multidimensional graph must be connected to avoid the "Cartesian Product" ([C6]). Moreover, it must be composed of valid edges giving rise to a path among **Cells** (factual data) and connected subgraphs of **Levels** (dimensional data) surrounding it.

Step 7: This step validates **Levels** subgraphs with regard to **Cells** placement: According to [C3], two different **Levels** in a subgraph can not be related to the same **Cell** (step 7b); to preserve [C4], **Level - Level** edges raising aggregation problems on **Cells** with **Measures** selected must be forbidden (step 7c), and finally, if we do not consider [C5], every subgraph must represent a valid **Dimension** hierarchy (i.e. not being used to select data). Thus, we must be able to point out two nodes in the subgraph representing the *top* and *bottom* **Levels** of the hierarchy, and if there are more than one alternative path between those nodes, they must be semantically equivalent (7a).

Step 8: **Cells** determine multidimensional data and they must be related somehow in the graph. Otherwise, they would not retrieve a single **Cube** of data. For every two **Cells** in the graph, we aim to validate those paths between them as a whole, inferring and validating the multiplicity raised as follows: (1) if exists a one-to-one correspondence between two **Cells**, we replace all relationships involved in that correspondence, by a one-to-one *context edge* between both **Cells** (i.e. a context edge replaces that subgraph representing the one-to-one correspondence). As depicted in figure 1.1, it means that there are a set of relationships linking, as a whole, a **Cell** CK, also linked by one-to-one paths to a whole CK of the other **Cell**. (2) Otherwise, if both CK's are related by means of one-to-many paths or the first CK matches the second one partially, we replace involved relationships by a one-to-many directed context edge. Finally, many-to-many relationships between **Cells** would invalidate the graph since they do not preserve disjointness.

Steps 9, 10 and 11: Previous step has validated the correspondences between **Cells** whereas these steps validate the **Cells** path (multidimensional data retrieved) as a whole: According to [C5], step 9 validates cycles in the path of **Cells** to assure they are not used to select data, similar to the **Levels** cycles

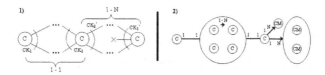

Fig. 1. Examples of **Cells** paths of context edges and nodes

validation. Once the cycle has been validated, **Cells** involved are clustered in a *context node* labeled with the cycle multiplicity, as showed in figure 1.2. Steps 10 and 11, according to [C4], look for potential aggregation problems. First one looks for **Cells** with **Measures** selected at the left side of a one-to-many context edge or node whereas second one looks for alternative branches with one-to-many context edges or nodes each, raising a forbidden many-to-many relationship between **Cells** involved (as depicted in figure 1.2).

5   A Practical Example

In this section, we present a practical example of the method introduced along this paper. We consider figure 2 (where CK's are underlined and FK's dash-underlined) to depict part of the operational schema of the organization. Therefore, given the following requirement: *"Retrieve benefits obtained with regard to supplier 'ABC', per month"*, it could be expressed in SQL as:

```
SELECT m.month, my.supplier, SUM(mp.profit)
FROM Month m, Monthly sales ms, Monthly supply my, Monthly profit mp, Supplier s, Prodtype pt, Product p
WHERE mp.month = ms.month AND mp.product = ms.product AND s.month = m.month AND ms.product = p.product AND my.month = m.month
AND my.supplier = s.supplier AND my.prodtype = pt.prodtype AND p.prodtype = pt.prodtype AND s.supplier = 'ABC'
GROUP BY m.month, my.supplier
ORDER BY m.month, my.supplier
```

We aim to decide if this query makes multidimensional sense. If it does, our method will propose the set of multidimensional schemas satisfying our multidimensional needs. First, we start constructing the multidimensional graph. In our case, we do not consider degenerate dimensions (see [C6]):

Step 1: We first create a node for each table in the FROM clause. Initially, they are labeled as unknown (?) nodes.

Step 2 and 3: For each attribute in the GROUP BY clause, we try to identify the role played by those tables which they belong to:

- m.month: This attribute belongs to the Month table. Since it is not part of a FK, we can directly label that node as a **Level**.
- my.supplier: This attribute belonging to the Monthly supply table is defined as a FK pointing to the supplier attribute in the Supplier table. This equality can be also found in the WHERE clause, and therefore, we can follow the FK chain up to the Supplier node, where the FK chain ends. Consequently, we label the Supplier node as a **Level**.

Finally, for each attribute in the SELECT not in the GROUP BY (i.e. mp.profit), we identify the node it belongs to as a **Cell** with **Measures** selected.

Step 4: In this step, we analyze the s.supplier = 'ABC' comparison clause. First, we extract the attribute compared (supplier) and identify the table it

```
Prodtype(prodtype)
Supplier(supplier, name, city)
Product(product, prodtype (→prodtype.prodtype), discount)
Month(month, numdays, season)
Monthly profit(month (→month.month), product(→product.product), profit)
Monthly sales(month (→month.month), product (→product.product), sales)
Monthly supply(month(→month.month),prodtype(→prodtype.prodtype),supplier(→supplier.supplier))
```

Fig. 2. The organizational relational database schema

belongs to (`Supplier`). Since it is not part of a FK, this table must be labeled as a **Level**. However, since it has been already labeled and there is no contradiction, the algorithm goes on without modifying the graph.

Step 5: For each join in the WHERE clause, we firstly infer the relationship multiplicity. For instance, `mp.month = ms.month` joins two attributes that are part of two CK's in their respective tables. Therefore, we first look if the whole CK's are linked. In this case, this is true since `mp.product = ms.product` also appears in the WHERE clause. Consequently, we are joining two CK's, raising up a 1 o-o 1 relationship. Since this relationship asks to preserve the multidimensional space due to zeros, at this moment, we should suggest to the user to outer-join properly both tables.

Secondly, according to the multiplicity inferred, we look at table 1 looking for those allowed multidimensional relationships between both nodes. That is, *C - C* or *L - L*. However, last alternative raises a contradiction, since it asks to label the `Monthly profit` node as a **Level** when it has been already labeled as a **Cell** with **Measures**. Consequently, it is eluded. Since the set of relationships allowed is not empty, we create an edge and we label it accordingly.

Finally, we propagate current knowledge. That is, according to that edge, the **Monthly sales** table must also be a **Cell**, and therefore, it is labeled as a **Cell** without selected **Measures**. After repeating this process for every join, we would obtain, at the end of this step, the graph depicted in figure 3.

To validate the graph, first, we check if the graph is connected (in this case, it is). Next, since some nodes have not been labeled, we find out all the valid alternatives by means of backtracking. For instance, if the `Product` node was labeled as a **Level**, according to the edge between `Product` and `Prodtype`, the latter should be also labeled as a **Level**. Moreover, the `Monthly supply` node may be labeled as a **Cell** or a **Level**. The backtracking algorithm ends retrieving all those non-contradictory labeling alternatives depicted in table 2 (those crossed out are eluded in this step since they raise up contradictions).

For each labeling retrieved by the backtracking algorithm, we try to validate the graph. For instance, we will follow in detail the validation algorithm for the first alternative, where all three unknown nodes are labeled as **Cells**:

– We validate each subgraph of **Levels** (namely those isolated **Levels** depicted in figure 3) with regard to **Cells**. Since they do not contain cycles (alternative paths) of **Levels**; there is neither two **Levels** in the same subgraph related to the same **Cell** nor forbidden **Level** - **Level** relationships, both are correct.
– Next, we create the context edges between **Cells**. In this case, we are not able to replace all the edges, since the `Monthly supply` and `Monthly sales`

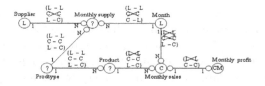

Fig. 3. The multidimensional graph deployed

unique correspondence (through the `Month` node) can not be replaced by a context edge (they are only linked through their **Month** field; i.e. joining two pieces of CK's and raising a forbidden many-to-many context edge).

Since we have found a contradiction, we elude this labeling and try the next one. Second labeling is forbidden because it raises a one-to-many **Level - Level** relationship (i.e. `Monthly supply - Month`) where the one side is related to a **Cell** with selected **Measures** (i.e. `Monthly profit`). Third alternative raises the same problem than the first one whereas the fourth one relates two **Levels** of the subgraph with the same **Cell**. Finally, the last alternative is valid, since we are able to replace `Monthly supply` and `Monthly sales` correspondence by a one-to-many directed context edge (in fact, they are related by joins raising a many-to-many relationship, but the comparison over the `supplier` field in the WHERE clause turns it into a one-to-many). Furthermore, the **Cells** path do not conform a cycle; **Cells** at the left side of the one-to-many context edge (i.e. `Monthly supply`) do not select **Measures**, and there are not alternative branches with one-to-many context edges or nodes each either.

Summing up, the algorithm would conclude that requirement is multidimensional and would propose the `Monthly supply`, `Monthly profit` and `Monthly sales` as factual data whereas `Supplier`, `Product` and `Prodtype`, and `Month` would conform the dimensional data.

6   Conclusions

Based on the criteria that an SQL query must enforce to make multidimensional sense, we have presented a method to validate multidimensional requirements expressed in terms of an SQL query. Our approach is divided into two main phases: first one creates the multidimensional graph storing relevant multidimensional information about the query, that will facilitate the query validation

Table 2. Labeling alternatives retrieved

Monthly supply	Prodtype	Product	Remarks
C	C	C	Illegal context edge
L	L	C	Invalid subgraph of Levels
C	L	C	Illegal context edge
L	L	L	Non-orthogonal dimensions
C	L	L	✓
C	C	L	×
L	C	C	×
L	C	L	×

along the second phase. Such graph represents tables involved in the query and its relationships, and our aim is to label each table as factual data or dimensional data. A correct labeling of all the tables gives rise to a multidimensional schema fulfilling the requirements expressed in the input query. Thus, if we are not able to generate any correct labeling, the input query would not represent multidimensional requirements. As future work, we will focus on how to conciliate those labeling proposed by our method for different multidimensional requirements.

Acknowledgments. This work has been partly supported by the Ministerio de Educación y Ciencia under project TIN 2005-05406.

References

1. A. Abelló, J. Samos, and F. Saltor. **YAM**^{2} (Yet Another Multidimensional Model): An extension of UML. *Information Systems*, 31(6):541–567, 2006.
2. M. Böhnlein and A. Ulbrich vom Ende. Deriving Initial Data Warehouse Structures from the Conceptual Data Models of the Underlying Operational Information Systems. In *Proc. of 2nd Int. Workshop on Data Warehousing and OLAP (DOLAP 1999)*, pages 15–21. ACM, 1999.
3. L. Cabibbo and R. Torlone. A Logical Approach to Multidimensional Databases. In *Proc. of 6th Int. Conf. on Extending Database Technology (EDBT 1998)*, volume 1377 of *LNCS*, pages 183–197. Springer, 1998.
4. D. Calvanese, L. Dragone, D. Nardi, R. Rosati, and S. Trisolini. Enterprise Modeling and Data Warehousing in TELECOM ITALIA. *Information Systems*, 2006.
5. P. Giorgini, S. Rizzi, and M. Garzetti. Goal-oriented requirement analysis for data warehouse design. In *Proc. of 8th Int. Workshop on Data Warehousing and OLAP (DOLAP 2005)*, pages 47–56. ACM Press, 2005.
6. M. Golfarelli, D. Maio, and S. Rizzi. The Dimensional Fact Model: A Conceptual Model for Data Warehouses. *Int. Journals of Cooperative Information Systems (IJCIS)*, 7(2-3):215–247, 1998.
7. B. Hüsemann, J. Lechtenbörger, and G. Vossen. Conceptual Data Warehouse Modeling. In *In Proc. of DMDW'00)*. CEUR-WS.org, 2000.
8. R. Kimball, L. Reeves, W. Thornthwaite, and M. Ross. *The Data Warehouse Lifecycle Toolkit: Expert Methods for Designing, Developing and Deploying Data Warehouses*. John Wiley & Sons, Inc., 1998.
9. H.J. Lenz and A. Shoshani. Summarizability in OLAP and Statistical Data Bases. In *Proc. of SSDBM'1997*. IEEE, 1997.
10. S. Luján-Mora and J. Trujillo. A comprehensive method for data warehouse design. In *In Proc. of DMDW'2003*, volume 77. CEUR-WS.org, 2003.
11. D.L. Moody and M.A. Kortink. From Enterprise Models to Dimensional Models: A Methodology for Data Warehouse and Data Mart Design. In *Proc. of DMDW'2000*. CEUR-WS.org, 2000.
12. R. Winter and B. Strauch. A Method for Demand-Driven Information Requirements Analysis in Data Warehousing Projects. In *In Proc. of HICSS'03*, pages 231–239. IEEE, 2003.

Extending Visual OLAP for Handling Irregular Dimensional Hierarchies

Svetlana Mansmann and Marc H. Scholl

University of Konstanz, P.O. Box D188, 78457 Konstanz, Germany
{Svetlana.Mansmann, Marc.Scholl}@uni-konstanz.de

Abstract. Comprehensive data analysis has become indispensable in a variety of environments. Standard OLAP (On-Line Analytical Processing) systems, designed for satisfying the reporting needs of the business, tend to perform poorly or even fail when applied in non-business domains such as medicine, science, or government. The underlying multidimensional data model is restricted to aggregating only over summarizable data, i.e. where each dimensional hierarchy is a balanced tree. This limitation, obviously too rigid for a number of applications, has to be overcome in order to provide adequate OLAP support for novel domains.

We present a framework for querying complex multidimensional data, with the major effort at the conceptual level as to transform irregular hierarchies to make them navigable in a uniform manner. We provide a classification of various behaviors in dimensional hierarchies, followed by our two-phase modeling method that proceeds by eliminating irregularities in the data with subsequent transformation of a complex hierarchical schema into a set of well-behaved sub-dimensions.

Mapping of the data to a visual OLAP browser relies solely on meta-data which captures the properties of facts and dimensions as well as the relationships across dimensional levels. Visual navigation is schema-based, i.e., users interact with dimensional levels and the data instances are displayed on-demand. The power of our approach is exemplified using a real-world study from the domain of academic administration.

1 Introduction

Data warehouse technology, initially introduced in the early 90s to support data analysis in business environments, has recently become popular in a variety of novel applications like medicine, education, research, government etc. End-users interact with the data using advanced visual interfaces that enable intuitive navigation to the desired data subset and granularity as well as its expressive presentation using a wide spectrum of visualization techniques.

Data warehouse systems adopt a *multidimensional data model* tackling the challenges of the On-Line Analytical Processing (OLAP) [2] via efficient execution of queries that aggregate over large data volumes. Analytical values within this model are referred to as *measures*, uniquely determined by descriptive values drawn from a set of *dimensions*. The values within a dimension are typically organized in a containment type hierarchy to support multiple granularities.

A Min Tjoa and J. Trujillo (Eds.): DaWaK 2006, LNCS 4081, pp. 95–105, 2006.

Standard OLAP ensures correct aggregation by enforcing *summarizability* in all dimensional hierarchies. The concept of *summarizability*, first introduced in [10] and further explored in [5] and [3], requires distributive aggregate functions and dimension hierarchy values, or informally, it requires that 1) facts map directly to the lowest-level dimension values and to only one value per dimension, and 2) dimensional hierarchies are balanced trees [5].

At the level of visual interfaces, summarizability is also crucial for generating a proper navigational hierarchy. Data browsers present each hierarchical dimension as recursively nested folders allowing users to browse either directly in the dimensional data, in which case each hierarchical entity can be expanded to see its child values, or in the dimensional attributes, where each hierarchical level is mapped to a sub-folder of its parent level's folder. Simple OLAP tools, e.g., Cognos PowerPlay [1], tend to provide only the data-based navigation whereas advanced interfaces, such as Tableau Software [13] and SAP NetWeaver BI [11], combine schema navigation with data display. Figure 1 shows the difference between data- and schema-based browsing for a hierarchical dimension Period.

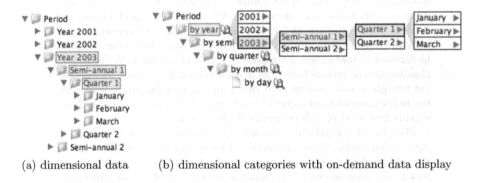

(a) dimensional data   (b) dimensional categories with on-demand data display

Fig. 1. Browsing in dimensional hierarchies: data vs. schema navigation

Analysts are frequently confronted with non-summarizable data which cannot be adequately supported by standard models and systems. To meet the challenges of novel applications, OLAP tools are to be extended at virtually all levels of the system architecture, from conceptual, logical and physical data transformation to adequately interfacing the data for visual querying and providing appropriate visualization techniques for comprehensive analysis.

This paper presents an OLAP framework capable of handling a wide spectrum of irregular dimensional hierarchies in a uniform and intuitive manner. All introduced extensions are supported by enriching the meta-data and providing algorithms for interfacing the data and mapping user interaction back to OLAP queries. The remainder of the paper is structured as follows: Section 2 sets the stage by describing related work and a motivating real-world case study from the area of academic administration. A classification of supported hierarchical patterns and re-modelling techniques for heterogeneous hierarchies are presented in Section 3, followed by the methods for data transformation and translating the multidimensional schema into a navigational framework in Section 4. We summarize our contribution and identify future research directions in Section 5.

2   Motivation and Related Work

2.1   Related Work on Multidimensional Data Modelling

A number of researchers have recognized the deficiencies of the traditional OLAP data model [15] and suggested a series of extensions at the conceptual level.

A powerful approach to modeling dimension hierarchies along with SQL query language extensions called SQL($\mathcal{H}$) was presented in [4]. SQL($\mathcal{H}$) does not require data hierarchies to be balanced or homogeneous. Niemi et al. [6] analyzed unbalanced and ragged data trees and demonstrated how dependency information can assist in designing summarizable hierarchies. Hurtado et al. [3] propose a framework for testing summarizability in heterogeneous dimensions.

Pedersen et al. have formulated further requirements an extended multidimensional data model should satisfy and evaluated 14 state-of-the-art models from both the research community and commercial systems in [9]. Since none of the existing models was even close to meeting most of the defined requirements, the authors proposed an extended model for capturing and querying complex multidimensional data. This model, supporting non-summarizable hierarchies, many-to-many relationships between facts and dimensions, handling temporal changes and imprecision, is by far the most powerful multidimensional data model of the current state of the art. A prototypical implementation of an OLAP engine called the Tree Scape System, which handles irregular hierarchies by normalizing them into summarizable ones, is described in [8].

To our best knowledge most of the extensions formalized by the above models have not been incorporated into any visual OLAP interface. In our previous work [14] we presented some insights into visual querying of heterogeneous and mixed-granularity dimensions. Our current contribution is an attempt to further reduce the gap between powerful concepts and deficient practices by designing a comprehensive framework for visual analytical querying of complex data.

2.2   Motivating Case Study

Our presented case study is concerned with the accumulated data on the expenditures within a university. Academic management wishes the data to be organized into an OLAP cube where the fact table *Expenditures* contains single orders with the measure attribute *amount* and dimensional characteristics *date*, *cost class*, *project*, *purchaser*, and *funding*. The values of each dimension are further arranged into hierarchies by defining the desired granularity levels, as illustrated by a diagram in ME/R notation (Multidimensional Entity/Relationship, introduced in [12]) shown in Figure 2.

We proceed by specifying various relationships within the dimensions of our case study and the requirements for their modeling.

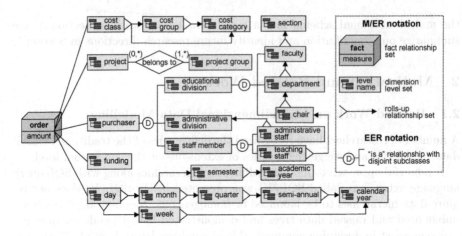

Fig. 2. University expenditures case study as ME/R Diagram

1. *Non-hierarchy*: A dimension with a single granularity, i.e. not involved in any incoming or outgoing rolls-up relationship, as is the case with funding.
2. *Strict hierarchy*: A dimension with only one outgoing rolls-up relationship per entity, i.e. with a many-to-one relationship towards each upper level of aggregation, for instance, chair → department → faculty → section.
3. *Non-strict hierarchy*: A dimension allows many-to-many relationships between its levels. In our example, the relationship between project and project group allows a single project to be associated with multiple project groups.
4. *Multiple hierarchies*: A single dimension may have several aggregation paths, as in period, where day may be grouped by month → quarter → semi-annual → calendar year, or by week → calendar year, or by month → semester → academic year. The former two paths are called alternative since they aggregate to the same top level.
5. *Heterogeneous hierarchy*: Consider the purchaser entity which is a super-class of educational division, administrative division, and staff member. Each sub-class has its own attributes and aggregation levels resulting in heterogeneous subtrees in the data hierarchy. Another example is staff member with sub-division into administrative staff and teaching staff.
6. *Non-covering hierarchy*: Strict hierarchy whose data tree is ragged due to allowing the links between data nodes to "skip" one or more levels. In terms of the ME/R diagram, such behavior occurs whenever the outgoing rolls-up relationship has more than one destinations level, as in cost class.
7. *Non-onto hierarchy*: Strict hierarchy that allows childless non-bottom nodes. For example, in the rolls-up relationship administrative staff → administrative division a division may appear to have no staff in purchaser role.
8. *Mixed-granularity hierarchy*: The data tree is unbalanced due to mixed granularity, as in the case of educational division whose sub-classes are, on the one hand, the end-instances of purchaser dimension, but, on the other hand, serve as aggregation levels in the hierarchy chair → department → faculty.

3   Extending the Multidimensional Data Model

In our work we rely on the terminology and formalization introduced by Petersen et al. in [9] since their model is the most powerful w.r.t. handling complex dimensional patterns like the ones identified in the previous section. However, we have also adopted some elements of the SQL($\mathcal{H}$) model [4] to enable heterogeneous hierarchies.

3.1   Basic Definitions

Intuitively, data hierarchy is a tree with each node being a tuple over a set of attributes. A dimensional hierarchy is based on a hierarchical attribute (the one directly referenced in the fact table), propagated to all levels of the tree.

Definition 3.1. A *hierarchical domain* is a non-empty set V_H with the only defined predicates = (identity), $\sqsubseteq$ (child/parent relationship), and $\sqsubseteq^*$ (transitive closure, or descendant/ancestor relationship) such that the graph $G_{\sqsubseteq}$ over the nodes $\{e_i\}$ of V_H is a tree. Attribute A of V_H is called a *hierarchical attribute*.

A hierarchy H is non-strict whenever $\exists (e_1, e_2, e_3 \in V_H) \wedge e_1 \sqsubseteq e_2 \wedge e_1 \sqsubseteq e_3 \wedge e_2 \neq e_3$, or, informally, if any node is allowed to have more than one parent.

Definition 3.2. A *hierarchy schema* $\mathcal{H}$ is a four-tuple $(\mathcal{C}, \sqsubseteq_{\mathcal{H}}, \top_{\mathcal{H}}, \bot_{\mathcal{H}})$, where $\mathcal{C} = \{\mathcal{C}_j, j = 1, \ldots, k\}$ are category types of $\mathcal{H}$, $\sqsubseteq_{\mathcal{H}}$ is a partial order on the $\mathcal{C}_j$'s, and $\top_{\mathcal{H}}$ and $\bot_{\mathcal{H}}$ are the top and bottom levels of the ordering, respectively.

$\mathcal{C}_j$ is said to be a category type in $\mathcal{H}$, denoted $\mathcal{C}_j \in \mathcal{H}$, if $\mathcal{C}_j \in \mathcal{C}$. Predicates $\sqsubset$ and $\sqsubset^*$ are used to define child/parent and descendant/ancestor relationship, respectively, between the category types in $\mathcal{C}$.

Definition 3.3. A *hierarchy (instance)* H associated with hierarchy schema $\mathcal{H}$ is a two-tuple $(C, \sqsubseteq)$, where $C = \{C_j\}$ is a set of categories such that $Type(C_j) = \mathcal{C}_j$ and $\sqsubseteq$ is a partial order on $\cup_j C_j$, the union of all dimensional values in the individual categories.

A category C_j is a set of dimensional values e such that $Type(e) = \mathcal{C}_j$; $|C_j|$ returns the number of values in set C_j. Hierarchy's data is stored in collection of tables with at most one table per schema node. Unlike in the original model of Jagadish et al. [4], we do not disallow tables with straddling levels in order to enable modeling of non-covering and mixed-granularity hierarchies.

We are now ready to formalize the notion of a homogeneous dimension.

Definition 3.4. A *homogeneous dimension* $\dot{D}$ is defined by its hierarchy schema $\mathcal{H} = (\mathcal{C}, \sqsubseteq_{\mathcal{H}}, \top_{\mathcal{H}}, \bot_{\mathcal{H}})$ and the respective hierarchy instance $H = (C, \sqsubseteq)$.

$\perp_{\mathcal{H}}$ is the type of $\dot{\mathcal{D}}$'s bottom category, i.e. the one containing the values of the finest granularity; $\top_{\mathcal{H}}$ corresponds to an abstract root node with a single value $\top$, also referred to as *ALL*.

A heterogeneous dimension is defined as consisting of multiple sub-dimensions, unified into a single hierarchy by means of super-classing:

> **Definition 3.5.** A *heterogeneous dimension* $\ddot{\mathcal{D}}$ is a pair $(\mathcal{D}, \top_{\mathcal{D}})$ where $\mathcal{D} = \{\mathcal{D}_i\}$ is a set of sub-dimensions and $\top_{\mathcal{D}}$ is an abstract super-class root node. Each sub-dimension $\mathcal{D}_i$ is of type $\dot{\mathcal{D}}$ or $\ddot{\mathcal{D}}$.

Figure 3 shows the resulting dimensional fact schema of our case study.

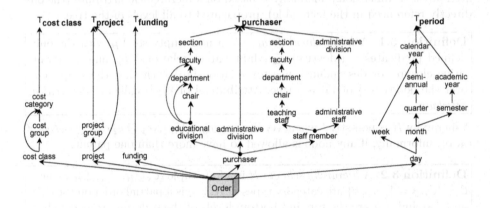

Fig. 3. University expenditures cube as 5-dimensional fact schema

3.2 Modeling Heterogeneous Hierarchies

At the conceptual level, heterogeneity corresponds to an *is_a* relationship, i.e. where the instances of a super-class are divided into sub-classes, each with its own attributes and aggregation levels. Logically, a super-class corresponds to an upper aggregation level w.r.t. its sub-class categories, but in the M/ER model super-classing is used for "homogenizing" heterogeneous entities and thus, a super-class ends up being a child of its sub-classes. Back to Figure 3, notice that super-classes purchaser, educational division, and staff member had to be placed underneath their respective sub-classes in the hierarchical schema.

From the logic of aggregation, the position of super-class entities is an obvious misplacement provoked by the requirement to have a single bottom granularity per dimension, so that it can be referenced by one foreign key in the fact table.

In Figure 4 we show the dimensional hierarchy of purchaser obtained by following the logic of dis-aggregation[1]. Notice how the heterogeneity of the dimensional

---

[1] Attached to each category node is the number of dimensional bottom-level values covered by that catergory. Unlike standard hierarchical categories, a sub-class of an *is_a* relationship contains just a fraction of its parent's values.

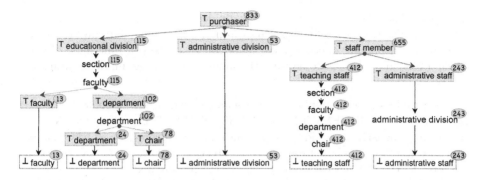

Fig. 4. Reshaping heterogeneous dimensions using abstract nodes

data has become obvious even at the bottom level. Using a straightforward intuition about hierarchically decomposing an aggregate, we can now derive a rule for modeling a *heterogeneous hierarchy*:

▷ the most general super-class serves as the root category $\top_{\mathcal{D}}$ whereas any further super-classes are normal categories;
▷ sub-classes are multiple child categories of their super-class category;
▷ sub-class category is of abstract type $\top_{\mathcal{D}_i}$ since it plays the role of an abstract root node for sub-dimension $\mathcal{D}_i$;
▷ sub-class entity is used repeatedly as a non-abstract bottom category $\bot_{\mathcal{D}_i}$ if it corresponds to the finest granularity of $\mathcal{D}_i$.

3.3   Modeling Mixed-Granularity Hierarchies

A special case of heterogeneity is a mixed-granularity hierarchy in which sub-classes of an *is_a* relationship are also used as hierarchy levels, as observed in educational institution where faculty and department are purchasers in their own right and also serve as aggregation categories for chair.

Our approach to modeling mixed-granularity is a straightforward mapping of the two-fold nature of its categories by means of sub-classing: mixed-granularity category is viewed as a heterogeneous dimension sub-divided into a non-hierarchical and a hierarchical sub-dimension, corresponding to its respective two roles. Further, the general rule of heterogeneous dimension modeling is applied. The resulting schema for educational division is shown in Figure 4.

4   Schema-Based Navigational Framework

Analysts interact with OLAP data in a predominantly "drill-down" fashion, starting with highly aggregated values and descending step-wise to the desired dimensionality and level of detail. The analyst's task can be thus reduced to a) selecting the measure and the aggregation function, b) browsing to the desired granularity in dimensional hierarchies, and c) filtering data to define the subset

to display. The visual OLAP interface is divided into two major areas of interaction: a navigation panel for browsing through dimensional data and the main
window for displaying query results. Selection of measures, functions, dimensional levels and values is done using the mouse, by clicking, marking, dragging
and so on.

A fact table is represented by a top-level folder (cube icon)
with sub-divisions DIMENSIONS and MEASURES. Each hierarchical dimension is a folder containing its schema categories as nested subfolders, from the root category $\top$ at the
top-level to the bottom category $\bot$, the latter represented
by a page icon. Non-abstract categories are supplied with a
button for displaying their actual data. Figure 5 shows the
navigational structure of our case study's OLAP cube.

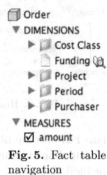

Fig. 5. Fact table navigation

In the remaining subsections we present the techniques
for mapping all types of dimensional hierarchies described
in section 2 to a schema-based navigational hierarchy.

4.1   Hierarchy Normalization Techniques

Schema-based navigation works correctly, if each data instance strictly adheres
to the schema of its respective hierarchy, or, formally, if for any two categories
C_j, C_i such that $C_i \sqsubseteq C_j$ the following summarizability conditions hold:

1. The mapping is *covering*: $\forall e_1 \in C_i : \exists e_2 \in C_j \land e_1 \sqsubseteq e_2$,
2. The mapping is *onto*[2]: $\forall e_2 \in C_j : (\exists e_1 \in C_i \lor (\exists e_1 \in C_k \land C_k \sqsubset C_j)) \land e_1 \sqsubseteq e_2$,
3. The mapping is *strict*: $\forall e_1 \in C_i : e_2, e_3 \in C_j \land e_1 \sqsubseteq e_2 \land e_1 \sqsubseteq e_3 \Rightarrow e_2 = e_1$.

Handling of non-summarizable data depends largely on the semantics behind
that data. If irregularity is caused by missing or imprecisely captured values and
it is crucial to produce imprecision-aware queries and results (e.g., in clinical
diagnosing or risk assessment), the approach of Pedersen et al. [9], in which the
original data remains un-normalized and imprecision is made explicit to the user
by providing a set of alternative queries, may be an appropriate solution.

However, if the data hierarchy is intrinsically irregular, as is project dimension,
where a project may be assigned to multiple groups or not assigned to any, such
data should be normalized to become navigable in a uniform way.

We adopt and modify the dimension transformation technique proposed by
Pedersen et al. in [7]. The original algorithm normalizes irregular hierarchies
by enforcing the summarizability conditions in the above order. The whole 3-
step transformation process, exemplified by normalizing the project dimension is
shown in Figure 6. In the second step, we provide options b) and c) in addition
to the original option a). *Onto* is enforced in the last step and can be omitted
altogether since missing bottom-level values are not relevant for navigability.

---

[2] By considering another child C_k we account for contingent heterogeneity of C_j.

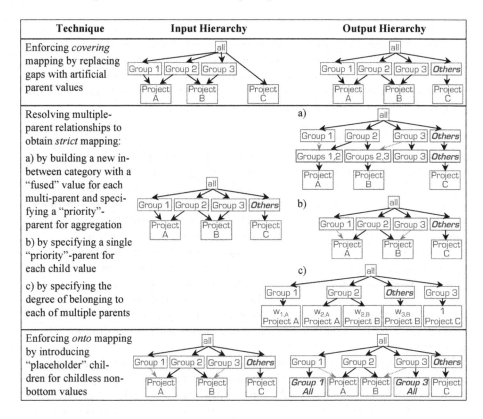

Fig. 6. 3-step normalization of the irregular dimension *project*

4.2   Schema Transformation Techniques

The navigational structure of a dimension is a recursive nesting of sub-dimensional nodes, where each node is used for drilling down to the respective granularity. The results of a drill-down are the sub-aggregates computed for each dimensional value. With respect to its underlying data hierarchy, the behavior of a sub-dimensional schema node can be reduced to the following types:

▷ *Non-hierarchical*, i.e bottom level, displayed as a non-expandable page icon;
▷ *Single-hierarchy* node is a folder containing a single subfolder of its child;
▷ *Multiple hierarchy* contains a subfolder for each of the alternative paths. These paths are mutually exclusive, so that once the user has selected one path, all others should be disabled for further interaction;
▷ *Super-class* is a folder containing all sub-class categories as subfolders. Since the super-class has no data of its own, there is no data display option. However, drill-down is possible and produces the aggregates of the sub-class categories. Sub-class folders are visually linked to each other, to be distinguished from the multiple hierarchy case since the former are not exclusive and, therefore, can be further explored in parallel;

▷ *Abstract Root*, node is a top-level folder with no data, used purely as a "wrapper" for the entire dimensional schema nested therein. Notice that abstract root is superfluous in case of a non-hierarchical (nothing to "wrap") or heterogeneous (abstract root already available) dimension.

▷ *Mixed-granularity* is a complex hierarchical node subdivided into a hierarchical and a bottom-level sub-dimensions.

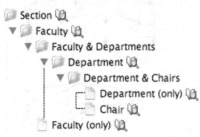

Fig. 7. Schema navigation hierarchy for a mixed-granularity fragment

Mixed-granularity deserves special attention due to its complexity. Figure 7 shows the resulting navigation for the fragment section → faculty → department → chair. Its structure is derived from the schema depicted in Figure 4, with the exception that the artificial sub-classes, such as $\top_{faculty}$ and $\top_{department}$ are merged into a common superclass node Faculty & Departments. This node is abstract and thus behaves as expected, i.e., its drill-down displays each of the two sub-class aggregates. The resulting navigation structure is rather complex, but it enables retrieval of a wide spectrum of aggregates with mere "drag-and-drop" interactions.

We have implemented the presented schema-based exploration approach for complex OLAP data as a Java application which connects to a specified database and allows user to navigate in OLAP cubes presenting the results as a pivot table, chart or a decomposition tree. At this stage, performance and scalability issues were left out of consideration.

5   Conclusion and Future Work

Inspired by the growing demand for OLAP applications in novel domains, confronted with irregular multidimensional data, we have presented a framework for modeling complex hierarchical dimensions and their seamless mapping to a schema-based navigational structure of a visual OLAP interface. Using a case study from the area of academic administration, we have provided a classification of dimensional behaviors, leading to non-summarizable hierarchies, such as ragged, unbalanced or non-strict data trees, as well as heterogeneous or mixed-granularity dimensional schema.

Our approach in based on a two-phase transformation of irregular dimensions: 1) enforcing summarizability within single homogeneous data hierarchies, and 2) reshaping complex hierarchical schemata into a set of well-behaved sub-dimensions. Our model does not introduce any query language extensions; it rather relies on the meta-data (e.g., dimension type, hierarchy schema, category type) for mapping OLAP data to a visual browser and translating user interaction back to the database operations.

Among our future research directions are to provide explicit handling of temporal and spatial aspects in modeling and querying OLAP data, to investigate the applicability of schema-based browsing for semi-structured and high-dimensional data, and to search for novel visualization and interaction techniques capable of presenting large volumes of complex data for explorative analysis.

References

1. "Cognos PowerPlay: Overview–OLAP Software," 2006. [Online]. Available: http://www.cognos.com/powerplay

2. E. F. Codd, S. B. Codd, and C. T. Salley, "Providing OLAP (on-line analytical processing) to user-analysts: An IT mandate," *Technical report, E.F.Codd & Associates*, 1993.

3. C. A. Hurtado and A. O. Mendelzon, "Reasoning about summarizability in heterogeneous multidimensional schemas," in *ICDT 2001, Proceedings of the 8th International Conference on Database Theory*, 2001, pp. 375–389.

4. H. V. Jagadish, L. V. S. Lakshmanan, and D. Srivastava, "What can hierarchies do for data warehouses?" in *VLDB '99, Proceedings of 25th International Conference on Very Large Data Bases*, 1999, pp. 530–541.

5. H.-J. Lenz and A. Shoshani, "Summarizability in OLAP and statistical data bases," in *Proceedings of 9th International Conference on Scientific and Statistical Database Management*, 1997, pp. 132–143.

6. T. Niemi, J. Nummenmaa, and P. Thanisch, "Logical multidimensional database design for ragged and unbalanced aggregation," in *Proceedings of 3rd International Workshop on Design and Management of Data Warehouses*, 2001, pp. 7.1–7.8.

7. T. B. Pedersen, C. S. Jensen, and C. E. Dyreson, "Extending practical pre-aggregation in on-line analytical processing," in *VLDB'99, Proceedings of 25th International Conference on Very Large Data Bases*, 1999, pp. 663–674.

8. ——, "The TreeScape system: Reuse of pre-computed aggregates over irregular OLAP hierarchies," in *VLDB 2000, Proceedings of 26th International Conference on Very Large Data Bases*, 2000.

9. ——, "A foundation for capturing and querying complex multidimensional data," *Information Systems*, vol. 26, no. 5, pp. 383–423, 2001.

10. M. Rafanelli and A. Shoshani, "STORM: A statistical object representation model," in *Proceedings of 5th International Conference on Statistical and Scientific Database Management*, 1990, pp. 14–29.

11. "SAP NetWeaver Business Intelligence," 2006. [Online]. Available: http://www.sap.com/solutions/netweaver/components/bi

12. C. Sapia, M. Blaschka, G. Höfling, and B. Dinter, "Extending the E/R model for the multidimensional paradigm," in *ER '98, Proceedings of the Workshops on Data Warehousing and Data Mining*, 1999, pp. 105–116.

13. "Tableau software," 2006. [Online]. Available: http://www.tableausoftware.com

14. S. Vinnik and F. Mansmann, "From analysis to interactive exploration: Building visual hierarchies from OLAP cubes," in *EDBT 2006, Proceedings of 10th International Conference on Extending Database Technology*, 2006, pp. 496–514.

15. T. Zurek and M. Sinnwell, "Datawarehousing has more colours than just black & white," in *VLDB '99, Proceedings of 25th International Conference on Very Large Data Bases*, 1999, pp. 726–729.

A Hierarchy-Driven Compression Technique for Advanced OLAP Visualization of Multidimensional Data Cubes

Alfredo Cuzzocrea[1], Domenico Saccà[1,2], and Paolo Serafino[1]

[1] Department of Electronics, Computer Science, and Systems
University of Calabria, I-87036 Cosenza, Italy
{cuzzocrea, sacca, serafino}@si.deis.unical.it
[2] Institute of High Performance Computing and Networks
Italian National Research Council, I-87036 Cosenza, Italy
sacca@icar.cnr.it

Abstract. In this paper, we investigate the problem of visualizing multidimensional data cubes, and propose a novel technique for supporting advanced OLAP visualization of such data structures. Founding on very efficient data compression solutions for two-dimensional data domains, the proposed technique relies on the amenity of generating "semantics-aware" compressed representation of two-dimensional OLAP views extracted from multidimensional data cubes via the so-called OLAP dimension flattening process. A wide set of experimental results conducted on several kind of synthetic two-dimensional OLAP views clearly confirm the effectiveness and the efficiency of our technique, also in comparison with state-of-the-art proposals.

1 Introduction

OLAP systems [7,8,19,22] have rapidly gained momentum in both the academic and research communities, mainly due to their capability of exploring and querying huge amounts of data sets in a multidimensional and multi-resolution way. Research-wise, three relevant challenges of OLAP have captured a lot of attention during the last years: (*i*) the *data querying* problem, which concerns with how data are accessed and queried to support summarized knowledge extraction from massive data cubes; (*ii*) the *data modeling* problem, which concerns with how data are represented and, thus, processed inside OLAP servers (e.g., during query evaluation); (*iii*) the *data visualization* problem, which concerns with how data are presented to OLAP users and decision makers in Data Warehousing environments. Indeed, research communities have mainly studied and investigated the first two problems, whereas the last one, even if important-with-practical-applications, has been very often neglected.

Approximate Query Answering (AQA) techniques address the first challenge, and can be justly considered as one of the most important topics in OLAP research. The main proposal of AQA techniques consists in providing approximate answers to resource-consuming OLAP queries (e.g., range queries [18]) instead of computing exact answers, as decimal precision is usually negligible in OLAP query and report activities (e.g., see [10]). Due to a relevant interest from the Data Warehousing research

A Min Tjoa and J. Trujillo (Eds.): DaWaK 2006, LNCS 4081, pp. 106–119, 2006.
© Springer-Verlag Berlin Heidelberg 2006

community, AQA techniques have been intensively investigated during the last years, also achieving important results. Among the others, *histograms* (e.g., [2,5,15]), *wavelets* ([32]), and *sampling* (e.g., [13]) are the most successful techniques, and they have also inducted several applications in even different contexts than OLAP. Summarizing, AQA techniques propose (*i*) computing compressed representations of multidimensional data cubes, and (*ii*) evaluating (approximate) answers against such representations via ad-hoc query algorithms that, usually, meaningfully take advantage from their hierarchical nature, which, in turn, is inherited from the one of input data cubes. *Conceptual data models* for OLAP are widely recognized as based on data cube concepts like *dimension, hierarchy, level, member,* and *measure,* first introduced by Gray *et al.* [14], which inspired various models for multidimensional databases and data cubes (e.g., [3,16,29,30,31]). Nevertheless, despite this effort, recently, several papers have put in evidence some formal limitations of accepted conceptual models for OLAP (e.g., [6]), or theoretical failures of popular data cube operations, like aggregation functions (e.g., [24,25,26]). Contrarily to the data querying and modeling issues, since *data presentation models* do not properly belong to the well-founded conceptual-logical-physical hierarchy for relational database models (which has also been inherited from multidimensional models), the problem of OLAP data visualization has been studied and investigated only so far [12,20,21,27,28]. On the other hand, being essentially OLAP a technology to support decision making, thus based on (sensitive) information exploration and browsing, it is easy to understand that, in future years, tools for advanced visualization of multidimensional data cubes will quickly conquest the OLAP research scene.

Starting from the fundamentals of the data cube compression and OLAP data visualization research issues, in this paper we argue to meaningfully exploit the main results coming from the first one and the goals of the second one in a combined manner, and propose *a novel technique for supporting advanced OLAP visualization of multidimensional data cubes.* The basic motivation of such an approach is realizing that (*i*) compressing data is an (efficient) way of visualizing data, and (*ii*) this intuition is well-founded at large (i.e., for any data-intensive system relying on massive data repositories), and, more specifically, it is particularly targeted to the OLAP context where accessing multidimensional data cubes can become a realistic bottleneck for Data Warehousing systems and applications.

Briefly, our proposed technique relies on two steps. The first one consists in generating a two-dimensional OLAP view D from the input multidimensional data cube A by means of an innovative approach that allows us to *flatten OLAP dimensions* (of A), and, as a consequence, effectively support exploration and browsing activities against A (via D), by overcoming the natural disorientation and refractoriness of human beings in dealing with hyper-spaces. Particularly, the (two) OLAP dimensions on which D is defined are built from the dimensions of A according to the analysis goals of the target OLAP user/application. The second step consists in generating a bucket-based compressed representation of D named as *Hierarchy-driven Indexed Quad-Tree Summary* (H-IQTS), and denoted by *H-IQTS(D)*, which meaningfully extends the compression technique for two-dimensional summary data domains presented in [4], by introducing the amenity of *generating semantics-aware buckets*, i.e. buckets that "follow" groups of the OLAP hierarchies of D. In other words, *we use the OLAP hierarchies defined on the dimensions of D to drive the compression process.* The latter step allows us to achieve space efficiency, while, at the same time, supporting approximate query answering and advanced OLAP visualization features. Similarly to [4], *H-IQTS(D)* is shaped as a quad-tree (thus, each "internal" bucket in *H-IQTS(D)* has four child sub-buckets), and the information stored in its buckets is still the sum of the items contained within them.

The technique we propose in this paper can be successfully applied to all those scenarios in which accessing and exploring massive multidimensional data cubes is a critical requirement. For instance, this is the case of *mobile OLAP systems and applications*, where users access corporate OLAP servers via handheld devices. In fact, mobile devices are usually characterized by specific properties (e.g., small storage space, small size of the display screen, discontinuance of the connection to the WLAN etc) that are often incompatible with the need of browsing and querying summarized information extracted from massive multidimensional data cubes made accessible through wireless networks. In such application scenarios, flattening multi-dimensional data cubes into two-dimensional OLAP views represents an effective solution yet an enabling technology for mobile OLAP, as, contrarily to what happens for hyper-spaces, handheld devices can easily visualize two-dimensional screens. This property, along with the realistic need of compressing data to be transmitted and processed by handheld devices, makes perfect sense to our idea of using data com-pression techniques as a way of visualizing OLAP data. Moreover, the amenity of driving the compression process by means of the OLAP hierarchies, thus meaning-fully generating semantics-aware buckets, further corroborates the application of our proposed technique to mobile OLAP environments, as the limited computational capabilities of handheld devices impose to definitively process useful knowledge, by discarding the useless one, being resource-consuming transactions infeasible for such kind of devices. For instance, these results can be successfully applied to the system *Hand-OLAP*, proposed by us in [11], which allows a handheld device to extract, browse and query compressed two-dimensional views (which are computed via the technique [4]) coming from a remote OLAP server. The basic idea which Hand-OLAP is based on is: rather than querying the original multidimensional data, it may be more convenient to generate a compressed view of them, store the view into the handheld device, and query it locally (off-line), thus obtaining approximate answers that, as well-understood, are perfectly suitable for OLAP goals (e.g., see [10]). Now, consider the benefits that can be achieved in Hand-OLAP thanks to the proposed technique. In Hand-OLAP, compressed views extracted from remote OLAP servers are mainly browsed via popular DRILL-DOWN OLAP operations (i.e., increasing the level of detail of OLAP data) implemented via splits over buckets of the view. Never-theless, letting b be the current bucket, since each split partitions b into four equal-size sub-buckets, the OLAP user could be required to perform many splits before to access the summarized knowledge he/she is interested in, as "wrong" buckets could be accessed during the exploration task. On the contrary, by admitting semantics-aware buckets, since OLAP analysis is subject-oriented [17], the OLAP user accesses the summarized knowledge of interest in a faster manner rather than the previous case, as each split partitions b into four sub-buckets computed over semantically-related OLAP data.

2   Fundamentals and Basic Definitions

In order to better understand our proposal, it is needed to introduce some fundamentals and basic definitions regarding the constructs of OLAP conceptual data model we adopt, along with the notation we use in the rest of the paper. These definitions are compatible with main results of previous popular models (e.g., [14]).

Given an OLAP dimension d_i, and its domain of *members* $\Psi(d_i)$, each of them denoted by ρ_j, a *hierarchy* defined on d_i, denoted by $H(d_i)$, can be represented as a general tree (i.e., such that each node of the tree has a number $N \geq 0$ of child nodes) built on the top of $\Psi(d_i)$. The tree $H(d_i)$ is usually built according to a bottom-up strategy by (*i*) setting as leaf nodes of $H(d_i)$ members in $\Psi(d_i)$, and (*ii*) iteratively aggregating sets of members in $\Psi(d_i)$ to obtain other (internal) members, each of them denoted by σ_j, which correspond to internal nodes in $H(d_i)$. In turn, internal members in $H(d_i)$ can be further aggregated to form other super-members until a unique aggregation of members is obtained; the latter corresponds to the root node of $H(d_i)$, and it is known in literature as the *aggregation ALL*. More precisely, ALL is only an artificial aggregation introduced to obtain a tree (i.e., $H(d_i)$) instead of a list of trees, each of them rooted in the second level internal nodes σ_j, which should be the "effective" upper-level partition of members in $\Psi(d_i)$. Each member in $H(d_i)$ is characterized by a *level* (of the hierarchy), denoted by L_j; as a consequence, we can define a level L_j in $H(d_i)$ as a collection of members. For each level L_j, the ordering of L_j, denoted by $O(L_j)$, is the one exposed by the OLAP server platform for the target data cube. Note that such ordering depends on how knowledge held in (OLAP) data is produced, processed, and delivered.

Given a multidimensional data cube A such that $Dim(A) = \{d_0, d_1, ..., d_{n-1}\}$ is the set of dimensions of A, and $Hie(A) = \{H(d_0), H(d_1), ..., H(d_{n-1})\}$ the set of hierarchies defined on the latter, being $H(d_i)$ the hierarchy defined on d_i, letting $L_j \geq 0$ be an integer, the collection of members σ_j at the level L_j (note that, when $L_j = 0$, $\sigma_j \equiv \rho_j$) of each hierarchy $H(d_i)$ in $Hie(A)$ univocally refers, in a multidimensional fashion, a certain (OLAP) data cell C_p in A *at the level* L_j (in other words, C_p is the OLAP aggregation of data cells in A *at the level* L_j). We name such collection as *j-level OLAP Metadata* (for C_p), and denote them as $J\text{-}M(C_p)$.

Given a member σ_j at the level L_j of the hierarchy $H(d_i)$ defined on an OLAP dimension d_i and the set of its child nodes $Child(\sigma_j)$, which are members at the level L_{j+1}, we define as the *Left Boundary Member* (LBM) of σ_j the child node of σ_j in $Child(\sigma_j)$ that is the *first* in the ordering $O(L_{j+1})$. Analogously, we define as the *Right Boundary Member* (RBM) of σ_j the child node of σ_j in $Child(\sigma_j)$ that is the *last* in the ordering $O(L_{j+1})$.

3   OLAP Dimension Flattening

The OLAP dimension flattening process is the first step of our technique for supporting advanced OLAP visualization of multidimensional data cubes. In more detail, we flatten dimensions of the input multidimensional data cube A into two specialized dimensions called *Visualization Dimensions* (VD) that support advanced OLAP visualization of A via constructing an ad-hoc two-dimensional OLAP view D defined on the VDs.

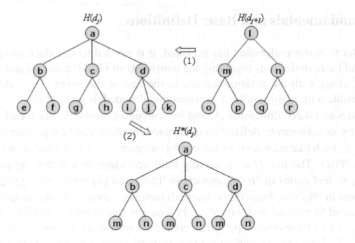

Fig. 1. Merging OLAP hierarchies

The process that allows us to obtain the two VDs from the dimensions of A works as follows. Letting $Dim(A)$ and $Hie(A)$ be the set of dimensions and the set of hierarchies of A respectively (formally defined as in Sect. 2), each VD is a tuple $v_i = \langle d_i, H^*(d_i) \rangle$ such that (i) d_i is the dimension selected by the target OLAP user/application, (ii) $H^*(d_i)$ is a hierarchy built from meaningfully merging the "original" hierarchy $H(d_i)$ of d_i with the hierarchies of other dimensions in A according to an ordered definition set $MD(v_i) = \{\langle HL_i, d_j, P_j \rangle, \langle HL_j, d_{j+1}, P_{j+1} \rangle, ..., \langle HL_{j+K-1}, d_{j+K}, P_{j+K} \rangle\}$, where $K = |MD(v_i)| - 1$. In more detail, for each couple of consecutive tuples $\langle\langle HL_j, d_{j+1}, P_{j+1} \rangle$, $\langle HL_{j+1}, d_{j+2}, P_{j+2} \rangle\rangle$ in $MD(v_i)$, the sub-tree of $H(d_{j+2})$ rooted in the root node of $H(d_{j+2})$ and having depth equal to P_{j+2}, denoted by $H_S^{P_{j+2}}(d_{j+2})$, is merged to $H(d_{j+1})$ by appending a *clone* of it to *each* member σ_{j+1} of the level HL_{j+1}, named as *hooking level*, in $H(d_{j+1})$. From the described approach, it follows that: (i) the ordering of items in $MD(v_i)$ defines the way of building $H^*(d_i)$; (ii) the first hierarchy to be processed is just $H(d_i)$. As an example of the flattening process of two OLAP dimensions into a new one, consider Fig. 1, where the hierarchy $H^*(d_j)$ is obtained by merging $H(d_{j+1})$ to $H(d_j)$ via setting $P_{j+1} = 1$ and $HL_j = 1$.

As regards data processing issues, it should be noted that, due to the above OLAP dimension flattening task, in order to finally compute D, it is needed to re-aggregate multidimensional data in A according to the new VDs.

4   Hierarchy-Driven Compression of Two-Dimensional OLAP Views

Compressing the two-dimensional OLAP view D (extracted from A according to the OLAP dimension flattening process presented in Sect. 3) is the second step of our proposed technique. Given D, for each step j of our compression algorithm, we need to (1) greedily select the leaf bucket b of $H\text{-}IQTS(D)$ having maximum *Sum of the*

Squared Errors (SSE), (2) split *b* in four sub-buckets through investigating, for each dimension d_k of *D*, levels of the hierarchy $H(d_k)$. The task (1) is similar to what proposed in [4] for two-dimensional summary data domains, whereas the novelty proposed in this paper consists in the task (2).

Formally, given the current bucket $b_j = D[l_{j,0}:u_{j,0}][l_{j,1}:u_{j,1}]$ to be split at the step *j* of our compression algorithm, such that $[l_{j,k}:u_{j,k}]$ is the range of b_j on the dimension d_k of *D*, the problem is finding, for each dimension d_k of *D*, a *splitting position* $S_{j,k}$ belonging to $[l_{j,k}:u_{j,k}]$. To this end, for each dimension d_k of *D*, our splitting strategy aims at (*i*) grouping items into buckets related to the same semantic domain, and (*ii*) maintaining as more balanced as possible the hierarchy $H(d_k)$. Particularly, the first aspect lets the benefits highlighted in Sect. 1; the second aspect allows us to sensitively improve query estimation capabilities as, on the basis of this approach, we finally obtain buckets with balanced "numerousness" (of items) that introduce a smaller approximation error in the evaluation of (OLAP) queries involving several buckets rather than the contrary case (see [4] for further investigations).

4.1 A Hierarchy-Driven Algorithm for Compressing Two-Dimensional OLAP Views

For the sake of simplicity, we will present our hierarchy-driven compression algorithm for two-dimensional OLAP views through showing how to handle the hierarchy of an OLAP dimension d_k (i.e., how to determine a splitting position $S_{j,k}$ on d_k). Obviously, this technique must be performed for both the dimensions of the target (two-dimensional) OLAP view *D*, thus obtaining, for each *couple* of splits at the step *j* of our algorithm (i.e., $S_{j,0}$ and $S_{j,1}$), four two-dimensional bucket to be added to the current partition of *D* (see Sect. 1).

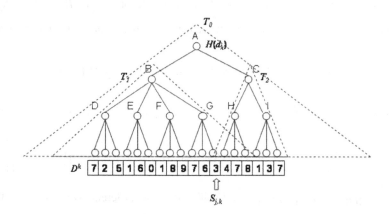

Fig. 2. Modeling the splitting strategy

Let $b_j = D[l_{j,0}:u_{j,0}][l_{j,1}:u_{j,1}]$ be the current bucket to be split at the step *j*. Consider the range $[l_{j,k}:u_{j,k}]$ of b_j on the dimension d_k of *D*. To determine $S_{j,k}$ on $[l_{j,k}:u_{j,k}]$, we denote as $T_{j,k}(l_{j,k}:u_{j,k})$ the sub-tree of $H(d_k)$ whose (*i*) leaf nodes are the members of the sets $0\text{-}M(C_w)$ defined on the data cells C_w in $D[l_{j,k}:u_{j,k}]$ (i.e., the one-dimensional bucket obtained by projecting b_j with respect to the dimension d_k), and (ii) the root node is the (single) member of the set P_k-$M(C_r)$ defined on the data cell C_r that is the aggregation of $D[l_{j,k}:u_{j,k}]$ at the level L_P of $H(d_k)$ (note that P_k is also the depth of $T_{j,k}(l_{j,k}:u_{j,k})$). To give an example, consider Fig. 2, where the one-dimensional OLAP view $D^k = D[0:|d_k| - 1]$, obtained by projecting D with respect to the dimension d_k, along with the hierarchy $H(d_k)$ are depicted. As shown in Fig. 2, the tree T_0, properly denoted by $T_{j,k}(0:17)$, is related to the whole OLAP view $D^k = D[0:17]$, and corresponds to the whole $H(d_k)$. At the step j, d_k is split in the position $S_{j,k} = 11$, thus generating the buckets $D[0:11]$ and $D[12:17]$. In consequence of this, the tree T_1, properly denoted by $T_{j+1,k}(0:11)$, is related to $D[0:11]$, whereas the tree T_2, properly denoted by $T_{j+1,k}(12:17)$, is related to $D[12:17]$.

Formally, let (i) d_k be the dimension of D to be processed; (ii) $H(d_k)$ the hierarchy defined on d_k, such that $P_k > 0$ is the depth of $H(d_k)$; (iii) $b_j = D[l_{j,k}:u_{j,k}]$ the current (one-dimensional) bucket to be split at the step j of our algorithm; (iv) $T_{j,k}(l_{j,k}:u_{j,k})$ the tree related to b_j. In order to select the splitting position $S_{j,k}$ on $[l_{j,k}:u_{j,k}]$, letting $T^1_{j,k}(l_{j,k}:u_{j,k})$ be the *second* level of $T_{j,k}(l_{j,k}:u_{j,k})$, we initially consider the data cell C_k in $D[l_{j,k}:u_{j,k}]$ whose indexer is in the middle of $D[l_{j,k}:u_{j,k}]$, denoted by $X_{j,D} = \left\lfloor \frac{1}{2} \cdot \left| D[l_{j,k}:u_{j,k}] \right| \right\rfloor$. It should be noted that processing the second level of $T_{j,k}(l_{j,k}:u_{j,k})$ (i.e., $T^1_{j,k}(l_{j,k}:u_{j,k})$) derives from the use of the aggregation ALL in OLAP conceptual models, which, in total, introduces an *additional* level in the general tree modeling an OLAP hierarchy (as discussed in Sect. 2).

Then, starting from ρ_k, being ρ_k the (only – see Sect. 2) member in the set 0-$M(C_k)$, we go up on $H(d_k)$ until the parent of ρ_k at the level $T^1_{j,k}(l_{j,k}:u_{j,k})$, denoted by σ_k, is reached, and we decide how to determine $S_{j,k}$ on the basis of the nature of σ_k. If σ_k is the LBM of the root node of $T_{j,k}(l_{j,k}:u_{j,k})$, denoted by $R_{j,k}$, then $S_{j,k} = \left\lfloor \frac{1}{2} \cdot \left| D[l_{j,k}:u_{j,k}] \right| \right\rfloor - 1$ and, as a consequence, we obtain the following two (one-dimensional) buckets as child buckets of b_j: $b'_{j+1} = \left[l_{j,k} : \left\lfloor \frac{1}{2} \cdot \left| D[l_{j,k}:u_{j,k}] \right| \right\rfloor - 1 \right]$ and $b''_{j+1} = \left[\left\lfloor \frac{1}{2} \cdot \left| D[l_{j,k}:u_{j,k}] \right| \right\rfloor : u_{j,k} \right]$. Otherwise, if σ_k is the RBM of $R_{j,k}$, then $S_{j,k} = \left\lfloor \frac{1}{2} \cdot \left| D[l_{j,k}:u_{j,k}] \right| \right\rfloor$ and, as a consequence, $b'_{j+1} = \left[l_{j,k} : \left\lfloor \frac{1}{2} \cdot \left| D[l_{j,k}:u_{j,k}] \right| \right\rfloor \right]$ and $b''_{j+1} = \left[\left\lfloor \frac{1}{2} \cdot \left| D[l_{j,k}:u_{j,k}] \right| \right\rfloor + 1 : u_{j,k} \right]$. Finally, if σ_k is different from both the LBM and the RBM of $R_{j,k}$, i.e. it *follows* the LBM of $R_{j,k}$ in the ordering $O(T^1_{j,k}(l_{j,k}:u_{j,k}))$ and *precedes* the RBM of $R_{j,k}$ in the ordering $O(T^1_{j,k}(l_{j,k}:u_{j,k}))$, we perform a finite number of shift operations on the indexers of $D[l_{j,k}:u_{j,k}]$ starting from the middle indexer $X_{j,D}$ and within the range $\Gamma_{j,k} = \left[\left\lfloor \frac{1}{2} \cdot \left| D[l_{j,k}:u_{j,k}] \right| \right\rfloor - \left\lfloor \frac{1}{3} \cdot \left| D[l_{j,k}:u_{j,k}] \right| \right\rfloor \right]$:

$$\left\lfloor \frac{1}{2} \cdot \left| D[l_{j,k}:u_{j,k}] \right| \right\rfloor + \left\lfloor \frac{1}{3} \cdot \left| D[l_{j,k}:u_{j,k}] \right| \right\rfloor \right\rfloor$$ until a data cell V_k in $D[l_{j,k}:u_{j,k}]$ such that the

corresponding member σ_k at the level $T^1_{j,k}(l_{j,k}:u_{j,k})$ is the LBM or the RBM of $R_{j,k}$, if exists, is found. It should be noted that admitting a maximum offset of

$\pm \left\lfloor \frac{1}{3} \cdot \left| D^k[l_{j,k}:u_{j,k}] \right| \right\rfloor$ with respect to the middle of the current bucket is coherent with

the aim of maintaining as more balanced as possible the hierarchy $H(d_k)$, which allows us to take advantages from the above-highlighted benefits (see Sect. 4).

To this end, starting from the middle of $\Gamma_{j,k}$ (which is equal to the one of $D[l_{j,k}:u_{j,k}]$, $X_{j,D}$), we iteratively consider indexers $I_{j,q}$ within $\Gamma_{j,k}$ defined by the following function:

$$I_{j,q} = \begin{cases} X_{j,D} & q = 0 \\ I_{j,q-1} + (-1)^q \cdot q & q > 1 \end{cases} \tag{1}$$

If such data cell V_k exists, then $S_{j,k}$ is set as equal to the so-determined indexer $I^*_{j,q}$, and, as a consequence, we obtain the couples of buckets $b'_{j+1} = \left\lfloor l_{j,k} : I^*_{j,q} - 1 \right\rfloor$ and $b''_{j+1} = \left\lfloor I^*_{j,q} : u_{j,k} \right\rfloor$ if $I^*_{j,q}$ is the LBM of $R_{j,k}$, or, alternatively, the couples of buckets $b'_{j+1} = \left\lfloor l_{j,k} : I^*_{j,q} \right\rfloor$ and $b''_{j+1} = \left\lfloor I^*_{j,q} + 1 : u_{j,k} \right\rfloor$ if $I^*_{j,q}$ is the RBM of $R_{j,k}$. On the contrary, if such data cell V_k does not exist, then we do not perform any split on $D[l_{j,k}:u_{j,k}]$, and we "remand" the splitting at the next step of the algorithm (i.e., $j + 1$) where the splitting position $S_{j+1,k}$ is determined by processing the *third* level $T^2_{j+1,k}(l_{j+1,k}:u_{j+1,k})$ of the tree $T_{j+1,k}(l_{j+1,k}:u_{j+1,k})$ (i.e., by decreasing the aggregation level of OLAP data with respect to the previous step). The latter approach is iteratively repeated until a data cell V_k verifying the above condition is found; otherwise, if the leaf level of $T_{j,k}(l_{j,k}:u_{j,k})$ is reached without finding any admissible splitting point, then $D[l_{j,k}:u_{j,k}]$ is added to the current partition of the OLAP view without being split. We point out that this way to do still pursues the aim of obtaining balanced partitions of the input OLAP view.

5 Experimental Study

5.1 Definitions and Metrics

In order to test the effectiveness of our proposed technique, we defined two kinds of experiments. The first one is oriented to probe the data cube *compression performances* (or, equally, the *accuracy*) of our technique, whereas the second one is instead oriented to probe the *visualization capabilities* of our technique in meaningfully supporting advanced OLAP visualization of multidimensional data cubes.

As regards the data layer of our experimental framework, we engineered two kinds of synthetic two-dimensional OLAP views (which, in turn, have been extracted from synthetic multidimensional data cubes via a random flattening process on the dimensions of the latter): (*i*) the view $D_C(L_1, L_2)$, for which data are uniformly distributed on a given range $[L_1, L_2]$ (i.e., the well-known *Continuous Values Assumption* (CVA) [9] holds), and (*ii*) the view $D_Z(z_{min}, z_{max})$, for which data are distributed according to a

Zipf distribution whose parameter z is randomly chosen on a given range $[z_{min}, z_{max}]$. Particularly, the latter realizes a totally random process for generating OLAP data and, as a consequence, closer to real-life views are obtained. Among other well-recognized benefits, using synthetic OLAP views allows us to completely control the variation of input parameters determining the nature of the OLAP data distributions as well as the one of the OLAP hierarchies (e.g., acting on the topology of the hierarchies etc), thus enriching the effectiveness of the analysis.

As regards the outcomes of our study, we defined the following metrics. For the first kind of experiments (i.e., that focused on the accuracy), given a population of synthetic range-SUM queries Q_S, we measure the *Average Relative Error* (ARE) between exact and approximate answers to queries in Q_S, i.e.

$$\bar{E}_{rel} = \frac{1}{|Q_S|} \cdot \sum_{k=0}^{|Q_S|-1} E_{rel}(Q_k), \text{ such that, for each query } Q_k \text{ in } Q_S, \; E_{rel}(Q_k) =$$

$$\frac{|A(Q_k) - \tilde{A}(Q_k)|}{A(Q_k)}, \text{ where } (i) \; A(Q_k) \text{ is the exact answer to } Q_k, \text{ and } (ii) \; \tilde{A}(Q_k) \text{ is the}$$

approximate answer to Q_k. Particularly, fixing a range sizes Δ_k for each dimension d_k of the target synthetic OLAP view D, we generate queries in Q_S through spanning D by means of the "seed" $\Delta_0 \times \Delta_1$ query Q^s.

For the second kind of experiments, we was inspired from the *Hierarchical Range Queries* (HRQ) introduced by Koudas *et al.* in [23]. In our implementation, a HRQ $Q_H(W_H, P_H)$ is a full tree such that: (*i*) the depth of such tree is equal to P_H; (*ii*) each internal node N_i has a fan-out degree equal to W_H; (*iii*) each node N_i stores the definition of a ("traditional") range-SUM query Q_i; (*iv*) for each node N_i in $Q_H(W_H, P_H)$, there not exists any sibling node N_j of N_i such that $Q_i \cap Q_j <> \emptyset$. Similarly to the previous kind of experiments, for each node N_i in $Q_H(W_H, P_H)$, the population of queries $Q_{S,i}$ to be used as input query set was generated by means of the above-described spanning technique (i.e., upon the seed query Q_i^s). In more detail, since, due the nature of HRQs, the selectivity of seed queries $Q_{i,k}^s$ of nodes N_i at the level k of $Q_H(W_H, P_H)$ *must* decreases as the depth P_k of $Q_H(W_H, P_H)$ increases, letting γ be an input parameter and $\|D\|$ the selectivity of the target OLAP view D, we first impose that the selectivity of the seed query of the root node N_0 in $Q_H(W_H, P_H)$, denoted by $\| Q_{0,0}^s \|$, is equal to the γ % of $\|D\|$, and then, for each internal node N_i in $Q_H(W_H, P_H)$ at level k, we randomly determine the seed queries of the child nodes of N_i by checking the following constraint: $\sum_{i=0}^{|(W_H)^{k+1}|-1} \| Q_{i,k+1}^s \| \leq \| Q_{i,k}^s \|$ and $Q_{i,k+1}^s \cap Q_{j,k+1}^s = \emptyset$ for each i and j in $[0, |(W_H)^{k+1}|-1]$, with $i <> j$, and adopting the criterion of maximizing each $\| Q_{i,k}^s \|$.

It should be noted that HRQs have a wide range of applications in OLAP systems (as also highlighted in [23]), since they allow us to extract "hierarchically-shaped" summarized knowledge from massive data cubes. Given a HRB $Q_H(W_H, P_H)$, we measure the *Average Accessed Bucket Number* (AABN), which models the average number of buckets accessed during the evaluation of $Q_H(W_H, P_H)$, and it is defined as follows: $AABN(Q_H(W_H,P_H)) = \sum_{k=0}^{P_H} \frac{1}{(W_H)^k} \cdot \sum_{\ell=0}^{|(W_H)^k|-1} AABN(N_\ell)$,   where, in turn,

AABN(N_ℓ) is the average number of buckets accessed during the evaluation of the population of queries $Q_{S,\ell}$ of the node N_ℓ in $Q_H(W_H,P_H)$, i.e. $AABN(N_\ell) =$

$\frac{1}{|Q_{S,\ell}|} \cdot \sum_{k=0}^{|Q_{S,\ell}|-1} ABN(Q_k)$, such that for each query Q_k in $Q_{S,\ell}$, ABN(Q_k) is the number

of buckets accessed during the evaluation of Q_k. Summarizing, given a compression technique T, AABN allows us to measure the capabilities of T in supporting advanced OLAP visualization of multidimensional data cubes as the number of buckets accessed can be reasonably considered as a measure of the computational cost needed to extract summarized knowledge, as a sort of measure of the *entropy* of the overall knowledge extraction process. As stated in Sect. 1, this aspect assumes a leading role in mobile OLAP settings (e.g., Hand-OLAP [11]).

5.2 Experimental Results

In our experimental study, we compared the performances of our proposed technique (under the two metrics defined above) against the following well-known histogram-based techniques for compressing data cubes: *MinSkew* by Acharya *et al.* [2], *GenHist* by Gunopulos *et al.* [15], and *STHoles* by Bruno *et al.* [5]. In more detail, having fixed the space budget G (i.e., the storage space available for housing the compressed representation of the input OLAP view), we derived, for each comparison technique, the configuration of the input parameters that the respective authors consider the best in their papers. This ensures a *fair* experimental analysis, i.e. an analysis such that each comparison technique provides its *best* performances.

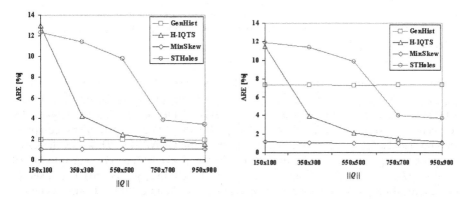

Fig. 3. Experimental results for the accuracy metrics with respect to the query selectivity ‖Q‖ on the 1.000 × 1.000 two-dimensional OLAP views $D_C(25,70)$ (left side) and $D_Z(0.5,1.5)$ (right side) with $r = 10$

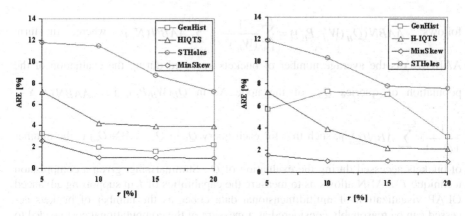

Fig. 4. Experimental results for the accuracy metrics with respect to the compression ratio r on the 1.000×1.000 two-dimensional OLAP views $D_C(25,70)$ (left side) and $D_Z(0.5,1.5)$ (right side) with $\|Q\| = 350 \times 300$

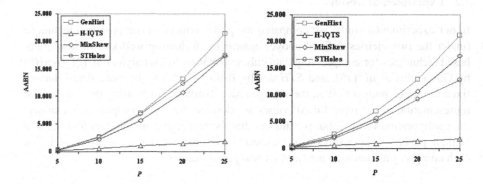

Fig. 5. Experimental results for the visualization metrics with respect to the depth of HRQs P on the 1.000×1.000 two-dimensional OLAP views $D_C(25,70)$ (left side) and $D_Z(0.5,1.5)$ (right side) with $W_H = 5$, $r = 10$, and $\gamma = 70$

Fig. 3 shows our experimental results for what regards the accuracy of the compression techniques with respect to the selectivity of queries in Q_S on the 1.000×1.000 two-dimensional OLAP views $D_C(25,70)$ (left side) and $D_Z(0.5,1.5)$ (right side) respectively. For all the comparison techniques, letting r be the parametric compression ratio and $size(D)$ the total occupancy of the input OLAP view D, we set the space budget G as equal to the r % of $size(D)$. For instance, $r = 10$ (i.e., G is equal to the 10 % of $size(D)$) is widely recognized as a reasonable setting (e.g., see [5]). Fig. 4 shows the results of the same experiment when ranging r on the interval [5,20] (i.e., G on the interval [5,20] % of $size(D)$), and fixing the selectivity of queries $\|Q\|$; this allows us to measure the *scalability* of the compression techniques, which is a critical aspect in OLAP systems (e.g., see [10]). Finally, Fig. 5 shows our experimental results for what regards the "visualization capabilities" of the comparison techniques (according to the guidelines drawn through the paper) with respect to the depth of HRQs (i.e., P_H) having fan-out degree W_H equal to 5 and the parameter γ equal to 70. The input two-dimensional OLAP views and the value of the parameter r are the same of the previous experiments.

From Fig. 3, 4 and 5, it follows that, with respect to the accuracy metrics, our proposed technique is comparable with *MinSkew*, which represents the best on two-dimensional views (indeed, as well-recognized-in-literature, *MinSkew* presents severe limitations on multidimensional domains); instead, with respect to the visualization metrics, our proposed technique overcomes the comparison techniques, thus confirming its suitability in efficiently supporting advanced OLAP visualization of multidimensional data cubes.

6 Conclusions and Future Work

In this paper, we have present an innovative technique for supporting advanced OLAP visualization of multidimensional data cubes, which is particularly suitable for mobile OLAP scenarios (like, for instance, those addressed by the system Hand-OLAP [11]). Founding on very efficient two-dimensional summary data domain compression solutions [4], our technique meaningfully exploits the data compression paradigm that, in this paper, has been proposed as a way of visualizing multidimensional OLAP domains to overcome the natural disorientation and refractoriness of human beings in dealing with hyper-spaces. In this direction, the OLAP dimension flattening process and the amenity of computing semantics-aware buckets are, to the best of our knowledge, innovative contributions to the state-of-the-art OLAP research. Finally, various experimental results performed on different kinds of synthetic two-dimensional OLAP views extracted from (synthetic) multidimensional data cubes, where characteristic parameters (such as the nature of distributions of OLAP data) can be easily controlled to improve the effectiveness of the analysis, have clearly confirmed the benefits of our proposed technique in the OLAP visualization context, also in comparison with well-known data cube compression techniques.

Future work is mainly focused on making the proposed technique capable of building m-dimensional OLAP views over massive n-dimensional data cubes, with $m \ll n$ and $m > 2$, by extending the algorithms presented in this paper. A possible solution could be found in the results coming from the *High-dimensional Data and Information Visualization* research area (e.g., see [1]), which are already suitable to be applied to the problem of visualizing multidimensional databases and data cubes.

References

1. 2D, 3D and High-dimensional Data and Information Visualization research group. University of Hannover (2005) available at http://www.iwi.uni-hannover.de/lv/seminar_ss05/bartke/home.htm
2. Acharya, S., Poosala, V., Ramaswamy, S.: Selectivity Estimation in Spatial Databases. Proc. of ACM SIGMOD (1999) 13-24
3. Agrawal, R. Gupta, A., Sarawagi, S.: Modeling Multidimensional Databases. Proc. of IEEE ICDE (1997) 232-243

4. Buccafurri, F., Furfaro, F., Saccà, D., Sirangelo, C.: A Quad-Tree Based Multiresolution Approach for Two-Dimensional Summary Data. Proc. of IEEE SSDBM (2003) 127-140

5. Bruno, N., Chaudhuri, S., Gravano, L.: STHoles: A Multidimensional Workload-Aware Histogram. Proc. of ACM SIGMOD (2001) 211-222

6. Cabibbo, L., Torlone, R.: From a Procedural to a Visual Query Language for OLAP. Proc. of IEEE SSDBM (1998) 74-83

7. Chaudhuri, S., Dayal, U.: An Overview of Data Warehousing and OLAP Technology. ACM SIGMOD Record, Vol. 26, No. 1 (1997) 65-74

8. Codd, E.F., Codd, S.B., Salley, C.T.: Providing OLAP to User-Analysts: An IT Mandate. E.F. Codd and Associates TR (1993)

9. Colliat, G.: OLAP, Relational, and Multidimensional Database Systems. SIGMOD Record, Vol. 25, No. 3 (1996) 64-69

10. Cuzzocrea, A.: Overcoming Limitations of Approximate Query Answering in OLAP. Proc. of IEEE IDEAS (2005) 200-209

11. Cuzzocrea, A., Furfaro, F., Saccà, D.: Hand-OLAP: A System for Delivering OLAP Services on Handheld Devices. Proc. IEEE ISADS (2003) 80-87

12. Gebhardt, M., Jarke, M., Jacobs, S.: A Toolkit for Negotiation Support Interfaces to Multi-Dimensional Data. Proc. of ACM SIGMOD (1997) 348-356

13. Gibbons, P.B., Matias, Y.: New Sampling-Based Summary Statistics for Improving Approximate Query Answers. Proc. of ACM SIGMOD (1998) 331-342

14. Gray, J., Chaudhuri, S., Bosworth, A., Layman, A., Reichart, D., Venkatrao, M.: Data Cube: A Relational Aggregation Operator Generalizing Group-By, Cross-Tab, and Sub-Totals. Data Mining and Knowledge Discovery, Vol. 1, No. 1 (1997) 29-53

15. Gunopulos, D., Kollios, G., Tsotras, V.J., Domeniconi, C.: Approximating Multi-Dimensional Aggregate Range Queries over Real Attributes. Proc. of ACM SIGMOD (2000) 463-474

16. Hacid, M.-S., Sattler, U.: Modeling Multidimensional Databases: A Formal Object-Centered Approach. Proc. of ECIS (1997)

17. Han, J., Kamber, M.: Data Mining: Concepts and Techniques. Morgan Kauffmann Publishers (2000)

18. Ho, C.-T., Agrawal, R., Megiddo, N., Srikant, R.: Range Queries in OLAP Data Cubes. Proc. of ACM SIGMOD (1997) 73-88

19. Inmon, W.H.: Building the Data Warehouse. John Wiley & Sons (1996)

20. Inselberg, A.: Visualization and Knowledge Discovery for High Dimensional Data. Proc. of IEEE UIDIS (2001) 5-24

21. Keim, D.A.: Visual Data Mining. Tutorial at VLDB (1997) available at http://www.dbs.informatik.uni-muenchen.de/daniel/VLDBTutorial.ps

22. Kimball, R.: The Data Warehouse Toolkit. John Wiley & Sons (1996)

23. Koudas N., Muthukrishnan S., Srivastava D.: Optimal Histograms for Hierarchical Range Queries. Proc. of ACM PODS (2000) 196-204

24. Lehner, W., Albrecht, J., Wedekind, H.: Normal Forms for Multivariate Databases. Proc. of IEEE SSDBM (1998) 63-72

25. Lenz, H.-J., Shoshani, A.: Summarizability in OLAP and Statistical Data Bases. Proc. of IEEE SSDBM (1997) 132-143

26. Lenz, H.-J., Thalheim, B.: OLAP Databases and Aggregation Functions. In Proc. of IEEE SSDBM (2001) 91-100

27. Maniatis, A., Vassiliadis, P., Skiadopoulos, S., Vassiliou, Y.: CPM: A Cube Presentation Model for OLAP. Proc. of DaWaK (2003) 4-13

28. Maniatis, A., Vassiliadis, P., Skiadopoulos, S., Vassiliou, Y.: Advanced Visualization for OLAP. Proc. of ACM DOLAP (2003) 9-16

29. Thanh Binh, N., Min Tjoa, A., Wagner, R.: An Object Oriented Multidimensional Data Model for OLAP. Proc. of WAIM (2000) 69-82
30. Tsois, A., Karayannidis, N., Sellis, T.: MAC: Conceptual Data Modeling for OLAP. Proc. of DMDW (2001) available at http://sunsite.informatik.rwth-aachen.de/Publications/ CEUR-WS/Vol-39/paper5.pdf
31. Vassiliadis, P.: Modeling Multidimensional Databases, Cubes and Cube Operations. Proc. of IEEE SSDBM (1998) 53-62
32. Vitter, J.S., Wang, M., Iyer, B.: Data Cube Approximation and Histograms via Wavelets. Proc. of ACM CIKM (1998) 96-104

Analysing Multi-dimensional Data Across Autonomous Data Warehouses

Stefan Berger and Michael Schrefl

Department of Business Informatics - Data & Knowledge Engineering (DKE),
University of Linz, Austria
{berger, schrefl}@dke.uni-linz.ac.at

Abstract. Business cooperations frequently require to analyse data across enterprises, where there is no central authority to combine and manage cross-enterprise data. Thus, rather than integrating independent data warehouses into a Distributed Data Warehouse (DDWH) for cross-enterprise analyses, this paper introduces a multi data warehouse OLAP language for integrating, combining, and analysing data from several, independent data warehouses (DWHs). The approach may be best compared to multi-database query languages for database integration. The key difference to these prior works is that they do not consider the multi-dimensional organisation of data warehouses.

The major problems addressed and solutions provided are: (1) a classification of DWH schema and instance heterogeneities at the fact and dimension level, (2) a methodology to combine independent data cubes taking into account the special characteristics of conceptual DWH schemata, i.e., OLAP dimension hierarchies and facts, and (3) a novel query language for bridging these heterogeneities in cross-DWH OLAP queries.

1 Introduction

Nowadays many companies use Data Warehouses (DWHs) and OLAP systems to analyze the performance of their business processes. The integration of autonomous DWHs is useful every time several enterprises cooperate in their business intelligence activities. The basic option for DWH integration is either to build a Distributed Datawarehouse System or a federation of several DWHs. Consequently, the existing and well-established DWH systems are replaced or migrated to implement a new, integrated schema, which are very labor-intensive tasks.

Multi Datawarehouse Systems (MDWHS) allow to analyze distributed multidimensional business data, overcoming the possible heterogeneities across several autonomous data cubes yet leaving the component systems unchanged. Notably, a MDWHS permits local decision and data management autonomy to the independent component DWHs in an architecture similar to "global-as-view" database integration environments [1]. Such a loose coupling of the local data cubes is advantageous for ad-hoc queries, especially if the permanent buildup of a common Distributed DWH is impossible. However, the integration of several multidimensional databases is a challenging task.

A Min Tjoa and J. Trujillo (Eds.): DaWaK 2006, LNCS 4081, pp. 120–133, 2006.

In this paper we propose a basic Multi Datawarehouse framework for the loosely coupled integration of data cubes. The resulting, integrated DWH schema is instantiated but not physically stored. This virtual instantiation of the integrated schema, denoted as *virtual datacube*, provides the basis for OLAP queries. In contrast, a tightly coupled MDWHS architecture instantiates the integrated DWH schema in a materialized datacube. The latter approach allows to easily integrate additional system components such as an OLAP server and an OLAP query tool to facilitate the analysts' work. The tightly coupled architecture is a subject of this paper.

Multidatabase Systems (MDBS) and Federated Database Systems (FDBS) provide successful examples of database integration [11,12,13]. A FDBS provides transparent access to the component databases through a global schema. In contrast, a MDBS allows users to access the (possibly heterogeneous) schemata of multiple databases directly. Thus, the coupling between the component databases is considerably tighter in FDBS than in MDBS [12]. The approach in this paper is inspired by MDBS architectures.

As part of the proposed framework, this paper classifies the possible heterogeneities among DWH schemata corresponding to the conceptual modelling constructs *fact* and *dimension*. Moreover, we provide a methodology for DWH schema integration, supported by the novel query language SQL-MDi, to deal with conflicts in *all* of the conceptual constructs. The major contributions of SQL-MDi are the following: (1) integration of dimension levels in a recursive manner; (2) design of a new or modification of an existing dimension hierarchy; (3) fine-grained conversion of attribute domains.

The main focus of our paper is to investigate the consequences of OLAP dimension *hierarchies* on the Data Warehouse integration process. The presence of hierarchical dimensions considerably complicates the consolidation of both dimensions *and* facts, as we show in Section 4. In contrast to previous work, our approach combines OLAP dimension and fact integration features with the support of dimension hierarchies.

The outline of this paper is as follows. Section 2 presents a case study to demonstrate the classes of heterogeneities among independent DWHs. Subsequently, Section 3 introduces the SQL-MDi language and briefly summarizes its syntax. In Section 4 we discuss our methodology and illustrate example SQL-MDi queries on the scenario of the case study. Section 5 discusses related work on multidimensional database integration. Finally, Section 6 concludes the paper and gives an outlook on our future research.

2   Case Study (Running Example)

As an illustrative example we assume the conceptual DWH schema of a health insurance organization, as given in Figure 1. The fictitious health insurance consists of independent suborganizations within several Federal States, governed by a federal association. For simplicity, our scenario considers only two suborganizations, both of which autonomously operate a Data Warehouse. The

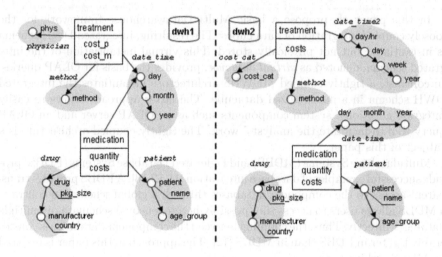

Fig. 1. Health insurance conceptual Data Warehouse schemata

schema is instantiated at two distinct nodes, dwh1 and dwh2, each of which hosts one DWH.

The schema in Figure 1 is specified in the DFM-notation proposed by [2]. In DFM, a conceptual DWH model consists of one or more *facts*, each of which is linked to one or more *dimensions*. A *datacube* is a fact together with the dimensions linked to it.

Our schema defines two cubes, treatment and medication, each with three dimensions describing the facts.[1] Thus, in Figure 1 the fact and dimension schema consist of {treatment, medication} and {method, drug, date_time, patient}, respectively. Note that DFM allows to "share" dimensions among multiple facts (as patient and date_time in Figure 1) [2]. An instantiation of our conceptual DWH schema at both sites dwh1 and dwh2 is specified in Figures 2 and 3, showing example fact and dimension instances.

Every dimension definition consists of (1) an arbitrary number of *aggregation levels*, including the implicit [ALL]-level, (2) a *roll-up hierarchy* between the levels, i.e. a partial order on the dimension's members, and (3) optional *non-dimensional attributes* to model the dimension instances more precisely. For example, the patient dimension is composed of (1) the levels patient and age_group, (2) the roll-up hierarchy {patient ↦ age_group ↦ ALL} and (3) the non-dimensional attribute name (of a patient).

In our running example, we assume a Relational OLAP (ROLAP) system be the physical platform for the implementation of the conceptual schema. ROLAP systems implement facts and dimensions as *fact tables* and *dimension tables*, respectively [3]. Foreign key constraints on tables in ROLAP systems either

---

[1] Later, both data cubes are used to exemplify conflicts on the schema and instance level. We only use two cubes for an easier presentation—all conflict categories could occur in a single cube.

associate facts with dimensions (e.g. *treatment—method*) or express an aggregation order on levels within a dimension (*roll-up hierarchy*, e.g. *day—month*).
The tuples of the fact and dimension tables contain, accordingly, the finite sets
of fact and dimension *instances*. The dimension instances are commonly denoted
as *dimension members* [3,4].

dwh1::medication

patient	drug	date_time	qty	cost
p1	'A'	25-01-06	1	68.4
p2	**'A'**	**03-02-06**	5	342.0
p3	'B'	17-02-06	4	728.0

dwh2::medication

patient	drug	date_time	qty	cost
p5	'AA'	03-02-06	2	148.0
p6	'B'	14-02-06	3	624.3
p2	**'A'**	**03-02-06**	1	70.8

dwh1::drug
[drug] $\mapsto$ [manufacturer] $\mapsto$ [ALL]

'A'	$\mapsto$	'Roche'	$\mapsto$	ALL
'B'	$\mapsto$	**'Sanchoz'**	$\mapsto$	ALL

dwh2::drug
[drug] $\mapsto$ [manufacturer] $\mapsto$ [ALL]

'A'	$\mapsto$	'Roche'	$\mapsto$	ALL
'B'	$\mapsto$	**'Bayer'**	$\mapsto$	ALL

Fig. 2. "Medication" fact tables of the case study

dwh1::treatment

method	date	phys	cost_p	cost_m
X-ray	23-02-06	'Dr.A'	356.0	425.0
CT	23-02-06	'Dr.C'	125.2	1742.0
CT	25-02-06	'Dr.F'	473.0	903.8

dwh2::treatment

method	date/hr	cost_cat	cost-$
X-ray	23-02-06 08:00	personnel	480.0
X-ray	23-02-06 09:00	material	613.0
CT	24-02-06 14:00	material	624.5

dwh1::date_time
[day] $\mapsto$ [month] $\mapsto$ [year] $\mapsto$ [ALL]

dwh2::date_time
[day/hr] $\mapsto$ [day] $\mapsto$ [week] $\mapsto$ [year] $\mapsto$ [ALL]

Fig. 3. "Treatment" fact tables of the case study

Summarizing, we regard a Data Warehouse as quadruple of distinct object
sets: *fact schemata, dimension schemata, fact instances, dimension instances*.
Every subset of DWH objects is a possible source of heterogeneities within the
Multi DWH System.

The example DWH instantiations (see Figures 2 and 3) demonstrate a situation that is commonly found in practice. Obviously, both DWHs model a similar
part of the real world. Nevertheless, it is easy to see that the medication and
treatment fact tables contain several heterogeneities. The conflicts contained in
the example are explained in detail below. A taxonomy of possible conflict classes
is briefly shown in Table 1. For a more detailed definition of the conflict classes
we refer the interested reader to [21].

The medication datacubes at dwh1 and dwh2 (see Fig. 2) conform to the
same ROLAP schema but contain numerous conflicts among their instance sets:
(1) a subset of the facts overlaps due to identical primary keys—given in bold
font (*overlapping facts*); (2) both drug dimensions contain an instance named
'A', which is, however, erroneously named 'AA' at dwh2 (*instance naming conflict*); (3) finally, the roll-up hierarchies of the dimension instances (shown at

Table 1. Overview of heterogeneities among Data Warehouses

	Facts	Dimensions
Instance level	– Overlapping facts – Disjoint fact subsets	– Naming conflicts – Overlapping members – Heterogeneous roll-up mappings
Schema level	– Different number of dimensions ("dimensionality") – Naming conflict (measures) – Domain conflict (measures)	– Diverse aggregation hierarchies – Inner level domain conflicts – Lowest level domain conflicts – Domain and/or naming conflicts (non-dimensional attributes)
Schema vs. instance	Fact context as dimension instances	Dimension members as contextualized facts

the bottom of Fig. 2) contain conflicting mappings for drug 'B' (different *roll-up hierarchies*).

The treatment datacubes at dwh1 and dwh2 (see Fig. 3) are heterogeneous due to several conflicts among their ROLAP schemata, but do not contain further conflicts in their instances: (1) whereas dwh1 uses two measures to distinguish cost categories (cost_p–personnel and cost_m–material), the treatment datacube at dwh2 defines the dimension cost_cat (*schema-instance conflict*); (2) ignoring the cost_cat dimension (contained as implicit information in cost_p and cost_m), the data cubes differ in their number of dimensions. The phys (physician) dimension of dwh1 is not modelled at dwh2 (*dimensionality conflict*); (3) the domain of the cost-attributes is incompatible among the treatment datacubes. We assume dwh1 to record cost figures in Euros, whereas dwh2 contains treatment costs in US-$ (*conflicting measure attribute domain*); (4) the level hierarchy of the date_time dimension contains four levels at dwh2, compared to three at dwh1. Moreover, the domains of the month and week levels are obviously different (conflicts in the *aggregation level hierarchy*); (5) finally, the lowest aggregation level of the date_time is more fine-grained at dwh2 (heterogeneous *lowest level domain*).

3   SQL-MDi—the Multi DWH OLAP Language

To integrate several autonomous Data Warehouses into a Multi DWH System, we propose a query language named SQL-MDi (*SQL for multi-dimensional integration*), supporting the methodology we present in Section 4. As its name suggests, SQL-MDi is based on the SQL standard [5]. SQL-MDi uses the basic *select – from – where – group by – having* structure, extended with various constructs to specify the virtual data cube. All cube definition language clauses precede the OLAP operations within the SELECT query part. Thus, the skeleton of an SQL-MDi query looks as follows:

```
DEFINE              <cube-definitions>
MERGE DIMENSIONS    <merge-dim-subclauses>
```

```
MERGE CUBES            <merge-cube-subclauses>
<standard sql-query>
```

The data definition part of an SQL-MDi query allows the following clauses: DEFINE CUBE contains a CUBE-declaration for every data cube to be merged into the virtual cube. Within this clause, the designer modifies the cube schemata and instances in order to be mutually compatible. Pivoting operations are available to restructure the multi-dimensional space of the integrated data cube. These operations also solve schema-instance conflicts among the individual DWHs. Further subclauses allow to specify either conversion functions or overriding instructions to resolve measure attribute conflicts. MERGE DIMENSIONS is the directive to bridge heterogeneities among the dimension schemata and instances of the independent DWHs. Within this clause the designer may (1) specify mappings between dimension levels (snowflake tables) of independent DWH schemata, (2) rename ambiguously named attributes, (3) convert attribute domains in dimension tables, (4) merge overlapping dimension instance sets, (5) resolve naming conflicts of dimension instances and (6) choose a roll-up hierarchy to use in the virtual cube. MERGE CUBES finally instructs the MDWHS to join the specified data cubes in order to compute the virtual cube. The designer fine-tunes the desired schema of the virtual cube (1) by choosing which dimensions to join over and (2) by specifying how the measures and dimensions of the virtual cube are derived from the component DWHs.

Most of the SQL-MDi clauses listed above require several subclauses to specify exactly how the virtual datacube is to be computed. In the remainder of the paper, we omit a detailed specification of all query subclauses. Instead we prefer to illustrate the expressive power of SQL-MDi using the various examples within Section 4. A complete reference to the SQL-MDi syntax is given in [21].

Due to lack of space, we further omit to formalize the semantics of our query language constructs and operators. Together with a query processing and execution model, the formalization of SQL-MDi is the topic of our current research.

4   Methodology for the Integration of Data Warehouses

In the following, we propose a DWH integration methodology, that accounts for all classes of conflicts defined in this paper. These conflicts can of course occur orthogonally in arbitrary combinations. To illustrate how SQL-MDi supports the proposed methodology, we give example queries and informally explain their semantics.

The integration methodology defines the consolidated multi-dimensional space to compute the virtual data cube. It must bridge heterogeneities at both the instance and schema level. Thus, the integration of heterogeneous DWHs consists of the following phases: (1) resolution of schema-instance conflicts, (2) schema integration, (3) instance consolidation, and finally (4) roll-up hierarchy design.

As preparatory step before integrating the dimension schemata, our methodology requires all dimensions of the autonomous DWHs to be converted to the snowflake schema. This representation reveals both the aggregation levels (tables) and the hierarchy mappings between dimensional attributes (foreign keys between levels) [3].

4.1 Resolve Schema-Instance Conflicts

The first phase of DWH integration achieves a uniform modelling of information within schema and instances. Schema transformation in multidimensional tables was investigated by Gingras and Lakshmanan [6]. They implemented several query constructs into nD-SQL, allowing the conversion of schema objects to schema information and vice versa. The nD-SQL constructs of "schema variables" and "complex columns" work well to restructure flat tables without dimension hierarchies.

Our query language, SQL-MDi, provides analogous constructs for fact table pivoting. However, SQL-MDi allows a more powerful restructuring of datacubes since it fully supports dimension hierarchies. Note that our language (in its current version) does not define schema object variables such as in nD-SQL [6].

The resolution of schema-instance conflicts is possible in two directions, depending on the desired virtual cube schema, as illustrated below. For the following two examples, assume dwh2::treatment with dimension date instead of date_time.

Example 1. Use an additional measure in dwh2::treatment:
    DEFINE CUBE dwh1::treatment AS c1, CUBE dwh2::treatment AS c2
        (MEASURE cost_pers IS cost WHEN cost_cat='personnel' DEFAULT 0,
        MEASURE cost_mat IS cost WHEN cost_cat='material' DEFAULT 0,
            DIM method, DIM date) MERGE TUPLES ON method, date
    MERGE CUBES c1,c2 INTO gdb::treatment AS c0 ON method, date
        (MEASURE cost_pers IS SUM(c1.cost_p, c2.cost_pers),
        MEASURE cost_mat IS SUM(c1.cost_m, c2.cost_mat), DIM method, DIM date)

Example 2. Use an additional dimension in dwh1::treatment:[2]
    DEFINE CUBE ...c2, CUBE ...c1 (MEASURE cost IS EITHER c1.cost_p, c1.cost_m,
        DIM cost_cat IS 'personnel' WHEN SOURCE(cost) = cost_p,
        'material' WHEN SOURCE(cost) = cost_m), DIM method, DIM date)
        SPLIT TUPLES FOR cost_p, cost_m DISCRIMINATE BY cost_cat
    MERGE CUBES c1,c2 INTO ...c0 ON method, date, cost_cat
        (MEASURE cost IS SUM(c1.cost, c2.cost))

The above examples model the information in dwh1 and dwh2 in a uniform way either as dimension instances or measures. Example 1 adapts c2's fact schema. The additional measure makes a merging of the facts necessary to avoid many '0' measure values. Every pair of facts with identical method and date/hr values is merged. Example 2 adds a dimension to c1, splits the facts adequately and converts the measures cost_pers and cost_mat to a unique cost-attribute.

---

[2] Let c1, c2 and c0 be defined as in example 1.

4.2   Integrate Dimension and Fact Schemata

In the second phase of our integration methodology the designer defines a common physical (ROLAP) schema for both dimension and fact tables. Note that the integration of dimensions has priority, since valid primary keys of the facts in the virtual datacube can only be determined by using consolidated dimensions. Previous approaches have already examined how to integrate OLAP dimensions [7,8] or fact tables [6] on the schema level. In our opinion, both steps must be combined, since mutual dependencies exist between the schemata of dimensions and facts.

Hierarchies within the dimensions are significant for the computation of both the base datacube and its aggregations (obtained by roll-up). Several previous approaches have already recognized the importance of dimension integration (e.g. [9,7,10]). Our methodology supports the integration of hierarchical OLAP dimensions at every aggregation level using mappings between compatible levels (similar to [9]).

Firstly, to identify common elements among dimension schemata, the designer defines mappings between equivalent levels. Using these explicit mappings, both an unequal number of dimension levels and granularity conflicts are resolved. If necessary, the lowest aggregated levels of heterogeneous dimensions are also harmonized.

Example 3. To define a common aggregation hierarchy for the date_time dimensions of the treatment fact tables, a roll-up of dwh2::date_time is necessary (cf. Figure 3):

DEFINE CUBE ...c1, CUBE...c2, CUBE ...c0 (ROLLUP c2.date/hr TO LEVEL day)
    MAP LEVEL gdb::date_time[day] IS dwh1::date_time[day], dwh2::date_time2[day],
        LEVEL gdb::date_time[year] IS dwh1::date_time[year], dwh2::date_time2[year]
MERGE DIMENSIONS c1.date AS d1, c2.date/hr AS d2 INTO c0.date AS d0
MERGE CUBES c1,c2 INTO ...c0 ON method, date

Additionally, this query maps compatible levels of d1 and d2. Note that merging directives for the other dimensions are unnecessary, since no conflicts exist among them.

Secondly, the designer completes the definition of the virtual cube schema by resolving heterogeneities among the fact schemata. The multi-dimensional space of the virtual datacube is based upon the integrated dimensions (defined previously). All additional dimensions defined in the component DWHs are automatically suppressed by rolling them up to [ALL]. Measure attributes are converted to the domain used in the virtual cube if necessary (if the component DWHs define heterogeneous domains). Thus, both dimensionality and measure attribute conflicts are solved.

Example 4. Define a homogeneous fact schema for the virtual treatment cube by converting the cost-measure (let the MAP LEVEL and MERGE DIMENSIONS clause be given as in Ex. 3):

```
DEFINE CUBE ...c1, CUBE ...c2 CUBE ...c0 (ROLLUP c2.date/hr TO LEVEL day)
    CONVERT MEASURES APPLY usd2eur() FOR c2.cost DEFAULT
    MAP LEVEL ... MERGE DIMENSIONS ...
    MERGE CUBES c1,c2 INTO c0 ON method, date
```

An important feature of our methodology is *fine-grained attribute conversion*. Sometimes a generalized conversion on all instances of an attribute (e.g. of c2.cost in the previous example) is not precise enough. Based on selection predicates, which may include dimensional attributes, the designer specifies an appropriate conversion function for only a subset of instances.

Example 5. Assume that all costs for tomography at dwh2 are stored in CHF, although this is inconsistent with the other cost figures. In this case, the conversion clause of the previous example is only appropriate if extended to a more fine-grained definition:

```
CONVERT MEASURES APPLY usd2eur() FOR c2.cost DEFAULT,
    chf2eur() FOR c2.cost WHERE method = 'CT'
```

Finally, attribute naming conflicts among either fact or dimension tables are resolved. Thus, the designer overcomes homonyms and synonyms in the conceptual schemata. Attribute mappings on the schema level are defined manually.

Example 6. Assume an additional non-dimensional attribute 'description' in dwh1:: method and 'desc' in dwh2::method. As both attributes equivalently model a textual description, they are mapped, extending Ex. 3 with an additional clause:

```
MERGE DIMENSIONS c1.method AS d4, c2.method AS d5 INTO c0.method AS d3
    MATCH ATTRIBUTES d3.desc IS d4.description, d5.desc
```

4.3   Consolidate Dimension and Fact Instances

The next DWH integration phase converts the instances of dimension and fact tables into the common schema defined previously—see 4.2. Similar to [8], we view dimension instances, together with the hierarchy between them, as a tree. These instance trees are consolidated by integrating the heterogeneous dimension instances. Analogously to the schema integration phase, dimension instances are processed before the facts.

The instance sets of every dimension in the virtual cube schema are integrated recursively among every common level along the aggregation hierarchy, beginning with the most fine-grained one. The designer performs the following operations with the instance sets of every level. (1) Resolve naming conflicts using explicit mappings between corresponding instances to reveal homonyms and synonyms. This way, subsets of corresponding and different dimension members are identified. (2) Specify which existing aggregation hierarchy to use in case of conflicting roll-up mappings. This ensures the referential integrity between aggregation levels which is given by foreign keys.

Alternatively, if no given dimension hierarchy is adequate, the designer may model a new one. The next subsection proposes a procedure for this purpose. If the designer elects to create a new dimension hierarchy, he only has to integrate the leaf instances of the given dimensions at this step. The roll-up consistency is ensured in the subsequent step of dimensional modelling. If needed, new roll-up mappings for only some selected dimension instances can also be defined.

Example 7. Manually mark the drug instance 'AA' at dwh2 as equivalent to instance 'A' at dwh1; moreover, define to use the roll-up mapping of dwh1::drug for c0:

```
DEFINE CUBE dwh2::medication AS c3, CUBE dwh1::medication AS c4
  (RENAME dg-id TO 'A' WHERE dg-id = 'AA'), CUBE gdb::medication AS m0
  RELATE dwh1::drug[drug] AS ds1, dwh2::drug[drug] AS ds2
    WHERE ds1.dg-id = ds2.dg-id USING HIERARCHY OF dwh1::drug
  MERGE DIMENSIONS c3.drug AS d3, c4.drug AS d4 INTO m0.drug AS d0
  MERGE CUBES c3,c4 INTO m0 ON patient, drug
```

Next, the facts from the component DWHs are arranged within the common multi-dimensional space. If fact subsets contain measures on the same real-world entities (often characterized by identical primary keys in different fact sets), these facts are said to *overlap*—otherwise, they are *disjoint*. Due to the conflicting information on the measures, overlapping facts must be merged adequately to compute meaningful results.

We distinguish two different semantic relationships between overlapping facts, determining the possible computation method(s) to obtain meaningful results:

- *Identical-relationship*: facts are *identical-related* if they describe the same real-world entities in the virtual datacube. Importantly, only one out of the given measure values can be true. The application of aggregation functions is meaningless.
- *Context-relationship*: matching facts are *context-related* if they describe one or more real-world entities in different contexts. This implies that the facts contain additional but hidden information, which may be made explicit. The other basic option is to aggregate the fact measures. Importantly, in some scenarios a subset of aggregation functions computes meaningless results, especially if the facts model information on different entities.

To merge overlapping facts, the designer identifies the semantical relationship between the facts and chooses an adequate merging strategy. Since the semantic relation between overlapping facts usually depends on subtle details, only a human designer can safely determine it. Subsequently, he or she defines the desired set operation to apply on the remaining, disjoint fact subsets.

Example 8. The overlapping medication-instances are *identical*. We assume the data of dwh1 to be more trustworthy than dwh2 and therefore specify to prefer the values received from dwh1. The *union* is computed of the remaining, disjoint subsets:[3]

```
DEFINE CUBE ...c3, CUBE ...c4  MERGE CUBES c3,c4 INTO ...m0 ON patient, drug
  PREFER c1.quantity DEFAULT    PREFER c1.cost DEFAULT
```

---

[3] Let c3, c4 and m0 be defined as in example 7.

Example 9. Let dwh3 be an additional DWH with the same schema as dwh2. Overlapping treatment-instances are clearly *context-related*. To compare cost figures between several DWHs, the fact context is extracted to an additional dimension as follows:

```
DEFINE CUBE dwh2::treatment AS c2, CUBE dwh3::treatment AS c3
MERGE CUBES c2,c3 INTO ...c0 ON method, date/hr
    TRACKING SOURCE AS DIMENSION state (state-id VARCHAR2(32))
    (MEASURE cost, DIM method, DIM date/hr, DIM state IS
    'state2' WHERE SOURCE() = c2, 'state3' WHERE SOURCE() = c3)
```

Finally, naming conflicts in non-dimensional attributes among the member sets are resolved. Attribute mappings are defined either manually or in a mapping table. This way, the designer overcomes homonyms and synonyms within the dimension instances.

Example 10. Assume the name attribute of patient instances contains several inconsistencies (not shown in Figure 2). They can be resolved using a mapping table:

```
DEFINE CUBE ...c3, CUBE ...c4
  (RENAME c4.patient.name USING MAPPINGTABLE pat-names TO c3.patient.name)
MERGE DIMENSIONS c3.drug AS d3, c4.drug AS d4 INTO m0.drug AS d0
```

The mapping table pat-names contains two attributes medication.patient.name, one for each DWH c1 and c2. Its tuples map pairs of different values modelling the same real world entities. The RENAME clause specifies the values desired in the virtual cube.

4.4   Design Roll-Up Hierarchies

If the integrated roll-up hierarchy of a dimension cannot satisfy the designer's needs, it is necessary to adapt these hierarchies. We propose a dimensional modelling approach that allows to specify arbitrary dimension levels and hierarchies. For this purpose, we slightly extend the snowflake schema to enhance its expressive power as follows.

Our framework models dimension hierarchies using snowflake tables [3] and the novel *roll-up tables*. Roll-up tables express a roll-up relationship between levels, amending foreign keys in the traditional snowflake model [2]. Note that predefined foreign keys are still valid, but a roll-up table definition may override it to express different roll-up relationships. If a predefined foreign key is appropriate for the integrated virtual cube, the (foreign key) constraint allows to compute the equivalent roll-up table automatically. Otherwise, the roll-up table is specified explicitly and populated manually.

Example 11. Retrieve the cost figures of the medication data cubes and define the additional level quarter for the date_time dimension:

```
DEFINE CUBE dwh1::treatment AS c1, CUBE dwh2::treatment AS c2
    (ROLLUP c2.date/hr TO LEVEL day), CUBE gdb::treatment AS c0
MERGE DIMENSIONS c1.date AS d1, c2.date/hr AS d2 INTO c0.date AS d0
    ADD LEVEL gdb::date.quarter(quarter-id VARCHAR2(32)),
    ADD ROLLUP gdb::date.month-quarter, ADD ROLLUP gdb::date.quarter-year
MERGE CUBES c1,c2 INTO ...c0 ON patient, date_time
```

(MEASURE cost IS c1.cost, c2.cost, DIM patient, DIM date_time IS
(SELECT 'q1-05', 'q2-05', 'q3-05', 'q4-05' FROM DUAL))
This statement inserts a new level quarter "between" month and year.

As demonstrated by the above example, our dimensional modelling approach provides two atomic operations: *add dimension level* and *add roll-up table*. Existing tables are never deleted. The atomic operations can be employed to perform the following complex dimensional modelling operations: (1) *Split or merge* existing dimension hierarchies (define dimension and roll-up tables; convert existing dimension instances and mappings to instances of the new dimension schema); (2) *Insert* an aggregation level into an existing hierarchy (define a new dimension table and the corresponding roll-up tables); (3) *Delete* an existing aggregation level (define a roll-up table "overriding" existing foreign-key constraints); (4) *Specify roll-up mappings* between dimension instances (insert a tuple into the appropriate roll-up table mapping both instances).

To finish dimensional modelling, the previously defined dimension and roll-up tables are populated with instances. Standard SQL statements are used for this purpose [5]. Dimension tables will most likely contain instances from within the predefined dimension schemata. Therefore, SQL statements populating the dimension tables can be embedded as subqueries into the SQL-MDi query (as shown in the above example). Due to their complexity, SQL statements to specify the contents of roll-up tables must be entered separately. For example, the roll-up table month-quarter would be filled with tuples that map every month in the month-table to the appropriate quarter.

5 Related Work

Query Languages for MDBS have received considerable attention in research and practice (e.g. MSQL [14,15,16], InterSQL [17] or SchemaSQL [18]). Multidatabase languageslike MSQL and SchemaSQL provide extensions to standard features to resolve data and schema conflicts [15,18]. Existing multidatabase languages cannot be applied to DWHs since they lack expressive power to handle the multidimensional data model.

Appropriate languages enabling queries to Multi DWH Systems are far from being mature. The first promising approach in this direction is nD-SQL [6], a language introducing schema transformation features, including multidimensional data. However, as the authors state themselves, the approach is still incomplete since the most recent nD-SQL version does not support aggregation hierarchies within dimensions [6].

A different approach extending standard SQL for OLAP applications is SQL_M [10]. The authors' main contribution is the formal definition of an OLAP data model together with a set of operations defined upon it. In contrast to our approach, the focus of SQL_M is primarily on irregularities in standalone OLAP systems. Although the integration of additional data sources (mainly from XML data) is addressed, SQL_M does not support the integration of multiple DWHs for OLAP purposes.

The DWH schema integration process itself still needs to be defined precisely to facilitate the design of MDWHS. A valuable approach addressing the integration of multidimensional databases is [9]. The authors elaborate on several techniques for dimension integration. However, they do not investigate any consequences on the computation of facts. While Cabibbo et al. concentrate on the development of the visual integration tool "DaWaII" [9,19], our work focuses on a declarative query language, that can also be used as definition language for DWH schema mappings.

Several approaches discuss how to exploit the common information of similar OLAP dimensions to optimize centralized or distributed DWH environments. Extended possibilities for drill-across queries based on similar dimensions are investigated by [7]. The approach of [8] proposes integrity constraints on OLAP dimensions as an attempt to establish design guidelines for multidimensional databases.

OLAP dimension hierarchies have received little attention in the research on data integration. Many approaches, including nD-SQL, assume flat, "degenerated" data cubes without aggregation hierarchies. A promising formal framework on dimension integration was developed by Cabibbo and Torlone [9], who propose both a dimension data model and algebra. Compared to the dimension algebra operators, the constructs of SQL-MDi provide an extended set of operations to manipulate schema or instance objects in DWHs. Dehne et al. [20] investigate how to deal with dimension hierarchies in parallel ROLAP systems. They focus, however, primarily on query processing whereas our paper discusses schema integration.

6   Conclusion and Future Work

We introduced a framework for the challenging problem of an OLAP query architecture for multiple independent Data Warehouses. This paper discussed a classification of heterogeneities to expect among distributed multidimensional databases. The proposed framework further consists of a methodology for the integration of autonomous data cubes, supported by a novel query language based on SQL.

Due to the complexity of possible data and schema conflicts, SQL-MDi queries are better suited for ad-hoc DWH integration scenarios. A Federated DWH System preserving the knowledge on virtual cube computation from the component DWHs is the subject of our current research. Moreover, we are currently investigating further interesting topics such as SQL-MDi (distributed) query optimization.

References

1. Lenzerini, M.: Data Integration: A Theoretical Perspective. In Popa, L., ed.: Proc. of PODS, ACM (2002) pp. 233–246.
2. Golfarelli, M., Maio, D., Rizzi, S.: The Dimensional Fact Model: a Conceptual Model for Data Warehouses. Int. J. Cooperative Inf. Syst. (7) (1998) pp. 215–247.

3. Vassiliadis, P., Sellis, T.K.: A Survey of Logical Models for OLAP Databases. SIGMOD Record (28) (1999) pp. 64–69.
4. Schrefl, M., Thalhammer, T.: On Making Data Warehouses Active. Proc. Intl. DaWaK Conf., LNCS Vol. 1874, Springer (2000) pp. 34–46.
5. International Organization for Standardization: (ISO/IEC 9075:1992: Information technology—Database languages—SQL).
6. Gingras, F., Lakshmanan, L.V.S.: nD-SQL: A Multi-dimensional Language for Interoperability and OLAP. In Gupta, A., Shmueli, O., Widom, J., eds.: VLDB, Morgan Kaufmann (1998) pp. 134–145.
7. Abelló, A., Samos, J., Saltor, F.: On Relationships Offering New Drill-across Possibilities. In Theodoratos, D., ed.: Proc. of DOLAP, ACM (2002) pp. 7–13.
8. Hurtado, C., Gutiérrez, C., Mendelzon, A.: Capturing Summarizability with Integrity Constraints in OLAP. ACM Trans. Database Syst. (30) (2005) pp. 854–886.
9. Cabibbo, L., Torlone, R.: Integrating Heterogeneous Multidimensional Databases. In Frew, J., ed.: Proc. of SSDBM. (2005) pp. 205–214.
10. Pedersen, D., Riis, K., Pedersen, T.B.: A Powerful and SQL-compatible Data Model and Query Language for OLAP. In Zhou, X., ed.: Australasian Database Conference. CRPIT (5) (2002).
11. Özsu, M.T., Valduriez, P.: Principles of Distributed Database Systems, Second Edition. Prentice-Hall (1999).
12. Litwin, W., Mark, L., Roussopoulos, N.: Interoperability of Multiple Autonomous Databases. ACM Comput. Surv. (22) (1990) pp. 267–293.
13. Sheth, A.P., Larson, J.A.: Federated Database Systems for Managing Distributed, Heterogeneous, and Autonomous Databases. ACM Comput. Surv. (22) (1990) pp. 183–236.
14. Grant, J., Litwin, W., Roussopoulos, N., Sellis, T.K.: Query Languages for Relational Multidatabases. VLDB Journal (2) (1993) pp. 153–171.
15. Litwin, W., Abdellatif, A., Zeroual, A., Nicolas, B., Vigier, P.: MSQL: A Multidatabase Language. Inf. Sci. (49) (1989) pp. 59–101.
16. Suardi, L., Rusinkiewicz, M., Litwin, W.: Execution of Extended Multidatabase SQL. In: ICDE, IEEE Computer Society (1993) pp. 641–650.
17. Mullen, J.G., Elmagarmid, A.K.: InterSQL: A Multidatabase Transaction Programming Language. In Beeri, C., Ohori, A., Shasha, D., eds.: DBPL. Workshops in Computing, Springer (1993) pp. 399–416.
18. Lakshmanan, L.V.S., Sadri, F., Subramanian, S.: SchemaSQL: An Extension to SQL for Multidatabase Interoperability. ACM Trans. Database Syst. (26) (2001) pp. 476–519.
19. Torlone, R., Panella, I.: Design and Development of a Tool for Integrating Heterogeneous Data Warehouses. Proc. Intl. DaWaK Conf., LNCS Vol. 3589, Springer (2005) pp. 105–114.
20. Dehne, F., Eavis, T., Rau-Chaplin, A.: Parallel Querying of ROLAP Cubes in the Presence of Hierarchies. In Song, I.Y., Trujillo, J., eds.: Proc. of DOLAP, ACM (2005) pp. 89–96.
21. Berger, S., Schrefl, M.: SQL-MDi Extended Syntax Reference. Technical report, available at http://www.dke.jku.at.

What Time Is It in the Data Warehouse?

Stefano Rizzi and Matteo Golfarelli

DEIS, University of Bologna, Viale Risorgimento 2, 40136 Italy

Abstract. Though in most data warehousing applications no relevance is given to the time when events are recorded, some domains call for a different behavior. In particular, whenever late registrations of events take place, and particularly when the events registered are subject to further updates, the traditional design solutions fail in preserving accountability and query consistency. In this paper we discuss the alternative design solutions that can be adopted, in presence of late registrations, to support different types of queries that enable meaningful historical analysis. These solutions are based on the enforcement of the distinction between transaction time and valid time within the model that represents the fact of interest. In particular, we show how late registrations can be differently supported depending on the flow or stock semantics given to events.

1   Introduction

Time is commonly understood as a key factor in data warehousing systems, since the decisional process often relies on computing historical trends and on comparing snapshots of the enterprise taken at different moments. Within the multidimensional model, time is typically a dimension of analysis: thus, the representation of the history of measure values across a given lapse of time, at a given granularity, is directly supported. On the other hand, though the multidimensional model does not inherently represent the history of attribute values within hierarchies, some ad hoc techniques are widely used to support the so-called *slowly-changing dimensions* [1]. In both cases, time is commonly meant as *valid time* in the terminology of temporal databases [2], i.e., it is meant as the time when the event or the change within a hierarchy *occurred* in the business domain [3]. *Transaction time*, meant as the time when the event or change was *registered* in the database, is typically given little or no importance in data warehouses, since it is not considered to be relevant for decision support.

One of the underlying assumptions in data warehouses is that, once an event has been stored, it is never modified, so that the only possible writing operation consists in appending new events as they occur. While this is acceptable for a wide variety of domains, some applications call for a different behaviour. In particular, the values of one or more measures for a given event may change over a period of time to be consolidated only *after* the event has been for the first time registered in the warehouse. In this context, if the current situation is to

A Min Tjoa and J. Trujillo (Eds.): DaWaK 2006, LNCS 4081, pp. 134–144, 2006.

be made timely visible to the decision maker, past events must be updated to reflect the incoming data.[1]

The need for updates typically arises when the early measurements made for events may be subject to errors (e.g., the amount of an invoice may be corrected after the invoice has been registered) or when events inherently evolve over time (e.g., notifications of university enrollments may be received and stored several days after they were issued). Unfortunately, if updates are carried out by physically overwriting past events, some problems may arise:

- Accountability and traceability require the capability of preserving the exact information the analyst based his/her decision upon. If old events are replaced by their "new" versions, past decisions can no longer be justified.
- In some applications, accessing only up-to-date versions of information is not sufficient to ensure the correctness of analysis. A typical case is that of queries requiring to compare the progress of an ongoing phenomenon with past occurrences of the same phenomenon: since the data recorded for the ongoing phenomenon are not consolidated yet, comparing them with past consolidated data may not be meaningful.

Note that the same problems may arise when events are registered in the data warehouse only once, but with a significant delay with respect to the time when they occurred: in fact, though no update is necessary, still valid time is not sufficient to guarantee accountability. Thus, in more general terms, we will call *late registration* any registration of events that is delayed with respect to the time when the event occurs in the application domain, with the tolerance of the natural delay related to the refresh interval of the data warehouse. A late registration may either imply an update or not.

In this paper we discuss the design solutions that can be adopted, in the presence of late registrations, to enable meaningful historical analysis aimed at preserving accountability and consistency. These solutions are based on the enforcement of the distinction between transaction time and valid time within the schema that represents the fact of interest. The paper contributions can be summarized as follows:

- Two possible semantics for events are distinguished, namely flow and stock, and it is shown how they can be applied to the events occurring in the application domain, to the events registered in the data warehouse for the first time, and to the events registered later to represent updates (Section 4).
- Three basic categories of queries are distinguished, from the point of view of their different temporal requirements in presence of late registrations (Section 5).
- A set of design solutions to support late registrations is introduced, and their relationship with the three categories of queries and with the two different semantics of events is discussed (Section 6).

---

[1] In the following, when using the term *update*, we will mean a *logical* update, which does not necessarily imply a *physical* update (i.e., an overwrite).

2   Related Literature

Several works concerning temporal data warehousing can be found in the literature. Most of them are related to consistently managing updates in dimension tables of relational data warehouses — the so-called *slowly-changing dimensions* (e.g., [4,5]). Some other works tackle the problem of temporal evolution and versioning of the data warehouse schema [6,7,8,9,10]. All these works are not related to ours, since there is no mention to the opportunity of representing transaction time in data warehouses in order to allow accountability and traceability in case of late registrations.

In [3] it is distinguished between *transient data*, that do not survive updates and deletions, and *periodic data*, that are never physically deleted from the data warehouse. In [1] two basic paradigms for representing inventory-like information in a data warehouse are introduced: the *transactional model*, where each increase and decrease in the inventory level is recorded as an event, and the *snapshot model*, where the current inventory level is periodically recorded. This distinction is relevant to our approach, and is recalled in Section 4.

In [11], the importance of advanced temporal support in data warehouses, with particular reference to medical applications, is recognized. In [12] the authors claim that there are important similarities between temporal databases and data warehouses, suggest that both valid time and transaction time should be modeled within data warehouses, and mention the importance of temporal queries. Finally, in [13] a storage structure for a bitemporal data warehouse (i.e., one supporting both valid and transaction time) is proposed. All these approaches suggest that transaction time should be modeled, but not with explicit reference to the problem of late registrations.

The approach that is most related to ours is the one presented in [14], where the authors discuss the problem of DW temporal consistency in consequence of delayed discovery of real-world changes and propose a solution based on transaction time and overlapped valid time. Although the paper discusses some issues related to late registrations, no emphasis is given to the influence that the semantics of the captured events and the querying scenarios pose on the feasibility of the different design solutions.

3   Motivating Examples

In the first example we provide, late registrations are motivated by the fact that the represented events inherently evolve over time. Consider a single fact modeling the student enrollments to university degrees; in a relational implementation, a simplified fact table for enrollments could have the following schema[2]:

FT_ENROLL(EnrollDate, Degree, AYear, City, Number)

where EnrollDate is the formal enrollment date (the one reported on the enrollment form). An enrollment is acknowledged by the University secretariat only

---

[2] For simplicity, we will assume that surrogate keys are not used.

when the entrance fee is paid; considering the variable delays due to the bank processing and transmitting the payment, the enrollment may be registered in the data warehouse even one month after the enrollment has been formally done. This is a case of late registrations. Besides: (i) notices of payments for the same enrollment date are spaced out over long periods, and (ii) after paying the fee, students may decide to switch their enrollment from one degree to another. Thus, updates are necessary in order to correctly track enrollments. The main reason why in this example the enrollment date may not be sufficient is related to the soundness of analysis. In fact, most queries on this fact will ask for evaluating the current trend of the number of enrollments as compared to last year. But if the current data on enrollments were compared to the consolidated ones at exactly one year ago, the user would wrongly infer that this year we are experiencing a negative trend for enrollments!

The second example, motivated by the delay in registering information and by wrong measurements, is that of a large shipping company with several warehouses spread around the country, that maintains a centralized inventory of its products:

FT_INVENTORY(InvDate, Product, Warehouse, Level)

We assume that the inventory fact is fed by weekly snapshots, coming from the different warehouses, of the inventory level for each product. In this scenario, delays in communicating the weekly levels and late corrections sent by the warehouses will produce late registrations, which in turn will raise problems with justifying the decisions made on previous reports.

4   The Semantics of Events

The aim of this section is to introduce the classification of events on which we will rely in Section 6 to discuss the applicability of the design solutions proposed.

As recognized in [1], from the point of view of the conceptual role given to events, facts basically conform to one of two possible models:

- *Transactional fact.* For a transactional fact, each event may either record a single transaction or summarize a set of transactions that occur during the same time interval. Most measures are *flow measures* [15]: they refer to a time interval and are cumulatively evaluated at the end of that period; thus, they are additive along all dimensions (i.e., their values can always be summed when aggregating).
- *Snapshot fact.* In this case, events correspond to periodical snapshots of the fact. Measures are mostly *stock measures* [15]: they refer to an instant in time and are evaluated at that instant; thus, they are non-additive along temporal dimensions (i.e., they cannot be summed when aggregating along time, while for instance they can be averaged).

This distinction is based on the semantics of the *stored events*, i.e., the events logically recorded in the data warehouse: in a transactional fact they are meant as *flow events*, while in a snapshot fact they are meant as *stock events*. Intuitively, while flow events model a "delta" for the fact, stock events measure its "level".

The choice of one model or another is influenced by the core workload the fact is subject to, but mainly depends on the semantics of the *domain events*, i.e., on how the events occurring in the application domain are measured: in the form of flows or in the form of stocks. In the first case, a transactional fact is the more proper choice, though also a snapshot fact can be used provided that (i) an aggregation function for composing the flow domain events into stock stored events is known, and (ii) events are not subject to updates — otherwise, after each update, all the related (stock) events would have to be updated accordingly, which may become quite costly. Conversely, if events are measured as stocks, a snapshot fact is the only possible choice, since adopting a transactional fact would require disaggregating the stock domain events into inflows and outflows — which, in the general case, cannot be done univocally.

A large percentage of facts in the business domain naturally conform to the transactional model. For instance, in an invoice fact, each (domain and stored) event typically represents a single line of an invoice, and its measures quantify some numerical aspects of that line — such as its quantity or amount. In theory, one could as well build an equivalent snapshot fact where each stored event models the cumulated sales made so far, computed by summing up the invoice lines: of course this would be quite impractical, since most query will focus on partial aggregations of invoice lines, that would have to be computed by subtraction of consecutive stored events.

Other facts naturally conform to the snapshot model: for instance a fact measuring, on each hour, the level of a river in different places along its course. Also the centralized inventory fact mentioned in Section 3 conforms to the snapshot model, since both its stored and domain events have stock semantics.

Finally, for some facts both models may reasonably fit: an example is the enrollment fact seen in Section 3, where two different interpretations can be given to events (and to measure Number accordingly) for the same schema. In the first (transactional) interpretation each (flow) event records the number of students from a given city who enrolled, on a given date, to a given degree course for a given academic year. In the second (snapshot) interpretation each (stock) event records, at a given date, the total number of students from a given city who enrolled to a given degree course for a given academic year so far. Two sample sets of events for enrollments according to the two interpretations are shown in Table 1; the designer will choose one or the other interpretation mainly according to the expected workload.

Table 1. Enrollment events for the transactional (left) and the snapshot (right) facts

EnrollDate	Degree	AYear	City	Number	EnrollDate	Degree	AYear	City	Number
Oct. 21, 2005	Elec. Eng.	05/06	Rome	5	Oct. 21, 2005	Elec. Eng.	05/06	Rome	5
Oct. 22, 2005	Elec. Eng.	05/06	Rome	2	Oct. 22, 2005	Elec. Eng.	05/06	Rome	7
Oct. 23, 2005	Elec. Eng.	05/06	Rome	3	Oct. 23, 2005	Elec. Eng.	05/06	Rome	10

5   Temporal Dimensions and Querying Scenarios

From a conceptual point of view, for every fact subject to late registrations, at least two different temporal dimensions may be distinguished. The first one refers to the time when events actually *take place* in the application domain, while the second one refers to the time when they are *perceived and recorded* in the data warehouse. In the literature on temporal databases, these two dimensions correspond, respectively, to valid time and transaction time [2]. Note that, for a fact that is not subject to late registrations, transaction time is implicitly considered to coincide with valid time (the natural delay due to the refresh interval in neglected).

While we take for granted that valid time must always be represented, since it is a mandatory coordinate for characterizing the event, the need for representing also transaction time depends on the nature of the expected workload. From this point of view, three types of queries can be distinguished (the terminology is inspired by [16]):

- *Up-to-date queries*, i.e., queries requiring the most recent value estimate for each measure. An example of up-to-date query on the enrollment fact is the one asking for the daily number of enrollments to a given degree made during last week. In fact, this query is solved correctly by considering the most up-to-date data available for the number of enrollments by enrollment dates. Representing transaction time is not necessary to solve this kind of queries, since they rely on valid time only.
- *Rollback queries*, i.e. queries requiring a past value estimate for each measure, as for instance the one asking for the current trend of the total number of enrollments for each faculty as compared to last year. In order to get consistent results, the comparison must be founded on registration dates rather than enrollment dates. Thus, this kind of query requires that transaction time is represented explicitly.
- *Historical queries*, i.e. queries requiring multiple value estimates for each measure. An example of historical query is the one asking for the day-by-day distribution of the enrollments registered overall for a given enrollment date. Also these queries require transaction time to be represented explicitly.

6   Design Solutions

In presence of late registrations, two types of design solution can be envisaged depending on the expected workload:

- *Monotemporal schema*, where only valid time is modeled as a dimension. This is the simplest solution: during each refresh cycle, as up-to-date values become available, a new set of events are recorded, which may imply updating events recorded at previous times. The time when the events are recorded is not represented, and no trace is left of past values in case of updates, so only up-to-date queries are supported.

- *Bitemporal schema*, where both valid and transaction time are modeled as dimensions. This is the most general solution, allowing for all three types of queries to be correctly answered. On each refresh cycle, new events for previous valid times may be added, and their registration time is traced; no overwriting of existing events is carried out, thus no data is lost.

The monotemporal schema for the enrollment example is exactly the one already shown in Section 3, where the only temporal dimension is EnrollDate. When further enrollments for a past enrollment date are to be registered, the events corresponding to that date are overwritten and the new values for measures are reported. Note that this solution can be equivalently adopted for both a transactional and a snapshot fact, and in neither case it supports accountability.

While the monotemporal schema deserves no additional comments, since it is the one commonly implemented for facts that either are not subject to late registrations or only require to support up-to-date queries, the bitemporal schema requires some further clarification. In fact, two specific solutions can be devised for a bitemporal schema, namely *delta solution* and *consolidated solution*, where the events used to represent updates have flow and stock semantics, respectively. These solutions are described in the following subsections.

6.1   The Delta Solution

In the delta solution:

1. each update is represented by a flow event that records a "delta" for the fact;
2. transaction time is modeled by adding to the fact a new temporal dimension, typically with the same grain of the temporal dimension that models the valid time, to represent when each event was recorded;
3. up-to-date queries are answered by aggregating events on all transaction times;
4. rollback queries at a given time t are answered by aggregating events on the transaction times before t;
5. historical queries are answered by slicing the events based on their transaction times.

This solution can easily be applied to a transactional fact: in this case, all stored events (those initially recorded and those representing further updates) have flow semantics. In particular, flow measures uniformly preserve their additive nature for all the events. Consider for instance the enrollment schema. If a delta solution is adopted, the schema is enriched as follows:

FT_ENROLL(EnrollDate, RegistrDate, Degree, AYear, City, Number)

where RegistrDate is the dimension added to model transaction time. Table 2 shows a possible set of events for a given city, degree, and year, including some positive and negative updates. With reference to these sample data, in the following we report some simple examples of queries of the three types together with their results, and show how they can be computed by aggregating events.

Table 2. Enrollment events in the delta solution applied to a transactional fact (events representing updates in italics)

EnrollDate	RegistrDate	Degree	AYear	City	Number
Oct. 21, 2005	Oct. 27, 2005	Elec. Eng.	05/06	Rome	5
Oct. 21, 2005	*Nov. 1, 2005*	*Elec. Eng.*	*05/06*	*Rome*	*8*
Oct. 21, 2005	*Nov. 5, 2005*	*Elec. Eng.*	*05/06*	*Rome*	*−2*
Oct. 22, 2005	Oct. 27, 2005	Elec. Eng.	05/06	Rome	2
Oct. 22, 2005	*Nov. 5, 2005*	*Elec. Eng.*	*05/06*	*Rome*	*4*
Oct. 23, 2005	Oct. 23, 2005	Elec. Eng.	05/06	Rome	3

1. q_1: *daily number of enrollments to Electric Engineering for academic year 05/06.* This up-to-date query is answered by summing up measure Number for all registration dates related to the same enrollment dates, and returns the following result:

EnrollDate	Degree	AYear	City	Number
Oct. 21, 2005	Elec. Eng.	05/06	Rome	11
Oct. 22, 2005	Elec. Eng.	05/06	Rome	6
Oct. 23, 2005	Elec. Eng.	05/06	Rome	3

2. q_2: *daily number of enrollments to Electric Engineering for academic year 05/06 as known on Nov. 2.* This rollback query is answered by summing up Number for all registration dates before Nov. 2:

EnrollDate	Degree	AYear	City	Number
Oct. 21, 2005	Elec. Eng.	05/06	Rome	13
Oct. 22, 2005	Elec. Eng.	05/06	Rome	2
Oct. 23, 2005	Elec. Eng.	05/06	Rome	3

3. q_3: *daily net number of registrations of enrollments to Electric Engineering for academic year 05/06.* This historical query is answered by summing up Number for all enrollment dates:

RegistrDate	Degree	AYear	City	Number
Oct. 23, 2005	Elec. Eng.	05/06	Rome	3
Oct. 27, 2005	Elec. Eng.	05/06	Rome	7
Nov. 1, 2005	Elec. Eng.	05/06	Rome	8
Nov. 5, 2005	Elec. Eng.	05/06	Rome	2

In case of a snapshot fact where the domain events have stock semantics, the delta solution is not necessarily the best one. See for instance Table 3, that with reference to the inventory example seen in Section 3 shows a possible set of events for a given week and product assuming that some data sent by local warehouses are subject to corrections. In this case, up-to-date and rollback queries that summarize the inventory level along valid time would have to be formulated as nested queries relying on different aggregation operators. For instance, the average monthly level for a warehouse is computed by first summing Level across RegistrDate for each InvDate, then averaging the partial results.

Table 3. Inventory events in the delta solution applied to a snapshot fact

InvDate	RegistrDate	Product	Warehouse	Level
Jan. 7, 2006	Jan. 8, 2006	LCD TV	Milan	10
Jan. 7, 2006	*Jan. 12, 2006*	*LCD TV*	*Milan*	*−1*
Jan. 7, 2006	Jan. 12, 2006	LCD TV	Rome	5
Jan. 7, 2006	Jan. 10, 2006	LCD TV	Venice	15
Jan. 7, 2006	*Jan. 14, 2006*	*LCD TV*	*Venice*	*2*

We close this section by considering the particular case of facts where registrations may be delayed but events, once registered, are *not* further updated. In this case accountability can be achieved, for both transactional and snapshot facts, by adding a single temporal dimension RegistrDate that models the transaction time. Up-to-date queries are solved without considering transaction times, while rollback queries require to select only the events recorded before a given transaction time. Historical queries make no sense in this context, since each event has only one logical "version". As a matter of fact, the solution adopted can be considered as a special case of delta solution where no update events are to be registered.

6.2   The Consolidated Solution

In the consolidated solution:

1. each update is represented by a stock event that records the consolidated version of the fact;
2. transaction time is modeled by adding to the fact two new temporal dimensions, used as timestamps to mark the time interval during which each event was current within the data warehouse (*currency interval*);
3. up-to-date queries are answered by slicing the events that are current today (those whose currency interval is still open);
4. rollback queries at a given time t are answered by slicing the events that were current at t (those whose currency interval includes t);
5. historical queries are answered by slicing the events based on their transaction times.

In the inventory example, if a consolidated solution is adopted, the schema is enriched as follows:

FT_INVENTORY(InvDate, CurrencyStart, CurrencyEnd, Product, Warehouse, Level)

Table 4 shows the consolidated solution for the same set of events reported in Table 3. An example of up-to-date query on these data is *"find the total number of LCDs available on Jan. 7"*, which returns 31. On the other hand, a rollback query is *"find the total number of LCDs available on Jan. 7, as known on Jan. 10"*, which returns 25. Finally, a historical query is *"find the fluctuation on the level of Jan. 7 for each warehouse"*, which requires to progressively compute the differences between subsequent events and returns −1, 0, and 2 for Milan,

Table 4. Inventory events in the consolidated solution applied to a snapshot fact

InvDate	CurrencyStart	CurrencyEnd	Product	Warehouse	Level
Jan. 7, 2006	Jan. 8, 2006	Jan. 11, 2006	LCD TV	Milan	10
Jan. 7, 2006	*Jan. 12, 2006*	–	*LCD TV*	*Milan*	*9*
Jan. 7, 2006	Jan. 12, 2006	–	LCD TV	Rome	5
Jan. 7, 2006	Jan. 10, 2006	Jan. 13, 2006	LCD TV	Venice	15
Jan. 7, 2006	*Jan. 14, 2006*	–	*LCD TV*	*Venice*	*17*

Table 5. Summary of the possible solutions (UQ and HQ stand for up-to-date and historical queries, respectively)

	transactional fact	*snapshot fact*	
	flow domain events	*flow domain events*	*stock domain events*
monotemporal schema	good but only supports UQ	good if no updates, else not recomm.	good but only supports UQ
delta sol. – no upd.	good	good	good
delta sol. – with upd.	good	not recomm. due to up-date propagation	fair due to nesting
consolidated solution	good but overhead on HQ	not recomm. due to up-date propagation	good but overhead on HQ

Rome, and Venice respectively. Thus, while up-to-date and rollback queries are very simply answered, historical queries may ask for some computation.

Similarly, for a transactional fact, applying the consolidated solution is possible though answering historical queries may be computationally more expensive than with a delta solution.

7   Conclusion

In this paper we have raised the problem of late registrations, meant as retrospective registrations of events in a data warehouse, and we have shown how conventional design solutions, that only take valid time into account, may fail to provide query accountability and consistency. Then, we have introduced some alternative design solutions that overcome this problem by modeling transaction time as an additional dimension of the fact, and we have discussed their applicability depending on the semantics of events. Table 5 summarizes the results obtained. Most noticeably, using a snapshot fact when domain events have flow semantics is not recommendable in case of updates, since they should then be propagated. Besides, for a transactional fact all solutions are fine, though the delta one is preferable since it adds no overhead for historical queries. Conversely, for a snapshot fact the consolidated solution is preferable since aggregation nesting is not required.

The overhead induced by the proposed solutions on the query response time and on the storage space obviously depends on the characteristics of the application domain and on the actual workload. Frequent updates determine a significant increase in the fact table size, but this may be due to a wrong choice of the designer, who promoted early recording of events that are not stable enough to be significant for decision support. The increase in the query response time may be contained by a proper use of materialized views and indexes: a materialized view aggregating events on all transaction times cuts down the time for answering up-to-date queries in the delta solution, while an index on transaction time enables efficient slicing of the events.

References

1. Kimball, R.: The data warehouse toolkit. Wiley Computer Publishing (1996)
2. Jensen, C., Clifford, J., Elmasri, R., Gadia, S.K., Hayes, P.J., Jajodia, S.: A consensus glossary of temporal database concepts. ACM SIGMOD Record **23** (1994) 52–64
3. Devlin, B.: Managing time in the data warehouse. InfoDB **11** (1997) 7–12
4. Letz, C., Henn, E., Vossen, G.: Consistency in data warehouse dimensions. In: Proc. IDEAS. (2002) 224–232
5. Yang, J.: Temporal data warehousing. PhD thesis, Stanford University (2001)
6. Bębel, B., Eder, J., Koncilia, C., Morzy, T., Wrembel, R.: Creation and management of versions in multiversion data warehouse. In: Proc. SAC, Nicosia, Cyprus (2004) 717–723
7. Blaschka, M., Sapia, C., Höfling, G.: On schema evolution in multidimensional databases. In: Proc. DaWaK. (1999) 153–164
8. Eder, J., Koncilia, C., Morzy, T.: The COMET metamodel for temporal data warehouses. In: Proc. CAiSE. (2002) 83–99
9. Golfarelli, M., Lechtenbörger, J., Rizzi, S., Vossen, G.: Schema versioning in data warehouses: Enabling cross-version querying via schema augmentation. Data and Knowledge Engineering (2006, To appear)
10. Quix, C.: Repository support for data warehouse evolution. In: Proc. DMDW. (1999)
11. Pedersen, T.B., Jensen, C.: Research issues in clinical data warehousing. In: Proc. SSDBM, Capri, Italy (1998) 43–52
12. Abelló, A., Martín, C.: The data warehouse: an object-oriented temporal database. In: Proc. JISBD 2003, Alicante, Spain (2003) 675–684
13. Abelló, A., Martín, C.: A bitemporal storage structure for a corporate data warehouse. In: Proc. ICEIS. (2003) 177–183
14. Bruckner, R., Tjoa, A.: Capturing delays and valid times in data warehouses - towards timely consistent analyses. Journ. Intell. Inf. Syst. **19** (2002) 169–190
15. Lenz, H.J., Shoshani, A.: Summarizability in OLAP and statistical databases. In: Proc. SSDBM. (1997) 132–143
16. Kim, J.S., Kim, M.H.: On effective data clustering in bitemporal databases. In: Proc. TIME. (1997) 54–61

Computing Iceberg Quotient Cubes with Bounding

Xiuzhen Zhang[1], Pauline Lienhua Chou[1], and Kotagiri Ramamohanarao[2]

[1] School of CS & IT, RMIT University, Australia
{zhang, lchou}@cs.rmit.edu.au
[2] Department of CSSE, The University of Melbourne, Australia
rao@csse.unimelb.edu.au

Abstract. In complex data warehouse applications, high dimensional data cubes can become very big. The quotient cube is attractive in that it not only summarizes the original cube but also it keeps the roll-up and drill-down semantics between cube cells. In this paper we study the problem of semantic summarization of iceberg cubes, which comprises only cells that satisfy given aggregation constraints. We propose a novel technique for identifying groups of cells based on *bounding* aggregates and an efficient algorithm for computing iceberg quotient cubes for monotone functions. Our experiments show that iceberg quotient cubes can reduce data cube sizes and our iceberg quotient cubing algorithm can be over 10-fold more efficient than the current approach.

1 Introduction

Since the introduction of the Cube operator [3], interests on data cube research has grown substantially. Several cube computation algorithms have been proposed, including relational approaches PipeHash and PipeSort [1], MemoryCube [7] and multiway array aggregation [13]. The number of cube cells grows exponentially with the number of dimensions. Large data cubes are difficult for storage and answering queries. Recent studies have focused on how to compute compressed data cubes, including Condensed Cube [9], Dwarf [8], Quotient Cube [5] and QC-Tree [6]. The quotient cube is especially attractive in that it compresses the original cube as well as keeps the roll-up/drill-down semantic among cells.

Iceberg cubes comprise cube cells whose aggregate value satisfies a given constraint. Many algorithms for iceberg cube computation have been proposed, including BUC [2], H-Cubing [4] and Star-Cubing [11]. Since cells failing the aggregation constraint are removed from the solution, there are "holes" in the lattice structure for iceberg cubes (shown in Fig. 1). It is interesting to see, with the presence of such "holes" of removed cells, whether semantic summarization can compress the original iceberg cubes. It is also interesting to study if iceberg cubes can be efficiently summarized while keeping the semantics. A tricky problem is how to incorporate effective pruning into summarization.

A Min Tjoa and J. Trujillo (Eds.): DaWaK 2006, LNCS 4081, pp. 145–154, 2006.

In this paper, we propose the concept of iceberg quotient cube and study its efficient computation. An iceberg quotient cube comprises classes of cells that satisfy a given constraint, and in each partition cells are of equal aggregate values and are connected by the roll-up/drill-down relationship. Obviously computing the iceberg cube first and then summarizing the resulting cells is a time-consuming approach. It is more efficient the iceberg quotient cubes are computed from base tables and pruning is applied with aggregation.

1.1   Main Ideas

We apply a novel technique *bounding* [12] for identifying lattices (of cells) of equal aggregates while pruning unqualified lattices.

In Table 1(a) Month, Product, SalesMan and City are dimensions, and Sale is the measure. Similarly Table 1(b) is a 4-dimensional dataset. A data cube of 4 dimensions comprises the 16 group-bys (including the empty group-by) from any subset of the 4 dimensions. With an aggregate function, each group-by in a data cube generates aggregations of the multi-set of measure values for partitions of tuples with the equal dimension-values, which we call *cells*. For example in Table 1(a) Min and Count are aggregate functions, and (Jan, Toy, John, Perth) is a cell with aggregations of Min(Sale) = 200 and Count(∗) = 5.

A data cube is a lattice with top and bottom cells respectively. The lattice on the left of Fig. 1 is the cube lattice for the toy dataset in Table 1(b). Cells are related by the super-cell/sub-cell relationship. Following the convention of BUC [2], a sub-cell (with more dimensions) are above its super-cells. The top cell for the lattice is False (not shown in Fig. 1), the empty cell that does not aggregate any tuples. The bottom cell is (∗, ∗, ∗, ∗), aggregating all tuples (∗ matches any value). The bounds for a lattice are computed from the most specific cells (MSCs) in the lattice under consideration. The MSCs can be viewed as the basic units for computing data cubes as all other cells can be computed from the MSCs. Table 1(a) shows a 4-dimensional dataset with 6 MSCs. Min(Sale) decreases monotonically with super-cells. The lower bound for the data cube is the minimum of Min(Sale) for all MSCs, which is 100. The upper bound for the cube is the maximum among all MSCs, which is 200. As will be seen later, a data cube can be decomposed into a set of sub-cubes and the bounding from MSCs applies to sub-cubes as well.

The 3 MSCs with "Month=March" form a sub-lattice, with (Mar, ∗, ∗, ∗) at the bottom and False at the top. What is special about this lattice is that its upper and lower bounds are both 100 (bounds are calculated as described before). So the lattice represents a class of cells with Min(Sale) = 100. If the aggregate value satisfies a given constraint, then it becomes a temporary class in the solution; otherwise the class is pruned. For monotone aggregate functions, such temporary classes are efficiently merged to produce the maximal partition of an iceberg data cube.

Table 1. Two sample dimensional datasets

Month	Product	SalesMan	City	Min(Sale)	Count(*)
Jan	Toy	John	Perth	200	5
Mar	TV	Peter	Perth	100	40
Mar	TV	John	Perth	100	20
Mar	TV	John	Sydney	100	10
Apr	TV	Peter	Perth	100	8
Apr	Toy	Peter	Sydney	100	5

(a) A sales dataset, partially aggregated

A	B	C	D	Sale
a_1	b_1	c_1	d_1	650
a_1	b_1	c_2	d_1	322
a_1	b_1	c_2	d_1	1087

(b) A toy dataset

1.2 Related Work

Our concept of iceberg quotient cube is motivated by the quotient cube [5]. We introduce semantic summarization into iceberg cubes. More importantly our approach of bound-based pruning and computing of iceberg quotient classes is different from the previous tuple-based approach [5]. A "jumping" method that can identify an equivalence class of cells without examining all cells in the class is essential for the efficiency of quotient cube computation. Based on BUC [2], Lakshmanan et al. [5] proposed a jumping method that involves examining every record in a partition of the underlying dataset. In contrast, our bound-based jumping method identifies an equivalence class of cells by examining MSCs; such an approach can improve the efficiency of quotient cube computation.

The QC-Tree is a data structure for storing quotient cubes. It is orthogonal to and can complement our work on iceberg quotient cubes.

The Dwarf Cube [8] and Iceberg Dwarf Cube [10] compresses the cube cells by exploiting shared prefixes and suffixes. The Condensed Cube [9] compresses a data cube by condensing the cells aggregated from the same set of base relation tuples into one cell. Nevertheless the focus of all these work are on compression and the semantics of data cubes are lost in the process.

Bound-prune cubing was proposed in our previous work to compute iceberg cubes [12]. In this work we apply bounding to summarization of data cubes.

2   Iceberg Quotient Cubes

The important roll-up and drill-down semantics on a data cube is the super-cell/sub-cell relationship among cells. Lakshmanan et al. [5] proposed the basic definitions for quotient cubes that preserve such semantics. Generally a data cube is partitioned into convex classes of cells with equal aggregates and cells in a class have the super-cell/sub-cell relationship.

Definition 1 Convex connected equivalence class. *All cells in a connected equivalence class are related by the super-cell(sub-cell) relationship and have equal aggregate values. In a convex class P, if a cell g and a sub-cell g' are in P, then cells that are sub-cells of g and super-cells of g' are also in P.*

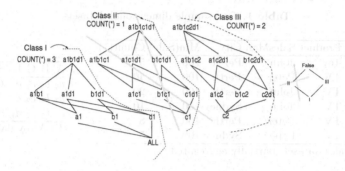

Fig. 1. The quotient cube of the function Count(∗) for the dataset in Table 1(b)

Definition 2 Quotient Cube Lattice. *A quotient cube lattice consists of convex connected equivalence classes of cells. Classes in the quotient lattice are connected by the super-class/sub-class relationship: a class C is super-class (sub-class) of another class D if there exist cells $c \in C$ and $d \in D$ such that c is a super-cell (sub-cell) of d. Each equivalence class is denoted as $[B, T]$, where B and T are the set of cells at the bottom and top of the class respectively.*

Example 1. *Consider the 4-dimensional dataset in Table 1(b). The original cube-lattice for* Count(∗) *has 24 cells, shown in Fig. 1. Cells can be summarized into 3 classes, which are represented by the bottom and top cells. Class I is* $[\{(\text{ALL})\}, \{(a_1, b_1, d_1)\}]$. $[\{(c_1)\}, \{(a_1, b_1, c_1, d_1)\}]$ *and* $[\{(c_2)\}, \{(a_1, b_1, c_2, d_1)\}]$ *are Class II and Class III respectively. Class II is a sub-class of class I. all cells in class II are sub-cells of some cells in Class I but not super-cells.*

Definition 3 Optimal Quotient Cube Lattice. *A quotient cube is optimal if all of its classes are maximal. A class is maximal if it contains the largest set of cells with equal aggregate values while satisfying connectivity and convexity.*

The aggregate value of a monotone aggregate function increases or decreases monotonically with respect to the super-cell relationship. For example, Count(∗) values increase with super-cells, whereas Min values decrease with super-cells. For monotone functions, there is a unique optimal quotient cube partition that coincides with the partition induced by connected equivalence partitions. In other words, if all connected cells with equal aggregate values are clustered in one class, the result is the optimal quotient cube. For non-monotone functions, a connected equivalence class is not necessarily convex, therefore, the optimal quotient cube cannot be induced solely from connected equivalence partitions.

Having all the basic definitions from [5], we are now ready to introduce our new definitions. The observation below emphasizes the following fact: For a given constraint, given that all cells in a class have the same aggregate value, a class is either pruned entirely or remains as a class, in other words, it is never split as the result of pruning by the aggregation constraint.

Observation 1. *Given a constraint, all cells failing the constraint form classes in the quotient cube. An iceberg cube consists of cells in the classes of the quotient cube whose aggregate values pass the constraint. The roll-up and drill-down semantics among the qualified classes are preserved.*

Definition 4 Iceberg Quotient Cube. *Let cells satisfying a given constraint be called iceberg cells. All iceberg cells are partitioned into convex and connected equivalence classes. The classes form an iceberg quotient cube.*

Example 2. *Continuing with Example 1, consider the constraint "Count($*$) $\geq$ 2". Class I and III in Fig. 1 remain while the entire Class II is pruned, as is denoted by the cross in Fig. 1. The semantics between Class I and III is kept.*

The crucial question to answer now is how to identify the equivalence classes of cells while effectively prune unpromising cells to achieve efficient iceberg quotient cubing. Our novel *Bounding* technique can solve both questions.

3   Computing Iceberg Quotient Cubes with Bounding

The naive approach of computing an iceberg cube first and then summarizing it into a quotient is obviously not an efficient approach. A more efficient approach of computing iceberg quotients is to compute iceberg quotients directly from input datasets, where aggregation, pruning with constraints and summarization is performed at the same time. Bounding can efficiently identify equivalence classes in a cube lattice with little extra cost. For monotone aggregate functions, the classes can then be easily merged to produce a set of maximal equivalence classes. We also present an efficient iceberg quotient cubing algorithm that incorporate all these ideas.

3.1   Bounding Aggregate Functions

Given a data cube on measure X and an aggregate function F, the tightest upper bound and lower bound are respectively reached by the largest and smallest aggregate values that can be produced by any set of MSCs of the data cube. However exhaustively checking the power set of MSCs is not computationally feasible. An aggregate function F is *boundable* [12] for a data cube if some upper and lower bounds of F can be determined by an algorithm with a single scan of some auxiliary aggregate values of MSCs of the data cube. We use an example to explain the main ideas of bounding. Details are described in [12].

Example 3. *Given measure X, Count(X) = Sum($\{$Count(X_i) $\mid i = 1..n\}$), where $X_1, ..., X_n$ are MSCs. The number of tuples in a cell of a data cube is no larger than the total number of tuples of all MSCs. Suppose g is a cube cell, Count(g) $\leq$ Sum($\{$Count(X_i) $\mid i = 1..n\}$). So Sum($\{$Count(X_i) $\mid i = 1..n\}$) is an upper for Count(X) of the data cube. On the other hand, to compute the lower bound, we also have Count(g) $\geq$ Min($\{$Count(X_i) $\mid i = 1..n\}$). As a result, the lower bound is Min($\{$Count(X_i) $\mid i = 1..n\}$). Both bounds can be obtained by one scan of MSCs and Count is boundable.*

Table 2. The bounds of SQL aggregate functions

F	upper bound ; lower bound
Count	$\underset{i}{\text{Sum}}\ \text{Count}(X_i); \underset{i}{\text{Min}}\ \text{Count}(X_i)$
Max	$\underset{i}{\text{Max}}\ \text{Max}(X_i); \underset{i}{\text{Min}}\ \text{Max}(X_i)$
Min	$\underset{i}{\text{Max}}\ \text{Min}(X_i); \underset{i}{\text{Min}}\ \text{Min}(X_i)$
Sum	$\underset{\text{Sum}(X_i)>0}{\text{Sum}}\ \text{Sum}(X_i)$ if (a) $\underset{\text{Sum}(X_i)<0}{\text{Sum}}\ \text{Sum}(X_i)$ if (b) $\underset{i}{\text{Max}}\ \text{Sum}(X_i)$ otherwise ; $\underset{i}{\text{Min}}\ \text{Sum}(X_i)$ otherwise
Average	$\underset{i}{\text{Max}}\ \text{Avg}(X_i); \underset{i}{\text{Min}}\ \text{Avg}(X_i)$

Given a dataset, X is the measure and X_1, ..., X_n are the MSCs.
(a): there is i such that $\text{Sum}(X_i) > 0$. (b): there is i such that $\text{Sum}(X_i) < 0$.

All SQL aggregate functions Count, Min, Max, Sum and Average are boundable, and their bounding algorithms are listed in Table 2. Note that Count, Max, Min, and Sum on non-negative (non-positive) measure values are monotone functions whereas Sum on arbitrary values and Average are non-monotone functions.

3.2   Identifying Equivalence Classes with Bounding

Observe that lattices are connected and convex. Bounding can be used to detect if a cell-lattice is an equivalence class as stated in the following proposition.

Proposition 1. *Given a lattice, all cells in the lattice have equal aggregate values if the upper and lower bounds of the lattice are equal.*

Proof. Proof of the proposition follows directly from that the aggregate values of cells in a lattice are bounded by the lower and upper bounds.

A data cube lattice can be partitioned into a set of sub-lattices each of which has equal aggregates. For all monotone functions, such a partition is easily achieved with single depth-first traversal of the G-tree (Section 3.3). If the bounds of a sub-lattice are equal and pass the constraint, it can be identified as one single class. The cells in the lattice do not need to be computed.

Although the temporary equivalence classes on a lattice is maximal with respect to a sub-lattice, to obtain the global maximal equivalence classes the temporary equivalence classes should be merged. Following Theorem 2 of [5], the following remark for monotone functions allows the merging process to produce maximal connected and convex equivalence classes based on the connectivity of classes and equality of their aggregate values.

Remark 1. For monotone functions, the unique optimal iceberg quotient cube is the partition induced by the connected equivalence classes.

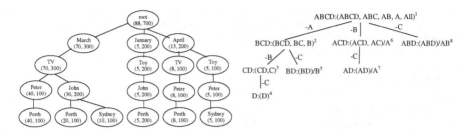

Fig. 2. The first G-tree Table 1(a) cube   **Fig. 3.** The G-trees for Cube(ABCD)

The following observation states how merging is achieved. The main idea is to derive more general and specific cells respectively from the bottom and top cells of lattices to be merged.

Observation 2. *For monotone functions, if two convex equivalence classes C_1 and C_2 are connected, the two classes can be merged into a coarser class C as follows: The bottom cells of C are the minimal set for the bottom cells of C_1 and C_2 with respect to the sub-cell relationship. The top cells of C are the maximal set for the top cells of C_1 and C_2 with respect to the sub-cell relationship.*

From Observation 2, to compute an iceberg quotient cube for a monotone function, two classes of equal aggregate values are merged as long as they have the super-cell/sub-cell relationship.

Example 4. *For simplicity * is omitted in cell notations. Consider merging*
$$C_1 = [\{(a_1, b_1, c_1)\}, \{(a_1, b_1, c_1, d_1)\}]$$
and
$$C_2 = [\{(b_1, c_1), (b_1, d_1)\}, \{(a_1, b_1, c_1), (a_1, b_1, d_1)\}].$$
The resulting class C is $\langle\{(b_1, c_1), (b_1, d_1)\}, \{(a_1, b_1, c_1, d_1)\}\rangle$. Among the bottom cells of C_1 and C_2, $\{(a_1, b_1, c_1), (b_1, c_1), (b_1, d_1)\}$, (b_1, c_1) is a super-cell of (a_1, b_1, c_1). So the minimal set is $\{(b_1, c_1), (b_1, d_1)\}$ and becomes the bottom cells of C. The top cells of C are similarly derived.

3.3   The G-Tree

The data structure for computing quotient cubes is the *G-tree* [12]. We use the first G-tree for cubing the dataset in Table 1(a) as an example to explain, which is shown in Fig. 2. In each node are the aggregates Sum(Sale) and Count(*). The aggregates in each node are for the cell with dimension-values on the path from the root to the node. For the leftmost path from the root of the G-tree, in the node (Peter) there are 40 tuples with Sum(Sale) = 100 in the (March, TV, Peter, *) partition. The leaf nodes give the MSCs for Cube(Month, Product, SalesMan, City).

To compute cells not represented on the first G-tree, sub-G-trees [3] are recursively constructed by collapsing dimensions. Fig. 3 shows the G-trees for

---

[3] Note that a sub-G-tree is not part of the original G-tree, but obtained from the original G-tree by collapsing a dimension.

Input: a) An N-dimensional dataset D with measure m.
  b) Aggregation constraint $C(F)$, where the aggregate function F is monotone.
Output: the Iceberg quotient cube Q, assumed global.
(1) Build the G-tree T from D for F.
(2) $Q = \phi$;
(3) **BIQC**(T, F, C);

Procedure BIQC (T, F, C)
(1) Let g be a conditional cell on T and L_g denote g's lattice of cells
(2) Compute the bounds $[B_1, B_2]$ for L_g;
(3) **if** (both B_1, B_2 violate C)
(4)   Skip the processing of L_g;
(5) **else if** ($B_1 == B_2$)
(6)   Merge the class from L_g to Q; //skip the processing of L_g, Section 3.2.
(7) **else**
(8) $S_L \leftarrow$ sub-lattices with equal bounds by depth-first traversal;// Section 3.1.
(9)   Merge classes in S_L to Q;
(10) **for each** dropping dimension D on T **do**
(11) $T_s \leftarrow$ the sub G-tree from collapsing D from T; //pruning, Section 3.4
(12)   **BIQC**(T_s, F, C);

Fig. 4. The Bound Iceberg Quotient Cubing Algorithm

Cube(ABCD). Each node represents a G-tree. For the ABCD-tree at the top, the corresponding group-bys are (A,B,C,D), (A,B,C), (A,B), (A) and (). The sub-G-trees of the ABCD-tree, which are the $(-A)$BCD, A$(-B)$CD, and AB$(-C)$D trees, are formed by collapsing on dimensions A, B, and C respectively. The dimensions after "/" in each node denote common prefix dimensions for the tree at the node and all its sub-trees. In the sub-G-tree construction process, we compute the bounds based on prefix dimensions and use them for pruning [12].

3.4   The Bound Iceberg Quotient Cubing Algorithm

Our bound iceberg quotient cubing (BIQC) algorithm is shown in Fig. 4. Line 1 of the algorithm denotes the following process of identifying temporary equivalence lattices: Following the depth-first traversal of T, at the node of a prefix cell g, a class C is formed and g is both the top and bottom cell of the class. If a descendent node g_d of g has equal aggregate value to that of g, then g_d is added as a top cell for G. Any sub-cell of g_d as a top cell is replaced by g_d. For any descendent cell $g_{d'}$, if the aggregate value is different from that of C, a new class C' with $g_{d'}$ as the bottom cell is created. On returning from the recursion to the bottom-cell of a class, the class is completed.

  Merging classes is at lines 6 and 9. When a lattice under consideration is not an equivalence class, it is partitioned into equivalence classes(Section 3.2). Pruning is applied at line 4 and line 11 on lattices whose bounds fail the constraints. Especially at line 11, all cells yet to be computed from the branches already included in an equivalence class or failing the constraint are pruned.

4   Experiments

We did experiments to study the compression effectiveness of iceberg quotient cubes and the efficiency of BIQC for the constraint "Count$(*) \geq \alpha$". We compare BIQC with BUC, the underlying iceberg cubing algorithm in [5]. To accurately compare computation cost, timing does not include the time for writing output.

Three datasets are used in our experiments. The US Census dataset [4] is dense and skewed: 88,443 tuples, 12 dimensions, and a cardinality range of 7–48. The TPC-R[5] dataset is relatively dense and random: 1000,000 tuples, 10 dimensions, and a cardinality range of 3–25. The Weather dataset [6] is extremely sparse: 100,000 tuples, 9 dimensions, and a cardinality range of 2–6505.

4.1   Compression Effectiveness of Iceberg Quotient Cubes

The compression ratio is the number of classes in a iceberg quotient as the proportion of number of cells in the original iceberg cube. A quotient cube with lower compression ratio is more effective in compressing the original data cube. With the constraint "support$(*) \geq \alpha$" (support is the relative Count in percentage), the compression ratio for the three datasets remains almost constant for $\alpha = 10\%..80\%$. On the sparse weather dataset, the compression ratio is around 80%. In contrast on the dense and skewed census dataset it is around 20%. This low ratio is in contrast to that of 70% on the random TPC-R dataset, It can be seen that iceberg quotient cube can more effectively reduce iceberg cube size on dense and skewed data.

4.2   Efficiency of Bound Iceberg Quotient Cubing

Fig. 5 shows the runtime of BIQC on computing the iceberg quotient cube with constraint "Count$(*) \geq \alpha$" in comparison to BUC on computing the original iceberg cube. BIQC is over 10-fold more efficient than BUC on Census and

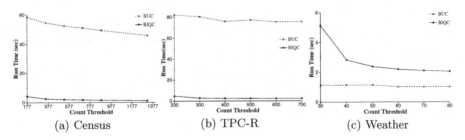

(a) Census   (b) TPC-R   (c) Weather

Fig. 5. Runtime comparison: BIQC vs. BUC with "Count$(*) \geq \alpha$"

---

[4] ftp://ftp.ipums.org/ipums/data/ip19001.Z.

[5] http://www.tpc.org/tpcr/.

[6] http://cdiac.ornl.gov/ftp/ndp026b/SEP85L.DAT.Z.

TPC-R for all Count thresholds. It is slower than BUC on the extremely sparse Weather data. The likely reason can be that on sparse data there are much more temporary equivalence classes while their sizes are smaller, which increase the cost for merging. BIQC scales relatively well with lower Count thresholds.

5 Conclusions

We have proposed the iceberg quotient cube for semantic summarization of iceberg cubes. We apply a novel technique bounding for efficient computation. Our experiments demonstrated that iceberg quotient cubes are effective for compressing iceberg cubes and our algorithm is significantly more efficient than the existing approach. Our future work will focus on the open problem of computing iceberg quotient cubes for complex aggregate functions [5].

References

1. S. Agarwal et. al. On the computation of multidimensional aggregates. In *Proc. VLDB*, 1996.
2. K Beyer and R Ramakrishnan. Bottom-up computation of sparse and iceberg cubes. In *Proc. SIGMOD*, 1999.
3. J Gray et al. Data cube: a relational aggregation operator generalizing group-by, cross-tab, and sub-totals. *Data Mining and Knowledge Discovery*, 1(1), 1997.
4. J Han et al. Efficient computation of iceberg cubes with complex measures. In *Proc. SIGMOD*, 2001.
5. L. Lakshmanan et al. Quotient cube: How to summarize the semantics of a data cube. In *Proc. VLDB*, 2002.
6. L. Lakshmanan et al. QC-trees: An efficient summary structure for semantic OLAP. In *Proc. SIGMOD*, 2003.
7. K. A. Ross and D. Srivastava. Fast computation of sparse data cubes. In *Proc. SIGMOD*, 1997.
8. Y. Sismanis et. al. Dwarf: Shrinking the petacube. In *Proc. SIGMOD*, 2002.
9. W. Wang et al. Condensed cube: An effective approach to reducing data cube size. In *Proc. ICDE*, 2002.
10. L. Xiang and Y. Feng. Fast computation of iceberg dwarf. In *Proc. SSDBM*, 2004.
11. D. Xin et al. Star-cubing: computing iceberg cubes by top-down and bottom-up integration. In *Proc. VLDB*, 2003.
12. X. Zhang, L. Chou and G. Dong. Efficient computation of iceberg cubes by bounding aggregate functions. *IEEE TKDE*, 2006. In submission.
13. Y. Zhao et al. An array-based algorithm for simultaneous multidimensional aggregates. In *Proc SIGMOD*, 1997.

An Effective Algorithm to Extract Dense Sub-cubes from a Large Sparse Cube*

Seok-Lyong Lee

School of Industrial and Information Engineering,
Hankuk University of Foreign Studies,
89 Wangsan-ri, Mohyun-myon, Yongin-shi, Kyungki-do 449-701, Korea
sllee@hufs.ac.kr

Abstract. A data cube provides aggregate information to support a class of queries such as a range-sum query. To process those queries efficiently, some auxiliary information, i.e. prefix sums, is pre-computed and maintained. In reality however most of high dimensional data cubes are very sparse, causing a serious space overhead. In this paper, we investigate an algorithm that extracts dense sub-cubes from a large sparse cube based on the density function. Instead of maintaining a large prefix-sum cube, a few dense sub-cubes are maintained to reduce the space overhead and to restrict the update propagation. We present an iterative method that identifies dense intervals in each dimension and constructs sub-cubes based on the intervals found. We show the effectiveness of our method through the analytic comparison and experiment with respect to various data sets and dimensions.

Keywords: Cube, Sub-cube, Data warehousing, Clustering.

1 Introduction

A range sum query over a data cube is popular in finding trends and relationships between attributes. It sums values of selected cells in a specified query range. A direct method to access the data cube causes a lot of cells to be accessed, incurring a severe processing overhead. To overcome this, the prefix sum approach [7] has been proposed. The main idea of this approach is to pre-compute prefix-sums of the cube. Any range-sum query can be answered by accessing 2^d appropriate prefix-sums, where d is the number of dimensions. Even though this method shows a considerable efficiency, it suffers from the update cost. In a current enterprise environment data elements of a cube are dynamically changed, which causes the update propagation to be an important issue. Another problem is the space overhead when a data cube is sparse. As the dimensionality becomes higher, the space to accommodate cells increases exponentially. In general the number of nonzero cells of the data cube is very small compared to the total number of cells. For example, consider real-world data from the U.S. Census Bureau using their Data Extraction System [1]. Only 11 attributes are chosen out of 372 attributes as follows: A measure attribute is *income*,

---

* This work was supported by Hankuk University of Foreign Studies Research Fund of 2006.

A Min Tjoa and J. Trujillo (Eds.): DaWaK 2006, LNCS 4081, pp. 155–164, 2006.

and functional attributes are *age, marital_status, sex, education, race, origin, family_type, detailed_household_summary, age_group,* and *class_of_worker.* Although the cube is ten-dimensional, it contains more than 16 million cells with only 15,985 nonzero elements [9]. Consequently the density of the cube is about 0.001. In reality many data warehouses contain multiple small regions of a clustered dense region, with points sparsely scattered over the rest of the space [4].

Various approaches to minimize the update propagation have been proposed since [7]. Geffner et el. [6] proposed the *relative prefix sum* (RPC) approach that tried to balance the query-update tradeoff between the direct method and the prefix sum approach. This approach is however impractical for high dimensionality and capacity since the update cost increases exponentially. Chan and Ioannidis [3] proposed a new class of cube representations called the hierarchical cubes. However, the index mapping from a high-level abstract to a low-level concrete cube is too complicate for implementation, and the analytical results of their method are not verified experimentally. Geffner et el. [5] proposed the *dynamic data cube* which was designed by decomposing the prefix sum cube recursively. But if the data cube is of high dimensions and high capacity, it is difficult to apply their approach since the tree becomes too large. These approaches based on RPC have the limitation in the context that the RPC is a slight transformation of the prefix-sum cube.

Chun et al. [2] proposed an index structure called the Δ-tree to reduce the update cost. However, the update speed-up of it is accomplished by the sacrifice of the retrieval efficiency. In many on-line analytic processing (OLAP) applications, it becomes an important issue to improve the update performance while minimizing the sacrifice of the retrieval efficiency. Furthermore, the methods mentioned above do not address much on the problem of the space reduction in a large data cube. More recently, Sismanis et al. [8] proposed Dwarf, a highly compressed structure which solves the storage space problem by identifying prefix and suffix redundancies in the structure of a cube and factoring them out of the store. It accomplishes the space reduction by eliminating these redundancies, not focusing on producing sub-cubes from a sparse cube. In this paper, we propose an effective algorithm that finds dense sub-cubes from a large sparse data cube to drastically reduce the space overhead. Those sub-cubes can be used to respond the range-sum query with minimizing the update propagation. Changing the value of a certain cell affects only a sub-cube in which the cell is contained, forcing the update propagation to be limited within the sub-cube.

Suppose a set of dimensions is $D = \{D_i \mid i = 1, 2, ..., d\}$, and the size of each dimension is represented by $|D_i|$, where the dimension D_i corresponds to a functional attribute. Then, a d-dimensional data cube is represented by $C[0:|D_1|-1]..[0:|D_d|-1]$ of size $|D_1| \times |D_2| \times \cdots \times |D_d|$. Each cell of C contains measure attributes and is denoted by $cl[j_1][j_2]..[j_d]$ where $0 \le j_i \le |D_i|-1$. The cube C may contain multiple *sub-cubes*, each of which is represented by $SC[l_1:h_1]..[l_d:h_d]$ where $0 \le l_i \le h_i \le |D_i|-1$. Then, the problem of finding sub-cubes is: Given a d-dimensional data cube $C[0:|D_1|-1]..[0:|D_d|-1]$, the minimum number of cells in a sub-cube (*minCells*), the density threshold for a histogram-bin (τ), and the density threshold for a sub-cube (δ), we are to find a set of dense sub-cubes SC's that satisfy the given condition. An input parameter *minCells* is needed to determine outliers, and two density thresholds, τ and δ, are used as conditional parameters to find dense sub-cubes.

2 Finding Dense Sub-cubes

We discuss our proposed method for finding dense sub-cubes from a given sparse data cube. The overall process of it is shown in Fig. 1. Phase 1 produces candidate sub-cubes from a given data cube. Dense intervals in each dimension are identified and an initial set of sub-cubes is formed by those dense intervals. For each sub-cube built, dense intervals within the sub-cube are identified again and sub-cubes of the identified sub-cube are built based on newly identified intervals. This procedure is applied repeatedly until a termination criterion is satisfied. In Phase 2, the sub-cubes produced in Phase 1 are refined with respect to the given density threshold. The sub-cubes that are closely placed are merged together in the enlarging step, while sparse surfaces of candidate sub-cubes are pruned in the shrinking step.

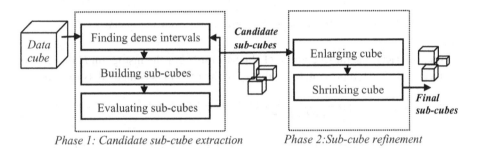

Phase 1: Candidate sub-cube extraction   *Phase 2:Sub-cube refinement*

Fig. 1. The overall sketch for finding dense sub-cubes

2.1 Candidate Sub-cube Extraction

Consider a 2-dimensional 16×16 data cube C with 33 non-empty cells in Fig.2, in which non-empty cells are marked. To find dense intervals from each dimension, we use the histogram flattening technique. A one-dimensional array is maintained for each dimension whose size is $|D_i|$. Each bin of the array holds the cardinality of non-empty cells. A bin is regarded as '*dense*' if it has more non-empty cells than the threshold. In Fig. 2, an array for D_1 has 16 bins and each bin contains the cardinality, say, 0 for the first bin, 1 for the second bin, 3 for the third bin, and so forth. These bins constitute a histogram. Let the i-th bin of a dimension have the value v_i. v_i is generated by the projection of the corresponding cells along with this dimension, representing the number of non-empty cells with respect to the bin. Now, let us compute a representative value of the bin using the histogram-flattening technique. We do not take v_i as the representative value of the bin i. Instead, we consider its neighboring bins as follows. Let f be the flattening factor and the representative value f bin i be v_i'. When $f = 0$, no flattening occurs. When $f = 1$, two neighbors of left and right sides, are involved in computing $v_i' = (v_{i-1} + v_i + v_{i+1}) / 3$. Similarly, when $f = 2$, four neighbors are involved. Thus, we get $v_i' = (v_{i-2} + v_{i-1} + v_i + v_{i+1} + v_{i+2}) / 5$. Considering the boundaries of the histogram, the representative value of the i-th bin is computed by Lemma 2.1.

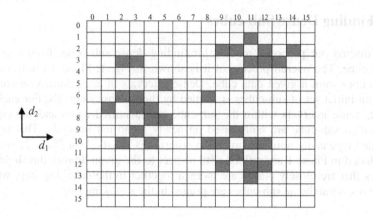

Fig. 2. A cube for a 2-dimensional 16×16 cube C with 33 non-empty cells

Lemma 2.1 (Representative value of the i-th bin): For the histogram H that covers the interval $[l{:}h]$, the representative value v_i' of the i-th bin is computed as follows:

$$v_i' = \begin{cases} \dfrac{1}{f+i-l+1}\cdot\displaystyle\sum_{t=l}^{i+f}v_t, & \text{when } h-l\geq f, l\leq i\leq l+f-1, \\[2mm] \dfrac{1}{2f+1}\cdot\displaystyle\sum_{t=i-f}^{i+f}v_t, & \text{when } h-l\geq f, l+f\leq i\leq h-f, \\[2mm] \dfrac{1}{f-i+h+1}\cdot\displaystyle\sum_{t=i-f}^{h}v_t, & \text{when } h-l\geq f, h-f+1\leq i\leq h, \\[2mm] \dfrac{1}{h-l+1}\cdot\displaystyle\sum_{t=l}^{h}v_t, & \text{when } h-l\geq f. \end{cases}$$

The value v_i' of the first and the last f bins, respectively, should be treated differently since the number of bins involved in computing v_i' is less than $2f+1$. For instance when $f=2$, the v_1' for the first bin is computed as $v_1' = (v_1 + v_2 + v_3) / 3$, and the v_2' for the second bin is computed as $v_2' = (v_1 + v_2 + v_3 + v_4) / 4$. After we get the flattened values for all bins, each value is evaluated with respect to the threshold τ, to determine whether the bin is dense or not. The histogram for the dimension 1 is computed as shown in Table 1 when $f = 0$, 1, and 2. We get dense intervals [1:5] and [8:14] for $f = 0$ and $\tau = 1$, [1:5] and [8:13] for $f = 1$ and $\tau = 1$, a single dense interval [1:14] for $f = 2$ and $\tau = 1$, [1:4] and [9:13] for $f = 2$ and $\tau = 2$.

Table 1. Histogram for the dimension 1 when $f = 0$, 1, and 2

bin / f	0	1	2	3	4	5	6	7	8	9	10	11	12	13	14	15
f = 0	0	1	3	4	3	2	0	0	2	3	4	5	4	1	1	0
f = 1	0.50	1.33	2.67	3.33	3.00	1.67	0.67	0.67	1.67	3.00	4.00	4.33	3.33	2.00	0.67	0.50
f = 2	1.33	2.00	2.20	2.60	2.40	1.80	1.40	1.40	1.80	2.80	3.60	3.40	3.00	2.20	1.50	0.67

Once we identify dense intervals in each dimension, we build sub-cubes based on the intervals. When $f = 0$ and $\tau = 1$, we get two dense intervals, [1:5] and [8:14] for D_1, and one interval [1:13] for D_2. Using these intervals, we are able to build two initial sub-cubes, $SC[1:5][1:13]$ and $SC[8:14][1:13]$. However, these sub-cubes still include sparse regions inside them. Thus, we apply again the process to find dense intervals with respect to each dimension within each sub-cube. For a sub-cube $SC[1:5]$ [1:13], we get one dense interval [1:5] for D_1 and two dense intervals, [3:3] and [5:10] for D_2, producing two sub-cubes, $SC[1:5][3]$ and $SC[1:5][5:10]$. Similarly, for a sub-cube $SC[8:14][1:13]$, we get one dense interval [8:14] for D_1 and three intervals, [1:4], [6:6], and [9:13] for D_2, producing three sub-cubes, $SC[8:14][1:4]$, $SC[8:14][6]$, and $SC[8:14][9:13]$. This process is iterative. We therefore need to determine a termination condition to stop the process. A cube is said to be *continuous* if and only if all edges of the cube are composed of dense intervals.

The iterative process terminates if an identified sub-cube is continuous. From a sub-cube $SC[1:5][3]$, we get the sub-cube $SC[2:3][3]$ by finding dense intervals in each dimension. Since this sub-cube is continuous, we stop repeating the process for this sub-cube. Similarly, we get the sub-cube $SC[1:5][5:10]$ that is continuous. We get $SC[9:14][1:4]$ from $SC[8:14][1:4]$, $SC[8][6]$ from $SC[8:14][6]$, and $SC[8:12][9:13]$ from $SC[8:14][9:13]$, respectively. The algorithms in Fig. 3 and 4 describe the procedures to find candidate dense sub-cubes.

Procedure_Create_SubCubes
Given: $C[l_1:h_1]..[l_d:h_d]$ (a given original cube)
Find: **SetSC** (a set of d-dimensional sub-cubes - $A_k[l_{1,k}:h_{1,k}]..[l_{d,k}:h_{d,k}]$)
/* Create d arrays from $C[l_1:h_1]..[l_d:h_d]$ by projection*/
        SetArr ← a set of d one-dimensional arrays for $C[l_1:h_1]..[l_d:h_d]$
/* Identify dense intervals from **SetArr** */
        for each one-dimensional array $a_i[l_i:h_i]$
            SetSI$_i$ ← a set of dense intervals for a_i
        end for
/* Create **SetSC** */
        Generate |**SetSI$_1$**|×|**SetSI$_2$**|×···×|**SetSI$_d$**| sub-cubes
            from dense intervals in each dimension
        SetSC ← sub-cubes created
/* Return a result **SetSC** */
        return SetSC

Fig. 3. Algorithm *Procedure_Create_SubCubes*

Procedure_Build_Dense_SubCubes
Given: $C[0:|D_1|-1]..[0:|D_d|-1]$ (a d-dimensional cube)
Find: **SetDSC** (a set of d-dimensional dense sub-cubes)
/* Create sub-cubes and push them into a stack STK */
        STK ← *Procedure_Create_SubCubes*(C)
/* Identifying dense sub-cubes */
        do while (STK is not empty)
            c ← pop(STK) /* c is a cube extracted from STK. */
            if (c is *continuous*) **then**

$$SetDSC \leftarrow SetDSC \cup \{ c \}$$
else
$$STK \leftarrow Procedure\_Create\_SubCubes(c)$$
end if
end while
/* Return a result **SetDSC** */
return SetDSC

Fig. 4. Algorithm *Procedure_Build_Dense_SubCubes*

2.2 Sub-cube Refinement

The candidate sub-cubes identified by the iterative process in the previous section are refined based on the density of a sub-cube. We start the discussion with defining the density of a cube.

Definition 2.2 (Density of a cube): Let the number of cells in a cube C be $numCells(C)$ and the number of dense cells in C be $numDenseCells(C)$. Then, the density of the cube C, $density(C)$, is defined as follows:

$$density(C) = \frac{numDenseCells(C)}{numCells(C)}$$

Enlarging sub-cubes. Two closely located sub-cubes are merged in this step if the merging satisfies a pre-specified condition. We call this step as an *'enlarging'* step since merging two cubes produces one larger cube. We first define a merging operator between two sub-cubes as follows:

Definition 2.3 (*Merging operator* $\oplus$): Consider two d-dimensional cubes, $A[l_{1,A}:h_{1,A}]..[l_{d,A}:h_{d,A}]$ and $B[l_{1,B}:h_{1,B}]..[l_{d,B}:h_{d,B}]$ to be merged. The merging operator $\oplus$ is defined as $A \oplus B = C[l_{1,C}:h_{1,C}]..[l_{d,C}:h_{d,C}]$ such that $l_{i,C} = min(l_{i,A}, l_{i,B})$ and $h_{i,C} = max(h_{i,A}, h_{i,B})$ for $i = 1, 2, ..., d$.

Let a d-dimensional cube $B[l_{1,B}:h_{1,B}]..[l_{d,B}:h_{d,B}]$ is to be merged to a cube $A[l_{1,A}:h_{1,A}]..[l_{d,A}:h_{d,A}]$. The number of cells increased by the merging is computed as $numCells(A \oplus B) - numCells(A)$, and the number of dense cells increased by merging two cubes is $numDenseCells(A \oplus B) - numDenseCells(A)$. Thus, the density of the increased portion, $density(\Delta_{A,B})$, of the merged cube is as follows:

$$density(\Delta_{A,B}) = \frac{numDenseCells(A \oplus B) - numDenseCells(A)}{numCells(A \oplus B) - numCells(A)}$$

In the previous example, consider that a sub-cube $SC[2:3][3]$ is merged to a sub-cube $SC[1:5][5:10]$. The merging operation, $SC[2:3][3] \oplus SC[1:5][5:10]$, produces a merged cube $SC[1:5][3:10]$. Thus the density of the increased portion, $density(\Delta)$, of the merged cube is $2/10 = 0.20$. Merging two cubes is allowed only when a pre-specified condition is satisfied. Let δ be a density threshold for a sub-cube, then the merging condition is defined as follows:

Definition 2.4 (*Merging condition*): When a cube B is to be merged to a cube A, the merging condition should be satisfied and is defined as follows:

$$density(\Delta_{A,B}) \geq \delta$$

The density threshold δ is determined depending on various application requirements and is given by a user. We however give some tips to determine the threshold. First, it can be chosen as the density of the merging cube, say, $\delta = density(A)$ when a cube B is to be merged to a cube A. Another choice can be the mean density $density_{mean}$ of sub-cubes identified by the previous process. Suppose that a sub-cube $SC[2:3][3]$ is merged to one of other sub-cubes. The $density(\Delta)$'s are 0.20 for $SC[1:5][5:10]$, 0.07 for $SC[9:14][1:4]$, 0.19 for $SC[8][6]$, and 0.17 for $SC[8:12][9:13]$, respectively. When we adopt the first case, the merging is not allowed to any sub-cube since $density()$'s for $SC[1:5][5:10]$, $SC[9:14][1:4]$, $SC[8][6]$, and $SC[8:12][9:13]$ are 0.37, 0.38, 1.00, and 0.40, respectively, and all these values do not meet the merging condition. When we adopt $density_{mean} = 0.54$ as the threshold, the merging does not occur, either. If a user specify the threshold explicitly, say, 0.15, then the sub-cube $SC[2:3][3]$ is merged to $SC[1:5][5:10]$, producing a new larger sub-cube $SC[1:5][3:10]$.

Shrinking sub-cubes. Even though sub-cubes are merged at the enlarging step under a pre-specified condition, newly produced sub-cubes may contain sparse portions in their surfaces. Thus, we evaluate each surface of them to prune it if its density is lower than the density threshold δ. A d-dimensional cube $C[l_1:h_1]...[l_d:h_d]$ has $2 \times d$ surfaces $(S_1[l_1:h_1][l_2:h_2]...[l_d], ..., S_{2d}[h_1][l_2:h_2]...[l_d:h_d])$. We call these surfaces *surface slices*. We evaluate the surface slices of each candidate sub-cube produced by the previous step. If the density of a slice is lower than δ, the slice is pruned from the cube, resulting in shrinking sub-cubes. Let us consider the sub-cube $SC[1:5][3:10]$ that has 4 surface slices, $S[1:5][3]$, $S[1:5][10]$, $S[1][3:10]$, and $S[5][3:10]$. The densities of these slices are 0.4, 0.4, 0.125, and 0.25, respectively. If we adopt $\delta = 0.15$ as the pruning threshold, then the surface slice $S[1][3:10]$ is pruned, producing the shrunken sub-cube $SC[2:5][3:10]$. This shrinking step is applied to the produced sub-cube $SC[2:5][3:10]$ until the shrinking does not occur any more. If $minCells = 16$, then the sub-cube $SC[8][6]$ is considered as an outlier. Finally, we get three sub-cubes, $SC[2:5][3:10]$, $SC[9:14][1:4]$, and $SC[8:12][9:13]$, and two outliers, $SC[2:3][3]$ and $SC[8][6]$.

3 Experiments

To show the effectiveness of our method we provide an analysis and experimental result on diverse data sets that are generated synthetically for various dimenionalities. Our experiment focuses on evaluating the space reduction, while mainaining the reasonable query execution time. The experiment was conducted using Pentium 4 1.7GHz processor with 1G MEM and 80G HDD. For the experiment, we have generated 16 sparse data cubes synthetically with the dimensionalities of 2, 3, 4, and 5, four cubes for each. The experiment was conducted for four dimensions ($d = 2,3,4,5$) for convenience, but our method does not restrict the dimensionality of data sets. These cubes are generated to have the clustered data distribution, in which the area within clusters is dense while the area outside clustered regions is sparse. From each data cube, we extracted dense sub-cubes using our method. For τ and δ, we chose the mean value of the histogram bins at each dimension and the mean density of sub-cubes, respectively. We have adopted 16 for *minCells*, leading all populated cells in the sub-cube that has cells less than 16 to be treated as outliers and stored in the table separated from the sub-cubes.

Space reduction. We present the space utilization of our method compared to the prefix-sum cube for a large sparse data cube. Consider a data cube C with a set of dimensions $D = \{D_i \mid i = 1, 2, ..., d\}$. The size of each dimension is represented by $|D_i|$, and the data cube is represented by $C[0:|D_1|-1]..[0:|D_d|-1]$. Then, the size of the cube $|C|$ is as follows:

$$|C| = |D_1| \times ... \times |D_d| = \prod_{i=1}^{d} |D_i|$$

Let $|D_1| = |D_2| = \cdots = |D_d| = N$ for the convenience. Then the $|C|$ is N^d. If the space that is needed to store a single cell of the cube (that is, a measure attribute) is c, the total amount of storage for C will be $c \cdot N^d$ when the cube is implemented by a multi-dimensional array. The space complexity will be $O(N^d)$. On the other hand, each dense sub-cube identified is implemented by a multi-dimensional array (MOLAP: Multi-dimensional OLAP), while outliers that is not contained in any sub-cube are stored in the relational table (ROLAP: Relational OLAP). Suppose that the method generates m sub-cubes (SC_j, for $1 \le j \le m$) and o outliers, and the size of an edge of SC_j with respect to d-dimension is $e_{j,d}$. Then, the size of sub-cubes identified, $size(SC)$, is as follows:

$$size(SC) = \sum_{j=1}^{m} |SC_j| = \sum_{j=1}^{m} |e_{j,1} \times ... \times e_{j,d}| = \sum_{j=1}^{m} \prod_{i=1}^{d} e_{j,i}$$

Let us assume that $e_{j,1} = e_{j,2} = ... = e_{j,d} = n$ and all sub-cubes are of equal-sizes for the comparative convenience. Then the total size to implement all sub-cubes is $m \cdot c \cdot n^d$. Each outlier is stored in the (*index*, *value*) form, where an *index* is a coordinate in the d-dimensional space and a *value* corresponds to a measure attribute. Thus, the space needed to store an outlier is $d \times I + c$, where I is the space that is needed to represent a coordinate of a single dimension. Without great loss of generality, we assume $I = c$. Therefore, the space needed to store all outliers is $o \cdot c \cdot (d+1)$. The space complexity of our method will be $O(m \cdot n^d + o \cdot d)$. Since m and o can be considered as constants and n is much smaller than N, we conclude that our approach demonstrates a significant space efficiency compared to the prefix-sum approach.

The space reduction in Fig. 5 shows 89.9-95.7 % compared to the data cube for dimension 2, 93.3-97.1 % for dimension 3, 95.4-97.3 % for dimension 4, and 96.3-97.6 % for dimension 5, respectively. We can observe that our method has achieved the high space efficiency, and that as the dimensionality becomes higher the space reduction increases. It means that the efficiency of storage saving is getting better in higher dimensions.

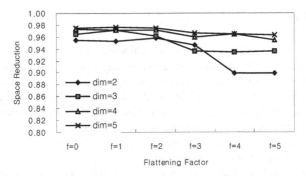

Fig. 5. Space reduction with respect to the dimensionality and flattening factor

Query efficiency. We have compared our method (*SC*) to the prefix-sum cube method (*PC*) [7] since it shows better performance than other methods in terms of the retrieval efficiency. The queries are grouped into three categories: *small, medium,* and *large.* In the *small* group, each edge length of query rectangles is smaller than 30% of the corresponding dimension length. And, 30-50% for the *medium* group and over 50% for the *large* group, respectively. We generated 20 queries for each group, and thus 60 queries were used for each dimension. To respond the query, our method takes the following two steps: (1) to search the sub-cubes in which most dense cells are contained, and (2) to search a tree structure called *delta(Δ)-tree*[2] in which outliers are stored. We do not describe how to store outliers in the tree due to the space limitation. Interested readers are referred to [2] for the details. The query performance is evaluated in term of the number of page I/O's since the computation time in the prefix-sum cube is negligible compared to the I/O time. Fig. 6 illustrates the comparison of query performance with respect to the query size and dimensionality. As we can observe from the figure, our method performs reasonably. In case of the small query group, the number of page I/O's is 5.7-18.4 in our method, and 4.1-14.7 in the prefix-sum method, which shows a little difference. For example, the page I/O ratio of our method versus the prefix-sum method is 1.02 to 1.39 for the small group, which is quite usable in a real business environment.

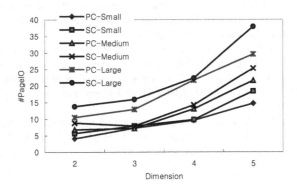

Fig. 6. Query efficiency with respect to the query size and dimensionality

4 Conclusion

In this paper, we have addressed the issue of finding dense sub-cubes from a sparse data cube. In a real OLAP environment, analysts may want to explore the relationship among attributes to find business trends and opportunities. A data cube for such analyses is generally very sparse. This is the motivation that we proposed a new technique. To solve the problem, we have first identified dense intervals in each dimension using the histogram-flattening technique, and constructed candidate sub-cubes based on the intervals. After the iterative process, those candidate sub-cubes are refined through enlarging and shrinking steps.

We have performed the analytic comparison and experiments to examine the space reduction and the query efficiency. It shows that our method drastically reduces the space requirement for a large sparse data cube, compared to the methods that use a large prefix-sum cube. The space reduction ratio is between 89.9 % and 97.6 %, and it becomes higher as the dimensionality increases, while maintaining the reasonable query performance. As a future work, we plan to study a multidimensional index structure to store both multiple sub-cubes and outliers to obtain better retrieval efficiency.

References

[1] U. S. Census Bureau, Census bureau databases. The online data are available on the web at http://www.census.gov/.

[2] S. J. Chun, C. W. Chung, J. H. Lee and S. L. Lee, Dynamic Update Cube for Range-Sum Queries, Proceedings of Int'l Conference on Very Large Data Bases, Italy, 2001, pp. 521-530.

[3] C. Y. Chan and Y. E. Ioannidis, Hierarchical cubes for range-sum queries, Proceedings of Int'l Conference on Very Large Data Bases, Scotland, 1999, pp. 675-686.

[4] D.W. Cheung, B. Zhou, B. Kao, H. Kan and S.D. Lee, Towards the building of a Dense-Region Based OLAP System, *Data and Knowledge Engineering*, Elsevier Science, V36, 1-27, 2001.

[5] S. Geffner, D. Agrawal, and A. El Abbadi, The Dynamic Data Cube, Proceedings of Int'l Conference on Extending Database Technology, Germany, 2000, pp.237-253.

[6] S. Geffner, D. Agrawal, and A. El Abbadi, T. Smith, Relative prefix sums: an efficient approach for quering dynamic OLAP Data Cubes, Proceedings of Int'l Conference on Data Engineering, Australia,1999, pp. 328-335.

[7] C. Ho, R. Agrawal, N. Megido, and R. Srikant, Range queries in OLAP Data Cubes, Proceedings of ACM SIGMOD Int'l Conference on Management of Data, 1997, pp. 73-88.

[8] Y. Sismanis, A. Deligiannakis, N. Roussopoulos, and Y. Kotidis, Dwarf: Shrinking the PetaCube, Proceedings of ACM SIGMOD Int'l Conference on Management of Data, 2002, pp. 464-475.

[9] J. S. Vitter and M. Wang, Approximate Computation of Multidimensional Aggregates of Sparse Data Using Wavelets, Proceedings of ACM SIGMOD Int'l Conference on Management of Data, Pennsylvania, 1999, pp. 193-204.

On the Computation of
Maximal-Correlated Cuboids Cells

Ronnie Alves[*] and Orlando Belo

Department of Informatics, School of Engineering, University of Minho
Campus de Gualtar, 4710-057 Braga, Portugal
{ronnie, obelo}@di.uminho.pt

Abstract. The main idea of iceberg data cubing methods relies on optimization techniques for computing only the cuboids cells above certain minimum support threshold. Even using such approach the curse of dimensionality remains, given the large number of cuboids to compute, which produces, as we know, huge outputs. However, more recently, some efforts have been done on computing only *closed cuboids*. Nevertheless, for some of the dense databases, which are considered in this paper, even the set of all closed cuboids will be too large. An alternative would be to compute only the *maximal cuboids*. However, a pure maximal approaching implies loosing some information, this is one can generate the complete set of cuboids cells from its maximal but without their respective aggregation value. To play with some "loss of information" we need to add an interesting measure, that we call the *correlated value of a cuboid cell*. In this paper, we propose a new notion for reducing cuboids aggregation by means of computing only the *maximal-correlated cuboids cells*, and present the M3C-Cubing algorithm that brings out those cuboids. Our evaluation study shows that the method followed is a promising candidate for scalable data cubing, reducing the number of cuboids by at least an order of magnitude or more in comparison with that of closed ones.

1 Introduction

Efficient computation of data cubes has been one of the focusing points in research since the introduction of data warehousing, OLAP, and the data cube operator [8]. Data cube computation can be formulated as a process that takes a set of tuples as input, computes with or without some auxiliary data structure, and materializes the aggregated results for all cells in all cuboids. Its size is usually much larger than the input database, since a table with n dimensions results in 2^n cuboids. Thus, most work is dedicated to reduce either the computation time or the final cube size, such as efficient cube computation [3, 14, 9], or cube compression [11, 15]. These cost reduction processes are all without loss of any information, while some others, like the approximation [1] or the iceberg-cube [5, 3, 14, 9] ones, reduce the costs by skipping trivial information.

---

[*] Supported by a Ph.D. Scholarship from FCT-Foundation of Science and Technology, Ministry of Science of Portugal.

A Min Tjoa and J. Trujillo (Eds.): DaWaK 2006, LNCS 4081, pp. 165–174, 2006.

The ideas of compressing cuboids cells in terms of classes of cells, or closed cells, seem to be an interesting approach to reduce size complexity, and also to explore optimally the semantics from the cube lattice. Nevertheless, for some of the dense databases we consider in this paper, even the set of all closed cuboids cells would grow to be too large. The only recourse may be to mine the maximal cuboids cells in such domains. However, a pure maximal approaching implies loosing some information - one can generate the complete set of cuboids cells from its maximal but without their respective aggregation value. To play with some loss of information we propose a new measure, that we called the *correlated value of a cuboid cell*. This measure is inspired on *all_confidence* measure [12], which has been successfully adopted for judging interesting patterns in association rule mining, and further exploited with confidence closed correlated pattern [10]. This measure must disclose true correlation (also dependence) relationship among cuboids cells and needs to hold the null-invariance property. Furthermore, real world databases tend to be correlated, i.e., dimensions values are usually dependent on each other. The main motivation of the proposed method emerged from the observation that real databases tend to be correlated, i.e., dimensions values are usually dependent on each other. For example, Store "Wallgreens" always sells Product "Nappy" or Store "Starbucks" always makes Product "Coffee". In addition, the result of correlated cells on the corresponding data cube is to generate a large number of cells with same aggregation values. The Range CUBE method was the first approach to explore correlation among dimensions values by using a range trie [6]. Although it does not compress the cube optimally and may not disclose true correlation relationship among cuboids cells holding the null-invariance property [12, 16, 10]. Inspired on the previous issues we raise a few questions to drive this work:

1. *Can we develop an algorithm which captures maximal correlated cuboids cells on dense/sparse databases?*
2. *How much such an approach can reduce the complete set of cuboids in comparison with the other approaches (i.e., pure maximal to closed ones)?*
3. *How about the data cubing costs?*

In this paper, we propose a new iceberg cube mining method for reducing cuboids aggregation by means of computing only the *maximal-correlated cuboids cells*, and present the M3C-Cubing algorithm that brings out those cuboids.

2 Maximal-Correlated Cuboids Cells

A cuboid is a multi-dimensional summarization of a subset of dimensions and contains a set of cells. A data cube can be viewed as a lattice of cuboids, which also integrates a set of cells.

Definition 1 – Cuboid Cell – In an n-dimension data cube, a cell $c = (i_1, i_2, ..., i_n : m)$ (where m is a measure) is called a k-dimensional cuboid cell (i.e., a cell in a k-dimensional cuboid), if and only if there are exactly k ($k \leq n$) values among $\{i_1, i_2, ..., i_n\}$ which are not * (i.e., all). We further denote $M(c) = m$ and $V(c) = (i_j, i_2, ..., i_n)$. In this paper, we assume that the measure *m* is count.

A cell is called *iceberg cell* if it satisfies a threshold constraint on the measure. For example, an iceberg constraint on measure count is $M(c) \geq min\_supp$ (where *min_supp* is a user-given threshold). Given two cells $c = (i_1, i_2, \ldots, i_n : m)$ and $c' = (i'_1, i'_2, \ldots, i'_n : m')$, we denote $V(c) \leq V(c')$ if for each i_j ($j = 1, \ldots, n$) which is not *, $i'_j = i_j$. A cell c is said to be covered by another cell c' if for each c" such that $V(c) \leq V(c'')$ $\leq V(c')$, $M(c'') = M(c')$. A cell is called a *closed cuboid cell* if it is not covered by any other cells. A cell is called a *maximal cuboid cell* if it is closed and has no other cell c which is superset of it (we have an *exception* just in case when its correlated value is higher than a minimum threshold).

Definition 2 – The Correlated Value of a Cuboid Cell – Given a cell c, the correlated value *3CV* of a V(c) is defined as,

$maxM(c) = \max \{ M(c_i) | \text{for each } c_i \in V(c) \}$ Eq.(1)
$3CV(c) = M(c) / maxM(c)$ Eq.(2)

Definition 3 – Maximal Correlated Cuboid Cell – A cell c is a *maximal-correlated cuboid cell* (M3C) if it is covered by a *maximal cuboid cell*, its M(c) value is higher than *min_supp* and its *3CV(c)* value is higher than *min_3CV* (where *min_3CV* is a user-given threshold for correlation)

From the last definition we allow a *correlated exception* for its supersets, where it is true when cell c is covered by another cell c' and $3CV(c')$ is higher than *min_3CV*.

Given the above definitions, the problem of computing the *maximal-correlated cuboids cells* is to compute all maximal cuboids cells which satisfy iceberg constraints and its *correlated exception* cells. An example of the maximal-correlated cuboids cells is given in Example 1.

Table 1. Example of Maximal Correlated Cuboids Cells

A	B	C	D
a1	b1	c1	d1
a1	b2	c2	d2
a1	b1	c1	d3
a1	b1	c1	d1
a2	b2	c2	d4

Example 1 - Maximal Correlated Cuboids Cells. Table 1 shows a table (with four attributes) in a relational database. Let the measure be count, the iceberg be count ≥ 2 and the correlated value 3CV ≥ 0.85. Then c1 = (a1,b1,c1,* : 3) and c2 = (a1,*,*,* : 4) are closed cells; c1 is a maximal cell; c3 = (a1,b1,*,* : 3) and c4 = (*,b1,c1,* : 3) are covered by c1; but c4 has a correlated exception (3CV=1); c5 = (a2,b2,c2,d4 : 1) does not satisfy the iceberg constraint. Therefore, c1 and c4 are maximal correlated cuboids' cells. The iceberg condition is *count* $\geq$ *min_sup* and *the correlated exception value* $\geq$ *min_3CV*.

3 M3C-Cubing

The proposed method for extraction of the Maximal-Correlated Cuboids Cells follows
the BUC data cubing ideas [3] – we call it as M3C-Cubing. The computation starts
from the smallest cuboids of the lattice, and works its way towards the larger, less
aggregated cuboids. Our method does not share the computation of aggregates
between parent and child cuboids, only the partitioning cost. Besides, as was verified
by BUC experimental results, partitioning is the major expense, not the aggregation
one.

We begin by defining the necessary terminology for describing the M3C-Cubing
algorithm. We consider a *base relation cell* to be a mapping $K(c) \rightarrow M(c)$, where K is
a composite key built from the grouping attributes values in $V(c)$ and $M(c)$ is also a
composite key with the value to be aggregated. From the base relation cell we can
extract several partitions; each partition has a subset of cells to aggregate. The
partition of a base relation cell is defined as $P(c) \rightarrow \{K(c) \rightarrow M(c)\}$, where $P(c)$ is the
partition key.

In order to get the *correlated value of a cuboid cell (3CV)* we need to keep the
aggregation value for each *1-D* cuboid. This is denoted as a mapping from $1-D(c) \rightarrow$
$M(c)$. We should note that the maximum value will occur when the subset $K(c)$
consists of a single grouping attribute (see *Definition 2*).

M3C-Cubing is guided by an SE-tree framework, first introduced by Rymon [13],
and adopted later by Mafia [4] and Max-miner[2]. In this work, we call as *M3C-tree*.
The *M3C-tree* is traversed by using a *pure depth-first* (DFS) order. Each node of the
M3C-tree provides *n-D* cuboids which will be further partitioned, aggregated and
checked if it is maximal or not (see *Definition 1*). In general, superset pruning works
better with DFS order since many least aggregated cuboids may already have been
discovered.

The strategies for pruning non-maximal correlated cuboids cells (*nonM3C*)
basically attempt to: test out iceberg condition, check if it is maximal and when is not,
check if it is a *correlation exception* (see *Definition 3*). They are just discarded in case
its *3CV* value is lower than a minimum threshold (*min_3CV*). Consequently, we
provide the complete set of interesting cuboids which are maximal-correlated cuboids.

M3C-Cubing also keeps the *current cuboids* aggregated and the *previous one* for
further pruning out of *nonM3C* cells. To speed up this process, we cannot remove an
entire branch of the *M3C-tree*, since we have to aggregate its related partitions in
order to validate the pruning conditions mentioned before. In this sense, we are just
able to prune out *nonM3C* cells by the time we expand the *M3C-tree* level-by-level.

Algorithm 3.1. M3C-Cubing: Computing maximal-correlated cuboids cells

Input: a table relation *trel*; *min_supp*; *min_3CV*.
Output   : the set of maximal-correlated cuboids cells.
Method :
1. Let *brel* be the base relation of *trel*.
2. Build the *M3C-tree* concerning the grouping attributes in *brel*.
3. Call M3C-Cubing (*min_supp*, *min_3CV*, *brel*, *M3C-tree*).

```
Procedure M3C-Cubing (min_supp, min_3CV, brel, M3C-tree)
 1: get 1-D cuboids from M3C-tree
 2: for each j in 1-D cuboids do
 3:     get its partition from brel on dimensions [n], and
           set part ←{K(c)→M(c)}
 4:     aggregate part and set agg ← {V(c)→M(c)} when M(c)>=min_supp
 5:     set allCbs ← {agg}; set 3cv-1d ← {allCbs}
 6: end for
 7: get n-D cuboids in DFS order from M3C-tree
 8: for each k in n-D cuboids do
 9:     get its partition from brel on dimensions [n-D],
           and set part ←{K(c)→M(c)}
10:     aggregate part and set agg ← {V(c)→M(c)} when M(c)>=min_supp
11:     set allCbs ← allCbs  ∪ {agg}; set currCbs ← {agg}
12:     set 3cv-nd ← 3cv-nd  ∪ {call 3cv-nd(3cv-1d, agg )}
13:     set maxCbs ← maxCbs ∪
                {call maxCorr (allCbs, currCbs, 3cv-nd, min_3CV )}
14: end for
Procedure maxCorr(allCbs, currCbs, 3cv-nd, min_3CV)
 1: set nonM3C ←{ }
 2: for each j in currCbs do
 3:     for each k in allCbs do
 4:         if dom(allCbs) is superset of dom(currCbs),
                nonM3C ← nonM3C ∪ {dom(currCbs)}
 4:     end for
 5: end for
 6: remove any nonM3C in allCbs where 3cv-nd(nonM3C)< min_3CV
 7: return allCbs

Procedure 3cv-nd(3cv-1d, agg)
 1: for each j in agg do
 2:     splits into 1-D cells; maxValue=0;
 3:     for each k in 1-D cells do
 4:         get its aggValue(3cv-1d)
 5:         if aggValue>=maxValue, maxValue=aggValue
 6:     end for
 7:     set 3cv=SI{agg}/ maxValue; set 3cv-nd ← {dom(agg) → 3cv}
 8: end for; return 3cv-nd
```

With the aim of evaluating how M3C-Cubing reduces the final set of cuboids, we have to do a few modifications to the main method to support both pure maximal cuboids and closed ones. Those modifications are available as two new procedures: One for pure maximal and other for closed cuboids. We omit here those procedures, but one can also follows the definitions on section 2.

To bring out the pure maximal we just need to re-write the line 6 in *maxCorr* Procedure. Thus, the conditional test on *3CV* value of the ancestor cuboids is set apart. Needless to say, that we cannot make any use of *3CV-nd* procedure either to get pure maximal or closed cuboids. To get just the closed cuboids we must verify the *closedness* property [15] among the cuboids, consequently we just have to check if its not covered by other cells.

3.1 Cover Equivalence in M3C-Cubing

The idea of grouping cover partitions cells into classes can also be explored by M3C-Cubing in order to shrink even more the final data cube. By definition 1, it is possible to group a set of cuboids cells by verifying those cells which are cover equivalent ones [11]. Thus, these cells essentially have the same value for any aggregate on any measure but with different degrees of correlation. For instance, in Example 1 the cells (a1,b1,c1,*) and (*,b1,c1,*) are cover equivalent cells. Next, we present a few concepts for guiding the grouping cover partition process with M3C-Cubing.

Cover partitions – The partition induced by cover equivalence is convex. Cover partitions can be grouped into a M3C class (*ji..jn*) (Figure 1). Each class in a cover partition has a unique maximal upper bound, and a unique lower bound (Table 2).

Upper bound cell – The upper bound for a particular class is the maximal cuboid cell contained in this class. Such as, in Example 1, the cell (a1,b1,c1,*) is the upper bound cell.

Lower bound cell – The lower bound cell for a particular class is the maximal 3CV value achieved by the correlated value of the cuboid cell (see *Definition 2*). Since M3C cubing allows catching all correlated exception cuboids, the lower bound cell will be that one with the highest 3CV value. E.g., in Example 1, the lower bound cell for class *j1* is given by (*,b1,c1,*).

To explore maximal correlation over those classes we have to define the *local_3CV* value for each class. The *local_3CV* value of a class is the maximum local value given by the lower bound cell of each class (Table 2).

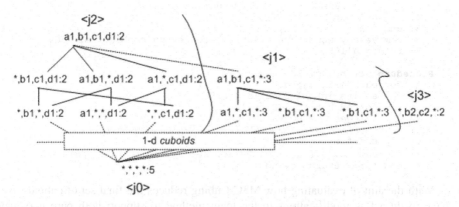

Fig. 1. The lattice formed by the cover partitions of the Example 1

Table 2. The set of classes from Example1

ClassID	UpBound	LoBound	Local_3CV	Lat_child	Agg
j0	(*,*,*,*)	(*,*,*,*)	0	-1	5
j1	(a1,b1,c1,*)	(*,b1,c1,*)	1	j0	3
j2	(a1,b1,c1,d1)	(*,b1,*,d1)	2/3	j0	2
j3	(*,b2,c2,*)	(*,b2,c2,*)	1	j0	2

4   Evaluation Study

In this section, we report our experimental results on the shrinking and performance aspects of each method (M3C=Maximal-Correlated, Max = pure Maximal and

Closed). The results are quite the same concerning to the performance point of view. This is true because those methods were developed having the basis on our main method (M3C). So, we can take those results only as an example of how much these modifications affect the whole time processing of the M3C-Cubing. On the other hand, reducing aspects of M3C-Cubing shows its viability by providing an interesting tradeoff between a pure maximal approaches to a closed one.

All the experiments were performed on a 3GHz Pentium IV with 1Gb of RAM memory, running Windows XP Professional. M3C-Cubing was coded with Java 1.5, and they were performed over eight synthetic datasets (Table 3). The values for columns *min_3CV%* and *min_supp* are provided for the tests when fixing one value and varying the other. The density column shows the degree(%)[1] of density/sparseness of each dataset. All datasets have a normal distribution.

Table 3. The overall information of each dataset

Dset	Tuples	Dims	Card.	Density	Min_3CV%	Min_Supp%
d1	100	3	3	27%	40%	2%
d2	250	5	3	97%	27%	0.80%
d3	500	3	5	25%	10%	0.60%
d4	750	4	5	83%	15%	0.67%
d5	1000	5	3	24%	17%	0.40%
d6	1250	4	6	100%	9%	0.16%
d7	3000	7	3	73%	35%	0.10%
d8	5000	6	4	82%	50%	0.04%

We first show that the complete set of maximal-correlated cuboids cells (M3C) is much smaller in comparison with both that of pure maximal (Max) and that of close ones (Closed). Figure 2 shows the number of cuboids generated by each approach from all datasets. The number of cuboids is plotted on a *log scale*. Figure 2(a) presents the number of cuboids generated when *min_3CV* is fixed and *min_supp*

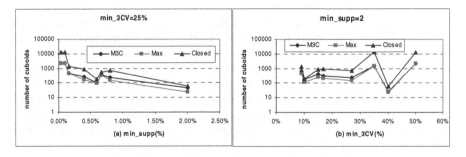

Fig. 2. Number of cuboids generated from all datasets

---

[1] The density degree of a dataset is calculated by the division: the product of each dimension (its cardinality value) by the number of tuples within the related dataset. The dataset is more dense when density degree is close to 100%.

varies, while figure 2(b) shows those cuboids the other way around, fixing *min_supp* and varying *min_3CV*. These figures show that the M3C generates much smaller cuboids under lower *min_supp* or lower *min_3CV*. They also illustrate how much bigger the closed cuboids are in comparison with the other two methods. These results also indicate that under higher density datasets the chances of reducing cuboids by M3C-Cubing is more effective. Furthermore, the distance between Max and M3C reveals the gap of cuboids which are discarded (higher correlated ones) when using a pure maximal approach.

The next two figures (figure 3(a) and figure 3(b)) show the performance aspects of M3C-Cubing from all datasets. These figures follow the same configuration properties from previous two (figure 2(a) and figure 2(b)). Figure 3(a) illustrate that under a fixed *min_supp*, the maximal-correlated cuboids are useful only with lower *3CV* thresholds. This is confirmed by the *downward property* [12] of *3CV_value* of a cuboid cell. By the time the data cubing process is getting closer to the least aggregated cuboids, the *3CV_value* also decreases, so the computation time is pretty close, because *3CV* is decreasing. Figure 3(b) points out the effectiveness of M3C-Cubing under lower *min_supp*, giving more likelihood to identify correlated-cuboids, increasing a little-bit the processing time to prune out *nonM3C* cells.

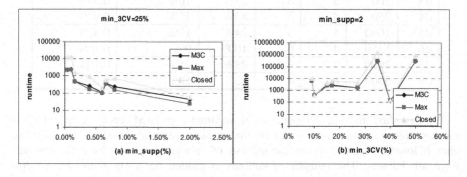

Fig. 3. The execution time from all datasets

Now, we are going to present a few examples concerning the reduction costs of computing the complete cube instead of a "partial" data cubing process. Figures ranging from figure 4(a) to figure 4(d) illustrate those results. Figure 4(a) and figure 4(b) shows the number of cuboids generated when *min_supp* varies and *min_3CV* is fixed, while figures 4(c), 4(d) present those when *min_3CV* varies and *min_supp* is fixed. Under any circumstances the final cube is quite closer to the closed one, which points out that even using such closed-reduction the cuboids size remains even bigger. It is also demonstrates how much M3C-Cubing can save in comparison with the other methods.

In summary, the experimental results show that the number of maximal-correlated cuboids is quite smaller in comparison with that of the closed ones. Even, with a few modifications to the main features of M3C-Cubing, it still performs competitively with the other ones. Moreover, we provide the set of all maximal-correlated cuboids.

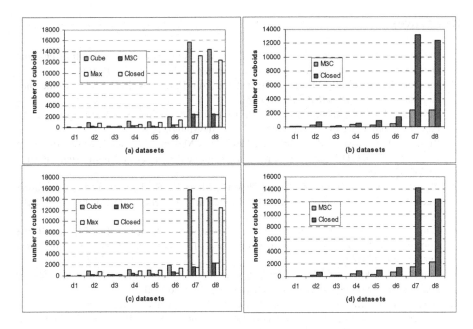

Fig. 4. Reductions cost of cubing over all datasets

5 Final Remarks

The motivation behind iceberg cube mining is tightly related to reducing the search space for computing aggregates. The classical methods either offer ways for sharing the computation among cuboids or for exploring the partition costs in order to reduce the large output size.

We have presented M3C-Cubing that effectively reduces the complete set of cuboids cells introducing a new notion called *maximal-correlated cuboids cells*. Through this cubing method we can find the maximal combinations among the grouping attributes and also keep its exceptional correlated cuboids, which can also indicates interesting changes on the cuboids during the cubing process.

We also have plans to investigate other aspects not addressed in this work such as: the application of *3CV* measure over other aggregate functions (average, min, max...) and the issues related to recover an aggregation value of subcells of an M3C cell.

For efficient mining of those cuboids we have devised M3C-Cubing which is guided by an *M3C-tree* with a pure DFS traversal order. In order to improve pruning, we must investigate the tail information of each node in the *M3C-tree* such as designed in [7, 17].

Finally, our evaluation study shows that maximal-correlated cuboids computation reduces the number of cuboids by at least an order of magnitude or more in comparison with the traditional approaches.

References

1. Barbara, D., Sullivan, M.: Quasi-cubes: Exploiting Approximations in Multidimensional Databases. In Proc. Int. Conference on Management of Data (SIGMOD), 1997.
2. Bayardo, R.: Efficiently Mining Long Patterns from Databases. In Proc. Int. Conference on Management of Data (SIGMOD), 1998.
3. Beyer, K., Ramakrishnan, R.: Bottom-up Computation of Sparse and Iceberg Cubes. In Proc. Int. Conference on Management of Data (SIGMOD), 1999.
4. Burdick, D., Calimlim, M., Gehrke, J.: MAFIA: A Maximal Frequent Itemset Algorithm for Transactional Databases. In Proc. Int. Conference on Data Engineering (ICDE), pp.443-452, 2001.
5. Fang, M., Shivakumar, N., Garcia-Molina, H., Motwani, R., Ullman, J., D.: Computing Iceberg Queries Efficiently. In Proc. Int. Conference on Very Large Databases (VLDB), 1998.
6. Feng, Y., Agrawal, D., Abbadi, A.-E., Metwally, A.: Range Cube: Efficient Cube Computation by Exploiting Data Correlation. In Proc. Int. Conference on Data Engineering (ICDE), 2004.
7. Gouda, K., Zaki, J.: GenMax : An Efficient Algorithm for Mining Maximal Frequent Itemsets. Data Mining and Knowledge Discovery, 11:1-20, 2005.
8. Gray, J., Bosworth, A., Layman, A., Pirahesh, A.: Data Cube: A Relational Aggregation Operator Generalizing Group-By, Cross-Tab, and Sub-Totals. In Proc. Int. Conference on Data Engineering (ICDE), 1996.
9. Han, J., Pei, J., Dong, G., Wank, K.: Efficient Computation of Iceberg Cubes with Complex Measures. In Proc. Int. Conference on Management of Data (SIGMOD), 2001.
10. Kim, W.-Y., Lee, Y.-K., Han, J.: CCMine: Efficient Mining of Confidence-Closed Correlated Patterns. In Proc. Int. Pacific-Asia Conference on Knowledge Discovery and Data Mining (PAKDD), 2004.
11. Lakshmanan, V.S., Pei, J., Han, J.: Quotient Cube: How to Summarize the Semantics of a Data Cube. In Proc. Int. Conference on Very Large Databases (VLDB), 2002.
12. Omiecinski. Alternative Interest Measures for Mining Associations. IEEE Trans. Knowledge and Data Engineering, 15:57-69, 2003.
13. Rymon, R.: Search through Systematic Set Enumeration. In Proc. Int. Conference on Principles of Knowledge Representation and Reasoning (KR), 539-550, 1992.
14. Shao, Z., Han, J., Xin, D.: MM-Cubing: Computing Iceberg Cubes by Factorizing the Lattice Space. In Proc. Int. Conference on Scientific and Statistical Database Management (SSDBM), 2004.
15. Xin, D., Han, J., Shao, Z., Liu, H.: C-Cubing: Efficient Computation of Closed Cubes by Aggregation-Based Checking. In Proc. Int. Conference on Data Engineering (ICDE), 2006.
16. Xiong, H., Tan, P.-N., Kumar, V. Mining Strong Affinity Associations Patterns in Data Sets with Skewed Support Distribution. In Proc. Int. Conference on Data Mining (ICDM), 2003.
17. Zou, Q., Chu, W.-W., Lu, B.: SmartMiner: A Depth First Algorithm Guided by Tail Information for Mining Maximal Frequent Itemsets. In Proc. Int. Conference on Data Mining (ICDM), 2002.

Warehousing Dynamic XML Documents

Laura Irina Rusu[1], Wenny Rahayu[2], and David Taniar[3]

[1,2] LaTrobe University, Department of Computer Science and Computer Engineering,
Bundoora, VIC 3086, Australia
lirusu@students.latrobe.edu.au, wenny@cs.latrobe.edu.au
[3] Monash University, School of Business Systems, Clayton, VIC 3800, Australia
David.Taniar@infotech.monash.edu.au

Abstract: Due to the increased popularity of using XML documents in exchanging information between diverse types of applications or in representing semi-structured data, the issue of warehousing large collections of XML documents has become strongly imperative. Furthermore, an efficient XML warehouse needs to be able to answer various user queries about its content or about the history of the warehoused documents. In this paper, we propose a methodology for warehousing dynamic XML documents, which allows a low degree of redundancy of the warehoused data, while preserving critical information.

Keywords: XML, dynamic XML, data warehouse, semi-structured data.

1 Introduction

Following the growing popularity of using XML documents in exchanging information between different legacy systems or in representing semi-structured data, warehousing XML documents have started to pose various issues to the researchers and industry people. One of the current research problems is to find out what type of warehouse is most suitable and efficient to store collections of XML documents, in such a way that they can be efficiently queried, either to answer user queries or to extract meaningful hidden knowledge.

In our research, we have identified two types of XML documents which could be included in a presumptive XML data warehouse: *static XML documents*, which do not change their content and structure (e.g. an XML document containing the papers published in a certain proceedings book) and *dynamic XML documents*, which change their structure or content in time, based on certain business processes (e.g. the content of an on-line bookshop, which might change daily, weekly or monthly, depending on e-customer behaviour). While the first category of XML documents has been the subject of intense research in the recent years, the topic of warehousing temporal versions of XML documents has started to be considered only lately [5].

In this paper, we look at the concepts related to the star-schema approach proposed in [6] for warehousing static XML documents and then we show how the multi-versioned XML documents might fit into this star-schema. In explaining the concepts involved in our proposal, we employ working examples throughout the paper and we use XQuery [8] for code examples. Note that the points discussed in this paper are not by any means exhaustive and they do not cover all the aspects and complexities involved in warehousing static or dynamic XML documents; it is part of our future

A Min Tjoa and J. Trujillo (Eds.): DaWaK 2006, LNCS 4081, pp. 175–184, 2006.
© Springer-Verlag Berlin Heidelberg 2006

research work to investigate any other issues which might arise from their implementation.

The rest of the paper is organized as follows: Section 2 studies the related work in the area of warehousing static and dynamic XML documents, Section 3 presents the proposed star-schema approach, for dynamic XML documents, Section 4 illustrates the benefits of the proposal in terms of querying and presents some performance tests results and finally, Section 5 gives some conclusions and highlights our future research on warehousing XML documents.

2 Related Work

A substantial amount of work has been carried out during the last few years to find efficient solutions to the problem of warehousing XML documents [1, 2, 3, 4]. A study on how to construct an XML data warehouse by analysing frequent patterns in user historical queries is provided in [4]. The authors start from determining which data sources are more frequently accessed by the users, transform those queries in *Query Path Transactions* and, after applying a rule mining technique, calculate the *Frequent Query Paths* which stay at the base of building data warehouse schema.

Another approach is proposed in [3], where an XML data warehouse is designed from XML schemas, proposing a semi-automated process. After pre-processing XML schema, creating and transforming schema graph, the authors choose facts for data warehouse and, for each fact, follow few steps in order to obtain star-schema.

With few exceptions, the common deficit of the most of existing research work in this area is its limitation to warehousing static XML documents, as separate pieces of information which needs to be stored using an organised and efficient format.

To our knowledge, our proposal is the first one to suggest a solution to the issue of warehousing dynamic documents. It concentrates on the specifics of multiple-versioned (i.e. dynamic) XML documents and their storage, with as less as possible redundancy, maintaining in the same time the critical information from the multiple versions of the documents, to allow rich and useful queries to be applied later on.

3 Proposed Approach

In this section, we will first recall the concepts related to building a star-schema warehouse (called SSW throughout the paper) for XML documents, as it is detailed in [6]. Then, we will look at how the critical information from multi-versioned XML documents are historically grouped using the consolidated delta [7] and how they can be stored in the SSW using the consolidated delta.

3.1 Building a Warehouse for Storing Static XML Documents

We proposed in [6] a generic process of building an XML data warehouse for static XML documents. Mainly, the process consists of the following steps: data cleaning and integration; data summarisation; creating intermediate XML documents; updating / linking existing documents and creating the complete data warehouse. A thoroughly set of explanations for the cleaning part of the warehousing process (i.e. minimizing the number of occurrences of dirty data, errors, duplications or inconsistencies from the raw XML data) can be found in [9].

For the purpose of our paper, we will exemplify the data summarization part, i.e. building the dimensions of the final warehouse, as new XML documents. Note that there are three types of dimensions proposed in [6], i.e. *constructed*, *extracted* or *partial-extracted*. The decision on which dimensions are required in the warehouse is taken only after the user-defined prerequisites have been analysed.

To exemplify, we consider the document in Fig.1, containing details of books in a library and we build three dimensions, i.e. "time", "authors" and "titles", which will become part of the data warehouse.

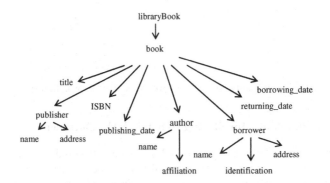

Fig. 1. Example of a static XML document

The code example for building the "time" dimension is given in Fig. 2. It uses the borrowing date to summarize the data, so the user will be able to extract the patterns of readers' borrowing behaviours in time; "Get-month-from-date" function also has a meaning of summarising data, by month, and it extracts the corresponding integer representing the month out of the raw borrowing date.

A "fact" document is also built, to store the core information extracted from the XML document (e.g. borrower details and returning date), together with links to the previously built dimensions. They will form the final static SSW, as shown in Fig. 3.

```
let $b:=0
document{
for $t in distinct-values
(doc("libraryBooks.xml")//borrowing_date)
        let $b:=$b+1
        return
           <borrowtime>
                <timeKey>{$b}</timekey>
                <borrowdate>{$t}</borrowdate>
                <month>{get-month-from-
date($t)}</month>
           </borrowtime>
}
```

Fig. 2. Example of XQuery code for building "time" dimensions in SSW

Each time a new document needs to be stored (e.g. daily borrowing details might be collected in an XML document stored in the SSW at the end of the month), the process will be repeated and it will add new items to the dimensions and new records in the fact document, for the new added information. While this is a logical and efficient process for the XML static documents which always brings *new* data to the warehouse, this might not be equally efficient for dynamic XML documents.

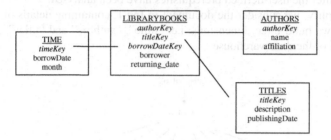

Fig. 3. Star schema of "LibraryBooks" XML data warehouse

3.2 Building a Warehouse for Storing Dynamic XML Documents

In this section, we show how the dynamic XML documents could be also warehoused using the star-schema approach. As exemplified in the "Introduction" section, a dynamic XML document could be the content of an on-line shop, which can change hourly/daily/weekly based on the users' behaviour and market forces. For example, new products can be added, some can become unavailable if sold out, prices can change due to promotional sales etc. Multiple versions of an XML document are not, by any means, just different XML documents and adding them, one by one, to the SSW, would be a redundant process, as there might be a large degree of similarity between successive versions.

A central piece in our proposal is the complex concept of *consolidated delta* [7], as an efficient way of representing multiple historical versions of the same XML document. It is built by appending the changes undergone by the document between two consecutive versions, to the previous version of the consolidated delta. Note that the initial version of the consolidated delta is actually the initial version of the dynamic XML document. We assign unique identifiers to the elements in the initial XML document, so at any time all the elements will be uniquely identified and we will be able to track their changes. We refer the reader to [7] for detailed steps in identifying changed elements and building the consolidated delta.

For example, consider a dynamic XML document representing the content of an on-line bookshop ("catalog.xml"), in four consecutive versions, i.e. the initial document at time T_0, followed by three versions with changes at times T_1, T_2 and T_3 (Fig. 4). After applying the steps of building the consolidated delta [7], the result (a new XML document) will contain details of changes for each element (i.e. the time of change, type of change and values for the inserted or modified elements), on top of the initial elements' values. At this point all the interesting and useful information extracted from the document's versions are "grouped" in the consolidated delta, so our intention is to warehouse only the information contained in it.

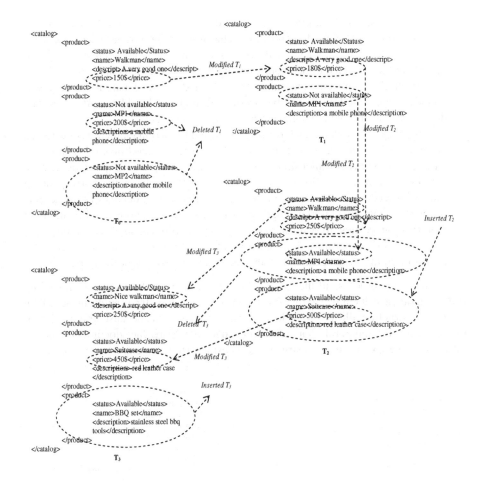

Fig. 4. The "catalog.xml" document in four consecutive versions

Referring to our working example again, suppose that after analysing user requirements, it was decided that the on-line products, their prices and their historic changes information need to be stored in the data warehouse. In our working example, we will build an extracted dimension, i.e. "products" (Fig. 5A), and three constructed dimensions, i.e. "price_ranges", "date_ranges" and "changes" (Fig. 5B, C and D).

After building the dimensions, the next stage is to extract the core information from the consolidated delta and to include it into the fact document, linking it to the dimensions. Few key steps must be observed for an efficient result, as follows:

(i)   Extract the elements to be stored, from the consolidated delta, as they exist at T_0 (i.e. the initial version of the document before any change) and add records to the fact document containing the core data to be warehoused, together with links to dimensions;

(ii) For each timestamp T_i, where i=1,2,...n, add the changes to the SSW, as follows:

a) check if any new elements have been inserted (products, in our case); add records to the fact document, with details on time & type of change and add records to the extracted dimensions with the new inserted elements;

b) check if any elements have been deleted - if one parent element was deleted, all its children would be considered as deleted; add record to the fact document, together with details on time & type of change;

c) check if any elements have been modified - a parent element is considered to be modified when any of its children is modified. If modification relates to a value in an extracted dimension (e.g. in our case prod_name & prod_descript in "products" dimension), do: (1) look it up by element_Id in the corresponding dimension and (2) add a record in the fact document with details of type & time of change for its children, together with its value before modification. If modification relates to values in a constructed dimension (e.g. in our case "price_ranges" dimension), only need to add a record in the fact document with details of child's type & time of change and its value after modification;

At the end of the process, all the extracted and the constructed dimensions, linked up to the central fact document will form the structure of the star-schema presented in Fig. 6. This structure allows a very low degree of redundancy, because only the initial document and the temporal changes are included; the XML fact document contains links up to the extracted / constructed dimensions (by element/change Id), which

```
Let $no:=0
Let $d:= doc("catalog.xml")
Document {
  <products>
  For $a in distinct-values ($d//product/name)
    Where last-stamp($a/../stamp)<>"deleted"
    Let $no:=$no +1
    Return
      <product>
        <prod_Id> {$no}</prod_Id>
        <prod_name>{$a}</prod_name>
        <prod_descript>{$a/../description}</prod_descript>
      </product>
  </products>
}                                    (A)
```

```
Document {
  <date_ranges>
  For $b in {1,2,...12)
  Return
    <date_range>
      <date_range_Id>{$b}</date_range_Id>
      <from_date>First-day-month ({$b}) </from_date>
      <to_date>First-day-month ({$b}+1)</to_date>
    </date_range>

  </date_ranges>
}                                    (C)
```

```
Document {
  <price_ranges>
  For $a in {1,2,...n)
  Return
    <price_range>
      <range_Id>{$a}</range_Id>
      <range>
        <from>50*({$a}-1)</from>
        <to>50 *{$a}</to>
      </range>
    </price_range>
  </price_ranges>
}                                    (B)
```

```
Document {
  <changes>
    <change>
      <change_Id>1</change_Id>
      <description>insert</description>
    </change>
    <change>
      <change_Id>2</change_Id>
      <description>modify</description>
    </change>
    <change>
      <change_Id>3</change_Id>
      <description>delete</description>
    </change>
  </changes> }                       (D)
```

Fig. 5. Building dimensions in the XML warehouse for dynamic documents

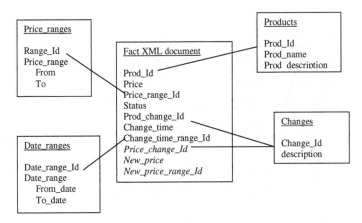

Fig. 6. Star-schema XML warehouse for multiple versions of an XML document

make temporal queries easy to be applied (see Section 4). In the same time, to avoid redundancy, for a timestamp T_i (i=1,2,…n.), the fact document will include only details of changes happened at T_i (e.g., if only price of a product was changed at time T_2, the only additional information stored in the fact document would be: price_change_Id, New_price and New_price_range_Id - italic in Fig. 6).

Surely, our working example is much simpler than any genuine situations which a user might work with, in real applications. The purpose of the example though, is to show, in clear steps, how our proposed approach works and how to build an XML data warehouse for dynamic XML documents, using the information stored in the consolidated delta, when warehousing each individual version is out of question, because of the redundancy.

4   Evaluation Against Temporal Queries

As stressed in the Introduction section, the rationale of any efficient data warehouse is to store the information as effective as possible for later use, making it easily available to be queried by the user. We argue that our proposed methodology of warehousing dynamic XML documents allows various temporal queries to be applied, with different degrees of complexity.

4.1   Validation on Ability to Answer Benchmark Temporal Queries

In our proposal, the timestamps, initially included in the consolidated delta and subsequently stored in the warehouse within time dimension(s), refers to the actual points in time when a change or another occurs, so the proposed SSW for dynamic XML documents is a *historical* (or *valid-time*) warehouse [10] for querying purposes.

In Fig. 7 we give an example of a query to be run on SSW; we look for modified products, where the timestamp of change varies between two limits; this is a temporal query returning a temporal result, as the date of change is included in the elements returned. If the date of change was not to be returned by the query, it would have been

```
Let $f:=doc("fact.xml")
Let $c:=doc("changes.xml")
Let $d:=doc("date_ranges.xml")
Let $pcId:={for $n in $c//change_Id where $n/../descript="modified" return $n}
Document {
for $a in distinct-values($f//prod_Id)
    for $h in $d//date_range_Id
    where $a/../prod_change_Id=$pcId
        and $a/../change_time_range_Id=$h
        and $h/../date_range/From_Date>=#01/01/2006#
        and $h/../date_range/To_Date<=#01/03/2006#
    return
        <prod_Id>{$a}</prod_Id>
        <date_of_change>{$a/../change_time}</date_of_change>
}
```

Fig. 7. Query: Extract all modified products in a date range

a temporal query with a non-temporal result, but involving a temporal element for processing (i.e. looking up change_time_range_Id in "date ranges" dimension).

4.2 Time Performance in Querying Star-Schema Warehouse

To analyse the time performance of the proposed method, we are looking at two main areas: (i) the time required for adding data from a new version of the XML document to the warehouse and (ii) the time required for running queries with temporal or non-temporal result on the XML data warehouse built before.

We constructed a number of versions for some initial documents of 10kB, 20kB, 63kB, 127kB and 509kB respectively (downloaded from the SIGMOD dataset [11]), by using a changes simulator implemented by us, where the percentages of deletions, additions or updates is controlled via a user-friendly interface and the elements to be changed are randomly chosen by the algorithm. Some of the tests results are as follows:

(a) In Fig. 8A, we show how the consolidated delta performs during 10 successive versions of a medium sized XML document (127kB), applying random 3% changes. Black bars represent the total size of versions, while white bars represent the size of the consolidated delta. As it can be noticed, the consolidated delta grows much more slowly than the sum of version sizes. Also, the time required to add the information for a new version from the consolidated delta to the data warehouse (the line running on top of the bars) has a linear growth.

(b) In Fig. 8B, we give the times for running three different queries (Y axis shows time in seconds) on warehouses of various sizes (i.e. 100kB, 250kB, s470kB, 530kB and 1400kB; X axis shows size in kB). The time for running the query exemplified in section 4.1 (middle one on graph), which involves temporal checks for all products in the warehouse, takes a little longer than the other two queries but overall all behave very well.

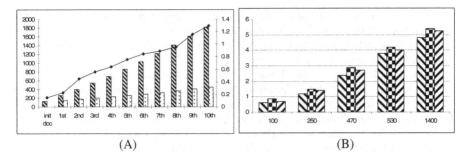

Fig. 8. Dynamic of the consolidated delta during 10 successive changes of a medium sized XML document (127kB) and the dynamic of time required for adding a new version's data to the warehouse

5   Conclusions and Future Work

In this paper we have presented a methodology for warehousing dynamic XML documents, i.e. documents which change their content in time. Storing multiple versions of the same document is not a feasible solution, because of the high degree of similarity and, consequently, of the high cost of processing each version. We have shown that the star-schema approach proposed in [6] to warehouse static XML documents is also applicable for dynamic XML documents and allows the user to store important information from the multiple versions (i.e. the actual initial data and the changes between versions), so that temporal or non-temporal queries can be run against it. As part of our future research work, we want to see how the consolidated delta can be used to mine interesting knowledge out of multiple versions of an XML document.

References

1. Widom, J., Data Management for XML: Research Directions, IEEE Data Engineering Bulletin, 22(3):44:52, Sept.1999
2. Goffarelli, M., Maio, D. and Rizzi, S., Conceptual design of data warehouses from E/R In Proceed. of Hawaii Intl. Conf. on System Sciences, vol. VII, Kona, Hawaii, pp. 334-343, 1998
3. Vrdoljak, B., Banek M. and Rizzi S., Designing Web Warehouses from XML Schema, Data Warehousing and Knowledge Discovery, 5th International Conference DaWak 2003, Prague, Czech Republic, Sept.3-5, 2003
4. Zhang J., Ling T.W., Bruckner R.M. and Tjoa A.M., Building XML Data Warehouse Based on Frequent Patterns in User Queries, Data Warehousing and Knowledge Discovery, 5th International Conference DaWak 2003, Prague, Czech Republic, Sept.3-5, 2003
5. Wang, F. and Zaniolo, C., Temporal queries in XML Document Archives and Web Warehouses, In *TIMEICTL*, 2003
6. Rusu, L.I., Rahayu, W. and Taniar, D. A methodology for Building XML Data Warehouses, International Journal of Data warehousing & Mining, 1(2), pp.67-92, April-June 2005

7. Rusu, L.I., Rahayu, W. and Taniar, D. Maintaining Versions of Dynamic XML Documents, In Proceed. of The 6th International Conference on Web Information Systems Engineering (WISE 2005), New York, NY, USA, November 20-22, 2005, pp.536-543
8. XQuery, http://www.w3.org/TR/xquery
9. Rusu, L.I., Rahayu, W. and Taniar, D. On Data Cleaning in Building XML Data Warehouses, The 6th Intl. Conference on Information Integration and Web-based Applications & Services (iiWAS2004), Jakarta, Indonesia, 797-807
10. P.P. Kalua, E.L. Robertson, Benchmark Queries for Temporal Databases, Technical Report TR379, Computer Science Department, Indiana University, 1993
11. www.cs.washington.edu/datasets - SIGMOD XML dataset

Integrating Different Grain Levels in a Medical Data Warehouse Federation

Marko Banek[1,*], A Min Tjoa[2], and Nevena Stolba[3,**]

[1] FER, University of Zagreb, HR-10000 Zagreb, Croatia
marko.banek@fer.hr
[2] Institute of Software Technology and Interactive Systems (ISIS),
Vienna University of Technology, Favoritenstr. 9-11/188, A-1040 Wien, Austria
amin@ifs.tuwien.ac.at
[3] Women's Postgraduate College for Internet Technologies (WIT)
Vienna University of Technology, Favoritenstr. 9-11/188, A-1040 Wien, Austria
stolba@wit.tuwien.ac.at

Abstract. Healthcare organizations practicing evidence-based medicine strive to unite their data resources in order to achieve a wider knowledge base for sophisticated research and matured decision support service. The central point of such an integrated system is a data warehouse, to which all participants have access. In order to insure a better protection of highly sensitive healthcare data, the warehouse is not created physically, but as a federated system. The paper describes the conceptual design of a health insurance data warehouse federation (HEWAF) aimed at supporting evidence-based medicine. We address a major domain-specific conceptual design issue: the integration of low-grained, time-segmented data into the traditional warehouse, whose basic grain level is higher than that of the time-segmented data. The conceptual model is based on a widely accepted international healthcare standard. We use ontologies of the data warehouse domain, as well as of the healthcare and pharmacy domains, to provide schema matching between the federation and the component warehouses.

1 Introduction

Evidence based medicine [14] successfully weaves the clinical decision process based on human knowledge and the most efficient and most accurate computer-supported research evidence. The application of its concepts speeds up the transfer of clinical research findings into practice, which finally leads to cost reduction both for patients and health insurance organisations, as well as the improvement of the healthcare process as whole. A data warehouse storing a huge amount of healthcare data is the central part of an information system that supports evidence-based medicine.

Healthcare institutions nowadays join their data into a single warehouse in order to achieve a broader and more comprehensive data foundation for knowledge discovery, to the benefit of all participants. However, laws insuring privacy protection forbid the

---

* "Ernst Mach" scholarship at ISIS funded by Austrian Fed. Ministry for Education, Science and Culture.
** Research partially funded by Austrian Fed. Ministry for Education, Science and Culture and the European Social Fund (ESF) under grant 31.963/46-VII/9/2002.

A Min Tjoa and J. Trujillo (Eds.): DaWaK 2006, LNCS 4081, pp. 185–194, 2006.
© Springer-Verlag Berlin Heidelberg 2006

confidential healthcare data to be copied and distributed outside the healthcare organizations. Instead of copying data physically into a new warehouse, a logical integration, a federated data warehouse [15] is created.

In this paper we propose a multidimensional conceptual model of a federated data
warehouse for the purpose of evidence-based medicine. The conceptual model of the
component warehouses offers a traditional view on financial measures, yet it does not
enable the processing of time-segmented medicine administration data (an important
topic in evidence based-medicine), whose grain level is even lower than the basic
grain level of the model. The contributions of our paper are the following: (1) we
develop a federated conceptual model that successfully integrates the low-level, time
segmented data but keeps the higher basic grain level. (2) Since the medicine administration quantities can be summed (like measures) and used as aggregation criteria
(like dimensions) they behave as a "cube in cube". We regard the time-segmented
data as a unique XML-like structure, extending the existing approaches for merging
OLAP systems with XML documents described in [12, 13].

The paper is structured as follows. In Section 2 the requirements to a warehouse
federation in healthcare domain are explained. Section 3 presents how the integration
of different grain levels into the federated model is achieved. The use of ontologies in
matching schemas for the federation is described in Section 4. An outline of the related work is given is Section 5. Finally, in Section 6 conclusions are drawn.

2   Federated Data Warehouse for Healthcare

A federated database is "a collection of cooperating database systems that are
autonomous and possibly heterogeneous" [15]. The existence of a federation must not
have any impact on the local users of a component database. A federated data warehouse is a functional data warehouse, a "big umbrella" [4]. No central, large data
warehouse collecting data from smaller component warehouses is created: heterogeneous data warehouses are integrated into one unit from the conceptual point of view.
A "common business model" [4] (i.e. common conceptual model) is needed, which
defines common facts and dimensions.

The paper describes how data warehouses of different health insurance organisations in Austria are merged in an evidence-based medicine collaboration project. The
case study of the federated data warehouse is called HEWAF (Healthcare Warehouse
Federation). A universal, simple and flexible common conceptual model is needed to
enable potential future integrations to be done seamlessly and with a minimum effort.
The conceptual model of HEWAF is based on the international healthcare standards
HL7 [21] in order to achieve a high level of generalisation and portability. Version 3
of HL7 standards defines the object-oriented Reference Information Model (RIM, the
starting point for all HL7 standards) and the Clinical Document Architecture (CDA),
an XML-based document mark-up standard, which specifies the structure and semantics of clinical documents used for their exchange. Comparing to other existing standards, we claim HL7 to be the most comprehensive. Other standards either have a too
strict format or allow too much semantic or structural ambiguity.

HEWAF will be used for OLAP queries and data mining. Therefore the conceptual
model of the federation will be subject-oriented and multidimensional. Dimensions

and facts should conform to HL7 RIM classes. Dimension attributes and measures should conform to attributes of HL7 classes and it must be possible to display each record (either at the basic-grain level of granularity, or an aggregated structure) as a CDA-conforming XML structure.

On the one hand, the federated warehouse will be used to find correlations between certain symptoms and diagnostic findings, to propose the best suitable therapy given the complete anamnesis status of a patient or to compare the efficiency of different medication products against the same disease. On the other hand, since health insurance organisations pay for therapy procedures and prescribed medications, they want to find possible unnecessary costs (e.g. medication therapies applied for a long time with no or very little effect) and to foster therapies that give the best possible efficiency for equal costs. Different from the patient-centred model based on the Electronic Patient Record, which is proposed in [9], our warehouse model is focused on three billable acts: patient encounters, therapies and prescriptions, which correspond to the HL7 RIM Act classes *PatientEncounter*, *Procedure* and *SubstanceAdministration*, respectively. In this way, all data relevant for a patient as well as financial data is captured.

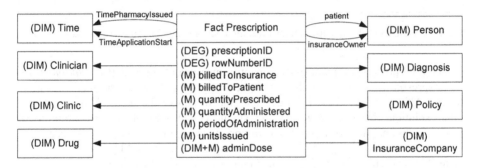

Fig. 1. The *Prescription* fact in HEWAF and its dimensions

The remainder of the paper describes the fact *Prescription* in the data warehouse star schema. The fact is characterized by eight standard dimensions (Fig. 1). The structures of the dimensions *Patient* and *InsuranceOwner* are identical, as they both provide a different view of personal data (if the treatment of a patient is carried by her/his own insurance policy, contents of both dimensions are the same). Analogously, there are two time dimensions of identical structure: *TimePharmacyIssued* and *TimeApplicationStart*. The value of the latter is often not exactly specified and in that case it is generally presumed to be equal to the value of the first. The other six dimensions are *Clinic, Clinician, Diagnosis* (only one, "main" diagnosis is specified in prescription documents), *Drug, Policy* and *InsuranceCompany*. There are two degenerate dimensions (i.e. single-attribute dimensions implemented as non-additive measures, [5]) corresponding to the serial numbers in the prescription document: *prescriptionID* and *rowNumberID* (Fig. 1). The fact contains two financial measures, *billedToInsurance* and *billedToPatient*, and four additional measures: *quantityPrescribed, quantityAdministered* (the prescribed quantity can be 10 pills, but we can buy only a package of 12 pills), *periodOfAdministration* and *unitsIssued*. Finally, there is an additional fact attribute, *adminDose*, which contains a sequence of time-labelled segments giving a detailed description of medical substance administration.

3 Low-Grained Medicine Administration Data

The fact *Prescription* gives us the ability to determine how different variants of prescription processes of the same drug substance can influence the patient's recovery and lead to a cost reduction. Several examples of the dosage instructions (also called *medicine administration* data) in the prescription document can be seen in Fig. 2.

---

1. Take 1 tablet each 8 hours for next 10 days
2. Take 600 mg each 12 hours for next 7 days
3. Take 2 tablets on the first day, and 1 on next four days (second tablet on the first day 12 hours after the first; tablet on the second day 12 hours after the last on the first day; later 24-hour periods)
4. Take 500 mg in the morning and 500 mg in the evening for next 7 days.

Fig. 2. Variants of dosage instructions (i.e. administration notes) in prescription documents

The total prescribed quantity (the quantity measure of the fact *Prescription*) is either expressed in units of weight or volume (for solid substances and liquids, respectively). Although it is possible to calculate the weight of the medical substance in a dilute solution, this is neither easy (we should collect data about concentrations of medical substance for all liquid drugs) nor practical (quantity is not additive across all levels of dimension *Drug*, similar to the number of units of sold goods in a grocery store [5]). Therefore the single attribute quantity consists of two parts: value and unit (which is in accordance with HL7).

All component data warehouses store administration instructions of prescriptions as a single attribute, *adminDose*, (Table 1, similar to the notation in Fig. 2), making them unsuitable for processing. Such a level of granularity also corresponds to the basic granularity of the fact *Prescription* in the federation model. However, the federation must enable administration data processing and putting queries at a detailed level. The grain level needed for their processing is lower than the basic grain level (i.e. the physical storage level) in the component warehouses. We argue that lowering the basic grain [5, 10] to the level of administration data is not an advisable solution for the following two reasons: (1) the semantics of the time dimension is different in the two cases, and fragmenting financial measures is meaningless; (2) the general focus of interest in the clinical decision making process is mainly aimed at prescription data (as in Fig. 1), not at the instructions for medicine administration.

We propose a federated conceptual model whose basic grain corresponds to that of the component warehouses and to the basic federate schema in Section 2, but enables the integration of data at an even lower grain level. We can observe the medicine administration data as a complex attribute of XML type in an object-relational database (Fig. 3). It is a union of separate dosage records, time-labelled segments similar to a kind of a patient's diary. Each record (*<dose>*) refers to a separate dose, an act of drug consumption at a different point in time. Every separate dose, a *<dose>* sub-element of *<adminDose>*, contains a sequence number attribute, *sn*, two attributes defining the timestamp: *ts* (value) and *tu* (unit), and two attributes defining the quantity *q* (value) and *u* (unit).

This kind of representation entirely follows the idea adopted by HL7, with only one *doseQuantity* attribute, defined as a sequence of partial dosage records [21] . On the contrary, the CDA representation of *doseQuantity* does not view a dose as an inseparable, atomic unit, but splits time and quantity data, thus not being able to reach as much expressive power as our model.

Table 1. Part of the prescription fact table in a relational component warehouse

drug ID	billed-ToIns ($)	qtyPrsc	qtyAdm	prdAdm	noUnits	adminDose
1234	23,50	7500 [mg]	8000 [mg]	10 [day]	2	1 t each 8 hours
1234	23,50	7000 [mg]	8000 [mg]	7 [day]	2	2 t each 10 hours

```
<adminDose>
    <dose sn="1" ts="0" tu="h" q="250" u="mg"/>
    <dose sn="2" ts="12" tu="h" q="250" u="mg"/>
    <dose sn="3" ts="1" tu="d" q="250" u="mg"/>
    <dose sn="4" ts="2" tu="d" q="250" u="mg"/>
    <dose sn="5" ts="3" tu="d" q="250" u="mg"/>
    <dose sn="6" ts="4" tu="d" q="250" u="mg"/>
</adminDose>
```

Fig. 3. Medicine administration data in an XML notation suitable for processing

3.1 Queries Containing Medicine Administration Data

Following the concept of HL7, we perceive *adminDose* as an XML-like structure that is a single attribute of the HEWAF prescription fact. In this Section we show how the dosage quantities can be aggregated as measures and used as selection or aggregation criteria like dimensions. Hence, we call the *adminDose* attribute a "cube in cube".

Querying the medicine administration data and associating it with other warehouse attributes follows the principles of XML-extended OLAP querying elaborated by D. Pedersen, Jensen and T.B. Pedersen [12, 13]. In their approach, a standard OLAP fact can have one or more XML structures as dimensions. The approach is based on an extended OLAP algebra and XPath [17] structures are added to SQL to fetch XML data (the language is called SQL_{XM}). They distinguish three different ways XML data can be included into OLAP queries. First, queries may be *decorated* with XML data. Second, external XML data may be used for *selection* (operation of restriction in relational algebra). Third, OLAP data may be grouped by the values of external XML data when aggregation is performed.

We adopt the basic principles of this approach, with one substantial difference: our "XML" data is part of the fact (a "cube in cube"), not dimensions. Therefore we must differentiate the *internal* aggregation, which processes data within the same fact record, and the *global* aggregation, which is described in [12, 13]. In HEWAF, *decoration* and *selection* queries can include internally aggregated data. Aggregation operators SUM, COUNT, MAX, MIN, AVG can be used, except for the constraint that quantities measured by weight and those measured by volume cannot be aggregated together. In the following queries we extend the principles of SQL_{XM}.

Decoration. Decoration means providing supplementary medicine administration data in the result of an OLAP query, without using it as selection (WHERE clause of an SQL query) or global aggregation (GROUP BY clause) criteria.

In Query 1 a decoration without internal aggregation is presented. For each patient who was prescribed 250 mg azithromycin capsules in May 2005, textual description of the cause diagnosis should be displayed, as well as the quantity (value and unit) of the first dosage portion and region where the patient lives.

Query 1: SELECT d.description, **fp.adminDose/dose[@sn="1"]/@q, adminDose/dose[@sn="1"]/@u,** p.region FROM FactPrescription fp, Diagnosis d, Time t, Drug dr, Patient p WHERE Time.month="05_2005" and Drug.drug_code= "(azithr_250mg_code)"

Selection. In Query 2 medicine administration data is part of the WHERE clause, i.e. determines selection. Also, it is aggregated internally, using the operator SUM. The result returns the (altogether) cost billed to insurance institutions for all prescribed antibiotics where the dosage on the first day (first 24 hours) is smaller than or equal to the fifth of the entire prescribed dose. The results are grouped by diagnosis (the second level of ICD-10 classification, [16]) and diagnosis ID, as well as diagnosis description are displayed.

Query 2: SELECT SUM(fp.billedToInsurance), d.level2ID, d.level2Desc FROM FactPrescription fp, Diagnosis d WHERE **SUM(fp.adminDose/dose[@ts<"24" and @tu="h"]/@q)**/(fp.quantityPrescribed)<=0.2 GROUP BY d.level2ID

Aggregation. Aggregation can be meaningfully performed over attributes with a discrete domain of values. Considering time-segmented dose records, serial number (*sn*) has a discrete domain, while timestamp (*ts*) and quantity (*q*) are typical features with continuous values. In general, continuous domains should be split into a finite set of groups and hierarchies created over the groups in order to perform aggregations.

We state one hour as the shortest periods of time during which aggregation can be performed. Larger periods are 3-hour, 6-hour, 12-hour, 24-hour, 2-day, 7-day, 14-day and 4-week period. Considering the dosage portions that are at the border of these intervals, we define a time interval from *a* to *b* as [*a*, *b*), meaning that the portion at the lower border (with timestamp *a*) is included in the interval while the upper border (with timestamp *b*) is not included.

Although the aggregation over a single (non-grouped) quantity value seems possible but meaningless, for most of the products sold as pills, capsules or tablets there is actually only a finite set of possible administration quantities. Moreover, medical standards for administering liquids also prescribe a finite number of possible quantities. For instance, we can aggregate dosage data if we constrain the value of attribute *basicProductForm* in dimension *Drug* only to "capsule" and "tablet" and restrict the query selection (WHERE clause) to the three lowest levels of the *Drug* dimension hierarchy (a packed factory product: Sumamed 250g, Zithromax 500g, a factory product: Sumamed, Zithromax or a substance: Azithromycin).

While in the approach described in [12, 13] the external XML dimension is used to define aggregation criteria, not changing the essence of the aggregation process, in our case the basic granularity of the *Prescription* fact is split to the level of an individual administration dose and then the aggregation is performed.

Query 3 selects only prescriptions of 250 mg Zithromax capsules, groups them according to the dosage quantities (quantity is the concatenation of quantity value and quantity unit) and counts the quantities, so that we can see which dosage quantity is preferred.

Query 3. SELECT **concat (fp.adminDose/dose/@q, fp.adminDose/dose/@u)**, COUNT(**fp.adminDose/dose/@q**) FROM FactPrescription fp, Drug d WHERE d.drug_code= "(zithromax_250mg_code)" and d.basicProductForm="capsule" GROUP BY **concat (fp.adminDose/dose/@q, fp.adminDose/dose/@u)**

4 Use of Ontologies in Achieving Federation

There have been many efforts during the last two decades to automate the process of integrating component database schemas, and, more recently, component warehouse schemas into a single federated schema. Sheth and Larson state that a completely automatic schema integration is not possible because of the inability of the semantic models to capture a real-world state completely, as well as the existence of multiple views and interpretations of a real-world state [15].

Recent research into ontologies and development of large lexical databases like WordNet [20] enables applications to "understand" the semantic relations between items. Ontologies organize terms of a certain domain into classes (e.g. wine and orange juice are both subclasses of drink and they are mutually disjoint) and state their relationships (e.g. colour is a property of wine). Lexical databases provide a thesaurus of synonyms, antonyms and homonyms.

Using ontologies and lexical databases in a rigorous manner could lead to a database federation schema matching process that would be almost fully automated. The application would deliver enough semantic information for the matching process, and the warehouse designer would only have to check its consistency. We briefly present the idea of an ontology-based warehouse schema matching, which is currently being implemented in W3C Web Ontology Language (OWL, [18]).

The role of ontologies in our approach is twofold. First, since there is no standard conceptual model of data warehouse, from which an ontology could be derived, we define our own "structural ontology" over the basic data warehousing constructs: cubes, dimensions, hierarchies, hierarchy levels, measures, dimensional attributes etc (the left side of Fig. 4). Ontology instances, which provide the structural schema of the federation and the component warehouses, can be automatically created from the warehouse metadata (the right side of Fig. 4). Second, additional ontologies must be used in order to match the structural components and accomplish the schema matching process. The ontologies correspond to domains described by the warehouse facts and dimensions. In our case we primarily need a healthcare and pharmacy ontology (which characterizes diseases, drugs, patients), but also other ontologies, referring to time (segments and units) or personal data. The use of WordNet should give a substantial support in building the ontologies. WordNet will also be used in cases when the query against ontologies produces no successful matching. Due to the lack of space, we plan to dedicate an entire future paper to the ideas described in this chapter.

```
<owl:Class rdf:ID="Attribute"/>

<owl:Class rdf:ID="DimAttribute">
  <rdfs:subClassOf
          rdf:resource="#Attribute"/>
</owl:Class>

<owl:Class rdf:ID="Level" />

<owl:ObjectProperty
rdf:ID="attributeOfLevel">
  <rdf:type
rdf:resource="&owl;FunctionalProperty"/>
  <rdfs:domain
rdf:resource="#DimAttribute"/>
    <rdfs:range  rdf:resource="#Level"/>
</owl:ObjectProperty>
```

```
<Level rdf:ID="ICDLevel2"/>

<DimAttribute
rdf:ID="level2Desc">
  <attributeOfLevel
rdf:resource="ICDLevel2">
  </DimAttribute>

<Dimension
rdf:ID="Diagnosis">
  <hasLevel
rdf:resource="ICDLevel1">
  <hasLevel
rdf:resource="ICDLevel2">
  <hasHierarchy
rdf:resource="DiagHierDef">
</Dimension>
```

Fig. 4. Ontology of the data warehouse domain

5 Related Work

One of the first scientific papers describing an accomplished clinical data warehouse development project is [3]. Differences between conventional, business-oriented data warehouses and clinical data warehouses are outlined in [9] and key research issues in clinical data warehousing identified. The warehouse outlined in [9] has the patient in the focus of its interest, while the approach in [10] is similar to ours, focusing on billable acts (encounters).

Some resemblance to our approach can be seen in [6], which illustrates an association rule mining technique over human sleep datasets. There is a macro-level dataset containing patient demographics, general and sleep-specific habits and sleep-related disorders, as well as a micro-level dataset consisting of detailed, time-series data obtained from sensors (data such as electro-encephalogram or electro-myogram).

A data warehouse federation is described in [1, 8]. XML Topic Maps (XTM) [19] is used to provide the integration framework. Various elements of the federation model and the component warehouses are described as topic map resources, providing an abstraction layer and thus seamlessly overcoming the semantic heterogeneity. However, the topics must be manually defined first.

In [11] an enterprise knowledge portal that integrates OLAP and information retrieval (IR) functionality is presented, with an RDF-based ontology as the core, which stores metadata for different resources. A similarity function for metadata search is defined, which treats two identical descriptions as a 100% match, while two completely unrelated descriptions are a 0% match. Construction of a federated spatial database, using OWL, is outlined in [7]. Spatial databases are defined by using a particular XML encoding for the transport and storage of geographic information. The ontology is derived from WordNet and the spatial data transfer standard. A self-medication information system, which proposes to patients information and services on mild clinical signs and associated treatments, is illustrated in [2]. Given the simplified patient's electronic health record as input, an ontology is used to infer the right treatment proposal out of the self-medication knowledge base.

6 Conclusion

This paper presents the conceptual model of HEWAF, a federated data warehouse for health insurance organizations practicing evidence-based medicine. The model is based on the widely adopted international standard HL7. The biggest challenge we addressed during the design process was the integration of time-segmented, low-grained medicine administration data into the standard conceptual multidimensional data warehouse model with financial measures. The medicine administration data is a complex attribute of the fact, which can be observed as an XML-like "cube in cube" and aggregated internally. The basic principles of OLAP-XML federation are adopted and extended to generate queries. In order to automate the schema matching process as much as possible, we developed a data warehouse domain ontology, and are currently working on developing a simplified domain ontology in the healthcare and pharmacy area.

References

[1] Bruckner, R.M., Tok, W.L., Mangisengi, O., Tjoa, A.M.: A Framework for a Multidimensional OLAP Model Using Topic Maps. In: Proc. Int. Conf. on Web Information Systems Engineering (WISE'01). IEEE Computer Society (2001) 109-118.

[2] Curé, O.: Ontology Interaction with a Patient Electronic Health Record. In: Proc. Symp. Computer-Based Medical Systems (CBMS'05). IEEE Computer Society (2005) 323-328

[3] Ewen, E.F., Medsker, C., Dusterhoft, L.E., Levan-Shultz, K., Smith, J.L., Gottschall, M.A.: Data Warehousing in an Integrated Health System: Building the Business Case. In: Proc. Int. Workshop on Data Warehousing and OLAP (DOLAP'98). ACM Press, New York (1998) 47-53

[4] Jindal, R., Acharya, A.: Federated Data warehouse Architecture, Wipro Technologies white paper, (2004) http://hosteddocs.ittoolbox.com/Federated%20data%20Warehouse%20Architecture.pdf (Last access: April 10, 2006)

[5] Kimball, R., Ross, M.: The Data Warehouse Toolkit, The Complete Guide to Dimensional Modeling. 2nd edn. John Wiley & Sons, New York (2002)

[6] Laxminarayan, P., Ruiz, C., Alvarez, S.A., Moonis, M.: Mining Associations over Human Sleep Time Series. In: Proc. Symp. Computer-Based Medical Systems (CBMS'05). IEEE Computer Society (2005) 323-328

[7] Morocho, V., Saltor, F., Pérez-Vidal, L.: Schema Integration on Federated Spatial DB across Ontologies. In: Proc. Int. Workshop on Engineering Federated Information Systems (EFIS'03). IOS Press (2003) 63-72

[8] Nguyen, T.B., Tjoa, A.M., Mangisengi, O.: MetaCube XTM: A Multidimensional Meta-data Approach for Semantic Web Warehousing Systems. In: Proc. Int. Conf. on Data Warehousing and Knowledge Discovery (DaWaK'03). Lecture Notes in Computer Science, Vol. 2737, Springer Verlag, Berlin Heidelberg New York (2003) 76-88

[9] Pedersen, T.B., Jensen, C.S.: Research Issues in Clinical Data Warehousing. In: Proc. Int. Conf. on Scientific and Statistical Database Management (SSDBM'98). IEEE Computer Society Press (2001) 43-52

[10] Song, I.-Y., Rowen, W., Medsker, C., Ewen, E.F.: An Analysis of Many-to-Many Relationships between the Fact and Dimension Tables in Dimensional Modeling. In: Proc. Int. Workshop on Design Management of Data Warehouses (DMDW'01), CEUR Workshop Proceedings, Vol. 39, CEUR WS-org (2001) 6(1-13)

[11] Priebe, T., Pernul G.: Ontology-based Integration of OLAP and Information Retrieval. In: Int. Workshop on Database and Expert Systems Applications (DEXA'03). IEEE Computer Society (2003) 610-614

[12] Pedersen, D., Riis, K., Pedersen, T.B.: XML Extended OLAP Querying. In: Proc. Int. Conf. on Scientific and Statistical Database Management (SSDBM'02). IEEE Computer Society (2002) 195-206

[13] Pedersen D., Riis, K., Pedersen, T.B.: A Powerful and SQL-Compatible Data Model and Query Language for OLAP. In: Database Technologies, Proc. Australasian Database Conference (ADC'02). Australian Computer Society (2002)

[14] Sackett, D.L., Rosenberg, W.M.C., Gray, J.A.M., Haynes, R.B., Richardson, W.S,: Evidence-Based Medicine: What It Is and What It Isn't. British Medical J., Vol. 312 (7032). BMJ Publishing Group (1996) 71-72

[15] Sheth, A.P., Larson, J.A.: Federated Database Systems for Managing Distributed, Heterogeneous, and Autonomous Databases. ACM Computing Surveys, Vol. 22 (3). ACM Press, New York (1990) 183-236

[16] World Health Organization (WHO): International Statistical Classification of Diseases and Related Health Problems, 10th Revision, Version for 2003 http://www3.who.int/icd/vol1htm2003/fr-icd.htm (Last access: April 10, 2006)

[17] World Wide Web Consortium: XML Path Language (XPath) v. 1.0. W3C recommendation (as of November 16, 1999). http://www.w3.org/TR/1999/REC-xpath-19991116

[18] World Wide Web Consortium: OWL Web Ontology Language. W3C Recommendation (as of February 10, 2004). http://www.w3.org/TR/2004/REC-owl-features-20040210/

[19] XML Topic Maps (XTM) 1.0, TopicMaps.Org Specification (as of June 6, 2001) http://www.topicmaps.org/xtm/1.0/xtm1-20010806.html

[20] Princeton University Cognitive Science Laboratory: WordNet, a lexical database for English language. http://wordnet.princeton.edu/ (Last access: April 10, 2006)

[21] Health Level Seven (HL7), www.hl7.org (Last access: April 10, 2006)

A Versioning Management Model for Ontology-Based Data Warehouses

Dung Nguyen Xuan, Ladjel Bellatreche, and Guy Pierra

LISI/ENSMA - Poitiers University - Futuroscope - France
{nguyenx, bellatreche, pierra}@ensma.fr

Abstract. More and more integration systems use ontologies to solve the problem of semantic heterogeneities between autonomous databases. To automate the integration process, a number of these systems suppose the existence of a shared domain ontology a priori referenced by the local ontologies embedded in the various sources. When the shared ontology evolves over the time, the evolution may concern (i) the ontology level, (2) the local schema level, and/or (3) the contents of sources. Since sources are autonomous and may evolve independently, managing the evolution of the integrated system turns to an *asynchronous versioning problem*. In this paper, we propose an approach and a model to deal with this problem in the context of a materialized integration system. To manage the changes of contents and schemas of sources, we adapt the existing solutions proposed in traditional databases. To support ontology changes, we propose the *principle of ontological continuity*. It supposes that an evolution of an ontology should not make false an axiom that was previously true. This principle allows the management of each old instance using the new version of ontology. With this assumption, we propose an approach, called *the floating version model*, that fully automate the whole integration process. Our proposed work has been validated by a prototype using ECCO environment and the EXPRESS language.

1 Introduction

As digital repositories of information are springing up everywhere and interconnectivity between computers around the world is being established, the construction and evolution management of data warehouse over such *autonomous*, *heterogeneous* and *distributed* data sources becomes crucial for a number of modern applications. A data warehouse can be seen as an integration system, where relevant data of various sources are extracted, transformed and materialized (contrary to the mediator architecture) in a warehouse. To facilitate the construction of a data warehouse, two main issues may be considered: (1) the resolution of different conflicts (naming conflicts, scaling conflicts, confounding conflicts and representation conflicts) caused by semantic and schematic heterogeneities [5] and (2) the schematic autonomy of sources, known as the receiver heterogeneity problem [5]. To deal with the first issue, more and more approaches associated to data an ontology [3]. An ontology is defined as a formal specification of a shared conceptualization [6]. The main contribution of these ontologies

A Min Tjoa and J. Trujillo (Eds.): DaWaK 2006, LNCS 4081, pp. 195–206, 2006.

is to formally represent the sense of instances of sources. In [3], we showed that when a shared (e.g., standardized) domain ontology exists, and each local source a priori references that ontology, an automatic integration becomes possible. Indeed, the articulation between the local ontologies and the shared one allows an automatic resolution of the different conflicts. Over the last years, a number of similar integration systems have been proposed following either mediator or warehouse architectures. In the materialized approach, several ontology-based data management systems like RDFsuite [1] and DLDB [11] have been developed. The main assumption of these systems is that all the sources use the same shared ontology.

Most of the sources participating in the integration process operate autonomously, they are free to modify their ontologies and/or schemas, remove some data without any prior "public" notification, or occasionally block access to the source for maintenance or other purposes. Moreover, they may not always be aware of or concerned by other sources referencing them or integration systems accessing them [13]. Consequently, the relation between the data warehouse and its sources is slightly coupled which causes anomalies of maintenance [4].

In the traditional databases, changes have two categories [12]: (1) content changes (insert/update/delete instances) and (2) schema changes (add/modify /drop attributes or tables). In order to tackle the problem of schema changes, two different ways are possible: *schema evolution* and *schema versioning* [9]. In ontology-based integration systems, the evolution management is more difficult. This difficulty is due to the presence of ontologies (shared and local) that may also (slowly) evolve. In order to ensure the schematic autonomy of sources, some ontology-based integration systems allow also each source to *refine* the shared ontology by adding new concepts [3].

When the shared ontology evolves over the time and none global clock exits enforcing all the sources and the warehouse to evolve at the same time, various sources to be integrated may reference the same shared ontology as it was at various points in time. Therefore, the problem of integration turns to an asynchronous versioning problem. In this paper, we address this problem by considering the ontology-based integration system developed in our laboratory [3]. This system is based on three major assumptions that reflect our point of view on large-scale integration: an automatic and a reliable integration of autonomous data sources is only possible if the source owners a priori agree on a common shared vocabulary. The only challenge is to define a mechanism that leaves as much as possible schematic autonomy of each source [3]. These assumptions are as follows: (1) Each data source participating in the integration process shall contain its own ontology. We call such a source an *ontology-based database* (OBDB) [3]. (2) Each local source a priori references a shared ontology by subsumption relationships "as much as possible" (i.e., each local class must reference its smallest subsuming class in the shared ontology). (3) A local ontology may restrict and extend the shared ontology as much as needed. The work proposed in this paper can be extended to others ontology-based integration systems. Although the evolution was largely studied [10], to the best of our knowledge, none of these systems considered the problem of asynchronous evolution of ontologies.

In order to manage asynchronous evolution, the following issues need to be addressed: (1) the management of the evolutions of ontologies in order to maintain the relations between ontologies and the data originating from various sources, (2) the management of the life cycle of the instances (periods where an instance was alive), and (3) the capability to interpret each instance of the data warehouse, even if it is described using a different set of properties than those defined in the current version of the ontology (some properties are added/deprecated).

This paper is divided in six sections: Section 2 proposes our semantic integration approach based on a priori articulation between the shared ontology and local ontologies. Section 3 presents our approach to manage evolution of contents and schemas of data sources. Section 4 describes our mechanism of managing ontology changes using the principle of ontological continuity, and presents our floating version model. Section 5 presents an implementation of our approach using the Express language and ECCO environment. Section 6 concludes the paper by summarizing the main results and suggesting future work.

2   An a Priori Integration Approach

In this section, we formalize the ontology-based integration process in order to facilitate the presentation of our proposed solution. Let $S = \{S_1, ..., S_n\}$ be a set of sources participating in the integration process. Note that each source S_i has a local ontology O_i that references/extends the shared ontology O. Formally, the ontology O can be defined as the 4-tuples $< C, P, Applic, Sub >$, where: (a) C is the set of the classes used to describe the concepts of a given domain, (b) P is the set of all properties used to describe the instances of the classes of C. Note that only a subset of P might be selected by any particular database [1], (c) $Applic$ is a function defined as $Applic : C \rightarrow 2^P$. It associates to each class of the ontology, the properties that are rigid (applicable) for each instance of this class and that may be used, in the database, for describing its instances. Note that for each $c_i \in C$, only a subset of $Applic(c_i)$ may be used in any particular database, for describing c_i instances, and (d) Sub is the subsumption function defined as $Sub : C \rightarrow 2^C$ [2], where for a class c_i of the ontology, it associates its direct subsumed classes [3]. Sub defines a partial order over C. In our model, there exists two kinds of subsumption relationships: $Sub = OOSub \cup OntoSub$, where: $OOSub$ is the usual object-oriented subsumption with the inheritance relationship. Through $OOSub$, applicable properties are inherited. $OOSub$ must define a single hierarchy. $OntoSub$ is a subsumption relationship without the inheritance. Through $OntoSub$ (also called case-of in the PLIB ontology model), properties of a subsuming class may be imported by a subsumed class.

---

[1] In our approach, each local ontology may also extend P.

[2] 2^C denotes the power set of C.

[3] C_1 subsumes C_2 iff $\forall x \in C_2, x \in C_1$.

OntoSub is also used as an *articulation operator* allowing to connect local ontologies into a shared ontology. Through this relationship, a local class may import or map all or some of the properties that are defined in the referenced class(es). In order to ensure the autonomy of sources, it may also define additional properties.

Now, we have all ingredients to define formally each source S_i as 5-tuples :
$< O_i, Sch_i, I_i, Pop_i, M_i >$, where:
(i) O_i is an ontology ($O_i :< C_i, P_i, Applic_i, Sub_i >$). (ii) $Sch_i : C_i \to 2^{P_i}$ associates to each ontology class $c_{i,j}$ of C_i the properties which are effectively used to describe the instances of the class $c_{i,j}$. This set may be any subset of $Appli(c_{ij})$ (as the role of an ontology is to conceptualize a domain, the role of a database schema is to select only those properties that are relevant for its target application). (iii) I_i is the set of instances of the source S_i. (iv) $Pop_i : C_i \to 2^{I_i}$ is the set of instances of each class. Finally, (v) the mapping M_i represents the *articulation* between the shared ontology O and the local ontology O_i. It is defined as a function: $M_i : C \to 2^{C_i}$, that defines the subsumption relationships without inheritance holding between C and C_i.

Several automatic integration scenarios may be defined in the above context [3]. For simplicity reason, we just outline below the *ExtendOnto* integration scenario, where the warehouse ontology consists of the shared ontology extended by the local ontologies of all the sources that have been added in the warehouse. Thanks to the articulation mappings (M_i), we note that all warehouse data that may be interpreted by the shared ontology (i.e., of which the class is subsumed by a shared ontology class) may be accessed through this ontology, whatever source they came from [4].

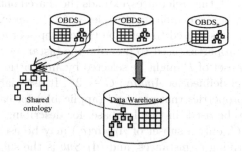

Fig. 1. The Structure of our Data Warehouse

The ontology-based data warehouse DW has the same source structure (Figure 1): $DW :< O_{DW}, Sch_{DW}, I_{DW}, Pop_{DW}, \phi >$, where:

1. O_{DW} is the warehouse ontology. It is computed by integrating local ontologies into the shared one. Its components are computed as follows:
   - $C_{DW} = C \cup (\cup_{1 \le i \le n} C_i)$.
   - $P_{DW} = P \cup (\cup_{1 \le i \le n} P_i)$.

---

[4] Another integration scenario, called *ProjOnto*, assumes that source instances are extracted after a projection operation on the shared ontology.

$$- \; Applic_{DW}(c) = \begin{cases} Applic(c), \text{ if } c \in C \\ Applic_i(c), \text{ if } c \in C_i \end{cases}$$

$$- \; Sub_{DW}(c) = \begin{cases} Sub(c) \cup M_i(c), \text{ if } c \in C \\ Sub_i(c), \text{ if } c \in C_i \end{cases}$$

2. $I_{DW} = \cup_{1 \leq i \leq n} I_i$.
3. The instances are stored in tables as in their sources.
   - $\forall c_i \in C_{DW} \wedge c_i \in C_i (1 \leq i \leq n)$:
     (a) $Sch_{DW}(c_i) = Sch_i(c_i)$,
     (b) $Pop_{DW}(c_i) = Pop_i(c_i)$
   - $\forall c \in C$
     (a) $Sch_{DW}(c) = Applic(c) \cap (Sch(c) \cup (\cup_{c_j \in Sub_{DW}(c)} Sch(c_j)))$.
     (b) $Pop_{DW}(c) = \cup_{c_j \in Sub(c)} Pop(c_j)$

3 Evolution Management of Contents and Schemas

In this section, we present a mechanism to identify classes, properties and instances and the life cycle of instances.

To identify classes and properties, we use the universal identifiers (UI) defined in the ontology [3]. We assume that the identifiers contain two parts separated by ":". The first and second parts represent, an UI and a version number, respectively. In order to recognize instances of the data warehouse, any source must define for each class having a population a *semantic key*. It is composed by the representation (in character string form) of values of one or several applicable properties of this class.

3.1 The Life Cycle of Instances

In some situations, it may be useful to know the existence of instances in the warehouse at any previous point in time. To do so, we do not need to archive also the versions of ontologies since the current version always allows to interpret old instances (see Section 4). This problem is known by "schema versioning" [15], where all versioned data of a table are saved. Two solutions are possible to satisfy this requirement: explicit storage and implicit storage approaches. In the *explicit storage* approach [2,15], all the versions of each table are explicitly stored. This solution has two advantages: (i) it is easy to implement and allows an automation of the process of updating of data, and (ii) query processing is straightforward. But it can be very important if the query needs an exploration of all versioned data of the warehouse. Another drawback is due to the storage of the replicated data. In the *implicit storage* approach [15], only one version of each table T is stored. This schema is obtained by making the *union* of all properties appearing in the various versions. On each data warehouse updating, one adds all existing instances of each source tables. Instances are supplemented by null values. This solution avoid the exploration of several versions of a given table. The major drawbacks of this solution are: (i) the problem of replicated data is still present, (ii) the implementation is more difficult than the previous one concerning the automatic computation of the schema of stored tables (the names of columns may have changed in the sources); (iii) the layout of the life cycle of data is difficult to implement (*"valid time"* [15]) and (iv) the semantics ambiguity of the null values.

Our solution follows the second approach and solves the problems as follows: (1) the problem of *replicated data* is solved thanks to the single semantic identification (value of the semantic key) of each instance of data, (2) the problem of the updating process of table schemata is solved through the use of universal identifiers (UI) for all the properties, (3) the problem of the representation of the instances life cycle is solved by a pair of properties: $(Version_{min}, Version_{max})$. It enables us to know the validation period of a given instance, and (4) the problem of the semantic ambiguity of the null values is handled by archiving the functions *Sch* of the various versions of each class. This archive enables us to determine the true schema of version of a table at any point in time, and thus the initial representation of each instance.

4   Ontology Evolution Management

4.1   Principle of Ontological Continuity

The constraints that may be defined in order to handle evolution of versioned ontology-based data sources result from the fundamental differences existing between the evolution of conceptual models and ontologies. A conceptual model is a model of a domain. This means, following the Minsky definition of a model [8], that it is an object allowing to respond to some particular questions on another object, namely, the target domain. When the questions change (when the organizational objectives of the target system are modified), its conceptual model is modified too, despite the fact that the target domain is in fact unchanged. Therefore, conceptual models are heavily depending upon the objectives assigned to the databases they are used to design. They evolve each time these objectives change. Contrary to conceptual models, an ontology is a conceptualization that is not linked with any particular objective of any particular computer system. It only aims to represent all the entities of a particular domain in a form that is consensual for a rather broad community having in mind a rather broad kind of problems. It is a logic theory of a part of the world, shared by a whole community, and allowing their members to understand each others. That can be, for example, the set theory (for mathematicians), mechanic (for mechanical engineers) or analytical counting (for accountants). For this type of conceptualizations, two changes may be identified: *normal evolution*, and *revolution*. A normal evolution of a theory is its deepening. New truths, more detailed are added to the old truths. But what was true yesterday remains true today. Concepts are never deleted contrary to [7].

It is also possible that axioms of a theory become false. In this case, it is not any more an evolution. It is a *revolution*, where two different logical systems will coexist or be opposed.

The ontologies that we are considered in our approach follow this philosophy. These ontologies are either standardized, for example at the international level, or defined by large size consortium which formalize in a stable way the knowledge of a technical domain. The changes in which we are interested are not those changes where all the shared knowledge of a domain is challenged by a new theory: we only address changes representing an *evolution* of the axioms of an ontology and not a *revolution*.

Therefore, we propose to impose to all manipulated ontologies (local and shared) to respect the following principle for ontology evolution:

Principle of ontological continuity: if we consider an ontology as a set of axioms, then ontology evolution must ensure that any true axiom for a certain version of an ontology will remain true for all its later versions. Changes that do not fulfill this requirement are called ontology revolution.

In the remaining paper, we only consider ontology evolution.

4.2   Constraints on the Evolution of Ontologies

In this section, we discuss the constraints for each kind of concept (classes, relation between classes, properties and instances) during ontology evolution. Let $O^k =< C^k, P^k, Sub^k, Applic^k >$ be the ontology in version k.

Permanence of the classes. Existence of a class could not be denied across evolution: $C^k \subset C^{k+1}$. To make the model more flexible, as it is the case non computerized ontology, a class may become obsolete. It will then be marked as "deprecated", but it will continue belong to the newer versions of the ontology. In addition, the definition of a class could be refined, but this should not exclude any instance that was member of the class in the previous version. This means:

- the definition of a class may evolve,
- each class definition is to be associated with a version number.
- for any instance $i, i \in C^k \Rightarrow i \in C^{k+1}$.

Permanence of properties. Similarly $P^k \subset P^{k+1}$. A property may become obsolete but neither its existence, nor its value for a particular instance may be modified. Similarly, a definition or value domain of a property may evolve. Taking into account the ontological principle of continuity, a value domain could be only increasing, certain values being eventually marked as obsolete.

Permanence of the Subsumption. Subsumption is also an ontological concept which could not be infirmed. Let $Sub^* : C \rightarrow 2^C$ be the transitive closure of the direct subsumption relation Sub. We have then:
$$\forall\, C \in C^k, Sub^{*k}(c) \subset Sub^{*k+1}(c).$$
This constraint allows obviously an evolution of the subsumption hierarchy, for example by intercalating intermediate classes between two classes linked by a subsumption relation.

Description of instances. The fact that a property $p \in Applic(c)$ means that this property is rigid for each instance of c. This is an axiom that cannot be infirmed: $\forall c \in C^k, Applic^{*k}(c) \subset Applic^{*k+1}(c)$.

Note that this does not require that same properties are always used to describe the instances of the same class. As described in section 4.1, schematic evolution does not depend only on ontology evolutions. It depends also, and mainly, on the organizational objectives of each particular database version.

4.3   Floating Version Model: A Global Access to Current Instances

Before presenting our floating version model, we indicate the updating scenario of our data warehouse: at given moments, chosen by the data warehouse administrator, the current version of a source S_i is loaded in the warehouse. This version includes its local ontology, the mapping M_i between local ontology O_i and the shared ontology O, and its current content (*certain instances eventually already exist in the warehouse, others are new, others are removed*). This scenario is common in the engineering domain, where an engineering data warehouse consolidates descriptions (i.e., electronic catalogues) of industrial components of a whole of suppliers. Therefore, in this scenario, the maintenance process is carried out each time that a new version of an electronic catalogue of a supplier is received.

Our floating version model is able to support two kind of user services: (i) it allows to provide an access via a single ontology to the set of all instances that have been recorded in the data warehouse over the time its ontology and/or (ii) it also allows to record the various versions of the ontologies (shared and local) and to trace the life cycle of instances (full multi-version management). In this section we discuss how these objectives will be achieved.

The principal difficulty due to source autonomy is that in some situations, when two different sources are loaded, let's say S_i and S_j, a same class c of shared ontology O can be referred by an articulation mapping (i.e., subsumption) in different versions. For example, classes c_i^n of S_i and c_j^p of S_j may refer to c^k (class c with version k) and c^{k+j} (class c with version $k + j$), respectively. According to the principle of ontological continuity, it is advisable to note that:

1. all applicable properties in c^k are also applicable in c^{k+j},
2. all subsumed classes by c^k are also subsumed by c^{k+j},

Thus, the subsumption relation between c^k and c_i^n could be replaced by a subsumption relation between c^{k+j} and c_i^n. Moreover, all the properties that were imported from c^k may also be imported from c^{k+j}. Therefore, the class c^k is not necessary to reach (as a subsuming class) instances of c_i^n.

This remark leads us to propose a model, called the *floating version model*, which enables to reach all the data in the data warehouse via only one version of each class of the warehouse ontology. This set of versioned classes, called the *"current version"* of the warehouse ontology is such that the current version of each class c^f is higher or equal to the largest version of that class referenced by a subsumption relationship at the time of any maintenance. In practice, this condition is satisfied as follows:

- if an articulation M_i references a class c^f with a version lower than f, then M_i is updated in order to reference c^f,
- if an articulation M_i references a class c^f with a version greater than f, then the warehouse connect itself to the shared ontology server, loads the last version of the shared ontology and migrates all references M_i $(i = 1..n)$ to new current versions.

Example 1. During the maintenance process of a class C_1 ((Figure 2)) that references the shared ontology class C with version 2 **(1)**, the version of C in current ontology is 1 **(2)**. In this case, the warehouse downloads the current version of the shared ontology **(3)**. This one being 3, class C_1 is modified to reference version 3 **(4)**.

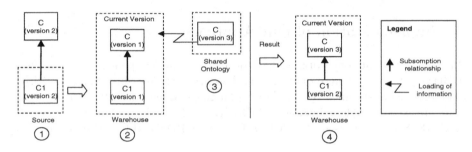

Fig. 2. A Model of the floating versions

We described below the two automatic maintenance processes that our floating version model makes possible.

Simplified Version Management. If the only requirements of users is to be able to browse the current instances of the data warehouse then, at each maintenance step: (1) ontology description of the various classes of the data warehouse ontology are possibly replaced by newer versions, and (2) the table associated to each class coming from a local ontology in the data warehouse is simply replaced by the corresponding current table in the local source.

A Full Multi-version Management. Note that in the previous case (Section 5.1), the articulation between a local ontology class and a shared ontology class stored in the current version of the data warehouse may not be its original definition (see the Figure 2). If the data warehouse user also wants to browse instances through the ontological definitions that existed when these instances were loaded, it is necessary to archive also all the versions of the warehouse ontology. This scenario may be useful, for example, to know the exact domain of an enumeration-valued property when the instance was defined. By implementing this possibility, we get a *multi-version data warehouse* which archives also all versions of classes having existed in the data warehouse life, and all the relations in their original forms. Note that the principle of ontological continuity seems to make seldom necessary this complex archive.

The multi-version data warehouse has three parts:

1. *current ontology.* It contains the current version of the warehouse ontology. It represents also a generic data access interface to all instance data, whenever they were introduced in the warehouse.
2. *Ontology archive.* It contains all versions of each class and property of the warehouse ontology. This part gives to users the true definitions of versions of each concept. Versions of table schema T_i are also historized by archiving the function $Sch^k(c_i)$ of each version k of c_i, where T_i corresponds to the class c_i.
3. *multi-versioned tables.* It contains all instances and their version_min and version_max.

5   Implementation of Our Approach

In order to validate our work, we have developed a prototype integrating several OBDSs (Figure 3), where ontologies and sources are described using the PLIB ontology model specified by the Express language. Such ontologies and instance data are exchangeable as instances of EXPRESS files ("physical file"). To process EXPRESS files, we used the ECCO Toolkit of PDTec [14]. An ontology and

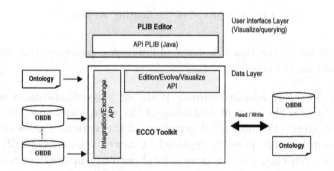

Fig. 3. Architecture of our Prototype

an OBDS may be created via an editor called PLIBEditor. It is used also to visualize, edit and update ontologies (both shared and local) and sources. It uses a set of PLIB API developed under ECCO.

We have developed a set of integration API allowing the automatic integration both in the simplified version management scenario, and in the full multi-version management scenario.

Figure 4 shows the view offered to users over the content of the data warehouse after integration. The shared ontology (left side) provides for hierarchical access

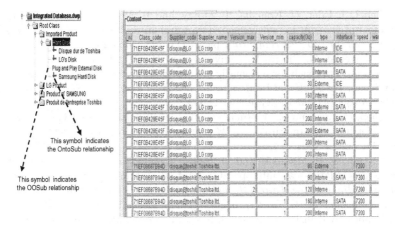

Fig. 4. Integrated hierarchical access and integrated querying over the data warehouse

and query over the data warehouse content: (i) a query over a shared ontology class allows to query all the classes subsumed either by the OOSub or by the OntoSub relationships, thus integrating instance data from all the integrated sources (see left side of Figure 4), and (ii) hierarchical access allows also to go down until classes that came from any particular ontology (see right side of Figure 4).

6   Conclusion

In this paper, we presented the problem of asynchronous versioning of a materialized integration system of heterogeneous and autonomous ontology-based data sources. The sources that we considered are those containing local ontologies referencing in an a priori manner a shared one by subsumption relationships. A difference between ontologies and database schemata is presented and we suggested to distinguish between *ontology evolution* and *ontology revolution*. To deal with ontology evolution, an ontological continuity principle is proposed. It allows the management of each old instance of the integrated system using a new version of the ontology. Following this assumption, two scenarios ensuring a fully automatic integration process have been proposed. Both scenarios are based on a floating version model, that needs only a single version of the warehouse ontology, called the current ontology. It allows the interpretation of all the instances of the warehouse. Our model was validated under ECCO by considering several local ontologies, where for each ontology, a set of sources instance data is defined. This approach allows, in particular, an automatic integration of electronic component catalogues in engineering.

References

1. S. Alexaki, V. Christophides, G. karvounarakis, D. Plexousakis, and K. Tolle. The ics-forth rdfsuite: Managing voluminous rdf description bases. *Proceedings of the Second International Workshop on the Semantic Web (SemWeb01)*, May 2001.

2. B. Bebel, J. Eder, C. Koncilia, T. Morzy, and R. Wrembel. Creation and management of versions in multiversion data warehouse. *Proceedings of the 2004 ACM symposium on Applied computing*, pages 717–723, June 2004.
3. L. Bellatreche, G. Pierra, D. Nguyen Xuan, H. Dehainsala, and Y. Ait Ameur. An a priori approach for automatic integration of heterogeneous and autonomous databases. *International Conference on Database and Expert Systems Applications (DEXA'04)*, (475-485), September 2004.
4. S. Chen, B. Liu, and E. A. Rundensteiner. Multiversion-based view maintenance over distributed data sources. *ACM Transactions on Database Systems*, 4(29):675–709, December 2004.
5. C. H. Goh, S. E. Madnick, and M. Siegel. Context interchange: Overcoming the challenges of large-scale interoperable database systems in a dynamic environment. *in Proceedings of the Third International Conference on Information and Knowledge Management (CIKM'94)*, pages 337–346, December 1994.
6. T. Gruber. A translation approach to portable ontology specification. *Knowledge Acquisition*, 5(2):199–220, 1995.
7. A. Maedche, B. Motik, L. Stojanovic, R. Studer, and R. Volz. Managing multiple ontologies and ontology evolution in ontologging. *Intelligent Information Processing*, pages 51–63, August 2002.
8. M. Minsky. Computer science and the representation of knowledge. *in The Computer Age: A Twenty-Year View, Michael Dertouzos and Joel Moses, MIT Press*, pages 392–421, 1979.
9. T. Morzy and R. Wrembel. Modeling a multiversion data warehouse : A formal approach. *International Conference on Entreprise Information Systems(ICEIS'03)*, 2003.
10. Natalya F. Noy and Michel Klein. Semantic integration: a survey of ontology-based approaches. *SIGMOD Record*, 33(4), December 2004.
11. Z. Pan and J. Heflin. Dldb: Extending relational databases to support semantic web queries. Technical report, Dept. of Computer Science and Engineering, Lehigh University, USA, 2004.
12. J. F. Roddick. A survey of schema versioning issues for database systems. *Information and Software Technology*, 37(7):383–393, 1995.
13. E.A. Rundensteiner, A. Koealler, and X. Zhang. Maintaining data warehouses over changing information sources. *Communications Of The ACM*, 43(6):57–62, June 2000.
14. G. Staub and M. Maier. Ecco tool kit - an environnement for the evaluation of express models and the development of step based it applications. *User Manual*, 1997.
15. Han-Chieh Wei and Ramez Elmasri. Study and comparison of schema versioning and database conversion techniques for bi-temporal databases. *Proceedings of the Sixth International Workshop on Temporal Representation and Reasoning (IEEE Computer)*, May 1999.

Data Warehouses in Grids with High QoS

Rogério Luís de Carvalho Costa and Pedro Furtado

University of Coimbra
Departamento de Engenharia Informática
Pólo II - Pinhal de Marrocos
3030 - 290 - Coimbra - Portugal
rogcosta@dei.uc.pt, pnf@dei.uc.pt

Abstract. Data warehouses are repositories of large amounts of historical data and are used primarily for decision support purposes. On the other hand, grids consist on the aggregation of distributed computational resources and presentation of these as a single service with a common interface. The deployment of distributed data warehouses on a grid architecture with QoS control strategies could lead to high levels of flexibility, scalability, reliability and efficiency. However, due to grids characteristics, it could also lead to great challenges. In this paper we investigate an efficient architecture to deploy large data warehouses in grids with high availability and good load balancing. We propose architecture and present experimental results.

1 Introduction

Data warehouses are repositories of large amounts of historical data from multiple sources and are used primarily for decision support purposes. They must ensure acceptable response time for complex analytical queries. Some works have been done in order to provide high performance for data warehouses. Usually, these involve materialized views [3], special index structures such as bitmap indices [22,23] and special operators [16].

On the other hand, the use of parallel and distributed data as a technique for improving performance in databases have been studied for some years. The majority of the studies are related to parallel join execution [10,17,18], placement [31] and query processing issues [7,8].

In this work we are especially concerned with the deployment and use of data warehouses in highly distributed environments such as grids and peer-to-peer networks.

Grid technology [11,12] consists on the aggregation of distributed computational resources and presentation of them as a single service with a common interface. Grids could lead to high levels of flexibility, scalability, reliability and efficiency. With careful partitioning and placement, the large computing power of a grid-like environment can be used to handle large data warehouses (which may reach in the order of hundreds of gigabytes or terabytes) efficiently.

Some of the key characteristics of a grid environment are: (1) processor capacities often differ, (2) processor loads change over time, (3) processors are

A Min Tjoa and J. Trujillo (Eds.): DaWaK 2006, LNCS 4081, pp. 207–217, 2006.

geographically distributed, and (4) network conditions are highly unpredictable. In fact, computers may connect and disconnect at any time, and their speeds may change over time. Due to these characteristics, the deployment and use of large data warehouses in grids leads to some challenges.

In this paper we propose a generic architecture to run the Node Partitioned Data Warehouse over a grid environment (GRID-NPDW) with efficient availability and load balancing mechanisms. Our discussion centers around fragmenting the data warehouse, placing and replicating it into sites and nodes within sites in a way that delivers availability with efficiency, that is, when nodes or entire sites are unreachable, the system performance degrades only slightly. We show that some skews could lead to the need of dynamic load balancing mechanisms. We propose and show experimental results for a load balancing policy for GRID-NPDW.

This paper is organized as follows: in Section 2 we present related work. Then we focus on fragmenting and replicating for availability in the grid context in Section 3. This basic data infrastructure is then used as the basis for the GRID-NPDW dynamic architecture discussed in Section 4. We present experimental results of the proposed approaches in Section 5. Finally, on Section 6, we present some conclusions and future work.

2   Related Work

Data warehouses are commonly organized as star schemas [4], which means that there are huge fact tables and multiple conformed dimensions. They are usually targeted at complex analytical queries. In fact, data warehouses are mostly read-only databases with periodic loads.

As one thinks on using parallelism with data warehouses, many questions arise. The first one is related to data allocation. Due to data warehouses' specialized schema and mostly read-only behaviour, replication and partitioning may be used simultaneously.

There have been some recent related works on data placement in distributed data warehouses. In [27], the authors present the multi-dimensional hierarchical fragmentation (MDHF) method. It is based on the fragmentation of the fact table considering several fragmentation attributes, each one referring to a different dimension. A fragment consists of all tuples belonging to one value range per fragmentation attribute. To each query submitted to the database are associated subqueries processing the different fragments. The authors show simulation results for a shared-disk architecture.

Node-Partitioned Data Warehouses (NPDW) are presented in [13] and extended in [14]. The author proposes that both facts and non-small dimension tables should be partitioned. Partitions are allocated to different processing nodes and dimension tables are hash-partitioned by their primary key. Fact tables are hash-partitioned by the most frequent equi-join attribute used by the relation. Small dimension tables are replicated in each processing node, because the processing burden for those relations is small. Dynamic repartitioning is also considered. In this strategy, each query submitted to the database must be modified in order to allow parallel processing by the nodes.

In [19] dynamic load balancing for parallel data warehouses is discussed. The authors present four strategies: *Logical, Partition, Size* and *Integrated*. All four strategies are evaluated in a shared-disk environment. The *Integrated* strategy, that considers either CPU and disk loads, has obtained the best performance. The authors claim that only the *Partition* strategy could be used in shared-nothing environments. Shared-disk servers are also considered in commercial products, like Oracle, as presented in [24].

On the other hand, grid technology is becoming more and more popular. Although today's typical data intensive science Grid application still uses flat files to process and store data [21], there are many works on the integration of database technology into the Grid. They consider different database related aspects, like distributed query processing [29], data placement [26] and data replication strategies and management [2,28].

Load balancing is another important issue when implementing distributed database systems. There are also some works on load balancing in Grids ([6,9,30]). Most of them use predictive data and algorithms to engineer local load balancing across multiple hosts.

Additionally, the technology of agent programming has emerged as a flexible and complementary way to manage resources of distributed systems due to the increased flexibility in adapting to the dynamically changing requirements of such systems [5]. The notion of agent has become popular in the Grid community, as exemplified by several publications on the use of agents in the grid [1,6,20,25].

In the next Section we discuss our fragmentation and replication approach as the basis for the architecture and high availability features of the GRID-NPDW.

3   Data Infrastructure and Efficient Availability in GRID-NPDW

There are many important challenges to be considered when implementing an application on a grid environment. In this paper we are especially interested in high availability and in high performance.

In grids, network conditions are highly unpredictable. It is usual that some nodes are not always available. As one cannot have total control of the environment, it is important to have some contingency plan in order to always be able to execute the requested application. Maintaining data replicas in several nodes could be one of the strategies.

Data Warehouses are usually deployed in relational databases using star schemas. These schemas are comprised of a few huge central fact relations and several smaller dimension relations [4], as shown in Figure 1. Each fact references a tuple in each dimension. For instance, facts may be sales measures and dimensions may include time, shop, customer, product the sales fact refers to. The NPDW is an architecture to process those data sets in parallel shared-nothing systems efficiently [13].

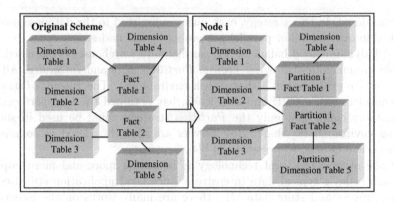

Fig. 1. Data allocation in NPDW

In NPDW, each relation can be partitioned (divided into partitions or fragments) or copied entirely into processing nodes (as also represented in Figure 1). Very large fact relations are workload-based partitioned and dimensions (which are small) are replicated into all sites. In this case most of the query processing can proceed in parallel between the nodes with only modest amounts of data being exchanged between nodes [14], except when differently-partitioned relations need to be joined.

In the case of a WAN-deployment, there is also the issue of latency between sites and the amount of data that needs to travel between sites may become a major issue. While in a LAN the partitioning of the central facts may be random or hash-based, in a geographically distributed environment such as the one we are considering, data origin is another logical option (e.g. a big multinational corporation has its data placed geographically, with a sub-grid in each continent).

In NPDW the decision to replicate relations is based on performance issues (to allow join processing without data migration between nodes) and also on the efficiently availability issue. In [15], several data replication strategies for efficient availability are presented and evaluated for NPDW.

One first approach (Full Replicas) could be to replicate an entire node (including all the partitions and replicas it has) into another node. Suppose *Node A* is replicated into *Node B*. *Node B* would have its own partitions and relations and *Node's A* partitions and relations. If *Node A* becomes unavailable or goes offline, *Node B* could take its place. However, using this strategy *Node B* would have to process twice as many data. If we assume homogeneous nodes for simplicity, this would result in double execution time even though only a single node was unavailable. So, this method is not efficient.

Partitioned Replica Groups (PRG) is shown as being the one that could lead to best results considering both efficiency and availability. The objective of PRG is twofold: to avoid the inefficiency of full replicas and still allow the system to keep on processing even when entire groups of nodes become unavailable. For partitioned relations, each *Node A* owns a partition. One or more replicas of that partition are created and divided into X slices, which are then copied into

X nodes that can replace *Node A* if *Node A* is unreachable. In case of failure of *Node A*, its replica is processed by the X other nodes without making a big imbalance of the load.

PRG also organizes processing nodes by groups, which allows some nodes to go offline simultaneously [15]. The idea is that partitions of all nodes participating in one group should always be (sliced and) replicated into nodes of a different group. No replicas of large table's data should be done in nodes of the same group. With this simple constraint, a whole group can be offline without stopping the whole system.

Suppose a fact table that is sliced into t fragments. In Figure 2 we show a possible configuration of PRG considering such fragments in an environment with six processing nodes. The nodes were organized into three groups of two nodes each. In the first node of each group, we have placed the first n fragments of the fact table. Fragments $n+1$ to t were replicated in the second node of each group. The replicas from Group 1 are placed on the Groups 2 and 3 (two sliced replicas). This way, no replicas of each fragment are placed in the same group and if Group 1 fails, the other groups will divide the corresponding data processing between them using the replicated fragments.

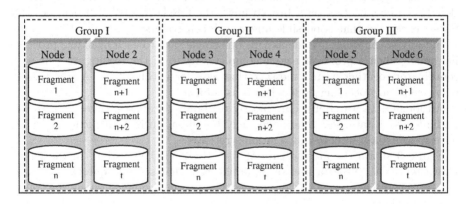

Fig. 2. Sample Group Configuration

This strategy can be adapted to the grid environment, where network conditions are highly unpredictable, with interesting solutions for efficient processing. Suppose we have a *GRID-NPDW* grid with nodes in four different locations: Lisbon, Paris, Madrid and London. In each location we may have several nodes. Consider that user's requests are made in Lisbon. It is more susceptible that a link from Lisbon to another location goes down (making all the nodes in this location offline for the Lisbon's server) then nodes within a single location.

This way, we propose the use of PRG in grids considering all the nodes in each geographical location as a group of nodes that should have its database sliced and replicated in other groups. But, due to grid's characteristics, some actions must be taken in order to achieve high levels of QoS, as it will be discussed in the next Sections.

4   Dynamic Architecture of the GRID-NPDW

NPDW is a data allocation strategy oriented for high performance on the execution of OLAP queries. But, as in grid's we do not have full control of the environment, which may have slow or broken network connections and may be highly heterogeneous, having different processor and memory capacities in each processing node, some dynamic policy must be used for load balancing.

We propose the use of an on-demand approach that distributes tasks (queries) to sites whenever these are available and idle. The PRG replication strategy used in GRID-NPDW implies that the system can assign the processing of a fragment to different nodes that already have the fragment, as every fragment is replicated into more than one node.

A task manager is responsible for assigning new tasks to nodes that are idle and ready to execute. A task is composed by a query to be executed and the identifier of the data group (table fragments on which the query should be executed). No task is pre-assigned to a node: if it happens that a given node is available or ready to execute another task, the system assigns a new task to it. This approach aims at allocating tasks dynamically and in a preventive manner. With this strategy, when some network connection is down or too slow (e.g. a slow backup connection on a broken link), the GRID-NPDW still provides the fastest execution that is possible under such constraints.

Initially, a *coordinator* node assigns one single task to each available processing node. When a processing node completes its task, the results are sent to a coordinator together with a message that asks for another task. A new task is only sent to a processing node when it asks for it.

Although data warehouses are mostly read-only databases, there are also periodic loads of data. As some nodes may be offline during data load, we must have specific data update propagation strategies.

Figure 3 shows the architecture of the GRID-NPDW system. In the figure *Client* represents either a user or an application that submits queries against a data warehouse and waits for an answer. The grid environment should be transparent to the *Client*. It always interacts with a *Coordinator node*. *Execution Manager* is the *Coordinator node's* component responsible for communication with clients, accepting requests and sending queries' answers to clients. *Task Manager* is the component responsible for sending tasks to computing nodes. *Task Manager* makes the necessary changes in clients' queries (i.e. adding subqueries) and sends the changed query and the indication of the fragment number on which the query should be executed to computing nodes. The *Task Manager* should know which computing node has each data fragment and replica, and if nodes' data is up to date or may be used in query execution according to QoS requirements. The information about data allocation and data freshness in each node is stored in a *Meta-Base*. Residing at each processing node is a *Processing Agent* (software agent), which is responsible for any processing node's related operations. These include the communications with the *Task Manager* and data manipulation (i.e. data replication). The *Data manager* is the *Coordinator Node's*

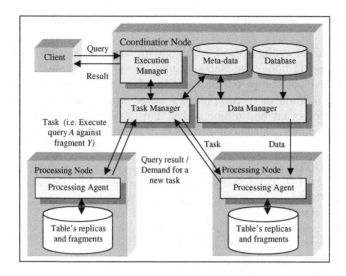

Fig. 3. Architecture of GRID-NPDW

component responsible to interact with processing nodes in order to control data allocation and replication (according to PRG).

5 Experimental Results

In this section we first present experimental results designed to test the efficient availability features of the GRID-NPDW system. Then, we show some results obtained on the use of the proposed dynamic load balancing policy.

Our experimental setup is composed of a master site, located in Rio de Janeiro, Brazil, and two execution sites, with 10 homogeneous processing nodes each, located at University of Coimbra, in Portugal. The schema and query 1 of the TPC-H benchmark is used in the experiments over an Oracle database engine. We have used a 25Gb database where tables *lineitem* and *orders* were sliced in 100 fragments.

First of all, we have tested the use of PRG for efficient availability. The number of fragments that each node needs to process depends on the number of unavailable sites. We have distributed the 100 fragments for execution in different configurations, testing both Full Replication and PRG in each configuration. Depending on the number of sites that are unavailable, we measure the actual execution time of the node considering that it has to process its own data plus replica fragments from unavailable site(s).

With all nodes online, each node has processed 5 fragments. Then, we have taken 2 nodes of each site offline. In this situation, using Full Replication, there are four nodes (two at each site) that will process 10 table fragments each, while other nodes will process 5 fragments each. Using PRG, four nodes (two at each site) will process 7 table fragments each, while other nodes will process 6 fragments each. The elapsed time [1] (min:secs) for each configuration is shown in Figure 4.

In the 20 nodes configuration, although we have the same number of tasks for each processing node, the elapsed times for each processing nodes are very different: node 1 has completed its tasks in 3.5 minutes while node 18 has consumed almost 7 minutes to complete its tasks. Similar skews have occurred in the configurations that had offline nodes. This leads to the needs of a dynamic load balancing policy, as the one proposed in the previous section.

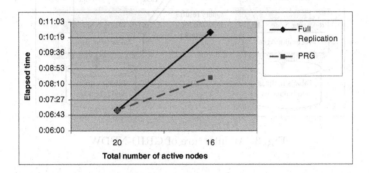

Fig. 4. NPDW-GRID with pre-determined number of tasks per node

We have tested the proposed policy using 10, 16 and 20 nodes. It has achieved good results. In Figure 5 we show execution time for each node in the 16 nodes configuration, considering Full Replication (FR), PRG and the demand driven policy (DD). In that Figure, the total execution time of each strategy is approximately the execution time of the slowest node (nodes 7 and 8). This means that FR took about (10 : 34), PRG took about (8 : 28) and DD took about (6 : 56) (i.e. DD's execution time was about only 65% of FR's execution time and about 82% of PRG's execution time).

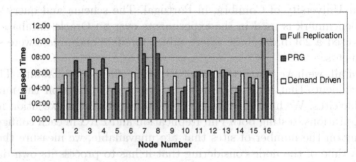

Fig. 5. Total execution time per node - 16 node configuration

The demand driven approach has lead to good results as it does not pre-assign tasks to nodes. In Figure 6 the number of tasks per node for the 16-node

---

[1] Execution time of the slowest active node

configuration is showed, considering Full Replication, PRG and the demand-driven policy. As showed in Figure 6, the demand driven approach has assigned different number of tasks for each node. The Figure shows the effect of the Demand Driven allocation of tasks, as the nodes that would end sooner under FR and PGR (e.g. node 1) execute more tasks under DD to balance the load, while on the other hand, the slowest nodes (nodes 7 and 8) execute less tasks in DD so that they do not slow the whole system as much.

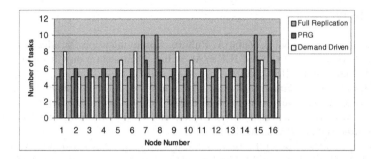

Fig. 6. Tasks per node - 16 node configuration

In fact, using Full Replication, as soon as a single node becomes unavailable, the whole system takes somewhere near to twice the time to answer a query, even though only a single node is delaying the whole system. On the other hand, the results also show that only by using PRG setup in grid environments could not always lead to the best results, not only because the nodes could have different processing powers but also because some skews (e.g. data and communication) may occur. The results have showed that the proposed architecture, including the dynamic load-balancing policy, could lead to good results when being used in the grid environment.

6   Conclusions and Future Work

In this paper we have proposed an efficient architecture for deploying and processing large data warehouses over a grid (GRID-NPDW). We focused mostly on data infrastructure, comprising fragmentation and replication into the grid, and dynamic processing over that infrastructure.

Considering grid's specifics characteristics, such as heterogeneous node processor capacities and unpredictable network conditions, we have adapted the partitioning and replication approach of a Node Partitioned Data Warehouse parallel architecture (NPDW) to the grid environment. By slicing and grouping replicas around grid sites and proposing a dynamic allocation of tasks into processing nodes, the strategy is able to deliver maximum efficiency in heterogeneous grids even when entire sites are unreachable or the link to those sites is too slow (e.g. slower backup connection).

Our experimental results focus on the efficient availability and load balancing issues, to show that dynamic policies are necessary and that the system performance could be increased with an on-demand load balancing policy.

Our future work focuses on the data freshness features, considering how data fragmentation and replication could be done automatically in grid environment, where some nodes could be temporarily offline. The future work also includes expanding the architecture to take care of users' specific QoS parameters.

References

1. D. Bruneo, M. Scarpa, A. Zaia, A. Puliato: Communication Paradigms for Mobile Grid Users, Procs. of the 3rd IEEE/ACM Intl. Symposium on Cluster Computing and the Grid (CCGRID), 2003
2. W. H. Bell, D. G. Cameron, R. Carvajal-Schiaffino, A. P. Millar, K. Stockinger, F. Zini: Evaluation of an Economy-Based File Replication Strategy for a Data Grid, In Intl. Workshop on Agent based Cluster and Grid Computing at CCGrid, IEEE Computer Society Press, 2003
3. E. Baralis, S. Paraboschi, E. Teniente: Materialzed View Selection in a Multidimensional Database. Proc. of 23rd Intl. Conf. on Very Large Databases (VLDB), 1997
4. S. Chaudhuri, U. Dayal: An Overview of Data Warehousing and OLAP Technology, SIGMOD Record 26(1), 1997.
5. A.L . Corte, A. Puliato, and O. Tomarchio: An agent-based framework for mobile users, in ERSADS'99, 1999.
6. J. Cao, D. P. Spooner, S. A. Jarvis, G. R. Nudd: Grid Load Balancing Using Intelligent Agents Future Generation Computer Systems special issue on Intelligent Grid Environments: Principles and Applications, 21(1) pp.135-149, 2005
7. DeWitt, D., et. al.: The Gamma Database Machine Project, IEEE Knowledge and Data Engineering, Vol. 2, No. 1, March, 1990.
8. D. J. DeWitt, Jim Gray, "Parallel Database Systems: The Future of High Performance Database Processing", Communications of the ACM, 1992.
9. M. Dobbera, G. Koolea, R. van der Mei: Dynamic Load Balancing Experiments in a Grid, Proc. of the 5th IEEE/ACM Intl. Symposium on Cluster Computing and the Grid (CCGrid 2005), 2005
10. D.J.DeWitt, J.F. Naughton, D.A.Schneider, S.Seshadri: Pratical Skew Handling in Parallel Joins, Proc. of 18ht Intl. Conf. on Very Large Databases (VLDB), pp.27-40, 1992
11. D.W.Erwin and D.F. Snelling: UNICORE: A Grid computing environment, Lecture Notes in Computer Science, vol.2150, 2001
12. I.Foster: The anatomy of the Grid: Enabling scalable virtual organizations, Concurrency and Computation: Practice and Experience, vol.13, 2001
13. P. Furtado: Workload-based Placement and Join Processing in Node-Partitioned Data Warehouses, in Intl. Conf. on Data Warehousing and Knownledge Discovery (Dawak), 2004.
14. P. Furtado: Experimental Evidence on Partitioning in Parallel Data Warehouses, Procs of the 7th ACM Intl. Workshop on Data Warehousing and OLAP (DOLAP), 2004
15. P. Furtado: Replication in Node Partitioned Data Warehouses, in VLDB Workshop on Design, Implementation, and Deployment of Database Replication (DIDDR), 2005

16. J. Gray et al: Data Cube: A Relational Aggregation Operator Generalizing Group-By, Cross-Tab and Sub-Totals. In: Data-Mining and Knowledge Discovery, 1997
17. K.A.Hua, H.C.Young: Desining a Highly Parallel Database Server Using Off-the-shelf Components, Procs. of the Int'l Computer Symposium, pp.47-54, 1990
18. H.Lu, K.Tan: Load-Balanced Join Processing in Shared-Nothing Systems, Journal of Parallel and Distributed Computing, 23, pp.382-398, 1994
19. H. MSrtens, E. Rahm, T. Sthr: Dynamic Query Scheduling in Parallel Data Warehouses, Procs of the 8th Intl. Euro-Par Conf. on Parallel Proc., pp.321 - 331, 2002
20. W. H. Min, W. Y. Wilson, Y. H. Ngi, W. Donghong, L. Zhixiang, L. K. Hong, Y. K. L.: Dynamic Storage Resource Management Framework for the Grid, Procs. of the 22nd IEEE/13th NASA Goddard Conf. on Mass Storage Systems and Technologies (MSST), 2005
21. M. A. Nieto-Santisteban, J. Gray, A. S. Szalay, J. Annis, A. R. Thakar, W. O'Mullane, When Database Systems Meet the Grid, Second Biennial Conf. on Innovative Data Systems Research (CIDR), Online Proceedings pp.154-161, 2005
22. P. O'Neil, G. Graefe: Multi-Table Joins Throug Bitmapped Join Indices, ACM SIGMOD Record 23(4), 1995
23. P. O'Neil, D. Quass: Improved Query Performance With Variant Indexes, Proc. of ACM SIGMOD Conf., 1995
24. M. Poess, R. K. Othayoth: Large Scale Data Warehouses on Grid: Oracle Database 10g and HP ProLiant Servers, Proc. of the 31st Intl. Conf. on Very Large Databases (VLDB), pp 1055-1066, 2005.
25. O. F. Rana, L. Moreau: Issues in Building Agent based Computational Grids, In Third Workshop of the UK Special Interest Group on Multi-Agent Systems (UKMAS'2000), 2000.
26. P. Watson: Databases in Grid Applications: Locality and Distribution, Proc. of the 22nd British National Conf. on Databases, BNCOD, LNCS 3567 pp. 1-16, 2005
27. T. Sthr, H. MSrtens, E. Rahm: Multi-Dimensional Database Allocation for Parallel Data Warehouses, Procs. of the 26th Intl. Conf. on Very Large Databases (VLDB), pp 273-284, 2000.
28. A. Shoshani, A. Sim, K. Stockinger: RRS: Replica Registration Service for Data Grids, VLDB Workshop on Data Management in Grids, 2005
29. J. smith, P. Watson, A. Gounaris, N. W. Paton, A. Fernandes, R. Sakellariou: Distributed Query Processing on the Grid, Intl. Journal of High Performance Computing Applications 17, pp.353-367, 2003
30. J. White, D. R. Thompson: Load Balancing on a Grid Using Data Characteristics, Proc. Int'l Conf. Grid Computing and Applications (GCA), pp. 184-188, 2005.
31. Zhou S., M.H. Williams: Data placement in parallel database systems, Parallel Database Techniques, IEEE Computer Society Press, 1997.

Mining Direct Marketing Data by Ensembles of Weak Learners and Rough Set Methods

Jerzy Błaszczyński[1], Krzysztof Dembczyński[1], Wojciech Kotłowski[1], and Mariusz Pawłowski[2]

[1] Institute of Computing Science, Poznań University of Technology,
60-965 Poznań, Poland
{jblaszczynski, kdembczynski, wkotlowski}@cs.put.poznan.pl
[2] Acxiom Polska, 02-672 Warszawa, Poland
mariusz.pawlowski@acxiom.com

Abstract. This paper describes problem of prediction that is based on direct marketing data coming from Nationwide Products and Services Questionnaire (NPSQ) prepared by Polish division of Acxiom Corporation. The problem that we analyze is stated as prediction of accessibility to Internet. Unit of the analysis corresponds to a group of individuals in certain age category living in a certain building located in Poland. We used several machine learning methods to build our prediction models. Particularly, we applied ensembles of weak learners and ModLEM algorithm that is based on rough set approach. Comparison of results generated by these methods is included in the paper. We also report some of problems that we encountered during the analysis.

1 Introduction

Direct marketing is one of the most popular form of promotion and selling. It is attractive, because its effectiveness can be measured, for example, by responses of customers to the promotion. Database of profiled customers is an important element in this type of marketing. From this database, one can select customers that with high probability will response to the promotion. To perform such a selection of customers one needs a prediction model. This model is derived from a sample of customers that are relatively well-known, for example, customers that fulfilled a special type of a questionnaire. Only attributes that are easily achieved for out-of-sample customers are used as predictors in the model. Acxiom is a company which aims in direct marketing technologies and is focused on integration data, services and technology to create innovative solutions that improve customer relationships. The mission of the company is to transform data collected from different sources (such as questionnaires, official registries) into marketing, actionable information, which helps to understand customer preferences, predict their behavior and increase effectiveness of direct marketing campaigns.

The problem considered in this paper consists in prediction of accessibility to Internet. Unit of the analysis corresponds to a group of individuals in certain age category living in a certain building located in Poland. The information

A Min Tjoa and J. Trujillo (Eds.): DaWaK 2006, LNCS 4081, pp. 218–227, 2006.

about access to Internet comes from Nationwide Products and Services Questionnaire (NPSQ) prepared by Polish division of Acxiom Corporation. Predictors are taken from different databases coming from Acxiom and official registries that we further describe in Section 2. From the business perspecitive, the most important factors indicating quality of constructed prediction models are precision and true positive ratios. The preliminary analysis has shown that the problem is hard and any small improvement of these ratios in comparison to the random classifier that takes into account distribution of classes will be acceptable.

We have used several machine learning methods to build our prediction models. Particularly, we have applied algorithms constructing ensembles of weak learners and ModLEM rule induction algorithm that is based on rough set approach. Ensembles of weak learners, sometimes called decision committees, have been successfully used to many real-world problems. Some of these methods are treated today as off-the-shelf methods-of-choice. Rough set approach has also proved to be a useful tool for solving classification problems. It allows to determine inconsistencies between analyzed objects (such as we have found in the analyzed database) and functional dependencies between subsets of attributes. Comparison of models built using these methods is included in the paper. First results of our analysis were very promising. However, due to a mistake made in the preparation of data, these results were overestimated. Results that we obtained on the fixed data are worse, but still acceptable.

The paper is organized as follows. In Section 2, the problem is formulated from business and machine learning perspectives. Data sources and project database schema is also described there. Section 3 includes general description of prediction methods used in the analysis. In Section 4, we describe problems faced during the analysis and show results of predictions. The last section concludes the paper.

2   Problem Statement

Acxiom in Poland collects data from many different sources, aggregated on different levels: individual person, household, building, statistical region, community. Since 1999 Acxiom is continuously running nationwide survey collecting information thru over 100 questions about lifestyle, shopping behavior, product and services preferences and also demographic profile of households and individuals. Survey database (NPSQ) consist of over 2.2 million household and is the biggest and the most comprehensive database of this kind. Even thou, this database cover only about 15% of all households in Poland. The challenge at this point is how to generate precise information about rest of the population. Collecting data thru survey would take long time, a lot of money with no guaranty that this project will ever succeed. One of the solutions is to look at the data available on market, integrate and analyze it and transform into information we are looking for. In the project described in this paper following data sources has been used:

- Database of buildings from registry of inhabitants (PESEL), which consist of data about over 5 millions of buildings in Poland with information of number of flats, inhabitants, age and sex structure,
- Database of statistical regions with demographic data (Acxiom),
- Regional Data Bank with information aggregated on community level including wide range of information about local markets (GUS BDR).

Aim of the project was to "translate" information from survey to the lowest possible level of aggregation based on data from sources listed above. The first step in this project was to define the most precise unit of analysis. Having data from PESEL database with age structure assigned to each building we decided to define unit of analysis as an age category within each building. This definition is the closest level of data aggregation to the level of individual person and thus allows describing individuals in the most precise way. This definition causes a simplification that each person, living under certain building in certain age brackets will be assigned the same characteristics mined out of all of the data sources used in this project. However, results of initial analysis shows that homogeneity of groups of individuals defined in this way is acceptable. We have assumed that the prediction model will be deterministic. It means that outputs of the model will indicate if a group of individuals in a certain age category living in a certain building has access to Internet or not. Alternatively, we could use a probabilistic model (i.e., in such a case outputs of the model will indicate distribution of access to Internet for the unit of analysis).

After defining basic unit of analysis the next task was to integrate all data sources. This process was simplified thanks to having complex reference database, which includes all relations between addresses, statistical regions and communities and also having the same standard of writing street names in PESEL and NPSQ database. Finally, after integration each record in PESEL database was assigned record id from NPSQ, Acxiom and GUS BDR databases. Combining databases thru joined id's allows building flat table including all data from all of the sources assigned to the final level of analysis.

The database used in the case study contains more than 200 000 records and totally 751 attributes (without counting key and auxiliary attributes). The database after integration process was transformed for analysis purposes to a model that is similar to star schema well-known in dimensional modelling. In our schema, fact table contains attributes taken from NPSQ database, dimensions are tables from PESEL, Acxiom and GUS BDR databases. The model is presented in Figure 1. Such a construction of the database improves performance and facilitates the analysis. For example, when we want to analyze impact of attributes from GUS BDR's dimension on accessibility to Internet, it is enough to join the fact table with this dimension, omitting all other data.

Let us define the prediction problem in the formal way. Concluding the above, the aim is to predict the unknown value of an attribute y (sometimes called *output, response variable* or *decision attribute*) that represents accessibility to Internet of individual person using the known joint values of other attributes (sometimes called *predictors, condition attributes* or *independent variables*)

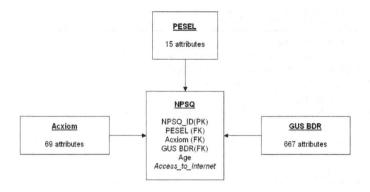

Fig. 1. Database schema used in case study

$\mathbf{x} = (x_1, x_2, \ldots, x_n)$. The goal of a learning task is to produce a function $F(\mathbf{x})$ from a set of training examples (or objects) $\{\mathbf{x_i}, y_i\}_1^N$ that predicts accurately y. Each training example corresponds to a responder of NPSQ, or, in other words, to a single record in NPSQ database. In the considered problem $y \in \{-1, 1\}$ indicates whether individual person has not or has access to Internet, respectively. In other words, all objects for which $y = -1$ constitute the decision class of individuals without Internet access, and all object for which $y = 1$ constitute the decision class of individuals with Internet access. These classes are denoted by Cl_{-1} and Cl_1, respectively. Condition attributes $\mathbf{x}$ refer, however, to the unit taken for the analysis, i.e., groups of individuals in a certain age category within certain building, because this information is easily achieved for individual persons that are not included in NPSQ database. The optimal classification procedure is given by:

$$F^*(\mathbf{x}) = \arg \min_{F(\mathbf{x})} E_{xy} L(y, F(\mathbf{x})) \tag{1}$$

where the expected value is over joint distribution of all attributes $(\mathbf{x}, y)$ for the data to be predicted. $L(y, F(\mathbf{x}))$ is loss or cost for predicting $F(\mathbf{x})$ when the actual value is y. The typical loss in classification tasks is:

$$L(y, F(\mathbf{x})) = \begin{cases} 0 & y = F(\mathbf{x}), \\ 1 & y \neq F(\mathbf{x}). \end{cases} \tag{2}$$

The learning procedure tries to construct $F(\mathbf{x})$ to be the best possible approximation of $F^*(\mathbf{x})$. The prediction model based on $F(\mathbf{x})$ is then applied to individual person described by attributes $\mathbf{x}$ referring, however, to certain age category within certain building to get information about her/his access to Internet.

3 Ensembles of Weak Learners and Rough Set Methods

To solve the defined problem we have used two types of algorithms: ensembles of weak learners (sometimes called decision committees) and rough set methods.

Algorithm 1. Ensemble of Weak Learners [4]

---

input : set of training examples $\{\mathbf{x}_i, y_i\}_1^N$
  M – number of weak learners to be generated.
output: ensemble of weak learners $\{f_m(\mathbf{x})\}_1^M$.
$F_0(\mathbf{x}) = \arg\min_{\alpha \in \Re} \sum_i^N L(y_i, \alpha)$;
for $m = 1$ *to* M **do**
  $\mathbf{p} = \arg\min_{\mathbf{p}} \sum_{i \in S_m(\eta)} L(y_i, F_{m-1}(\mathbf{x}_i) + f(\mathbf{x}_i, \mathbf{p}))$;
  $f_m(\mathbf{x}) = f(\mathbf{x}, \mathbf{p})$;
  $F_m(\mathbf{x}) = F_{m-1}(\mathbf{x}) + \nu \cdot f_m(\mathbf{x})$;
end
$ensemble = \{f_m(\mathbf{x})\}_1^M$;

The first algorithm forms an ensemble of subsidiary classifiers that are simple learning and classification procedures often referred to as weak learners. The ensemble members are applied to classification task and their individual outputs are then aggregated to one output of the whole ensemble. The aggregation is computed as a linear combination of outputs or a simple majority vote. The most popular methods that are used as weak learners are decision tree induction procedures, for example C4.5 [7] or CART [3]. There are several approaches to create ensembles of weak learners. The most popular are bagging [2] and boosting [9]. In [4], Friedman and Popescu have formulated a general schema of algorithm that can simulate these two approaches. The schema is presented as Algorithm 1. In this procedure, $L(y_i, F(\mathbf{x}_i))$ is a loss function, $f_m(\mathbf{x}_i, \mathbf{p})$ is the weak learner characterized by a set of parameters $\mathbf{p}$ and M is a number of weak learners to be generated. $S_m(\eta)$ represents a different subsample of size $\eta \leq N$ randomly drawn with or without replacement from the original training data. ν is so called "shrinkage" parameter, usually $0 \leq \nu \leq 1$. Values of ν determine the degree to which previously generated weak learners $f_k(\mathbf{x}, \mathbf{p})$, $k = 1..m$, effect the generation of a successive one in the sequence, i.e., $f_{m+1}(\mathbf{x}, \mathbf{p})$.

Classification procedure is performed according to:

$$F(\mathbf{x}) = sign(a_0 + \sum_{m=1}^{M} a_m f_m(\mathbf{x}, \mathbf{p})). \tag{3}$$

$F(\mathbf{x})$ is a linear classifier in a very high dimensional space of derived variables that are highly nonlinear functions of the original predictors $\mathbf{x}$. These functions are induced by weak learners, for example, they are decision trees. Parameters $\{a_m\}_0^M$ can be obtained in many ways. For example, they can be set to fixed values (for example, $a_0=0$ and $\{a_m = 1/M\}_1^M$), computed by some optimization techniques, fitted in cross-validation experiments or estimated in the process of constructing an ensemble (like in AdaBoost [9]).

According to Friedman and Popescu [4], bagging method [2] may be represented by Algorithm 1 and classification procedure (3) by setting $\nu = 0$, subsamples $S_m(\eta)$ are drawn randomly with replacement, where η is given by a user, $a_0 = 0$ and $\{a_m = 1/M\}_0^M$. AdaBoost uses exponential loss, $L(y, F(\mathbf{x})) = exp(-y \cdot F(\mathbf{x}))$, for $y \in \{-1, 1\}$, and corresponds to Algorithm 1 by setting $\nu = 1$ and $S_m(\eta)$ to be a whole set of training examples.

ModLEM [5] is a rule induction procedure that is based on rough set approach [6]. Decision rules are simple logical statements of a form: "*if* [conditions], *then* [decision]". The induction of rules in rough set approach consists of the two following phases: calculation of lower and upper approximations of decision classes, and induction of certain rules from lower approximations and possible rules from upper approximations. The first phase is useful to show inconsistencies in the data. Inconsistencies that we consider arise when objects with the same values of condition attributes are assigned to different decision classes. Lower approximation of a class is composed of all its objects that are consistent. Upper approximation holds also inconsistent objects. In the second phase, calculated approximations are used in rule induction process to obtain rules that represent certain knowledge (i.e., certain rules) and rules that represent possible knowledge (i.e., possible rules). In our problem, we expected that further insight into inconsistencies in groups of individuals that define units of analysis will allow us to obtain more precise classification results.

ModLEM is a specialized version of a general procedure that is known as *sequential covering*, very often used in rule induction systems. In fact, this procedure can be presented (see Algorithm 2) in a similar manner to Algorithm 1. One can remark on this basis that a set of decision rules may be then treated as an ensemble of decision rules that are very simple classifiers. Let us notice that Friedman and Popescu [4] has recently also developed a variant of Algorithm 1 that constructs an ensemble of decision rules. These rules are created in a specific way from a decision tree induced in each iteration of the algorithm. In sequential covering procedure, positive and negative examples are distinguished. Rules are built in such a way that they cover only positive examples. For certain rules assigning examples to a given class Cl_i, $i \in \{-1, 1\}$ positive examples are those from lower approximation of this class. Analogously, positive examples for possible rules are those from upper approximation of this class. A set of positive examples is denoted by $\hat{X}$. A rule parameterized by $\mathbf{c}$ is defined as:

$$f(\mathbf{x}, \mathbf{c}) = \begin{cases} 1 & \text{if } \mathbf{x} \text{ is covered by conditions } \mathbf{c} \text{ and rule assigns to } Cl_1, \\ 0 & \text{if } \mathbf{x} \text{ is not covered by conditions } \mathbf{c}, \\ -1 & \text{if } \mathbf{x} \text{ is covered by conditions } \mathbf{c} \text{ and rule assigns to } Cl_{-1}. \end{cases} \quad (4)$$

Loss function is defined as:

$$L(y, F_m(\mathbf{x})) = \begin{cases} 0 & y = sign(F_m(\mathbf{x})), \\ 1 & y \neq sign(F_m(\mathbf{x})). \end{cases} \quad (5)$$

Procedure of constructing a decision rule consists in a greedy heuristic that minimize $\sum_{i \in \hat{X}} L(y_i, F_m(\mathbf{x}_i) + f(\mathbf{x}_i, \mathbf{c}))$.

Classification procedure is performed according to a distance-based version of the bucket brigade algorithm [1]. The decision to which class the classified object is assigned depends on three factors: *strength* (*str*), *specificity* (*spe*) and *matching* (*mat*) factor. All those factors are computed for rule $f(\mathbf{x}, \mathbf{c})$. *Strength*

Algorithm 2. Sequential covering

> **input** : set of training examples $X = \{\mathbf{x}_i, y_i\}_1^N$
> set of positive examples $\hat{X} \subset X$.
> **output**: set of rules $\{f_m(\mathbf{x})\}_1^M$.
> $m = 1$;
> **while** $\sum_{i \in \hat{X}} L(y_i, f(\mathbf{x}_i, \mathbf{c})) \neq 0$ **do**
> $\quad\quad c = \arg\min_{\mathbf{c}} \sum_{i \in \hat{X}} L(y_i, F_m(\mathbf{x}_i) + f(\mathbf{x}_i, \mathbf{c}))$;
> $\quad\quad f_m(\mathbf{x}) = f(\mathbf{x}, \mathbf{c})$;
> $\quad\quad F_m(\mathbf{x}) = F_{m-1}(\mathbf{x}) + f_m(\mathbf{x})$;
> $\quad\quad m = m + 1$;
> **end**
> $M = m$; $rules = \{f_m(\mathbf{x})\}_1^M$;

is a total number of training examples classified correctly by the rule. *Specificity* is number of conditions of the rule. *Matching* factor reflects number of selectors of the rule matched by object x.

$$F(\mathbf{x}) = \arg\max_y \sum_{f(\mathbf{x}, \mathbf{c}) = y} str(f(\mathbf{x}, \mathbf{c})) \cdot spe(f(\mathbf{x}, \mathbf{c})) \cdot mat(f(\mathbf{x}, \mathbf{c})). \quad\quad (6)$$

For more detailed description of ModLEM algorithm refer to [5].

4 Problems Indicated and Experimental Results

The first problem, that we encountered, was the size of the database. It contained over 200 000 examples, described by 751 attributes. To succeed with our analysis we decreased the number of attributes using filter method based on information gain criterion [7]. We have sorted all attributes with respect to this criterion and chosen 139 attributes, for which the value of information gain was on acceptable level. Unfortunately, majority of attributes has this value very close to zero and the highest value was also very small, what shows that the problem is very hard. To make learning process more efficient, we decided to divide the database into smaller data bins. We have decided to split the database with respect to values of one of the attributes. The chosen attribute is "the number of individuals in a building" denoted as R later in this paper. We decided to use this attribute since we expected to obtain different prediction models, depending on the type of the building considered (e.g. family houses, blocks of flats, etc.). The database was then split into 21 bins of similar size, but with different consecutive values of R in each bin. To check impact of this type of splitting on the resulting models, we have also randomly splited the database into 20 bins of equal size. Then, we have compared accuracy of models resulting from these two splittings. The results of the comparison are presented later in the paper.

For purpose of our experiments, the database has been divided into two balanced sets. The one that is used to train and to validate prediction models. The second is a test set used in a final verification of built models. Computations

Table 1. First results obtained in the case study on test file

Classifier	Bagging with j48			ModLEM		
	Class	True positive	Precision	Class	True positive	Precision
	-1	0.843	0.868	-1	0.844	0.871
	1	0.463	0.409	1	0.451	0.4

were performed using Weka package [11] for ensembles methods and ROSE program [8] for ModLEM. The problem of prediction of accessibility to Internet is imbalanced. Only approximately 20% of NPSQ records indicate access to Internet. To deal with it, we have used CostSensitiveClassifier in each computations performed in Weka. ModLEM algorithm is less prone to imbalancement of data sets and it performed without cost sensitive adaptation.

From the business perspective, the most important factors indicating quality of models are precision and true positive ratios. They are defined for each decision class Cl as follows:

$$precision(Cl) = \frac{|\text{set of examples correctly classified to } Cl|}{|\text{set of all examples classified to } Cl|},$$

$$true\_positive(Cl) = \frac{|\text{set of examples correctly classified to } Cl|}{|\text{set of all examples from } Cl|},$$

where $|A|$ denotes a number of examples in set A.

To get the idea about improvement of constructed models, one can compare them to random classifier that takes into account distribution of classes. In our problem, where we have two decision classes, Cl_{-1} and Cl_1, it is easy to estimate the probability of error for such a random classifier. In our case 80% of examples belong to class Cl_{-1}, 20% to class Cl_1. Random algorithm would classify correctly 68% of objects (64% from class Cl_{-1} and 4% from class Cl_1). The precision in class Cl_1 would be 20%, and the true positive ratio would be also 20%, etc. While analyzing hard problems as it is in our case, we do not expect to get high improvement of precision and true positive ratios as compared to random classifier. Usually, even small improvements are acceptable. In our problem, we expected that improvement around 10 percent points would be a good result.

First experiments shown very promising results. We have obtained the best results on the test set using ModLEM algorithm and Bagging ($\eta = N$) with j48 that is Weka implementation of C4.5 [7]. These results are presented in Table 1. The parameters of j48 and ModLEM were fitted in cross-validation experiments, and it was striking for us that the best models were obtained using parameters that causes decision trees to be very detailed and high number of long decision rules. Unfortunately, the results presented in Table 1 are overestimated. It was caused by a mistake that we have made in preparation of data for the experiment. This mistake consists in presence of duplicated record in NPSQ. In some cases there were two records for a household for which there were no difference on condition and decision attributes. In many cases, one record from such a pair

Table 2. Revised results obtained in the case study

Classifier		Bagging with j48			AdaBoost with DS	
Type of split	Class	True positive	Precision	Class	True positive	Precision
Random	-1	0.596	0.852	-1	0.579	0.851
	1	0.582	0.262	1	0.59	0.258
by R	-1	0.595	0.855	-1	0.591	0.85
	1	0.591	0.265	1	0.577	0.258
for $R < 4$	-1	0.555	0.875	-1	0.556	0.875
	1	0.716	0.31	1	0.717	0.311
test set,	-1	0.574	0.846	-1	0.569	0.846
split by R	1	0.614	0.281	1	0.618	0.280
Classifier		Bagging with SVM			ModLEM	
Random	-1	0.591	0.855	-1	0.899	0.808
	1	0.593	0.265	1	0.141	0.259
by R	-1	0.597	0.858	-1	0.829	0.818
	1	0.599	0.268	1	0.235	0.248
for $R < 4$	-1	0.529	0.873	-1	0.869	0.797
	1	0.725	0.301	1	0.226	0.333
test set,	-1	0.574	0.848	-1	0.777	0.808
split by R	1	0.621	0.283	1	0.323	0.284

was placed in the training set, and other record from such a pair was placed in the test set. In total there were 17% of such redundant records.

Results on fixed data are much worse, but still acceptable. The algorithms that performed best are: bagging ($\eta = N$) with j48, bagging ($\eta = N/10$) with linear Support Vector Machines (SVM) [10], AdaBoost with decision stumps (DS) (i.e., one level decision trees). Results obtained by ModLEM are worse. We expect that it is caused by higher imbalance between decision classes and increased overall level of inconsistencies between examples for which R was high. We expect also that an approach to classification that is more focused on objects from areas of inconsistency that are detected by rough set approach will provide better results. Table 2 contains detailed results of experiments. These results come from 10-fold cross-validation for each bin, averaging these results over bins. In cross-validation experiments we have used two types of splitting. We present also results for the bin in which R is lower than 4. Finally, we present results on test set, where split by R was used.

We used t-test to check whether the constructed models increase significantly precision and true positive ratios. These tests shown that there are significant improvements between results of models as compared to results achieved by random classifier. When it comes to check, whether splitting with respect to R impacts accuracy of predicted models, there are almost no differences between this type of splitting and random split. Division with respect to R parameter does not influence considerably overall values of these factors. Let us underline that usage of this type of splitting gives further insight into the problem. For bins with small R, the results are better than for the whole data set. It is worth noting that in the case of data with duplicates, there was a large difference of model quality factors between these two types of splitting. This difference is in favor of models built on bins created with respect to R.

5 Conclusions

In this paper we have described project that concerns a real-world problem of mining direct marketing data. We have applied several machine learning methods to predict accessibility to Internet. When solving such problems one should be very careful at initial stages of preparing data for the experiment. Mistake that was made at this stage lead us to overestimation of obtained results. The results that we have obtained after correction of the prepared data are worse but still acceptable. The best results were obtained by application of ensembles of weak learners. There is slight advantage of bagging with linear SVM, where subsamples were of size $N/10$. In our opinion, the results of ModLEM can be improved if we apply more sophisticated strategy for objects from areas of inconsistency that are detected by rough set approach. It is included in our further research plans.

References

1. Booker, L. B., Goldberg, D. E., Holland, J. F.: Classifier systems and genetic algorithms. In Carbonell, J. G. (ed.): Machine Learning. Paradigms and Methods. Cambridge, MA: The MIT Press, (1990) 235–282
2. Breiman, L.: Bagging Predictors. Machine Learning 2 **24** (1996) 123-140
3. Breiman, L., Friedman, J. H., Olshen, R. A., Stone, C. J.: Classification and Regression Trees. Wadsworth (1984)
4. Friedman, J. H., Popescu, B. E.: Predictive Learning via Rule Ensembles. Research Report, Stanford University, `http://www-stat.stanford.edu/~jhf/` (last access: 1.06.2006), February (2005)
5. Grzymala-Busse, J. W., Stefanowski, J.: Three discretization methods for rule induction. International Journal of Intelligent Systems 1 **16** (2001) 29–38
6. Pawlak, Z.: Rough Sets. Theoretical Aspects of Reasoning about Data. Kluwer Academic Publishers, Dordrecht (1991)
7. Quinlan, J. R.: C4.5: Programs for Machine Learning, Morgan Kaufmann (1993)
8. Rough Sets Data Explorer (ROSE2), `http://idss.cs.put.poznan.pl/site/rose.html` (last access: 1.06.2006)
9. Schapire, R. E., Freund, Y., Bartlett, P, Lee, W. E.: Boosting the margin: A new explanation for the effectiveness of voting methods. The Annals of Statistics 5 **26** (1998) 1651–1686
10. Vapnik, V.: The Nature of Statistical Learning Theory. Springer-Verlag, New York (1995)
11. Witten, I., H., Frank, E.: Data Mining: Practical machine learning tools and techniques, 2nd Edition. Morgan Kaufmann, San Francisco (2005)

Efficient Mining of Dissociation Rules

Mikołaj Morzy

Institute of Computing Science
Poznań University of Technology
Piotrowo 2, 60-965 Poznań, Poland
Mikolaj.Morzy@put.poznan.pl

Abstract. Association rule mining is one of the most popular data mining techniques. Significant work has been done to extend the basic association rule framework to allow for mining rules with negation. Negative association rules indicate the presence of negative correlation between items and can reveal valuable knowledge about examined dataset. Unfortunately, the sparsity of the input data significantly reduces practical usability of negative association rules, even if additional pruning of discovered rules is performed. In this paper we introduce the concept of dissociation rules. Dissociation rules present a significant simplification over sophisticated negative association rule framework, while keeping the set of returned patterns concise and actionable. A new formulation of the problem allows us to present an efficient algorithm for mining dissociation rules. Experiments conducted on synthetic datasets prove the effectiveness of the proposed solution.

1 Introduction

Operational databases and enterprise data warehouses contain limitless volumes of data. Valuable knowledge is hidden in these data under the form of trends, regularities, correlations, and outliers. Traditional database and data warehouse querying models are not sufficient to extract this knowledge. The value of the data, as provided by traditional databases, can be greatly increased by adding the means to automatically discover useful knowledge from large volumes of gathered data. Data mining, a novel research discipline, aims at the discovery and extraction of useful, previously unknown, non-trivial, and ultimately understandable patterns from large databases and data warehouses [1]. Data mining uses methods from statistics, machine learning, artificial intelligence, databases, and other related disciplines to extract unknown, utilitarian, and interesting rules and regularities in order to assist users in informed decision making.

One of the most successful and widely used data mining techniques is association rule mining. Association rules [3] represent the patterns of co-occurrence of items in a large collection of sets. An example of an association rule is an expression of the form *'wine'* ∧ *'grapes'* ⇒ *'cheese'* ∧ *'white bread'*, which represents the fact that purchasing wine and grapes implies purchasing cheese and white bread in the same transaction. Association rules can be easily applied to

A Min Tjoa and J. Trujillo (Eds.): DaWaK 2006, LNCS 4081, pp. 228–237, 2006.

countless application domains. For instance, in market basket analysis the collection of sets corresponds to the database of customer transactions and each set corresponds to a set of products purchased by a customer during a single visit to the store. Discovered rules can be used for organizing cross-sales, designing mail catalogs, or reorganizing shelf layout.

Association rules capture only the "positive knowledge", i.e., sets of items comprising associations are always positively associated. One might be interested in discovering "negative knowledge" expressed as negative associations between items. An example of such pattern is an expression of the form *'FC Barcelona jersey'* $\Rightarrow \neg$ *'Real Madrid cap'* $\wedge \neg$ *'Real Madrid scarf'*, which represents the fact, that a customer who purchases an FC Barcelona jersey will almost never buy either a cap or a scarf with Real Madrid logo. Another type of a pattern conveying "negative knowledge" is an expression where only certain elements in the antecedent or consequent are negated. An example of such an expression is *'beer'* $\wedge$ *'sausage'* $\Rightarrow$ *'mustard'* $\wedge \neg$ *'red wine'* , which represents the fact, that transactions containing beer and sausages usually contain mustard and do not contain red wine. Negative associations can be successfully used in several application domains to identify conflicting or complementary sets of products.

Unfortunately, incorporating negation into association rule framework is very difficult. Due to the sparsity of data measured as the ratio of the average number of items per transaction to the total number of possible items, the number of possible association rules with negation is huge. Discovered patterns are valid, if they are useful and utilitarian. For association rules with negation the number of rules is unmanageable, thus not feasible in practice. This phenomenon can be easily explained as follows: in an average transaction, only a small fraction of items is present. At the same time, almost all possible items are not present in every transaction. Therefore, each transaction supports a huge number of patterns containing negation. Post-processing of association rules with negation and pruning coincidental rules is also a difficult and tedious task.

In our opinion, the main problem of previously proposed solutions is the complexity and the size of models, which effectively hinder the usefulness and practical applicability of these sophisticated models. In this paper we introduce a novel concept of dissociation rules. Our goal is to allow users to find negatively associated sets of items while keeping the number of discovered patterns low. We concentrate on such formulation of the problem, which results in a compact and usable set of patterns. By simplifying the model we sacrifice the abundance of discovered patterns for the simplicity and intelligibility of the result, making our model attractive for end users. Our main contribution includes the introduction of dissociation rules and the development of the DI-Apriori algorithm for mining dissociation rules. We conduct several experiments on synthetic datasets that compare our algorithm to a straightforward naive approach. The results of the experimental evaluation prove the feasibility of the presented proposal.

The paper is organized as follows. In Sect. 2 we review the related work on the subject. We present basic definitions used throughout the paper in Sect. 3. The naive approach and the DI-Apriori family of algorithms are presented in Sect. 4.

Section 5 contains the results of the experimental evaluation of the proposed solution. The paper concludes in Sect. 6 with the future work agenda.

2 Related Work

The first proposal to discover strong, exact, and approximate rules over the tuples contained in a relational table was formulated in [12]. The notion of association rule mining was introduced in [3]. In [4] the authors introduced the Apriori algorithm that quickly became the seed for many other algorithms for discovering frequent itemsets. The idea of mining "negative" information was first presented in [5] where the authors introduce the concept of excluding associations. They present a versatile method for finding associations of the form $A \wedge B \wedge \neg C \Rightarrow D$, where $A \wedge B \Rightarrow D$ does not hold due to insufficient confidence. Such a rule represents the fact that "A and B imply D when C does not occur". Their solution is to transform the database into a trie structure and extract both positive association rules and excluding association rules directly from the trie.

An algorithm for discovering strong negative association rules using taxonomy of domain knowledge was presented in [13]. This fundamental work introduced the concept of the interestingness of a rule measured in terms of the unexpectedness of the rule. A rule is unexpected if its support significantly deviates from the expected support. The authors propose to use the taxonomy of items along with the uniformity assumption to discover itemsets with support significantly lower than the expected support computed from the taxonomy. Another method for mining both positive and negative association rules is presented in [14]. The authors define a new measure for rule importance that combines support, confidence, and interestingness of a rule. Using this measure the authors introduce novel concepts of frequent and infrequent itemsets of potential interest that are used for mining positive and negative association rules.

An interesting algorithm for mining both positive and negative association rules is presented in [6]. The authors constrain themselves to finding confined negative association rules of the form $\neg X \Rightarrow Y$, $\neg X \Rightarrow \neg Y$, or $X \Rightarrow \neg Y$, where the entire antecedent or consequent is a conjunction of only negated or a conjunction of only non-negated terms. These rules are a subset of the generalized negative association rules, for which its antecedents or consequents can be expressed as a conjunction of negated or non-negated terms. The authors acknowledge that their approach is not general enough to capture all types of negative rules. However, limiting the algorithm to the discovery of confined negative association rules only allows the authors to develop an efficient method based on the correlation coefficient analysis.

The problem of mining generalized negative association rules has been attacked in [9]. Itemsets are divided into derivable and non-derivable based on the existence of certain rules (functional dependencies) in the dataset. The authors present an efficient method of concise representation of a huge number of patterns with negation using negative border and rule generators. Furthermore, an efficient algorithm for mining rules with negation is presented that uses variations of candidate itemsets and error counts of rules. Finally, [8] discusses inverse Apriori-like method for mining sporadic rules, which are rules with very low support and high confidence.

Somehow related to the negative association rule mining is the problem of discovering unexpected patterns [11]. The authors propose to use prior background knowledge acquired from domain experts to serve as a set of expectations and beliefs about the domain. They combine this prior knowledge with association rule mining algorithm to discover patterns that contradict expert expectations. Similar research on exception rules was conducted in [7,10]. Exception rules, sometimes also referred to as surprising patterns, represent an unexpected deviation from a well-established fact and allow negated terms to appear in patterns.

3   Basic Definitions

Let $L = \{l_1, l_2, \ldots, l_n\}$ be a set of literals called *items*. Let D be a database of variable-length transactions, and $\forall t_i \in D : t_i \subseteq L$. A transaction t_i supports an item x if $x \in t_i$. A transaction t_i supports an itemset X if $\forall x \in X : x \in t_i$. The *support* of an itemset X, denoted as $support_D(X)$, is the ratio of the number of transactions in D that support X to the total number of transactions in D. Given two itemsets $X, Y \subset L$, the support of the itemset $X \cup Y$ is called the *join* of X and Y. An itemset containing k items is called a *k-itemset*. An itemset with the support higher than the user-defined threshold *minsup* is called a *frequent itemset*. Let L_D denote the set of all frequent itemsets discovered in the database D. The *negative border* of the collection of frequent itemsets, denoted as $Bd^-(L_D)$, consists of minimal itemsets not contained in the collection of frequent itemsets. Formally, $Bd^-(L_D) = \{X : X \notin L_D \wedge \forall\, Y \subset X, Y \in L_D\}$.

Given user-defined thresholds of minimum support and maximum join, denoted as *minsup* and *maxjoin*, respectively, where *minsup* > *maxjoin*. An itemset Z is a *dissociation itemset*, if $support_D(Z) \leq maxjoin$ and Z can be divided into disjoint itemsets X,Y, such that $X \cup Y = Z$, $support_D(X) \geq minsup$, and $support_D(Y) \geq minsup$. Dissociation itemsets are used to generate dissociation rules. A dissociation rule is an expression of the form $X \not\Rightarrow Y$, where $X \subset L$, $Y \subset L$, and $X \cap Y = \emptyset$. Furthermore, $support_D(X \cup Y) \leq maxjoin$, $support_D(X) \geq minsup$, and $support_D(Y) \geq minsup$. X is called the antecedent of the rule and Y is called the consequent of the rule. A dissociation rule $X \not\Rightarrow Y$ represents the fact that, although items contained in X and items contained in Y often occur together when X and Y are considered separately, items contained in $X \cup Y$ occur together very rarely. A dissociation rule $X \not\Rightarrow Y$ is *minimal*, if $\nexists X' \subseteq X, Y' \subseteq Y$ such, that $X' \not\Rightarrow Y'$ is a valid dissociation rule.

Three statistical measures are used to describe the statistical significance and strength of the rule. The *support* of the rule $X \not\Rightarrow Y$ is the smaller ratio of the number of transactions that support either the antecedent or the consequent of the rule to the total number of transactions.

$$support_D(X \not\Rightarrow Y) = \min\{support_D(X), support_D(Y)\}$$

We decide to redefine the notion of rule support purposely. The support of the rule is used mainly for post-processing of discovered rules to select rules of interest. In this case, users are likely to be interested in selecting rules that pertain to statistically significant itemsets contained in either the antecedent or the consequent of the rule. The *join* of the rule is used to measure the quality of the rule expressed as the rarity of the rule,

$$join_D (X \nRightarrow Y) = support_D(X \cup Y)$$

Again, we choose to use the term *join* for the measure known as the support of the rule in traditional association rule mining. We decide to do so in order to avoid confusion, as the relative importance of a rule increases with the increase of the traditional support of the rule, whereas in the case of dissociation rules the most important rules are the ones with very low values of the join measure.

The confidence of the rule $X \nRightarrow Y$ is the ratio of the number of transactions that support the antecedent and do not support the consequent of the rule to the number of transactions that support the antecedent of the rule.

$$confidence_D (X \nRightarrow Y) = \frac{support_D (X) - support_D(X \cup Y)}{support_D (X)} =$$
$$= 1 - \frac{join_D (X \nRightarrow Y)}{support_D (X)}$$

The problem of discovering dissociation rules can be formulated as follows. Given a database D and thresholds of minimum support, confidence, and maximum join, called *minsup*, *minconf*, and *maxjoin*, respectively. Find all dissociation rules valid in the database D with respect to the above mentioned thresholds. The thresholds are used in the following way. The *minsup* is used to select statistically significant itemsets for antecedents and consequent of generated rules. The *maxjoin* threshold provides an upper limit of how often the elements constituting the antecedent and the consequent of the rule are allowed to appear together in the database D. Finally, the *minconf* threshold is used only for the post-processing of rules and selecting the strongest rules. Note that given the values of *minsup* and *maxjoin*, the confidence of each generated dissociation rule has a lower bound $confidence_D = (1 - maxjoin/minsup)$.

4   Algorithm

The generation of dissociation rules is based on the following lemmas.

Lemma 1. *Let L_D denote the set of all frequent itemsets discovered in the database D. If $X \nRightarrow Y$ is a valid dissociation rule, then $(X \cup Y) \notin L_D$.*

Lemma 1 is trivial. $X \nRightarrow Y$ implies that $support_D (X \cup Y) \leq maxjoin \leq minsup$, from which follows that $(X \cup Y) \notin L_D$.

Lemma 2. *If* $X \nRightarrow Y$ *is a valid dissociation rule, then* $\forall X' \supseteq X, Y' \supseteq Y$ *such, that* $X' \in L_D \wedge Y' \in L_D$, $X' \nRightarrow Y'$ *is a valid dissociation rule.*

From the fact that $X' \supseteq X$ and $Y' \supseteq Y$ follows that $support_D (X' \cup Y') \leq support_D (X \cup Y)$. Because $support_D (X \cup Y) \leq maxjoin$ and both X' and Y' are frequent, $X' \nRightarrow Y'$ is a dissociation rule.

Lemma 3. $\forall X, Y$ *such, that* $X \nRightarrow Y$ *is a valid dissociation rule, there exists* $Z \in Bd^- (L_D)$ *such, that* $(X \cup Y) \supseteq Z$.

From the definition of the negative border follows that, for each set X, either X is frequent, or X belongs to the negative border, or one of its proper subsets belongs to the negative border. Since $X \nRightarrow Y$ is a valid dissociation rule, either $(X \cup Y) \in Bd^- (L_D)$ (and all its proper subsets are frequent), or $(X \cup Y) \notin Bd^- (L_D)$ and it has a proper subset in $Bd^- (L_D)$. Otherwise, $(X \cup Y)$ would have to be frequent and $X \nRightarrow Y$ would not be a valid dissociation rule. Lemma 3 is particularly important, because it allows to find all dissociation rules by exploring and extending the negative border of the collection of frequent itemsets.

Similarly to traditional association rule mining, the problem of mining dissociation rules can be divided into two subproblems. The first problem consists in discovering all dissociation itemsets, given thresholds of *minsup* and *maxjoin*. The second problem consists in using discovered dissociation itemsets to generate dissociation rules. The naive approach to generating dissociation rules is the following. First, all frequent itemsets are discovered using the Apriori algorithm [4]. Next, all possible pairs of frequent itemsets are joined to generate candidate dissociation itemsets. Candidate dissociation itemsets that are contained in L_D are pruned based on Lemma 1. Actual support counts of candidate dissociation itemsets are found during a full database scan. This approach is highly ineffective. The number of candidate dissociation itemsets can be large, especially for low values of *minsup* threshold. Pruning performed based on Lemma 1 does not eliminate many candidate dissociation itemsets and many candidates are unnecessarily verified. However, the advantage of the naive algorithm is exactly one database scan to determine all valid dissociation itemsets and dissociation rules.

In order to efficiently discover dissociation rules, we propose the following procedure. We conclude from Lemma 2 that it is sufficient to discover only minimal dissociation rules. All remaining dissociation rules can be generated by extending antecedents and consequents of minimal dissociation rules with frequent supersets. Therefore, we reduce the problem of mining dissociation rules to the problem of mining minimal dissociation rules. We use Lemma 3 to limit the search space of candidate dissociation itemsets to supersets of sets contained in the negative border of the collection of frequent itemsets. Indeed, each set contained in the negative border $Bd^- (L_D)$ is either a candidate dissociation itemset, or is the seed set for a candidate dissociation itemset. Let us assume that the set $\{m, n, o\}$ is contained in the negative border $Bd^- (L_D)$. If $support_D (\{m, n, o\}) \geq maxjoin$, then $\{m, n, o\}$ is extended with all frequent

1-itemsets $\{p_i\}$, such that $\{p_i\} \cup \{m, n, o\}$ can be divided into two disjoint frequent itemsets. Let L_D^1 denote the set of all frequent 1-itemsets. Let $C_{\not\Rightarrow}$ denote the set of pairs of frequent itemsets that are candidates for joining into a dissociation itemset, and let $D_{\not\Rightarrow}$ denote the set of pairs of frequent itemsets that form valid dissociation itemsets. The outline of the DI-Apriori algorithm is presented in Figure 1.

Require: L_D, the collection of all frequent itemsets
Require: L_D^1, the collection of all frequent 1-itemsets
 1: $D_{\not\Rightarrow} = \{(X, Y) : \{X \cup Y\} \in Bd^-(L_D) \wedge (X, Y).support \leq maxjoin$
 2: $C_{\not\Rightarrow} = \{(X, Y) : \{X \cup Y\} \in Bd^-(L_D) \wedge (X, Y) \notin D_{\not\Rightarrow}\}$
 3: **while** $C_{\not\Rightarrow}$ grows **do**
 4:     **for all** $(X, Y) \in C_{\not\Rightarrow}$ **do**
 5:         **for all** $l \in L_D^1$ **do**
 6:             **if** $\{X \cup l\} \in L_D \wedge \{Y \cup l\} \in L_D \wedge \{X \cup Y \cup l\} \notin L_D$ **then**
 7:                 $C_{\not\Rightarrow} = C_{\not\Rightarrow} \cup \{X \cup Y \cup l\}$
 8:             **end if**
 9:         **end for**
10:     **end for**
11:     **for all** $(X, Y) \in C_{\not\Rightarrow}$ **do**
12:         compute $support_D(X \cup Y)$
13:     **end for**
14: **end while**
15: $D_{\not\Rightarrow} = \{(X, Y) \in C_{\not\Rightarrow} : (X, Y).support \leq maxjoin\}$
16: **for all** $(X, Y) \in D_{\not\Rightarrow}$ **do**
17:     **for all** $X' \in L_D : X' \supseteq X$, $Y' \in L_D : Y' \supseteq Y$ **do**
18:         $D_{\not\Rightarrow} = D_{\not\Rightarrow} \cup \{(X', Y')\}$
19:     **end for**
20: **end for**
21: **for all** $(X', Y') \in D_{\not\Rightarrow}$ for which the support is unknown **do**
22:     compute $support_D(X' \cup Y')$
23: **end for**
24: **for all** $(X, Y) \in D_{\not\Rightarrow}$ **do**
25:     **if** $1 - \frac{support_D(X \cup Y)}{support_D(X)} \geq minconf$ **then**
26:         output $X \not\Rightarrow Y$
27:     **else if** $1 - \frac{support_D(X \cup Y)}{support_D(Y)} \geq minconf$ **then**
28:         output $Y \not\Rightarrow X$
29:     **end if**
30: **end for**

Fig. 1. DI-Apriori

The DI-Apriori algorithm proceeds as follows. First, the negative border is examined and all itemsets with support less than *maxjoin* are added to the set of valid dissociation itemsets. The remaining itemsets in the negative border form the seed set of candidate dissociation itemsets. While the collection of candidate dissociation itemsets grows, we repeat the following steps. Each candidate dissociation itemset is extended with frequent 1-itemsets that allow to split the candidate dissociation itemset into a frequent antecedent and consequent. All candidates are verified during a single database pass and their support counts are determined. Candidate dissociation itemsets with support lower than *maxjoin* are added to the set of valid dissociation itemsets. Discovered minimal dissociation itemsets are used to generate the remaining dissociation itemsets by replacing antecedents and consequents by their frequent supersets (lines 16–20). Also, the join measure for newly created dissociation itemsets is computed (lines 21–23). Finally, all dissociation itemsets are used to produce dissociation rules with respect to the provided *minconf* threshold.

Our implementation of the DI-Apriori algorithm uses a specialized physical data structure, the DI-tree. DI-tree is a lattice of dissociation itemsets, where each node of the lattice corresponds to a single dissociation itemset (either candidate or valid). DI-tree structure is optimized for fast lookup of dissociation itemsets and their components. On the physical level we have devised two modifications to the original method of the DI-tree traversal (these modifications are dubbed DI*-Apriori and DI⁻-Apriori, we do not describe them in detail due to the lack of space). The main advantage of DI-Apriori is the fact that the number of generated candidate dissociation itemsets is significantly smaller than when using the naive approach. Table 1 summarizes the number of frequent and candidate itemsets processed during the invocation of the naive algorithm in comparison with the number of itemsets tested by the DI-Apriori. The drawback of DI-Apriori is the fact that several database scans are required to compute the supports of dissociation itemsets. We present the results of the experimental evaluation of the proposed algorithm in the next section.

Table 1. Number of itemsets processed by Basic Apriori vs. DI-Apriori

		Basic Apriori		DI-Apriori
minsup	*maxjoin*	frequent itemsets	candidate itemsets	
5%	1%	83	396	264
4%	1%	214	2496	1494
3%	1%	655	16848	4971

5   Experimental Results

All experiments have been conducted on synthetic datasets generated using the generator from IBM's Quest Project [2]. Experiments presented in this section use a dataset consisting of 20 000 transactions with an average size of 10 items, the *minsup* threshold is set to 5%, the number of patterns built into the dataset is 300 with an average size of 4 items. The *maxjoin* threshold is set to 3% if not stated otherwise. Figure 2 presents the number of dissociation rules and the number of frequent itemsets discovered when varying the *minsup* threshold. In this experiment the *maxjoin* threshold is always kept 4% below the *minsup* threshold. We can see a strong correspondence between the number of dissociation rules and frequent itemsets (note the logarithmic scale on the y-axis).

The execution time of algorithms when varying the average length of transactions is depicted in Figure 3. We do not observe any significant differences in the execution times of variations of DI-Apriori. Furthermore, all variations of DI-Apriori outperform the naive algorithm (again, note the logarithmic scale on the y-axis). Figure 4 shows the scaling capabilities of DI-Apriori. We are glad to notice that the algorithm scales almost linearly with the size of the database. Finally, Figure 5 presents the execution time relative to the difference between *minsup* and *maxjoin* thresholds. Obviously, the execution time of the naive algorithm does not depend on this parameter. The DI-Apriori algorithms perform slightly better for larger gaps between *minsup* and *maxjoin* thresholds, but the difference in execution times is not significant. We attribute this behavior to the fact that for larger gaps between *minsup* and *maxjoin* thresholds, although the number of dissociation itemsets drops, the number of intermediate itemsets (itemsets that are neither frequent nor rare) increases, thus keeping the size of the DI-tree structure approximately constant.

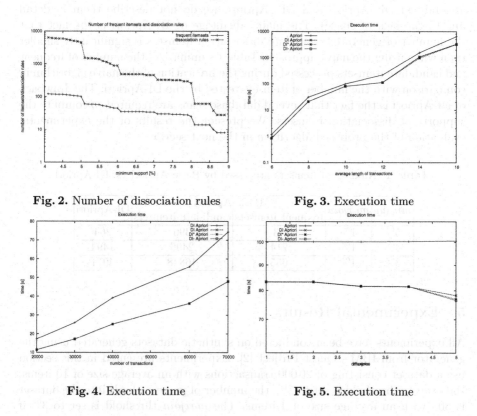

Fig. 2. Number of dissociation rules   **Fig. 3.** Execution time

Fig. 4. Execution time   **Fig. 5.** Execution time

6 Conclusions

This paper initiates the research on dissociation rules. It is a simple model that successfully captures the "negative knowledge" hidden in the data, while keeping the number of discovered patterns low. Main advantages of the proposal are the simplicity, practical feasibility, and usability of the model. Our future work agenda includes further investigation of the properties of the model. One of the most urgent research directions is an experimental comparison of dissociation rules with other types of "negative" association rule models presented in Sect. 2. We are also eager to see how dissociation rules behave on real-world market basket datasets. Finally, we plan to refine the algorithm to scale to very large databases and we intend to develop concise and compact representations for collections of discovered dissociation rules.

References

1. *Advances in Knowledge Discovery and Data Mining.* AAAI/MIT Press, 1996.
2. R. Agrawal, M. J. Carey, and C. F. et al. Quest: A project on database mining. In *Proceedings of the 1994 ACM SIGMOD International Conference on Management of Data, Minneapolis, Minnesota, May 24-27, 1994*, page 514. ACM Press, 1994.
3. R. Agrawal, T. Imielinski, and A. N. Swami. Mining association rules between sets of items in large databases. In *1993 ACM SIGMOD, Washington, D.C., May 26-28*, pages 207–216. ACM Press, 1993.
4. R. Agrawal and R. Srikant. Fast algorithms for mining association rules in large databases. In *VLDB 1994, September 12-15, Santiago de Chile*, pages 487–499.
5. A. Amir, R. Feldman, and R. Kashi. A new versatile method for association generation. In *Princ. of Data Mining and Knowledge Disc.*, pages 221–231, 1997.
6. M.-L. Antonie and O. R. Zaiane. Mining positive and negative association rules: An approach for confined rules. Technical Report TR04-07, Department of Computing Science, University of Alberta, 2004.
7. F. Hussain, H. Liu, E. Suzuki, and H. Lu. Exception rule mining with a relative interestingness measure. In *PADKK 2000, Kyoto, Japan, April 18-20*, pages 86–97.
8. Y. S. Koh and N. Rountree. Finding sporadic rules using apriori-inverse. In *PAKDD 2005, Hanoi, Vietnam, May 18-20*, pages 97–106, 2005.
9. M. Kryszkiewicz and K. Cichoń. Support oriented discovery of generalized disjunction-free representation of frequent patterns with negation. In *PAKDD 2005, Hanoi, Vietnam, May 18-20*, pages 672–682, 2005.
10. H. Liu, H. Lu, L. Feng, and F. Hussain. Efficient search of reliable exceptions. In *PAKDD 1999, Beijing, China, April 26-28*, volume 1574, pages 194–203, 1999.
11. B. Padmanabhan and A. Tuzhilin. A belief-driven method for discovering unexpected patterns. In *KDD 1998, August 27-31, New York City, New York, USA*, pages 94–100. AAAI Press, 1998.
12. G. Piatetsky-Shapiro. Discovery, analysis, and presentation of strong rules. In *Knowledge Discovery in Databases*, pages 229–248. AAAI/MIT Press, 1991.
13. A. Savasere, E. Omiecinski, and S. B. Navathe. Mining for strong negative associations in a large database of customer transactions. In *ICDE 1998, February 23-27, Orlando, Florida, USA*, pages 494–502. IEEE Computer Society, 1998.
14. X. Wu, C. Zhang, and S. Zhang. Efficient mining of both positive and negative association rules. *ACM Transactions on Information Systems*, 22(3):381–405, 2004.

Optimized Rule Mining Through a Unified Framework for Interestingness Measures

Céline Hébert and Bruno Crémilleux

GREYC, CNRS - UMR 6072, Université de Caen
Campus Côte de Nacre
F-14032 Caen Cédex France
Forename.Surname@info.unicaen.fr

Abstract. The large amount of association rules resulting from a KDD process makes the exploitation of the patterns embedded in the database difficult even impossible. In order to address this problem, various interestingness measures were proposed for selecting the most relevant rules. Nevertheless, the choice of an appropriate measure remains a hard task and the use of several measures may lead to conflicting information. In this paper, we propose a unified framework for a set of interestingness measures $\mathcal{M}$ and prove that most of the usual objective measures behave in a similar way. In the context of classification rules, we show that each measure of $\mathcal{M}$ admits a lower bound on condition that a minimal frequency threshold and a maximal number of exceptions are considered. Furthermore, our framework enables to characterize the whole collection of the rules simultaneously optimizing all the measures of $\mathcal{M}$. We finally provide a method to mine a rule cover of this collection.

1 Introduction

Exploring and analyzing relationships between features is a central task in KDD processes. Agrawal et al. [1] define association rules as the implications $X \rightarrow Y$ where X and Y represent one or several features (or attributes). However, among the overwhelming number of rules resulting from practical applications, it is difficult to determine the most relevant rules [9]. An essential task is to assist the user in selecting interesting rules. In this paper, we focus on classification rules i.e. rules concluding on a class label. These rules are useful for producing emerging patterns [5], characterizing classes [4] and building classifiers [10].

This paper is about the use of interestingness measures for classification rules. Such measures are numerous. The Support and the Confidence measures are probably the most famous ones, but there are more specific ones such as the Lift [3] or the Sebag and Schoenauer's measure [14]. In practice, choosing a suitable measure and determining an appropriate threshold for this measure is a challenge for the end user. Combining results coming from several measures is even much more difficult. Thus an important issue is to compare existing interestingness measures in order to highlight their similarities and differences and understand better their behaviors [13, 2]. Even if most of the usual measures

A Min Tjoa and J. Trujillo (Eds.): DaWaK 2006, LNCS 4081, pp. 238–247, 2006.

are based on the rule antecedent frequency and the rule number of exceptions, there is a lack of generic results and this observation was the starting point of this work.

Contributions. In this paper, we design an original framework grouping together a large set $\mathcal{M}$ of measures (also called δ-dependent measures) having a similar behavior. This framework points out the minimal frequency threshold γ and the maximal number of exceptions of a rule δ as two parameters highly characterizing the rule quality. We provide lower bounds according to γ and δ for any measure in $\mathcal{M}$. This result guarantees a minimal quality for the rules. We show that all the measures $\mathcal{M}$ can be simultaneously optimized, which ensures to produce the best rules according to these measures. We finally provide a method to mine a rule cover of these rules, making our approach efficient in practice.

Organization. The paper is organized as follows. Section 2 discusses related work and gives preliminary definitions. Section 3 describes our framework and the relationship with the parameters γ and δ. Section 4 shows how to optimize the measures $\mathcal{M}$ and obtain a rule cover of all the rules optimizing simultaneously these measures. Section 5 gives experimental results about the quality of the mined rules.

2 Preliminaries

2.1 Covering and Selecting the Most Interesting Rules

Lossless cover. It is well known that the whole set of association rules contains a lot of redundant rules [1]. So several approaches propose to extract a cover of the rules [19] like the *informative rules* [11]. Such a rule has a minimal antecedent and a maximal consequence. They are lossless since we can regenerate the whole set of rules according to both minimal support and confidence thresholds. In Section 4.3, we extend this result by proving that the informative classification rules are a cover of all the rules optimizing simultaneously the measures $\mathcal{M}$.

Deficiencies in selecting the most interesting rules. A lot of works address the selection of relevant rules by means of interestingness measures. It requires to define properties characterizing "good" interestingness measures [9, 12]. Piatetsky-Shapiro [12] proposes a framework with three properties and we set our work with respect to it. Other works compare interestingness measures to determine their differences and similarities, either in an experimental manner [16] or in a theoretical one [15, 7]. There are also attempts to combine several measures to benefit from their joint qualities [6]. However it should be underlined that choosing and using a measure remain a hard task.

This paper deals with the previously mentionned aspects of the rule selection problem. By defining a large set of measures $\mathcal{M}$ behaving in a similar way, choosing one of these measures becomes a secondary issue. We intend to exhibit the minimal properties that a measure must satisfy in order to get the most generic framework. We combine their qualities by showing that they can be simultaneously optimized. To avoid redundancy, we give a method to produce only a cover of the rules optimizing $\mathcal{M}$, i.e. the informative classification rules.

2.2 Definitions

Basic definitions. A database $\mathcal{D}$ is a relation $\mathcal{R}$ between a set $\mathcal{A}$ of *attributes* and a set $\mathcal{O}$ of *objects*: for $a \in \mathcal{A}, o \in \mathcal{O}$, $a\mathcal{R}o$ if and only if the object o contains the attribute a. A *pattern* is a subset of $\mathcal{A}$. The frequency of a pattern X is the number of objects in $\mathcal{D}$ containing X; it is denoted by $\mathcal{F}(X)$. Let $\mathcal{C} = \{c_1, \ldots, c_n\}$ be a set of class values. Each object in $\mathcal{D}$ is assigned a class label in $\mathcal{C}$. $\mathcal{D}_i$ corresponds to the set of the objects labeled by c_i. Table 1 shows an example of database containing 8 objects and two labels c_1 and c_2.

Table 1. An example of database $\mathcal{D}$

$\mathcal{D}$	Attributes								Classes		
Objects	A	B	C	D	E	F	G	H	c_1	c_2	
o_1	1	0	1	0	1	0	1	0	1	0	
o_2	0	1	1	0	1	0	1	1	1	0	
o_3	1	0	1	0	1	0	0	1	1	0	$\mathcal{D}_1$
o_4	1	0	1	0	1	0	0	1	1	0	
o_5	0	1	1	0	1	1	0	0	0	1	
o_6	1	0	0	1	0	1	0	1	0	1	
o_7	0	1	1	0	1	1	0	1	0	1	$\mathcal{D}_2$
o_8	1	0	1	0	0	0	1	0	0	1	

Classification rules. A rule $r : X \to c_i$ where X is a pattern and c_i a class label is a *classification rule*. X is the *antecedent* of r and c_i its *consequence*. $\mathcal{F}(Xc_i)$ is the frequency of r and $\mathcal{F}(X)$ the frequency of its antecedent. For instance, $r_1 : F \to c_2$ and $r_2 : EH \to c_1$ are classification rules in $\mathcal{D}$ (cf. Table 1). $\mathcal{F}(X) - \mathcal{F}(Xc_i)$ is the *number of exceptions* of r, i.e., the number of objects containing X which are not labeled by c_i. The rule r_2 admits 1 exception (object o_7) and the frequency of its antecedent is equal to 4.

Evaluating objective measures. An interestingness measure is a function which assigns a value to a rule according to its quality. We recall here the well-known Piatetsky-Shapiro's properties [12] which aim at specifying what a "good" measure is. As this paper focuses on classification rules, we formulate them in this context.

Definition 1 (Piatetsky-Shapiro's properties). *Let $r : X \to c_i$ be a classification rule and M an interestingness measure.*

- *P1: $M(r) = 0$ if X and c_i are statistically independent;*
- *P2: When $\mathcal{F}(X)$ and $|\mathcal{D}_i|$ remain unchanged, $M(r)$ monotonically increases with $\mathcal{F}(Xc_i)$;*
- *P3: When $\mathcal{F}(Xc_i)$ and $\mathcal{F}(X)$ (resp. $|\mathcal{D}_i|$) remain unchanged, $M(r)$ monotonically decreases with $|\mathcal{D}_i|$ (resp. $\mathcal{F}(X)$).*

P2 ensures the increase of M with the rule frequency. Most of the usual measures satisfy P2 (e.g., support, confidence, interest, conviction). However, there are a few exceptions (e.g., J-measure, Goodman-Kruskal, Gini index). In the next section, we will use P2 to define our framework.

3   A Unified Framework for Objective Measures

This section defines our framework gathering various measures in a set $\mathcal{M}$. The key idea is to express a measure according to two parameters: the minimal frequency γ for the rule antecedent and the maximal number of rule exceptions δ. Then, we formalize the influence of δ by associating a δ-dependent function to each measure.

3.1   Dependency on the Parameter δ

Definition 2 indicates that a measure M can be expressed as a two-variable function of the rule frequency and the frequency of its antecedent.

Definition 2 (Associated Function). *Let M be an interestingness measure and $r : X \rightarrow c_i$ a classification rule. $\Psi_M(x, y)$ is the function associated to M i.e. it is equal to $M(r)$ where $x = \mathcal{F}(X)$ and $y = \mathcal{F}(Xc_i)$.*

For instance, when M is the Growth Rate, we obtain: $\Psi_{GR}(x, y) = \frac{y}{x-y} \times \frac{|\mathcal{D} \backslash \mathcal{D}_i|}{|\mathcal{D}_i|}$.
Using Ψ_M, the Piatetsky-Shapiro's properties P2 and P3 (cf. Section 2.2) can be formulated as: "Ψ_M monotonically increases with y" and "Ψ_M monotonically decreases with x".

Figure 1 plots $\mathcal{F}(Xc_i)$ according to $\mathcal{F}(X)$ for a classification rule $r : X \rightarrow c_i$. The gray area depicts the condition imposed by γ on the rule antecedent. The hatched area of width δ illustrates the link between the variables $x = \mathcal{F}(X)$ and $y = \mathcal{F}(Xc_i)$ of Ψ_M: bounding the rule number of exceptions by δ ensures that $\mathcal{F}(Xc_i)$ is close to $\mathcal{F}(X)$.

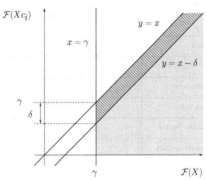

Fig. 1. Dependency between $x = \mathcal{F}(X)$ and $y = \mathcal{F}(Xc_i)$

Definition 3 explicitly expresses this link by defining the now called δ-dependent function $\Psi_{M,\delta}$.

Definition 3 (δ-dependent function). *Let M be an interestingness measure. The δ-dependent function $\Psi_{M,\delta}$ is the one-variable function obtained by the change of variable $y = x - \delta$ in Ψ_M i.e., $\Psi_{M,\delta}(x) = \Psi_M(x, x - \delta)$.*

Pursuing the example of the Growth Rate, we get: $\Psi_{GR,\delta}(x) = \frac{x-\delta}{\delta} \times \frac{|\mathcal{D}| - |\mathcal{D}_i|}{|\mathcal{D}_i|}$

3.2   The Set $\mathcal{M}$ of δ-Dependent Measures

We think that the link between $\mathcal{F}(Xc_i)$ and $\mathcal{F}(X)$ highlighted above is an important feature when studying the behavior of an interestingness measure M. That is the reason why we propose a new Property P4 which takes this link into account. P4 imposes that M increases with the variable x of $\Psi_{M,\delta}$.

Definition 4 (P4 : Property of δ-dependent growth). *Let M be an interestingness measure. When δ remains unchanged, $\Psi_{M,\delta}$ increases with x.*

Table 2. Examples of δ-Dependent Measures

Measure	Definition for classification rules	Lower bound
Support	$\dfrac{\mathcal{F}(Xc_i)}{|\mathcal{D}|}$	$\dfrac{\gamma - \delta}{|\mathcal{D}|}$
Confidence	$\dfrac{\mathcal{F}(Xc_i)}{\mathcal{F}(X)}$	$1 - \dfrac{\delta}{\gamma}$
Sensitivity	$\dfrac{\mathcal{F}(Xc_i)}{|\mathcal{D}_i|}$	$\dfrac{\gamma - \delta}{|\mathcal{D}_i|}$
Specificity	$1 - \dfrac{\mathcal{F}(X) - \mathcal{F}(Xc_i)}{|\mathcal{D}| - |\mathcal{D}_i|}$	$1 - \dfrac{\delta}{|\mathcal{D}| - |\mathcal{D}_i|}$
Success Rate	$\dfrac{|\mathcal{D}| - |\mathcal{D}_i| - \mathcal{F}(X) + 2\mathcal{F}(Xc_i)}{|\mathcal{D}|}$	$1 + \dfrac{\gamma - 2\delta - |\mathcal{D}_i|}{|\mathcal{D}|}$
Lift	$\dfrac{|\mathcal{D}| \times \mathcal{F}(Xc_i)}{|\mathcal{D}_i| \times \mathcal{F}(X)}$	$(1 - \dfrac{\delta}{\gamma}) \times \dfrac{|\mathcal{D}|}{|\mathcal{D}_i|}$
Piatetsky-Shapiro	$\dfrac{\mathcal{F}(Xc_i)}{|\mathcal{D}|} - \dfrac{|\mathcal{D}_i| \times \mathcal{F}(X)}{|\mathcal{D}|^2}$	$[\gamma \times (1 - \dfrac{|\mathcal{D}_i|}{|\mathcal{D}|}) - \delta] \times \dfrac{1}{|\mathcal{D}|}$
Laplace (k=2)	$\dfrac{\mathcal{F}(Xc_i) + 1}{\mathcal{F}(X) + 2}$	$\dfrac{\gamma - \delta + 1}{\gamma + 2}$
Odds ratio	$\dfrac{\mathcal{F}(Xc_i)}{\mathcal{F}(X) - \mathcal{F}(Xc_i)} \times \dfrac{|\mathcal{D}| - |\mathcal{D}_i| - \mathcal{F}(X) + \mathcal{F}(Xc_i)}{|\mathcal{D}_i| - \mathcal{F}(Xc_i)}$	$[\dfrac{\gamma - \delta}{|\mathcal{D}_i| - \gamma + \delta}] \times [\dfrac{|\mathcal{D}| - |\mathcal{D}_i| - \delta}{\delta}]$
Growth rate	$\dfrac{\mathcal{F}(Xc_i)}{\mathcal{F}(X) - \mathcal{F}(Xc_i)} \times \dfrac{|\mathcal{D}| - |\mathcal{D}_i|}{|\mathcal{D}_i|}$	$\dfrac{\gamma - \delta}{\delta} \times \dfrac{|\mathcal{D}| - |\mathcal{D}_i|}{|\mathcal{D}_i|}$
Sebag & Schoenauer	$\dfrac{\mathcal{F}(Xc_i)}{\mathcal{F}(X) - \mathcal{F}(Xc_i)}$	$\dfrac{\gamma - \delta}{\delta}$
Jaccard	$\dfrac{\mathcal{F}(Xc_i)}{|\mathcal{D}_i| + \mathcal{F}(X) - \mathcal{F}(Xc_i)}$	$\dfrac{\gamma - \delta}{|\mathcal{D}_i| + \delta}$
Conviction	$\dfrac{|\mathcal{D}| - |\mathcal{D}_i|}{|\mathcal{D}|} \times \dfrac{\mathcal{F}(X)}{\mathcal{F}(X) - \mathcal{F}(Xc_i)}$	$\dfrac{|\mathcal{D}| - |\mathcal{D}_i|}{|\mathcal{D}|} \times \dfrac{\gamma}{\delta}$
ϕ-coefficient	$\dfrac{|\mathcal{D}| \times \mathcal{F}(Xc_i) - |\mathcal{D}_i| \times \mathcal{F}(X)}{\sqrt{\mathcal{F}(X) \times |\mathcal{D}_i| \times (|\mathcal{D}| - \mathcal{F}(X)) \times (|\mathcal{D}| - |\mathcal{D}_i|)}}$	$\dfrac{\gamma \times (|\mathcal{D}| - |\mathcal{D}_i|) - \delta \times |\mathcal{D}|}{\sqrt{\gamma \times (|\mathcal{D}| - \gamma) \times |\mathcal{D}_i| \times (|\mathcal{D}| - |\mathcal{D}_i|)}}$
Added Value	$\dfrac{\mathcal{F}(Xc_i)}{\mathcal{F}(X)} - \dfrac{|\mathcal{D}|}{|\mathcal{D}_i|}$	$\dfrac{\gamma - \delta}{\gamma} - \dfrac{|\mathcal{D}_i|}{|\mathcal{D}|}$
Certainty Factor	$\dfrac{\mathcal{F}(Xc_i) \times |\mathcal{D}| - \mathcal{F}(X) \times |\mathcal{D}_i|}{\mathcal{F}(X) \times (|\mathcal{D}| - |\mathcal{D}_i|)}$	$\dfrac{\gamma \times (|\mathcal{D}| - |\mathcal{D}_i|) - \delta \times |\mathcal{D}|}{\gamma \times (|\mathcal{D}| - |\mathcal{D}_i|)}$
Information Gain	$\log \left(\dfrac{\mathcal{F}(Xc_i)}{\mathcal{F}(X)} \times \dfrac{|\mathcal{D}|}{|\mathcal{D}_i|} \right)$	$\log \left(\dfrac{\gamma - \delta}{\gamma} \times \dfrac{|\mathcal{D}|}{|\mathcal{D}_i|} \right)$

We claim that P4 captures an important characteristic of an interestingness measure M: the behavior of M with respect to the joint development of the rule antecedent frequency and the rule number of exceptions. This characteristic is not found in Piatetsky-Shapiro's framework. Table 2 provides a sample of measures fulfilling P4 (see their definitions in [15, 17]).

We define now the set $\mathcal{M}$ of δ-dependent measures:

Definition 5 ($\mathcal{M}$: Set of δ-dependent measures). *The set of δ-dependent measures $\mathcal{M}$ is the set of measures satisfying P2 and P4.*

Definition 5 does not require a δ-dependent measure to also satisfy P1 or P3. Remember that our aim is to define the most generic framework. Contrary to P2 and P3, P4 does not impose on $\Psi_{M,\delta}$ to monotonically increase and thus, the Conviction is a δ-dependent measure. A lot of measures belong to $\mathcal{M}$: for instance, all the measures in Table 2 are in $\mathcal{M}$. As $\mathcal{M}$ is defined in intension, it is an infinite set. The next section shows how to bound and optimize these measures.

4   Simultaneous Optimization of the δ-Dependent Measures

4.1   Lower Bounds and Optimization

For any measure of $\mathcal{M}$, Theorem 1 explicits a lower bound depending on γ and δ ($|\mathcal{D}|$ and $|\mathcal{D}_i|$ are constant values).

Theorem 1 (Lower bounds). *Let $r : X \to c_i$ be a classification rule. Assume that $\mathcal{F}(X) \geq \gamma$ and r admits less than δ exceptions. Thus, for each measure M in $\mathcal{M}$, $\Psi_{M,\delta}(\gamma)$ is a lower bound of $M(r)$.*

Proof. Since r has less than δ exceptions, we immediately have $\mathcal{F}(Xc_i) \geq \mathcal{F}(X) - \delta$. From P2, $\Psi_M(x,y)$ increases with y and thus $\Psi_M(x,y) \geq \Psi_M(x, x - \delta) = \Psi_{M,\delta}(x)$. We know that x is greater than or equal to γ and M satisfies P4. Consequently, $\Psi_{M,\delta}(\gamma)$ is a lower bound for $\Psi_{M,\delta}(x)$. $\square$

Theorem 1 means that the quality of any rule r whose antecedent is a γ-frequent pattern and having less than δ exceptions, is greater than or equal to $\Psi_{M,\delta}(\gamma)$. As this result is true for any measure in $\mathcal{M}$, r satisfies a minimal quality for each measure of $\mathcal{M}$, thus we get a set of rules of good quality according to $\mathcal{M}$. The lower bounds only depends on δ and γ and constant values on $\mathcal{D}$. They can be computed (see the last column in Table 2) to quantify the minimal quality of rules. Intuitively, the more the antecedent frequencies increase and the numbers of exceptions decrease, the higher the global quality of a set of rules is. Due to the properties P2 and P4 of the δ-dependent measures, for all measures M in $\mathcal{M}$, $\Psi_{M,\delta}(\gamma)$ increases with γ and decreases with δ. Property 1 (proved in [8]) shows that the lower bound of any measure M in $\mathcal{M}$ can tend towards its upper bound. The conjunction of Theorem 1 and Property 1 proves that the rules with a γ-frequent antecedent and having less than δ exceptions optimize all the measures in $\mathcal{M}$.

Property 1 *The optimal value of $\Psi_{M,\delta}(\gamma)$ is obtained when $\gamma \to |\mathcal{D}|$ and $\delta \to 0$.*

4.2   Completeness

Theorem 2 indicates that any classification rule r optimizing the set of measures $\mathcal{M}$ (i.e., $\forall M \in \mathcal{M}$, $M(r) \geq \Psi_{M,\delta}(\gamma)$) is a rule whose antecedent is frequent and having less than δ exceptions.

Theorem 2 (Completeness). *Let $r : X \to c_i$ a classification rule. Assume that $M(r) \geq \Psi_{M,\delta}(\gamma)$ for all measures M in $\mathcal{M}$. Then $\mathcal{F}(X) \geq \gamma$ and r admits less than δ exceptions.*

Proof. We prove the completeness by reducing it to the absurd. We denote by *Spe* the Specificity and by *Sup* the Support (see Table 2 for their definitions). Assume that r admits δ' exceptions with $\delta' > \delta$. We have $-\frac{\delta'}{|\mathcal{D}|-|\mathcal{D}_i|} < -\frac{\delta}{|\mathcal{D}|-|\mathcal{D}_i|}$

followed by $Spe(r) < \Psi_{Spe,\delta}(\gamma)$, which is in contradiction with our hypothesis. Thus r has less than δ exceptions.

Suppose that $\mathcal{F}(X) = \gamma' < \gamma$. We have $Sup(r) < \frac{\gamma'-\delta}{|\mathcal{D}|} < \Psi_{Sup,\delta}(\gamma)$ and this is in contradiction with our hypothesis as well. Thus, the antecedent frequency is greater than γ. □

The assumption $M(r) \geq \Psi_{M,\delta}(\gamma)$ for $M \in \{Support, Specificity\}$ is sufficient to establish this proof. However, it is necessary to assume $M(r) \geq \Psi_{M,\delta}(\gamma)$ for all measures M in $\mathcal{M}$ in Theorem 2 to demonstrate the completeness of our approach. So, this theorem is the reverse of Theorem 1. Combining Theorems 1 and 2 results in an equality between the set of classification rules with a γ-frequent antecedent and a number of exceptions under δ and the set of classification rules r whose value is greater than or equal to the lower bounds for any measure M in $\mathcal{M}$. Theorem 2 ensures the completeness when mining the rules optimizing the set $\mathcal{M}$ by extracting the classification rules according to the thresholds γ and δ. The next section shows that we can reduce even more the set of rules to mine without any loss.

4.3 Reduction to a Rule Cover

We have introduced in Section 2.1 the rule cover based on informative rules. This cover enables to restore the whole collection of association rules with their exact frequencies and confidence [11]. In this section, we extend this result for the classification rules optimizing simultaneously the measures $\mathcal{M}$. By analogy with informative rules, we call *informative classification rule* a classification rule having a free[1] pattern as antecedent and concluding on a class label. Theorem 3 proves that the informative classification rules having γ-frequent antecedents and less than δ exceptions constitute a cover of the classification rules optimizing all the measures in $\mathcal{M}$.

Theorem 3 (Rule cover). *The set of informative classification rules having γ-frequent antecedents and less than δ exceptions enables to generate the whole set of classification rules r with $M(r) \geq \Psi_{M,\delta}(\gamma)$ for each measure M in $\mathcal{M}$.*

Proof. Assume that $X \rightarrow c_i$ is an informative classification rule and $h(X)$ is the closure of X (see [18] for a definition of the closure). From X and $h(X)$, it is possible to build the set of patterns Y containing X and included in $h(X)$. The rules $Y \rightarrow c_i$ constitute the whole set of rules optimizing $\mathcal{M}$. We demonstrate that:
(1) *A rule* $Y \rightarrow c_i$ *optimizes all the measures of* $\mathcal{M}$. Due to the properties of the closure, $\mathcal{F}(Y) = \mathcal{F}(X) = \mathcal{F}(h(X))$. Thus, Y is γ-frequent. Moreover, since X and Y appear in the same objects of $\mathcal{D}$, we have $\mathcal{F}(Xc_i) = \mathcal{F}(Yc_i)$. This ensures that the rules $X \rightarrow c_i$ and $Y \rightarrow c_i$ have an identical number of exceptions i.e. less than δ. This proves the first point.

---

[1] Free (or key) patterns are defined in [11]. They have interesting properties of minimality in lattices and enable to build rules with minimal antecedents.

(2) *All the rules optimizing $\mathcal{M}$ are generated.* Suppose the rule $Z \rightarrow c_i$ optimizes $\mathcal{M}$ but is not generated by our method. Let X' be the largest free pattern containing Z. $X' \rightarrow c_i$ is not an informative rule (otherwise, $Z \rightarrow c_i$ would have been generated) thus we consider two cases: either X' is not frequent but this implies that Z is not frequent (Contradiction) or $X' \rightarrow c_i$ has more than δ exceptions and thus, $Z \rightarrow c_i$ has more than δ exceptions as well (Contradiction). $\square$

For any classification rule r, the cover always contains a rule having the same quality as r for all the measures in $\mathcal{M}$. As there are efficient algorithms to extract the free (or key) patterns [11] which are the antecedents of the informative rules, Theorem 3 is precious to mine in practice the informative classification rules. We have designed the CLARMINER prototype [8] which produces the whole set of informative classification rules.

5   Rule Quality Testing

The aim of the experiments is twofold. We quantify the quality of the rules mined in practice according to the set of measures given in Table 2 and the reduction brought by the informative classification rule cover. Experiments are carried out on the MUSHROOM data set from the UCI Machine Learning Repository[2] with a 2.20 GHz Pentium IV processor with Linux operating system by using 3Gb of RAM memory.

Overview of the mined rules. We focus on the quality of the informative classification rules with $\gamma = 812$ and $\delta = 40$. These values correspond to a relative frequency of 10% and a relative number of exceptions under 5%. The mining produces 1598 rules with antecedents containing a maximum of 7 attributes. Table 3 gives for each measure: its lower bound, the average value and the ratio $\frac{avg - \Psi_{M,\delta}(\gamma)}{\Psi_{M,\delta}(\gamma)}$ (called *difference* in Table 3). For instance, the average value for the set of rules is 0.252 for the Sensitivity (the lower bound is 0.184) and 74.65 for the Sebag & Schoenauer's measure (the lower bound is 19.3). For the Sebag & Schoenauer's measure, the average value is 286.81% above the lower bound. Remark that the difference is less important for other measures but the lower bound for these measures is really close to their maximum. For instance, the difference is 4.3% for the Confidence and the lower bound is 0.951 with an optimal value equal to 1.

Table 3. Lower bound, average value and difference (%)

Measure	Support	Confidence	Sensitivity	Specificity	Success Rate	Lift	PS	Laplace	Odds Ratio
Lower bound	0.095	0.951	0.184	0.990	0.572	1.835	0.043	0.950	21.771
Average	0.128	0.992	0.252	0.998	0.620	1.958	0.063	0.991	29.603
Difference	34.74	4.3	37.33	0.81	8.39	6.70	45.63	4.3	35.97

Measure	GR	S & S	Jaccard	Conviction	ϕ-coefficient	AV	Certainty Factor	GI	
Lower bound	17.961	19.30	0.185	9.785	0.289	0.433	0.898	0.607	
Average	71.178	74.654	0.252	36.901	0.72	0.485	0.984	0.671	
Difference	296.29	286.81	36.22	277.12	28.72	12.01	9.58	10.54	

---

[2] http://www.ics.uci.edu/~mlearn/MLSummary.html

Table 4. Ratio number of rules/number of informative rules

γ	812	812	812	1500	1500	1500	2000	2000	2000
δ	25	50	100	50	100	200	75	150	300
Ratio	178.8	143.0	110.5	108.4	64.2	50.8	6.8	6.3	8.9

Comparison between informative rules and the whole set of rules. Table 4 shows that considering only informative rules instead of all the rules optimizing the measures $\mathcal{M}$ significantly reduces the number of rules: according to γ and δ, the cover only contains from 0.6% to 15.9% of the whole rule collection.

6   Conclusions and Future Work

In this paper, we have designed an original framework gathering most of the usual interestingness measures for classification rules. The measures belonging to this framework are shown to behave the same way and choosing "the" appropriate measure appears to be a secondary issue. We have established that all the measures of this framework can be simultaneously optimized, thus enabling the production of the best rules. A cover of these rules can be efficiently mined and experiments indicate that the number of produced rules is significantly reduced.

This work could be extended in many directions. We are working on generalizing our framework to any association rule. One key point of our approach is that the rule consequence is a class label and its frequency is known. The generalization is not obvious because *no information is provided* about the consequence frequency when considering any association rule. Another objective is to automatically determine the couples of parameters (δ, γ) to mine the rules satisfying measure thresholds fixed by the user to combine the various semantics conveyed by the measures. A third extension is the study of measures that do not belong to our framework.

Acknowledgements. This work has been partially funded by the ACI "masse de données" (French Ministry of research), Bingo project (MD 46, 2004-2007).

References

[1] R. Agrawal, T. Imielinski, and A. N. Swami. Mining association rules between sets of items in large databases. In P. Buneman and S. Jajodia, editors, *SIGMOD'93 Conference*, pages 207–216. ACM Press, 1993.

[2] J. R. J. Bayardo and R. Agrawal. Mining the most interesting rules. In *KDD'99*, pages 145–154, 1999.

[3] S. Brin, R. Motwani, and C. Silverstein. Beyond market baskets: Generalizing association rules to correlations. In J. Peckham, editor, *SIGMOD 1997, Proceedings ACM SIGMOD International Conference on Management of Data, May 13-15, 1997, Tucson, Arizona, USA*, pages 265–276. ACM Press, 1997.

[4] B. Crémilleux and J.-F. Boulicaut. Simplest rules characterizing classes generated by delta-free sets. In *22nd Int. Conf. on Knowledge Based Systems and Applied Artificial Intelligence (ES'02)*, pages 33–46, Cambridge, UK, December 2002.

[5] G. Dong and J. Li. Efficient mining of emerging patterns: discovering trends and differences. In *proceedings of the Fifth International Conference on Knowledge Discovery and Data Mining (ACM SIGKDD'99)*, pages 43–52, San Diego, CA, 1999. ACM Press.

[6] D. Francisci and M. Collard. Multi-criteria evaluation of interesting dependencies according to a data mining approach. In *Congress on Evolutionary Computation*, pages 1568–1574, Canberra, Australia, 12 2003. IEEE Press,.

[7] J. Fürnkranz and P. A. Flach. Roc 'n' rule learning-towards a better understanding of covering algorithms. *Machine Learning*, 58(1):39–77, 2005.

[8] C. Hébert and B. Crémilleux. Obtention de règles optimisant un ensemble de mesures. In *Conférence francophone sur l'apprentissage automatique (CAp'06)*, Trégastel, France, 2006.

[9] R. J. Hilderman and H. J. Hamilton. Measuring the interestingness of discovered knowledge: A principled approach. *Intell. Data Anal.*, 7(4):347–382, 2003.

[10] B. Liu, W. Hsu, and Y. Ma. Integrating classification and association rules mining. In *proceedings of Fourth International Conference on Knowledge Discovery & Data Mining (KDD'98)*, pages 80–86, New York, August 1998. AAAI Press.

[11] N. Pasquier, Y. Bastide, R. Taouil, and L. Lakhal. Discovering frequent closed itemsets for association rules. In *proceedings of 7th International Conference on Database Theory (ICDT'99)*, volume 1331 of *Lecture notes in artificial intelligence*, pages 299–312, Jerusalem, Israel, 1999. Springer Verlag.

[12] G. Piatetsky-Shapiro. Discovery, analysis, and presentation of strong rules. In *Knowledge Discovery in Databases*, pages 229–248. AAAI/MIT Press, 1991.

[13] M. Plasse, N. Niang, G. Saporta, and L. Leblond. Une comparaison de certains indices de pertinence des règles d'association. In G. Ritschard and C. Djeraba, editors, *EGC*, volume RNTI-E-6 of *Revue des Nouvelles Technologies de l'Information*, pages 561–568. Cépaduès-Éditions, 2006.

[14] M. Sebag and M. Schoenauer. Generation of rules with certainty and con dence factors from incomplete and incoherent learning bases. In M. L. J. Boose, B. Gaines, editor, *European Knowledge Acquisistion Workshop, EKAW'88*, pages 28-1-28-20, 1988.

[15] P.-N. Tan, V. Kumar, and J. Srivastava. Selecting the right interestingness measure for association patterns. In *KDD*, pages 32–41. ACM, 2002.

[16] B. Vaillant, P. Lenca, and S. Lallich. A clustering of interestingness measures. In *The 7th International Conference on Discovery Science*, pages 290–297, 10 2004.

[17] B. Vaillant, P. Meyer, E. Prudhomme, S. Lallich, P. Lenca, and S. Bigaret. Mesurer l'intérêt des règles d'association. In *EGC*, pages 421–426, 2005.

[18] R. Wille. *Ordered sets*, chapter Restructuring lattice theory: an approach based on hierachies of concepts, pages 445–470. Reidel, Dordrecht, 1982.

[19] M. J. Zaki. Generating non-redundant association rules. In *KDD'00*, pages 34–43, 2000.

An Information-Theoretic Framework for Process Structure and Data Mining

Antonio D. Chiaravalloti[2], Gianluigi Greco[1], Antonella Guzzo[2], and Luigi Pontieri[2]

Dept. of Mathematics[1], UNICAL, Via P. Bucci 30B, 87036, Rende, Italy
ICAR, CNR[2], Via Pietro Bucci 41C, 87036 Rende, Italy
ggreco@mat.unical.it, {chiaravalloti, guzzo,
pontieri}@icar.cnr.it

Abstract. Process-oriented systems have been increasingly attracting data mining community, due to the opportunities the application of inductive *process mining* techniques to log data can open to both the analysis of complex processes and the design of new process models. Currently, these techniques focus on structural aspects of the process and disregard data that are kept by many real systems, such as information about activity executors, parameter values, and time-stamps.

In this paper, an enhanced process mining approach is presented, where different process variants (use cases) can be discovered by clustering log traces, based on both structural aspects and performance measures. To this aim, an information-theoretic framework is used, where the structural information as well as performance measures are represented by a proper domain, which is correlated to the "central domain" of logged process instances. Then, the clustering of log traces is performed synergically with that of the correlated domains. Eventually, each cluster is equipped with a specific model, so providing the analyst with a compact and handy description of the execution paths characterizing each process variant.

Keywords: process mining, workflow management, coclustering, mutual information

1 Introduction

Process mining is a key technology for advanced Business Process Management aimed at supporting the (re)design phase of process-oriented systems. In fact, based on the log data that are gathered by these systems, process mining techniques (e.g., [9,6,7,8]) are devoted to discover the underlying process model and the constraints explaining the episodes recorded. The "mined" model, providing the user with a summarized view on process operations, can be profitably exploited in designing or re-engineering a concrete workflow schema that will efficiently support the enactment of the process.

While mining a complex process, possibly involving hundreds of activities, it is often convenient to first single out its variants, i.e., its use cases, and then equip each of them with a specialized schema (as in [10,5]). By this way, one can avoid generating an overly-detailed and inaccurate description of the process, which mixes up semantically different scenarios. Technically, such variants can be discovered by properly partitioning traces into clusters, as informally discussed in the following running example.

A Min Tjoa and J. Trujillo (Eds.): DaWaK 2006, LNCS 4081, pp. 248–259, 2006.
© Springer-Verlag Berlin Heidelberg 2006

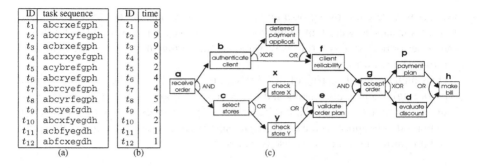

ID	task sequence
t_1	abcrxefgph
t_2	abcrxyfegph
t_3	acbrxefgph
t_4	abcrxyefgph
t_5	acybrefgph
t_6	abcryefgph
t_7	abrcyefgph
t_8	abcyrfegph
t_9	abcyefgdh
t_{10}	abcxfyegdh
t_{11}	acbfyegdh
t_{12}	abfcxegdh

ID	time
t_1	8
t_2	9
t_3	9
t_4	8
t_5	2
t_6	4
t_7	4
t_8	5
t_9	4
t_{10}	2
t_{11}	1
t_{12}	1

(a)   (b)   (c)

Fig. 1. Log traces (a), metrics values (b) and a workflow schema (c) for process HANDLEORDER

Example 1. As a sample applicative scenario, consider the toy HANDLEORDER process for handling customers' orders in a business company, which is graphically illustrated in Fig. 1.(c). An example log data for the process is shown in Fig. 1.(a), where each execution trace is registered as a sequence of activity identifiers.

Note that a, b, c, e, f, g and h are executed in all the instances of HANDLEORDER, while the other ones appear in a subset of them only. Moreover, every trace containing r also includes p and does not contain d; conversely, d appears any time r does not. Based on these observations, we can recognize two (*structurally*) homogeneous clusters of traces, each one representing a variant of the process: $\{t_1, ..., t_8\}$ (orders with deferred payment) and $\{t_9, ..., t_{12}\}$ (orders with immediate payment).

By equipping each cluster with a specific workflow schema, we can get a more accurate representation than the one in Fig. 1.(c), actually mixing up different usage patterns and models spurious executions – e.g., traces containing both r and p, as well as traces where neither r or d appear.   ◁

Despite the efforts spent in the design of process mining techniques, their actual impact in the industry is endangered by some simplifying assumptions. For instance, most of the approaches in the literature are *propositional* in that they exploit an abstraction of logs as a set of task identifiers, thereby completely disregarding all *non-structural* data that are still kept by many real systems, such as information about activity executors, time-stamps, parameter values, as well as different performance measures.

In this paper, an enhanced process mining approach is presented which allows to discover different process variants, by clustering log traces based on to both structural and non-structural aspects. To this aim, beside the list of activity identifiers, we equip each trace with a number of *metrics*, which are meant to characterize some performance measures for the enactment at hand, such as the total processing time. As an example, for each trace in the log of the HANDLEORDER process, the total execution time is shown in Fig. 1.(b). One can note that instances including both r and x take longer than the others, as a result, e.g., of some additional verification procedure done at store X whenever the ordered goods are being payed in a deferred way.

In order to take care of the different execution facets in the clustering, we introduce and discuss an information-theoretic framework that extends previous formalizations in [3,2],in a way that the structural information as well as each of the performance measures is represented by a proper domain, which is correlated to the "central domain" of process instances according to the contents of the log. The clustering of log traces is then performed in a synergic way w.r.t. the clustering of structural elements and performance measures.

The simultaneous clustering of *two* different types of objects (short: bi-dimensional *co-clustering*), such as documents and terms in text corpora [1,12] or genes and conditions in micro-array data [11], has become a very active research area. However, in order to profitably apply such a co-clustering approach in a process mining setting, we extend it in different respects, as discussed below.

- First, in order to deal with both the structural information (activities) and the performance measures, we consider co-clustering over (at least) three different domains, which has been marginally addressed in the literature. In fact, an earlier work [4] faced this problem through a spectral approach applied in a simplified setting, where each domain can be clustered into two clusters only. Importantly, [4] asked for both removing this assumption and assessing whether the information-theoretic approach of [3] can be used in this setting. The research work illustrated in Section 3 precisely faces both of these issues.
- Second, in Section 4, we tackle the co-clustering problem in a scenario where some domains consists of numerical (ordered) values. This problem has been not investigated before and requires the definition of ad-hoc techniques to mine numerical (co)clusters as non-overlapping ranges of values. To this aim, we propose and study an exact (but time-consuming) partitioning method, as well as a faster, greedy, heuristic that provides an approximate solution to the problem.

We conclude by pointing out that all the algorithms proposed in the paper have been implemented and tested. Discussion on experimental results are reported in Section 5.

2   Formal Framework

Process Modeling: Schemas and Performance Measures. The *control flow graph* of a process P is a tuple $\langle D_A, E, a_0, F \rangle$, where D_A is a finite set of *activities*, $E \subseteq (D_A - F) \times (D_A - \{a_0\})$ is a relation of precedences between activities, $a_0 \in D_A$ is the starting activity, $F \subseteq D_A$ is the set of final activities. A control flow graph is usually extended by specifying, for each activity, cardinality constraints on the number of adjacent activities that can/must be performed.

Example 2. For example, the control flow graph for our running example is shown in Fig. 1.(c). Here, constraints are specified by suitable labels next the activity nodes – e.g., g is an *and-join* activity as it must be notified by its predecessors that both the client is reliable and the order can be supplied correctly.   ◁

A *trace* for P is a string over the alphabet D_A, representing an ordered sequence of activity occurrences. A *process log* $\mathcal{L}$ for P (over D_A) is a tuple $\langle D_A, D_T, \mathcal{F}_{Z^1}, ..., \mathcal{F}_{Z^N} \rangle$ such that: **(1)** D_T is a set of trace (over D_A) identifiers, and **(2)** $\mathcal{F}_{Z^i}$, with $i = 1..N$, is a performance measure associating a trace in D_T with a real value, [1] i.e., $\mathcal{F}_{Z^i}$: $D_T \mapsto \mathbb{R}$.

For each performance measure $\mathcal{F}_{Z^i}$ with $i = 1..N$, we define its *active domain*, denoted by D_{Z^i}, as the image of $\mathcal{F}_{Z^i}$ over the set of traces D_T, i.e., $D_{Z^i} = \{\mathcal{F}_{Z^i}(t_j) \mid t_j \in D_T\}$, where for any trace t_j in D_T, $\mathcal{F}_{Z^i}(t_j)$ is the value that t_j is assigned by the i-th function $\mathcal{F}_{Z^i}$. As an example, in the HANDLEORDER process, we have $D_T = \{t_1, ..., t_{12}\}$, while the active domain over the timings is $D_Z = \{1, 2, 4, 5, 8, 9\}$.

The Information-Theoretic Framework. Based on the data stored in $\mathcal{L}$, we can establish some correlations among the *central domain* D_T, representing a set of logged process instances, and the *auxiliary* domains $D_A, D_{Z^1}, ..., D_{Z^N}$. Specifically, correlations can be modelled by considering a random variable T ranging over D_T, along with a random variable X associated with each auxiliary D_X, where X is a placeholder for any of the auxiliary variables $A, Z^1, ..., Z^N$. Then, we use $p(T, X)$ to denote the joint-probability distribution between T and X; in particular, $p(t_j, x)$ is the probability for the event that T is the trace t_j *and* X takes the value $x \in D_X$.

Assume that traces in D_T (resp., values in D_A, and in D_{Z^i}) have to be clustered into m^T (resp., m^A, m^i) clusters, say $\widehat{D}_T = \{\hat{t}_1, ..., \hat{t}_{m^T}\}$ (resp., $\widehat{D}_A = \{\hat{a}_1, \hat{a}_2, ..., \hat{a}_{m^A}\}$, $\widehat{D}_{Z^i} = \{\hat{z}^i_1, \hat{z}^i_2, ..., \hat{z}^i_{m^i}\}$). Then, a *co-clustering* of the log $\mathcal{L}$ is a tuple $C = \langle C_T, C_A, C_{Z^1}, ..., C_{Z^N}\rangle$, such that $C_T : D_T \mapsto \widehat{D}_T$, $C_A : D_A \mapsto \widehat{D}_A$ and $C_Z : D_{Z^i} \mapsto \widehat{D}_{Z^i}$, for $i = 1...N$.[2]

As firstly observed in [3], in order to find "good" co-clusters, for any auxiliary domain D_X, one can minimize the *loss in mutual information* $\Delta I_X(C_T, C_X) = I(T; X) - I(\widehat{T}_{C_T}; \widehat{X}_{C_X})$ (or, shortly, ΔI_X) between the random variables T and X and their clustered versions. Indeed, by minimizing the loss in mutual information, one can expect that the random variables $\widehat{T}$ and $\widehat{X}$ retain as much information as possible from the original distributions T and X.

An algorithm for the *bi-dimensional* co-clustering (cf. only one auxiliary domain X must be co-clustered along with T) was proposed in [3], based on the observation that ΔI_X can be expressed as a dissimilarity between the original distribution $p(T, X)$ and a function $q(T, X)$ approximating it. More precisely: $\Delta I_X = \mathcal{D}(p(T, X) \| q(T, X))$, where $\mathcal{D}(\cdot \| \cdot)$ denotes the Kullback-Leibler (KL) divergence, and $q(T, X) = p(\widehat{T}, \widehat{X}) \cdot p(T|\widehat{T}) \cdot p(X|\widehat{X})$ is a function preserving the marginals of $p(T, X)$. In particular, ΔI_X can be expressed in terms of "individual" loss contributes measuring the (KL-based) dissimilarity between each element in D_X (or, D_T) and the cluster it was assigned to:

$$\Delta I_X = \sum_{x \in D_X} \delta_T(x, C_X(x)) = \sum_{t \in D_T} \delta_X(t, C_T(t)) \quad (1)$$

where $\delta_T(x, \hat{x}) = p(x) \cdot \mathcal{D}(p(T|x) \| q(T|\hat{x}))$, for each $x \in D_X$, and $\delta_X(t, \hat{t}) = p(t) \cdot \mathcal{D}(p(X|t) \| q(X|\hat{t}))$, for each $t \in D_T$.

---

[1] With no substantial modifications, $\mathcal{F}_{Z^i}$ can be defined as a multi-valued function that groups the metrics of different trace identifiers referring to the same sequence of activities.

[2] The notation $\widehat{X}_{C_X}$ will be shortened as $\widehat{X}$ whenever C_X is clear from the context.

In fact, the algorithm in [3] searches for the function $q(T, X)$ that is most similar to $p(T, X)$, according to $\mathcal{D}$, by means of an alternate minimization, which considers one dimension per time, and assigns each element in D_X (resp., D_T) to the cluster which is the "most similar" to it, according to coefficient δ_T (resp., δ_X). A similar strategy is also exploited in the multi-dimensional co-clustering approach, introduced in the following.

3   Multidimensional Co-clustering of Workflow Logs

When more than one auxiliary domains are considered, the ultimate goal is to discover a clustering function for each of them, so that a low value for all the pairwise information loss functions is obtained. A major problem, in this multi-dimensional extension, is that there may well exists two auxiliary dimensions $X, X' \in \{A, Z^1, ...Z^N\}$, with $X \neq X'$, such that the best co-clustering solution for the pair D_T and D_X does not conform with the best co-clustering for D_T and $D_{X'}$, as concerns the partitions of traces in D_T.

Our solution to jointly optimize all the pairwise loss functions is to linearly combine them into a global one, by using $N + 1$ weights $\beta_A, \beta_1, ..., \beta_N$, with $\beta_A + \sum_{i=1}^{N} \beta_i = 1$, which are meant to quantify the relevance that the corresponding auxiliary domain should have in determining the co-clustering of the whole log data. Therefore, the co-clustering problem for the log $\mathcal{L}$ can be rephrased into finding the set of clusters that minimize the quantity $\beta_A \cdot \Delta I_A + \sum_{i=1}^{N} \beta_i \cdot \Delta I_{Z^i}$.

Definition 1. Let $\mathcal{L} = \langle D_A, D_T, \mathcal{F}_{Z^1}, ..., \mathcal{F}_{Z^N} \rangle$ be a process log, and $\beta_A, \beta_1..., \beta_N$ be real numbers, such that $\beta_A + \sum_{i=1}^{N} \beta_i = 1$. Then, a co-clustering $C = \langle C_T, C_A, C_{Z^1}, ..., C_{Z^N} \rangle$ of $\mathcal{L}$ is *optimal* if, for each co-clustering C' of $\mathcal{L}$, it holds:

$$\beta_A \Delta I_A(C_T, C_A) + \sum_{i=1}^{N} \beta_i \Delta I_{Z^i}(C_T, C_{Z^i}) \geq \beta_A \Delta I_A(C_T', C_A') + \sum_{i=1}^{N} \beta_i \Delta I_{Z^i}(C_T', C_{Z^i}')$$

Algorithm LogCC, shown in Fig. 2, computes an optimal co-clustering, by receiving in input a log $\mathcal{L} = \langle D_A, D_T, \mathcal{F}_{Z^1}, ..., \mathcal{F}_{Z^N} \rangle$, weights $\beta_A, \beta_1, ..., \beta_N$, and cluster sizes.

First, an initial co-clustering $\langle C_T^0, C_A^0, C_{Z^1}^0, ..., C_{Z^N}^0 \rangle$ is computed, which is eventually refined in the main loop. The refinement is carried out in an alternate manner. Indeed, at each repetition, say s, a (locally) optimal clustering $C_A^{(s)}$ (resp., $C_{Z^i}^{(s)}$) is computed for the activity domain D_A (resp., for each metrics domain Z^i, with $1 \leq i \leq N$), based on the current clustering of the traces in T. Specifically, the cluster assigned to each activity $a \in D_A$ is computed according to the formula:

$$C_A^{(s)}(a) = \arg \min_{\hat{a} \in \hat{D}_A} \mathcal{D}(p(T|a) || q^{(s-1)}(T|\hat{a})) \tag{2}$$

where $q(T, A)$ is a distribution approximating $p(T, A)$, and preserving its marginals.

Note that the clustering $C_{Z^i}^{(s)}$, for each (ordered) numerical domain Z^i, is computed by function Partition, which splits the domain into a number of intervals, and assign each of them to one cluster in $\hat{D}_{Z^i}$. The function, discussed later on, also takes as input the distribution $q^{(s-1)}$, accounting for the current co-clustering solution.

Based on the clusters of $A, Z^1, ..., Z^N$, an optimal clustering $C_T^{(s)}$ is computed as:

$$C_T^{(s)}(t) = \arg \min_{\hat{t} \in \hat{D}_T} \beta_A \cdot \mathcal{D}(p(A|t) || q^{(s-1)}(A|\hat{t})) + \sum_{i=1}^{N} \beta_i \cdot \mathcal{D}(p(Z^i|t) || q^{(s-1)}(Z^i|\hat{t})) \tag{3}$$

Input: A process log $\mathcal{L} = \langle D_T, D_A, \mathcal{F}_{Z^1}, ..., \mathcal{F}_{Z^N} \rangle$,
 real nums $\beta_A, \beta_1, ..., \beta_N$, and cardinal nums $m^T, m^A, m^1, ..., m^N$
Output: A co-clustering for $\mathcal{L}$, and a set of workflow schemas $\mathcal{W}$;

Extract joint probability functions $p(T, A), p(T, Z^1), ..., p(T, Z^N)$, out of $\mathcal{L}$;
Define an arbitrary co-clustering $\langle C_T^0, C_A^0, C_{Z^1}^0, ..., C_{Z^N}^0 \rangle$ for $\mathcal{L}$;
Compute $q^{(0)}(T, A)$, and $q^{(0)}(T, Z^i)$ for $= 1 ... N$;
let $s = 0$, $\Delta I_A^{(0)} = \mathcal{D}(p(T, A) || q^{(0)}(T, Z^i))$, and $\Delta I_i^{(0)} = \mathcal{D}(p(T, Z^i) || q^{(0)}(T, Z^i))$;
repeat
    Compute $q^{(s)}(T, A), q^{(s)}(T, Z^i)$ for $i = 1 ... N$, and **set** $s = s + 1$;
    for each $a \in D_A$ **do**
        $C_A^{(s)}(a) := \arg\min_{\widehat{a} \in \widehat{D}_A} \delta_T(a, \widehat{a})$;
    for each Z^i **do**
        $C_{Z^i}^{(s)} := \texttt{Partition}(D_{Z^i}, \widehat{D}_{Z^i}, q^{(s-1)}(T, Z^i))$;
    Compute $q^{(s)}(T, A), q^{(s)}(T, Z^i)$ for $i = 1 ... N$, and **set** $s = s + 1$;
    for each $t \in D_T$ **do**
        $C_T^{(s)}(t) := \arg\min_{\widehat{t} \in \widehat{D}_T} \left(\beta_A \delta_A(t, \widehat{t}) + \sum_{i=1}^N \beta_i \delta_{Z^i}(t, \widehat{t}) \right)$;
    let $\Delta I_A^{(s)} = \mathcal{D}(p(T, A)^{(s-1)} || q(T, A)^{(s-1)}))$:
    let $\Delta I_i^{(s)} = \mathcal{D}(p(T, Z^i)^{(s-1)} || q(T, Z^i)^{(s-1)})), \forall Z^i$;
while $\beta_A \Delta I_A^{(s)} + \sum_{i=1}^N \beta_i \Delta I_i^{(s)} < \beta_A \Delta I_A^{(s-2)} + \sum_{i=1}^N \beta_i \Delta I_i^{(s-2)}$;
$C_T^* := C_T^{(s-2)}$, $C_A^* = C_A^{(s-3)}$, $C_{Z^1}^* = C_{Z^i}^{(s-3)}$, for $= 1 ... N$;
for each $\widehat{t} \in \widehat{D}_T$ **do**
    $W(\widehat{t}) := \texttt{MineSchema}(\{\widehat{t} \in \widehat{D}_T \mid C_T^*(t) = \widehat{t}\})$;
return $\langle C_X^*, C_{Y^1}^*, ..., C_{Y^N}^* \rangle$ and $\mathcal{W} = \{W(\widehat{t}) \mid \widehat{t} \in \widehat{D}_T\}$;

Fig. 2. Algorithm `LogCC`: Discovery of co-clusters over workflow traces and correlated data

Each cluster is then equipped with a workflow schema, by function `MineSchema` implementing some standard process mining algorithm [9,6,8,9].

Note that when applied to domains $D_T, D_A, D_{Z^1}, ..., D_{Z^N}$, `LogCC` cannot generally ensure that every information loss function ΔI_X monotonically decreases, for each $X \in \{A, Z_1, ..., Z_N\}$. Conversely, the (global) objective function (i.e., $\beta_A \cdot \Delta I_A + \sum_{i=1}^N \beta_i \cdot \Delta I_i$) is guaranteed to converge to a local optimum, under some technical conditions on the implementation of `Partition`, which are discussed below.

Let D_Z denote a numerical domain, $\widehat{D}_Z$ a set of cluster labels for it, and let $C_Z : D_Z \mapsto \widehat{D}_Z$ and $C_T : D_T \mapsto \widehat{D}_T$ denote two clustering functions for D_Z and, resp., D_T. Moreover, let $q^{C_T, C_Z}(T, Z)$ be a distribution preserving the marginals of $p(T, Z)$. Then a *split function* $\mathcal{P}$ computing a clustering from D_Z to $\widehat{D}_Z$, based on q^{C_T, C_Z}, is said *loss-safe* if for any $D_Z, \widehat{D}_Z, C_T, C_Z$ it is $\Delta I_Z(C_T, \mathcal{P}(D_Z, \widehat{D}_Z, q^{C_T, C_Z})) \leq \Delta I_Z(C_T, C_Z)$.

Theorem 1. *Provided that the split function* `Partition` *is loss-safe, algorithm* `LogCC` *converges to a local optimum, i.e., to a co-clustering for $\mathcal{L}$ such that for any other co-clustering $C' = \langle C_T', C_A', C_{Z^1}', ... C_{Z^N}' \rangle$ of $\mathcal{L}$ it is:*

(a) $\Delta I_X(C_T, C_X') \geq \Delta I_X(C_T, C_X), \forall X \in \{A, Z^i, ..., Z^N\}$, *and*

(b) $\beta_A \Delta I_A(C_T', C_A) + \sum_{i=1}^N \beta_i \Delta I_{Z^i}(C_T', C_{Z^i}) \geq \beta_A \Delta I_A(C_T, C_A) + \sum_{i=1}^N \beta_i \Delta I_i(C_T, C_{Z^i})$,

---

Input: A domain D_Z, a set of clusters $\widehat{D}_Z = \{\widehat{z}_1, ..., \widehat{z}_m\}$;
Output: A clustering function from D_Z to $\widehat{D}_Z$;

Compute $c_l(i) = \sum_{0 < i \leq u} \delta_T(z_i, \widehat{z}_l)$, $\forall i \in [1..n]$ and $\forall l \in [1..m]$;
$g(1, i) := c_1(i)$, $\forall i \in [1..n]$;
for $s = 2..m$ **do**
    for $i = 1..n$ **do**
        $g(s, i) := \min_{\mu \in [1..i]}(\, g(s-1, \mu) + c_s(i) - c_s(\mu)\,)$;
        $h(s, i) := \arg\min_{\mu \in [1..i]}(\, g(s-1, \mu) + c_s(i) - c_s(\mu)\,)$;
    end for
Let $b_m = n + 1$, and $b_0 = 1$;
for $l = 1..m$ **do**
    Let $b_{m-l} = h(m - l + 1, b_{m-l+1})$;
Set $C_Z(z_i) := \widehat{z}_l$ for each $l \in [1..m]$ and for each $i \in [b_{l-1} + 1..b_l]$;
return C_Z;

Fig. 3. Algorithm NDP-OPT: A dynamic programming implementation of Partition

4   Clustering Numerical Domains: Function Partition

This section discusses two possible implementations of function Partition, used by LogCC, which is aimed at computing a new clustering function C_Z from a numerical domain $D_Z = \{z_1, ..., z_n\}$ to a given set of clusters $\widehat{D}_Z = \{\widehat{z}_1, ..., \widehat{z}_m\}$.

Differently from the case of generic domains, values in D_Z are disposed in an ordered way (i.e., $z_u < z_v$ for each u, v such that $u < v$), and this ordering must still hold among the clusters, i.e., $\forall \widehat{z}_k, \widehat{z}_l \in \widehat{D}_Z$ s.t. $k < l$, any value assigned to $\widehat{z}_k$ precedes all the values assigned to $\widehat{z}_l$. To make the above requirement clearer, we next define the *Numerical Domain Partitioning* (short: NDP).

Let $b_1, ..., b_{m-1}$ be $m - 1$ boundary indexes such that $1 \leq b_r \leq b_s \leq n + 1$ for every r, s, and $1 \leq r < s < m$. A clustering function C_Z can be extracted out of these indexes as follows: $C_Z(z_i) = \widehat{z}_l$ iff $b_{l-1} \leq i < b_l$, where for notation convenience two fixed, additional bounds are considered: $b_0 = 1$ and $b_m = n + 1$. Then, problem NDP consists in finding $m - 1$ boundary indexes such that the resulting clustering function C_Z gets the minimum value for $\mathcal{G}^{C_Z}(D_Z, \widehat{D}_Z) = \sum_{\widehat{z}_l \in \widehat{D}_Z} \sum_{i=b_{l-1}}^{b_l - 1} \delta(z_i, \widehat{z}_l)$. From now on, the term $\mathcal{G}^{C_Z}(D_Z, \widehat{D}_Z)$ will be referred to as the *partition cost* of C_Z.

Clearly enough, the above formulation makes inappropriate the scheme proposed in [3] (and used in algorithm LogCC for clustering the "non-numerical" domains D_A and D_T), where elements in the domain are clustered independently of each other. Thus, some specialized algorithms are needed to face NDP, which are discussed below.

A dynamic programming algorithm for Partition. The algorithm shown in Fig. 3 computes an exact solution to problem NDP. The underlying idea is to consider the problem of clustering a range $D_Z^{[u,v]} = \{z_u, ..., z_v\}$ of D_Z, by using a range $\widehat{D}_Z^{[r,s]} = \{\widehat{z}_r, ..., \widehat{z}_s\}$ of $\widehat{D}_Z$. Based on the result below, this sub-problem can be solved by finding a function $C_Z^{[u,v]} : D_Z^{[u,v]} \mapsto \widehat{D}_Z^{[r,s]}$ minimizing $\mathcal{G}^{C_Z^{[u,v]}}(D_Z^{[u,v]}, \widehat{D}_Z^{[r,s]})$.

Theorem 2. *Let* $\mathcal{G}^*(D_Z^{[u,v]}, \widehat{D}_Z^{[r,s]}) = \min_{C_Z^{[u,v]}} \mathcal{G}^{C_Z^{[u,v]}}(D_Z^{[u,v]}, \widehat{D}_Z^{[r,s]})$. *Then it holds:*

$$\mathcal{G}^*(D_Z^{[u,v]}, \widehat{D}_Z^{[r,s]}) = \min_{u \leq \mu \leq v} \left[\mathcal{G}^*(D_Z^{[u,\mu]}, \widehat{D}_Z^{[r,s-1]}) + \mathcal{G}^*(D_Z^{[\mu+1,v]}, \widehat{D}_Z^{[s,s]}) \right]$$

noticing that $\mathcal{G}^*(D_Z^{[\mu+1,v]}, \widehat{D}_Z^{[s,s]}) = \sum_{i=\mu+1}^{v} \delta(z_i, \widehat{z}_s)$.

Algorithm NDP-OPT is, in fact, a dynamic-programming implementation of Theorem 2. Indeed, at each step, $g(s, i)$ will store the minimal partition cost of splitting the first i values in D_Z among the first s clusters, i.e., $g(s, i) = \mathcal{G}^*(D_Z^{[1,i]}, \widehat{D}_Z^{[1,s]})$. These costs are computed in increasing order of s and, for each s, in increasing order of i, for $s = 1..m$ and $i = 1..n$. As a basic case, for every range $D_Z^{[1,i]}$ the algorithm stores in $g(1, i)$ the cost that results from assigning all the values in $D_Z^{[1,i]}$ to the sole cluster $\widehat{z}_1$. Moreover, to efficiently evaluate the cost of assigning all the values in $D_Z^{u,v}$ to any cluster $\widehat{z}_l$, all prefix-sum $c_l(u) = \sum_{0<i\leq u} \delta(i, l)$ are preliminary computed — note that, in fact, it holds: $\mathcal{G}^*(D_Z^{[u,v]}, \{\widehat{z}_l\}) = c_l(v) - c_l(u-1)$.

In more detail, the optimal split cost $g(s, i) = \mathcal{G}^*(D_Z^{[1,i]}, \widehat{D}_Z^{[1,s]})$ is singled out by evaluating, for each index $\mu < i$, the value $\mathcal{G}^*(D_Z^{[1,\mu]}, \widehat{D}_Z^{[1,s-1]})$, stored in $g(s-1, \mu)$, along with $\mathcal{G}^*(D_Z^{[\mu+1,i]}, \widehat{D}_Z^{[s,s]})$, which can be derived from $c_s(\cdot)$. In addition, the boundary index leading to this optimal split is kept in $h(s, i)$. In the next step, the optimal $m-1$ boundary indexes, which ensure the minimum value (stored in $g(m, n)$) of the whole objective function, are extracted out of table h. Finally, a clustering function is built out of these boundaries, and returned as output. Note that the correctness of the algorithm stems from the fact that each term $g(s, i)$ coincides with the partial solution $\mathcal{G}^*(D_Z^{[1,i]}, \widehat{D}_Z^{[1,s]})$, and is correctly computed according to the recursive formulation in Theorem 2. Consequently, the approach leads to a loss-safe partitioning, since the solution found by NDP-OPT gets the minimal information loss among all possible splits of D_Z, including, in particular, the one found in the previous step of algorithm LogCC.

Let $n = |D_Z|$, $m = |\widehat{D}_Z|$, with $1 < m < n$ and $P_{T,Z}$ be the size of the contingency table over D_Z and D_T, i.e., the number of non-zero values in the distribution $p(T, Z)$. Then, it can be shown that NDP-OPT is loss-safe, and computes in $O(n^2 \times m + P_{T,Z})$ an exact solution to problem NDP.

A greedy algorithm for function Partition. A serious drawback of algorithm NDP-OPT is the quadratic dependency on $|D_Z|$, which makes it unviable in many important real world application scenarios. Hence, we next investigate an alternative, greedy, approach to NDP, which consumes linear time in $|D_Z|$ only.

The algorithm, shown in Fig. 4, iteratively performs a binary split on both D_Z and $\widehat{D}_Z$, where every range $D_Z^{[u,v]} = \{z_u, ..., z_v\}$ of values from D_Z is associated with a suitable range $\widehat{D}_Z^{[r,s]} = \{\widehat{z}_r, ..., \widehat{z}_s\}$ of clusters from $\widehat{D}_Z$. For any pair of intervals $D_Z^{[u,v]}$ and $\widehat{D}_Z^{[r,s]}$, we keep trace of the associated index ranges by storing $\langle u, v, r, s \rangle$ in R.

Starting with only one cluster, which encompasses the whole $\widehat{D}_Z$ and is assigned to all values in D_Z, the algorithm iteratively selects a cluster $\widehat{D}_Z^{[\overline{r},\overline{s}]}$, spanning over at least two clusters of $\widehat{D}_Z$ (i.e., $\overline{s} > \overline{r}$), along with its associated interval $D_Z^{[\overline{u},\overline{v}]}$, and acts

---

Input: A domain D_Z, a set of clusters $\widehat{D}_Z = \{\widehat{z_1}, ..., \widehat{z_m}\}$;
Output: A clustering function from D_Z to $\widehat{D}_Z$;

$c(u, s) := \sum_{0 < i \leq u} \sum_{0 < l \leq r} \delta_T(z_u, \widehat{z_r})$, $\forall u \in [1..n]$ and $\forall r \in [1..m]$;
Let $\Theta(u, v, r, s) = (\, c(v, s) - c(u - 1, s) - c(v, r - 1) + c(u - 1, r - 1) \,)\,/(s - r + 1)$;
$R := \{\langle 1, m, 1, n \rangle\}$;
while $R \neq \emptyset$ **do**
    Let $\langle \overline{u}, \overline{v}, \overline{r}, \overline{s} \rangle$ be a tuple in R, and $\tau = \left\lfloor \frac{s+r}{2} \right\rfloor$;
    if $\overline{r} = \overline{s}$ **then**
        Set $C_Z(z_i) := \widehat{z_\tau}$ for each i in $[\overline{u}..l^*]$;
    else
        Let $l^* = \arg\min_{\mu \in [\overline{u}..\overline{v}]}(\,(\, \Theta(\overline{u}, \mu, \overline{r}, \tau) + \Theta(\mu + 1, \overline{v}, \tau + 1, \overline{s})\,)\,)$;
        $R := R \cup \{\langle \overline{u}, l^*, \overline{r}, \tau \rangle, \langle l^* + 1, \overline{v}, \tau + 1, \overline{s} \rangle\}$;
    end if;
end while;
return C_Z;

Fig. 4. Algorithm `NDP-GR`: A greedy implementation for `Partition`

a binary partition on both of them. While the cluster range $[\overline{r}, \overline{s}]$ is divided into two equi-numerous sub-ranges, $[\overline{u}..\overline{v}]$ is split in a greedy way, based on the cost function Θ, defined as follows: $\Theta(u, v, r, s) = \frac{1}{s-r+1} \cdot \sum_{l=r}^{s} \sum_{i=u}^{v} \delta(i, l)$. Roughly, $\Theta(u, v, r, s)$ provides a pessimistic estimation for the contribution given by values $z_u, ..., z_v$ to the final mutual information loss, when they are required to only be assigned to some of the clusters $\widehat{z_r}, ..., \widehat{z_s}$ – it is indeed an upper bound for $\mathcal{G}^*(D_Z^{[u,v]}, \widehat{D}_Z^{[r,s]})$.

Specifically, the selected interval $[\overline{u}..\overline{v}]$ is split in correspondence of the index μ^* that guarantees the lowest value for $\Theta(\overline{u}, \mu^*, \overline{r}, \tau) + \Theta(\mu^* + 1, \overline{v}, \tau + 1, \overline{s})$ – estimating the loss in mutual information that will arise by assigning $z_{\overline{u}}, ..., z_{\mu^*}$ (resp., $z_{\mu^*+1}, ..., z_{\overline{v}}$) to some clusters in $\widehat{z_{\overline{r}}}, ..., \widehat{z_\tau}$ (resp., $\widehat{z_{\tau+1}}, ..., \widehat{z_{\overline{s}}}$). Then, R is updated accordingly, by replacing tuple $\langle \overline{u}, \overline{v}, \overline{r}, \overline{s} \rangle$ with those representing the new clusters originated from it: $\langle \overline{u}, \mu^*, \overline{r}, \tau^* \rangle$ and $\langle \mu^* + 1, \overline{v}, \tau^* + 1, \overline{s} \rangle$. As a special case, when the tuple extracted from R spots just a single cluster $\widehat{z_{\overline{r}}}$ in $\widehat{D}_Z$, the algorithm updates the function C_Z, eventually returned as output, by assigning all the values in $D_Z^{[u,v]}$ to $\widehat{z_{\overline{r}}}$.

It is easy to see that algorithm `NDP-GR` takes $O(n \times m + P_{T,Z})$ only. This makes the algorithm `NDP-GR` an efficient tool for clustering even large numerical domains. However, as a price for its efficiency, we do not have any guarantee about the loss-safe property, instead enjoyed by `NDP-OPT`. Yet, a number of experiments (discussed in Section 5) evidenced that `NDP-GR` finds nearly-optimal solutions in many practical cases, hence ensuring reasonable computation time for the whole co-clustering process.

5   Experiments

The approach discussed in the paper has been tested against several synthesized log data, obtained by an ad-hoc Java generator, according to the following procedure. Given a workflow schema, its activities are randomly partitioned into clusters. For each activity cluster, a number of traces are randomly generated according to the schema, yet requiring that all the activities in the cluster occur. Conversely, a set of metric values are generated according to a uniform distribution, and then ordered and divided into a

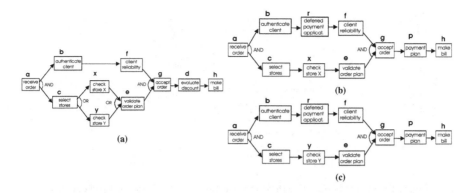

Fig. 5. Workflow schemas for three trace clusters mined from a log of process HANDLEORDER

given number of intervals. Each such interval is made to correspond to a trace cluster, and all the traces in the latter are randomly associated with some values in the interval. Finally, all correlation tables are altered with some noise, by flipping a fraction θ of their entries, and turned into valid joint probability matrices, by a normalization step.

Qualitative results on the running example. We start our analysis by discussing the results of LogCC on a syntectic log data we have randomly generated over the schema in Fig. 1.(c). Specifically, to reflect the semantics of the application, we generated 2000 traces in a way that task d does not occur in any trace including r, and that p appears in any trace not containing r. In order to cluster the log according to both structure and the performances, three correlated dimensions are considered: traces (T), activities (A) and durations (Z). For each dimension, we applied algorithm LogCC by requiring 3 clusters (i.e., $m^T = 3$, $m^A = 3$ and $m^Z = 3$). Moreover, we used the greedy implementation of function Partition (cf. algorithm NDP-GR), and gave the same weight to both auxiliary dimensions (i.e., $\beta_A = \beta_Z = 0.5$).

Fig. 5 shows the schemas associated with the discovered clusters, corresponding to three different use case of the process. Indeed, Fig. 5.(a) describes a schema for managing orders without deferred payment (task r does not appear at all), where discount evaluation (task d) is done mandatorily. Conversely, the two other schemas (Fig. 5.(b) and 5.(c)) concern orders with deferred payment, which are, in their turn, split in two different clusters, based on the presence of task x. Note that such a finer grain partition of the traces, which could not have been obtained by considering their structural aspects only, allows to recognize a specific usage case, quite relevant to performance analysis: deferred-payment orders requiring a check over store X (cf. Fig. 5.(b)), which clearly distinguish from the remaining process instances (cf. Fig. 5.(c)) for higher duration.

Quantitative results on synthesized data. In order to make scalability tests, we fixed a workflow schema of 200 activities, with 100 of them left optional, and we defined metrics to take values from the range 0..500. Several datasets have been generated, with different numbers of traces (up to 2000), by using a fixed noise factor $\theta = 0.2$. In each test, the number of required clusters (made varying up to 16) was set the same for all dimensions (e.g., traces, activities, metrics).

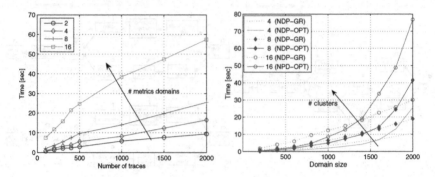

Fig. 6. Total computation time (left) and partitioning time (right) on synthetic data

n^Z	m^Z	Loss NDP-OPT	Loss NDP-GR	#steps NDP-GR	#steps NDP-OPT
400	2	2,548656681	2,548751835	193,67	19052,33
800	2	2,571874636	2,571863359	382	73545
1200	2	2,58146775	2,581462137	576,67	167161,33
1600	2	2,585506739	2,58550221	771,67	298920,67
2000	2	2,589513452	2,589513266	967	469104,33
400	4	2,542673346	2,542453391	378,67	55205
800	4	2,574832966	2,574787792	764,67	222167
1200	4	2,582005478	2,582005276	1146	496971
1600	4	2,586112494	2,586100372	1555,33	913054
2000	4	2,590549195	2,590555083	1955,33	1441242
400	8	2,546683739	2,54598238	579	136089,33
800	8	2,574457027	2,574144555	1144	520352
1200	8	2,580460745	2,580369062	1737	1190361,67
1600	8	2,586304248	2,586284432	2349	2169104
2000	8	2,589181461	2,589158344	2905	3310708,33

Fig. 7. Loss in mutual information: NDP-OPT vs NDP-GR

The total computation time of algorithm LogCC, equipped with the greedy version of function Partition, is depicted in the left side of Fig. 6. These results – confirmed in a wider series of tests not illustrated here for space reasons – prove the scalability of the approach, by showing a linear dependence of the computation time on both the number of traces and the number of domains considered.

The right-side of Fig. 6 shows, instead, results for a comparison between NDP-OPT (solid lines) and NDP-GR (dashed lines), for different number of clusters and sizes of the partitioned domain. As expected from the theoretical analysis provided in Section 4, one may notice that algorithm NDP-GR scales linearly w.r.t. the number of elements in the domain, while algorithm NDP-OPT suffers from a quadratic dependence, which is needed to provide an optimal solution for the partitioning problem. Further insights on this behavior can be achieved from 7, where the number of steps (formally, the number of times an element of the domain is considered for being a boundary) of both the algorithms is reported, averaged on 4 executions.

Note that yet being an approximate solution that does not enjoy the *loss-safe* property, NDP-GR is effective to clustering numerical domains, as it appears from Fig. 7, which also compares the loss in mutual information produced by NDP-OPT and NDP-GR, for different numbers of elements and numbers of asked clusters.

6   Conclusions

We have devised a novel process mining approach that substantially differs from previous works in taking account performance measures on log traces, beside mere "structural" information on task timing. The approach founds on an information-theoretic framework, where log traces are co-clustered along with their structural elements and metrics values. Each cluster of traces is eventually provided with a workflow schema, which hence models a specific use case of the process.

Notably, we extend the framework of [3] by considering more than two domains for the clustering, and by introducing numerical domains to be split into non-overlapping ranges. To face the latter issue, we have proposed two alternative implementations of the splitting procedure, based on an exact dynamic-programming approach and on an efficient greedy heuristic, respectively. Encouraging results were obtained by testing the approach on synthesized data, even when using the greedy procedure.

As directions of future work, we intend to carry out a more extensive empirical analysis of the approach on real process logs, as well as to devise some strategy for supporting the user in properly setting the parameters of the algorithm.

References

1. I. S. Dhillon. Co-clustering documents and words using bipartite spectral graph partitioning. In *Proc. Intl. Conf. on Knowledge Discovery and Data Mining (KDD01)*, pp. 269–274, 2001.
2. P. Berkhin and J. D. Becher. Learning simple relations: Theory and applications. In *Proc. SIAM Intl. Conf. on Data Mining (SDM02)*, 2002.
3. I. S. Dhillon, S. Mallela, and D. S. Modha. Information-theoretic co-clustering. In *Proc. Intl. Conf. on Knowledge Discovery and Data Mining (KDD03)*, pp. 89–98, 2003.
4. B. Gao, T.-Y. Liu, X. Zheng, Q.-S. Cheng, and W.-Y. Ma. Consistent bipartite graph co-partitioning for star-structured high-order heterogeneous data co-clustering. In *Proc. Intl. Conf. on Knowledge Discovery and Data mining (KDD05))*, pp. 41–50, 2005.
5. G. Greco, A. Guzzo, L. Pontieri, and D. Saccà. Mining expressive process models by clustering workflow traces. In *Proc. Pacific-Asia Conference (PAKDD'04)*, pp. 52–62, 2004.
6. J. Herbst and D. Karagiannis. Integrating machine learning and workflow management to support acquisition and adaptation of workflow models. *Journal of Intelligent Systems in Accounting, Finance and Management*, 9:67–92, 2000.
7. S. Hwang and W. Yang. On the discovery of process models from their instances. *Decision Support Systems*, 34(1):41–57, 2002.
8. G. Schimm. Mining most specific workflow models from event-based data. In *Proc. Intl. Conf. on Business Process Management*, pp. 25–40, 2003.
9. W. van der Aalst, A. Weijters, and L. Maruster. Workflow mining: Discovering process models from event logs. *IEEE Transactions on Knowledge and Data Engineering (TKDE)*, 16(9):1128–1142, 2004.
10. B. van Dongen and W. van der Aalst. Multi-phase process mining: Aggregating instance graphs into EPCs and Petri nets. In *Proc. Intl. Work. on Applications of Petri Nets to Coordination, Worklflow and Business Process Management (PNCWB) at the ICATPN'05*, 2005.
11. S. Madeira and A. Oliveira. Biclustering algorithms for biological data analysis: a survey. *IEEE/ACM Transactions on Computational Biology and Bioinformatics*, 1:24–45.
12. H. Zha, X. He, C. Ding, H. Simon, and M. Gu. Bipartite graph partitioning and data clustering. In *Proc. Intl. Conf. on Information and Knowledge Management (CIKM'01)*, pp. 25–32, 2001.

Mixed Decision Trees:
An Evolutionary Approach

Marek Krętowski and Marek Grześ

Faculty of Computer Science, Białystok Technical University
Wiejska 45a, 15-351 Białystok, Poland
{mkret, marekg}@ii.pb.bialystok.pl

Abstract. In the paper, a new evolutionary algorithm (EA) for mixed tree learning is proposed. In non-terminal nodes of a mixed decision tree different types of tests can be placed, ranging from a typical univariate inequality test up to a multivariate test based on a splitting hyperplane. In contrast to classical top-down methods, our system searches for an optimal tree in a global manner, i.e. it learns a tree structure and tests in one run of the EA. Specialized genetic operators allow for generating new sub-trees, pruning existing ones as well as changing the node type and the tests. The proposed approach was experimentally verified on both artificial and real-life data and preliminary results are promising.

1 Introduction

Decision trees [18] are one of the most frequently applied data mining approaches. There exist many induction algorithms which can differ in several more or less important elements, like for example the way for tree construction (i.e. top-down versus global) or the way for test selection. From a users point of view, one of the most important features of a decision tree is a test representation in the internal nodes. In typical univariate trees two types of tests are usually permitted. For a nominal attribute, the mutually exclusive sets of feature values are associated with each branch, whereas for a continuous valued feature inequality tests are applied. In case of multivariate trees more than one feature can be used to create a test. Linear (oblique) tests based on a splitting hyper-plane are specific and the most widely used form of the multivariate test. It should be noticed that most of the DT-based systems are homogeneous, which means that they take advantage of only one type of test (i.e. univariate or oblique).

The term *mixed decision trees* was proposed by Llora and Wilson in [15] to describe trees in which different types of tests can be exploited. One of the first and best-known examples of such an approach is the *CART* system [3]. This system is able to search for a linear combination of non-nominal features in each node and it compares the obtained test with the best univariate test. However, it should be noted that *CART* has a strong preference to simpler tests and it results in very rare use of more elaborate splits. Another form of the hybrid classifier is proposed by Brodley in [4]. Her *MCS* system combines univariate

A Min Tjoa and J. Trujillo (Eds.): DaWaK 2006, LNCS 4081, pp. 260–269, 2006.

tests, linear machines and instance-based classifiers (k-NN) and during the top-down generation of a tree classifier it recursively applies automatic bias selection. Recently, a fine grain parallel model $GALE$ [15] was applied to generate decision trees which employ inequality and oblique tests.

Evolutionary techniques [16] are known to be useful in many data mining tasks [9]. They were successfully applied to learning univariate (e.g. [10,19,20]) and linear trees (e.g. [6,2,5]). Regardless of the tree types there are two main approaches to the induction: top-down and global. The first one is based on a greedy recursive procedure of test searching and sub-node creation until a stopping condition is met. In contrast to this classical method, the global algorithm searches for both the tree structure and tests at the same time.

The global approach based on evolutionary algorithms for decision tree induction was investigated in our previous papers. We showed that homogeneous trees (univariate [12] or oblique [13,14]) can be effectively induced and we demonstrated that globally generated classifiers are generally less complex with at least comparable accuracy. In this paper, we want to merge the two developed methods in one system, which will be able to induce mixed trees.

The rest of the paper is organized as follows. In the next section our global system for induction of mixed decision trees is presented. Preliminary experimental validation of the approach on both artificial and real-life datasets are presented in section 3. The paper is concluded in the last section.

2   Global Induction of Mixed Decision Trees

The general structure of the proposed algorithm follows a typical evolutionary framework [16]. As the presented approach is a continuation and unification of our work on the global induction of homogeneous decision trees [12,13,14], in this section we described only these issues that are specific to mixed trees.

Representation and initialization. A mixed decision tree is a complicated tree structure, in which the number of nodes, test types and even the number of test outcomes are not known in advance for a given learning set. Moreover additional information, e.g. about feature vectors associated with each node, should be accessible during the induction. As a result, decision trees are not specially encoded in individuals and they are represented in their actual form.

There are three possible test types in internal nodes: two univariate and one multivariate. In case of univariate tests, a test representation depends on the considered attribute type. For nominal attributes at least one attribute value is associated with each branch starting in the node, which means that an internal disjunction is implemented. For continuous-valued features typical inequality tests with two outcomes are used. In order to speed up the search process only boundary thresholds[1] as potential splits are considered and they are calculated

---

[1] A boundary threshold for the given attribute is defined as a midpoint between such a successive pair of examples in the sequence sorted by the increasing value of the attribute, in which the examples belong to two different classes.

before starting the EA. Finally, an oblique test with binary outcome can be also applied as a multivariate test. A splitting hyperplane is represented by a fixed-size table of real values corresponding to the weight vector and the threshold. The inner product is calculated to decide where an example is routed.

Before starting the actual evolution, the initial population is created. All initial trees are homogeneous, but half of the population is initialized with univariate tests and the other part with oblique tests. A simple top-down algorithm is applied to generate all individuals. In each potential internal node it chooses randomly a pair of objects from different classes and searches for a test which separates them to distinct sub-trees. In case of a univariate tree, such a test can be directly constructed for any feature with different feature values. When an oblique test is necessary, the splitting hyperplane is perpendicular to the segment connecting the two drawn objects and placed in a halfway position.

The algorithm terminates when the fitness of the best individual does not improve during a fixed number of generations (default value is equal 1000) or the maximum number of generations (default value: 10000) is reached.

Genetic operators. There are two specialized genetic operators corresponding to the classical mutation and cross-over. Application of both operators can result in changes of the tree structure and tests in non-terminal nodes.

A mutation-like operator is applied with a given probability to a tree (default value is 0.5) and it guarantees that at least one node of the selected individual is mutated [14]. Modifications performed by this operator depend on the node type (i.e. if the considered node is a leaf node or an internal node). For a non-terminal node a few possibilities exist:

- a completely new test of the same or different type can be drawn; new tests are created in the same way as described for the initialization,
- the existing test can be altered by shifting the splitting threshold (continuous-valued feature), by re-grouping feature values (nominal features) or by shifting the hyperplane (oblique test); these modifications can be purely random or can be performed according to the adapted dipolar operator [11],
- the test can be replaced by another test or tests can be interchanged,
- one sub-tree can be replaced by another sub-tree from the same node,
- the node can be transformed into a leaf.

Modifying a leaf makes sense only if it contains objects from different classes. The leaf is transformed into an internal node and a new test is randomly chosen. The search for effective tests can be recursively repeated for all descendants.

There are also several variants of cross-over operators (applied with a default probability 0.2). One node is randomly chosen in each of two affected individuals and an exchange encompasses sub-trees or is limited only to nodes (their tests). The order of sub-trees can be also altered during the cross-over.

The application of any genetic operator can result in a necessity for relocation of the input vectors between parts of the tree rooted in the modified node. Additionally the local maximization of the fitness is performed by pruning lower parts of the sub-tree on the condition that it improves the value of the fitness.

Fitness function. A fitness function drives the evolutionary search process and is the most important and sensitive component of the algorithm. When concerning a classification task it is well-known that the direct optimization of the classifier accuracy measured on the learning set leads to an over-fitting problem. In a typical top-down induction of decision trees, the over-specialization problem is mitigated by defining a stopping condition and by applying a post-pruning [8]. In our approach, the search for an optimal structure is embedded into the evolutionary algorithm by incorporating a complexity term in the fitness function. The fitness function is maximized and has the following form:

$$Fitness(T) = Q_{Reclass}(T) - \alpha \cdot (Comp(T) - 1.0), \tag{1}$$

where $Q_{Reclass}(T)$ is a reclassification quality and α is the relative importance of the classifier complexity (default value is 0.005). In the simplest form the tree complexity $Comp(T)$ can be defined as the classifier size which is usually equal to the number of nodes. The penalty associated with the classifier complexity increases proportionally with the tree size and prevents classifier over-specialization. Subtracting 1.0 eliminates the penalty when the tree is composed of only one leaf (in majority voting).

This simple complexity definition is surely adequate for a homogeneous tree composed of only univariate tests. However, when linear tests are also considered, it seems that a more elaborate solution is necessary. It is rather straightforward that an oblique split based on a few features is more complex than a univariate test and that we should apply preference to simpler tests as an inductive bias. As a consequence the tree complexity should also reflect the complexity of the tests. However it is not easy to definitely decide how to balance different test complexities because it depends on the problem solved and user preferences. In such a situation we decided to define the tree complexity $Comp(T)$ in a flexible way and allow the user to tune its final form:

$$Comp(T) = |N_{leaf}(T)| + \sum_{n \in N_{int}(T)} (1 + \beta \cdot (F(n) - 1)), \tag{2}$$

where $N_{leaf}(T)$ and $N_{int}(T)$ are sets of leaves and internal nodes correspondingly, $F(n)$ is the number of features used in the test associated with the node n and $\beta \in [0, 1]$ is the relative importance of the test complexity (default value 0.2). The complexity of the tree is defined as a sum of the complexities of the nodes and it is assumed that for leaves and internal nodes with univariate tests the node complexity is always equal to 1.0. It can be also observed that when $\beta = 1$ the number of features used in a test is applied as the test complexity, whereas when $\beta = 0$ the complexity of a test is completely ignored.

3   Experimental Results

The proposed approach to learning mixed decision trees is assessed on both artificial and real life datasets and is compared to the well-known top-down

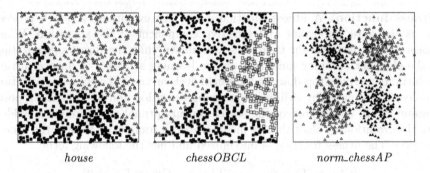

house   chessOBCL   norm_chessAP

Fig. 1. Examples of artificial datasets

univariate ($C4.5$ [21]) and oblique ($OC1$ [17]) decision tree systems. It is also compared to two homogenous versions of our global GDT system: univariate - GDT-AP [12] and oblique GDT-OB [14]. All prepared artificial datasets comprise training and testing parts. In case of data from a UCI repository [1] for which testing data is not provided, 10-fold stratified cross-validation was employed. Each experiment on all stochastic algorithms (i.e. all except $C4.5$) was performed 10 times and the average result of such an evaluation was presented. The $OC1$ system was run with different values of the seed that initializes the random number generator. Our system is initialized by the system time.

A statistical analysis of the obtained results was done by the Friedman test with the corresponding Dunn's multiple comparison test (significance level equal to 0.05) as recommended by Demsar [7].

Artificial datasets. A range of artificial datasets suited to axis-parallel or oblique tests was generated to assess the universality of the proposed approach. Most of the datasets have two continuous-valued features (see examples in Fig. 1) and only the $LS10$ (Linearly Separable) dataset has 10 features. The number of examples was varied and depends on the number of distinct regions. In the training part it ranged from 1000 (for simple 2-dimensional problems) to 4000 (for $LS10$). The testing part is twofold larger in each case.

There was also prepared a special dataset (see Fig. 2a) to validate the performance of the proposed mixed decision tree system. This dataset is the three class problem that contains three descriptive features. Two of them (x and y) are continuous-valued and the last one (z) is nominal with two binary values. This experiment was intended to check whether our system can deal with such a problem in which the best separability of classes can be achieved by incorporating all three types of splits. A hyperplane and an inequality test separate observations on two planes and one nominal test provides additional separation between those planes. In Fig. 2b the decision tree learned by the GDT-Mix system is presented. It is the best solution to this problem. The most important thing is that the algorithm was able to select correctly different types of tests and apply them to build the optimal tree structure. This experiment shows

Table 1. Results on artificial data

Dataset	C4.5		OC1		GDT-Mix		GDT-AP		GDT-OB	
	size	quality	size	quality	size	quality	size	quality	size	quality
chess2x2	1	50	10.1	89.3	4.0	99.7	4	99.75	4	99.34
chess2x2x2	1	50	23.8	71.0	8.0	98.5	8	99.72	8.2	97.00
chess3x3	9	99.7	21.1	73.7	9.0	98.8	9	99.73	9.9	97.08
chessOB2CL	33	95.6	7	77.3	4.3	98.0	17.9	92.64	4.7	99.05
chessOB4CL	35	94.6	4.3	49.8	4.0	97.9	18	92.14	4.4	98.41
house	21	97.4	8.2	92.8	4.0	96.0	13.3	96.62	4	96.71
ls10	284	77.3	7.3	95.3	2.0	95.7	18.8	70.68	2	97.20
ls2	22	97	2	99.7	2.0	99.8	14	95.68	2	99.93
normal	5	90	7.3	87.9	3.6	89.5	25.7	86.85	4	90.01
norm_chessAP	1	50	11.2	85.5	4.0	95.4	4.2	95.53	4	95.42
norm_chessOB	19	93	11	83.3	4.0	93.7	9.3	92.59	4	93.58
norm_wave	15	94	8.4	90.3	4.0	94.5	9.1	93.45	4	94.87
zebra1	25	95.3	3	83.5	3.3	99.1	15.3	94.64	3	99.28
zebra2	2	59.5	4.8	94.1	4.0	98.5	21.4	91.63	4.4	98.70
zebra3	57	91.2	8.2	24.3	8.8	95.4	31.5	88.80	8.8	96.76

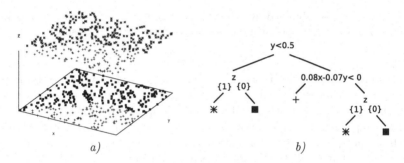

a)   b)

Fig. 2. A graphical representation of the dataset which can be optimally separated only with all three test types and the tree obtained by *GDT-Mix* system

that when such compound relationships will exist in the real data our algorithm may tackle them successfully revealing invaluable information for specialists in a certain domain to which it might have been applied.

The results on the range of datasets designed for this investigation are collected in Table 1. Because we analyze artificial data in this experiment, we know how, in terms of the type of tests used in the tree, the optimal solution can be represented. There are certain classification tasks, like for instance the classical chessboard problem, that suit very well univariate decision trees. There are also linearly separable datasets (like e.g. *LS*10) for which splits based on hyperplanes are highly recommended to avoid a staircase-like structure. The main aim of our endeavor in this work is to show that *GDT-Mix* can easily adjust to the specific problem. The analysis of Table 1 proved that the *GDT-Mix* inducer performs better on axis parallel data while compared to oblique systems

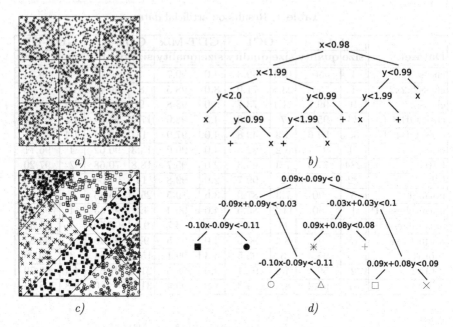

Fig. 3. Decision trees obtained by *GDT-Mix* system for *chess3x3* and *zebra3* datasets (*b*) and *d*)) and the corresponding dataset scatterplots with drawn splits (*a*) and *c*))

and on linearly separable data while compared to axis parallel systems. It is also important that statistical analysis does not show significant differences between the *GDT-Mix* algorithm and the systems specialized for certain problems when a comparison is made on such problems. Our universal system performs as well as the specialized systems, that is its very strong point. The statistical test indicates that *GDT-OB* is significantly better in terms of quality than *C4.5*, *OC1* and *GDT-AP*. As for *GDT-Mix*, it is statistically better than *OC1*. The comparisons based on the second measure (the tree size) are also favorable. Statistical analysis reveals that *GDT-Mix* produces significantly smaller trees than *C4.5* and *GDT-AP*. This score is easily justified, because in the case of problems which require oblique splits our *GDT-Mix* system takes advantage of such splits.

Discussed results show that the proposed algorithm is more flexible in terms of representation which can be modified during the induction. For that reason more detailed analysis of these results aims at investigating the obtained decision trees. Such trees for relatively complex axis parallel and linearly separable classification tasks are presented in Fig. 3. These trees present a promising result because the *GDT-Mix* system managed to find the type of tests that suit the data in the best way and was able to apply them to build trees that perform very competitively while comparing to results of specialized systems. In Fig. 3a and 3c splits from decision trees are additionally drawn to present how the input space is partitioned by the global inducer. These splits show that trees obtained

Table 2. Results on real datasets with only continuous attributes

Dataset	OC1		GDT-Mix		GDT-OB	
	size	quality	size	quality	size	quality
balance-scale	5.4	90.0	2.8	89.3	3.2	89.1
bcw	4.7	91.2	2.0	97.1	2.0	96.9
bupa	5.8	65.6	3.6	69.5	3.0	71.3
glass	4.5	55.7	13.4	69.9	11.6	68.8
page-blocks	15.6	96.6	3.0	94.9	3.0	95.3
pima	6.5	69.6	2.4	75.0	2.1	75.3
sat	58.3	78.9	6.0	83.0	7.0	83.1
vehicle	21.6	66.4	8.8	67.7	7.7	65.7
waveform	10.5	77.4	4.2	81.2	4.2	82.2
wine	3.2	87.0	4.2	89.3	4.8	90.9

Table 3. Results on real datasets with both continuous and nominal attributes

Dataset	C4.5		GDT-Mix		GDT-AP	
	size	quality	size	quality	size	quality
australian	39	87	2.0	86.5	22.8	84.6
cars	31	97.7	3.6	97.9	4.0	98.7
cmc	136.8	52.2	4.0	55.1	13.1	53.8
german	77	73.3	3.8	72.0	16.5	73.4
golf	5	60	4.9	70.5	4.7	72.5
heart	22	77.1	6.1	75.3	44.9	74.2
solar	20	73.1	5.8	70.7	33.7	73.6
vote	5	97	2.0	97.0	13.5	95.6

in this experiment have an optimal structure (the empirical superiority of global induction).

Real-life data. Results on real-life data are divided into two groups. In the first one, $GDT - Mix$ is compared with $OC1$ and $GDT - OB$ systems, which are designed for applications where the instances have only numeric (continuous) feature values (Table 2). In the second group, the proposed system is compared with univariate tree induction algorithms on datasets that have both nominal and continuous attributes (Table 3).

The analysis of these results shows that there are no statistically significant differences in the quality between compared algorithms on all datasets. It is very favorable result. It means that the *GDT-Mix* system, which is designed to be universal to different kinds of tasks, performs as good as specialized counterparts. In the case of the size of the tree the same statistical analysis of the Table 3 indicates that *GDT-Mix* produces significantly smaller trees than *C4.5*. A detailed inspection of this table shows that there are some datasets (e.g. *heart*) for which there is evident difference in the tree size which shows the superiority

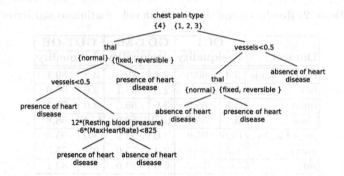

Fig. 4. The decision tree for *heart* data found by *GDT-Mix*

of the *GDT-Mix* algorithm. This is a very useful feature of mixed trees. As for the Table 2 there is a statistical difference in terms of the tree size ($p = 0.046$) but Dunn's test failed to detect it.

More detailed analysis of decision trees obtained for real-life *heart* data is presented in Figure 4. This dataset was chosen for investigation because it contains both nominal and continuous attributes and represents a quite easily understood problem (at least in terms of outcomes of the classifier). Figure 4 presents one of decision trees (there were 10 runs of the algorithm on each dataset) that were gained in our experiment for *heart* data. In the presented tree all three types of possible tests are used. This example underlines the advantage of decision trees of being self explanatory and easy to understand. In mixed decision trees we can have tests both on nominal and continuous attributes what present interesting features of this system in terms of practical applications.

4   Conclusion and Future Works

In the paper a new evolutionary algorithm for global induction of mixed decision trees is proposed. In the unified framework both univariate and oblique tests are searched and applied in not-terminal nodes for optimal data splitting. The flexible defined fitness function enables the controlling of the inductive biases. Even preliminary validation shows that the algorithm is able to adapt to the problem being solved and to locally choose the most suitable test representation.

The presented approach is still under development and currently we are working on introducing more specialized mutation variants. They will allow the system e.g. to switch from an oblique hyper-plane to the closest axis-parallel test and analogously to slightly incline an original univariate test. We also consider introducing additional test types, especially multivariate tests. Furthermore, the fitness function and especially the impact of the definition of the complexity term on the resulting decision tree will be studied in more detail.

Acknowledgments. This work was supported by the grant W/WI/5/05 from Białystok Technical University.

References

1. Blake, C., Keogh, E., Merz, C.: *UCI repository of machine learning databases*, Irvine, CA: University of California, Dept. of Computer Science (1998).
2. Bot, M., Langdon, W.: Application of genetic programming to induction of linear classification trees. In *EuroGP 2000*. Springer LNCS 1802 (2000) 247–258.
3. Breiman, L., Friedman, J., Olshen, R., Stone C.: *Classification and Regression Trees*. Wadsworth Int. Group (1984).
4. Brodley, C.: Recursive automatic bias selection for classifier construction, *Machine Learning* 20 (1995) 63-94.
5. Cantu-Paz, E., Kamath, C.: Inducing oblique decision trees with evolutionary algorithms. *IEEE Transactions on Evolutionary Computation* **7**(1) (2003) 54–68.
6. Chai, B., Huang, T., Zhuang, X., Zhao, Y., Sklansky, J.: Piecewise-linear classifiers using binary tree structure and genetic algorithm. *Pattern Recognition* **29**(11) (1996) 1905–1917.
7. Demsar, J.: Statistical comparisons of classifiers over multiple data sets. *Journal of Machine Learning Research* 7 (2006) 1–30.
8. Esposito, F., Malerba, D., Semeraro, G.: A comparative analysis of methods for pruning decision trees. *IEEE Transactions on Pattern Analysis and Machine Intelligence* **19**(5) (1997) 476–491.
9. Freitas A.: *Data Mining and Knowledge Discovery with Evolutionary Algorithms*. Springer (2002).
10. Koza, J.: Concept formation and decision tree induction using genetic programming paradigm, In *Proc. of PPSN 1.*, Springer LNCS 496 (1991) 124–128.
11. Krętowski, M.: An evolutionary algorithm for oblique decision tree induction, In: *Proc. of ICAISC'04*, Springer LNCS 3070 (2004) 432–437.
12. Krętowski, M., Grześ, M.: Global learning of decision trees by an evolutionary algorithm, In: *Information Processing and Security Sys.*, Springer, (2005) 401–410.
13. Krętowski, M., Grześ, M.: Global induction of oblique decision trees: an evolutionary approach, In: *Proc. of IIPWM'05.*, Springer, (2005) 309–318.
14. Krętowski, M., Grześ, M.: Evolutionary learning of linear trees with embedded feature selection, In: *Proc. of ICAISC'06*, Springer LNCS 4029 (2006).
15. Llora, X., Wilson, S.: Mixed decision trees: Minimizing knowledge representation bias in LCS, In: *Proc. of GECCO'04*, Springer LNCS 3103 (2004) 797–809.
16. Michalewicz, Z.: *Genetic Algorithms + Data Structures = Evolution Programs*. 3rd edn. Springer (1996).
17. Murthy, S., Kasif, S., Salzberg, S.: A system for induction of oblique decision trees. *Journal of Artificial Intelligence Research* 2 (1994) 1–33.
18. Murthy, S.: Automatic construction of decision trees from data: A multidisciplinary survey. *Data Mining and Knowledge Discovery* 2 (1998) 345–389.
19. Nikolaev, N., Slavov, V.: Inductive genetic programming with decision trees. *Intelligent Data Analysis* 2 (1998) 31–44.
20. Papagelis, A., Kalles, D.: Breeding decision trees using evolutionary techniques. In: *Proc. of ICML'01.*, Morgan Kaufmann (2001) 393–400.
21. Quinlan, J.: *C4.5: Programs for Machine Learning*. Morgan Kaufmann (1993).

ITER: An Algorithm for Predictive Regression Rule Extraction

Johan Huysmans[1], Bart Baesens[1,2] and Jan Vanthienen[1]

[1] K.U.Leuven, Dept. of Decision Sciences and Information Management,
Naamsestraat 69, B-3000 Leuven, Belgium
[2] School of Management, University of Southampton, Southampton, SO17 1BJ,
United Kingdom

Abstract. Various benchmarking studies have shown that artificial neural networks and support vector machines have a superior performance when compared to more traditional machine learning techniques. The main resistance against these newer techniques is based on their lack of interpretability: it is difficult for the human analyst to understand the motivation behind these models' decisions. Various rule extraction techniques have been proposed to overcome this opacity restriction. However, most of these extraction techniques are devised for classification and only few algorithms can deal with regression problems.

In this paper, we present ITER, a new algorithm for pedagogical regression rule extraction. Based on a trained 'black box' model, ITER is able to extract human-understandable regression rules. Experiments show that the extracted model performs well in comparison with CART regression trees and various other techniques.

1 Introduction

While newer machine learning techniques, like artificial neural networks and support vector machines, have shown superior performance in various benchmarking studies [1,10] the application of these techniques remains largely restricted to research environments. A more widespread adoption of these techniques is foiled by their lack of explanation capability which is required in some application areas, like medical diagnosis or credit scoring. To overcome this restriction, various algorithms [2,4,5,6,8] have been proposed to extract meaningful rules from such trained 'black box' models. These algorithms' dual goal is to mimic the behavior of the black box as closely as possible with a minimal amount of rules. The main part of these extraction algorithms focus on classification problems, with only a few exceptions devised especially for regression.

In this paper, we present ITER, a new algorithm for pedagogical regression rule extraction. Based on a trained 'black box' model ITER is able to extract human-understandable regression rules. The algorithm works by iteratively expanding a number of hypercubes until the entire input space is covered.

In the next section, a small overview of related research is given. While algorithms for classification rule extraction are more widespread, we will cover

A Min Tjoa and J. Trujillo (Eds.): DaWaK 2006, LNCS 4081, pp. 270–279, 2006.
© Springer-Verlag Berlin Heidelberg 2006

some techniques that are able to extract regression rules either directly from the data points or from an underlying 'black box' regressor. In the third section, the inner workings of the ITER algorithm are explained in great detail and the performance of this algorithm is compared with other machine learning techniques.

2   Related Research

Regression trees [3,7] are usually constructed directly from the available training observations and are therefore not considered to be rule extraction techniques in the strict sense of the word. A CART regression tree [3] is a binary tree with conditions specified next to each non-leaf node. Classifying a new observation is done by following the path from the root towards a leaf node, choosing the left node when the condition is satisfied and the right node otherwise, and assigning the observation the value below the leaf node. This value below the leaf nodes equals the average y-value of training observations falling into this leaf node.

The regression tree is constructed by iteratively splitting nodes, starting from only the root node, so as to minimize an impurity measure. Often, the impurity measure of a node t is calculated as:

$$R(t) = \frac{1}{N} \sum_{\mathbf{x}_n \in t} (y_n - \overline{y}(t))^2 \qquad (1)$$

with $(\mathbf{x}_n, y_n)$ the training observations and $\overline{y}(t)$ the average y-value for observations falling into node t. The best split for a leaf-node of the tree is chosen such that it minimizes the impurity of the newly created nodes. Mathematically, the best split s* of a node t is that split s which maximizes:

$$\Delta R(s,t) = R(t) - p_L R(t_L) - p_R R(t_R) \qquad (2)$$

with t_L and t_R the newly created nodes. Construction of the tree is terminated when certain stopping criteria are met. Pruning of the nodes is performed afterwards to improve generalization behavior of the constructed tree.

Although most regression tree algorithms can be applied directly on the training data, it is also possible to apply these techniques for pedagogical rule extraction. Instead of using the original targets, the target values are provided by a trained black box model and the regression tree is constructed on these new data points. In our empirical experiments, we will use CART with both approaches.

3   ITER

3.1   Description

The pedagogical ITER-algorithm[1] can be used to build predictive regression rules from a trained regression model (e.g., a neural network or support vector

---

[1] Iter=latin for 'journey'.

machine). With minor adaptations it is suitable for classification problems as well. The main idea of the algorithm is to iteratively expand a number of (hyper)cubes until they cover the entire input space. Each of these cubes can then be converted into a rule of the following format:

if Var 1 $\in$ [Value$_1^{Low}$, Value$_1^{High}$] and Var 2 $\in$ [Value$_2^{Low}$, Value$_2^{High}$]

...and Var M $\in$ [Value$_M^{Low}$, Value$_M^{High}$] then predict some Constant

with M the dimension of the input space. The algorithm starts with the creation of a user-defined number of random starting cubes. These cubes are infinitesimally small and therefore correspond to points in the input space. Afterwards, these initial cubes are gradually expanded until they cover the entire input space or until they can no longer be expanded. During each update the following steps are executed:

1. For each hypercube i=1,...,N and for each dimension j=1,...,M calculate how far the cube can be expanded to both extremes of the dimension before it intersects with another cube, call these distances $LowerLimit_i^j$ and $UpperLimit_i^j$.
2. For each hypercube i=1,...,N and for each dimension j=1,...,M calculate the size of the update. The update equals $MinUpdate_j$, a user-specified constant, unless this size would result in overlapping cubes. If this is the case then the update is smaller such that the two blocks become adjacent. Mathematically: $LowerUpdate_i^j=$ minimum{$LowerLimit_i^j$, $MinUpdate_j$} and $UpperUpdate_i^j=$ minimum{$UpperLimit_i^j$, $MinUpdate_j$}
3. For each hypercube i=1,...,N and for each dimension j=1,...,M create two temporary cubes adjacent to the original cube along the opposite sides of dimension j with a width of respectively $LowerUpdate_i^j$ and $UpperUpdate_i^j$. For each of both cubes, create a number of random points lying within the cube and calculate the mean prediction for these points according to the trained continuous regression model. Call the difference between each of both means and the mean prediction for the original cube respectively $LowerDiff_i^j$ and $UpperDiff_i^j$.
4. Find the global minimum over all cubes of these differences and combine the temporary cube for which the difference was minimal with its original cube. Update the mean prediction for this cube and remove all other temporary cubes.

A small example will help to clarify the above procedure. In Figure 1, a two-dimensional input space (M=2) is shown with two cubes (N=2). We have chosen $MinUpdate_1$ equal to $MinUpdate_2$, a small positive constant. The numbers within the cubes are the mean predictions of the continuous black box model for points lying within that cube.

For both cubes we create four new cubes that surround the original cube. In Figure 1, these cubes are dark-shaded. The height of the cubes on the top and bottom (expanding along Y-dimension) equals $MinUpdate_2$. Similarly, the

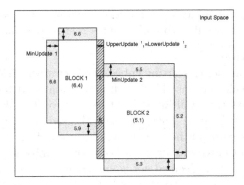

Fig. 1. Example for Iter-algorithm

width of the cubes on the left and right equals $MinUpdate_1$. However, if the first cube is expanded $MinUpdate_1$ units to the right, it would overlap with the second cube. Therefore the update to the right is smaller so that the two blocks become adjacent and non-overlapping. The same situation occurs with the update of the second block to the left (striped regions in Figure 1). For each of the dark shaded cubes, a number of random observations lying within that cube are generated and the predictions of the original 'black box' model for these data points are averaged. Finally, we select the shaded cube for which the difference between this average and the average prediction for the original cube is minimal. In the example, this is the shaded cube most to the right with a difference of 0.1. This cube is then combined with its original cube and the mean prediction for this cube is updated. The above steps are iterated until no further updates are possible.

3.2 Discussion

Size of Input Space. Before the first iteration of the algorithm, ITER calculates the size of the surrounding hypercube, i.e. the cube that surrounds all of the training observations. When calculating the allowed update size, ITER takes this surrounding cube into consideration and never creates cubes that lie outside the surrounding cube. The surrounding cube is also used to retrieve default values for the $MinUpdate_j$'s. Unless the user specifies otherwise, the defaults equal a twentieth of the size of each dimension. For example, if the values of the training observations for some dimension lie within the interval $[0,1]$ then $MinUpdate=0.05$.

Non-exhaustivity
While ITER creates rules that are non-overlapping, it is not always able to cover the entire input space. With other words, the rules created by ITER are exclusive but not necessarily exhaustive. In Figure 4(f), a small example of this situation is given. None of the four cubes can expand towards the middle because each cube is blocked by another cube. The shaded area will therefore not be covered by any rule. To ensure exhaustivity, we have to add a number of cubes that cover

the remaining gaps. Fortunately, from initial experiments we have observed that generally the number of cubes to add remains relatively small.

New Cube Creation

By specifying the number of starting cubes, the user automatically indicates the desired number of rules because ITER will never create extra cubes during execution. Only to make the resulting rule set exhaustive, the algorithm is allowed to construct additional cubes. There are several disadvantages, such as a strong dependence of the results on the number and location of the starting cubes, that make it worthwhile to give the algorithm the opportunity to create a new cube when the current update is deemed not 'good' enough. In this definition, we consider an update to be 'good' when the global minimum of step 4 is smaller than a user-specified threshold. We will therefore modify step 4 of the algorithm to:

New Step 4

Find the global minimum over all cubes of these differences.

- If this global minimum is smaller than the threshold then combine the temporary cube for which the difference was minimal with its original cube. Update the mean prediction for this cube and remove all other temporary cubes.
- If this global minimum is larger than the threshold then create a new cube on the position of the temporary cube for which the difference was the global minimum. The size of each side of the hypercube equals $MinimumUpdate_j$ (smaller if this results in overlapping cubes)

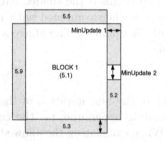

Fig. 2. New Cube Creation

By setting the threshold to a very large value, all updates will be considered good and the results of the updated step 4 will be similar to the original. In Figure 2, the creation of a new cube is shown. When the threshold is smaller than 0.1, a new cube will be created at the right hand side of the original cube. The size of each dimension of this new cube equals $MinUpdate_j$.

4 Empirical Results

In this section, ITER is applied to several artificial datasets with 2 continuous inputs from the interval [0,1]. Each of the datasets consists of 1000 observations, 500 for training and 500 for testing, and implements the following rules:

Table 1. Datasets

ARTI1	ARTI2
if x $\leq$ 0.5 and y $\leq$ 0.5 then z=0.7 + α RAND	if x $\leq$ 0.5 and y $\leq$ 0.5 then z=0 + α RAND
if x $\leq$ 0.5 and y > 0.5 then z=0.4 + α RAND	if x $\leq$ 0.5 and y > 0.5 then z=1 + α RAND
if x > 0.5 and y $\leq$ 0.5 then z=0.3 + α RAND	if x > 0.5 and y $\leq$ 0.5 then z=1 + α RAND
if x > 0.5 and y > 0.5 then z=0.0 + α RAND	if x > 0.5 and y > 0.5 then z=0 + α RAND

ARTI3	ARTI4
z= x + y + α RAND	z= $1 - (x - 0.5)^2 - (y - 0.5)^2 + \alpha$ RAND
a linear function	a parabole

with RAND a uniform random number in the interval [-1,1] and α a parameter to control the amount of randomness in the data. Although ARTI1 and ARTI2 may seem very similar, the symmetry in ARTI2 will cause considerable problems for a greedy algorithm like CART.

Several models are evaluated for each of these datasets and the influence of noise is tested by applying different values for α. The different models are Linear Regression (LR), K-Nearest Neighbor (KNN), Least-Squares Support Vector Machines (LS-SVM) [9] and CART. For the LS-SVMs we use a RBF-kernel with regularization and kernel parameters selected by a gridsearch procedure as described in [9]. CART trees were applied both directly on the data and as a pedagogical algorithm. For the pedagogical approach, we replace the original targets with values provided by the best performing 'black box', usually a LS-SVM model. Subsequent pruning of the tree is performed by minimizing the 10-fold cross-validation error on the training data to improve generalization behavior of the tree.

For a comparison of ITER with the other models, we initialize the algorithm with one random start cube and the default update sizes. For the selection of an appropriate threshold value, a simple trial-and-error approach was followed. For different values of the threshold we plot the average number of extracted rules and the performance on the training data over 100 independent trials. In Figure 3, we show this plot for ARTI 1 with α set to 0. It can be observed that small values for the threshold result in better performance but that it comes at the cost of an increased number of rules. A threshold somewhere between 0.1 and 0.25 might be preferred as it provides both interpretability and accuracy. Notice

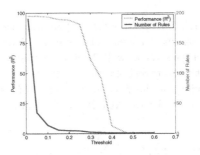

Fig. 3. ITER (ARTI1 with α=0)

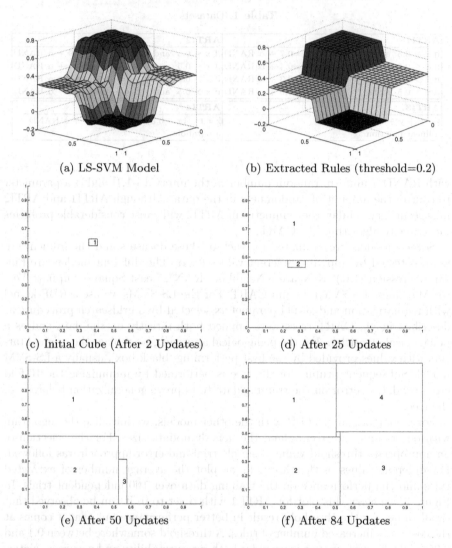

(a) LS-SVM Model

(b) Extracted Rules (threshold=0.2)

(c) Initial Cube (After 2 Updates)

(d) After 25 Updates

(e) After 50 Updates

(f) After 84 Updates

Fig. 4. Original LS-SVM Model (a) and extracted rules (b) for ARTI1 ($\alpha = 0$)

that the choice for a small threshold will result in rules that better approximate the underlying 'black box' model but that it will not lead to overfitting as long as the underlying model generalizes well. In Figure 4, execution of the algorithm is shown for ARTI1 with the threshold set to 0.2.

In Table 2, an overview of the results is given. For each of the models, we calculate the Mean Absolute Error (MAE) and R^2 value as follows:

$$MAE = \frac{1}{N} \sum_{i=1}^{N} \mid y_i - \hat{y}_i \mid \tag{3}$$

$$R^2 = 1 - \frac{\sum_{i=1}^{N}(y_i - \hat{y}_i)^2}{\sum_{i=1}^{N}(y_i - \bar{y})^2} \quad (4)$$

with N the number of observations, y_i and $\hat{y}_i$ respectively the target value and model prediction for observation i and $\bar{y}$ the mean target value. For the rule extraction techniques, MAE Fidelity and R^2 Fidelity show to what extent the extracted rules mimic the behavior of the underlying model. The same formulas (3) and (4) were used to calculate these measures, but with y_i and $\hat{y}_i$ representing the model prediction of respectively the 'black box' model and the extracted rules.

From Table 2, one can conclude that ITER is able to mimic accurately the behavior of the underlying models with only a limited amount of rules. For several of the experiments, ITER even achieves the same level of performance

Table 2. Overview of Out-of-Sample Performance

	MAE	R^2	# Rules	MAE Fidel.	R^2 Fidel.	MAE	R^2	# Rules	MAE Fidel.	R^2 Fidel.
ARTI1 ($\alpha=0$)						**ARTI1 ($\alpha=0.5$)**				
LR	0.11	74.79				0.27	32.61			
KNN(k=5)	0.02	93.10				0.27	27.90			
LS-SVM	0.03	94.93				0.27	35.28			
$CART_{direct}$	**0.00**	**99.52**	4			0.26	37.99	4		
$CART_{LS-SVM}$	0.01	97.41	12.95	0.02	97.80	0.26	36.26	51.31	0.03	97.47
$ITER_{LS-SVM}^{threshold=0.05}$	0.02	94.93	36.25	0.02	98.61	0.26	35.73	73.33	0.03	97.45
$ITER_{LS-SVM}^{threshold=0.1}$	0.02	95.12	12.94	0.02	97.75	0.26	35.74	16.40	0.05	91.19
$ITER_{LS-SVM}^{threshold=0.2}$	0.03	90.73	4.50	0.04	93.54	0.27	32.30	4.98	0.08	79.90
ARTI2 ($\alpha=0$)						**ARTI2 ($\alpha=0.5$)**				
LR	0.50	-0.65				0.48	-0.45			
KNN(k=5)	0.05	92.18				0.30	59.15			
LS-SVM	0.01	95.20				0.29	61.75			
$CART_{direct}$	**0.00**	**98.40**	11.96			0.27	68.15	11.01		
$CART_{LS-SVM}$	0.01	97.11	11.35	0.01	96.15	0.28	65.38	41.20	0.07	96.27
$ITER_{LS-SVM}^{threshold=0.1}$	0.04	92.85	31.55	0.03	93.51	0.29	62.13	82.59	0.07	96.36
$ITER_{LS-SVM}^{threshold=0.15}$	0.04	92.94	26.72	0.03	93.43	0.29	63.48	35.64	0.08	94.31
$ITER_{LS-SVM}^{threshold=0.20}$	0.04	92.79	21.20	0.04	93.31	0.29	63.03	18.88	0.10	91.56
ARTI3 ($\alpha=0$)						**ARTI3 ($\alpha=0.5$)**				
LR	**0.02**	**99.50**				0.26	63.81			
KNN(k=5)	0.03	99.17				0.28	56.74			
LS-SVM	0.03	99.49				0.26	63.75			
$CART_{direct}$	0.05	97.48	86.41			0.28	55.65	15.11		
$CART_{LS-SVM}$	0.06	97.09	74.88	0.05	97.75	0.26	63.68	77.10	0.04	98.19
$ITER_{LS-SVM}^{threshold=0.05}$	0.04	98.63	190.25	0.03	99.16	0.26	63.18	162.31	0.03	99.08
$ITER_{LS-SVM}^{threshold=0.10}$	0.07	96.08	51.90	0.06	96.61	0.27	61.54	44.58	0.06	96.35
$ITER_{LS-SVM}^{threshold=0.15}$	0.09	92.24	25.00	0.09	92.76	0.27	58.51	22.33	0.09	92.27
$ITER_{LS-SVM}^{threshold=0.2}$	0.12	87.02	15.34	0.12	87.53	0.28	54.98	13.39	0.11	87.11
ARTI4 ($\alpha=0$)						**ARTI4 ($\alpha=0.25$)**				
LR	0.08	-0.39				0.14	0.52			
KNN(k=5)	0.01	98.22				0.14	17.76			
LS-SVM	**0.00**	**100.00**				**0.13**	**26.70**			
$CART_{direct}$	0.02	94.27	92.08			0.14	17.56	14.48		
$CART_{LS-SVM}$	0.02	93.49	59.15	0.02	93.50	0.13	24.35	65.09	0.02	94.59
$ITER_{LS-SVM}^{threshold=0.04}$	0.02	92.58	68.60	0.02	92.59	0.13	24.57	75.02	0.02	93.68
$ITER_{LS-SVM}^{threshold=0.05}$	0.03	88.71	44.82	0.03	88.71	0.13	23.22	49.00	0.03	90.24
$ITER_{LS-SVM}^{threshold=0.1}$	0.05	63.32	10.99	0.05	63.33	0.14	17.72	11.97	0.05	67.32

as the underlying black box models. However, one can also observe that ITER has difficulties with finding the exact boundaries when the update size is chosen too large. For example, in Figure 4(f) ITER makes the first cube too large along the Y-axis because it uses the default update size of 0.05. A smaller update size would allow for better performance but at the cost of an increase in iterations and computation time. We are therefore looking into the use of adaptive update sizes so that larger updates are applied when the underlying 'black box' function is flat and smaller update sizes when the algorithm encounters slopes.

The results show that CART slightly outperforms ITER on most datasets, but what can not be observed from the results is the advantage of ITER's non-greedy approach for the interpretability of the extracted rules. For example, CART will fail to find good rules for ARTI2 because it is unable to find a split for the root node that significantly decreases impurity. It will therefore choose a more-or-less random split, $x2<0.95$, that does not correspond to any of the optimal splits ($x1<0.5$ or $x2<0.5$). ITER's expanding of hypercubes does not face this problem of looking only one step ahead and will be able to find rules that correspond more closely to those of Table 1.

5   Conclusion

In this paper, we presented a new algorithm for regression rule extraction and compared its performance with CART regression trees and several 'black box' regression techniques. While we believe that ITER can become a worthwhile alternative to CART's recursive partitioning approach, there is one major improvement recommended before ITER is able to assume this role. The use of adaptive update sizes can increase performance of the extracted rules in combination with a reduction of the required number of iterations. Our current work is focused on the implementation of this adaptive update rates. Future research will expand the algorithm to allow nominal variables as inputs and consequents for the rules that can be linear functions of the inputs.

References

1. B. Baesens, T. Van Gestel, S. Viaene, M. Stepanova, J. Suykens, and J. Vanthienen. Benchmarking state of the art classification algorithms for credit scoring. *Journal of the Operational Research Society*, 54(6):627–635, 2003.
2. N. Barakat and J. Diederich. Eclectic rule-extraction from support vector machines. *International Journal of Computational Intelligence*, 2(1):59–62, 2005.
3. L. Breiman, J.H. Friedman, R.A. Olsen, and C.J. Stone. *Classification and Regression Trees*. Wadsworth and Brooks, 1984.
4. G. Fung, S. Sandilya, and R.B. Rao. Rule extraction from linear support vector machines. In *11th ACM SIGKDD international conference on Knowledge discovery in data mining*, pages 32–40, 2005.
5. D. Martens, B. Baesens, T. Van Gestel, and J. Vanthienen. Adding comprehensibility to support vector machines using rule extraction techniques. In *Credit Scoring and Credit Control IX*, 2005.

6. H. Núñez, C. Angulo, and A. Català. Rule extraction from support vector machines. In *European Symposium on Artificial Neural Networks (ESANN)*, pages 107–112, 2002.

7. J.R. Quinlan. Learning with Continuous Classes. In *5th Australian Joint Conference on Artificial Intelligence*, pages 343–348, 1992.

8. R. Setiono, W.K. Leow, and J.M. Zurada. Extraction of rules from artificial neural networks for nonlinear regression. *IEEE Transactions on Neural Networks*, 13(3):564–577, 2002.

9. J.A.K. Suykens, T. Van Gestel, J. De Brabanter, B. De Moor, and J. Vandewalle. *Least Squares Support Vector Machines*. World Scientific, Singapore, 2002.

10. S. Viaene, R. Derrig, B. Baesens, and G. Dedene. A comparison of state-of-the-art classification techniques for expert automobile insurance fraud detection. *Journal of Risk And Insurance (Special Issue on Fraud Detection)*, 69(3):433–443, 2002.

COBRA: Closed Sequential Pattern Mining Using Bi-phase Reduction Approach

Kuo-Yu Huang, Chia-Hui Chang*, Jiun-Hung Tung, and Cheng-Tao Ho

Department of Computer Science and Information Engineering,
National Central University, Chung-Li, Taiwan 320
{want, ginhong, ctho}@db.csie.ncu.edu.tw, *chia@csie.ncu.edu.tw

Abstract. In this work, we study the problem of closed sequential pattern mining. We propose a novel approach which extends a frequent sequence with closed itemsets instead of single items. The motivation is that closed sequential patterns are composed of only closed itemsets. Hence, unnecessary item extensions which generates non-closed sequential patterns can be avoided. Experimental evaluation shows that the proposed approach is two orders of magnitude faster than previous works with a modest memory cost.

1 Introduction

Sequential pattern mining is a fundamental data mining task that has broad applications, including user behavior analysis, network intrusion detection and tandem repeats in DNA sequences. Ever since Agrawal et al. [6,7] introduced the concept of sequential pattern mining in 1995, this problem has received a great deal of attention [2,12,1,5]. Mining sequential pattern is more complex than frequent itemsets, since the permutations of items needs to be considered. Thus, instead of mining the complete set of frequent sequential patterns, we have stronger motive to mine closed sequential patterns, i.e. those containing no super-sequence with the same support. Mining closed sequential patterns not only reduce the number of sequences presented to users but also increase the mining efficiency by pruning the enumeration space.

Although mining closed subsequences shares a similar problem setting with mining closed itemsets [3,4], the techniques developed in closed itemset mining cannot work for frequent subsequence mining directly because subsequence testing requires ordered matching which is more difficult than simple subset testing. To the best of our knowledge, there are only two algorithms in closed sequential pattern mining, including CloSpan [10] and BIDE [9]. CloSpan takes the approach which generates a candidate set for closed sequential patterns and conducts post-pruning on it. The idea is that if a new discovered sequence s' is a sub-sequence or super-sequence of an existing sequence s and the projected database of s and s' is equal (closure checking), then we can stop searching any descendant of s' in the prefix search tree (thus pruning the search space) since for all γ the support of sequence $s' \diamond \gamma$ is equal to that of $s \diamond \gamma$. What makes the concept works is that the equivalence of the projected databases can be implemented by comparing the size of the databases. Furthermore, the size of the projected databases

A Min Tjoa and J. Trujillo (Eds.): DaWaK 2006, LNCS 4081, pp. 280–291, 2006.

can be used as the hash key to improve subsequence/supersequence checking more efficiently. However, the candidate maintenance-and-test paradigm suffers the inherent drawback in scalability.

Therefore, Wang et al. propose an alternative solution without candidate maintenance. It adopts a sequence closure-checking scheme called BIDE. From definition, we know that if a sequence $S = < s_1, s_2, \ldots, s_n >$ is not a closed sequence, there must exist at least an event e' which can be used to extend sequence S to a new sequence S' with the same support. The sequence S can be extended from the right most direction (after s_n), the left most direction (before s_1) or in the middle of the sequence (between s_i and s_{i+1}). If no such event exists, then S must be a closed sequence. Thus, the proposed BIDE scheme is to scan for common items from the sequence database, which might exist between s_i and s_{i+1}. As for search space pruning, they propose the *BackScan* pruning method to stop growing unnecessary patterns if the current prefix can not be closed. Again, they have defined the subsequences where the common items are searched for this BackScan closure checking. Although BIDE do not keep track of any historical closed sequential patterns (or candidate) for a new pattern's closure checking, it is a computational consuming approach since it needs multiple database scans for the bi-direction closure checking and the backscan pruning.

Both algorithms adopt the framework of PrefixSpan [5] which grows patterns by itemset extension and sequence extension, i.e. the last transaction of the current sequence is extended with a frequent item in the same transaction (item extension or I-step, denoted by $\diamond_i$) or different transaction (sequence extension or S-step, denoted by $\diamond_s$). However this pattern-growth strategy has two drawbacks: duplicate item extensions (To find the closed sequence $<\{A, B\}, \{A, B\}, \{A, B\}>$, we need three item extensions.) and expensive matching cost. In this paper, we have come up with a novel approach which conducts only sequence extensions by adding frequent closed itemsets to overcome these drawbacks. Frequent closed itemsets, as proved in the next section, are in fact the basic components of frequent closed sequences. They can be used to remove duplicate item enumeration as well as to reduce the matching cost for finding locally frequent items for I-extension.

The rest of this paper is organized as follows. We define the problem of closed sequential pattern mining in Section 2. Section 3 presents our algorithm. Experiments are reported in Section 4. Finally, conclusions are made in Section 5.

2 Problem Definition

Given a database SD of customer transactions, where each transaction consists of the following fields: customer-id, transaction-time, and the items purchased in the transaction. No customer has more than one transaction with the same transaction-time. Let $I = \{i_1, i_2, \ldots, i_N\}$ denote the set of items. A customer sequence can be represented by an ordered lists of itemsets, i.e., $S=<t_1, \ldots, t_n>$, where each itemset t_j is a nonempty subset of I, denoting the items bought in one transaction. The number of itemsets in a sequence is called the length of the sequence and a sequence with length l is called an l-sequence. A sequence $\alpha=<a_1, \ldots, a_m>$ is a **sub-sequence** of another sequence

$\beta = <b_1, \ldots, b_n>$, if and only if each a_j $(1 \leq j \leq m)$ can be mapped by b_{i_j} $(a_j \subseteq b_{i_j})$ and preserve its order $(1 \leq i_1 < i_2 < \ldots < i_m \leq n)$. We say β is super-sequence of α and β contains α.

A sequence database $SD = \{S_1, \ldots, S_{|SD|}\}$ is a set of sequences. Each sequence is associated with a *sid*. $|SD|$ represents the number of sequences in the database SD. The **absolute support** of a sequence α in a sequence database SD is the number of sequences in SD which contain α.

Given two sequences α and β. If α is a super-sequence of β and their supports are the same, we say α **absorbs** β. A sequential pattern β is a **closed sequential pattern** if there exists no proper sequence α that absorb β. The problem of closed sequential pattern mining is formulated as follows: given a minimum support level $minsup$, our task is to mine all closed sequential patterns in the sequence database with support greater than $minsup$, i.e. the **frequent** sequential patterns.

Table 1. An example sequence database SDB

SID	Sequence
1	$(C)(A, B, C)(B, C)(A, B, C)$
2	$(B, C)(A, B, C)(C)$
3	$(B, C)(A)(D, F)(A, B, C)(C)$
4	$(C)(A)(D, E)(A, B, C)$

To make connection between closed itemsets with closed sequential patterns, we define transaction support and sequence support of an itemset as follows. The transaction support of an itemset ρ is defined as the number of transactions that contain ρ while the sequence support of ρ is the number of sequences that contain the 1-sequence ρ. As usual, an itemset ρ is closed if there exist no superset of ρ with the same transaction support. However, an itemset ρ is frequent in a sequence database SD if the sequence support of ρ is greater than $minsup$. Thus, ρ is a frequent closed itemset if the sequence support is greater than $minsup$ and there exists no superset with the same transaction support.

Example 1. Given $minsup = 3$, all subsets of $\{A, B, C\}$ are frequent in the example sequence database in Table 1 since each itemset has sequence support 4. However, only $\{A\}$, $\{C\}$, $\{B, C\}$, and $\{A, B, C\}$ are frequent closed itemsets. Itemset $\{B\}$ is not a closed itemset since it has the same transaction support 8 as itemset $\{B, C\}$. Similarly, itemsets $\{A, B\}$ and $\{A, C\}$ are absorbed by $\{A, B, C\}$ since they have the same transaction support 5.

3   The COBRA Algorithm

In this section, we present an important observation and prove that a frequent closed sequential pattern is composed of only frequent closed itemsets. Thus, we devise a bi-phase reduction approach which mines frequent closed itemsets first and enumerate frequent closed sequential patterns by conducting sequence extensions. Before introducing the pruning strategy, we first define some terms.

Definition 1. *Given a sequence $S = <s_1, \ldots, s_n>$, the **First Matched Transaction** (**FMT**) of a 1-sequence $<p_1>$ is defined as the transactional ID of the first instance of the itemset p_1. Recursively, we can define the FMT of a $(m + 1)$-sequence $<p_1 \ldots p_m p_{m+1}>$ from the FMT of the m-sequence $<p_1 \ldots p_m>$ as (the transaction ID of) the first appearance of itemset p_{m+1} which occurs after the FMT of the m-sequence $<p_1 \ldots p_m>$. Given a sequence database SD (each transaction in SD has a unique ID), the **First Matched transaction List** (**FML**) of a prefix sequence $\alpha=<p_1 \ldots p_n>$ is defined as the list of first matched transactions of the sequences in SD w.r.t. α. Similarly, the **SID List** of α is a list of sequence IDs that support α.*

Given an itemset p, let $c(p)$ denote the closed itemset which contains p and has the same transaction support as p. If p is closed, then $c(p) = p$. By definition, $c(p)$ and p have the same transaction support and the FML are the same (denoted as $p.FML = c(p).FML$).

Lemma 1. *Given three sequential patterns α, β and γ, if $\alpha.FML = \beta.FML$ then $\alpha \diamond_s \gamma.FML = \beta \diamond_s \gamma.FML$ and $\alpha \diamond_s \gamma.SIDList = \alpha \diamond_s \gamma.SIDList$ (Definition 1).*

Theorem 1. *A closed sequential pattern is composed of only closed itemsets.*

Proof. Assume $\alpha = p_1 \diamond_s \ldots \diamond_s p_n$ is a closed sequential pattern, but some of the p_is are non-closed itemsets. Consider a sequential pattern $\beta = c(p_1) \diamond_s p_2 \diamond_s \ldots \diamond_s p_n$, $\alpha.SIDList = \beta.SIDList$ since $p_1.FML = c(p_1).FML$ (Lemma 1). Recursively, we can find a sequential pattern $\delta = c(p_1) \diamond_s \ldots \diamond_s c(p_n)$ such that $\alpha.FML = \delta.FML$. Therefore, α is not a closed sequential pattern. We thus have a contradiction to the original assumption that α is a closed sequential pattern and thus conclude that "all closed sequential patterns α are composed of only closed itemsets."

Theorem 1 is an important property as it provides a different view of mining closed sequential patterns. Instead of extending a prefix by I-steps and S-steps alternatively, we can mine closed frequent itemsets before mining closed sequential patterns and extends a prefix sequence by only S-steps. Therefore, we have come up with a three phase algorithm. In the first phase, we find all frequent closed itemsets and denote each of them by a unique C.F.I. *code*. To avoid the need to match closed frequent itemsets in a sequence in the enumeration phase, the original database is transformed into another database where the items in each sequence are replaced by C.F.I. *codes* that are contained in the transactions. Finally, the closed sequential patterns are enumerated in the third phase.

To illustrate, the example database SDB (Table 1) can be transformed into Figure 2 given the C.F.I. *codes* shown in Figure 1. This transformation retains the horizontal format of the original database. Note that the transactions are renumbered to eliminate empty transactions due to the removal of non-frequent items (e.g. D, E, F). Figure 1 also shows the location lists of each closed frequent itemset, which represent the vertical format of the original database.

We refer this as a bi-phase reduction approach since we mine C.F.I. for first phase reduction then mine closed sequences for second phase reduction. This approach not only reduces the search spaces and duplicate combinations but also avoids the matching

Code	C.F.I.	FML	LocationList (SID,TID)
#1	ABC	2, 6, 10,14	(1,2), (1,4), (2,6), (3,10), (4,14)
#2	BC	2, 5, 8, 14	(1,2),(1,3), (1,4), (2,5), (2,6), (3,8), (3,10), (4,14)
#3	A	2, 6, 9, 13	(1,2), (1,4), (2,6), (3,9), (3,10), (4,13), (4,14)
#4	C	1, 5, 8, 12	(1,1), (1,2), (1,3), (1,4), (2,5), (2,6), (2,7), (3,8), (3,10), (3,11), (4,12), (4,14)

Fig. 1. Vertical-based LocationList and FML

TID	1	2	3	4	5	6	7	8	9	10	11	12	13	14
SID	1	1	1	1	2	2	2	3	3	3	3	4	4	4
Code	#4	#1	#2	#1	#2	#1	#4	#2	#3	#1	#4	#4	#3	#1
		#2	#4	#2		#4	#2		#4	#2				#2
		#3		#3			#3			#3				#3
		#4		#4			#4			#4				#4

Fig. 2. Horizontal Encoded Database EDB

costs in item extension process. A similar framework has also been adopted in [8] for inter-transaction association mining. However, applying such a framework in closed pattern mining is much more economic than regular pattern mining since the number of frequent itemsets are larger than that of frequent closed itemsets. In the next section, we will discuss how to further prune the search space by **LayerPruning** and **ExtPruning**.

3.1 Pruning Strategies

Although the number of closed itemsets can be larger than the number of items, which seems to harm the mining process, lots of them can be ignored without consideration by layer pruning. As a contrast to previous works which only prune a branch of a non-closed pattern, layer pruning removes several non-closed branches at once and reduces the costs in pattern checking. Before introducing the pruning strategy, we first define the order of two first match lists.

Definition 2. *(The Order of FML) Given two FMLs*
$S_1.FML = \{a_1, a_2, \ldots, a_m\}$ *and* $S_2.FML = \{b_1, b_2, \ldots, b_n\}$ $(m \geq n)$*, we say that* $S_1.FML <_L S_2.FML$ *if and only if there exists* $i_1, i_2, \ldots, i_n$ *such that* $a_{i_j}.SID = b_j.SID$ *and* $a_{i_j} < b_j$ *for all* j $(1 \leq j \leq n)$*. The equal signs hold* $(S.FML =_L S'.FML)$ *when* $m = n$ *and* $a_j = b_j$ *for all* j, $(1 \leq j \leq m)$.

Example 2. Consider the example database SDB again, Figure 1 shows the first matched transaction list (FML) for the frequent closed itemsets which are also 1-sequences. The FML for C.F.I. *codes* #1, #2, #3, #4 are $\{2,6,10,14\}$, $\{2,5,8,14\}$, $\{2,6,9,13\}$ and $\{1,5,8,12\}$, respectively. The orders between these FMLs are #1. $FML >_L$ #4.FML and #3.$FML >_L$ #4.FML.

LayerPruning: For two C.F.I. p_1 and p_2 that can be a sequence extension of a prefix sequence $\alpha = <s_1, \ldots, s_n>$ in form of $S_1 = \alpha \diamond_s p_1$ and $S_2 = \alpha \diamond_s p_2$, the LayerPruning works as follows:

1. If $S_1.FML <_L S_2.FML$, then remove p_2. Vice versa.
2. If $S_1.FML =_L S_2.FML$, then if (a) $p_1 \subseteq p_2$, then remove p_1; (b) $p_2 \subseteq p_1$, then remove p_2; (c) neither $p_1 \subset p_2$ nor $p_1 \supset p_2$, then remove both p_1 and p_2.

For instance in our running example, we can completely skip prefix #1 and #3 from root since $\#1.FML >_L \#4.FML$ and $\#3.FML >_L \#4.FML$. Thus, the Layer-Pruning technique removes non-closed patterns in the same layer since the pruning is invoked within a local search of a prefix pattern. The correctness of the pruning technique can be proven by the following lemma and theorems.

Theorem 2. *Let two C.F.I. p_1 and p_2 that can be a sequence extension of a prefix sequence $\alpha=<s_1,\ldots,s_n>$ in form of $S_1 = \alpha \diamond_s p_1$ and $S_2 = \alpha \diamond_s p_2$. If $S_1.FML <_L S_2.FML$, then all extensions of S_2 must not be closed.*

Proof. By definition (Definition 1), the FML of α is smaller than that of its extensions, therefore, $\alpha.FML <_L S_1.FML$. Since $S_1.FML <_L S_2.FML$, wherever $p2$ occurs, $p1$ will also occur in the interval between $\alpha.FML$ and $S_2.FML$. Thus, the super-sequence $S' = \alpha \diamond_s p_1 \diamond_s p_2$ of S_2 has the same FML as S_2, and $S'.SIDList = S_2.SIDLis$ (Lemma 1). Therefore, S_2 is not a closed sequential pattern.

Theorem 3. *Let two C.F.I. p_1 and p_2 that can be a sequence extension of a prefix sequence $\alpha=<s_1,\ldots,s_n>$ in form of $S_1 = \alpha\diamond_s p_1$ and $S_2 = \alpha\diamond_s p_2$, and $S_1.FML =_L S_2.FML$. (a) If $p_1 \subset p_2$, then all extensions of S_1 must not be closed. (b) If neither $p_1 \subset p_2$ nor $p_1 \supset p_2$, then all extensions of p_1 and p_2 must not be closed.*

Proof. (a) First, S_1 is a subsequence of S_2 since p_1 is a subset of p_2. Second, S_1 and S_2 have the same support since $S_1.FML =_L S_2.FML$. Therefore, S_1 is not a closed sequential pattern.

(b) Consider the sequential pattern $\beta = \alpha \diamond_s p_1 \diamond_i p_2=<s_1,\ldots,s_n,p_1 \cup p_2>$. Since $S_1.FML =_L S_2.FML$ and $\beta.FML =_L S_1.FML \cap S_2.FML$, we have $\beta.FML =_L S_1.FML =_L S_2.FML$. Therefore, for any extension S_1 and S_2 of α, there exists β, such that β is a super sequence of S_1 and S_2, and $\beta.SIDList = S_1.SIDList = S_2.SIDList$. Therefore, S_1 and S_2 are not the closed sequential pattern.

Although LayerPruning can prune non-closed sequences during sequence extension step of a prefix sequence, there are still some non-closed sequential patterns that can be generated in different layer. Therefore, we need a checking step to remove non-closed sequential patterns, we refer to this pruning as ExtPruning.

ExtPruning: For two sequential patterns α and β, the rule of ExtPruning states that

1. If $\alpha.FML =_L \beta.FML$ and α is a super sequence of β, then remove β and vice versa.
2. If $Sup(\alpha) = Sup(\beta)$ and α is a super sequence of β, then β is not closed pattern, vice versa.

The first rule of ExtPruning holds according to Theorem 3, while the second rule follows the definition of closed sequential patterns.

3.2   COBRA: Design and Implementation

In this section, we discuss the implementation of the COBRA algorithm. COBRA can be outlined as three major phases: (I) Mining Closed Frequent Itemset; (II) Database Encoding; and (III) Mining Closed Sequential Pattern. Figure 3 shows the pseudo code of the COBRA algorithm. Line 1 calls a modified CHARM [11] to mine frequent closed itemsets. Line 2-3 associates each C.F.I. with a unique *code* and constructs the encoded database EDB using the *code*s of the C.F.I. Line 4-21 mines the set of all frequent closed sequential patterns. Details are described below.

There are already many closed frequent itemset mining algorithms. We prefer using a vertical-based mining algorithm in the first phase (e.g., CHARM[11]) since the vertical format records the locations (TIDList) of C.F.I.s which can be used to construct the transformed database in the second phase. Recall that frequent closed itemsets in a sequence database are defined by both sequence supports and transaction support, therefore, transaction ids are replaced by a 2-tuple (SID, TID) location to facilitate the counting of sequence supports and transaction supports.

In the second phase, we associate each C.F.I. with a unique *code* and construct the encoded database in horizontal format based on the location lists of the C.F.I. Note that C.F.I.s are sorted by their length in a decreasing order such that super-sequences are generated earlier to reduce update cost in the third phase. Once the encoded database is constructed, we can release the memory space of *LocationList* for all C.F.I.s.

Procedure **COBRA(sequence database** SD, $minsup$)
1. **Call mCHARM() to find the set of all C.F.I.;**
2. **Associate each C.F.I. with an** *code*, **and let** CS **denotes the set of** *code*s.
3. **Construct the encoded DB** EDB **using** CS;
4. CS = **LayerPruning(**CS**);**
5. **for each** $code_i$ **in** CS **do**
6.   **cobraDFS(**$code_i, code.FML$**);**

Subprocedure **cobraDFS(**α, FML**)**
7. **Compute Extended List** EL **of** FML;
8. **if (** $|EL| < minsup$ **) then**
9.   **ExtPruning(**α**); return;**
10. **end**
11. **if (** $|EL| < |FML|$ **) then**
12.   **if (ExtPruning(**α,FML**)) then return;**
13. LC = **Local Frequent Codes in** $\alpha.PDB$;
14. LC = **LayerPruning(**LC**);**
15. **if (** $|EL| = |FML|$ **) then**
16. FEI = **All** LC_is **with** $|LC_i.FML| = |FML|$;
17.   **if (** $FEI == \phi$ **) then**
18.   **if (ExtPruning(**α,FML**)) then return;**
19. **end**
20. **for each** LC_i **in** LC **do**
21.   **cobraDFS(**$\alpha \diamond_s LC_i, LC_i.FML$**);**

Fig. 3. COBRA Algorithm

Furthermore, we can remove transactions without any frequent items to reduce the size of storage. Then, the first match transaction list for each C.F.I. (also the frequent 1-sequences) is constructed for the use in the third phase.

The mining process follows the idea of PrefixSpan to look for locally frequent (extendable) *code*s in the projected database of a prefix sequence. Starting with an empty sequence, the extendable *code*s are the frequent C.F.I.s. However, before the enumeration, we first apply the $LayerPruning$ strategy to remove unnecessary enumeration in the same layer (line 4). To reduce the cost of comparing any two FMLs (a total of $O(|C.F.I.|^2)$ comparisons), we devise a hash structure which uses Equation (1) as its hash function (pNo is chosen to be a prime number. $HSize$ is the size of the hash table.). Equation (1) has more uniformly distributed keys than simple $|SIDList|$ can do. Only C.F.I.s that are hashed to the same bucket are compared to each other. Extendable C.F.I. that are not able to produce closed sequential patterns are then removed based on Theorem 2 and 3. In the pseudo code, the procedure $LayerPruning$, which implements the above idea, takes $\{\#1, \#2, \#3, \#4\}$ as an input and returns $\{\#2, \#4\}$ since $\#4.FML <_L \#1.FML$ and $\#4.FML <_L \#3.FML$.

$$h(SIDList) = (|SIDList| + \sum_{Sid \in SIDList} Sid * pNo) mod HSize \qquad (1)$$

In the procedure cobraDFS, with a new pattern α and its FML $\alpha.FML = \{t_1, \ldots, t_n\}$, we first compute the extended position list (EL) by looking at the next transaction of t_i, which has the same sequence id with t_i. For example, the EL of *code* $\#2$ in Figure 1 is $\{3, 6, 9\}$ (transaction 15 is discarded for it does not have a sequence id as transaction 14). The number of transactions in the EL represents the largest support an extended sequence of α can have. Thus, if $|EL|$ is less than $minsup$, then we can skip all extensions of the prefix α (line 8-10); otherwise we do the extension of α (lines 11-21). In the later case, we compute the projected database of α (line 13) and find all locally frequent *code*s (denoted by LC). Again, before extension, $LayerPruning$ is applied to remove unnecessary *code*s (line 14). Formally, we define the extended list (EL) and projected database (PDB) of a pattern as follows.

Definition 3. *Given a sequence α and its $FML = \{t_1, \ldots, t_n\}$, the **Extended List** (EL) of α is defined as a list of extended position t_i' where $t_i' = t_i + 1$ and $t_i'.SID = t_i.SID$.*

Definition 4. *Given the extended list of a sequential pattern α, with extended list $\alpha.EL = \{t_1, \ldots, t_n\}$, the **Projected Database** (PDB) of α is defined as $\alpha.PDB = \{t_1', \ldots, t_m'\}$ where $t_i'.SID = t_j.SID$ for some t_j and $t_j < t_i' \leq t_{|SD|}$, where $|SD|$ denotes the number of transactions in the extended databases.*

For example, the projected database for $\alpha = \#2$ (with $\#2.EL = \{3, 6, 9\}$) in Figure 2 is $\#2.PDB = \{3, 4, 6, 7, 9, 10, 11\}$.

Definition 5. *Given a sequence $\alpha = <s_1, \ldots, s_n>$, the **Forward Extended Itemset** (FEI) of α is defined as the set of extended codes of α which have the same SIDList as α, i.e. $\alpha.SIDList = \alpha \diamond_s p_i'.SIDList$.*

We output the new prefix sequence α only when it has the chance to be a closed sequential pattern. This includes the following three cases: (1) $|EL| < minsup$ (line 8) (2) $|EL| < |FML|$ (line 11-12) (3) $|FEL| = \phi$ (line 17-18). In the first case, no super-sequence of α can be generated as frequent patterns. In the second case, the supports of all super-sequences of α are less than α. In the third case, there are no extendable *codes* with the same support as α. This is equivalent to check for common *codes* that can be extended from the right direction (one of the two directions in BIDE). However, non closed sequential patterns still can be generated. Therefore, we should make a closure checking to verify if α is a closed sequential pattern or not. This is implemented by *ExtPruning* which maintains the set of generated sequences.

Similar to *LayerPruning*, *ExtPruning* also uses Equation 1 as the hash function. The hash table for *ExtPruning* is called *CSTab*. A sequence α is only compared to sequences with the same SIDLists. The return value of *ExtPruning* indicates whether the extension of prefix α should go on. If α is a sub-sequence of an existing pattern β in the hash table and $\alpha.FML = \beta.FML$, then we simply discard α and return $True$ to stop the extension of prefix α (line 12,18).

Theorem 4. *The COBRA algorithm generates all closed sequential patterns.*

Proof. First of all, the anti-monotone property "if a pattern is not frequent, all its super-patterns must be infrequent" is sustained for closed sequential patterns. According to Theorem 1, the search space composed by only closed frequent itemset covers all closed sequential patterns. COBRA's search is based on a complete set enumeration space. The only branches that are pruned as those that do not have sufficient support. The *LayerPruning* only removes unnecessary enumerations (Theorem 2 and 3). On the other hand, *ExtPruning* remove only non-closed sequential patterns. Therefore, the COBRA algorithm generates all frequent and only closed sequential patterns.

The proposed algorithm, COBRA, is basically a memory-based algorithm since the number of closed itemsets can be larger than the number of items. If the data is too large to fit in the memory space, the partition-and-validation strategy can be used to handle such a case. Two alternative partition strategies are proposed here: prefix-based partition and horizontal-based partition (see [?] for details).

4   Experimental Result

In this section, we report the performance study of the proposed algorithms on synthetic data set as used in [10,?]. All the experiments are performed on a 3.2GHz Pentium PC with 3 Gigabytes main memory, running Microsoft Windows XP. All the programs are written in Microsoft/Visual C++ 6.0. In the following experiments, the size of hash table is set to 100.

Scalability Test. The synthetic sequence data is generated on the basis of the description in [6]. We start by looking at the performance of COBRA with default parameter $minsup = 0.5\%$. Figure 4(a) shows the scalability of the algorithms with varying data size. COBRA is two orders of magnitude faster than BIDE for 50K sequences. The scaling of COBRA with database size was linear. Because BIDE needs more scanning time as the data size increases, BIDE has exponential scalability in terms of data size. However, COBRA consumes more memory space than BIDE as shown in Figure 4(b). The main reason is that COBRA maintain the encoded database which is composed by C.F.I.s instead of simple items. For example, COBRA costs approximately 6.6MB for the encoded database maintenance at $|D| = 50K$ and FML costs approximately 10MB.

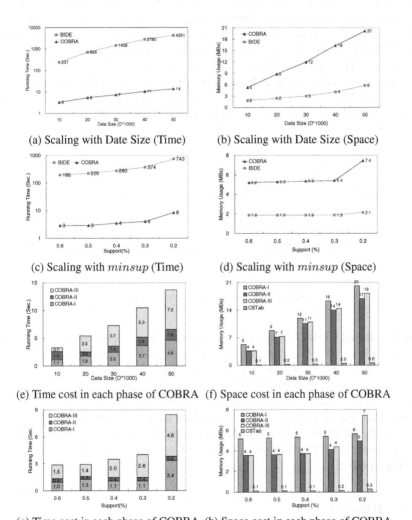

(a) Scaling with Date Size (Time)   (b) Scaling with Date Size (Space)

(c) Scaling with $minsup$ (Time)   (d) Scaling with $minsup$ (Space)

(e) Time cost in each phase of COBRA (f) Space cost in each phase of COBRA

(g) Time cost in each phase of COBRA (h) Space cost in each phase of COBRA

Fig. 4. Scalability Test

The runtime of COBRA and BIDE on the default data set with varying minimum support threshold, $minsup$, from 0.2% to 0.6% is shown in Figure 4(c). COBRA is faster (90 times) and more scalable than BIDE since the number of sequences checked in the backward extension of BIDE grows rapidly as the $minsup$ decreases, while CO-BRA only compare the maintained patterns with the newly found pattern. Again, the memory requirement for COBRA increases as $minsup$ decreases since the number of C.F.I.s increases as $minsup$ decreases (see Figure 4(d)). In short, the performance study shows that the COBRA algorithm is efficient and scalable for closed sequential pattern mining with acceptable memory cost.

To better understand the algorithm, Figure 4(e)(f)(g)(h) demonstrates the time and space expense in each phase. Roughly speaking, the time costs for the three phases are 40%, 10%, and 50%, respectively. As shown in the Figure 4(e)(g), Phase I (the memory-based CHARM) consumes the most time and space since it maintains the (SID, TID) pairs for each closed frequent itemsets. The space requirement for each phase does not vary much since each of them includes both the horizontal encoded database EDB and the vertical database FML. The space requirement for maintaining closed sequential patterns $CSTab$ (by $ExtPruning$) in phase III is also shown in Figure 4(f)(h) for reference.

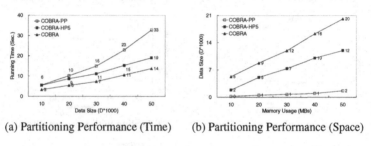

(a) Partitioning Performance (Time)   (b) Partitioning Performance (Space)

Fig. 5. Partition-based COBRA: Synthetic Data

Partition-Based COBRA. Figure 5 demonstrates the memory reduction by partition-based COBRA. Prefix-based partition (COBRA-PP) has less memory requirement than horizontal-based partition (COBRA-HP 5 partitions). Since COBRA-PP divides more partitions than COBRA-HP5, COBRA-PP needs more time in pattern validation than COBRA-HP5. However, experimental result shows that both partition-and-validation strategies are not only more efficient than BIDE but also reduce the memory require-ments of the COBRA. Thus, while we are trading more space for speed in time, the basic principle is worth trying since the memory cost can be well reduced by partition-based approaches.

5   Conclusion

In this paper, we propose a bi-phase reduction approach algorithm for closed sequen-tial pattern mining. Different from previous studies, we first conduct item extension and then do sequence extension, which overcomes some drawbacks in typical pattern-growth method. The mining process is divided into 3-phases: (I) Mining Closed Fre-quent Itemset; (II) Database Encoding and (III) Mining Closed Sequential Pattern. The proposed algorithm uses both vertical (FML) and horizontal (EDB) database formats to reduce the searching time in the mining process. Basically, the proposed algorithm is a memory-based algorithm, and its efficiency comes from the removal of database scans and compressed strategy of bi-phase reduction approach. Although COBRA consumes more memory space than BIDE, the gain in time cost shows the advantage of COBRA. Besides, memory space cost can be further reduced by partition-and-validation strategies or post (disk-based) $ExtPruning$.

Acknowledgement

This work was sponsored by National Science Council, Taiwan under grant NSC94-2213-E-008-020.

References

1. M. N. Garofalakis, R. Rastogi, and K. Shim. Spirit: Sequential pattern mining with regular expression of constraints. *IEEE Transactions on Knowledge and Data Engineering (TKDE)*, 14(3):530–552, 2002.
2. J. Han, J. Pei, B. Mortazavi-Asl, Q. Chen, U. Dayal, and M. Hsu. Freespan: Frequent pattern-projected sequential pattern mining. In *Proceedings of the 6th ACM SIGKDD International Conference on Knowledge Discovery and Data Mining (KDD'00)*, pages 355–359, 2000.
3. J. Han, J. Wang, Y. Lu, and P. Tzvetkov. Mining top-k frequent closed patterns without minimum support. In *Proceedings of the 2002 IEEE International Conference on Data Mining (ICDM'02)*, 2002.
4. J. Pei, G. Dong, W. Zou, and Jiawei Han. On computing condensed frequent pattern bases. In *Proceedings of International Conference on Data Mining (ICDM'02)*, 2002.
5. J. Pei, J. Han, B. Mortazavi-Asl, J. Wang, H. Pinto, Q. Chen, U. Dayal, and M. Hsu. Mining sequential patterns by pattern-growth: The prefixspan approach. *IEEE Transaction on Knowledge Data Engineering*, 16(11):1424–1440, 2004.
6. R. Agrawal and R. Srikant. Mining sequential patterns. In *Proceedings of the 11th International Conference on Data Engineering (ICDE'95)*, pages 3–14, 1995.
7. R. Srikant and R. Agrawal. Mining sequential patterns: Generalizations and performance improvements. In *Proceedings of the 5th International Conference on Extending Database Technology (EDBT'96)*, volume 1057 of *Lecture Notes in Computer Science*, pages 3–17. Springer, 1996.
8. A. K.H. Tung, H. Lu, J. Han, and L. Feng. Efficient mining of intertransaction association rules. *IEEE Transactions on Knowledge and Data Engineering (TKDE)*, 15(1):43–56, 2003.
9. J. Wang and J. Han. Bide: Efficient mining of frequent closed sequences. In *Proceedings of the 20th International Conference on Data Engineering (ICDE'04)*, pages 79–90, 2004.
10. X. Yan and R. Afshar J. Han. Clospan: Mining closed sequential patterns in large datasets. In *Proceedings of the Third SIAM International Conference on Data Mining (SDM)*, 2003.
11. M. J. Zaki and C.J. Hsiao. Charm: An efficient algorithm for closed itemset mining. In *Proceedings of the 2nd SIAM International Conference on Data Mining (SDM'02)*, 2002.
12. M.J. Zaki. Spade: An efficient algorithm for mining frequent sequences. *Machine Learning*, 42(1/2):31–60, 2001.

A Greedy Approach to Concurrent Processing of Frequent Itemset Queries

Pawel Boinski, Marek Wojciechowski, and Maciej Zakrzewicz

Poznan University of Technology
Institute of Computing Science
ul. Piotrowo 2, 60-965 Poznan, Poland
{pawel.boinski, marek, mzakrz}@cs.put.poznan.pl

Abstract. We consider the problem of concurrent execution of multiple frequent itemset queries. If such data mining queries operate on overlapping parts of the database, then their overall I/O cost can be reduced by integrating their dataset scans. The integration requires that data structures of many data mining queries are present in memory at the same time. If the memory size is not sufficient to hold all the data mining queries, then the queries must be scheduled into multiple phases of loading and processing. Since finding the optimal assignment of queries to phases is infeasible for large batches of queries due to the size of the search space, heuristic algorithms have to be applied. In this paper we formulate the problem of assigning the queries to phases as a particular case of hypergraph partitioning. To solve the problem, we propose and experimentally evaluate two greedy optimization algorithms.

1 Introduction

Multiple Query Optimization (MQO) [16] is a database research area that focuses on optimizing sets of queries together by executing their common expressions only once in order to save query execution time. Many exhaustive and heuristic algorithms have been proposed for traditional MQO. A specific type of a database query is a Data Mining Query (DMQ) [10], which describes a data mining task. It defines constraints on the data to be mined and constraints on the patterns to be discovered. Existing data mining systems execute DMQs serially and do not try to share any common expressions between different DMQs.

DMQs can be processed in batches, executed during low user activity time. If source datasets of the batched queries overlap, serial execution will result in reading certain parts of the database more times than necessary. If I/O steps of batched DMQs were integrated, then it would be possible to decrease the overall execution cost and time of the whole batch. One of the methods to process batches of DMQs is Common Counting, focused on frequent itemset discovery queries [1]. It is based on Apriori algorithm [3] and it integrates the steps of candidate support counting – all candidate hash trees for multiple DMQs are loaded into memory and the database is scanned only once. Basic Common Counting [17] assumes that all DMQs fit in memory, which is not the common case, at least for initial Apriori iterations. If the memory can

A Min Tjoa and J. Trujillo (Eds.): DaWaK 2006, LNCS 4081, pp. 292–301, 2006.

hold only a subset of all DMQs, then it is necessary to partition/schedule the DMQs into subsets called phases. The best query scheduling algorithms proposed so far are: *CCAgglomerative* [19] and its extension called *CCAgglomerativeNoise* [6]. In this paper we propose and experimentally evaluate two new greedy optimization algorithms: *CCGreedy* and *CCSemiGreedy*. *CCGreedy* implements a pure greedy strategy, and *CCSemiGreedy* is its extension following a semi-greedy heuristics [9].

2 Related Work

Multiple-query optimization has been extensively studied in the context of database systems (see e.g. [16]), however very little work has been done on optimizing sets of data mining queries. To the best of our knowledge, apart from the Common Counting method discussed in this paper, the only other multiple data mining query processing scheme is Mine Merge, presented in one of our previous papers [18].

As an introduction to multiple data mining query optimization, we can regard techniques of reusing results of previous queries to answer a new query [5][7][11] [14]. As we have shown in [15], these methods can be used to optimize processing of batches of data mining queries after appropriate ordering of the queries. However, such an approach is applicable just in a small fraction of cases that Common Counting can successfully handle.

Hypergraph partitioning has been extensively studied particularly in the domain of VLSI design [4]. In data mining context it has been proposed as a clustering technique in [13]. Many formulations of the hypergraph partitioning problem have been considered, differing in partitioning constraints and objectives (see e.g. [4] or [12]). Our formulation differs from typical approaches because we do not have any balance constraint on the sizes of resulting partitions, only a strict upper bound on the on the sum of weights of vertices in a partition, reflecting the memory limit.

3 Background

3.1 Basic Definitions

Frequent itemset query. A *frequent itemset query* is a tuple $dmq = (R, a, \Sigma, \Phi, \beta)$, where R is a relation, a is a set-valued attribute of R, Σ is a condition involving the attributes of R, Φ is a condition involving discovered itemsets, and β is the minimum support threshold. The result of dmq is a set of itemsets discovered in $\pi_a \sigma_\Sigma R$, satisfying Φ, and having support $\geq \beta$ (π and σ denote projection and selection).

Elementary data selection predicates. The set $S=\{s_1, s_2, ..., s_k\}$ of data selection predicates over the relation R is a set of *elementary data selection predicates* for a set of frequent itemset queries $DMQ = \{dmq_1, dmq_2, ..., dmq_n\}$ if for all u, v we have $\sigma_{s_u} R \cap \sigma_{s_v} R = \varnothing$ and for each dmq_i there exist integers a, b, ..., m such that $\sigma_\Sigma R = \sigma_{s_a} R \cup \sigma_{s_b} R \cup .. \cup \sigma_{s_m} R$.

3.2 Review of Common Counting

Common Counting is so far the best algorithm for multiple-query optimization in frequent itemset mining. It consists in concurrent execution of a set of frequent itemset queries using the Apriori algorithm and integrating their dataset scans. The algorithm iteratively generates and counts candidates for all the data mining queries, storing candidates generated for each query in a separate hash-tree structure. For each distinct data selection formula, its corresponding database partition is scanned once per iteration, and candidates for all the queries referring to that partition are counted.

Basic Common Counting assumes that memory is unlimited and therefore the candidate hash-trees for all queries can completely fit in memory. If, however, the memory is limited, Common Counting execution must be divided into multiple *phases*, so that in each phase only a subset of queries is processed. In general, many assignments of queries to phases are possible, differing in the reduction of I/O costs. The task of assigning queries to phases in a way minimizing the overall I/O cost is called *query scheduling*.

Since the sizes of candidate hash-trees change between Apriori iterations, the scheduling has to be performed at the beginning of every Apriori iteration. A scheduling algorithm requires that sizes of candidate hash-trees are known in advance. Therefore, in each iteration of Common Counting, we first generate all the candidate hash-trees, measure their sizes, save them to disk, schedule the data mining queries, and then load the hash-trees from disk when they are needed. The exhaustive search for an optimal assignment of queries to Common Counting phases is inapplicable for large batches of queries due to the size of the search space (expressed by a Bell number). Therefore, several scheduling heuristics have been proposed.

4 Frequent Itemset Query Scheduling by Hypergraph Partitioning

4.1 Data Sharing Hypergraph

A set of frequent itemset queries $DMQ = \{dmq_1, dmq_2, ..., dmq_n\}$ can be modeled as a weighted hypergraph whose vertices represent queries and hyperedges represent elementary data selection predicates. A hyperedge in the hypergraph corresponds to a database partition and connects the queries whose source datasets *share* that partition.

Formally, a *data sharing hypergraph* for the set of data mining queries $DMQ = \{dmq_1, dmq_2, ..., dmq_n\}$ and its corresponding set of elementary data selection predicates $S=\{s_1, s_2, ..., s_k\}$ is a hypergraph $DSG=(V,E)$, where $V=DMQ$, $E=S$, and a vertex $dmq_i \in DMQ$ is incident with an hyperedge $s_j \in S$ iff $\sigma_{s_j}R \subseteq \sigma_{\Sigma}R$. Each vertex dmq_i has an associated weight $w(dmq_i)$ representing the amount of memory consumed by data structures of the query dmq_i. Each hyperedge s_j has an associated weight $w(s_j)$ representing the size of the database partition returned by the elementary data selection predicate s_j.

Note that the above definition of a data sharing hypergraph allows hyperedges incident with only one vertex in order to represent database partitions read by only one query.

Example. Given three frequent itemset queries operating on the relation $R_1 = (a_1, a_2)$: $dmq_1=(R_1, "a_2", "5<a_1<20", \emptyset, 3\%)$, $dmq_2=(R_1, "a_2", "10<a_1<30", \emptyset, 5\%)$, $dmq_3=(R_1, "a_2", "15<a_1<40", \emptyset, 4\%)$. The set of elementary data selection predicates for the set of frequent itemset queries $DMQ=\{dmq_1, dmq_2, dmq_3\}$ is $S=\{"5<a_1<10", "10<a_1<15", "15<a_1<20", "20<a_1<30", "30<a_1<40"\}$. The data sharing hypergraph for DMQ is shown in Fig. 1.

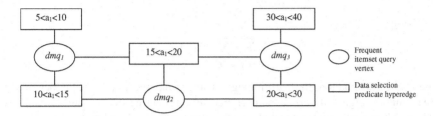

Fig. 1. Example data sharing hypergraph

4.2 Hypergraph Partitioning Problem Formulation

The goal of query scheduling for Common Counting is assigning queries to phases fitting into main memory in a way minimizing the overall I/O cost. Each of the phases returned by the scheduling algorithm is a set of frequent itemset queries for which a data sharing hypergraph can be constructed. Thus, query scheduling for Common Counting can be interpreted as a particular case of hypergraph partitioning.

After partitioning, elementary data selection predicates corresponding to database partitions shared by queries that have been assigned to different phases will be represented as hyperedges in more then one resulting hypergraph. In other words, a hyperedge that is cut by the partitioning will be partitioned into a number of hyperedges connecting subsets of vertices previously connected by the original hyperedge. One of the possible partitionings of the data sharing hypergraph from Fig. 1, representing scheduling into two phases is shown in Fig. 2. Hyperedges that have been cut (partitioned) are presented in bold.

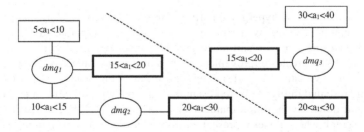

Fig. 2. Example partitioning of the data sharing hypergraph from Fig. 1

In terms of hypergraph partitioning, the goal of query scheduling for Common Counting can be stated as follows:

Problem Statement. Given a data sharing hypergraph for the set of frequent itemsets queries $DSG = (V,E)$ and the amount of available main memory $MEMSIZE$, the goal is to partition the vertices of the hypergraph into k disjoint subsets $V_1, V_2, ..., V_k$, and their corresponding data sharing hypergraphs $DSG_1 = (V_1,E_1)$, $DSG_2 = (V_2,E_2)$, ..., $DSG_k = (V_k,E_k)$ such that

$$\underset{x=1..k}{\forall} \sum_{dmq_i \in V_x} w(dmq_i) \leq MEMSIZE$$

minimizing

$$\sum_{x=1..k} \sum_{s_j \in E_x} w(s_j).$$

In the above formulation, the partitioning constraint has the form of an upper bound on the sum of weights of vertices in each partition, reflecting the amount of available memory, while the partitioning objective is to minimize the total sum of weights of hyperedges across all the partitions, representing the overall I/O cost of the Common Counting iteration. It should be noted that the number of resulting partitions (i.e. Common Counting phases) is not known a priori, and there is no lower bound on the sum of weights of vertices in each partition. Informally, the latter means that we do not require that the resulting partitions are of similar sizes.

According to the classification from [12], the partitioning objective in our problem formulation is equivalent to minimizing the k-1 metric, where the goal is to minimize the size of the hyperedge cut to which each cut hyperedge contributes k-1 times its weight.

Our hypergraph partitioning problem is NP-hard since if we consider only hypergraphs with hyperedges connecting exactly two vertices, its decision version will restrict itself to the classic graph partitioning problem formulation from [8] (proof of NP-completeness by restriction). Taking that into account, for large number of vertices (frequent itemset queries) heuristic approaches have to be applied to solve the problem, resulting in possibly suboptimal solutions.

5 Greedy Approach to Query Scheduling

We propose to solve the hypergraph partitioning problem representing query scheduling for Common Counting by starting with each query in a separate partition and then iteratively merging pairs of partitions, greedily choosing the two partitions whose merging results in greater improvement of the partitioning objective and at the same time does not violate the partitioning constraint. This leads to the *CCGreedy* algorithm presented in Fig. 3. To represent the gain in the partitioning objective for all pairs of partitions the algorithm maintains a *gain graph* $GG=(V, E)$, which is a fully connected graph whose nodes represent partitions and each edge weight represents the gain thanks to merging a pair of partitions connected by the edge. The gain is computed as the difference between the values of partitioning objectives after and before merging a given pair of queries. Limited by space we omit the formal description of initial gain graph generation.

```
CCGreedy(GG=(V,E)):
begin
  while (true) begin
    sort E in desc. order with respect to eᵢ.gain,  ignore edges with zero gains
    newPartition = ∅
    for each eᵢ = {vₓ, vᵧ} in E do
      if (treesize(eᵢ) ≤ MEMSIZE) then
        newPartition = vₓ ∪ vᵧ
        V = V \ {vₓ, vᵧ};       V = V ∪ {newPartition};       E = E \ eᵢ
        for each v in V do begin
          newEdge = {v, newPartition}, compute newEdge.gain
          E = E ∪ {newEdge}
        end
        break
      end if
    end
    if newPartition = ∅ then break end if
  end
  return V
end
```

Fig. 3. *CCGreedy* algorithm

An obvious problem with greedy algorithms like *CCGreedy* is that the locally optimal choice in each operation may not lead to the globally optimal solution. To increase the chances of finding the optimal partitioning we modify *CCGreedy* by applying a semi-greedy strategy to it. The result is the *CCSemiGreedy* algorithm depicted in Fig.4.

```
CCSemiGreedy(GG=(V,E), RCLLen):
begin
  while (true) begin
    sort E in desc. order wrt. eᵢ.gain,
    ignore edges with zero gains
    newPartition = ∅
    RCL = genRCL(GG, RCLLen)
    if length(RCL) = 0 then break end if
    randomly choose eᵢ = {vₓ, vᵧ} from RCL
    newPartition = vₓ ∪ vᵧ
    V = V \ {vₓ, vᵧ}; V = V ∪ {newPartition};  E = E \ eᵢ
    for each v in V do begin
      newEdge = {v, newPartition}
      compute newEdge.gain
      E = E ∪ {newEdge}
    end
  end
  return V
end
```

```
function genRCL(GG=(V,E), RCLLen):
begin
  RCL = nil
  for each eᵢ = {vₓ, vᵧ}  in E do
    if (treesize(eᵢ) ≤ MEMSIZE) then
      RCL = append(RCL, eᵢ)
      if length(RCL) = RCLLen then
        break
      end if
    end if
  end
  return RCL
end
```

Fig. 4. *CCSemiGreedy* algorithm

CCSemiGreedy differs from *CCGreedy* in the step of choosing the partitions to merge. *CCSemiGreedy* uses restricted candidate list (*RCL*) which is returned by the function *genRCL*. This procedure iterates over the gain graph and checks if hash trees of all the queries from a given pair of partitions fit together in memory. If this condition is satisfied, the current edge is added to the *RCL*. Generation of the *RCL* is stopped when the list reaches the length of *RCLLen* (set by a user). In *CCSemiGreedy* we check the length of the *RCL*. If it is zero, there is no possible merge, otherwise an edge (for partition merging) is chosen randomly from the *RCL*. Other steps of the *CCSemiGreedy* algorithm are the same as those described for *CCGreedy* algorithm.

In practice, *CCSemiGreedy* should be applied to query scheduling in the following way: Firstly, an initial schedule should be generated with *CCGreedy*. Then, *CCSemiGreedy* should be executed a user-defined number of times. In the end, the best of the generated schedules should be used for Common Counting.

6   Experimental Evaluation

We implemented our algorithms in C# and conducted experiments on a PC with Intel Pentium IV 2.53GHz processor and 512MB of RAM, running Windows XP.

In the first series of experiments, we performed simulations to determine influence of *CCSemiGreedy* parameters (RCL length and number of attempts) on its effectiveness. We simulated batches of data mining queries by randomly generating the database predicate and size of the candidate tree for each query. Size of available memory was randomly generated in such way that at least every single query could fit into memory. Series of simulations consisted of 500 iterations to get average values and were applied to batches of queries ranging from 3 to 50 queries per batch.

Figure 5 presents the influence of chosen RCL length on the number of disk blocks read by *CCSemiGreedy*. The experiments indicate that the length of the RCL should be very small but greater than 2 items. Best results were obtained for 3 to 6 items. For further experiments we have chosen the length of RCL equal to 3.

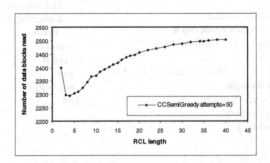

Fig. 5. Influence of the RCL length on the overall accuracy of *CCSemiGreedy*

Figure 6 presents influence of the second parameter of *CCSemiGreedy*, which is the number of attempts to generate schedule. It is obvious that more attempts generally will result in better schedules but at the expense of increasing the scheduling time.

Results indicate that after more than fifty attempts there is no significant improvement in the quality of the schedule.

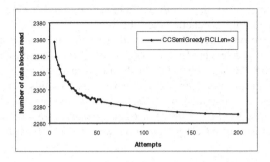

Fig. 6. Influence of the number of attempts on the overall accuracy of *CCSemiGreedy*

In the second series of experiments we compared *CCGreedy* and *CCSemiGreedy* scheduling algorithms with previously proposed *CCAgglomerative* and *CCAgglomerativeNoise* in terms of effectiveness (quality of generated schedules) and efficiency (scheduling times). These experiments were performed on a synthetic dataset generated with GEN [2]. The dataset had the following characteristics: number of transactions = 500000, average number of items in a transaction = 4, number of different items = 10000, number of patterns = 1000. The data resided in a local *PostgreSQL* database. We randomly generated batches of 5 to 30 queries, operating on subsets of the test database.

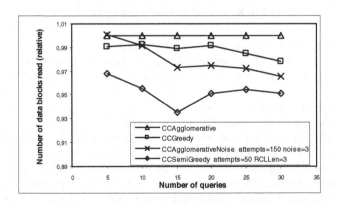

Fig. 7. Amounts of data read by different schedules

Figure 7 presents how the accuracy of the scheduling algorithms changes with the number of queries. To improve readability of the chart, we present relative amount of data blocks read by schedules generated by *CCGreedy*, *CCSemiGreedy* and *CCAgglomerativeNoise* wrt. *CCAgglomerative*. *CCAgglomerativeNoise* iteratively tries to improve the schedule generated by *CCAgglomerative* in a similar way as

CCSemiGreedy extends *CCGreedy*. We used the optimal value (3%) of the noise parameter of *CCAgglomerativeNoise*, determined in similar simulations to those carried for *CCSemiGreedy*. The number of attempts (150) for *CCAgglomerativeNoise* was chosen in such way that both *CCSemiGreedy* and *CCAgglomerativeNoise* algorithms had equal time to generate the schedule.

Experiments were performed for three values of the main memory limit (90, 120 and 150kB) and for four levels of the average overlapping of datasets read by queries in the set (20%, 40%, 60%, 80%). Due to limited space we present results that are averages taken over all the conducted experiments. Results show that the most effective schedules are generated by *CCSemiGreedy* and are about 5% better than those generated by *CCAgglomerative*. For *CCAgglomerativeNoise* and *CCGreedy* the measured improvement over *CCAgglomerative* was 2% and 1% respectively.

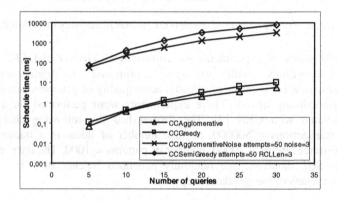

Fig. 8. Scheduling times (logarithmic scale)

Figure 8 presents scheduling times for the considered algorithms. This time for *CCSemiGreedy* and *CCAgglomerativeNoise* numbers of attempts were fixed at the same level (50). Execution times of *CCAgglomerative* and *CCGreedy* are negligible, with *CCGreedy* requiring at most twice as much time as *CCAgglomerative*. Execution times of *CCSemiGreedy* are up to three times longer than those of *CCAgglomerative Noise* and the gap increases with the number of queries.

The results of our experiments show that *CCGreedy* is more effective than *CCAgglomerative*, and properly parameterized *CCSemiGreedy* generates better schedules than *CCAgglomerativeNoise*, which makes it the best scheduling algorithm for Common Counting. The execution times of the new algorithms are longer but in typical situations the increase in scheduling time will be dominated by the reduction of the time spent on disk operations thanks to better schedules.

7 Summary

In this paper we considered the problem of concurrent execution of frequent itemset queries. We introduced two new heuristic query scheduling algorithms for the Common Counting method: *CCGreedy* and *CCSemiGreedy*. Our experiments show that the new algorithms offer a significant improvement in accuracy over the existing solutions while providing acceptable scheduling times.

CCGreedy and *CCSemiGreedy* assume that the set of data mining queries to execute is static. However, in a real system, new queries may arrive while the other queries are being executed. In the future we plan to extend our approach to allow for dynamic scheduling of arriving queries.

References

1. Agrawal R., Imielinski T., Swami A: Mining Association Rules Between Sets of Items in Large Databases. Proc. of the 1993 ACM SIGMOD Conf. on Management of Data (1993)
2. Agrawal R., Mehta M., Shafer J., Srikant R., Arning A., Bollinger T.: The Quest Data Mining System. Proc. of the 2nd KDD Conference (1996)
3. Agrawal R., Srikant R.: Fast Algorithms for Mining Association Rules. Proc. of the 20th Int'l Conf. on Very Large Data Bases (1994)
4. Alpert C.J., Kahng A.B.: Recent Directions in Netlist Partitioning: A Survey. Integration: The VLSI Journal 19 (1995)
5. Baralis E., Psaila G.: Incremental Refinement of Mining Queries. Proceedings of the 1st DaWaK Conference (1999)
6. Boinski P., Jozwiak K., Wojciechowski M., Zakrzewicz M.: Improving Quality of Agglomerative Scheduling in Concurrent Processing of Frequent Itemset Queries. Proc. of the International IIS: IIPWM'06 Conference (2006)
7. Cheung D.W., Han J., Ng V., Wong C.Y.: Maintenance of Discovered Association Rules in Large Databases: An Incremental Updating Technique. Proc. of the 12th ICDE (1996)
8. Garey M.R., Johnson D.S.: Computers and Intractability. A Guide to the Theory of NP-Completeness. WH Freeman and Company (1979)
9. Hart J.P., Shogan A.W.: Semi-greedy Heuristics: An Empirical Study. Operations Research Letters, Vol. 6 (1987)
10. Imielinski T., Mannila H.: A Database Perspective on Knowledge Discovery. Communications of the ACM, Vol. 39, No. 11 (1996)
11. Jeudy B., Boulicaut J-F.: Using Condensed Representations for Interactive Association Rule Mining. Proceedings of the 6th PKDD Conference (2002)
12. Karypis G.: Multilevel Hypergraph Partitioning. In: Cong J., Shinnerl J. (eds.): Multilevel Optimization Methods for VLSI, Kluwer Academic Publishers (2002)
13. Karypis G., Han E., Kumar V.: Chameleon: A Hierarchical Clustering Algorithm Using Dynamic Modeling. IEEE Computer, Vol. 32, No. 8 (1999)
14. Meo R.: Optimization of a Language for Data Mining. Proc. of the ACM Symposium on Applied Computing - Data Mining Track (2003)
15. Morzy M., Wojciechowski M., Zakrzewicz M.: Optimizing a Sequence of Frequent Pattern Queries. Proc. of the 7th DaWaK Conference (2005)
16. Sellis T.: Multiple Query Optimization. ACM Transactions on Database Systems, Vol. 13, No. 1 (1988)
17. Wojciechowski M., Zakrzewicz M.: Evaluation of Common Counting Method for Concurrent Data Mining Queries. Proc. of the 7th ADBIS Conference (2003)
18. Wojciechowski M., Zakrzewicz M.: Evaluation of the Mine Merge Method for Data Mining Query Processing. Proc. of the 8th ADBIS Conference (2004)
19. Wojciechowski M., Zakrzewicz M.: On Multiple Query Optimization in Data Mining. Proc. of the 9th Pacific-Asia Conference on Knowledge Discovery and Data Mining (2005)

Two New Techniques for Hiding Sensitive Itemsets and Their Empirical Evaluation

Ahmed HajYasien and Vladimir Estivill-Castro

Faculty of Engineering and Information Technology, Griffith University

Abstract. Many privacy preserving data mining algorithms attempt to selectively hide what database owners consider as sensitive. Specifically, in the association-rules domain, many of these algorithms are based on item-restriction methods; that is, removing items from some transactions in order to hide sensitive frequent itemsets.

The infancy of this area has not produced clear methods neither evaluated those few available. However, determining what is most effective in protecting sensitive itemsets while not hiding non-sensitive ones as a side effect remains a crucial research issue. This paper introduces two new techniques that deal with scenarios where many itemsets of different sizes are sensitive. We empirically evaluate our two sanitization techniques and compare their efficiency as well as which has the minimum effect on the non-sensitive frequent itemsets.

Keywords: Privacy preserving data mining, association rules, sanitizing algorithms, data sanitization, sensitive itemsets.

1 Introduction

In the context of data mining and in particular association rules, the process of hiding sensitive patterns is called data sanitization [4]. Data sanitization is defined as the process of making sensitive information in non-production databases safe for wider visibility [8]. The problem of sanitizing the knowledge in order to protect privacy of individuals or parties during a mining process is called Privacy Preserving Data Mining (PPDM) [6]. Privacy preserving data mining allows individuals or parties to collectively discover knowledge without disclosing what is considered private. Privacy preserving data mining can be attempted at three levels (see Fig. 1). The first level is either raw data or databases where transactions reside. The second level is data mining algorithms and techniques. The third level is at the output of different data mining algorithms and techniques. **This paper works on Level 1; that is, sanitizing the database in order to hide a set of sensitive itemsets specified by the database owners.** Typically this process has followed the path of processing a database to produce another one so that sensitive itemsets are now hidden. Selecting the right technique to hide sensitive itemsets is important for an effective data sanitization process. Hiding an item or itemset means reducing its support below a privacy support threshold provided by the user. We use the word "attack" to indicate

A Min Tjoa and J. Trujillo (Eds.): DaWaK 2006, LNCS 4081, pp. 302–311, 2006.

that we modify the records about an item or itemset. This attack aims at reducing the support of the item in order to hide it. In this paper, we introduce a
comparison between two techniques that hide sensitive itemsets.

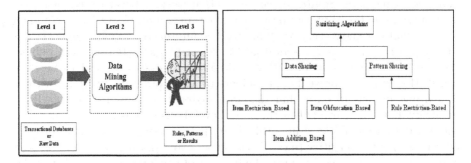

Fig. 1. We can attempt privacy preserving data mining at three major levels. However,
others [14] have suggested a taxonomy of sanitizing algorithms.

2 Background

The task of mining association rules over market basket data [2] is considered
a core knowledge discovery activity. Association rule mining provides a useful mechanism for discovering correlations among items belonging to customer
transactions in a market basket database. Let D be the database of transactions
and $J = \{J_1, ..., J_n\}$ be the set of items. A transaction T includes one or more
items in J (*i.e.*, $T \subseteq J$). An association rule has the form $X \to Y$, where X and
Y are non-empty sets of items (*i.e.* $X \subseteq J$, $Y \subseteq J$) such that $X \cap Y = \emptyset$. A
set of items is called an itemset, while X is called the antecedent. The support
$sprt_D(x)$ of an item (or itemset) x is the percentage of transactions from D in
which that item or itemset occurs in the database. In other words, the support s
of an association rule $X \to Y$ is the percentage of transactions T in a database
where $X \cup Y \subseteq T$. The confidence or strength c for an association rule $X \to Y$
is the ratio of the number of transactions that contain $X \cup Y$ to the number of
transactions that contain X. An itemset $X \subseteq J$ is frequent if at least a fraction
s of the transaction in a database contains X. Frequent itemsets are important
because they are the building blocks to obtain association rules with a given
confidence and support. Typically, algorithms to find frequent itemsets use the
anti-monotonicity property, and therefore, find first all frequent itemset of size
k before proceeding to find all itemsets of size $k + 1$. We will refer to the set of
all frequent itemsets of size k as depth k.

  We assume a context where parties are interested in releasing some data but
they also aim to keeping some patterns private. We identify patterns with frequent itemsets. Patterns represent different forms of correlation between items in
a database. *Sensitive itemsets* are all the itemsets that are not to be disclosed to
others. While no sensitive itemset is to become public, the non-sensitive itemsets

are to be released. One could keep all itemsets private, but this would not share any knowledge. The aim is to release as many non-sensitive itemsets as possible while keeping sensitive itemsets private. This is an effort to balance privacy with knowledge discovery. It seems that discovery of itemsets is in conflict with hiding sensitive data. *Sanitizing algorithms* that work at Level 1 take (as input) a database D and modify it to produce (as output) a database D' where mining for rules will not show sensitive itemsets. The alternative scenario at Level 3 is to remove the sensitive itemsets from the set of frequent itemsets and publish the rest. This scenario implies that a database D does not need to be published. However, this prevents data miners to apply other discovery algorithms of learning models to data, and therefore, reduces the options for knowledge discovery. Pattern-sharing algorithms are Level 3 algorithms and are also called rule restriction-based algorithms [14]. Here, parties usually share a set of rules after removing the sensitive rules. Thus, parties avoid sharing data and it is been argued that this approach reduces the hazards of concluding any sensitive rules or discovering private data. However, they are typically over-protected. They correspond to the approach in statistical databases where data is released from a data generator based on learned model. While the learned model is based on the original data, users of the generated data can only learn the generator model and therefore may miss many patterns in the data.

Thus, this paper considers sanitizing algorithms. Oliveira et al. [14] refer to existing sanitizing algorithms mostly as data-sharing techniques Data-sharing techniques correspond to Level 1 in our taxonomy and has been addressed in the literature [4,7,12,13,15]. The data-sharing techniques have been divided into three categories (see Fig. 1). First, (item restriction)-based algorithms reduce either the support or confidence to a safe zone (below a given privacy support threshold) by deleting transactions or items from a database to hide sensitive rules that can be derived from that database. Second, (item addition)-based algorithms add imaginary items to the existing transactions. Usually the addition is performed in the antecedent part of the rule. As a result, the confidence of such a rule is reduced and enters the safe zone. The problem with this approach is that the addition of new items will create new rules and parties could share untrue knowledge (sets of items that are not frequent itemsets appear as such). Third, (item obfuscation)-based algorithms replace some items with a question mark in some transactions to avoid the exposure of sensitive rules. Unlike the (item addition)-based, with (item obfuscation)-based, no false rules are passed to any party. Our algorithms here are (item restriction)-based, since again, these minimise the risk of discovery knowledge that it is not valid.

3   Statement of the Problem

Let J be a finite set of items, $D \subseteq 2^J$ a set of transactions. Consider a fixed support, and let F be the set of frequent itemsets in D, $B \subseteq F$ a set of sensitive itemsets, $A = F \setminus B$ a set of non-sensitive itemsets, and $t \geq 0$ an integer to represent the privacy support threshold.

Let X be the set of items that form the itemsets in B, and Y be the set of items that form the itemsets in A. Note that while $A \cap B = \emptyset$, usually $X \cap Y$ is not empty. Typically we would like to attack items in X since these would reduce the support of itemsets in B while we would like to preserve the support of items in Y. We assume that we have a well posed problem in that we assume no element of A is a subset of an element of B and vice versa, and that for all $a \in A$ or $b \in B$, $\sigma_D(a) \geq t$ and $\sigma_D(b) \geq t$ respectively (where $\sigma_D(a), \sigma_D(b)$ are the support of a and b respectively in D).

Formally, the problem receives as input D, B, A, and t. The task is to lower the support of the itemsets in B below t and keep the impact on the non-sensitive itemsets $A = F \setminus B$ at a minimum. This problem has been proven to be NP-hard [4,9]. Even though, an heuristic algorithm has been proposed [4], such algorithm works only in the case $\|B\| = 1$. That is, only one itemset can be hidden. While the algorithm can be applied to the case $\|B\| > 1$ by repeating the algorithm on each $b \in B$, no details are provided on how to select and iterate over the itemsets in B. Even when $B = \{b\}$, some ambiguity exists in the description for what item in b to attack.

4 Our New Two Heuristics

Our two new heuristics focus on building an itemset g so that attacking items in g would affect the support of sensitive itemsets. We first describe the process of attacking items from $g \subset J$. Note that g is not necessarily sensitive itself; that is, we do not require $g \in B$. In fact, it may be that g is not even frequent. We describe two ways of selecting transactions to attack, these will be called methods. We also describe two ways of building the set g, and we refer to these as techniques. We present the methods first.

4.1 The Methods

The methods presented here determine what item and what transaction to attack given an itemset $g \subset J$. The two methods hide one sensitive itemset related to itemset g. How sensitive itemsets are related to g will become clear in the next subsection. Suffice it to say, for now that g will contain items that have high support in sensitive itemsets (and hopefully low support in non-sensitive itemsets). In both methods, we attack an item $x \in g$ until one itemset $b \in B$ becomes hidden. Then, a new itemset g is selected. We perform the attack on sensitive itemsets by attacking the item $x \in g$ with the highest support. We determine the list of transactions $L_g \subseteq D$ that support g (i.e. $L_g = \{T \in D | g \subset T\}$. We remove the item x from the transactions $T \in L_g$ until the support of some $b \in B$ is below the required privacy support threshold. The difference between our two methods is that the transactions $T \in L_g$ are sorted in two different orders. Thus, which transactions are attacked and which ones are left untouched, even though they include x is different for the two methods.

Method 1 sorts the transactions $T \in L_g$ in ascending order based on $\|T \setminus g\|$ (the number of items in T not in g). Notice that $\|T \setminus g\|$ can be zero. The guiding principle is that if $\|T \setminus g\|$ is small, then removing x from T would impact the support of sensitive itemsets but rarely the support of other itemsets, thus non-sensitive itemsets will remain mostly untouched. Method 2 sorts the transactions $T \in L_g$ in ascending order based on $\|(Y \cap T) \setminus g\|$ (recall that Y is all items in A and A is all the non-sensitive frequent itemsets). Again, $\|(Y \cap T) \setminus g\|$ can be zero. The second method makes even a stronger effort to make sure that those transactions that are attacked have very few items involved in non-sensitive itemsets.

4.2   How to Select the Itemset g — The Techniques

We present here the techniques to prioritize the order in which itemsets $b \in B$ are attacked so that their support is below t. The techniques build the itemset g used by the methods described before.

Technique 1 (Item Count)

1. First sort the items in X based on how many itemsets in B contain the item. Recall that $X \subset J$ is all items in the sensitive itemsets. Thus, this sorts the items in X is according to

$$Item\_Count(x) = \sum_{b \in B} \|\{x\} \cap b\|.$$

   Let $x_0 \in X$ be the item with the highest count. If we have more than one item with the same $Item\_Count(x)$ value, we select the item with the highest support. If the tie persists, we select arbitrarily. Then,

$$g = \bigcup_{b \in B \text{ and } x_0 \in b} b.$$

   That is, g is the union of sensitive itemsets that include the item x_0.
2. If the construction of g results in hiding a sensitive itemset (either using Method 1 or Method 2), then the hidden itemset is removed from B.
   (a) If B is empty, then the technique stops.
   (b) Otherwise the technique is applied again, building a new g from the very beginning.
3. If the construction of g does not result in hiding a sensitive itemset, we find $x \in g$ with lowest support, and replace g with $g \setminus \{x\}$. We then re-apply Method 1 or Method 2 again (whichever of the two methods has been selected).

An illustrative example using Method 1: Suppose $B = \{(v_1 v_2 v_4), (v_2 v_4), (v_1 v_5), (v_2 v_3 v_4)\}$. To hide these itemsets based on the item count technique, first we need to sort the items based on their number of sensitive itemsets they participate in (refer to Table 1(a)). The next step is to attack v_4 in the transactions where v_4 appears with v_1, v_2 and v_3. This is because v_4 is involved in the largest number of sensitive itemsets (3) and the union of all sensitive itemsets that contain v_4 results in $g = \{v_1, v_2, v_3\}$. Once we have this g, we find that the item with highest support in g is again v_4. If attacking v_4 was not enough to hide any itemset in B, then we attack v_4 in the transactions where v_4 appears with v_1 and v_2. We exclude v_3 to create a new g because it is the item with the lowest support that appears with v_4 in B. Again, if that attack was insufficient to hide any itemset in B, we keep excluding the next item with the lowest support. The attack on v_4 persists until at least one itemset in B is hidden (note that this must eventually happen). Then, we remove this itemset from B and repeat the process until all itemsets in B are hidden. Because in this example we are using the item count technique with Method 1, these transactions should be sorted based on the number of items that appear in each transaction excluding v_1, v_2, v_3 and v_4. Transaction with nothing extra besides v_1, v_2, v_3 and v_4 will be attacked first.

Table 1. Examples for the two techniques

(a) The first step in item count is to sort items.

item	# of occurrence	support
v_4	3	56%
v_2	3	48%
v_1	2	28%
v_3	1	17%
v_5	1	11%

(b) Increasing cardinality: itemsets sorted by support.

itemset cardinality	support
$v_2 v_4$	15%
$v_1 v_5$	10%
$v_2 v_3 v_4$	6%
$v_1 v_2 v_4$	5%

Technique 2 (Increasing Cardinality): The technique first sorts the itemsets in B based on their cardinality. Starting from the smallest cardinality, the technique selects an itemset g that in this case is an itemset $b \in B$. The technique can then have a Method 1 variant or a Method 2 variant. If we have more than one itemset of the same cardinality, we attack the itemset with the highest support. This technique also iterates until all sensitive itemsets are hidden. Every time an itemset b is hidden, a new g is calculated. Note that because $g \in B$, the entire application of Method 1 or Method 2, must result in g being hidden, and therefore a sensitive itemset is hidden.

An illustrative example using Method 2: Suppose $Y = \{v_1, v_2, v_3, v_4, v_5, v_6, v_7\}$, $B = \{(v_1 v_2 v_4), (v_2 v_4), (v_1 v_5), (v_2 v_3 v_4)\}$. To hide these itemsets based on the increasing cardinality technique, first we need to sort the itemsets in B based on their itemset cardinality (refer to Table 1(b)). Then, we start by attacking the itemsets in the smallest cardinality (that is cardinality 2 in this example). We let g be the itemset with highest support. As both Method 1 and Method 2 attack the item with highest support in g, and let us say that v_2 has the highest support, then based on Method 2, v_2 will be attacked in the transactions where v_2 appear with v_4. These transactions should be sorted based on those who have fewest number of items in Y excluding items in g (that is, excluding v_2 and v_4).

4.3 Data Structures and Algorithms

There are famous algorithms used to mine data and produce the frequent item-sets like the Apriori algorithm [3] or the FP-tree growth algorithm [11]. The sanitization of the database departs from results of a frequent itemset calculation; thus, we do not include in the cost of sanitization the first computation of frequent itemsets. However, a naive implementation of our methods and techniques would require that we recalculate the support of itemsets in A and B after each itemset in B is hidden. This would be very expensive. From the mining of the database for the first time, we have the support of each frequent itemset. We store this in a dictionary abstract data type $SUPPORT$, where we use the frequent itemset as the key, and the support as the information. We chose a hash table as the concrete data structure, to efficiently retrieve and update $SUPPORT(b)$. We also build an additional data structure by extracting all transactions that support each of the frequent itemsets in A and B. For each frequent itemset, we have a list of IDs for transaction (those transactions that support the itemset). Note that the attack of an item on a transaction corresponds to removing the item of the transaction. It is easy to identify which frequent itemsets b see their support reduced by one. The dictionary information $SUPPOSRT(b)$ is updated as $SUPPORT(b) \leftarrow SUPPOT(b) - 1$. What is costly in the methods is the sorting of L_g. Note that the criteria by which the sorting is performed changes every cycle when we hide a sensitive itemset. For Technique 2, the computational cost is small. In this technique, we sort the frequent itemsets in B once and only once, and the criteria is their cardinality. And we always remove the itemset at the front of the list. This technique is very efficient. Technique 1 is more sophisticated, and those, more CPU intensive. In fact, because it creates an itemset g that may not be sensitive, we may require a pass through the original database to construct L_g.

5 Experimental Results and Comparison

Experiments on both techniques were carried out based on the first $20,000$ transactions from the "Frequent Itemset Mining Dataset Repository" (retail.gz dataset) [1]. The dataset was donated by Tom Brijs and includes sales transactions acquired from a fully-automated convenience store over a period of 5.5 months in 1998 [5]. We used the "A-priori algorithm" [10] to obtain the frequent itemsets. We performed the experiments with three different privacy support thresholds ($\sigma = 5\%, \sigma = 4\%$, and $\sigma = 3\%$).

For each technique, we ran the experiment 10 times for each privacy support threshold with different random selection of size-2 and size-3 itemsets among the frequent itemsets (in this way we are sure we are not selecting favorable instances to any of the two techniques). We ran the experiments once selecting randomly 3 itemsets and once selecting randomly 5 itemsets. Our results are presented in Fig 2, Fig. 3, Fig. 4, and Fig. 5. It is clear that in terms of minimizing the impact on non-sensitive itemsets, item count is superior to the technique based on increasing cardinality. While item count has more CPU requirements, and

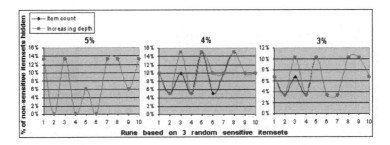

Fig. 2. Item count vs. increasing cardinality, hiding 3 itemsets using method 1

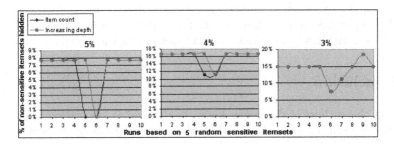

Fig. 3. Item count vs. increasing cardinality, hiding 3 itemsets using method 2

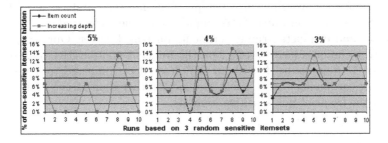

Fig. 4. Item count vs. increasing cardinality, hiding 5 itemsets using method 1

potentially its complexity could imply a new scan of the original database, we found that this additional scan did not occur in our experiments. Moreover, two aspects diminish the potential disadvantage of item count as more costly. First, most of the computational cost is not on the techniques but on the methods when they sort L_g. Note that they are doing this for all itemsets which hold the items x_0 being attacked. Thus, it is not only one list, but several lists that are sorted. Therefore, the difference between techniques is really not influential. Second, if the technique item count were to perform a scan of the database, this is very seldom, and moreover, as we produce the sanitized database, we scan

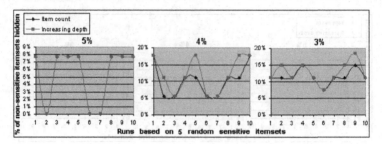

Fig. 5. Item count vs. increasing cardinality, hiding 5 itemsets using method 2

the original database. This production of the sanitized database at the conclusion of both techniques implies that if item count does scan the database once or twice, this is within a competitive constant factor with the item count technique.

6   Conclusion

As far as the authors of this paper know, in the field of association-rule mining, there is no existing methodology that discuss the best ways to hide a set of itemsets using item-restriction methods. We have presented in this paper two techniques based on item-restriction that hide sensitive itemsets. We also showed that rather simple new data structures implement these techniques with acceptable cost since we avoid expensive steps of mining the database several times during the sanitization process. We implemented the code needed to test both techniques and conducted the experiments on real data set. Our results show that both techniques have an effect on the frequent non-sensitive itemsets but, Technique 1 (item count) has about 25% less effect compared to Technique 2 (increasing cardinality). Also, using Method 2 rather than Method 1 lowers the effect on the frequent non-sensitive itemsets.

References

1. Frequent itemset mining dataset repository. http://fimi.cs.helsinki.fi/data/.
2. R. Agrawal, T. Imielinski, and A. Swami. Mining association rules between sets of items in large databases. In *Proc. of the ACM SIGMOD Conference on Management of Data*, pages 207–216, Washington D.C., USA, May 1993.
3. R. Agrawal and R. Srikant. Fast algorithms for mining association rules. In Jorge B. Bocca, Matthias Jarke, and Carlo Zaniolo, editors, *Proc. 20th Int. Conf. Very Large Data Bases, VLDB*, pages 487–499. Morgan Kaufmann, December 1994.
4. M. Atallah, E. Bertino, A. Elmagarmid, M. Ibrahim, and V. Verykios. Disclosure limitation of sensitive rules. In *Proc. of 1999 IEEE Knowledge and Data Engineering Exchange Workshop (KDEX'99)*, pages 45–52, Chicago, IL., November 1999.
5. T. Brijs, G. Swinnen, K. Vanhoof, and G. Wets. Using association rules for product assortment decisions: A case study. In *Knowledge Discovery and Data Mining*, pages 254–260, 1999.

6. C. Clifton, M. Kantarcioglu, and J. Vaidya. Defining privacy for data mining. In *Proc. of the National Science Foundation Workshop on Next Generation Data Mining*, pages 126–133, Baltimore, MD, USA, November 2002.

7. E. Dasseni, V. S. Verykios, A. K. Elmagarmid, and E. Bertino. Hiding association rules by using confidence and support. In *Proc. of the 4th Information Hiding Workshop*, pages 369–383, Pittsburg,PA, April 2001.

8. D. Edgar. Data sanitization techniques. White Papers, 2004.

9. A. HajYasien, V. Estivill-castro, and R. Topor. Sanitization of databases for refined privacy trade-offs. In *Proc. of the IEEE International Conference on Intelligence and Security Informatics (ISI 2006)*, San Diego, USA, May 2006. Springer LNCS.

10. J. Han and M. Kamber. *Data mining:Concepts and Techniques.* 2001.

11. J. Han, J. Pei, and Y. Yin. Mining frequent patterns without candidate generation. In Weidong Chen, Jeffrey Naughton, and Philip A. Bernstein, editors, *ACM SIGMOD Intl. Conference on Management of Data*, pages 1–12, Dallas, May 2000. ACM Press.

12. S. R. M. Oliveira and O. R. Zaiane. Privacy preserving frequent itemset mining. In *Proc. of the IEEE ICDM Workshop on Privacy, Security, and Data Mining*, pages 43–54, Maebashi City, Japan, December 2002.

13. S. R. M. Oliveira and O. R. Zaiane. Algorithms for balancing privacy and knowledge discovery in association rule mining. In *Proc. of the 7th International Database Engineering and Applications Symposium*, pages 54–63, China, July 2003.

14. S.R.M. Oliveira, O.R. Zaiane, and Y. Saygin. Secure association rule sharing. In *Proc. of the 8th PAKDD Conference*, pages 74–85, Sydney, Australia, May 2004. Springer Verlag Lecture Notes in Artificial Intelligence 3056.

15. Y. Saygin, V. S. Verykios, and C. Clifton. Using unknowns to prevent discovery of association rules. *SIGMOD Record*, 30(4):45–54, December 2001.

EStream: Online Mining of Frequent Sets with Precise Error Guarantee

Xuan Hong Dang[1], Wee-Keong Ng[1], and Kok-Leong Ong[2]

[1] School of Computer Engineering, Nanyang Technological University, Singapore
{dang0008, awkng}@ntu.edu.sg

[2] School of Engineering & IT, Deakin University, Australia
leong@deakin.edu.au

Abstract. In data stream applications, a good approximation obtained in a timely manner is often better than the exact answer that's delayed beyond the window of opportunity. Of course, the quality of the approximate is as important as its timely delivery. Unfortunately, algorithms capable of online processing do not conform strictly to a precise error guarantee. Since online processing is essential and so is the precision of the error, it is necessary that stream algorithms meet both criteria. Yet, this is not the case for mining frequent sets in data streams. We present EStream, a novel algorithm that allows online processing while producing results strictly within the error bound. Our theoretical and experimental results show that EStream is a better candidate for finding frequent sets in data streams, when both constraints need to be satisfied.

1 Introduction

In recent years, we are seeing a new class of applications that changed the traditional view of databases as a static store of information. These applications are commonly characterized by the high-speed data streams they generate (or receive), and the need to analyze them in real-time over limited computing resources [8,2]. Further, stream data can be lost under high speed conditions, become outdated in the analysis context, or intentionally dropped through techniques like sampling [3] or load shedding [12]. This makes it imperative to design algorithms that compute the answer in an online fashion with only one scan of the data stream whilst operating under the resource limitations. Consequently, this makes it impossible to compute an exact answer for the complex queries often found in data analysis.

Fortunately, approximate answers are usually sufficient for these applications. While approximates are desirable in the context of data stream applications, it is important to remember that the quality of the approximation is equally important as the timely processing of its query. Consider the case of processing financial data streams. Clearly, if a large error margin exist in the approximated answers, there will be serious financial consequences despite delivering the results within the given timeframe. Therefore, while approximate answers are sufficient, keeping the accuracy to within some error bound is necessary.

A Min Tjoa and J. Trujillo (Eds.): DaWaK 2006, LNCS 4081, pp. 312–321, 2006.

In the existing literature (e.g., [9,11,14]) the quality of the approximate answer is often governed by an error parameter. Although this defines the allowable error margin in the approximate answer, we observed that this is only the case when the algorithms analyze the data stream in batch mode. In other words, algorithms that are capable of online processing do not conform strictly to a precise error guarantee. Since online processing is essential to these applications *and* so is the precision of the error guarantee, it is essential that algorithms for data streams meet both criteria. Yet, this is not the case especially on the discovery of frequent sets in transactional data streams.

The goal of discovering frequent sets is to find the set of a collection of items (or any objects), whose occurrence count is at least greater than a certain threshold based on a fraction of the stream seen so far. So given a domain of m distinct items, there are 2^m distinct collections (or itemsets) that may appear in the data stream. Practically, it is impossible to enumerate and count all collections for each of the incoming transactions in the stream – given limited space and the need for real-time analysis. Hence, the downward closure property is exploited by delaying the counting of larger collections until all its subsets are found to be above the given threshold [5,13,4]. The implication of that is a bigger error margin on collections of larger sizes. As a result, existing methods cannot guarantee the same error threshold for frequent sets of different length.

We present EStream, our solution to finding frequent sets along with their estimated supports and error guarantees. Underpinning the design of EStream is the ability to give a precise error estimation on the support of frequent sets based on their length *during online processing*. Specifically, our proposal ensures that (i) there is no error in counting 1-itemsets; (ii) for 2-itemsets, the error in the estimate is no more than ϵ; and (iii) for itemsets of length $k > 2$, the error is no more than 2ϵ; where ϵ is the preset error threshold and k is the maximal length of the frequent set in the stream.

Next in Section 2, we introduce the preliminaries of discovering frequent sets in the context of data streams. We then present EStream's data structure and algorithm together with the error analysis. Section 3 is where we report our empirical results, and Section 4 will follow with a discussion of related works. Finally, we conclude our discussion in Section 5.

2 EStream: Data Structure and Algorithm

Let $\mathcal{DS} = \{t_1, \ldots, t_n, \ldots\}$ be a transactional data stream, where each transaction t_i contains items (or objects) drawn from $I = \{a_i, \ldots, a_m\}$. Without lost of generality, let n be the logical timestamp for each transaction, and thus n is also the number of transactions seen so far in $\mathcal{DS}$. The *frequency* of an itemset X, denoted $freq(X)$, is therefore the occurrence count of X in $\mathcal{DS}$ up to the nth transaction, and the *support* of X, denoted $supp(X)$, is thus the ratio of $freq(X)$ to n, i.e., $supp(X) = freq(X) \times n^{-1}$.

We further define that an itemset is *frequent* at time n if $supp(X)$ is no less than $\sigma \in (0, 1]$, the minimum support. It is an *infrequent* pattern if

$supp(X) \leqslant 2\epsilon$, where $\epsilon \in (0, 0.5\sigma]$ is the error parameter. Otherwise, it is a *sub-frequent* pattern. Collectively, both frequent and sub-frequent patterns are also called *significant* patterns. Further, let $k > 2$ be the maximal length of the patterns to discover from the stream. Then, the objective of our algorithm is to find, at any instant, all the frequent patterns up to length k with the error guarantees mentioned earlier.

2.1   Data Structure

In order to capture potentially frequent patterns, a trie-like data structure is used. A *trie* is a tree structure organized using key-space decomposition. Here, the key range is equally subdivided and the split within the key range for each node in the trie is predefined. A typical trie is the *alphabet trie* that stores a dictionary of words. In EStream, we adopt a variation of the alphabet trie.

First, let us elaborate that the set of items $I = \{a_1, \ldots, a_m\}$ is ordered such that any two items $a_i \in I, a_j \in I$ $(1 \leqslant i, j, \leqslant m)$, $a_i \prec a_j$ if and only if $i < j$. Similarly, we assume that any transaction $t \subseteq I$ has the items ordered in the same way. We can now define the following.

Definition 1. *A **TrieIT** (a.k.a. Trie Itemset) is a set of tree nodes where each node w is a 2-tuple (w_l, w_c) such that $w_l \in I$ is the node's label, and w_c is the frequency. Since each node corresponds to an item $a_i \in I$, we also use w_i (for brevity) to refer to a node that corresponds to $a_i \in I$. Then, the following conditions hold: (1) Let $C(w_i)$ be an ordered set of children nodes of w_i. If $C(w_i) \neq \varnothing$, then $C(w_i) \subseteq \{w_{i+1}, w_{i+2}, ..., w_m\}$; (2) For a node w_i, let $w_\ell, w_{\ell+1}, ..., w_{i-1}(1 \leqslant \ell \leqslant i - 1)$ be the set of nodes on the path from the root to the parent of w_i, then w_c is the frequency of the itemset $\{a_\ell, a_{\ell+1}, ..., a_i\}$.*

Each TrieIT $\mathcal{W}_i$ corresponds to some $a_i \in I$ whose root node is also labeled a_i.

Definition 2. *A **STrieIT** (a.k.a. Significant TrieIT) is a set of TrieITs that maintains the significant itemsets found in the stream. It has a special root node that references the root node of each TrieIT. Except for the root node, each node in the STrieIT is a 4-tuple $\langle w_\ell, Ccnt, Acnt, Wid \rangle$, where $w_\ell \in I$ is the node label; Ccnt is the frequency of the itemset $\{..., w_\ell\}$ in the current 'condow'[1]; Acnt is its accumulated frequency before the current 'condow'; and Wid indexes the 'condow' at which the itemset is inserted into the STrieIT.*

2.2   Algorithm

We next describe EStream given in Algorithm 1. In addition to the data stream, the analyst needs to specify three parameters: σ, ϵ, and k for each analysis. Since the processing is *online*, starting and attaching multiple instances of EStream to the data stream are possible, where each EStream instance will utilize a separate

---

[1] The *conceptual* win*dow*, i.e., condow, will become clearer as we present our EStream algorithm in the next section.

STrieIT as its synopsis (denoted $\mathcal{S}$ in the algorithm) to maintain the frequent set candidates based on the given parameters.

EStream processes each transaction on the fly and discards it immediately from memory after processing. As each transaction arrives, the algorithm inserts each frequent set candidate identified from the transaction into $\mathcal{S}$. After processing Δ transactions, the algorithm scans $\mathcal{S}$ to remove those itemsets that now become infrequent. In the algorithm, Δ is determined by $2^{k-2} \times \epsilon^{-1}$, which defines the size of the conceptual window (or *condow*). Since transactions are processed one by one, each condow provides a conceptual grouping for the transactions, and a logical time for scanning $\mathcal{S}$.

For each itemset of length ℓ ($1 \leqslant \ell \leqslant k$), we identify a corresponding minimal frequency threshold. This threshold is used to specify whether a ℓ-itemset can be generated as a potentially frequent set in the current condow. More specifically, a ℓ-itemset is inserted into $\mathcal{S}$ if the frequencies of all its immediate subsets in the condow are above this threshold. In the algorithm, the minimum thresholds of every pattern length is stored in a arr of k elements. Element j^{th} of arr is determined by $arr[j] = \Delta\epsilon \sum_{i=2}^{j}(1/2^{i-2})$ for $2 \leqslant j \leqslant k$; and $arr[1]$ is set to 0 for 1-itemsets since they have no subsets (except for $\{\varnothing\}$).

Let us denote the index of the current condow by $w_{crr} = \lceil n/\Delta \rceil$. Whenever a new transaction t_n arrives, the algorithm processes it as follows.

Increment. If an itemset X appearing in t_n is also maintained in $\mathcal{S}$, then increase $Ccnt$ by 1.

Insert. For every $X \subseteq t_n$ not in $\mathcal{S}$, insert X into $\mathcal{S}$ with initial values of $\langle X, 1, 0, w_{crr}\rangle$ if X is a singleton [2]; otherwise, let Y be any immediate subset of X, then X is inserted into $\mathcal{S}$ if all the following conditions hold:

- All immediate subsets of X are in $\mathcal{S}$;
- $\nexists Y$ such that $Acnt(Y) \neq 0$ and $Ccnt(Y) \leqslant arr[\|X\|]$; i.e., there are no Y being inserted into $\mathcal{S}$ from previous condows whose frequency in the current condow is insufficiently significant;
- $\nexists Y$ such that $Acnt(Y) = 0$ and $Ccnt(Y) \leqslant (arr[\|X\|] - arr[\|Y\|])$; i.e., there are no Y that has just been inserted into $\mathcal{S}$ in the current condow but after that its frequency is no more than $(arr[\|X\|] - arr[\|Y\|])$.

In cases where X is not inserted into $\mathcal{S}$, all its supersets in t_n need not be further checked.

Prune. This step is invoked each time $n \equiv 0 \bmod \Delta$ and after t_n is processed. The algorithm prunes $\mathcal{S}$ by removing all but 1-itemsets that satisfy $Ccnt(X) + Acnt(X) + X.Wid \times arr[\|X\|] \leqslant w_{crr} \times arr[\|X\|]$. Consequently, if an itemset is removed, all its supersets are also removed. An exception are those itemsets recently inserted into $\mathcal{S}$ in the current condow. These itemsets are generated after their immediate subsets became sufficiently frequent. Also in this step, for each remaining itemset X, its accumulated frequency is updated by $Acnt(X) = Acnt(X) + Ccnt(X)$ and then reset $Ccnt(X) = 0$.

---

[2] Recall that the immediate subsets of a 1-itemset is $\{\varnothing\}$ which appears in every transaction, all 1-itemsets are therefore inserted into $\mathcal{S}$ without conditions. For the same reason, they are also not pruned from $\mathcal{S}$.

At any instant upon the request of the analyst, the algorithm scans S to produce all 1-itemsets satisfying $Ccnt(X) + Acnt(X) \geqslant \sigma \times n$ and those ℓ-itemsets satifying $Ccnt(X) + Acnt(X) + X.Wid \times arr[|X|] \geqslant \sigma \times n$.

Algorithm 1. EStream: Finds frequent sets from transactions sighted in $\mathcal{DS}$.

Input

$\mathcal{DS}$	: data stream of transactions;
$\sigma \in (0,1]$	: minimum support threshold;
$\epsilon \in (0, 0.5\sigma]$	: maximum error allowable in σ;
k	: the longest frequent patterns to find;

Output

At anytime on demand, all estimated frequent sets seen in the stream.

1: $\Delta = 2^{(k-2)} \times \epsilon^{-1}$; $w_{crr} = 1$; $a[1] = 0$;
2: **for** $j = 2; j \leqslant k; j++$ **do** $arr[j] = \Delta\epsilon \sum_{i=2}^{j}(1/2^{i-2})$
3: **for each** $t_n \in \mathcal{DS}$ **do**
4:     **for each** 1-itemset $X \in t_n$ **do**
5:        **if** $X \in S$ **then** $Ccnt(X)++$ **else** Insert $(X, 1, 0, w_{crr})$ to S;
6:        **for each** itemset $X \subseteq t_n$ **do**
7:           **if** $X \in S$ **then**
8:              $Ccnt(X)++$
9:           **else**
10:              **if** $((\nexists Y \mid (Acnt(Y) \neq 0) \wedge (Ccnt(Y) \leqslant arr[|X|]))$ **and** $(\nexists Y \mid (Acnt(Y) = 0) \wedge (Ccnt(Y) \leqslant (arr[|X|] - arr[|Y|]))$ **and** $(\forall Y \mid Y \subset X \wedge Y \in S)$ **then**
11:                 Insert $(X, 1, 0, w_{crr})$ to S
12:              **end if**
13:           **end if**
14:           **if** X cannot be inserted into S **then**
15:              $t_n = t_n - \{C \subseteq t_n \mid C$ is a superset of $X\}$
16:           **end if**
17:        **end for**
18:        **if** $i \equiv 0 \bmod \Delta$ **then**
19:           Scan S to prune all nodes X such that $(|X| \geqslant 2) \wedge (Ccnt(X) + Acnt(X) \leqslant (w_{curr} - X.Wid) \times arr[|X|])$;
20:           $Acnt(X) = Acnt(X) + Ccnt(X)$; $Ccnt(X) = 0$;
21:        **end if**
22:        **return** $\{X \mid Ccnt(X) + Acnt(X) + X.Wid \times arr[|X|] \geqslant \sigma \times n\}$ upon request;
23: **end for**

Of interest to the reader is that EStream does not rely on the frequencies of all its subsets seen in the stream to generate a new candidate. Instead, only those frequencies in the current condow are considered. This can be understood by the fact that frequencies of itemsets are not uniformly distributed in all parts of the stream. Further, shorter itemsets often gain higher frequency counts than those of longer itemsets. Over a longer period of time, they are often have significant frequencies. Thus, their frequencies will always support the generation of longer candidates according to the downward closure property.

Yet, the frequencies of these new itemsets are very close to the threshold used to eliminate infrequent itemsets. Therefore, they are likely to be deleted again due to time-variation in many streams. In view of this, EStream records the variations on the frequency of each itemset X in different parts of the stream by separating its frequency in the current condow ($Ccnt$) and the accumulated one in previous condows ($Acnt$). This helps identify significant itemsets in the entire stream seen so far but not in the current condow. As a result, EStream efficiently reduces the generation of redundant itemsets and thus improve its performance.

2.3   Error Analysis

For each itemset X, we denote its *true frequency* by $freq_T(X)$ and *estimated frequency* by $freq_E(X) = Acnt(X) + Ccnt(X)$ using the synopsis S. Respectively, $supp_T(X)$ and $supp_E(X)$ denote its *true* and *estimated support*.

Lemma 1. *If an itemset X is deleted in the current condow w_{crr}, then its true frequency $freq_T(X)$ seen so far in the stream is no more than $w_{crr} \times arr[\|X\|]$.*

Lemma 2. *The true frequency of any itemset X in S is with the limits of $freq_E(X) \leqslant freq_T(X) \leqslant freq_E(X) + arr[\|X\|] \times X.Wid$.*

Theorem 1. *If n is the number of transactions seen so far and X is a 2-itemset, then $supp_E(X) \leqslant supp_T(X) \leqslant supp_E(X) + \epsilon$.*

Theorem 2. *If n is the number of transactions seen so far and X is a k-itemset, then $supp_E(X) \leqslant supp_T(X) < supp_E(X) + 2\epsilon$.*

Due to space constraints, the proof of the above lemmas and theorems is presented in [7].

3   Performance Evaluation

We implemented our algorithm in C++ and performed our experiments on a 1.9GHz Pentium machine with 1GB of memory running Windows XP. We utilized the method described in [1] to generate datasets and followed a similar naming convention for these datasets.

3.1   Scalability Studies

To test scalability, we evaluated our algorithm on a number of datasets with varying characteristics. For space reasons, we reported two representative datasets having opposite characteristics (see [7] for discussion of other datasets). In the first, the transaction has an average of 8 items with frequent sets whose length averages at 4. This dataset contains 5,000 distinct items. In the other, the transaction has an average of 5 items with frequent sets whose length averages at 3

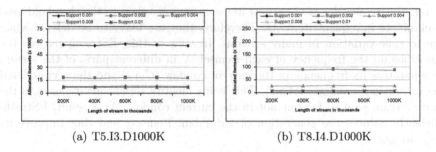

(a) T5.I3.D1000K   (b) T8.I4.D1000K

Fig. 1. Memory usage on two representative datasets of opposite characteristics. The scalability tests on other datasets can be obtained in [7].

but contains 10,000 distinct items. In both streams, we have 1 million transactions. We measured two parameters that is important for stream applications: (i) the execution time; and (ii) the memory consumption.

To simulate an online data stream, transactions are processed individually and discarded immediately. This leaves the available memory for the synopsis S. Figure 1 shows the memory usage on the two datasets using EStream. The usage levels indicated in the figure represents the maximum number of itemsets being generated during processing. This is equivalent to the maximum number of nodes allocated in S before pruning. We measure the usage levels over a number of minimum supports, ranging σ from 0.1% to 1% (and $\epsilon = 0.1\sigma$) after 200,000 transactions[3]. As expected a drop in the minimum support increases the memory usage. Nevertheless, the interesting point here is that the memory usage remains constant at any given support threshold throughout the lifetime of processing the stream. This happens because EStream is designed to maintain only potentially frequent sets in S; and by the pruning step, all insignificant candidates are removed periodically after each condow.

Figure 2 shows the execution times on the two selected datasets. Again, with the same range of support thresholds, we see that the cumulative execution time of EStream grows linearly – which indicates the uniform processing time over each condow; or uniform processing time for each transaction arriving from the stream. This stable execution time is also important in a data stream environment where the size of the stream is potentially unbounded.

3.2   Time-Varying Studies

In the previous experiments, we have excluded the time-variation parameter which has an effect on the memory consumption and execution time. In this section, we evaluate the impact and show how EStream addresses this issue effectively in its design.

---

[3] Since Δ is determined by $2^{k-2} \times \epsilon^{-1}$ and σ is varied from 0.1% to 1% (with $\epsilon = 0.1\sigma$), Δ is thus changed accordingly. Here, we took the measurement at the condow around this value, which is 200K transactions.

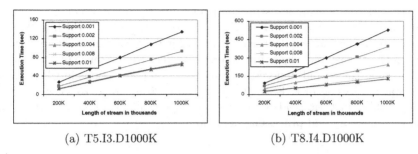

(a) T5.I3.D1000K   (b) T8.I4.D1000K

Fig. 2. Execution time on two representative datasets

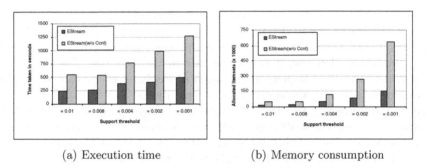

(a) Execution time   (b) Memory consumption

Fig. 3. Experiment results on a time-varying data streams

We have mentioned that the data stream distribution may change over time. In Estream, we separate the counting of itemsets in the current condow from the previous ones. New itemsets are generated only based on the presence of significant subsets in the current condow. Consequently, a large scale of redundant candidates are reduced. While we have discussed this at the end of Section 2.2, we confirm the practicality of this approach in the experiments below.

Using T8.I4.D1000K, the effect of time-variation is simulated on the dataset using the method proposed by Giannella *et. al.* [9], where an item mapping table is utilized. Here, 20% of items are randomly chosen for itemset generation with low frequencies; and periodically after every 50,000 transactions, random permutations among all items are applied to the table. To test the difference, we have a variation of EStream that generates candidates using all condows since starting the algorithm, i.e., relying on *Acnt* only. We denote this variant as EStream (w/o *Ccnt*). With the same range of support thersholds, Figure 3 shows the comparison in terms of execution and memory usage of EStream and its variant that uses only the cumulative counts, i.e., EStream (w/o *Ccnt*). Although a decrease in support threshold causes both to increase their number of nodes used in $\mathcal{S}$, we see that the memory utilization grows sharply in the case of EStream (w/o *Ccnt*). This happens as 1-itemsets are often significant if considering their frequency in the entire data stream but may not be sufficiently frequent in some condows due to time-variations.

In the case of EStream, a distinction is made through the use of *Acnt* (which is the cumulative frequencies of previous condows) and *Ccnt* (which is the frequencies of the current condow). By distinguishing the frequencies of itemsets in the current condow, our algorithm is able to detect the presence of such spurious items and thus avoid unnecessary processing on transactions in which those items appear. In contrast, EStream (w/o *Ccnt*) would tend to view them as frequent which in turn, leads to the generation of longer itemsets causing an increase in memory and processing demand.

4   Related Work

We can classify the problem of frequency counting into two categories: finding frequent singletons (e.g., [11,6]), and finding frequent sets (e.g., [5,14]). In the former category, the solutions have online processing capabilities and precise error guarantees. However, it is not the case in the later one. The main difficulty stems from the exponential explosion of itemsets, which caused existing algorithms to approach the constraints in separation.

Hidber [10] proposed the first online processing algorithm called CARMA. In CARMA, the error on an itemset's frequency is based on the highest frequency error among its subsets. This estimation is often too conservative as itemsets are frequently deleted and inserted throughout the runtime of the algorithm. More importantly, a loose estimate on smaller itemsets results in a looser estimate in their supersets. This is why a vast majority ($>$ 95%) of the itemsets generated in CARMA turns out to be false positives. Chang *et al.* [5] recently introduced an extension of CARMA in a forgetful model. In Chang's extension, the weights on older transactions are gradually decreased as new ones arrive in the stream. Despite this non-uniform threshold, the maximum error of a new itemset is derived by choosing the highest frequency error from its subsets. Consequently, the error guarantee varies for each pattern.

In contrast, EStream's strategy is not based on the highest error among subsets. Rather, a set of frequency thresholds are specified in advance for every itemset of specific lengths. These thresholds are then used to identify the candidates within each condow. If an itemset is not generated, its frequency in the condow is guaranteed to be no more than the corresponding threshold. Since the thresholds and the condow size are pre-specified, the support of each itemset is guaranteed within the same error. Work of Manku and Motwani, the Lossy-Counting [11], is the first attempt to guarantee a precise error on the patterns it discovers. Our algorithm is similar to theirs by the virtue that both find all frequent itemsets and guarantees the error on each itemset to be within the user-specified limits. In order to achieve this however, their work has to process transactions in batches and thus, results cannot be produced online due to buffering. Another work that gives error guarantees on mining results is the FDPM [14]. Jeffery *et. al.*'s work divides the stream into buckets, where the size of each bucket is determined by the Chernoff bound and a user-specified error. Each bucket is then processed separately and the results are updated into a global data structure recording the overall frequent patterns. Like the Lossy-Counting, FDPM is also a batch-processing algorithm. Furthermore, the lossy nature of FDPM causes truly frequent patterns to be missed in the final result. On the other hand, EStream guarantees that all patterns (if truly frequent) will be discovered while operating in online-processing mode.

5 Conclusions

We argue the need for critical stream applications, e.g., financial analysis, to both satisfy the online processing requirements and a strict error guarantee in their estimated results. We demonstrated this using the case of finding frequent sets on transactional streams in which the algorithms in existence address either the problem of online discovery and error guarantees *separately*. EStream represents our first effort to address these two constraints simultaneously in a single solution. As shown through theoretical analysis and empirical results, EStream accomplishes this goal while capturing the inherent characteristics of time-variation common in many data streams. We believe this will be an important step towards effective data stream applications.

References

1. R. Agrawal and R. Srikant. Fast algorithms for mining association rules in large databases. In *VLDB Conference*, pages 487–499, 1994.
2. B. Babcock, S. Babu, M. Datar, R. Motwani, and J. Widom. Models and issues in data stream systems. In *PODS Conference*, pages 1–16, 2002.
3. B. Babcock, M. Datar, and R. Motwani. Sampling from a moving window over streaming data. In *ACM-SIAM Symposium on Discrete Algorithms*, 2002.
4. J.H. Chang and W.S. Lee. Estwin: Adaptively monitoring the recent change of frequent itemsets over online data streams. In *CIKM Conference*, 2003.
5. J.H. Chang and W.S. Lee. Finding recent frequent itemsets adaptively over online data streams. In *ACM SIGKDD Conference*, pages 487–492, 2003.
6. Graham Cormode and S. Muthukrishnan. What's hot and what's not: tracking most frequent items dynamically. *ACM Trans. Database Syst.*, 30(1):249–278, 2005.
7. X.H. Dang, W.K. Ng, and K.L. Ong. Online mining of frequent patterns with precise error guarantees. Technical Report, Nanyang Technological University.
8. M. Garofalakis, J. Gehrke, and R. Rastogi. Querying and mining data streams: you only get one look a tutorial. In *ACM SIGMOD Conference*, 2002.
9. C. Giannella, J. Han, J. Pei, X. Yan, and P.S. Yu. *Mining Frequent Patterns in Data Streams at Multiple Time Granularities*. AAAI/MIT, 2003.
10. C. Hidber. Online association rule mining. In *SIGMOD Conference*, 1999.
11. G.S. Manku and R. Motwani. Approximate frequency counts over data streams. In *VLDB Conference*, pages 346–357, 2002.
12. N. Tatbul, U. Çetintemel, S.B. Zdonik, M. Cherniack, and M. Stonebraker. Load shedding in a data stream manager. In *VLDB Conference*, pages 309–320, 2003.
13. W.G. Teng, M.S. Chen, and P.S. Yu. A regression-based temporal pattern mining scheme for data streams. In *VLDB Conference*, pages 93–104, 2003.
14. J.X. Yu, Z.C., H. Lu, and A. Zhou. False positive or false negative: Mining frequent itemsets from high speed transactional data streams. In *VLDB Conference*, 2004.

Granularity Adaptive Density Estimation and on Demand Clustering of Concept-Drifting Data Streams*

Weiheng Zhu[1], Jian Pei[2], Jian Yin[1], and Yihuang Xie[1]

[1] Zhongshan University, China
gz_zwh@263.net, issjyin@mail.sysu.edu.cn, lion21@163.com
[2] Simon Fraser University, Canada
jpei@cs.sfu.ca

Abstract. Clustering data streams has found a few important applications. While many previous studies focus on clustering objects arriving in a data stream, in this paper, we consider the novel problem of *on demand clustering concept drifting data streams*. In order to characterize concept drifting data streams, we propose an effective method to estimate densities of data streams. One unique feature of our new method is that its granularity of estimation is adaptive to the available computation resource, which is critical for processing data streams of unpredictable input rates. Moreover, we can apply any clustering method to on demand cluster data streams using their density estimations. A performance study on synthetic data sets is reported to verify our design, which clearly shows that our method obtains results comparable to CluStream [3] on clustering single stream, and much better results than COD [8] when clustering multiple streams.

1 Introduction

Recently, clustering data streams has found a few important applications, such as stock market and financial data analysis, sensor networks, wireless communication, and network traffic management. A data stream can be regarded as a (potentially endless) list of data entries. Typically, data streams are assumed arriving continuously and rapidly.

In this paper, we study the problem of *on demand clustering concept drifting data streams*, which is illustrated in the following example.

Example 1 (Motivation). In a coal mine, thousands of sensors are deployed in pits to monitor the temperature, the humidity, and the concentrations of oxygen and gas. Each sensor keeps reporting the observed data, and thus generates a data stream. Typically,

---

* This work was supported by the National Natural Science Foundation of China (60573097) , Natural Science Foundation of Guangdong Province (05200302, 04300462), Research Foundation of National Science and Technology Plan Project (2004BA721A02), Research Foundation of Science and Technology Plan Project in Guangdong Province (2005B10101032), Research Foundation of Disciplines Leading to Doctorate degree of Chinese Universities(20050558017), the NSERC Grants 312194-05 and 614067, and the NSF Grant IIS-0308001. All opinions, findings, conclusions and recommendations in this paper are those of the authors and do not necessarily reflect the views of the funding agencies.

A Min Tjoa and J. Trujillo (Eds.): DaWaK 2006, LNCS 4081, pp. 322–331, 2006.

the sensors are not synchronized. That is, the rate that a sensor reports data is independent of the others. Generally, such surveillance data streams are concept drifting. That is, the distribution of a stream may evolve over time.

Clustering the surveillance data streams is important to monitor the working conditions in pits. However, due to the nature of sensors and the detection environment, the data collected is often noisy. It is not surprising at all that about 30% of data in a large sensor network is noise. Data records may be lost on their way to the servers. Apparently, clustering the objects (i.e., records of (temperature, humidity, oxygen concentration, gas concentration)) in a data stream does not make good sense. Instead, if we can characterize the distributions of temperature, humidity, oxygen concentration, and gas concentration of sensors, we should cluster the sensors according to their distributions.   ∎

To tackle the problem of on demand clustering concept drifting data streams motivated in Example 1, we need to address some challenges.

Challenge 1: *How we can characterize the distributions of noisy data streams?*

Our contribution. We propose to characterize a data stream using its *kernel density estimation* [15]. Accordingly, data streams should be clustered by their densities. Although kernel density estimation is also used in [2] to estimate the changes in a data stream, to the best of our knowledge, this is the first paper to apply kernel density estimation to cluster multiple data streams.

Challenge 2: *When the number of fast data streams is large, how can we develop an efficient and scalable method to maintain the density estimations adaptively?*

Our contribution. Many previous methods employ load-shedding, i.e., dropping some data, to handle workload heavier than their capabilities. However, load-shedding may lose some important information. Here, we propose a load-skimming approach, which lowers down the granularity of the kernel density estimation adaptively but still captures every incoming data entry. Our load-skimming approach can provide a solid bound on the quality of density estimation.

Challenge 3: Concept drifting may happen in a data stream. *How can we capture the concept drifting effectively?*

Our contribution. We develop an effective approach to detect significant changes of the density of a data stream. The general idea is to monitor the top-k densest regions in a data stream, and catch the changes. Comparing to the existing methods of change detection, our method is simple and efficient, and thus can be used to handle a large number of fast data streams.

The rest of the paper is organized as follows. In Section 2, we formulate the problem and review the related work. The granularity adaptive density estimation method is proposed in Section 3. We develop the notion of top-k synopsis and the concept drifting detection method in Section 4. The experimental results are reported in Section 5. Section 6 concludes the paper.

2 Problem Definition and Related Work

In this section, we first present the model of on demand clustering of data streams according to their kernel densities. Then, we review related work.

2.1 The Model

Without loss of generality, we consider *data space* $\mathcal{D}^n$, where $\mathcal{D} = [\alpha, \beta] \subset \mathcal{R}$ is a range of real numbers. A data stream S is a sequence of vectors v_j $(j = 1, 2, \ldots)$ such that each vector $v_j \in \mathcal{D}^n$. A vector is also called an *entry*.

To characterize a data stream S, the distribution of the vectors in the data space can be used. Let f be the density function of data stream S. Conceptually, stream S is generated by sampling an infinite data set generated by f.

A data stream S is call *concept drifting* if the density function f of S evolves over time. In this paper, we consider a set of concept drifting data streams $S_1, \ldots, S_m$. We assume that the data streams in question are not synchronized. In other words, the j-th vector v_j^1 in stream S_1 and the j-th vector v_j^2 in S_2 may not arrive at the same time or at the same time slot. This assumption reflects the application scenarios where the input rates of data streams may vary from stream to stream, and from time to time.

Essentially, the similarity between two streams S_1 and S_2 can be measured by the similarity between their density functions f_1 and f_2. Therefore, we can cluster the streams according to their densities.

Problem definition. Given a set of concept drifting data streams $S_1, \ldots, S_m$ in the data space $\mathcal{D}^n$, the problem of *on demand clustering* the data streams is to continuously maintain the density functions $f_1, \ldots, f_m$ for the streams, and cluster the streams on demand according to the similarity among their density functions.   ■

The on demand clustering of data streams consists of two steps: continuous density estimation and on demand clustering. In the continuous density estimation step, data streams are summarized using density functions. In the clustering step, any clustering method can be used, such as k-means employed in our experimental study. In the rest of the paper, we shall focus on the continuous density estimation step.

2.2 Related Work

Clustering has been studied extensively in both statistics and computer science literature. Jain et al. [10] provides a nice survey.

Clustering data streams has been studied in depth recently (e.g., [1,3,2,5,9,14]). In real applications, clustering analysis may be conducted under different models. For example, many of the previous studies (e.g., [1,3,5,9,14]) focus on clustering data objects in one stream. That is, an entry in the data stream in question represents a data object. The task is to cluster the objects, probably with some constraints such as considering only objects arriving in a sliding window, or finding clusters in subspaces. As another example, some studies (e.g., [12,17]) maintain clusters of moving objects over time.

Some methods have also been developed to detect changes of clusters. For example, Aggarwal [2] uses velocity density estimation to capture and visualize changes in an evolving data stream. Bursts are often considered as an important type of changes. Burst-detection in data streams has been studied in [11,13,18].

When the input rates of streams exceed the capacity, load shedding techniques can be used. Essentially, a load shedder samples the input data streams, and the stream processing methods are applied on the samples only instead of the raw streams. Therefore, load shedding can improve the latency of the data analysis result by trading off the answer quality. Various load shedding strategies for data stream processing have been studied, such as [4,7,16].

The critical difference between load shedding and load skimming developed in this paper is that load skimming still processes every observation instead of sampling the incoming streams. Load skimming adapts to changing input rates of streams by adjusting the granularity of the data analysis.

Recently, clustering data streams on demand has been studied in [3,8]. In [3], Aggarwal et al. use micro-clusters to summarize objects in a data stream. Then, clustering on demand is conducted using the micro-clusters instead of the original data. CluStream [3] clusters objects in a single data stream, and does not address the problem of clustering multiple data streams and clustering using densities. In [8], Dai et al. assume that each data stream is an infinite time series and the data streams are synchronized in entry arrival. COD [8] approximates the time series and use the approximation to conduct clustering on demand. In our model, a stream is not a time series and streams are not synchronized in arrival. In Section 5, we shall experimentally compare our approach and CluStream [3] and COD [8].

3   Granularity Adaptive Density Estimation

In this section, we discuss how to estimate the kernel density function for a data stream. We assume that concept drifting does not happen. Section 4 will address how to handle concept drifting.

3.1   Kernel Density Estimation

To estimate the density function f from a data stream, we adopt the *kernel density estimation* method [15].

Consider estimating the density function f for a data stream S that has no concept drifting. At a point p in the data space, $f(p)$ is the density at the point. Suppose the density function f is in Gaussian distribution. Then, $f(p)$ can be estimated by

$$f(p) = \frac{1}{k} \sum_{j=1}^{k} \left(\frac{1}{\sqrt{2\pi}} \cdot e^{-\frac{dist(p,v)^2}{2h^2}} \right), \tag{1}$$

where k is the number of entries in the data stream arrived so far, $dist(p,v)$ is the Euclidian distance between p and v, and h is a parameter to describe the influence of a data point in its neighborhood. The intuition is that an entry can be regarded as being generated by different points in the data space according to the density function, and the density function at a point can thus be estimated by the sum of the contributions of all the entries.

Generally, we can use any kernel functions for density estimation. In this paper, we use the Gaussian kernel due to its simplicity and its universal applicability in applications. Our approach can still be applied using other kernel functions.

3.2   Grid-Based Estimation

To estimate a continuous density function for a data stream is difficult. In practice, we can approximate a continuous density function by a discrete representation. Intuitively, by estimating the densities of a large number of probe points evenly distributed in the data space $\mathcal{D}^n$, we can achieve a good estimation of the continuous density function. For any point q in the data space, $f(q)$ can be estimated by $f(p)$ where p is the probe point closest to q.

Technically, we can organize the probe points as a grid in the data space $\mathcal{D}^n$. Let l be a *granularity parameter* specified by the user. Recall that $\mathcal{D} = [\alpha, \beta]$ is the range in each dimension. Let $\omega = \frac{\beta - \alpha}{l}$. Then, we deploy $(l+1)^n$ probe points $(\alpha + i_1 \omega, \ldots, \alpha + i_n \omega)$ in the data space, where $0 \leq i_1, \ldots, i_n \leq l$. That is, on each dimension we have $(l+1)$ probe point coordinate values evenly distributed. We call $(l+1)^{-n}$ the *granularity* of the probe grid. The smaller the granularity, the better the estimation quality.

When a new entry v in the data stream comes, for each probe point p, we shall update the density function $f(p)$ according to Equation 1.

3.3   Granularity Adaptive Estimation

Clearly, the complexity of updating the density estimation for each new entry in a stream is $O(l^n)$. To control the cost in practice, we propose two methods: granularity adapting discussed here and localized estimation introduced in Section 3.4.

The input rate of a data stream may change over time. When the input rate of a data stream increases and becomes so fast that the density estimation cost exceeds the capacity of the stream mining system, updating every probe point in the grid may become infeasible or unacceptable.

In order to still process every new observation point in the upcoming stream, we can lower down the granularity of the probe grid. In other words, we can make the granularity adaptive to the input rate of the data stream.

Technically, we can adjust the granularity parameter l. By reducing l, we can reduce the number of probe point coordinates in each dimension, and thus reduce the granularity. Suppose the new granularity parameter is l'. then, the reduction on the granularity is $((l+1)^n - (l'+1)^n)$. The following result help to set the granularity parameter l properly.

Theorem 1. *Let update time of the density estimation for a probe point be t, the input rate of a stream be ν, and the fraction of runtime allocated to processing the stream be a. Then, the granularity is minimized when the granularity parameter $l = \lfloor (\frac{a}{\nu t})^{\frac{1}{n}} \rfloor - 1$.*

Proof. The maximum number of probe points that can be processed in a unit time is $\frac{a}{\nu t}$. l must be an integer and satisfy inequality $\frac{a}{\nu t} \geq (l+1)^n$. The theorem follows.   ∎

In implementation, adjusting granularity parameters frequently can be very costly. Instead, we use a granularity upgrade rate $\psi > 1$. Let the current granularity parameter be l. When the input rate of a data stream exceeds the capacity of the system, the granularity parameter is reduced to $\frac{l}{\psi}$. On the other hand, when the available resource is sufficient to support a finer granularity of parameter at least $l \cdot \psi$, then the granularity is lowered down.

When the granularity parameter is changed, a new probe point may not be a probe point in the previous probe grid. To avoid loss of historical data, a new probe point that is not in the previous probe grid inherits the density function estimation from the closest probe point that is in the previous probe grid.

3.4 Localized Estimation

As analyzed before, when the granularity is small, updating the density estimation at each probe point for a new entry in a data stream can be costly. From Equation 1, we can observe that the effect of a new entry on a remote probe point can be very small. The effect decreases exponentially with respect to the distance between the entry and the probe point: the larger the distance, the smaller the effect.

This observation motivates the localized estimation method as follows. We can ignore the effect on the probe points that are far away from the new entry. Technically, we can neglect probe points that are of distance at least δh from the observation point. We can prove the following.

Theorem 2 (Error bound). *For a probe point p, if all entries q in the data stream such that $dist(p, q) > \delta h$ are ignored, the error on the estimation of $f(p)$ is bound by*

$$E = \frac{1}{k} \sum_{q, dist(p,q) > \delta h} e^{-\frac{dist(p,q)^2}{2h^2}} \leq \frac{|\{q | dist(p, q) \geq \delta h\}|}{k} \cdot e^{-\frac{\delta^2}{2}},$$

where k is the total number of entries arrived so far in the data stream. ∎

By Theorem 2, we can update only the probe points around a newly arrived entry in a data stream. In practice, the error can be much smaller than the upper bound when the granularity is not too rough.

3.5 Summary

We can use a probe grid to estimate a discrete representation of the density function of a data stream. By localized estimation, when a new entry arrives, we only need to update the density estimation of the probe points around the entry, and the accumulated error is bound by Theorem 2. To address the change of input rate of a data stream, we can adjust the granularity parameter adaptively.

4 Tracing Concept Drifting and on Demand Clustering

Section 3 presents an adaptive method to estimate densities of data streams. When concept drifting happens, a data stream evolves and its density function changes over time. How can we handle concept drifting data streams effectively and timely?

4.1 Tracing Drifting by Decaying

When concept drifting happens in a data stream, the density of the stream in a recent window is different from the density in the long term history, as elaborated in Figure 1.

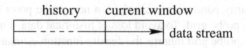

Fig. 1. Concept drifting

Therefore, to handle concept drifting, we shall trace the drifting concepts by finding the current density. Here, we propose two methods.

Critically, to trace the current density, we need a mechanism to eliminate stale data gradually. Decaying is a typical and effective strategy, which is also used in some previous studies on data streams, such as [6]. Essentially, each data entry carries a weight which decays over time. More recent data has higher weights than older data.

In the context of this study, we use a decay factor ρ, which is a value between 0 and 1. Periodically, the density estimation of each probe point is decayed by factor ρ, i.e., $f(p) = \rho f(p)$. In implementation, decaying can be conducted lazily. That is, each probe point p carries a time stamp τ_p. When the probe point p is updated due to a new entry in the stream, τ_p is compared with the system current time stamp τ. The density estimation $f(p)$ should be decayed to $f(p) \cdot \rho^{\tau - \tau_p}$ before the effect of the new entry is added in.

Alternatively, to capture the current density distribution, we can use a window W of size τ, where τ is a user-specified parameter. We estimate the density distribution in W. When the window is full (i.e., τ new entries arrive), the density distribution in W is compared with the historical density distribution. If the difference between the two distributions is minor, then no concept drifting happens and the density distribution in W can be added to the historical density distribution, since the density distribution is addable. On the other hand, if the difference is substantial, then the concept drifting happens. We should use the distribution in W to replace the historical distribution.

4.2 On Demand Clustering

We can compare two data streams using their densities. Let f_1 and f_2 be the estimated density functions of data streams S_1 and S_2, respectively. Then, the similarity between S_1 and S_2 can be measured as

$$sim(S_1, S_2) = \sqrt{\int_{\mathcal{D}^n} (f_1(p) - f_2(p))^2 dp} \tag{2}$$

With the probe grids, Equation 2 can be approximated by

$$sim(S_1, S_2) = \sqrt{\sum_{\text{probe point } p} (f_1(p) - f_2(p))^2} \tag{3}$$

We can apply any clustering algorithms on demand to find clusters of the data streams.

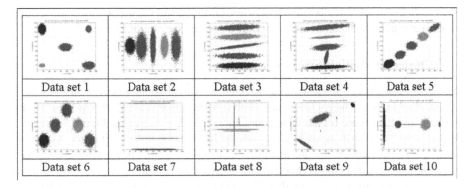

Fig. 2. The 10 data sets used in Section 5.1

Table 1. The sum of squares of distances to means on the 10 synthetic data sets

Method	D_1	D_2	D_3	D_4	D_5	D_6	D_7	D_8	D_9	D_{10}
CluStream	**32394.9**	69811.6	73561.5	**49371.7**	42980.7	53675.6	**21952.9**	**29070.7**	43029.2	**34900.2**
Our method	33887.7	**66779.9**	**68583.9**	58816.3	**37240.7**	**47000.1**	51351.3	49511.2	**32093.4**	68476.9

5   Experimental Results

To verify the clustering method proposed in this paper, we conduct an extensive performance study using synthetic data sets. Limited by space, we can only report some results on selected aspects here. More experimental results can be found in the full version of the paper.

5.1   Clustering One Data Stream

First, we examine whether clustering using density estimation can be competent with other clustering methods on mining one data stream. We use 10 synthetic data sets as shown in Figure 2. Each data set contains $50,000$ entries of 5 clusters in a 2-dimensional data space.

On each data set, we run CluStream [3] our density estimation algorithms, respectively. CluStream uses $10,000$ entries to initialize $5,000$ micro-clusters. Our density estimation algorithm uses a 200×200 probe grid (i.e., the granularity parameter is set to 19), and $h = 10$ in localized estimation (Section 3.4). Both methods scan the data set only once. Then, micro-clusters and probe points are clustered by k-means, where the number of clusters in clustering is set to 5. To compare the quality of clusters found, we compute the sum of squares (SSQ) of distances between entries in the clusters and the corresponding means. The results are shown in Table 1.

We observe that each method obtains the better clustering results on 5 data sets, respectively. Interestingly, on data sets D_7, D_8 and D_{10} where some clusters distributed in a long stripe, CluStream performs substantially better. In such cases, micro-clusters are capable to capture the stripe structures and thus the situations are to the advantage of CluStream. In the other data sets, our method achieves better or comparable results.

The runtime of computing micro-clusters in CluStream and the density estimation time in our method are also comparable. Limited by space, we omit the details.

5.2 Clustering Multiple Streams

We generate synthetic data streams in Gaussian distribution. Each stream contains 10, 000 data entries. The experimental results on 100 streams are shown in Figure 3. In this test, 10 clusters are found, which contain 2, 3, 8, 2, 7, 11, 14, 3, 43, and 7 streams, respectively. The distribution of the streams are listed in the order of clusters. As can be seen, streams in each cluster are of similar distribution. To the best of our knowledge, there exists no other methods that can also cluster multiple streams according to their density distributions. Please note that COD [8] treats each stream as a time series, and thus cannot identify clusters properly in this test. In fact, COD outputs a cluster of 91 streams and 9 clusters each of 1 stream in this experiment.

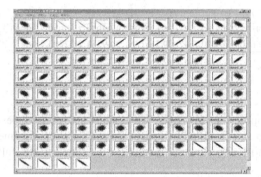

Fig. 3. Clustering multiple streams

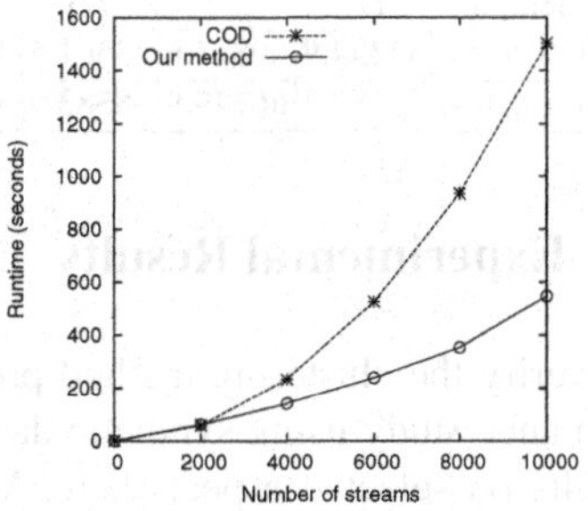

Fig. 4. Scalability of clustering multiple streams

Since COD also cluster multiple streams, we compare the runtime of our method and that of COD. The result is shown in Figure 4. As can be seen, our method is scalable with respect to the number of data streams. When there are many streams, our method is clearly more efficient than COD.

6   Conclusions

In this paper, we propose a simple yet effective method for on demand clustering multiple concept drifting data streams. The central idea is to characterize concept drifting data streams by estimating densities. Our new method is adaptive to the available computation resource, which is critical for processing data streams of unpredictable input rates. Moreover, we can apply any clustering method to on demand cluster data streams using their density estimations. We report a performance study on synthetic data sets to verify our design. The experimental results clearly show that our method can obtain clusters of good quality and is scalable in mining a large number of data streams.

References

1. C. Aggarwal, et al. A framework for projected clustering of high dimensional data streams. In *Proceedings of the 30th International Conference on Very Large Data Bases (VLDB'04)*, Toronto, ON, Canada, August 2004.
2. C. C. Aggarwal. A framework for diagnosing changes in evolving data streams. In *Proceedings of the 2003 ACM SIGMOD international conference on Management of data*, pages 575–586. ACM Press, 2003.
3. C. C. Aggarwal, et al. A framework for clustering evolving data streams. In *Proc.the 19th Int. Conf. on Very Large Data Bases (VLDB'03)*, Berlin, Germany, September 2003.
4. B. Babcock, et al. Load shedding techniques for data stream systems. In *Proceedings of the 2003 Workshop on Management and Processing of Data Streams (MPDS 2003)*, San Diego, California, June 2003.
5. B. Babcock, et al. Maintaining variance and k-medians over data stream windows. In *Proceedings of the twenty-second ACM SIGMOD-SIGACT-SIGART symposium on Principles of database systems (PODS'03)*, pages 234–243, New York, NY, USA, 2003. ACM Press.
6. J. H. Chang and W. S. Lee. Finding recent frequent itemsets adaptively over online data streams. In *KDD '03: Proceedings of the ninth ACM SIGKDD international conference on Knowledge discovery and data mining*, pages 487–492. ACM Press, 2003.
7. Y. Chi, et al. Loadstar: A load shedding scheme for classifying data streams. In *Proc. 2005 SIAM Int. Conf. Data Mining*, New Port Beach, CA, April 2005.
8. B-R Dai, et al. Clustering on demand for multiple data streams. In *Proceedings of the Fourth IEEE International Conference on Data Mining (ICDM'04)*, pages 367–370. IEEE, November 2004.
9. S. Guha, et al. Clustering data streams. In *Proc. IEEE Symposium on Foundations of Computer Science (FOCS'00)*, pages 359–366, Redondo Beach, CA, 2000.
10. A. K. Jain, et al. Data clustering: A survey. *ACM Comput. Surv.*, 31:264–323, 1999.
11. J. Kleinberg. Bursty and hierarchical structure in streams. In *KDD '02: Proceedings of the eighth ACM SIGKDD international conference on Knowledge discovery and data mining*, pages 91–101, New York, NY, USA, 2002. ACM Press.
12. Y. Li, et al. Clustering moving objects. In *KDD '04: Proceedings of the tenth ACM SIGKDD international conference on Knowledge discovery and data mining*, pages 617–622, New York, NY, USA, 2004. ACM Press.
13. J. Ma and S. Perkins. Online novelty detection on temporal sequences. In *KDD '03: Proceedings of the ninth ACM SIGKDD international conference on Knowledge discovery and data mining*, pages 613–618, New York, NY, USA, 2003. ACM Press.
14. L. O'Callaghan, et al. High-performance clustering of streams and large data sets. In *Proc. 2002 Int. Conf. Data Engineering (ICDE'02)*, San Fransisco, CA, April 2002.
15. B. W. Silverman. *Density Estimation for Statistics and Data Analysis*. Chapman and Hall, 1986.
16. N. Tatbul, et al. Load shedding in a data stream manager. In *VLDB*, pages 309–320, 2003.
17. Q. Zhang and X. Lin. Clustering moving objects for spatio-temporal selectivity estimation. In *Proceedings of the fifteenth conference on Australasian database (CRPIT'04)*, pages 123–130, Darlinghurst, Australia, Australia, 2004. Australian Computer Society, Inc.
18. Y. Zhu and D. Shasha. Efficient elastic burst detection in data streams. In *Proceedings of the ninth ACM SIGKDD international conference on Knowledge discovery and data mining*, pages 336–345. ACM Press, 2003.

Classification of Hidden Network Streams

Matthew Gebski, Alex Penev, and Raymond K. Wong

National ICT Australia
and School of Computer Science & Engineering
University of New South Wales
Sydney, NSW 2052
Australia

Abstract. Traffic analysis is an important issue for network monitoring and security. We focus on identifying protocols for network traffic by analysing the size, timing and direction of network packets. By using these network stream characteristics, we propose a technique for modelling the behaviour of various TCP protocols. This model can be used for recognising protocols even when running under encrypted tunnels. This is complemented with experimental evaluation on real world network data.

1 Introduction

Computer security and intrusion detection have become important problems in computer science. One interesting area of security is that of misuse detection, in which we attempt to discern inappropriate behaviour by users who (seemingly) have legitimate access to a system. With the increase in importance of the web over the past 10 years, so too has there been an increase in the number of ways that appropriate network access can be abused. For instance, users may attempt to abuse their privileges and resources by tunneling or proxying file sharing software connections over HTTP or SSH to mask the inappropriate activity by using an acceptable protocol.

In this paper, we address the problem of protocol identification in which, from a network stream, we attempt to identify the underlying protocol that applications are using for communication. Unlike some previous approaches, we restrict ourselves to limited information about the traffic, using only the timing and size of observed packets. There are numerous scenarios where the amount of information for identification is limited to these attributes. Consider the problem of classifying encrypted traffic based on the protocol. The traffic may be flowing over an SSH stream or may be encrypted in some other manner. Examples of malicious activity include access to websites that may generally be prevented due to the company's firewall, or running filesharing programs.

To a third party observer, the only information that may be ascertained is the timing between packets and the size of the packets themselves. Unlike many instances where the packets may be available to an administrator, we are unable to extract the protocol information directly from the headers of the packets. Furthermore, it is not possible even to discern the ports to which the connections

A Min Tjoa and J. Trujillo (Eds.): DaWaK 2006, LNCS 4081, pp. 332–341, 2006.

are being made as this information is hidden at the client end and reconstructed at the server end of the tunnel.

Our aim is to develop a model based on the traffic structure that is visible externally. This is then used to evaluate the likelihood of a new stream matching each of the previously observed protocols. In addition to being able to discriminate between protocols with high accuracy, we are able to determine certain websites based on their idiosyncratic behaviour (i.e. GMail). Our technique is based around the construction of a bipartite graph representing outgoing and incoming packets. From this graph, we weight edges between outgoing and incoming nodes based on the likelihood of the ratios of the transmitted and received packet sizes. This allows us to classify new connection sequences based on particularly indicative sub-sequences.

The remainder of this paper is organised as follows. We begin in section 2 by discussing the existing work for intrusion detection, focusing on work that is related to the problem of protocol identification. Following this, in section 3 we present our approach. In section 4 we discuss our experimental evaluation and we conclude in section 5.

2   Related Work

There is a large amount of research for network security. In particular, the area of *intrusion detection* focuses on discerning aberrant behaviour which may indicate malicious or inappropriate use of a system. Many approaches to intrusion detection use pattern matching [7,1,2], but they often require significant human effort in constructing rules to specify what constitutes inappropriate behaviour. Recently, more "automatic" approaches such as neural networks have been used for intrusion detection [11], in addition to other data mining techniques such as frequent item analysis [10], episode rules [6] and root cause analysis [5].

Related to intrusion detection is the problem of *misuse detection*. Misuse detection involves determining if a legitimate user is abusing the system, such as attempting to disguise their illegitimate actions as legitimate actions. We should note that it is possible that the a malicious third party may have gained unauthorised access to a user's account resulting in the misuse.

Our previous work [4] into misuse detection has focused on detecting unusual user behaviour (in particular for UNIX shell commands). It is possible to model commands that users enter, and using a tree-based system, generate a score indicating the likelihood of a new sequence of commands having been entered by that user (or by an intruder). Unfortunately, this technique can not be applied to the problem of protocol identification as incoming sequences were compared to one particular user whereas for protocol identification, there are numerous relevant protocols and user behavioural patterns. Other work on misuse detection include Lane and Brodley's instance based learning approach [8,9], and Sequeira and Zaki's clustering approach, ADMIT [12].

In this paper, we focus on the identification of network protocols as an indication of misuse. This identification should be applicable even when ports have been disguised by tunneling or encrypting data. The naive technique for protocol identification is to simply examine the outgoing and incoming ports — connections on port 80 are classified as HTTP, on port 22 as SSH and so forth. This is trivially circumvented by proxy servers, tunnels or port remapping. In [3], Early et al. used a decision tree for identification of HTTP, FTP, Telnet, SMTP and SSH traffic without using port numbers. The C5.0 classification algorithm was used, and although their classification accuracy ranged from 82-100%, their method heavily relied on the SYN, ACK, PSH and FIN flags in TCP frames. Each of these fields is unavailable if the traffic has been encrypted or tunneled.

For the related problem of classifying webpages over a secure socket layer connection (SSL), Sun et al [13] constructed signatures of approximately 100,000 sites using the number and the sizes of referenced HTTP objects. By comparing signatures, they were able to identify 80% of return visits to the sites with a false positive rate of under 5%. While identification for static pages was accurate, dynamic pages were virtually "non-identifiable". This approach is unsuitable for our problem because few TCP sessions are consistent in their packet counts, which makes protocol identification closer in nature to dynamic pages.

More recently, Wright et al. [14] considered encrypted tunnels, and noted that only three packet-level data were available to a protocol classifier: delta time between session packets, direction of packets and block rounded sizes. Based on these limitations, their Hidden Markov Model approach aimed to solve a sequence alignment problem with 4 states (Insert, Delete, and two Match states to model client-server crosstalk). Training was done on 9 protocols to determine parameters and transitional probabilities of their profile HMMs. Test sessions were classified as the protocol responsible for the best-matching HMM profile. Despite not using TCP-headers, their results were comparable to [3]. However, the approach had sub-optimal accuracy for interactive protocols such as SSH and FTP, and it is unclear how their model will perform for protocols such as BitTorrent.

3   Our Approach

3.1   Preliminaries

We will assume that we are dealing with sets of incoming/outgoing sequences comprised of tuples summarising a packet. Each tuple is of the form $< time, size, direction >$. We will use S to denote a session with S_{out} and S_{in} for the outgoing and incoming packets respectively. $S_{out}[i]$ will be used to refer to the ith tuple in S_{out}. For simplicity and clarity we do not consider the ACK acknowledgement packets (although our model can be adjusted to accommodate the existence of the acknowledgement packets).

For the construction of our model, we take into account the source and destination hosts and ports in addition to the time and size. This host and port information is *not* used for the identification of the protocols in the testing stage. Although the source and destination ports would aid in the identification, these fields are not used as the information would no longer be available if the user

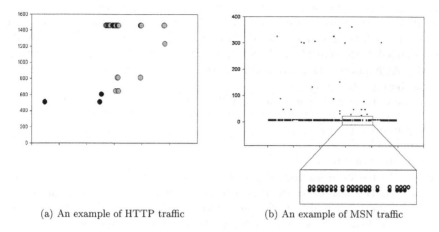

(a) An example of HTTP traffic   (b) An example of MSN traffic

Fig. 1. Two examples of network traffic

tunnels their connection. While it may not be possible to determine the actual destination host or port for a tunneled connection, we only require the direction for incoming/outgoing packets. After training, we can classify an unknown stream using only the time, size and direction of its packets.

3.2   Model

The primary assumption that we make in regards to the traffic structure relates to request and responses. From the sequences S_{out} and S_{in}, we create a set of forward/backward pairs. Physically, the first value of these pairs corresponds with a request made from the client machine while the second corresponds with a response from the remote server. Of course, either the request or the response may require multiple packets in order to transmit all the intended information. An example of this may be a client requesting an image via HTTP — the request is typically only a few packets. However, the HTTP response often may require numerous packets. Figure 1 demonstrates this concept, the horizontal axis represents packet observation times (transmission times for outgoing packets and arrival times for incoming packets) while the vertical axis represents packet size. Figure 1a shows an HTTP session with the black dots indicating client side traffic (outgoing) and the grey dots indicating server responses. We can see that there are only three request packets followed by a number of large reply packets. Conversely, Figure 1b displays a portion of an MSN session. Again black dots indicate outgoing transmissions while the white dots indicate server replies. We can observe the primary communication consists of 'keep alive' packets from the client followed by a reply from the server accepting the keep alive request. This concept is highlighted in the enlarged region where we can clearly see a small (6 bytes) outgoing transmission followed by a slightly larger reply (8 bytes).

With this flow structure in mind, a bipartite graph is constructed to represent each session. We use two sets of nodes, *OutgoingNodes* and *IncomingNodes* to represent the outgoing nodes respectively. Multiple transmissions or responses without an intervening packet are combined to contain the information from subsequent packets. This means that if the image used in the previous example is transmitted using multiple packets without any response from the client (other than the *ACK* packets that are ignored), the image will be represented as one node in the bipartite graph.

Graph construction is performed as follows:

1. $OutgoingNodes = \emptyset$
2. $IncomingNodes = \emptyset$
3. For each packet in the session:
   - (a) If the packet is an outgoing packet:
     - i. If the last observed packet was incoming, create a new incoming node and add it to *IncomingNodes*. Create an edge between this node and the second most recently created outgoing node.
     - ii. If the last observed packet was outgoing, add this packet to the node storing the previously observed packet
   - (b) If the packet is an incoming packet:
     - i. If the last observed packet was outgoing, create a new outgoing node and add it to *OutgoingNodes*. Create an edge between this node and the most recently created outgoing node.
     - ii. If the last observed packet was incoming, add this packet to the node storing the previously observed packet.

3.3 Edge Weighting

Once we have constructed the graphs representing the incoming and outgoing packets for various sessions, we are now motivated to summarise these graphs so that they may be used for our analysis. Furthermore, we wish to weight the edges of this summary graph to represent the strengths of various relationships between transmissions of varying sizes.

There are two cases that are of particular interest:

1. Given an outgoing node N_{out} of size $N_{out}.s$, we wish to determine the likelihood of receiving return information (that is, an incoming node) with packets of size $N_{in}.s$. An example of where this would be of assistance would be in the identification of HTTP connections as the request is often relatively small while the reply is typically much larger.
2. Given an outgoing node N_{out} and corresponding return packet, we wish to be able to represent if either more outgoing packets are likely to be transmitted or if N_{out} is likely to be the last. For instance, HTTP connections are typically shorter, while MSN sessions are kept alive longer with many request/response pairs.

For the first of these cases, the weights are determined based on the outgoing packet size and the return sizes. For each outgoing packet size, we consider the likelihood of receiving each of the corresponding return sizes. Let us denote

R_s as the set of outgoing nodes with a size of s. Then we compute the set $R_{in} = \{N_{in} | N_{in}$ has an edge to a node in $R_s\}$ for any given s. We then calculate the weight for a return packet of size s' having transmitted a packet of size s as

$$W(s, s') = \frac{count(s') * R_{in}^{-1}}{argmax_{r \in R_{in}}(count(s')) * |R_{in}|^{-1})}$$

That is, the weights are the ratio to the previous number of observations for that packet size to the maximum number of observed packets. In the case of a particular value for s' typically following a value of s, other values of s' will be given low weights. In the case where a given transmission size may have many values of s' for the reply, there will be little contribution. Additionally, we also take into account $\overline{R_{in}}$ and $\sigma(R_{in})$. There are a number of reasons why the scores produced by this weighting system are beneficial. Firstly, if we have a large spread of values, $\sigma(R_{in})$ will be large; the spread of relevant values which s' may take result in a good rating will also be large. This may happen with the previously mentioned HTTP image example. We would expect a reasonably high variance for the replies in addition to a mean that is typically higher than the size of the request. In contrast, MSN sessions will often have small outgoing packets for keep-alive messages along with small replies. The ratio between the outgoing and incoming packets is close to 1 and the variance will be small. In this case, with low variance, if s' is not very close to the mean of R_{in}, it will be marked as being not relevant to the protocol in question.

To improve consistency in terms of sizes, we remove outliers from the return sizes. For a given size s with corresponding return set R, we remove the top and bottom 1% entries in R when sorted by size. This removes outliers that greatly affect the mean and variance and in turn would lead to a decrease in accuracy.

3.4   Protocol Identification

As with the model construction, we consider outgoing/incoming tuples. Once we have the pairs, we match each against the previously observed outgoing nodes. For each matching node, we weight the pair currently being considered by the likelihood of it being from the protocol under consideration. Once the pair has been scored, we consider the following pair. In addition to calculating the score for the following pair, we also examine the likelihood of the size of the following pair given the current pair.

We calculate the score for a session as:

$$score(S) = \frac{1}{|Pairs|} \sum_{pair \in Pairs} W(pair.outsize, pair.insize) * W'(pair, previous)$$

Where $Pairs$ is the set of outgoing-incoming node pairs created by building the bipartite graph with no outgoing-outgoing edges (i.e. the set of request/response pairs). $pair.outsize$ and $pair.insize$ correspond to the outgoing and incoming nodes sizes respectively. Finally, W' corresponds to the likelihood of an outgoing packet of the size of $pair.outsize$ following the previous outgoing packet. That is, the score is the average score obtained by weighting each node based on the request/response sizes and the size of the following previous nodes.

This technique for scoring does not take into account sizes that have not been previously observed. Consider the case of a model being constructed for a set of HTTP connections with request sizes of 453, 454 and 456, each with a large response. If we then try to identify a connection with a single outgoing transmission of size 455 and a large response, we will have no corresponding outgoing size for weighting.

In order to account for this, we use binning to divide the existing outgoing values. These bins are then used for determining the corresponding outgoing packets for the scoring of the session of interest.

4   Experimental Analysis

4.1   Experimental Structure

Our data has been collected from TCP logs from a number of users in our organisation, over the course of approximately 6 weeks. From the raw log files, we determine individual protocol connections using source/destination host and port pairs, and sequence numbers. This allows us to construct entire connections of related packets, even if they were to time-out or advertise out-of-sequence numbers. While we use data from the TCP/IP frames for construction of our model, we do not use this data during classification.

Almost 35,000 successful host-host connections occurred, a total of 2.4m packets averaging 69 per connection. Of these, we initially discarded zero-sized packets (e.g. ACK, SYN/FIN) in addition to packets for protocols for incidental connections such as SMB and IMAP. We then ignored connections with less than 5 packets. Connections which were already established when logging began were also discarded.

The remaining 15,000 connections focused heavily on our protocols of interest. Approximately 2,800 of these constitute our main data set with the remaining 12,500 being related to failed network intrusion attempts (which we consider later, please see Table 4). The distribution of the protocols is: HTTP (38%), BitTorrent (59%), MSN (2%) and SSH (1%). The MSN and SSH sessions were infrequent in number but generally lasted a very long time, while peer BitTorrent connections and HTTP tend to have a shorter lifespan.

4.2   Experimental Results

Table 1 shows the results on the raw session information collected (although, we should mention that *no* information other than the size, time and directions of packets was used). As we can see, the accuracy is consistently high with all but HTTP and SSH sessions being identified correctly more than 90% of the time. Closer inspection reveals that these sessions are often mistaken for BitTorrent packets due to repeated communication with the server in question.

Of those HTTP sessions that were incorrectly identified, we observe that often the incoming data was particularly large which is consistent with some of the observed BitTorrent connections. Additionally, the SSH packets are generally

Table 1. Results for standard identification

Protocol	SSH	BitTorrent	MSN	HTTP
SSH	86.96%	13.04%	0.0%	0.0%
BitTorrent	0.06%	98.90%	0.0%	0.98
MSN	0.0%	2.04%	97.96%	0.0%
HTTP	0.0%	13.09%	0.0%	86.91%

classified correctly. The SSH protocol was the one on which performance was least optimal in [14].

Our second set of experiments analyse the performance of our approach on connection data with the block size rounded to simulate the effect of encryption. Once again we did not use any information other than size, time and direction of the packets. The blocks were padded to the next highest multiple of 16 bytes.

Conceptually, we would expect a reduction in the quality of our approach. The rounding of the packet sizes further obfuscates the limited information originally available to us. This is supported by our results as shown in Table 2. The two protocols to be most seriously affected are the HTTP and BitTorrent protocols. In both cases, packets are now misclassified.

Despite this, the accuracy is still reasonable. The HTTP packets are classified correctly approximately 83% of the time while the accuracy for the BitTorrent connections is marginally under 80% (78.6%). In fact, for the SSH streams, there is a slight increase in the accuracy of the identification (this is due to a lower score being given by the BitTorrent model as opposed to an improvement in the quality of the SSH model.

Table 2. Results for identification with simulated encrypted block sizes

Protocol	SSH	BitTorrent	MSN	HTTP
SSH	86.96%	13.04%	0.0%	0.0%
BitTorrent	5.86%	78.5%	11.9%	3.60%
MSN	0.0%	4.08%	95.9%	0.0%
HTTP	0.97%	16.0%	0.0%	82.9%

Our third set of experiments again uses the rounded packet sizes. However we also add the task of identifying a particular website (GMail [1]). Table 3 depicts the results for these experiments. GMail is somewhat 'interactive' in that the webpage is updated and draft emails automatically saved. As such, some smaller BitTorrent sessions were classified as GMail sessions. Overall, GMail sessions were identified correctly slightly over 80% the time. However, the misclassified GMail sessions were classified as HTTP sessions, which is technically correct but does not provide us with the granularity in analysis that we desire.

Our final set of experiments incorporate a number of failed SSH connections from unauthorized parties attempting access for which network traffic was being

---

[1] http://www.gmail.com

Table 3. Results for identification with simulated encrypted block sizes and separate GMail packets

Protocol	SSH	BitTorrent	MSN	HTTP	GMail
SSH	95.6%	4.34%	0.0%	0.0%	0.0%
BitTorrent	5.86%	78.5%	11.9%	3.35%	0.24%
MSN	0.0%	4.08%	95.9%	0.0%	0.0%
HTTP	1.01%	16.6%	0.0%	79.2%	3.03%
GMail	0.0%	0.0%	0.0%	17.4%	82.5%

Table 4. Results for identification with simulated encrypted block sizes and intrusion attempts

Protocol	SSH	BitTorrent	MSN	HTTP	GMail	SSH Intr. Attempts
SSH	82.6%	4.34%	0.0%	0.0%	0.0%	13.0%
BitTorrent	5.85%	78.4%	12.0%	3.35%	0.24%	0.12%
MSN	0.0%	2.04%	95.9%	0.0%	2.04%	0.0%
HTTP	1.01%	16.6%	0.0%	79.2%	3.03%	0.0%
GMail	0.0%	0.0%	0.0%	17.4%	82.5%	0.0%
SSH Intr. Attempts	0.02%	0.0%	0.0%	0.0%	0.0%	99.9%

monitored. There were 12465 of these connections. Detecting such sessions would be particularly useful as it provides a means by which it would be possible to identify the computer being used as a tool for intrusion detection on a third party system.

Table 4 shows the results for the SSH intrusion attempt experiments. We can see these sessions are consistently identified correctly with only 3 classified incorrectly. Furthermore, these incorrectly identified sessions were classified as SSH connections. We may notice some SSH sessions being incorrectly — this is due to being very short in length and similarity with the signature for an 'average' SSH session is lower than the similarity with a short exchange of keys and authentication information. The intrusion SSH model is very 'tight' as the intrusion attempts are very consistent with each other, with only the attempt to set up an SSH connection. This contrast with the other profiles contributes to the very high accuracy.

5   Conclusions and Future Work

In this paper, we have presented an approach for modelling and identifying protocols based on encrypted streams of network traffic. More specifically, we are able to perform this identification using only the timing and size of observed packets, as opposed to using any information contained within the packets themselves. We believe that the presented results are indeed promising and can be applied for network monitoring and security even under various encryption schemes.

We are currently working towards extending our system for real-time monitoring of network traffic including a more rigorous system for classifying access to certain webpages over tunnels. Furthermore, this work will incorporate work on determining particular network behaviours that may be illegal (such as using the system as a base for intrusion of third party systems).

References

1. S. Antonatos, K. Anagnostakis, M. Polychronakis, and E. Markatos. Performance analysis of content matching intrusion detection systems, 2004.
2. C. R. Clark and D. E. Schimmel.   A pattern-matching co-processor for network intrusion detection systems.   In *IEEE International Conference on Field-Programmable Technology (FPT)*, pages 68–74, Tokyo, Japan, 2003.
3. J. P. Early, C. E. Brodley, and C. Rosenberg. Behavioral authentication of server flows. In *ACSAC '03: Proceedings of the 19th Annual Computer Security Applications Conference*, page 46, Washington, DC, USA, 2003. IEEE Computer Society.
4. M. Gebski and R. K. Wong. Intrusion detection via analysis and modelling of user commands. In *Data Warehousing and Knowledge Discovery*, pages 388–397, 2005.
5. K. Julisch. Clustering intrusion detection alarms to support root cause analysis. *ACM Trans. Inf. Syst. Secur.*, 6(4):443–471, 2003.
6. K. Julisch and M. Dacier. Mining intrusion detection alarms for actionable knowledge. In *KDD '02: Proceedings of the eighth ACM SIGKDD international conference on Knowledge discovery and data mining*, pages 366–375, New York, NY, USA, 2002. ACM Press.
7. S. Kumar and E. H. Spafford. A Pattern Matching Model for Misuse Intrusion Detection. In *Proceedings of the 17th National Computer Security Conference*, pages 11–21, 1994.
8. T. Lane and C. E. Brodley. Approaches to online learning and concept drift for user identification in computer security. In *Knowledge Discovery and Data Mining*, pages 259–263, 1998.
9. T. Lane and C. E. Brodley. Temporal sequence learning and data reduction for anomaly detection. *ACM Trans. Inf. Syst. Secur.*, 2(3):295–331, 1999.
10. W. Lee. Applying data mining to intrusion detection: the quest for automation, efficiency, and credibility. *SIGKDD Explor. Newsl.*, 4(2):35–42, 2002.
11. J. Ryan, M.-J. Lin, and R. Miikkulainen. Intrusion detection with neural networks. In M. I. Jordan, M. J. Kearns, and S. A. Solla, editors, *Advances in Neural Information Processing Systems*, volume 10. The MIT Press, 1998.
12. K. Sequeira and M. Zaki. Admit: anomaly-based data mining for intrusions. In *Proceedings of the eighth ACM SIGKDD international conference on Knowledge discovery and data mining*, pages 386–395. ACM Press, 2002.
13. Q. Sun, D. R. Simon, Y.-M. Wang, W. Russell, V. N. Padmanabhan, and L. Qiu. Statistical identification of encrypted web browsing traffic. In *IEEE Symposium on Security and Privacy*, pages 19–30, 2002.
14. C. Wright, F. Monrose, and G. M. Masson. Hmm profiles for network traffic classification. In *VizSEC/DMSEC '04: Proceedings of the 2004 ACM workshop on Visualization and data mining for computer security*, pages 9–15, New York, NY, USA, 2004. ACM Press.

Adaptive Load Shedding for Mining Frequent Patterns from Data Streams

Xuan Hong Dang[1], Wee-Keong Ng[1], and Kok-Leong Ong[2]

[1] School of Computer Engineering, Nanyang Technological University, Singapore
{dang0008, awkng}@ntu.edu.sg
[2] School of Engineering & IT, Deakin University, Australia
leong@deakin.edu.au

Abstract. Most algorithms that focus on discovering frequent patterns from data streams assumed that the machinery is capable of managing all the incoming transactions without any delay; or without the need to drop transactions. However, this assumption is often impractical due to the inherent characteristics of data stream environments. Especially under high load conditions, there is often a shortage of system resources to process the incoming transactions. This causes unwanted latencies that in turn, affects the applicability of the data mining models produced – which often has a small window of opportunity. We propose a load shedding algorithm to address this issue. The algorithm adaptively detects overload situations and drops transactions from data streams using a probabilistic model. We tested our algorithm on both synthetic and real-life datasets to verify the feasibility of our algorithm.

1 Introduction

Recently, data streams have emerged as a new data type that has attracted much attention from the data mining community. They arise naturally in a number of applications, including financial services (e.g., stock ticker, financial monitoring), sensor networks (e.g., earth sensing satellites, astronomical observatories), web tracking and personalization (e.g., web log entries or web-click streams) [2]. These stream applications share three distinguishing characteristics that limit the applicability of most traditional algorithms: (i) data continuously arrive at high and unpredictable arrival rate; (ii) the volume of data is unbounded, making it impractical to store the entire data stream; (iii) on the basic of the data, decisions are arrived at and acted upon in close to real time. Consequently, the main challenge in mining data streams is to develop adaptive algorithms that support the processing of stream data in one-pass manner with constraints on system resources.

Finding frequent item(set)s (or patterns) plays an important role in analyzing data streams [11]. Given a stream of transactions, the goal is to compute all itemsets that occur in at least a fraction of the stream. To address this problem, many algorithms have been reported in the literature [11,5,13,8,15,10]. A common characteristics among them, however, is the focus on memory management while assuming that the machinery itself is fast enough to handle all

A Min Tjoa and J. Trujillo (Eds.): DaWaK 2006, LNCS 4081, pp. 342–351, 2006.

incoming transactions without incurring any unwanted latencies. In practice, this assumption is impractical, e.g., data streams generated from a large number of bio-sensors embedded in the soldiers' uniforms [12]; data streams generated by large scale multi-player online games [4]. These applications are characterized by a large number of push-based data sources and more importantly, the data rates can be very high and unpredictable. For instance, the arrival rate of data in a network game is not easy to be predicted due to volatility in the number of players as well as the game-state of each player [4]. In [12,3], the authors have shown that the arrival rate of data streams usually exceeds the system capacity despite all the efforts in scaling up processing algorithms. For the problem of mining frequent itemsets, this issue is even more serious due to the huge number of itemsets that needs frequency updates. Given a transaction of length m, the number of frequent patterns can exponentially increase to 2^m. It is obvious that completely processing all incoming transactions is generally impractical under high load conditions. Therefore, algorithms mining from data streams must cope with system overload situations.

In this paper, we study the problem of mining frequent patterns over data streams under the assumption that the CPU is a limited resource. When the CPU capacity is overloaded, the system will not be able to keep up with newly arrived data, so *load shedding* – discarding some fraction of unprocessed data – becomes necessary. We propose an algorithm to detect overload situations, and selectively drops a fraction of the transactions from data streams. Specifically, we address and provide solutions to the following questions: (i) How to determine overload situations? (ii) How much load to shed? (ii) How to approximate frequent patterns under the introduction of load shedding? We adopt an adaptive and self-regulating approach to these questions. The current statistics of data streams are periodically evaluated to detect overload conditions. An adaptive dropping strategy, based on the Hoeffding bound, is then applied to discard transactions from the data stream. We have conducted a set of experiments on both synthetic and real-life datasets to evaluate the efficiency of our approach. The results were very encouraging even when the data rate exceeds an order of magnitude over the CPU capacity and that the underlying distribution is constantly changing.

Next in Section 2, we formally formulate the problem of load shedding in mining frequent patterns from data streams. The proposed approach to the problem is described in Section 3. The experimental results are reported in Section 4. In Section 5, we review related work. Finally, our conclusion is given in Section 6.

2   Problem Formulation

Let $I = \{a_1, a_2, ..., a_m\}$ be a set of literals called *items*. Let $\mathcal{DS} = \{t_1, t_2, ..., t_N, ...\}$ be a data stream where each transaction t_i contains a set of items $(t_i \subseteq I)$; t_N is the current transaction and thus N is the current length (or timestamp) of the stream. We denote the *frequency* of an itemset X by $freq(X)$, which is the occurrence count of X in $\mathcal{DS}$ up to the Nth transaction, and the *support* of X, denoted $supp(X)$, is the ratio of $freq(X)$ to N; i.e., $supp(X) = freq(X) \times N^{-1}$. X is called a *frequent itemset* at the point of output timestamp N if $supp(X)$ is no less than $\sigma \in (0,1]$, the minimum support; it is called a *maximal frequent itemset* (MFI) if none of its immediate supersets are frequent. We formulate the load shedding problem for finding frequent patterns over data streams as follows.

We are given a processing capacity (CPU) C of a mining system and a data stream $\mathcal{DS}$ with arbitrary high arrival rates. Let $Load(\mathcal{DS})$ indicate the workload of the system. Then a load shedding is invoked when $Load(\mathcal{DS}) > C$. The objective is to construct an adaptive algorithm that can detect and drop a fraction of transactions to guarantee $Load(\mathcal{DS}) \leqslant C$ and yet discover a set of patterns that closely approximates to the set of actual frequent itemsets from the data stream.

3 Adaptive Load Shedding in Data Streams

3.1 Overload Detection

It is obvious that the system workload is dependent on the time to process each transaction, which in turns mainly depends on the number of itemsets contained in the transaction whose frequencies must be updated. Unfortunately, we may not know how much time is needed to process a transaction if we do not know exactly the number of frequent itemsets in the transaction. The difficulty lies in the fact that we are not be able to process all transactions under a high-speed data stream. Thus, to quickly estimate the system workload, we propose an approximate method that is relied on maximal frequent itemsets (MFIs). There are three main reasons that we may utilize MFIs for this task. First, it is known that the set of MFIs also contains all frequent itemsets. Therefore, updating a MFI also updates all its subsets that are also frequent. Second, the number of MFIs is significantly smaller than the number of frequent itemsets [14]. Actually, it provides the most compact representation for all frequent patterns. Third, according to the definition, the support of MFIs is always closest to σ. Consequently, the set of MFIs essentially reflects the current content of the data stream.

Let k be the number of MFIs in a transaction and X_i, $1 \leqslant i \leqslant k$, be a MFI. We derive estimated time (i.e., load coefficient) to process one transaction:

$$L = \sum_{i=1}^{k} 2^{|X_i|} - \sum_{i,j=1}^{k} 2^{|X_i \cap X_j|} \tag{1}$$

The first summation in the equation estimates the number of frequent itemsets within each MFI. The second one estimates the common itemsets sharing among MFIs. In practice, we can ignore all MFIs whose length is only 1 or 2. This is because the number of itemsets in each of these short MFIs is very negligible compared to those in a longer one. For example, if a transaction contains a MFI of length 10, the total number of itemsets need to update frequencies is at least $2^{10} - 1$, whereas if the transaction contains only MFIs of length 1, this number is at most equal to the transaction length. Therefore, we can quickly estimate processing time of a transaction by comparing it with a small set of MFIs. Suppose we measure the above statistics for n transactions over one time unit. Let r be the current rate of the data stream (i.e., the number of transactions arriving in one time unit), we introduce the following inequality:

$$r \times \frac{\sum_{i=1}^{n} L_i}{n} \leqslant C \tag{2}$$

The left hand side gives the estimated workload during one time unit. L_i is calculated from Equation 1. C, as formulated above, is the processing capacity of the mining system. We assume that when this inequality is not held, the mining system is overloaded.

3.2 Load Shedding by Sampling Transactions

In order to estimate how much load to shed, we rely on Inequality 2. Let P be a parameter expressing the fraction of transactions that should be discarded. Then P must satisfy:

$$P \times r \times \frac{\sum_{i=1}^{n} L_i}{n} \leqslant C \tag{3}$$

If $P = 1$, there is no need to shed load. Otherwise, a maximal value of P is identified such that the inequality still holds. Suppose $P < 1$, then we may use the following approach to discard transactions and to approximate frequent patterns. We apply one of statistical results, the Hoeffding bound [9].

Consider the situation that we randomly draw n transactions from a dataset and estimate the true support p of itemset X in this dataset (i.e., $supp(X) = p$). We assume that the occurrence of X in a transaction is a *Bernoulli trial* and denote a random variable $A_i = 1$ if X occurs in the ith transaction and $A_i = 0$ if not. Obviously, $\Pr(A_i = 1) = p$ and $\Pr(A_i = 0) = 1 - p$.[1] Hence, n randomly drawing transactions are regarded as n independent Bernoulli trials. Let r be the number of times that $X_i = 1$ occurs in these n transactions; r is called a *binomial* random variable and thus, its expectation is np. Then, the Hoeffding bound states that for any ϵ, $0 < \epsilon < 1$:

$$\Pr\{|r - np| \geqslant n\epsilon\} \leqslant 2e^{-2n\epsilon^2} \tag{4}$$

Let $supp_E(X) = r/n$ be the estimated support of X computed from n sampling transactions. Equation 4 gives us the probability that the true support $supp(X)$ of X is deviated from its estimated support $supp_E(X)$ by an amount of $\pm\epsilon$. If we want this probability to be no more than δ, then the required number of sampling transactions is at least (by setting $\delta = 2e^{-2n_0\epsilon^2}$):

$$n_0 = \frac{1}{2\epsilon^2} \ln \frac{2}{\delta} \tag{5}$$

---

[1] We use $\Pr(.)$ to denote the probability of a condition being met.

It is obvious that if the data stream is uniformly distributed, then n_0 transactions can reflect the same statistical information about the entire data stream. Hence, processing these n_0 transactions gives us a set of patterns that closely approximates (within (ϵ, δ)) the set of actual frequent itemsets over the entire data stream. Unfortunately, this assumption is often unrealistic in stream environments. Rather, when the data rate significantly varied, we often expect that the underlying distribution also changes as well. When the workload changes, the corresponding value of P must be detected. Then, each incoming transaction is chosen with probability P until we sample enough n_0 transactions, which is called a *sample batch*. All frequent itemsets in this sample batch are then discovered. We call them *local* patterns because they are found only within part of the stream. This procedure is repeated until the system workload changes to another level. By the Hoeffding bound, we are guaranteed that the true support of each local pattern is close to its estimated support computed in these n_0 transactions.

We now address the problem of how to report the global frequent itemsets in the entire data stream. For ease of explanation, we ignore the error produced by applying the Hoeffding bound (i.e., $\epsilon = \delta = 0$). It is easy to prove that a global pattern must be locally frequent in at least one part of the data stream. Therefore, we can safely report all local frequent itemsets as an approximate set of all global patterns. However, due to the non-uniform distribution of the stream, this approximation clearly will result in many false global patterns that are locally frequent only. One way to reduce this number is to control the maximal support error of each pattern within a threshold σ_0 ($< \sigma$) called *significant support* and further classify itemset X to be *frequent* if $supp(X) \geqslant \sigma$; *infrequent* if $supp(X) \leqslant \sigma_0$; otherwise, X is *sub-frequent*. Collectively, both frequent and sub-frequent itemsets are also called *significant* patterns.

With the introduction of σ_0, we need to revisit the problem of identifying n_0. So far, n_0 is computed from Equation 5. However, it is clear that this value cannot be chosen arbitrarily because if ϵ is too small, n_0 will be very large. For instance, with $\epsilon = 0.001$ and $\delta = 0.01$, $n_0 \approx 2,600,000$ transactions, making it too huge to buffer in main memory. On the other hand, n_0 cannot be too small since it depends on σ_0, which is used to control the number of significant patterns. For instance, we assume that each itemset appearing more than 0.01% of the sample batch size will be significant and if $n_0 = 10,000$, then every itemset will be chosen. Certainly, this number is extremely huge due to the nature of exponential explosion of itemsets. In view of this, we select $n_0 = Max\{\frac{\beta}{\sigma_0}; \frac{1}{2\epsilon^2} \ln \frac{2}{\delta}\}$, where β is an integer that must be greater than 1.

3.3   The Algorithm

With the above analysis, this section presents our algorithm named *Load Shedding* for mining *Frequent Itemsets* (LSFI). We use a prefix tree S to maintain significant itemsets. Initially, S is empty. Each node in S corresponds to an itemset X and has the following fields: (1) *Item*: The last item of X and thus X is represented by the set of items on the path from the root to the node; (2) *Acnt*:

The accumulated frequency of X seen so far in the data stream;(3) *Bid*: The index of the sample batch at which X is inserted into S.

The algorithm receives the following parameters: processing capacity C; data stream $\mathcal{DS}$; minimum support threshold σ and significant support threshold $\sigma_0 \in (0, \sigma]$. Load shedding is invoked when the system workload exceeds C. On demand, the algorithm returns an approximate set of frequent itemsets seen so far in the data stream. LSFI includes the following steps:

1. Before processing the data stream, the algorithm initializes the sample batch index $b_{crr} = 0$ and computes the sampling size $n_0 = Max\{\frac{\beta}{\sigma_0}; \frac{1}{2\epsilon^2} \ln \frac{2}{\delta}\}$.
2. Periodically, it estimates the workload of the system and identifies an appropriate sampling rate P. If the workload is no more than C, set this value to 1. Otherwise, choose P such that Inequality 3 is satisfied.
3. Each time when t_N arrives, LSFI samples it with probability P.
4. When n_0 transactions has been sampled:
   - LSFI firstly increases the index of sample batch by 1.
   - Then, all significant itemsets from this sample batch are mined. Any X whose frequency in this batch, denoted by $Ccnt(X)$, is greater than $\lceil \sigma_0 \times n_0 \rceil$ will be viewed as a significant itemset.
   - For each such itemset X:
     - If X is already maintained in S, update $Acnt(X)$ by adding an amount of $\lceil 1/P \times Ccnt(X) \rceil$. Note that to compensate for the dropping transactions caused by P, the frequency of each itemset must be scaled up appropriately by $1/P$ to approximate its true frequency in the current part of the stream.
     - Otherwise, if X is not in S, create a new node for X with $Acnt(X) = \lceil 1/P \times Ccnt(X) \rceil$ and $X.Bid = b_{curr}$.
   - After that, LSFI travels S to prune all infrequent itemsets whose $Acnt(X) \leqslant (b_{crr} - X.Bid) \times \lceil \sigma_0 \times n_0 \rceil$. To be clear with this condition, we need to clarify some points. First, the minimum frequency needed to make X significant in each sampling batch n_0 is at least more than $\lceil \sigma_0 \times n_0 \rceil$. Since X was inserted at $X.Bid$, the frequency it must accumulate to continue staying significant until the current sample batch must be more than $(b_{crr} - X.Bid) \times \lceil \sigma_0 \times n_0 \rceil$. On the other hand, $Acnt(X)$ is its true frequency since inserted at $X.Bid$. Therefore, if this value is no more than $(b_{crr} - X.Bid) \times \lceil \sigma_0 \times n_0 \rceil$, X is no longer significant. In case X is removed, all its supersets are also removed.
   - For the next sample batch index, LSFI updates it by $b_{crr} = \lceil N/n_0 \rceil$.
5. When a user requests for the results, LSFI scans $\mathcal{S}$ and produces all itemsets X whose $Acnt(X) + X.Bid \times \lceil \sigma_0 \times n_0 \rceil \geqslant \sigma \times N$. It is worth to note that $X.Bid \times \lceil \sigma_0 \times n_0 \rceil$ is X's maximal frequency lost caused by the pruning step described above.

4   Performance Results

We implemented LSFI in C++ and performed experiments on a 1.9GHz Pentium machine with 1GB of main memory running Windows XP. To verify the feasibility of LSFI, both synthetic and real-life datasets are utilized. Using method described in [1], we generate two datasets of size 1 million transactions using 10,000 unique items. The first one has an average transaction size of 5 items with an average pattern size of 3. The second one has average transaction size 8 with an average pattern size of 4. We denote two datasets respectively by T5.I3.D1000K and T8.I4.D1000K. For a real-life dataset, the KDD Cup 2000 "BMS-POS" dataset is used that contains 515,597 transactions with 1,657 distinct items and the average number of items per transactions is 6.5.

Since our algorithm is probabilistic, both recall and precision measures will be used. For the same reason, each experiment is repeated 10 times for each parameter combination and the results are reported using their average values.

4.1 Accuracy Measurements

In our experiments, we fix $\epsilon = 0.01, \delta = 0.01$, Accordingly, $n_0 \approx 25K$. We also select $\beta = 4$ and $\sigma_0 = 0.1\sigma$. Thus, the last value n_0 is $Max\{\frac{\beta}{0.1\sigma}; 25K\}$. For each experiment, C is fixed but the system workload, expressed as a multiple of CPU capacity, is varied from 2 to 10. For example, a workload of 2 corresponds to a stream rate that is twice as high as the CPU capacity when no load shedding is needed.

Figure 1 shows our experiment results on the three selected datasets where σ is varied from 0.1% to 0.8%. For two synthetic datasets, there are no (or a few) frequent itemsets found at $\sigma > 0.4\%$. Hence, only σ less than those is considered. As expected, at lower levels of workload, LSFI generates a higher number of true frequent patterns indicated by the high value of recall, and a smaller number of false frequent patterns shown by the high precision value. Nevertheless, the interesting point is that, at all levels of σ, the algorithm still finds more than 92% of all the true frequent itemsets and retains the percentage of false frequent itemsets below 10% even when the system workload is 10 times higher than C.

With the same range of σ, more detail results are reported in Figure 2 where we plot precision and recall for each itemset length. Due to space constraints, only results on the real-life dataset (with pattern length $\leqslant 4$) are reported (see [7] for results on other datasets). It is observed from the figure that as the length of itemsets increases, the precision decreases. This happens because, for longer itemsets, their support tends to be closer to σ. According to our approximation, all itemsets whose support is greater than $(\sigma - \sigma_0)$ are reported as frequent patterns. Therefore, the precision is often lower for longer patterns due to many of them having true support in the range $(\sigma - \sigma_0, \sigma)$. This observation can be realized more clearly when σ is set smaller (indicated by the slope is higher). As with lower supports we find more of longer frequent patterns. Note that the recall is not affected by this approximation as the true frequency of patterns is guaranteed by the Hoeffding bound, which is generally dependent on the number of sampling transactions. When the level of workload is 2, the recall is always found to be higher than 97% for every itemset length.

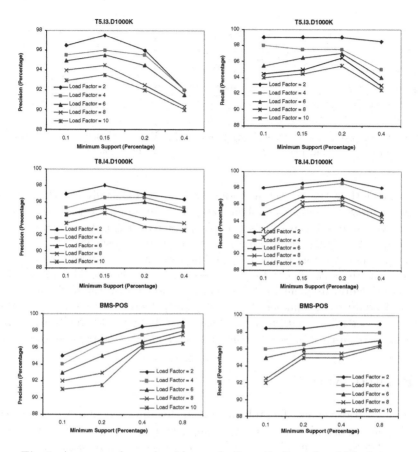

Fig. 1. Accuracy of our algorithm on both synthetic and real-life datasets

4.2 Adaptability

To test the ability of LSFI to adapt to changes, we generate dataset T5T8. D1000K where the first part includes 200K transactions taken from T5.I3. D1000K, and the second one includes 800K transactions from T8.I4.D1000K.

We send the dataset to the system at a rate just below the CPU capacity. When the algorithm progresses to the second part of the dataset, the set of MFIs changes significantly. For example, at $\sigma = 0.1\%$, the number of MFIs of length 5 increased from 14 to 40 and the number of MFIs of length 6 increased from 5 to 9. Furthermore, we also found 1 MFI of length 7 and 2 MFIs of length 8 that did not appear in the first part of the dataset. This is due to the length of transactions increasing from 5 to 8 also increasing the number of longer MFIs. Consequently, the system needs more time to process these transactions. With this detection, P was adjusted correspondingly. Figure 3 shows the accuracy of LSFI in this experiment. We observe that the recall at all σ thresholds is still very high ($\geq 95\%$) and is likely the same. Nevertheless, the precision is

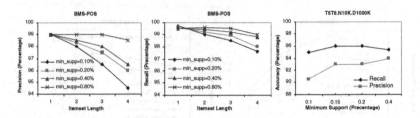

Fig. 2. Accuracy vs. Itemset Length for BMS-POS dataset at Load Factor 2

Fig. 3. Accuracy on dataset T5T8.D1000k

slightly lower than that in the uniform dataset T8.I4.D1000K (which occupies 80% of our new dataset). To explain this point, we note that when the size of transactions increases, LSFI finds more frequent patterns in the second part of the dataset. According to our approximation where we estimate σ_0 to be the maximum support error of any frequent pattern, a small fraction of itemsets discovered in the second part have over-estimated frequency. This means that they were (locally) frequent in the second part, but not in the first part of the dataset. To reduce this number of false frequent patterns, we can set σ_0 smaller. However, by setting $\sigma_0 = 0.1\sigma$, the precision is still above 90% in all cases. That means the percentage of false frequent patterns is guaranteed no more than 10%.

5   Related Works

In querying data streams, the problem of load shedding is defined as the process of finding an optimal plan for inserting dropping operations along existing arcs of a query network. Aurora [12] is one of the first projects addressing this issue by utilizing different QoS graphs representing various important levels of querying objects. Based on that, transactions will be dropped progressively starting from those that contain information about the lowest important objects. STREAM [3] is another project where a load shedding scheme based on sampling is proposed for aggregate queries. It modifies the query network by inserting load shedder operators together with sampling rates in such a way that the total sampling rate eliminates sufficient amount of dropping data. This work is similar to ours in that the random sampling is used as a means of load shedding. In stream mining, Loadstar [6] is the first work addressing the load shedding problem for classification by utilizing a set of Quality of Decision metrics.

Recent work on mining frequent patterns over data streams can be classified into three models:(i) *Landmark* model where patterns are discovered between a particular point of time and the current time. Lossy Counting [11] and FDPM [15] are typical algorithms; (ii) *Time-fading* model where transactions are weighted based on the time arrival. Works on this model include estDec [5] and FP-Stream [8]; (iii) *Sliding-window* model where it further considers the elimination of transactions. As a new transaction arrives, the oldest one in the window is retired. FTP-DS [13], TSSW [10] are some algorithms. All these works just address only the problem of memory limitation in data streams. Our work (on landmark model) further addresses the load shedding problem.

6   Conclusions

In this paper, we address the problem of finding frequent patterns from data streams where the mining system may not keep up with the arrival rate of the stream. We have proposed an approach to detect the overload situation based on a small set of maximal frequent itemsets. By adopting the Hoeffding bound, we have developed an algorithm that sheds load by discarding a fraction of incoming transactions adaptively under overload situations. Experiments both on real-life and synthetic datasets have been conducted to evaluate the proposed algorithm. The results showed that both the precision and recall are guaranteed in very high values even when the arrival rate of data streams is much higher than the capacity of the mining system and the skew of data streams is simulated.

References

1. R. Agrawal and R. Srikant. Fast algorithms for mining association rules in large databases. In *VLDB Conference*, pages 487–499, 1994.
2. B. Babcock, S. Babu, M. Datar, R. Motwani, and J. Widom. Models and issues in data stream systems. In *PODS Conference*, pages 1–16, 2002.
3. B. Babcock, M. Datar, and R. Motwani. Load shedding for aggregation queries over data streams. In *ICDE Conference*, pages 350–361, 2004.
4. C. Chambers, W. Feng, S. Sahu, and D. Saha. Measurement-based characterization of a collection of on-line games. In *IMC Conference*, pages 1–14, 2005.
5. J.H. Chang and W.S. Lee. Finding recent frequent itemsets adaptively over online data streams. In *ACM SIGKDD Conference*, pages 487–492, 2003.
6. Y. Chi, P.S. Yu, H. Wang, and R. R.Muntz. Loadstar: A load shedding scheme for classifying data streams. In *SIAM Conference*, pages 346–357, 2005.
7. X.H. Dang, W.K. Ng, and K.L. Ong. Adaptive load shedding for mining frequent patterns from data streams. Technical Report, Nanyang Technological University.
8. C. Giannella, J. Han, J. Pei, X. Yan, and P.S. Yu. *Mining Frequent Patterns in Data Streams at Multiple Time Granularities.* AAAI/MIT, 2003.
9. W. Hoeffding. Probability inequalities for sums of bounded random variables. *Journal of the American Statistical Association*, 58(301):13–30, 1963.
10. C.H. Lin, D.Y. Chiu, Y.H. Wu, and A.L.P. Chen. Mining frequent itemsets from data streams with a time-sensitive sliding window. In *SIAM Conference*, 2005.
11. G.S. Manku and R. Motwani. Approximate frequency counts over data streams. In *VLDB Conference*, pages 346–357, 2002.
12. N. Tatbul, U. Çetintemel, S.B. Zdonik, M. Cherniack, and M. Stonebraker. Load shedding in a data stream manager. In *VLDB Conference*, pages 309–320, 2003.
13. W.G. Teng, M.S. Chen, and P.S. Yu. A regression-based temporal pattern mining scheme for data streams. In *VLDB Conference*, pages 93–104, 2003.
14. G. Yang. The complexity of mining maximal frequent itemsets and maximal frequent patterns. In *ACM SIGKDD Conference*, pages 344–353, 2004.
15. J.X. Yu, Z.C., H. Lu, and A. Zhou. False positive or false negative: Mining frequent itemsets from high speed transactional data streams. In *VLDB Conference*, 2004.

An Approximate Approach for Mining Recently Frequent Itemsets from Data Streams[*]

Jia-Ling Koh and Shu-Ning Shin

Department of Computer Science and Information Engineering
National Taiwan Normal University
Taipei, Taiwan 106, R.O.C
jlkoh@ntnu.edu.tw

Abstract. Recently, the data stream, which is an unbounded sequence of data elements generated at a rapid rate, provides a dynamic environment for collecting data sources. It is likely that the embedded knowledge in a data stream will change quickly as time goes by. Therefore, catching the recent trend of data is an important issue when mining frequent itemsets from data streams. Although the sliding window model proposed a good solution for this problem, the appearing information of the patterns within the sliding window has to be maintained completely in the traditional approach. In this paper, for estimating the approximate supports of patterns within the current sliding window, two data structures are proposed to maintain the average time stamps and frequency changing points of patterns, respectively. The experiment results show that our approach will reduce the run-time memory usage significantly. Moreover, the proposed FCP algorithm achieves high accuracy of mining results and guarantees no false dismissal occurring.

1 Introduction

The strategies for mining frequent itemsets in static databases have been widely studied over the last decade such as the Apriori[1], DHP[3], and FP-growth[2]. Recently, the data stream, which is an unbounded sequence of data elements generated at a rapid rate, provides a dynamic environment for collecting data sources. It is considered that the main restrictions of mining data streams include scanning the data in one pass and performing the mining within a limited memory usage.

Since it is not feasible to store the past data in data streams completely, a method for providing the approximate answers with accuracy guarantees is required. Lossy-counting is the representative approach for mining frequent itemsets from data streams[7]. Given an error tolerance parameter ε, the Lossy-counting algorithm prunes the patterns with support being less than ε from the pool of monitored patterns such that the required memory usage is reduced. Consequently, the frequency of a pattern is estimated by compensating the maximum number of times that the pattern

[*] This work was partially supported by the R.O.C. N.S.C. under Contract No. 94-2213-E-003-010 and 94-2524-S-003-014.

A Min Tjoa and J. Trujillo (Eds.): DaWaK 2006, LNCS 4081, pp. 352–362, 2006.

could have occurred before being inserted into the monitored patterns. It is proved no false dismissal occurs with Lossy-counting algorithm and the frequency error is guaranteed not to exceed a given error tolerance parameter. The hash-based approach was proposed in [4], in which each item in a data stream owns a respective list of counters in a hash table, and each counter may be shared by many items. A new novel algorithm, called hCount, was provided to maintain frequent items over a data stream and support both insertion and deletion of items with a less memory space.

Although the restriction of memory usage was considered in the two works introduced previously, the time sensitivity issue is another important issue when mining frequent itemsets from data streams. It is likely that the embedded knowledge in a data stream will change quickly as time goes by. In order to catch the recent trend of data, the *estDec* algorithm [5] decayed the old occurrences of itemsets as time goes by to diminish the effect of old transactions on the mining result of frequent itemsets in the data steam.

The above approach provided time-sensitive mining for long-term data. However, in certain applications, it is interested only the frequent patterns mined from the recently arriving data within a fixed time period. The sliding window method [6] attempted to solve this problem, in which the current sliding window was defined to be the most recently coming W transactions in a data stream by a given window size W. Accordingly, the recently frequent itemsets were defined to be the frequent itemsets mined from the current sliding window. Meanwhile, the Loosy-counting strategy was applied to reduce the number of maintained patterns. Consequently, the processing of the sliding window approach is characterized into two phases: window initialization phase and window sliding phase. The window initialization phase is activated when the sliding window is not full. In this phase, the occurrences of patterns in a newly coming transaction are maintained in a lattice structure at each time point. After the sliding window has become full, the window sliding phase is activated. In addition to maintain the occurrence for the new transaction, the oldest transaction has to be removed from the sliding window. However, all the transactions in the current sliding window need to be maintained in order to remove their effects on the current mining result when they are beyond the scope in the window.

To prevent from storing the whole transaction data in current transaction window, two data representation methods, named **average time stamps (ATS)** and **frequency changing points (FCP)**, respectively, are provided in this paper for monitoring the recent occurrence of itemsets in data streams. Moreover, a FP-tree-like data structure is adopted to store the monitored patterns for further reducing the memory usage. Accordingly, ATS and FCP algorithms are proposed for maintaining the corresponding monitoring data structures. The experimental results show that our approach will reduce the run-time memory usage significantly. Moreover, the proposed FCP algorithm achieves high accuracy of mining results and guarantees no false dismissal occurring.

This paper is organized as follows. The related terms used in this paper are defined in Section 2 first. The two provided methods for approximately monitoring recently frequent patterns in a data stream are introduced in Section 3 and Section 4, respectively. The performance evaluation on the proposed algorithms and a related work is reported in Section 5. Finally, in Section 6, we conclude this paper.

2 Preliminaries

Let $I = \{i_1, i_2, ..., i_m\}$ denote the set of items in the specific application domain and a transaction be composed of a bucket of items inputted within a fixed time unit. A data stream, $DS = [T_1, T_2, ..., T_t)$, is an infinite sequence of transactions, where each transaction T_i is associated with an time identifier i, and t denotes the time identifier of the latest transaction currently. Let the set of transactions in DS from time i to j be denoted as $DS[i,j]$. Under a predefined window size w, the **current transaction window** at time t, denoted as CTW_t, is $DS[t\text{-}w+1, t]$. The time identifier of the first transaction in CTW_t is denoted as CTW_t^{first}, that is $t\text{-}w+1$.

An itemset (or a pattern) is a set consisting of one or more items in I, that is, a nonempty subset of I. If itemset e is a subset of transaction T, we call T **contains** e. The number of transactions in CTW_t which contain e is named the **recent support count** of e in DS_t, denoted as $RC_t(e)$. The **recent support** of e, denotes as $Rsup_t(e)$, is obtained from $RC_t(e) \, / \, w$. Given a user specified minimum support value between 0 and 1, denoted as S_{min}, and a maximum support error threshold value between 0 and S_{min}, denoted as ε, an itemset e is called a **recently frequent** itemset in DS_t if $Rsup_t(e) \geq S_{min}$. If $S_{min} \geq Rsup_t(e) \geq \varepsilon$, e is called a **recently potential frequent** itemset in DS_t. Otherwise, $Rsup_t(e) < \varepsilon$ and e is a **recently infrequent** itemset in DS_t.

3 Average Time Stamps Method

3.1 ATS Monitoring Data Structure

In our model of data streams, each transaction T_i, has a corresponding time identifier i. For an itemset p contained in T_i, i is named an **appearing time stamp** of p. The **average time stamp(ATS)** of an itemset p is the average of all the appearing time stamps of p from the first time p appears in the data stream.

In the ATS monitoring data structure, each entry maintains a 3-tuple (t_s, f, sum) for its corresponding itemset p as described as the following.

1) t_s: time of the first occurring of p to be counted into the accumulated support count;
2) f: the accumulated support count of p in $DS[t_s, t]$;
3) sum: the sum of appearing time stamps of p in $DS[t_s, t]$.

Consequently, the average time stamp of a pattern p, denoted as $avg_t(p)$, is obtained by performing $p.sum \, / \, p.f$.

3.2 ATS Algorithm

In the window initialization phase, for each newly coming transaction T_t at time t, the work for maintaining T_t in the *ATS* monitoring data structure is described as follows. For each subset p of T_t, if the corresponding record is stored in the monitoring data structure, the record is updated to be: $p.f = p.f+1$ and $p.sum = p.sum+t$. Otherwise, a record for p is inserted into the data structure with $p.f = 1$, $p.t_s = t$ and $p.sum = t$.

Similar to the window sliding phase proposed by [6], in addition to append the new transaction, the first transaction in CTW_{t-1} has to be removed from the current transaction window. However, the transactions in CTW_{t-1} are not maintained in our approach. Instead, the average time stamps of itemsets are estimated according to the stored information. If $p.t_s < CTW_t^{first}$ and $avg_t(p) < p.t_s +(CTW_t^{first} - p.t_s)/2$, it implies most of the occurrences of p are beyond the period of CTW_t under the uniform distribution assumption. Therefore, such a pattern is pruned from the monitoring data structure. Otherwise, p is still active in CTW_t and the corresponding record remains.

Moreover, in order to reduce the memory requirement, the records of recently infrequent patterns are pruned from the monitoring data structure every m time identifiers. The recent support of a pattern p is estimated according to the following equation:

If $p.t_s > CTW_t^{first}$, $Rsup_t(p)=(p.f + \lfloor((p.t_s\ div\ m)\times m - CTW_t^{first}) \times \varepsilon \rfloor)/w;$ ---- <1>
Else $Rsup_t(p)= p.f / (t- p.t_s +1).$ ---- <2>

Based on the information cashed in the monitoring data structure, the structure is traversed to find all the patterns p with $Rsup_t (p) \geq S_{min}$ whenever needing to mine the recently frequent itemsets.

4 Frequency Changing Points Method

4.1 FCP Monitoring Data Structure

With the average time stamp method described in Section 3, for each pattern p, $p.f$ is used to accumulate the occurrences of p from $p.t_s$ to current time t. If a pattern p was never being pruned from the monitoring data structure, $p.t_s$ denotes the first time identifier when p appeared in the data stream. There are two cases to be analyzed according to the relationship between $p.t_s$ and CTW_t^{first}:

(1) $p.t_s \geq CTW_t^{first}$: it is implied that $p.f$ accumulates the actual support count of p in CTW_t. Thus, $Rsup_t(p)$ is obtained from $(p.f / w)$ accurately.
(2) $p.t_s < CTW_t^{first}$: it is implied that $p.f$ accumulates the support count of p not only in CTW_t but also in $DS[p.t_s, CTW_t^{first}-1]$. The cases that whether a pattern p is frequent in $DS[p.t_s, CTW_t^{first}-1]$, in CTW_t, and in $DS[p.t_s, t]$ are summarized in Table 1.

Table 1. The case analysis of a frequent pattern in DS during different time intervals

Interval	$DS[p.t_s, CTW_t^{first}-1]$	CTW_t	$DS[p.t_s, t]$
Case 1	p is frequent	p is frequent	p is frequent
Case 2	p is frequent	p is infrequent	p is frequent or infrequent
Case 3	p is infrequent	p is frequent	p is frequent or infrequent
Case 4	p is infrequent	p is infrequent	p is infrequent

According to Case 2 and Case 3, to decide whether p is frequent in CTW_t according to its support in $DS[p.t_s, t]$ may cause false alarm and false dismissal, respectively. The false alarm occurring in Case 2 dues to p becomes sparser in CTW_t. The recent support of p in CTW_t is estimated according the count in $DS[p.t_s, t]$ such that p is evaluated to be recently frequent incorrectly. Similarly, in the situation of Case 3, the false dismissal occurring because a frequent pattern p in CTW_t is judged to be infrequent wrongly if p appears sparsely in $DS[p.t_s, CTW_t^{first}-1]$.

According to the cases discussed above, it is a critical point when the appearing frequency of a pattern becomes sparser. Let t' denote the last time identifier when a pattern p appeared previously. If p appears at current time t and $(t-t') > (1/S_{min})$, t is named a *frequency changing point(FCP)* of p. It means p is infrequent in $DS[t'+1, t]$. The frequency changing points of a pattern p are being used to adjust the boundaries of intervals for accumulating the support counts of p. When $p.t_s$ is beyond the corresponding time interval of CTW_t, $p.t_s$ is adjusted to be a frequency changing point of p as close to CTW_t^{first} as possible. Accordingly, the estimated recent support of p will approach the actual recent support of p in CTW_t.

In the monitoring data structure of frequency changing point, for an itemset p, each entry maintains a 5-tuple $(t_s, f, t_e, C_d, Rqueue)$ as described as the following.

(1) t_s: the starting time of p to be counted into the accumulated support count;
(2) f: the accumulated support count of p in $DS[t_s, t]$;
(3) t_e: the time identifier of the most recent transaction that contains p;
(4) C_d: the accumulated support count of p in $DS[t_s, t_e-1]$;
(5) $Rqueue$: a queue consists of a sequence of (ct_1, ac_1), (ct_2, ac_2), ..., (ct_n, ac_n) pairs, in which ct_i is a frequency changing point of p for $i=1,...,n$. Besides, ac_1 denotes the support count of p in $DS[t_s, ct_1-1]$ and ac_i denotes the support count of p in $DS[ct_{i-1}, ct_i-1]$ for $i=2,...,n$.

4.2 FCP Algorithm

In the window initialization phase, each subset p in a new transaction is appended into the FCP monitoring data structure (FCP_MDS). The maintained information of p includes its frequency changing points and the accumulated support counts between the changing points. The corresponding pseudo code is shown below.

Procedure AppendNew_FCP()
```
{If p is in FCP_MDS
    { p.f= p.f+1;
      If t-p.te > (1/Smin) /* a frequency changing point */
        {n = the number of elements in p.Rqueue ; n=n+1;
        ctn=t, acn= (p.f - 1)- p.Cd;
        append (ctn, acn) into p.Rqueue;  p.Cd= p.f - 1; }
      p.te =t;}
   else { p.f=1; p.ts= t ; p.te= t; p.Cd=0; p.Rqueue=null;
        insert p into FCP_MDS;}}
```

In the window sliding phase, in addition to perform procedure AppendNew_ FCP(), it is necessary to adjust the starting point of support count accumulation for the monitored pattern p if $p.t_s$ is less than CTW_t^{first}. If $p.Rqueue$ is empty for such a pattern p, it implies p remains frequent during the accumulation interval as Case 1 enumerated in Table 1. Therefore, no false dismissal occurs when discovering recently frequent patterns according to the support count of p in $DS[p.t_s, t]$ and there is no need to adjust $p.t_s$. On the other hand, it implies there is one or more frequency changing points of p occurring if $p.Rqueue$ is not empty. Then the frequency changing points of p are checked one by one to adjust its starting time of support count accumulation. It is applicable to adjust $p.t_s$ in the following three situations:

(1) The changing point $ct_l \leq CTW_t^{first}$: it implies the support count accumulated in ac_l is beyond the scope of CTW_t.

(2) The changing point $ct_l > CTW_t^{first}$ and $ac_l=1$: it implies the occurring of p before ct_l is at $p.t_s$ only which is out of the time period covered by CTW_t.

(3) The changing point $ct_l > CTW_t^{first}$, $ac_l>1$, and the previous time point when p appears before ct_l, denoted as t_e', is less than CTW_t^{first}: although the value of t_e' is not maintained, the largest value of t_e' is derivable from ct_l and $p.t_s$. Because ct_l is a frequency changing point, $ct_l - t_e'>1/S_{min}$. Thus, $t_e'< (ct_l -1/S_{min})$. Moreover, ac_l keeps the support count accumulated in $DS[p.t_s, ct_l-1]$ and no changing point occurs in this period. In other words, the interval of every two adjacent appearing time among the ac_l times of occurring must be less than or equal to $1/S_{min}$. Thus, $t_e' \leq p.t_s+ (ac_l-1)\times(1/S_{min})$ and $t_e'< p.t_s+ (ac_l-1)\times(1/S_{min})+1$ is derived. By combining these two inequalities, the largest value of t_e', denoted as $t_e'\_max$, is derived to be $\min((ct_l -1/S_{min}), p.t_s+ (ac_l-1)\times(1/S_{min})+1)-1$. If $t_e'\_max$ is less than CTW_t^{first}, it implies the support count accumulated in ac_l has been expired.

When satisfying each one of the situations enumerated above, the changing point pair (ct_l,ac_l) is removed from $p.Rqueue$, $p.t_s$ is adjusted to be ct_l; and the accumulated support counts $p.f$ and $p.C_d$ are modified accordingly. Then the following changing points are examined similarly. The corresponding code is shown below.

Procedure AdjustStart_FCP()
```
{For each p in FCP_MDS
    If p.ts < CTWt^first
    If Rqueue≠null {
        i=1; Adjust = True;
        While (Adjust) {
                If (cti ≤ CTWt^first)
                Else if ((cti > CTWt^first )∧( aci=1))
                Else {te'_max = min((ctl -1/Smin), p.ts+ (acl-1)×(1/Smin)+1) − 1;
                      If (te'_max ≥ CTWt^first) Adjust = False;}
                If (Adust) {
                Remove (cti,aci) from p.Rqueue;
                p.ts = cti; p.f= p.f-aci; p.Cd= p.Cd-aci. ;  i= i +1; }
                }/*end while */
        } /* end If */ }
```

Moreover, it is indicated that a pattern p does not appear in CTW_t if $p.f$ becomes 0 or t_e is less than CTW_t^{first}. Therefore, such a pattern is pruned to prevent from storing the unnecessary patterns in the monitoring data structure.

The situation that $p.t_s$ and $p.f$ are not adjusted occurs when $p.Rqueue$ is not empty and the changing point ct_l in $p.Rqueue$ does not satisfy the three situations enumerated above. It is implied that $ct_l>CTW_t^{first}$, $ac_l>1$, and $t_e'\_max \geq CTW_t^{first}$. In this case, p is frequent in $DS[p.t_s, CTW_t^{first}-1]$ because there is not any frequency changing point appearing between $p.t_s$ and ct_1. When judging whether p is recently frequent in CTW_t according to its support estimated from $DS[p.t_s, t]$, even though false alarm may occur, it is certain that no false dismissal will occur.

Similar to the ATS algorithm, the recently infrequent patterns are pruned periodically to avoid the monitoring data structure glowing huge. The recent support of a pattern is estimated also according to equation <1> and <2> defined in ATS method.

[Example 1]

Table 2. Data stream sample

Time	1	2	3	4	5	6	7	8	9	10	11	12	13	14	15
Itemset	AB	AB	D	A	AB	AC	AE	AC	E	AE	AD	B	AE	B	AE

Table 2 shows a sample of data stream. Suppose S_{min} is set to be 0.5, ε is 0.25, and window size w is 10. Under the assumption that the infrequent patterns are pruned every 5 time identifiers, the process of constructing the monitoring data structure of frequency changing points is described as the following.

From time t_1 to t_4, there was not any frequency changing point occurring for those monitored patterns. The corresponding constructed monitoring data structure at t_4 is shown in Figure 1(a). After that, time t_5 is a frequency changing point of AB. Thus, the changing point entry (5, 2) is appended into AB.$Rqueue$. After pruning the infrequent pattern D, whose estimated recent support is less than 0.2, the resultant monitoring data structure is shown in Figure 1(b). Continuing the similar processing, the resultant monitoring data structure at t_{10} after the patterns in T_{10} have been appended into the data structure is shown in Figure 1(c). Then the following process starting at t_{11} changes into the window sliding phase. The values of $p.t_s$ and. $p.f$ are going to be adjusted if $p.t_s$ is less than CTW_t^{first}. For example, after the patterns in T_{12} are processed, both B.t_s and AB.t_s are less than CTW_{12}^{first}, and their corresponding $Rqueues$ are not empty. By satisfying the third case among the three conditions of adjustment, B.t_s is adjusted to be 5 and B.f= B.f -2. Similarly, AB.t_s is set to be 5 and AB.f= AB.f-2. The obtained result is shown in Figure 1(d). After the patterns in T_{15} are appended to the monitoring data structure at time t_{15}, the information of pattern B is adjusted. Then pattern AB is removed because the last time it appeared is out of the range of CTW_{15}. After pruning the infrequent itemsets C, D, and AC, the monitoring data structure is shown as Figure 1(e). From the result shown in Figure 1(e), the recent supports of A, B, E, and AE are estimated to be 0.73(11/15=0.73), 0.3((2+1/10=0.3), 0.5(5/10=0.5), and 0.4(4/10 =0.4). Therefore, the discovered recent frequent patterns are A and E.

For compressing the FCP monitoring data structure in the implementation, the FP-tree-like structure is adopted to store the 5-tuples of patterns. However, to prevent from two scans over the data set, the items in a transaction are sorted according to their alphanumeric order instead of their frequency-descending order. Moreover, the mining algorithm on FP-tree is performed on FCP_MDS to find all the patterns p with $Rsup_t(p) \geq S_{min}$ on demand.

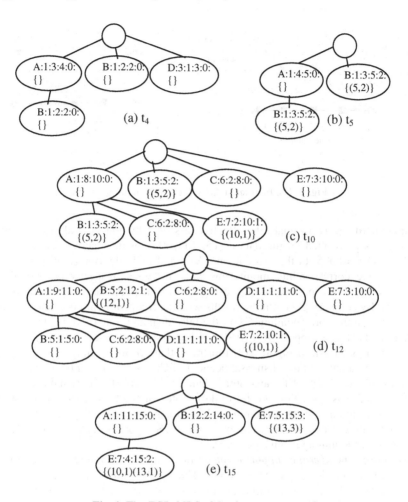

Fig. 1. The *FCP_MDS* of the data stream sample

5   Performance Study

The proposed algorithms and Sliding Window method (SW algorithm in short) [6] are implemented using Visual C++ 6.0. The TD_FP_Growth algorithm[8] is applied to discover recently frequent patterns from the FCP monitoring data structure. The experiments have been performed on a 3.4GHz Intel Pentium IV machine with 512 megabytes main memory and running Microsoft XP Professional. Moreover, the data sets are generated from the IBM data generator [1], where each dataset simulates a data stream with a transaction coming within each time unit. In the first part of experiments, the false dismissal rates/ false alarm rates are measured to indicate the effectiveness of the proposed methods. Furthermore, the execution time and memory usage is measured in the second part of experiments to show the efficiency of the proposed FCP algorithm by comparing with the ones of SW algorithm.

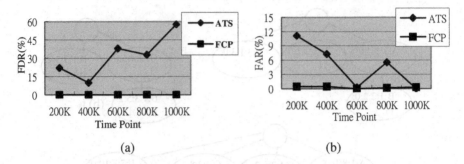

Fig. 2. The FDR and FAR values of the mining results

[Experiment 1]. To evaluate the effectiveness of ATS and FCP algorithms, an experiment is performed on the dataset T5.I4.D1000K with window size=20000, S_{min} =0.01, and ε =0.005. In this experiment, ATS and FCP algorithms are performed to maintain the corresponding monitoring data structures, respectively, and TD_FP-Growth algorithm is performed once every 200K time points to find recently frequent itemsets. By comparing the mining results with the frequent itemsets found by Apriori Algorithm on the corresponding CTW_t, the false dismissal rate (FDR), false alarm rate (FAR), and average support error (ASE) of the two algorithms are measured.

The results shown in Figure 2(a) illustrates that all the recently frequent patterns are discovered and no false dismissal occurs in FCP algorithm. On the other hand, the false dismissal rate of ATS algorithm changes dramatically, it is indicated that its mining quality is unstable. The false alarm rates of the two proposed algorithm at various time points are shown in Figure 2(b). It is reported that the false alarm rate of FCP algorithm is below 0.5%. Although the ATS algorithm has higher FAR, more than 88% of the mining results are accurate.

Moreover, the *average support error* defined in [7] is also used to model the relative accuracy of the proposed methods. The results show that ASEs($R_{FCP}|R_{Apriori}$) keeps under 3×10^{-5} at different time points; ASEs($R_{FCP}|R_{Apriori}$) are less than 3×10^{-3} but with variations from time to time.

[Experiment 2]. In this experiment, FCP and SW algorithms are compared on their accumulated execution time and maximum memory usage used for maintaining the monitored patterns (the mining time is not included). This experiment is performed on the dataset T5.I4D1000K with S_{min}=0.01 and ε =0.005. When the window size is varied from 10000, 20000, to 30000, the results of accumulated execution time and maximum memory usage are shown in Figure 3(a) and 3(b), respectively. Although the accumulated execution time increases as the window size is raised, the efficiency of FCP algorithm is comparable to the one of SW algorithm. In contrast with SW algorithm, the memory usage of FCP is significantly reduced without being sensitive to the window size. Moreover, it verifies that FCP is feasible for the streaming environment with a small memory. By varying the setting of ε, Figure 3(c) and 3(d) show the results of accumulated execution time and maximum memory usage, respectively. It is indicated that the execution time of FCP is not sensitive to ε. In addition, the maximum memory usage of FCP keeps steady, which is limited within 15 MB.

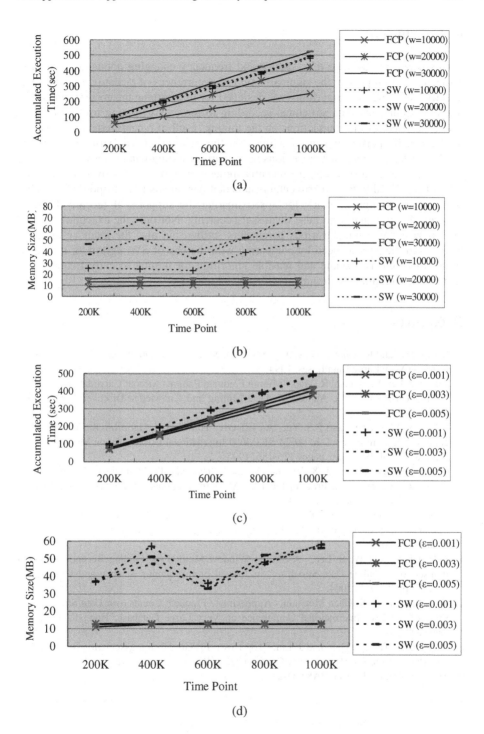

Fig. 3. The execution time and memory usage of FCP and SW algorithms

6 Conclusion

In this paper, the average time stamps and frequency changing points are proposed, respectively, to represent the summarization of occurrences of recent patterns. Consequently, ATS and FCP algorithms are designed for maintaining the corresponding FP-tree-like monitoring data structures according to the newly coming transaction. Besides, the effect of old transactions on the mining result of recent frequent itemsets is diminished by performing pruning rules on the monitoring data structures without needing to keep the whole transactions in the current sliding window physically. From the monitoring data structure, the recently frequent patterns are discovered efficiently at any time. Finally, the experimental results demonstrate that the proposed FCP algorithm achieves high accuracy for approximating the supports of recently frequent patterns and guarantees no false dismissal occurring. Not only the execution time of FCP is acceptable under various parameters setting, but also the memory usage of FCP is significantly reduced by comparing with the one of SW algorithm. It demonstrates that FCP is a stable and feasible algorithm for mining recently frequent patterns in the streaming environment with a small memory.

References

1. R. Agrawal and R. Srikant, "Fast Algorithms for Mining Association Rules," in Proc. of Int. Conf. on Very Large Data Bases, 1994.
2. J. Han, J. Pei, Y. Yin and R. Mao, "Mining Frequent Patterns without Candidate Generation: A Frequent-Pattern Tree Approach", Data Mining and Knowledge Discovery, 8(1):53-87, 2004.
3. J.S. Park, M.S. Chen, and P.S. Yu, "An Effective Hash-based Algorithm for Mining Association Rules," in Proc. of the ACM SIGMOD International Conference on Management of Data (SIGMOD'95), May, pages 175-186, 1995.
4. C. Jin, W. Qian, C. Sha, J. X. Yu, and A. Zhou, "Dynamically Maintaining Frequent Items Over a Data Stream," in Proc. of the 12th ACM International Conference on Information and Knowledge Management, 2003.
5. J. H, Chang and W.S. Lee, "Finding Recent Frequent Itemsets Adaptively over Online Data Streams, " in Proc. of the 9th ACM International Conference on Knowledge Discovery and Data Ming, 2003.
6. J. H. Chang and W. S. Lee, "A Sliding Window Method for Finding Recently Frequent Itemsets over Online Data Streams, " in Journal of Information Science and Engineering Vol. 20, pp753-762, 2004.
7. G. S. Manku and R. Chen Motwani, "Approximate Frequent Counts over Data Streams, " in Proc. of the 28th International Conference on Very Large Database, Hong Kong, China Aug, 2002.
8. K Wang, L. Tang, J. Han, and J. Liu, "Top Down FP-Growth for Association Rule Mining, " in Proc. of the 6th Pacific Area Conference on Knowledge Discovery and Data Mining, May 6-8, Taipei, Taiwan, PAKDD-2002.

Learning Classifiers from Distributed, Ontology-Extended Data Sources

Doina Caragea, Jun Zhang, Jyotishman Pathak, and Vasant Honavar

AI Research Lab, Department of Computer Science, Iowa State University
226 Atanasoff Hall, Ames, IA 50011
{dcaragea, zhang, jpathak, honavar}@cs.iastate.edu

Abstract. There is an urgent need for sound approaches to integrative and collaborative analysis of large, autonomous (and hence, inevitably semantically heterogeneous) data sources in several increasingly data-rich application domains. In this paper, we precisely formulate and solve the problem of learning classifiers from such data sources, in a setting where each data source has a hierarchical ontology associated with it and semantic correspondences between data source ontologies and a user ontology are supplied. The proposed approach yields algorithms for learning a broad class of classifiers (including Bayesian networks, decision trees, etc.) from semantically heterogeneous distributed data with strong performance guarantees relative to their centralized counterparts. We illustrate the application of the proposed approach in the case of learning Naive Bayes classifiers from distributed, ontology-extended data sources.

1 Introduction

The availability of large amounts of data in many application domains has resulted in unprecedented opportunities for data driven knowledge discovery. However, the massive size, the distributed nature of the data sources and the inevitability of semantic differences between independently managed data repositories present significant hurdles in our ability to fully exploit such data sources in knowledge discovery. The Semantic Web enterprise [1] is aimed at supporting seamless and flexible access and use of semantically heterogeneous data sources by associating meta-data (e.g., ontologies) with data available in many application domains. The work described in this paper is aimed at the development of algorithms for learning concise and accurate classifiers from semantically heterogeneous, distributed data sets for applications in which integration of data from multiple sources into a centralized repository is not feasible (e.g., because of the enormous size of the data sources).

The problem that we seek to address is best illustrated by an example: Consider two academic departments that independently collect information about their *Students* in connection to *Internships*. Suppose a data set D_1 collected by the first department is described by the attributes *ID, Advisor Position, Student Level, Monthly Income* and *Internship* and it is stored into a table as the one corresponding to D_1 in Table 1. Suppose a second data set D_2 collected by the second department is described by the attributes *Student ID, Advisor Rank, Student Program, Hourly Income* and *Intern* and it is stored into a table as the one corresponding to D_2 in Table 1.

A Min Tjoa and J. Trujillo (Eds.): DaWaK 2006, LNCS 4081, pp. 363–373, 2006.

Consider a user, e.g., a university statistician, who wants to draw some inferences about the two departments of interest from the user's perspective, where the representative attributes are *Student SSN, Advisor Status, Student Status, Yearly Income* and *Internship*. For example, the statistician may want to infer a model that can be used to find out whether a student in the statistician's data (D_U in Table 1) has completed an internship or not.

This requires the ability to perform queries over the two data sources associated with the departments of interest from the user's perspective (e.g., *number of doctorate students who did an internship*). However, we notice that the two data sources differ in terms of semantics from the user's perspective. In order to cope with this heterogeneity of semantics, the user must observe that the attributes *ID* in the first data source and *Student ID* in the second data source are similar to the attribute *Student SSN* in the user data; the attributes *Advisor Position* and *Advisor Rank* are similar to the

Table 1. Student data collected by two departments and a statistician

	ID	Adv.Pos.	St.Level	M.Inc.	Intern.
	34	Associate	M.S.	1530	yes
D_1	49	None	1st Year	600	no
	23	Professor	Ph.D.	1800	no
	SID	Adv.Rank	St.Prog.	H.Inc.	Intern
	1	Assistant	Master	14	yes
D_2	2	Professor	Doctoral	17	no
	3	Associate	Undergrad	8	yes
	SSN	Adv.Status	St.Status	Y.Inc.	Intern
	475	Assistant	Master	16000	?
D_U	287	Professor	Doctorate	18000	?
	530	Associate	Undergrad	7000	?

attribute *Advisor Status*; the attributes *Student Level* and *Student Program* are similar to the attribute *Student Status*, etc.

To establish the correspondence between values that two similar attributes can take, we need to associate types with attributes and to map the domain of the type of an attribute to the domain of the type of the corresponding attribute (e.g., *Hourly Income* to *Yearly Income* or *Student Level* to *Student Status*). We assume that the type of an attribute can be a standard type such as String, Integer, etc. or it can be given by a simple hierarchical ontology. Figure 1 shows examples of attribute value hierarchies for the attributes *Student Level, Student Program,* and *Student Status* in the data sources D_1, D_2 and the user data D_U, respectively. Examples of semantical correspondences in this case could be: *Graduate* in D_2 is equivalent to *Grad* in D_U, *1st Year* in D_1 is equivalent to *Freshman* in D_U, *M.S.* in D_2 is smaller than (or hierarchically below) *Master* in D_U, etc.

In this paper, our main focus is on learning classifiers from such semantically heterogeneous data sources. Learning typically requires extracting relevant statistics from data. When the data sources are semantically heterogeneous, because of differences in the levels of abstraction at which data in different data sources are specified relative to the user's perspective, we are presented with the problem of learning classifiers from partially specified data. Previous work [2] has shown how to exploit a set of hierarchically structured ontologies in the form of *isa* hierarchies over attribute values in a single data source to learn classifiers from partially specified data. Against this background, this paper aims to address the problem of *learning concise and accurate classifiers from semantically heterogeneous distributed data sources*.

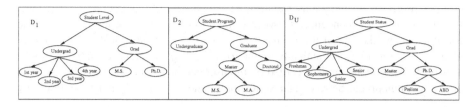

Fig. 1. Hierarchical ontologies associated with the attributes *Student Level, Student Program* and *Student Status* that appear in the two data sources of interest D_1 and D_2 and in user data D_U, respectively

The rest of the paper is organized as follows: Section 2 provides a more precise formulation of the problem of learning compact and concise classifiers from semantically heterogeneous distributed data; Section 3 presents a general approach to solving this problem, illustrates its application in the case of Naive Bayes classifiers and presents theoretical guarantees associated with the proposed algorithm; and Section 4 concludes with a summary and discussion.

2   Problem Formulation

2.1   Ontology-Extended Data Sources

Suppose that the data of interest are distributed over the data sources $D_1, \cdots, D_p$, where each data source D_i contains only a fragment of the whole data D. Two common types of data fragmentation are *horizontal fragmentation*, where each data fragment contains a subset of data tuples and *vertical fragmentation*, where each data fragment contains subtuples of data tuples [3].

Let D_i be a distributed data source described by the set of attributes $\{A_1^i, \cdots, A_n^i\}$ and $O_i = \{A_1^i, \cdots, A_n^i\}$ a simple ontology associated with this data. The element $A_j^i \in O_i$ corresponds to the attribute A_j^i and describes the type of that particular attribute. The type of an attribute can be a (possibly restricted) standard type (e.g., Positive Integer or String) or a hierarchical type. A hierarchical type is defined as an ordering of a set of terms [4] (e.g., the values of an attribute). Of special interest to us are tree structured *isa hierarchies* over the values of the attributes that describe a data source, also called *attribute value taxonomies* (see Figure 1).

The schema S_i of a data source D_i is given by the set of attributes $\{A_1^i, \cdots, A_n^i\}$ used to describe the data together with their respective types $\{A_1^i, \cdots, A_n^i\}$ described by the ontology O_i. We define an *ontology-extended data source* as a tuple $\mathcal{D}_\rangle = <D_i, S_i, O_i>$, where D_i is the actual data in the data source, S_i is the schema of the data source and O_i is the ontology associated with the data source.

2.2   Complete Data from a User Perspective

Let $<D_1, S_1, O_1>, \cdots, <D_p, S_p, O_p>$ be an ordered set of p ontology-extended data sources and U a user that poses queries against these heterogeneous data sources. A user perspective is given by a user ontology O_U and a set of interoperation constraints IC that define correspondences between terms in $O_1, \cdots, O_p$ and terms in O_U. The constraints can take one of the forms: $x{:}O_i \equiv y{:}O_U$ (x is semantically *equivalent* to y), $x{:}O_i \leq y{:}O_U$ (x is semantically *below* y), $x{:}O_i \geq y{:}O_U$ (x is semantically *above* y) [4]. The set of constraints specified by the user can be used to (semi-automatically) infer a set of mappings between data source ontologies $O_1, \cdots, O_p$ and a user ontology O_U.

Let $\Gamma = \Gamma(O_U)$ be a cut through the user ontology. If $\Lambda_j^U \in O_U$ is a standard (linear) type, then the cut $\Gamma(\Lambda_j^U)$ through the domain Λ_j^U is the domain itself. However, if Λ_j^U is a hierarchical type, then $\Gamma(\Lambda_j^U)$ defines the level of abstraction at which the user queries are formulated. For example, $\{Undergrad, Master, Ph.D.\}$ is a level of abstraction in the hierarchy associated with the attribute *Student Status* in the user perspective in our example (Figure 1). Any value above this cut implies a higher level of abstraction (e.g., $Grad$), while a value below the cut (e.g., ABD) implies a lower level of abstraction, when used to specify instances. A user level of abstraction Γ determines a level of abstraction $\Gamma_i = \Gamma(O_i)$ in each distributed data source D_i (by applying the corresponding mappings). Let $x = (v(A_1^i), \cdots, v(A_n^i))$ be an instance in D_i. We say that the instance x is:

- *Fully specified* if for all $1 \leq j \leq n$, the value $v(A_j^i)$ is on or below the cut Γ_i. If $v(A_j^i)$ is on the cut Γ_i, we say that $v(A_j^i)$ is an *exactly specified* value; if $v(A_j^i)$ is below the cut Γ_i, we say that $v(A_j^i)$ is an *over-specified* value.
- *Partially specified* if there exist at least one attribute value $v(A_j^i)$ which is above the cut Γ_i. We say that $v(A_j^i)$ is an *under-specified* value.

Given a cut Γ through the user ontology, the available data sources $D_1, \cdots, D_p$ could be seen as a complete virtual data set D, whose instances are specified at the level of abstraction corresponding to the cut Γ. More precisely, D is defined as the multi-set union (i.e., duplicates are allowed) of the distributed instances, appropiately mapped to the user ontology by mapping each attribute value to the corresponding value in the user ontology. Note that the complete data cannot always be constructed in practice (e.g., when the user cut results in under-specified data in the distributed data sources), thus making impossible the application of standard centralized machine learning algorithms. However, under specific assumptions about the distribution of the under-specified data (e.g., all the under-specified values are equally likely), certain statistics about data (e.g., counts of data) can be easily estimated.

2.3 Learning Compact and Accurate Classifiers from Distributed, Ontology-Extended Data Sources

The problem of learning classifiers from data can be summarized as follows [5]: Given a data set D of labeled examples, a hypothesis class H, and a performance criterion P, the learning algorithm L outputs a hypothesis $h \in H$ that optimizes P. In pattern classification applications, h is a classifier (e.g., a Naive Bayes classifiers, a Decision Tree, a Support Vector Machine, etc.). Under appropriate assumptions, the resulting classifier is likely to accurately classify unlabeled instances.

A distributed setting typically imposes a set of constraints Z on the learner that are absent in the centralized setting. In this paper, we assume that the constraints Z prohibit the transfer of raw data from each of the sites to a central location while allowing the learner to obtain certain statistics from the individual sites (e.g., counts of instances that have specified values for some subset of attributes). Thus, the problem of learning compact and accurate classifiers from distributed, semantically heterogeneous data sources can be formulated as follows: Given a collection of ontology-extended data sources $<D_1, S_1, O_1>, \cdots, <D_p, S_p, O_p>$, a user perspective (O_U, IC), a set of constraints Z, a hypothesis class H and a performance criterion P, the task of the learner L_d is to output a hypothesis $h \in H$ that optimizes P using only operations allowed by Z.

We say that an algorithm L_d for learning from distributed, semantically heterogeneous data sets $D_1, \cdots, D_p$ is *exact* relative to its centralized counterpart L if the hypothesis produced by L_d is identical to that obtained by L from the complete data set D obtained by appropriately integrating the data sets $D_1, \cdots, D_p$ according to the user perspective, as defined in the previous section.

3   Sufficient Statistics Based Solution

We want to design algorithms for learning compact and accurate classifiers from distributed, semantically heterogeneous data sources. Our approach is based on a general strategy for transforming algorithms for learning classifiers from data into algorithms for learning classifiers from distributed data [6].

This strategy relies on the decomposition of the learning task into two components [7]: an *information gathering* component, in which the information needed for learning is identified and gathered from the distributed data sources, and a *hypothesis generation* component which uses this information to generate or refine a partially constructed hypothesis. The information gathering component involves a procedure for specify-

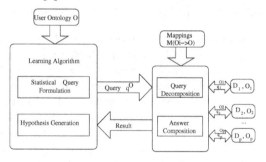

Fig. 2. Learning from semantically heterogeneous data sources

ing the information needed for learning as a *query* and a procedure for answering this query from distributed data. The procedure for answering queries from distributed data entails the decomposition of a posed query into sub-queries that the individual data sources can answer, followed by the composition of the partial answers into a final answer to the initial query. If the distributed data sources are also semantically heterogeneous, mappings between the data sources ontologies and a user ontology need to be applied in the process of query answering to reconcile the semantic differences [6] (Figure 2).

The strategy described can be applied to a large class of learning algorithms (e.g., naive Bayes, decision trees, Bayesian networks, etc.). To illustrate it, we will use Naive

Bayes algorithms as an example. Zhang and Honavar [8] proposed an algorithm (AVT-NBL) for learning compact and accurate Naive Bayes classifiers from a data set in the presence of an associated ontology. In the remaining of this section we identify the information requirements (*sufficient statistics*) of AVT-NBL algorithm, and we show how to transform it into an algorithm for learning compact and accurate Naive Bayes classifiers from distributed, semantically heterogeneous data sources.

3.1 Sufficient Statistics for AVT-NBL

A statistic $s(D)$ is called a *sufficient statistic* for a parameter θ if $s(D)$ captures all the information about the parameter θ contained in the data D [9]. Caragea et al. [6] generalized this notion of a sufficient statistic for a parameter θ to yield the notion of a sufficient statistic $s_L(D)$ for learning a hypothesis h using a learning algorithm L applied to a data set D. Thus, a statistic $s_L(D)$ is a *sufficient statistic for learning* a hypothesis h using a learning algorithm L applied to a data set D if there exists a procedure that takes $s_L(D)$ as input and outputs h.

Consider for example, the Naive Bayes classifier that operates under the assumption that each attribute is independent of the others given the class. Thus, the joint class conditional probability of an instance can be written as the product of individual class conditional probabilities corresponding to each attribute defining the instance. The Bayesian approach to classifying an instance $x = \{v_1, \cdots, v_n\}$ is to assign it to the most probable class $c_{MAP}(x)$. Thus, we have: $c_{MAP}(x) = \underset{c_j \in C}{\mathrm{argmax}}\, p(v_1, \cdots, v_n | c_j) p(c_j) = \underset{c_j \in C}{\mathrm{argmax}}\, p(c_j) \prod_i p(v_i | c_j)$. Therefore, the task of the Naive Bayes Learner (NBL) is to estimate the class probabilities $p(c_j)$ and the class conditional probabilities $p(v_i | c_j)$, for all classes $c_j \in \mathbf{C}$ and for all attribute values $v_i \in dom(A_i)$. These probabilities can be estimated from a training set D using standard probability estimation methods [5] based on relative frequency counts. We denote by $\sigma(v_i | c_j)$ the frequency count of the value v_i of the attribute A_i given the class label c_j, and by $\sigma(c_j)$ the frequency count of the class label c_j in a training set D. These frequency counts completely summarize the information needed for constructing a Naive Bayes classifier from D, and thus, they constitute *sufficient statistics* for Naive Bayes learner.

While the sufficient statistics required for constructing a classifier can be computed in one step in some simple cases (e.g., Naive Bayes), in general, this may require interleaved execution of the information gathering and hypothesis generation components of the algorithm over several steps with each step yielding *refinement sufficient statistics* that are used to refine a partially construsted classifier. More precisely, $s_L(D, h_i \to h_{i+1})$ is a sufficient statistic for the refinement of h_i into h_{i+1} if there exists a procedure R that takes h_i and $s_L(D, h_i \to h_{i+1})$ as inputs and outputs h_{i+1} [3].

We next identify the refinement sufficient statistics for the AVT-NBL algorithm [8]. AVT-NBL efficiently expoits taxonomies defined over values of each attribute in the data set to find a Naive Bayes classifier that optimizes the Conditional Minimum Description Length (CMDL) score [10]. The CMDL score provides a means of trading off the error of the classifier against its complexity. If we denote by

$|D|$ the size of the data set, Γ a cut through the AVT associated with this data, $h = h(\Gamma)$ the Naive Bayes classifier corresponding to the cut Γ, $size(h)$ the number of probabilities used to describe h and $CLL(h|D)$ the conditional log-likelihood of the hypothesis h given the data D, then the $CMDL$ score can be written as $CMDL(h|D) = \left(\dfrac{\log|D|}{2}\right) size(h) - |D|CLL(h|D)$. Here, $CLL(h|D) =$

$|D| \displaystyle\sum_{i=1}^{|D|} \log p_h(c_i|v_{i1}\cdots v_{in})$, where $p_h(c_i|v_{i1}\cdots v_{in})$ represents the conditional probability assigned to the class $c_i \in C$ associated with the example $x_i = (v_{i1}, \cdots, v_{in})$. Because each attribute is assumed to be independent of the others given the class, we

can write $CLL(h|D) = |D| \displaystyle\sum_{i=1}^{|D|} \log \left(\dfrac{p(c_i) \prod_j p_h(v_{ij}|c_i)}{\sum_{k=1}^{|C|} p(c_k) \prod_j p_h(v_{ij}|c_k)} \right).$

AVT-NBL starts with a Naive Bayes classifier corresponding to the most abstract cut in the attribute value taxonomy associated with the data (most general classifier) and it iteratively refines the cut by searching in a greedy fashion through the space of possible cuts, until a best cut, according to the performance criterion, is found. More precisely, let h_i be the current hypothesis corresponding to the current cut Γ (i.e., $h_i = h(\Gamma)$) and Γ' a (one-step) refinement of Γ (see Figure 3).

Let $h(\Gamma')$ be the Naive Bayes classifier corresponding to the cut Γ' and let $CMDL(\Gamma|D)$ and $CMDL(\Gamma'|D)$ be the CMDL scores corresponding to the hypotheses $h(\Gamma)$ and $h(\Gamma')$, respectively. If $CMDL(\Gamma) > CMDL(\Gamma')$ then $h_{i+1} = h(\Gamma')$, otherwise $h_{i+1} = h(\Gamma)$. This

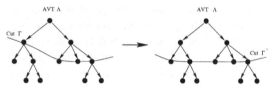

Fig. 3. The refinement of a cut Γ through an attribute value taxonomy Λ

procedure is repeated until the differences $|CMDL(\Gamma) - CMDL(\Gamma')|$ approaches zero for all (one-step) refinements Γ' of Γ. The last hypothesis constructed is the output of the AVT-NBL algorithm.

Therefore, the final classifier that the AVT-NBL outputs is obtained from the most general classifier through a sequence of refinement operations. Each refinement operation corresponds to the refinement of the current cut and it is based on the $CMDL$ score. Thus, the sufficient statistics for learning AVT-NBL classifiers can be seen as refinement sufficient statistics, which are identified below.

Let h_i be the current hypothesis corresponding to a cut Γ and $CLDM(\Gamma|D)$ its score. If Γ' is a refinement of the cut Γ, then the refinement sufficient statistics needed to construct h_{i+1} are given by the frequency counts needed to construct $h(\Gamma')$ together with the probabilities needed to compute $CLL(h(\Gamma')|D)$ (calculated once we know $h(\Gamma')$). If we denote by $dom_{\Gamma'}(A_i)$ the domain of the attribute A_i when the cut Γ' is considered, then the frequency counts needed to construct $h(\Gamma')$ are $\sigma(v_i|c_j)$ for all values $v_i \in dom_{\Gamma'}(A_i)$ of all attributes A_i and for all class values $c_j \in dom_{\Gamma'}(C)$, and

$\sigma(c_j)$ for all class values $c_j \in dom_{\Gamma'}(C)$. To compute $CLL(h(\Gamma')|D)$ the products $\prod_j p_{h(\Gamma')}(v_{ij}|c_k)$ for all examples $x_i = (v_{i1}, \cdots, v_{in})$ and for all classes $c_k \in C$ are needed.

The step $i + 1$ of the algorithm corresponding to the cut Γ' can be briefly described in terms of information gathering and hypothesis generation components as follows:

1) Compute $\sigma(v_i|c_j)$ and $\sigma(c_j)$ corresponding to the cut Γ' from the training data D
2) Generate the NB classifier $h(\Gamma')$
3) Compute $\prod_j p_{h(\Gamma')}(v_{ij}|c_k)$ from D
4) Generate the hypothesis h_{i+1}

3.2 Naive Bayes Classifiers from Semantically Heterogeneous Data

Let $<D_1, S_1, O_1>, \cdots, <D_p, S_p, O_p>$ be a set of p ontology-extended data sources and O_U a user ontology. Let Γ be a cut through the user ontology.

The step $i + 1$ (corresponding to the cut Γ' in the user ontology) of the algorithm for learning Naive Bayes classifiers from distributed, semantically heterogeneous data sources $D_1, \cdots, D_p$ is similar to the step $i + 1$ of the algorithm for learning from a single data set (described above), except that the sufficient statistics are computed from the distributed data sources $D_1, \cdots, D_p$.

Thus, we have reduced the problem of learning Naive Bayes classifiers from distributed, ontology-extended data sources, to the problem of gathering the statistics $s_L(D, h_i \rightarrow h_{i+1})$ from such data sources. Next, we show how to answer statistical queries $q(s_L(D, h_i \rightarrow h_{i+1}))$ that return statistics $s_L(D, h_i \rightarrow h_{i+1})$, from horizontally and vertically fragmented distributed, semantically heterogeneous data sources.

Horizontally Fragmented Data. If the data are horizontally fragmented, the examples are distributed among the data sources of interest. Thus, the user query $q(\sigma(v_i|c_j))$ can be decomposed into the sub-queries $q_1(\sigma(v_i^1|c_j^1)), \cdots, q_p(\sigma(v_i^p|c_j^p))$ corresponding to the distributed data sources $D_1, \cdots, D_p$, where v_i^k and c_j^k are the values in O_k that map to the values v_i and c_j in O_U. Once the queries $q_1(\sigma(v_i^1|c_j^1)), \cdots, q_p(\sigma(v_i^p|c_j^p))$ have been answered, the answer to the initial query can be obtained by adding up the individual answers into a final count $\sigma(v_i|c_j) = \sigma(v_i^1|c_j^1) + \cdots + \sigma(v_i^p|c_j^p)$. Similarly, we compute the counts $\sigma(c_j)$. Once the counts $\sigma(v_i|c_j)$ and $\sigma(c_j)$ have been computed, the Naive Bayes classifier $h' = h(\Gamma')$ corresponding to the cut Γ' can be generated. The next query that needs to be answered is $q(\prod_j p_{h'}(v_{ij}|c_k))$ corresponding to each (virtual) example $x_i = (v_{i1}, \cdots, v_{in})$ (in the complete data set) and each class c_k based on the probabilities that define h'. Because all the attributes of an example are at the same location in the case of the horizontal data fragmentation, each query $q(\prod_j p_{h'}(v_{ij}|c_k))$ is answered by the data source that contains the actual example x_i. When all such queries have been answered, the score $CMDL$ can be computed and thus the hypothesis that will be output at this step can be generated.

If any of the values v_i^k or c_j^k are partially specified in O_k, we "fill in" the partially specified values and increment the count accordingly. Traditional methods for dealing with missing data, as well as new statistical methods designed specifically for partially specified data can be used to "fill in" partially specified values. In this paper, we assume that the user specifies a distribution over partially specified values or that such a distribution is inferred based on the corresponding specified values in a different data source.

Vertically Fragmented Data. If the data is vertically fragmented, the attributes are distributed among the data sources of interest, but all the values of an attribute are found at the same location. Therefore, a user query $q(\sigma(v_i|c_j))$ can be answered by a particular data source that contains the attribute A_i. However, the user query $q(\prod_j p_h(v_{ij}|c_k))$ is decomposed into sub-queries according to the distributed data sources and the final answer is obtained by multiplying the individual answers.

3.3 Theoretical Analysis

Theorem 1 (Exactness). *The algorithm for learning Naive Bayes classifiers from a set of horizontally (or vertically) fragmented distributed, ontology-extended data sources $<D_1,S_1,O_1>,\cdots,<D_p,S_p,O_p>$, from a user perspective $<O_U,IC>$, in the presence of the inferred mappings $\psi_1,\cdots,\psi_p$, is exact with respect to the algorithm for learning Naive Bayes classifiers from the complete data set D, obtained (in principle) by integrating the data sources $D_1,\cdots,D_p$ according to mappings $\psi_1,\cdots,\psi_p$.*

Proof sketch: Because of the information gathering and hypothesis generation decomposition of the the AVT-NBL algorithm, the exactness of the algorithm for learning from distributed, semantically heterogeneous data sources depends on the correctness of the procedures for decomposing a user query q into sub-queries $q_1,\cdots,q_p$ corresponding to the distributed data sources $D_1,\cdots,D_p$ and for composing the individual answers to the queries $q_1,\cdots,q_p$ into a final answer to the query q. More precisely, we need to show that the condition $q(D) = \mathcal{C}(q_1(D_1),\cdots,q_p(D_p))$ (*exactness condition*) is satisfied, where $q(D),q_1(D_1),\cdots,q_p(D_p)$ represent the answers to the queries $q,q_1,\cdots,q_p$, respectively, and $\mathcal{C}$ is a procedure for combining the individual answers. When data is horizontally fragmented the query $q(\sigma(v_i|c_j))$ is decomposed into sub-queries $q_1(\sigma(v_i^1|c_j^1)),\cdots,q_p(\sigma(v_i^p|c_j^p))$ corresponding to the distributed data sources $D_1,\cdots,D_p$ and the final answer is $\sigma(v_i|c_j)(D_1,\cdots,D_p) = \sigma(v_i^1|c_j^1)(D_1) + \cdots + \sigma(v_i^p|c_j^p)(D_p)$. If we denote by $\sigma(v_i|c_j)(D)$ the answer to the query $q(\sigma(v_i|c_j))$ posed to the complete data set D, we need to show that $\sigma(v_i|c_j)(D_1,\cdots,D_p) = \sigma(v_i|c_j)(D)$. This is obviously true when the data sources $D_1,\cdots,D_p$ are homogeneous because the addition operation is associative. The equality holds also when the data sources are heterogeneous, due to the way we compute the counts (by simulating the construction of the complete data set D). A similar argument can be made for the exactness condition in the case of the query $q(\sigma(c_j))$. Because the answer to the query $q(\prod_j p_h(v_{ij}|c_k))$ is obtained from a single data source and no combination procedure is needed, the exactness condition is trivially satisfied in this case. Similarly we can prove the exactness of the algorithm for leaning from vertically fragmented distributed data, which completes the proof of the exactness theorem.

4 Summary and Discussion

There is an urgent need for algorithms for learning classifiers from distributed, autonomous (and hence inevitably, semantically heterogeneous) data sources in several increasingly data-rich application domains such as bioinformatics, environmental informatics, medical informatics, social informatics, security informatics, among others.

In this paper, we have precisely formulated the problem of learning classifiers from distributed, *ontology-extended data sources*, which make explicit (the typically implicit) ontologies associated with autonomous data sources. User-specified semantic correspondences (mappings between the data source ontologies and the user ontology) are used to answer statistical queries that provide the information needed for learning classifiers, from such data sources. The resulting framework yields algorithms for learning classifiers from distributed, ontology-extended data sources. These algorithms are provably exact relative to their centralized counterparts in the case of the family of learning classifiers for which the information needed for constructing the classifier can be broken down into a set of queries for sufficient statistics that take the form of counts of instances satisfying certain constraints on the values of the attributes. Such classifiers include decision trees, Bayesian network classifiers, classifiers based on a broad class of probabilistic models including generalized linear models, among others. We have illustrated the proposed approach in the case of learning Naive Bayes classifiers from horizontally fragmented distributed, ontology-extended data sources.

There is a large body of literature on distributed learning (See [11] for a survey). However, with the exception of [3], most algorithms for learning classifiers from distributed data do not offer performance guarantees (e.g., exactness) relative to their centralized counterparts. Integration of semantically heterogeneous data has received significant attention in the literature (see [12] for a survey). Most of this work has focused on bridging semantic differences between schemas and ontologies associated with the individual data sources and answering (typically relational) queries from such data sources.

Caragea et al. [6] present an approach to semantic integration of data from multiple sources when data are described in terms of different ontologies and briefly outline some ideas on extending this approach to solve the problem of learning from semantically heterogeneous data. In contrast, this paper precisely formulates and provides a solution to this problem in the important special case where each data source has an AVT ontology associated with it.

The algorithm and the analysis presented in this paper, together with results like those presented in [6] represent important steps towards a problem of significant current interest that cuts across multiple areas of AI (such as informtion integration, machine learning, knowledge representation, etc.).

References

1. Berners-Lee, T., Hendler, J., Lassila, O.: The Semantic Web. Scientific American (2001)
2. Zhang, J., Caragea, D., , Honavar, V.: Learning ontology-aware classifiers. In: Proceedings of the Eight International Conference on Discovery Science (DS 2005). (2005) 308–321

3. Caragea, D., Silvescu, A., Honavar, V.: A framework for learning from distributed data using sufficient statistics and its application to learning decision trees. International Journal of Hybrid Intelligent Systems **1** (2004)

4. Bonatti, P., Deng, Y., Subrahmanian, V.: An ontology-extended relational algebra. In: Proceedings of the IEEE Conference on Information Integration and Reuse, IEEE Press (2003) 192–199

5. Mitchell, T.: Machine Learning. McGraw Hill (1997)

6. Caragea, D., Pathak, J., Honavar, V.: Learning classifiers from semantically heterogeneous data. In: Proceedings of the International Conference on Ontologies, Databases, and Applications of Semantics for Large Scale Information Systems. (2004)

7. Kearns, M.: Efficient noise-tolerant learning from statistical queries. Journal of the ACM **45** (1998) 983–1006

8. Zhang, J., Honavar, V.: AVT-NBL: An algorithm for learning compact and accurate naive bayes classifiers from attribute value taxonomies and data. In: Proceedings of the Fourth IEEE International Conference on Data Mining, Brighton, UK (2004)

9. Casella, G., Berger, R.: Statistical Inference. Duxbury Press, Belmont, CA (2001)

10. Friedman, N., Geiger, D., Goldszmidt, M.: Bayesian network classifiers. Machine Learning **29** (1997)

11. Kargupta, H., Chan, P.: Advances in Distributed and Parallel Knowledge Discovery. AAAI/MIT (2000)

12. Doan, A., Halevy, A.: Semantic Integration Research in the Database Community: A Brief Survey. AI Magazine, Special Issue on Semantic Integration **26** (2005) 83–94

A Coherent Biomedical Literature Clustering and Summarization Approach Through Ontology-Enriched Graphical Representations

Illhoi Yoo[1], Xiaohua Hu[2], and Il-Yeol Song[2]

[1] Department of Health Management and Informatics, School of Medicine, University of Missouri-Columbia, Columbia, MO, 65211, USA
MU.Prof.Yoo@gmail.com
[2] College of Information Science and Technology, Drexel University, Philadelphia, PA, 19104, USA
{thu@cis, song} @drexel.edu

Abstract. In this paper, we introduce a coherent biomedical literature clustering and summarization approach that employs a graphical representation method for text using a biomedical ontology. The key of the approach is to construct document cluster models as semantic chunks capturing the core semantic relationships in the ontology-enriched scale-free graphical representation of documents. These document cluster models are used for both document clustering and text summarization by constructing Text Semantic Interaction Network (TSIN). Our extensive experimental results indicate our approach shows 45% cluster quality improvement and 72% clustering reliability improvement, in terms of misclassification index, over Bisecting K-means as a leading document clustering approach. In addition, our approach provides concise but rich text summary in key concepts and sentences. The primary contribution of this paper is we introduce a coherent biomedical literature clustering and summarization approach that takes advantage of ontology-enriched graphical representations. Our approach significantly improves the quality of document clusters and understandability of documents through summaries.

Keywords: Document clustering, text summarization, ontology, scale-free network, MEDLINE.

1 Introduction

A huge amount of textual information has been produced and collected in text databases or digital libraries for decades because the most natural form to store information is text. For example, MEDLINE, the largest biomedical bibliographic text database, has more than 16 million articles and more than 10,000 articles are weekly added to MEDLINE. In order to tackle this pressing text information overload problem, document clustering and text summarization together have been used as a solution. This is because document clustering enables us to group similar text information and then text summarization provides condensed text information for the similar text by extracting the most important text content from a similar document set

A Min Tjoa and J. Trujillo (Eds.): DaWaK 2006, LNCS 4081, pp. 374–383, 2006.

or a document cluster. For this reason, document clustering and text summarization can be used for important components of information retrieval system. Document clustering improves information retrieval (IR) performance because similar documents grouped by document clustering tend to be relevant to the same user queries [13] [14]. Text summarization helps IR users identify which documents satisfy their needs the best by providing summaries of the retrieved documents.

In this paper, we introduce a coherent biomedical literature clustering and summarization approach. The coherence of document clustering and text summarization is required because a set of documents are usually multiple-topics. For this reason text summarization does not yield high-quality summary without document clustering. On the other hand, document clustering is not very useful for users to understand a set of documents if the explanation for document categorization or the summaries for each document cluster is not provided. In other words, document clustering and text summarization are complementary. This is the primary motivation for the coherent approach of document clustering and text summarization.

The primary contribution of this paper is we introduce a coherent biomedical literature clustering and summarization approach that takes advantage of ontology-enriched graphical representations of documents. Our approach significantly improves the quality of document clusters and understandability of documents through summaries for each document cluster.

The rest of the paper is organized as follows. Section 2 surveys the related works. In Section 3, we propose a novel graph-based document clustering approach that uses domain knowledge in an ontology and text summarization using Text Semantic Interaction Network using the semantic relationships in the document cluster model. An extensive experimental evaluation on MEDLINE articles is conducted and the results are reported in Section 4. Section 5 concludes our paper.

2 Related Works

Document Clustering: A number of document clustering approaches have been developed for several decades. Most of these document clustering approaches are based on the vector space representation and apply various clustering algorithms to the representation. Thus, the approaches can be categorized as hierarchical or partitional.

Hierarchical agglomerative clustering algorithms were used for document clustering. The algorithms successively merge the most similar objects based on the pairwise distances between objects until a termination condition holds. Thus, the algorithms can be classified by the way they select the pair of objects for calculating the similarity measure (e.g., single-link, complete-link, and average-link). An advantage of the algorithms is that they generate a document hierarchy so that users can drill up and drill down for specific topics of interest. However, due to their cubic time complexity, they are limited for a very large number of documents.

Partitional clustering algorithms (especially K-means) are the most widely-used algorithms in document clustering [10]. Most of the algorithms first randomly select k centroids and then decompose the objects into k disjoint groups through iteratively relocating objects based on the similarity between the centroids and the objects. As one of the most widely-used partitional algorithms, K-means minimizes the sum of squared distances between the objects and their corresponding cluster centroids. As a variation of K-means, BiSecting K-means [10] first selects a cluster (normally the biggest one) to split and then splits the objects into two groups (i.e. $k = 2$) using K-means. One major drawback of partitional algorithms is that clustering results are heavily sensitive to the initial centroids because the centroids are randomly selected.

Recently, Hotho et al. introduced the semantic document clustering approach that uses background knowledge [7]. The authors apply an ontology during the construction of a vector space representation by mapping terms in documents to ontology concepts and then aggregating concepts based on the concept hierarchy, which is called concept selection and aggregation (COSA). As a result of COSA, they resolve a synonym problem and introduce more general concepts in the vector space to easily identify related topics [7]. Their method, however, cannot reduce the dimensionality (i.e. the document features) in the vector space; it still suffers from the "*Curse of Dimensionality*".

While all the approaches mentioned above represent documents as a feature vector, Suffix Tree Clustering (STC) [16] does not rely on the vector space model. STC does not treat a document as "a set of words". One of major drawbacks of STC is that semantically similar nodes may be distant within a suffix tree, because STC does not consider the semantic relationships among phrases (nodes or base clusters). In addition, some common expressions may lead to combine unrelated documents.

Text Summarization: Text summarization has been studied since Luhn's work in 1958 [9]. Since then, a variety of summarization approaches have been introduced. For instance, there are statistical methods based on the bag-of-words model, linguistic methods using natural language processing, knowledge-based methods using concepts and their relations, and summary generation methods. The first three approaches try to seek the most important information (usually sentences or terms) for a condensed version of documents while the last approach generates completely a new summary that consists of informative terms, phrases, clauses and sentences. The main difficulty of the last approach is to figure out how to combine them to make sentences that are grammatically correct.

In the bioinformatics/biomedical field many multi-document summarization systems have also been introduced. TextQuest [8] is designed to summarize documents retrieved in response to a keyword(s) based search on PubMed. However, it does not retain the association between the genes and the retrieved documents. MedMiner [12] can provide summarized literature information on genes but it is limited when finding relations between two genes only. In addition, it returns a few hundred sentences as the summary. Shatkey et al. [11] suggested a system, which attempts to find functional relations among genes on a genome-wide scale. However, this system requires the user to specify a representative document for each gene which describes the gene very well. Looking for the representative document may take a lot of time, effort and knowledge on the part of the user. In addition, as genes have multiple biological functions, it is very rare to find a document that covers all aspects of a gene across various biological domains. GEISHA [3] is based on the comparison of the frequency of abstracts linked to different gene clusters. Interpretation by the end user of the biological meaning of the terms is facilitated by embedding them in the corresponding significant sentences and abstracts and by establishing relations with other, equally significant terms.

3   The Proposed Approach: CSUGAR

We present a novel coherent document clustering and summarization approach, called *C*lustering and *SU*mmarization with *Gr*A*p*hical *R*epresentation for documents (CSUGAR). The proposed approach consists of two components, document clustering and text summarization as shown in Figure 1. Each step is discussed in detail below; see the circled numbers in Figure 1. Note the steps 1 to 3 correspond to document clustering and the steps 4 to 6 correspond to text summarization.

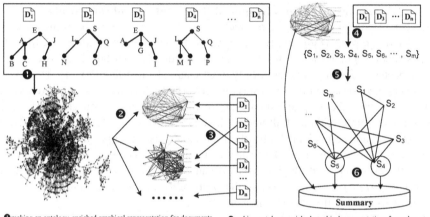

❶ making an ontology-enriched graphical representation for documents
❷ graph clustering for a graphical representation of documents
❸ assigning documents to clusters based on the document cluster models

❹ making ontology-enriched graphical representations for each sentence
❺ constructing Text Semantic Interaction Network (TSIN)
❻ selecting significant text contents for summary

Fig. 1. The Dataflow of the CSUGAR

Step1 - Ontology-enriched Graphical Representation for Documents through Concept Mapping
The idea of the use of ontology-enriched graphical representation for documents for document clustering was first introduced in our previous work [15]. Here, we briefly introduce the graphical representation method.

The first step of all document clustering methods is to convert documents into a proper format. Since we recognize documents as a set of concepts that have their complex internal semantic relationships, we represent each document as a graph structure using the MeSH ontology. The primarily motivations behind the graphical representation of documents are the following. First, the graphical representation of documents is a very natural way to portray the contents of documents because the semantic relationship information about the concepts in documents remains on the representation while the vector space representation loses all the information. Second, the graphical representation method provides *document representation independence*.

This means that the graphical representation of a document does not affect other representations. In the vector space representation, the addition of a single document usually requires the changes of every document representation. Third, the graphical representation guarantees better scalability than vector space model. Because a document representation is an actual data structure on text processing, its size should be as small as possible for better scalability. As the number of documents to be processed increases, a corpus-level graphical representation at most linearly expands or keeps its size with only some changes on edge weights, while a vector space representation (i.e. document*word matrix) at least linearly grows or increases by $n*t$ where n is the number of documents and t is the number of distinct terms in documents. For the detailed description about the graphical representation method for documents, refer to [15].

Step 2 - Graph Clustering for a Graphical Representation of Documents

A number of phenomena or systems, such as the Internet [2] have been modeled as networks or graphs. Traditionally those networks were interpreted with Erdos & Rényi's random graph theory, where nodes are randomly distributed and two nodes are connected randomly and uniformly (i.e. Gaussian distribution) [4]. However, researchers have observed that a variety of networks such as those mentioned above, deviate from the random graph theory [1] in that a few most connected nodes are connected to a high fraction of all nodes (there are a few *hub* nodes). However, these *hub* nodes cannot be explained with the traditional random graph theory. Recently, Barabasi and Albert introduced the scale-free network [2]. The scale-free network can explain the *hub* nodes with high degrees because its degree distribution decays as a power law, $P(k) \sim k^{-\gamma}$, where $P(k)$ is the probability that a vertex interacts with k other vertices and γ is the degree exponent [2].

Recently, Ferrer-Cancho and Solé have observed that the graph connecting words in English text follows a scale-free network [5]. Thus, the graphical representation of documents belongs to a highly heterogeneous family of scale-free networks. Our Scale Free Graph Clustering (SFGC) algorithm is based on the scale-free nature (i.e. the existence of a few hub vertices (concepts) in the graphical representation). SFGC starts detecting k hub vertex sets (HVSs) as the centroids of k graph clusters and then assigns the remaining vertices to graph clusters based on the relationships between the remaining objects and k hub vertex sets. For the detailed description of SFGC algorithm, refer to [15].

Step3 - Model-based Document Assignment

In this section, we explain how to assign each document to document clusters. In order to decide which document belongs to which document cluster, CSUGAR matches the graphical representation of each document with each of the graph clusters as models. Here, we might adopt graph similarity mechanisms, such as edit distance (the minimum number of primitive operations for structural modifications on a graph). However, these mechanisms are not appropriate for this task because individual document graphs and graph clusters are too different in terms of the number of vertices and edges. As an alternative to graph similarity mechanisms we take a vote mechanism. This mechanism is based on the classification (HVS or non-HVS) of the vertices in the graph clusters according to their salient scores. This classification leads to different votes. To this end, each vertex of each individual document graph casts two different numbers of votes for document clusters based on whether the vertex belongs to HVS or non-HVS. Each document is assigned to the document cluster that has the majority of votes in the document clusters.

The next three steps correspond to text summarization. Text summarization is to condense information in a set of documents into a concise text. This text summarization problem has been addressed by selecting and ordering sentences in documents based on a salient score mechanism. We address the problem by analyzing the semantic interaction of sentences (as summary elements). This semantic structure of sentences is called Text Semantic Interaction Network (TSIN), where vertices are sentences. We select sentences (vertices in the network) as summary elements based on degree centrality. Unlike traditional approaches, we do not use linguistic features for summarization for MEDLINE abstracts since they usually consist of only single paragraphs.

Step 4 - Making Ontology-enriched Graphical Representations for Each Sentence
The first step of the graphical representation for sentences is basically the same as the graphical representation method for documents except concept extension and individual graph integration. In this step the concepts in sentences are extended using the relationships in relevant document cluster models rather than the entire concept hierarchy. In other words, we extend concepts within relevant semantic field.

Step 5 - Constructing Text Semantic Interaction Network (TSIN)
The key process of text summarization is how to select "salient" sentences (or paragraphs in some approaches) as summary elements. We assume that the sentences becoming summary have the strong semantic relationships with other sentences because summary sentences cover the main points of a set of documents and comprise

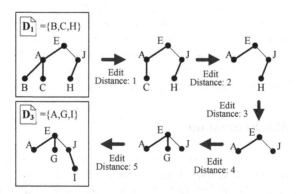

Fig. 2. Edit Distance between Two Graphical Representations of D_1 and D_2

a condensed version of the set. In order to represent the semantic relationship among sentences, we construct Text Semantic Interaction Network (TSIN), where vertices are sentences, edges are the semantic relationship between them, and edge weights indicate the degree of the relationships.

In order to deal with the semantic relationships between sentences and calculate the similarities (as edge weight in the network) between them, we use edit distance between the graphical representations of sentences. The edit distance between G1 and G2 is defined as the minimum number of structural modification required to become G1 into G2, where structural modification is one of vertex insertion, vertex deletion, and vertex update. For example, the edit distance between the two graphical representations of D_1 and D_2 in Figure 2 is 5.

Step 6 - Selecting Significant Text Contents for Summary

A number of approaches have been introduced to identify "important" nodes (vertices) in networks (or graphs) for decades. These approaches are normally categorized into degree centrality based approaches and between centrality based approaches. The degree centrality based approaches assume that nodes that have more relationships with others are more likely to be regarded as important in the network because they can directly relate to more other nodes. In other words, the more relationships the nodes in the network have, the more important they are. The betweenness centrality based approaches views a node as being in a favored position to the extent that the node falls on the geodesic paths between other pairs of nodes in the network [6]. In other words, the more nodes rely on a node to make connections with other nodes, the more important the node is.

These two approaches have their own advantages and disadvantages. For example, betweenness centrality based approaches yield better experiment results to find cluster centroids than other relevant approaches, while they require cubic running times so that they are not appropriate for very large graphs. Degree centrality based approaches have been criticized because they only take into account the immediate relationships for each node while they require the linear running time and provide comparable output quality with betweenness centrality based approaches.

To this end, we adopt degree centrality to measure the centrality of sentences in TSIN because of its linear computational time. In order to overcome its disadvantage, mentioned above, we measure, for each node, the semantic relationships with all other nodes (i.e., pairwise similarities for every pair of nodes) so that both immediate and distant relationships that each node has are considered while using degree centrality.

4   Experimental Evaluation

In order to measure the effectiveness of CSUGAR, we conducted extensive experiments on public MEDLINE abstracts. For the extensive experiments, first we collected document sets related to various diseases from MEDLINE. We use

"MajorTopic" tag along with the disease-related MeSH terms as queries to MEDLINE. After retrieving the base data sets, we generate various document combinations whose numbers of classes are 2 to 9 by randomly mixing the document sets. The document sets used for generating the combinations are later used as answer keys on the performance measure. For the detailed description about the document sets, the evaluation method, and the experimental setting, refer to [15].

Document Clustering

Because the full detailed experiment results are too big to be depicted in this paper, we average the clustering evaluation metric values and show the standard deviations (σ) for them to indicate how consistent a clustering approach yields document clusters (simply, the reliability of each approach). The σ would be a very important document clustering evaluation factor because document clustering is performed in the circumstance where the information about documents is unknown. Table 1 summarizes the statistical information about clustering results. From the table, we notice the following observations:

- CSUGAR outperforms the nine document clustering methods.
- CSUGAR has the most stable clustering performance regardless of test corpora, while CLUTO Bisecting K-means and K-means do not always show stable clustering performance.
- Hierarchical approaches have a serious scalability problem.
- STC and the original Bisecting K-means have a scalability problem.
- MeSH Ontology improves the clustering solutions of STC.

We observe that CSUGAR has the best performance, yields the most stable clustering results and scales very well. More specifically, CSUGAR shows 45% cluster quality improvement and 72% clustering reliability improvement, in terms of MI, over Bisecting K-means with the best parameters.

Table 1. Summary of Overall Experiment Results on MEDLINE Document Sets

	STC		K-means	Original Bisecting K-means [10]	CLUTO Bisecting K-means		CSUGAR
	word strings	concept strings			Largest	LOS	
MI	μ: 0.429 σ: 0.238	μ: 0.359 σ: 0.149	μ: 0.128 σ: 0.148	μ: 0.395 σ: 0.193	μ: 0.161 σ: 0.139	μ: 0.096 σ: 0.112	**μ: 0.053** **σ: 0.031**
Purity	μ: 0.601 σ: 0.214	μ: 0.731 σ: 0.098	μ: 0.932 σ: 0.080	μ: 0.666 σ: 0.154	μ: 0.918 σ: 0.064	μ: 0.944 σ: 0.056	**μ: 0.947** **σ: 0.030**
F-measure	μ: 0.499 σ: 0.285	μ: 0.512 σ: 0.198	μ: 0.828 σ: 0.206	μ: 0.532 σ: 0.236	μ: 0.780 σ: 0.180	μ: 0.880 σ: 0.139	**μ: 0.926** **σ: 0.062**

LOS: selecting the cluster (to be bisected) with the least overall similarity and Largest: selecting the largest cluster to be bisected. MI: the smaller, the better clustering quality. Purity and F-measure: the bigger, the better clustering quality

Text Summarization
Table 2 shows the experiment result for text summarization for a document cluster called "Alzheimer Disease"; due to the page limitation only a document cluster is presented. We believe that its document cluster model in HVS and Top 7 sentences as summary significantly help users understand the document cluster.

Table 2. Experiment Results for Text Summarization: For the Alzheimer Disease document cluster its document cluster model and key sentences as summary are shown

Document Cluster Model (HVS sets)	
Top 7 Sentences as Summary for the Document Cluster	• Tau protein extracted from filaments of familial multiple system tauopathy with presenile dementia shows a minor 72-kDa band and two major bands of 64 and 68 kDa that contain mainly hyperphosphorylated four-repeat tau isoforms of 383 and 412 amino acids. • The central pathological cause of Alzheimer disease (AD) is hypothesized to be an excess of beta-amyloid (Abeta) which accumulates into toxic fibrillar deposits within extracellular areas of the brain.These deposits disrupt neural and synaptic function and ultimately lead to neuronal degeneration and dementia • In dementia of Alzheimer type (DAT), cerebral glucose metabolism is reduced in vivo, and enzymes involved in glucose breakdown are impaired in post-mortem brain tissue • Alzheimer's disease (AD), a progressive, degenerative disorder of the brain, is believed to be the most common cause of dementia amongst the elderly • The fundamental cause of Alzheimer dementia is proposed to be Alzheimer disease, i.e. the neurobiological abnormalities in Alzheimer brain • Alzheimer's disease (AD) is a degenerative disease of the brain, and the most common form of dementia • Regional quantitative analysis of NFT in brains of non-demented elderly persons: comparisons with findings in brains of late-onset Alzheimer's disease and limbic NFT dementia.

5 Conclusion

The primary contribution of this paper is we introduce a coherent biomedical literature clustering and summarization approach that takes advantage of ontology-enriched graphical representations of documents. Our approach significantly improves the quality of document clusters and understandability of documents through summaries for each document cluster.

Acknowledgments. This research work is supported in part from the NSF Career grant (NSF IIS 0448023) NSF CCF 0514679 and the PA Dept of Health Tobacco Settlement Formula Grant (#240205, 240196).

References

1. Amaral, L.A.N., Scala, A., Barthélémy, M. and Stanley, H.E. *Proc. Nat. Ac. Sci USA, 97*, 2000, 11149-11152.
2. Barabasi, A.L., Albert, R. Emergence of scaling in random networks, *Science, 286*, 1999, 509.
3. Blaschke C, Oliveros JC, Valencia A (2001) Mining Functional Information Associated With Expression Arrays. *Funct. Integr. Genomics, Vol. 1, No. 4*, pp. 256-268
4. Erdos, P. and Rényi, A. On the Evolution of Random Graphs. *Publ. Math. Inst. Hungar. Acad. Sci. 5*, 1960, 17-61.
5. Ferrer-Cancho, R., and Solé, R.V., The small world of human language. In *Proceedings of the Royal Society of London, 268*, 1482, 2001, 2261–2266.
6. Hanneman, R. A., Riddle, M. 2005. Introduction to social network methods [online]. *University of California*. Available from: http://faculty.ucr.edu/~hanneman/
7. Hotho, A., Maedche A., and Staab S. Text Clustering Based on Good Aggregations. *Künstliche Intelligenz (KI), 16*, 4, 2002, 48-54.
8. Iliopoulos I, Enright AJ, Ouzounis CA (2001). Textquest: document clustering of Medline abstracts for concept discovery in molecular biology. *PSB 2001*, pp. 384-395
9. Luhn, H.P. (1958) The automatic creation of literature abstracts. *IBM Journal of Research and Development, Vol. 2, No. 2*, pp. 159-165
10. Shatkey, H., Edwards, S., Wilbur, W.J. and Boguski, M. (2000) Genes, Themes and Microarrays: Using Information Retrieval For Large-Scale Gene Analysis. The 8th International Confer-ence on Intelligent Systems Molecular Biology (ISMB 2000), La Jolla, pp. 317-328
11. Steinbach, M., Karypis, G., and Kumar, V. *A Comparison of Document Clustering Techniques*. Technical Report #00-034. University of Minnesota, 2000.
12. Tanabe, L., Scherf, U., Smith, L.H., Lee, J.K., Hunter, L., and Weinstein, J.N (1999) MedMiner: An Internet Text-Mining Tool for Biomedical Information, with Application to Gene Expression Profiling. *Biotechniques, Vol. 27, No. 6*, pp. 1210-1217
13. van Rijsbergen, C. J. *Information Retrieval, 2nd edition*, London: Buttersworth, 1979.
14. Willett, P. Recent trends in hierarchical document clustering: A critical review. *Information Processing & Management, 24*, 5, 1988, 577-597.
15. Yoo I., Hu X., and Song I.Y., Clustering Ontology-enriched Graph Representation for Biomedical Documents based on Scale-Free Network Theory, accepted in the *IEEE Conference on Intelligent Systems (IEEE IS'06)*, Sept 4-6, 2006.
16. Zamir, O., and Etzioni O. Web Document Clustering: A Feasibility Demonstration, In *Proceedings of SIGIR 98*, 1998, 46-54.

Automatic Extraction for Creating a Lexical Repository of Abbreviations in the Biomedical Literature

Min Song[1], Il-Yeol Song[2], and Ki Jung Lee[2]

[1] Information Systems Department, New Jersey Institute of Technology
University Heights, Newark, NJ 07102-1982, 01,
min.song,@njit.edu
[2] College of Information Science & Technology, Drexel University
Philadelphia, PA 19104
(215) 895-2474, 01
{song, leekijung}@drexel.edu

Abstract. The sheer volume of biomedical text is growing at an exponential rate. This growth creates challenges for both human readers and automatic text processing algorithms. One such challenge arises from common and uncontrolled usages of abbreviations in the biomedical literature. This, in turn, requires that biomedical lexical ontologies be continuously updated. In this paper, we propose a hybrid approach combining lexical analysis techniques and the Support Vector Machine (SVM) to create an automatically generated and maintained lexicon of abbreviations. The proposed technique is differentiated from others in the following aspects: 1) It incorporates lexical analysis techniques to supervised learning for extracting abbreviations. 2) It makes use of text chunking techniques to identify long forms of abbreviations. 3) It significantly improves Recall compared to other techniques. The experimental results show that our approach outperforms the leading abbreviation algorithms, ExtractAbbrev and ALICE, at least by 6% and 13.9%, respectively, in both Precision and Recall on the Gold Standard Development corpus.

1 Introduction

In parallel with the growth of the increase in the biomedical literature, the growth in biomedical terminology has been significantly increased. Since multiple names and abbreviations exist in many biomedical entities, it is desirable to have an automated means to collect these synonyms and abbreviations to help users conduct literature searches. In addition, automatic extraction of synonyms and abbreviations would facilitate text mining tasks if all of the synonyms and abbreviations for an entity could be mapped to a single term representing the context. A typical task in this line of research on information extraction is to uncover gene name synonyms and biomedical term abbreviations [4].

Understanding of abbreviations in documents is a challenging task for human readers and computers, particularly in the situation where large amounts of data to be digested increases at an exponential rate. The task of abbreviation extraction was reported to affect knowledge-intensive systems, such as information retrieval systems and information systems in the biomedical domains [2].

A Min Tjoa and J. Trujillo (Eds.): DaWaK 2006, LNCS 4081, pp. 384–393, 2006.

An abbreviation database would help users to understand and digest the content provided in the biomedical domain if the database lists abbreviations together with their senses and it is automatically updated periodically. Constructing abbreviation databases manually is a time-consuming and labor intensive task. In addition, manual maintenance and further extension are increasingly complex. As an effective and alternative approach, automatic construction of an abbreviation database has been proposed [2; 7].

There are several compelling reasons for why abbreviation extraction is a difficult task. First, an automatic method to associate an abbreviation to its corresponding expansion in the context is required, with an assumption that the authors define abbreviations when they are first introduced in a specific domain for the less well-known senses of abbreviations. Second, well-known senses of abbreviations are not always defined in the document where abbreviation is presented. Third, it requires a method to identify senses in documents, a method to group textual variants of the same sense together, and a method to link them to the proper sense in the corresponding sense inventory. Additionally, abbreviations are highly ambiguous: one abbreviation may represent dozens of senses. A method to resolve the sense ambiguity is needed.

In this paper, we propose a hybrid approach combining lexical analysis techniques and the Support Vector Machine (SVM) to create an automatically generated and maintained lexicon of abbreviations. The proposed technique is differentiated from others in the following aspects. 1) It incorporates lexical analysis techniques to supervised learning for extracting abbreviations. 2) It makes use of text chunking techniques to identify long forms of abbreviations. 3) It significantly improves recall compared to other techniques.

The rest of this paper is organized as follows: Section 2 summarizes the related work. Section 3 describes the overall architecture and methodology of our techniques. Section 4 describes the evaluation. Section 5 concludes the paper.

2 Related Work

In this section, we review existing studies on extracting abbreviations. Many studies use rule based algorithms and detection of parentheses as the core part of extracting valid abbreviated terms and matching them with appropriate expanded expressions.

Chang et al. [3] use an algorithm with a logistic regression technique to extract abbreviations. Their algorithm scores abbreviation expansions based on the similarity to a training set of human-annotated abbreviations from MEDLINE abstracts. Their system locates candidate abbreviations by identifying parentheses and set basis of its approach on the resemblance to a training set of human-annotated abbreviations. The algorithm is reported to have a maximum recall of 83% at 80% precision. Major limitations of their approach are that an abbreviation must be enclosed in parentheses and a set of rules applied to abbreviation extraction was not comprehensive compared to other rule-based extraction techniques.

Yu et al. [10] present a system (i.e., AbbRE) with a rule-based algorithm. Their system contains pattern-matching rules for mapping abbreviations to their full forms in biomedical text. AbbRE is reported to have an average 70% recall and 95%

precision for defined abbreviations. However, their experimental setup was limited to defined abbreviations which constitute only 25 percent of total abbreviations in biomedical articles as their own statistics identify.

Liu and Friedman [8] propose an algorithm based system to extract a set of related terms from the biomedical literature. The recall of the algorithm was around 88.5%, and its precision was 96.3%. The limitation of their approach is that the system is not suitable for identifying expansions that occur only once in a text.

Schwartz and Hearst [9] report a system with a simple algorithm based on the use of parentheses and ad hoc rules for identifying abbreviations' definitions in biomedical texts. It, first, extracts "short form-long form" pair candidates from a text and then identifies the correct long-form from the sentence that the paired short-form is enclosed. Their simple algorithm processes the extraction beginning from the end of both the short-form and the long-form, moves from right to left, checking the shortest long-form that matches the short-form. In order to be a valid extraction, each and every letter in the short-form must match a character in the long-form, while the matched characters in the long-form must be in the same order as the characters in the short-form. The algorithm has an experimental result of 82% of recall and a precision of 96%.

Ao and Takagi [1] describe an ad hoc algorithm called ALICE. ALICE identifies and extracts pairs of abbreviations and their expansions by using parentheses-searching and heuristic pattern-matching rules. In addition to the strategies used by Yu et al. [11] and Schwartz and Hearst [9], this algorithm uses manually expanded patterns, rules, and stop word lists. The authors argue that their system can potentially validate 320 abbreviation-expansion patterns as combinations of the rules. It is reported that the system achieved 95% recall and 97% precision on randomly selected titles and abstracts from the MEDLINE database. ALICE is reported to be limited to disambiguate synonyms and expansions.

Major drawback of presented studies is that they depend on heuristic rule for extraction of abbreviations and matching them with proper expanded expressions. By adopting a technique that identifies phrase groups by the SVM-based text chunking technique, our approach of abbreviation extraction is not limited to structural dependency of algorithms that looks for parenthetical expressions in a sentence. Moreover, pattern matching algorithm based on distance calculation provides more scalable process of abbreviation-expansion matching.

3   The Hybrid Abbreviation Extraction System

In this section, we describe the proposed hybrid abbreviation extraction system, called AbbrevExtractor, combining the Support Vector Machine-based noun chunking technique with pattern matching techniques. In Section 3.1, we present the system architecture of AbbrevExtractor. In Section 3.2, we discuss the noun chunking technique. Finally, Section 3.3 explains our abbreviation extraction algorithm.

3.1   The System Architecture

The system architecture of our hybrid abbreviation extraction system, AbbrevExtractor, is illustrated in Fig. 1. AbbrevExtractor consists of five major components: 1) data reader, 2) sentence parser, 3) noun chunker, 4)abbreviation matcher, 5) best-match selector component.

The Noun Chunker component applies a SVM-based text chunking technique. A typical text chunking algorithm seeks a complete partitioning of a sentence into chunks of different types [6]. Since our chunking technique requires identifying POS (Part-Of-Speech) tags for individual words, we incorporate Brill's POS Tagger into AbbrevExtractor. Brill's technique is one of the high quality POS tagging techniques.

The Best-Match Selector component identifies the correct long form from a set of candidate long forms within the sentence by computing the proximity of candidate long forms to a short form.

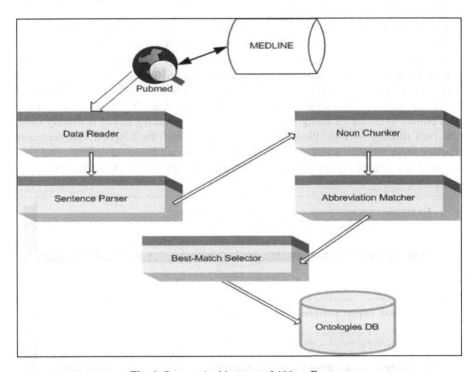

Fig. 1. System Architecture of AbbrevExtrator

The outline of the approach described in Figure 1 is as follows:
1) A query is submitted to Pubmed to retrieve MEDLINE documents.
2) A set of retrieved documents is read into AbbrevExtractor in the XML format.
3) Sentences are identified and parsed by the Sentence Parser component.
4) Each sentence is split into phrase groups by the SVM-based noun chunking component.
5) Short forms and candidate long forms are identified by the pattern matching-based Abbreviation Matcher component.

6) Correct long forms are determined and selected from candidate long forms by the best match selector component.

7) A pair of a short form and a long form is inserted into the database of Ontologies for abbreviations.

3.2 Sentence Chunking by SVM component

Text chunking is defined as dividing a text into syntactically correlated parts of words [6]. Chunking is recognized as a series of processes – first, identifying proper chunks from a sequence of tokens, and second, classifying these chunks into some grammatical classes. Major advantages of using text chunking over full parsing techniques are that partial parsing such as text chunking is much faster, more robust, yet sufficient for abbreviation extraction.

Support Vector Machine (SVM) based text chunking was reported to produce the highest accuracy in the text chunking task [6]. The SVMs-based approach such as other inductive-learning approaches takes as input a set of training example and finds a classification function that maps them to a class. SVMs are known to robustly handle large features [5]. This makes them an ideal model for abbreviation extraction. SVMs are particularly useful for real world data sets that often contain inseparable data points. Although training is generally slow, the resulting model is usually small and runs quickly as only the patterns that help define the function that separates positive from negative examples. In addition, SVMs are binary classifiers, and thus we need to combine several SVM models to obtain a multiclass classifier. Due to the

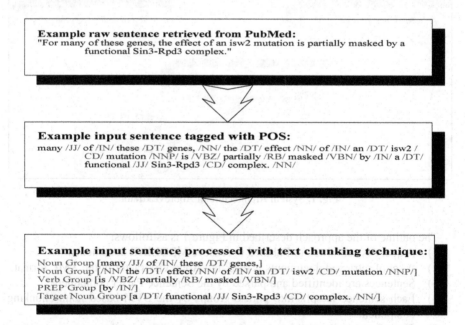

Fig. 2. A Procedure of Sentence Parsing (JJ denotes adjective, IN denotes preposition, DT denotes determiner, CD cardinal number, NN denotes singular noun, NNP denotes proper noun, VBZ and VBN denote verb, RB denotes adverb.)

nature of the SVM as a binary classifier it is necessary in a multi-class task to consider the strategy for combining several classifiers. In this paper, we use Tiny SVM [6] in that Tiny SVM performs well in handling a multi-class task.

Figure 2 illustrates the procedure of converting a raw sentence from PubMed to the phrase-based units grouped by the SVM text-chunking technique. The top box shows a sentence that is part of abstracts retrieved from PubMed. The middle box illustrates the parsed sentence by POS taggers. The bottom box shows the final conversion made to the POS tagged sentence by the SVM based text chunking technique.

3.3 Determination of Correct Short and Long Forms

AbbrevExtractor selects a short and candidate long forms within noun phrase groups. Given this prerequisite, AbbrevExtractor applies pattern matching-based rules to identify short forms and long forms, similar to ExtractAbbrev and ALICE.

In ExtractAbbrev, short forms are selected if the following conditions are satisfied: 1) it consists of at most two terms, and its length is between two to ten characters, at least one of the characters is a letter, and the first character is alphanumeric. Finding correct long forms is based on starting from the end of both the short form and the long form, moving right to left, trying to find the shortest long form that matches the short form. In ALICE, short forms are determined by the rules of nine discard conditions and four acceptance conditions. Long forms are selected by five discard conditions and 16 templates.

Compared to these ExtractAbbrev and ALICE, AbbrevXtractor identifies correct short and long forms within noun phrase groups. The selection rules for short forms are adapted from ExtractAbbrev [9]. The selection rules for candidate long forms are as follows: 1) The first word of the candidate long form is not in the first word list of candidate long forms. 2) The candidate long forms do not consist of only one word in the long form list. 3) The number of words in a noun group less than 10. 4) The characters in short forms are matched in capitalized characters in candidate long forms. 5) Candidate long forms are one word and the name of its POS is CD.

Once all the candidate long forms are identified, we compute distance between short form and candidate long forms, based on order it is presented in the sentence. Figure 3 shows how candidate long forms and a short form are located in a sentence. A candidate long form in the shortest distance with a short form is selected as the best matched long form.

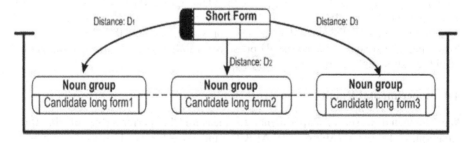

Fig. 3. Topology of Short and Candidate Long forms

4 Evaluation

In this section, we present the data collections used for the experiments, the experimental methods, and the other abbreviation extraction techniques for comparison. To evaluate AbbrevExtractor, we compare it with two other query expansion techniques: 1) ExtractAbbrev, a simple pattern-matching rule-based, 2) ALICE, a heuristic rule-based. Performance of these techniques is measured by the precision, recall, and F-measure. The data used for experiments are the Gold Standard Development and Evaluation corpus and ALICE corpus.

4.1 Data Collection

To evaluate our technique, we use ALICE corpus [1]. ALICE corpus was built with 1000 abstracts with titles that were randomly selected from the MEDLINE (PMID: 12500000 – 12599999). ALICE corpus was manually tagged with pairs of abbreviations and their expansions by experts. There were 1095 tagged abbreviation-expansion pairs.

We also use the Medstract Gold Standard Evaluation Corpus. The gold standard was created to help evaluate the algorithms used for information extraction and data mining in bioinformatics for the task of acronym identification. The gold standard is publicly available as an XML file at <http://www.medstract.org/gold-standards. html>.

4.2 ExtractAbbrev

We chose ExtractAbbrev to compare the performance of our technique in extracting abbreviations from MEDLINE. ExtractAbbrev is a pattern matching-based extraction system. It implements a simple algorithm for extracting abbreviations and their definitions from the biomedical text. It extracts abbreviation-definition candidates adjacent to parentheses. It finds correct definitions by matching characters in the abbreviation to characters in the definition, starting from the right. The first character in the abbreviation must match a character at the beginning of a word in the definition.

4.3 ALICE

We also compared our technique with ALICE [1]. ALICE is a rule-based extraction system that builds by searching parentheses and extracting pairs of abbreviations and their expansions by using heuristic pattern-matching rules. ALICE is composed of three phases, that is, the Inner Search (IS), the Outer Extraction (OE), and the Validity Judgment (VJ). The IS phase is for searching a candidate abbreviation and recognizing whether the candidate is an abbreviation or not, the OE phase is for extracting of its expansion, and the VJ phase is for judging the propriety of the pair of an abbreviation and its expansion.

4.4 Experimental Results

We conducted a set of experiments to measure the performance of the three techniques: 1) ExtractAbbrev, 2) ALICE, and 3) AbbrEx. F-measure combines precision and recall in order to provide a single number measurement for information extraction systems (1).

$$F_b = \frac{(b^2+1)\,PR}{b^2 P + R} \tag{1}$$

Here, P is precision and R is recall. If b=0, F becomes precision. If b= ∞, F becomes recall. Last, b=1 means that recall and precision are equally weighted. If b=0.5, it means that recall is half as important as precision. If b=2.0, it means recall is twice as important as precision. Because $0 \leq P, R \leq 1$, a larger value in the denominator means a smaller value overall. We also use recall and precision which are prevalent evaluation methods in IE.

Table 3, 4 and 5 respectively shows the overall performance of the three algorithms on Gold Standard Development and Evaluation data and ALICE corpus. The results indicate the improvements in precision and recall of each algorithm compared to its preceding algorithm. Among the algorithms, AbbrevExtractor in precision and recall shows the best improvement among the algorithms.

Table 3 shows the results of the performance among these three techniques on the Gold Standard Development data. As shown in Table 3, AbbrevExtractor outperforms the other two techniques from 8.8% to 13.2% better in F-measure. In precision, AbbrevExtractor is higher than the other two by 13.9% and 19.4%. In recall, AbbrevExtractor is higher than the other two by 6% and 9%. The second best technique is ALICE. ExtractAbbrev turns out to be ranked last.

Table 3. Results Obtained Using the Gold Standard Development Corpus

Algorithm	Gold Standard Development Corpus		
	Recall	Precision	F-measure
ExtractAbbrev	0.61	0.58	0.59
ALICE	0.63	0.62	0.62
AbbrevXtractor	0.67	0.72	0.68

Table 4 demonstrates that AbbrevExtractor outperforms the other two techniques from 4.2% to 5.6% higher in F-measure. In precision, AbbrevExtractor is higher than the other two by 3.8% and 14%. In recall, AbbrevExtractor is higher than the other two by 7.2% and 8.7%.

Table 4. Results Obtained Using the Gold Standard Development Corpus

Algorithm	Gold Standard Evaluation Corpus		
	Recall	Precision	F-measure
ExtractAbbrev	0.64	0.76	0.69
ALICE	0.63	0.68	0.68
AbbrevXtractor	0.69	0.79	0.72

Table 5 shows the results of the performance among these three techniques on ALICE data. As shown in Table 5, AbbrevExtractor outperforms ExtractAbbrev by 5.2% in F-measure. In precision, AbbrevExtractor outperforms ExtractAbbrev by 4.1%. In terms of F-measure and precision, AbbrevExtractor is equivalent to ALICE. In recall, AbbrevExtractor outperforms the other two by 2% and 8.2%.

Table 5. Results Obtained Using Gold Standard Development Corpus

Algorithm	ALICE Corpus		
	Recall	Precision	F-measure
ExtractAbbrev	0.89	0.93	0.91
ALICE	0.95	0.97	0.96
AbbrevXtractor	0.97	0.97	0.96

Overall, the results of the experiments show that AbbrevEXtractor achieves the best performance in Precision, Recall and F-measure.

5   Conclusion

We proposed a novel effective abbreviation extraction (AE) technique, called AbbrevExtractor. AbbrevExtractor is a hybrid AE technique that applies the SVM-based noun chunking with pattern matching-based rules to the abbreviation extraction problem. Our approach automatically identifies pairs of best long forms with its short forms (i.e., abbreviations).

The proposed technique is differentiated from others in the following aspects. 1) It incorporates lexical analysis techniques to supervised learning for extracting abbreviations. 2) It makes use of text chunking techniques to identify long forms of abbreviations. 3) It significantly improves recall compared to other techniques.

We also demonstrated our approach consistently performs better than the other two well-received systems for abbreviation extraction, ExtractAbbrev and ALICE. In terms of F-measure, AbbrevExtractor performed better than the other two by 4.1% to 14.1%. In terms of Precision and Recall, our technique outperforms ExtractAbbrev and ALICE by 3.8% to 19.4% and 2% to 9%, respectively.

As a follow-up study, we are developing an abbreviation server that connects to the PubMed server to retrieve MEDLINE records and extract abbreviations from the result sets. We are also conducting a series of experimental tests with a much bigger size of data to investigate whether the size of data influences on accuracy of extraction.

References

1. 1. Ao, H. and Takagi, T. (2005) ALICE: An algorithm to extract abbreviations from MEDLINE, *Journal of the American Medical Informatics Association*, 12: 576-586.
2. Aronson, A.R. (2001) Effective Mapping of Biomedical Text to the UMLS Metathesaurus: the MetaMap Program, *Proceedings of the AMIA Symposium*: 17-21.

3. Chang, J.T., Schütze, H. and Altman, R.B. (2002) Creating an Online Dictionary of Abbreviations from MEDLINE, *The Journal of the American Medical Informatics Association*, 9: 612-620.
4. Cohen, A. and Hersh, W. (2005) A Survey of Current Work in Biomedical Text Mining, *Briefing in Bioinformatics*, 6: 57-71.
5. Cortes, C. and Vapnik, V. (1995) Support-vector Networks, *Machine Learning*, 20: 273-297.
6. Kudo, T. and Matsumoto, Y. (2000) Use of Support Vector Learning for Chunk Identification, *Proceedings of the CoNLL-2000 and LLL-2000*: 142-144.
7. Liu, H., Aronson, A.R. and Friedman, C. (2002) A Study of Abbreviations in MEDLINE Abstracts, *Proceedings of the AMIA Annual Fall Symposium*: 64-69.
8. Liu, H. and Friedman, C. (2003) Mining Terminological Knowledge in Large Biomedical Corpora, *Proceedings of the Pacific Symposium on Biocomputing*, 8: 415-426.
9. Schwartz, A.S. and Hearst, M.A. (2003) A simple algorithm for identifying abbreviation definitions in biomedical text, *Proceedings of the Pacific Symposium on Biocomputing*, 8: 451-462.
10. Yu, H., Hripcsak, G. and Friedman, C. (2002) Mapping abbreviations to full forms in biomedical articles, *Journal of the American Medical Informatics Association*, 9: 162-172.
11. Yu, Z., Tsuruoka, Y. and Tsujii, J. (2003) Automatic Resolution of Ambiguous Abbreviations in Biomedical Texts using Support Vector Machines and One Sense Per Discourse Hypothesis, *Proceedings of the SIGIR*.

Priority-Based k-Anonymity Accomplished by Weighted Generalisation Structures

Konrad Stark[1], Johann Eder[2], and Kurt Zatloukal[1]

[1] Medical University Graz, Institute of Pathology, Auenbruggerplatz 25, A-8036 Graz
[2] University of Vienna, Department of Knowledge and Business Engineering, Rathausstrae 19/9 A-1010 Wien

Abstract. Biobanks are gaining in importance by storing large collections of patient's clinical data (e.g. disease history, laboratory parameters, diagnosis, life style) together with biological materials such as tissue samples, blood or other body fluids. When releasing these patient-specific data for medical studies privacy protection has to be guaranteed for ethical and legal reasons. k-anonymity may be used to ensure privacy by generalising and suppressing attributes in order to release sufficient data twins that mask patients' identities. However, data transformation techniques like generalisation may produce anonymised data unusable for medical studies because some attributes become too coarse-grained. We propose a priority-driven anonymisation technique that allows to specify the degree of acceptable information loss for each attribute separately. We use generalisation and suppression of attributes together with a weighting-scheme for quantifying generalisation steps. Our approach handles both numerical and categorical attributes and provides a data anonymisation based on priorities and weights. The anonymisation algorithm described in this paper has been implemented and tested on a carcinoma data set. We discuss some general privacy protecting methods for medical data and show some medical-relevant use cases that benefit from our anonymisation technique.

1 Introduction

When using patient-related data in medical research, the protection of patient privacy is of highest priority. Whenever data records containing sensitive patient data are released, the risk of patient reidentification has to be considered and suitable measures for data protection have to be found. To do this we use a concept of k-anonymity [7] which assures that each record describing a person contained in a released data set has at least k-1 data twins (similar records) in this set. Following the concept of k-anonymity various approaches ([4], [9], [10], [5], [6]) exist for transforming data in such a way as to avoid identification. On the one hand generalisations are used to transform attribute values to aggregated values depending on hierarchical structures. On the other hand, attribute values that may unmask individuals are simply suppressed. Each of these techniques provides privacy protection at the cost of data quality, since each transformation is associated with an *information loss*. This loss may be quantified [8], [2] in

A Min Tjoa and J. Trujillo (Eds.): DaWaK 2006, LNCS 4081, pp. 394–404, 2006.

order to detect an anonymisation providing the least information loss. However, the acceptable information loss may differ as the case arises. Some attributes should be generalised as little as possible while others may be transformed to more general values. Therefore, we propose a novel anonymisation technique that takes into account data quality requirements. We propose a hierarchical generalisation model that includes information loss quantifiers. Depending on the overall degree of information loss, a suitable generalisation solution can be found. Furthermore, the output of the anonymisation algorithm is strongly influenced by customizable priorities. By assigning priorities to attributes, the degree of preferred anonymisation is defined. Additionally, maximal generalisation limits guarantee that the transformed data set is applicable to subsequent processing. We use descriptive meta-data information of the data set to be released in order to check for data twins. The concept was developed in the context of the Austrian Genome Programme GEN-AU [3] and as preliminary work for the biobank initiative of the Medical University Graz [1]. We developed a virtual data warehouse solution where patient data (personal data, anamnesis, lifestyle data, clinical analysis data) and gene expression data is integrated and materialized in a data mart which then supports analytical queries. A critical part of this system is the support of tissue and patient data selection and the anonymisation of data. The released data should not allow the identification of the individual and the anonymisation process should generate data that is still applicable for medical research. Our anonymisation technique manages to fulfill both demands if possible: Released records meet the k-anonymity requirement and the degree of acceptable information loss may be specified by user-defined priorities. The rest of the paper is organized as follows: We introduce our meta data model in section 2 and show what kind of meta data about the released data set and hierarchies is needed. In section 3 preprocessing work for medical data is described. The anonymisation algorithm and its various parameters are presented in section 4. Finally, we give a short overview of our prototype implementation in 5 and a summary and an outlook on our future activities in 6.

2   Meta-data Model

A record set R is a table containing a set of tuples $t(id, \nu_1, .., \nu_n)$ where id is the unique tuple id and n is the number of table attributes. Let QI be the set of table attributes and a single attribute is denoted as $\alpha_i \in QI$. The concept of k-anonymity [4] requires that each distinct value combination of quasi-identifying attributes occurs at least k times in the released data ($|(\nu_1, .., \nu_n)| \geq k$). Hence, we determine each distinct value combination in the following way: Let $R*$ be the multiset accomplished by the projection of $[R - id]$. Then an equivalence relation 'equal values for all α_i' may be defined on $R*$. That relation defines a partition on $R*$ in equivalence classes. Each equivalence class $[class_i]$ is generated for a certain attribute value combination $(\nu_1, .., \nu_n)$ and has an associated cardinality c_i counting the number of its elements. We store the set of $[class_i]$ in the *aggregated data table* T_{Agg} to check the k-anonymity constraint for a certain attribute value combination. Each attribute α_i has an associated generalisation hierarchy that allows to transform an attribute value to a more general value. Each transformation is denoted as **generalisation step**. Formally, a generalisation step may be defined as a function $generalise : \Upsilon \mapsto \Upsilon'$. Record set $\Upsilon \subseteq R$ is transformed to record set Υ' in the following way:

$\forall\, t \in \Upsilon,\, t = t(id, \nu_1, .., \nu_n) \bullet \exists\, t' \in \Upsilon',\, t' = t(id, \nu'_1, .., \nu'_n)$ that satisfies following conditions:

1. $\exists\, i,\, 1 < i < n \bullet \nu'_i = generalisedValue(\nu_i)$
2. $\forall\, j \neq i \bullet \nu'_j = \nu_j$

In other words, each tuple is transformed by replacing an attribute value of a certain α_i with a more general value. We distinguish between a **dimension hierarchy** that describes the hierarchical scheme of an attribute and a **member hierarchy** describing the hierarchy of attribute values. While the member hierarchy is used to transform record values to generalised values, the dimensional hierarchy is used for evaluation of generalisation steps.

2.1   Dimensional Hierarchy

A dimensional hierarchy is composed of generalisation levels. Let the lowest generalisation level be L_0, at that level all attribute values remain unchanged. Let L_{max} be the maximal generalisation level for a certain α_i. At this level, all values of an attribute α_i are combined to a single generalised value. The highest generalisation level corresponds to the suppression of the attribute, since a general *all* value has as much information as a masked out attribute. Generalisations are always associated with an **information loss**, since an attribute value is transformed to a less specific value. By applying a sequence of consecutive generalisation steps, the information loss is accumulated. However, the data quality decrease is not necessarily equal for each generalisation step along the hierarchy. For instance, consider the generalisation of patient age values 10, 12, 16, 20. If 10 and 12 are generalised to [10-15] and 16 and 20 are generalised to [16-20], less information is lost than by generalising all four values to [10-20]. Table 1 shows another example from the medical research domain. Tumour staging T specifies the size of the tumour and its local spread. Stage T is a numeric value in the range from 1-4 combined with prefixes for subclassification, such as 'a', 'b', 'c' or 'mic'. By applying two generalisation steps value classification "1a" is transformed into "1-2". Staging T is determined by the size of the primary tumour. While for instance in breast cancer, tumours with a greatest dimension of 2 cm

Table 1. Staging T

$$"1a", "1b" \mapsto ["1"] \qquad L_0 \mapsto L_1$$
$$"2a", "2b", "2c" \mapsto ["2"] \quad L_0 \mapsto L_1$$
$$"1", "2" \mapsto ["1-2"] \qquad L_1 \mapsto L_2$$

are classified as T1, tumours with a greatest dimension of minimal 2 and maximal 5 cm are classified as T2. The transformation from $L_0 \mapsto L_1$ is of different quality than transformation $L_1 \mapsto L_2$, since the difference among the subclassifications "1a","1b" and "1c" is smaller than the one among the classifications "1" and "2". In order to weight data transformations we introduced a quality criterion for each generalisation step. φ is an estimation metric specifying how the goodness of information is affected by a generalisation step. It measures the information loss for attribute α_i at a certain generalisation level. We will refer to φ also as *penalty*. It is 0 at L_0 and 1 at L_{max}. Information loss quantifiers φ_j are assigned to all intermediate generalisation levels L_j, $0 < j < max$. Each attribute hierarchy has to be evaluated separately by carefully choosing ascending values that appropriately reflect the data quality at each step. Penalties are included in the dimension hierarchy which consists of simple level relationships modelling the generalisation levels: $step(\alpha_i, L_{Parent}, L_{Child}, \varphi)$. Attribute α_i is subject to an incremental informational loss when being generalised from level *Child* to level *Parent*, whereas the total accumulated information loss compared to L_0 is given in φ. The accumulated information loss φ_{Parent} for attribute α_i and level L_{Parent} is calculated as follows: Let ψ be the relative (subjectively chosen) information loss between levels *Parent* and *Child* then if there is a relation $step(\alpha_i, L_{Child}, L_{Child-1}, \varphi_{Child})$, $\varphi_{Parent} = \psi + \varphi_{Child}$, else $\varphi_{Parent} = \psi$. We assume an equal information loss for each generalisation level. That is, penalties need not be included in the member hierarchy. By assigning penalties generalisation steps become weighted and comparable to each other. The anonymisation algorithm is capable of searching within a weighted graph and can create generalisations on basis of minimal information loss.

2.2   Member Hierarchy

Each attribute α_i ($\alpha_i \in QI$) takes its values from a certain domain D_i. Generally, we distinguish two types of domains: *Nominal/ordinal* domains and *numeric* domains. Depending on the type of domain different generalisation strategies are applicable. Attributes with nominal or ordinal data types are typically generalised using a predefined generalisation hierarchy. Attributes of numeric domain type may also be generalised with a predefined (interval-based) hierarchy. Additionally, numeric values may be mapped to categories (e.g.: blood pressure) or they could be aggregated dynamically without predefined hierarchies. A set of relations model a member hierarchy for one attribute. Formally, a hierarchical member relation is defined as follows: $parent(\alpha_i, Parent, Child)$. The attribute identifier α_i has to be unique, *Parent* is the generalised value of *Child*, whereas *Child* could be either a generalised value itself or a value from the attribute domain. Alternative hierarchies may be modelled in the same way as multiple parents are assignable to the same child. For numerical attributes with predefined intervals additional relations are necessary: $interval(Ident, From, To)$. *Ident* corresponds to a generalised *Parent* value of the above-mentioned relation. *From* and *To* specify the interval borders. Intervals do not need an explicit assignment from attribute values to certain intervals, since the membership to a range may be easily calculated on-the-fly. A possible interval mapping for patients' age could be as follows:

$parent(patientAge, "0 - 40", "0 - 20")$
$parent(patientAge, "0 - 40", "20 - 40")$
$parent(patientAge, "40 +", "40 - 60")$
$parent(patientAge, "40 +", "60 +")$
$interval("0 - 20", 0, 20)$
$interval("20 - 40", 21, 40)$
$interval("40 - 60", 41, 60)$
$interval("60 +", 61, \infty)$
$interval("0 - 40", 0, 40$
$interval("40 +", 41, \infty)$

We assume predefined intervals as disjunctive, that is, each attribute value is mapped to exactly one interval on the same generalisation level.

3   Preprocessing Steps

Attributes that are not obviously linked to individuals still have to be investigated carefully. An unique value for one or a set of non-sensitive attributes allows reidentification of an individual. For instance, if the surgery date, height and weight of a certain patient are known, this information may be matched against a released table of the surgery. It is unlikely that a large patient collective with the same characteristics is operated on the same day. Hence, the patient's individuality could not be preserved and additional individual information like blood parameters and diagnosis could be unveiled. In order to limit the disclosure risk some attributes may be transformed preemptively to less specific values. This, however, requires that there is no relevant information loss for each transformed attribute in the domain of application. Therefore, the attribute set of the table to be released has to be scanned thoroughly to identify attributes with low or no information content at all. While superfluous attributes are simply skipped, domain-relevant attributes may be recoded. That is, the values range of one (*single attribute recoding*) or the combination of multiple attributes (*attribute combination recoding*) is mapped to either a computed or categorical range. In the following application-specific examples for preprocessing a medical data set are given.

Attribute elimination: Attributes that are immediately related to patients' identities are removed from the released data set. First name, surname, day of birth and address of the patient are eliminated. While sensitive information is necessary for daily medical routine activities, there is no need to disclose such private data to medical studies.

Substitution: Before filtering the patient's birthday, the relative age of the patient is determined by calculating the period of time between a medical relevant event and the day of birth. For instance a medical study monitoring different courses of disease for liver carcinoma is interested in the patient age at the moment the initial diagnosis was made. Further, the period of time between tumour resection and local recurrence should be used in statistical analysis. In both cases date types are transformed to relative values: patient age at initial diagnosis = initial diagnosis date - day of birth, disease free survival = local recurrence date - tumour resection date.

Categorical recoding: Attributes with a broad range easily permit reidentification of individuals if only a few or no data twins at all are available for distinctive attribute values. By standardising/categorising those attributes the information content is preserved and privacy protection could be facilitated. Medical diagnoses frequently have a variety of notations and abbreviations for describing identical diseases. Typically, diagnoses are stored in large free text fields allowing different spellings, abbreviations and synonyms. Thus, even in huge patient collectives diagnosis texts may be unique for one patient. This problem can be solved by introducing international codes like ICD-N (International Classification of Diseases) or ICD-O (International Classification for Oncology). In addition to privacy protection the use of classifiers facilitates data queries and makes individual cases more comparable with each other.

Attribute combination recoding: In some cases multiple attributes may be summarized to one code. Individual-related characteristics like height and weight are combinable to a BMI (body mass index) measure. Furthermore, blood pressure and age may be mapped to the categories of low, normal and high.

4   Anonymisation Algorithm

The aim of the algorithm is to find a suitable anonymisation solution that satisfies k-anonymity and user-specific requirements. That is, the search takes into account quality aspects of attribute generalisations mentioned in section 2.1 and is driven by contextual preferences.

4.1   Priorities and Limits

Priorities are used to specify the degree of desired anonymisation of attributes. In some cases exact values for a specific attribute may be favored while the generalisation degree of others is negligible. By specifying priorities the user is able to determine the degree of generalisation and information loss he is willing to cope with. Attributes with lower priorities are generalised first while attributes with higher priorities are only generalised when no other solution may be found. A priority p_i is assigned to each attribute α_i. Priorities have values in the range $[0, .., 1]$. The most important attribute has the highest priority value and all differences between any two consecutive priorities values are equal. The following example illustrates the equally scaled priority values:
$StagingT \hookleftarrow 0.2$, $StagingN \hookleftarrow 0.4$, $StagingM \hookleftarrow 0.6$, $PatientAge \hookleftarrow 0.8$

Priorities are used to weight the information loss quantifiers of generalised attribute values. Hence, in the final generalisation solution the information loss for attribute *PatientAge* should be much smaller than for attribute *StagingT*. In other words, attribute *StagingT* might be transformed to a more general value than attribute *PatientAge*. In some cases, attributes should be generalised only up to a certain degree or not transformed at all. Otherwise, their values become useless for an application domain. Therefore, it's crucial to allow definition of maximal limits for information loss, someone is willing to cope with. If an attribute value should be excluded from generalisation its limit is set to L_0.

4.2   Search Space

Generally, an anonymisation algorithm looks for an acceptable generalisation solution by trying various combinations of single attribute generalisations. Since no information about the attributes' value distribution may be deduced from the member hierarchy, a blind search would try all possible combinations of single attribute generalisations. The total number of possible generalisations may be calculated as follows: $\prod_{i=1}^{n} Lmax_i$, where $Lmax_i$ is the maximal generalisation level for attribute α_i and n is the number of all attributes. The set of possible generalisations form a search space lattice, where each search node contains generalisation levels of all attributes $\alpha_i \in QI$. In the initial node, each α_i is at generalisation level L_0, while the end node consists of generalisation levels $(Lmax_1,..,Lmax_n)$. Let η be the set of search nodes and let the search nodes be connected to each other by edges. Then, $\forall\ n_p, n_q \in \eta,\ n_p \neq n_q,\ n_p = (lp_1,..,lp_n) \wedge n_q = (lq_1,..,lq_n) \bullet edge(n_p, n_q) \rightarrow (\exists\ i \bullet lp_i = L_x \wedge lq_i = L_{x+1}) \wedge (\forall\ j \neq i \bullet lp_j = lq_j)$
The search space lattice defined above allows anonymisation of a certain tuple set by performing a sequence of generalisation steps until the k-anonymity condition holds. Each edge of the lattice stands for one generalisation step and each search node represents the state after the generalisation step has been applied. Without any additional information, a standard breadth-first search would look for a generalisation solution by simply concatenating anonymisation steps between nodes. Finally, it would return the first found generalisation solution that satisfies k-anonymity. The breadth-first algorithm guarantees to find a generalisation solution if one exists. Though, there is no way of ranking all generalisation solutions that could be created. Therefore, our anonymisation algorithm utilizes a combination of actual generalisation levels and user-defined priorities for ranking paths in the search space.

4.3   Match Operator

Generalisation steps aim at increasing the number of data twins of a released record set. In order to calculate the number of data twins a generalised tuple has we introduce a match operator. That operator determines a set of matched tuples MS for a given tuple t and record set RS: $matchedSet(t, RS) \rightarrow MS$. We search for matched tuples in the aggregated table T_{Agg} defined in section 2, whereas the cardinality column is not considered in the search. Two tuples t and

Table 2.

MATCH	STAGINGT	STAGINGN	STAGINGM	COUNTER
	"1a"	"1"	"1"	1
X	"1b"	"2"	"1"	1
	"1c"	"1"	"1"	1
	"1a"	"2"	"1"	2
	"1b"	"2"	"1"	1

Table 3.

MATCH	STAGINGT	STAGINGN	STAGINGM	COUNTER
	"1a"	"1"	"1"	1
X	"1b"	"2"	"1"	1
	"1c"	"1"	"1"	1
X	"1a"	"2"	"1"	2
	"1a","1b","1c"	"2"	"1"	3

t' can be matched if their corresponding attribute values can be unified. Two attribute values ν and ν' can be unified $\nu \doteq \nu'$ if one of the following conditions holds:

1. $\nu = \nu'$
2. ν is a generalised value of ν' along the member hierarchy

That is, $t = (\nu_1, .., \nu_n)$ matches $t' = (\nu'_1, .., \nu'_n)$ if $\forall \, \nu_i, \nu'_i, 1 \leq i \leq n \bullet \nu_i \doteq \nu'_i$. To determine the set of tuples that match a certain tuple a search pattern P_t may be defined. P_t is a list of sets $(S_1, .., S_n)$ that is defined for a certain tuple $t = (\nu_1, .., \nu_n)$ as follows: If ν_i is a generalised value then S_i is the set of its leaf nodes in the member hierarchy, otherwise $S_i = \{\nu_i\}$. Hence, we can define a set of tuples $t' \in MS$ that may be matched with tuple t if

1. $t' = (\nu'_1, .., \nu'_n)$
2. $P_t = (S_1, .., S_n)$
3. $\forall \, \nu'_i \, 1 \leq i \leq n \bullet \nu'_i \in S_i$

Consider the following example: Table 2 shows an aggregated table T_{Agg} with 4 entries $(vk_1, .., vk_4)$. Tuple $t_1 = t("1b", "2", "1")$ should be released. The number of data twins of t_1 is assessed by looking for an entry in T_{Agg} that match with t_1. The last row in table 2 specifies the *search pattern* for t_1. Entry vk_2 shows that t_1 has no data twin. Hence, t_1 is generalised by applying the generalisation step "1b" $\mapsto$ ["1"]) on staging T attribute. Now, vk_1 and vk_3 match with t_1 and two addionally data twin were generated as shown in table 3. When staging M is generalised by generalisation step "1" $\mapsto$ ["1 − 2"], t_1 has 4 data twins (table 4).

Table 4.

Match	StagingT	StagingN	StagingM	Counter
X	"1a"	"1"	"1"	1
X	"1b"	"2"	"1"	1
X	"1c"	"1"	"1"	1
X	"1a"	"2"	"1"	2
	"1a","1b","1c"	"1","2"	"1"	5

4.4 Algorithm Specification

```
Input:   Record set to be released, PriorityList,
         Limits, k-anonymity parameter
Output: Anonymised record set
```

1. Determine k-anonymity violating records

   Let Υ be the record set to be released, k the anonymity parameter. Let $priorV = (p_1, .., p_n)$ be the vector of priorities and let $limV = (lim_1, .., lim_n)$ the vector of limits for n attributes. Vector $costV = (cost_1, .., cost_n)$ stores the generalisation cost for each attribute. Let $v[attributeName]$ be the projection operation to access the associated value for attribute $attributeName$ in structure v (could be vector or tuple). For lack of space we do not include the treatment of alternative hierarchies. Let vk_i be an entry of the aggregated table T_{Agg}, then Γ is the record set that violates the k-anonymity constraint:

   $\forall\, t_i \in \Gamma \bullet t_i \in \Upsilon \wedge t_i = (\nu_1, .., \nu_n) \wedge \exists\, vk_i = (\nu_1, .., \nu_n, c_i) \wedge c_i < k$

2. Initialize the generalisation level vector

   The generalisation level vector $levelV = (l_1, .., l_n)$ reflects the current generalisation levels for all n attributes. Initially, all levels are set to 0.

   $while(\Gamma \neq \emptyset)$

   $do\ steps\ 3, 4, 5$

3. Determine attribute to be generalised

   α_g is the attribute to be generalized and is determined by the function $minimum(costV)$. Among all attributes, α_g is the attribute that has the minimal weighted information loss after being transformed to the next generalization level.

   $for\ all\ \alpha_i \in QI$

       $cl = levelV\,[\alpha_i]$

       $step(\alpha_i, L_{pl}, L_{cl}, \varphi)$

       $if(pl \geq limV\,[\alpha_i])$

           $costV\,[\alpha_i] = \infty$

       $else$

           $costV\,[\alpha_i] = \varphi * priorV\,[\alpha_i]$

   $end\ for$

   $\alpha_g = minimum(costV)$

If all costs of *costV* are ∞, no solution on the basis of given priorities and limits can be found. The anonymisation has to be started with a different parameter setting.

4. Generalise Γ

   The generalisation step is applied to all $t_i \in \Gamma$. In every tuple α_g value is replaced by its generalised value.

   for all $t_i \in \Gamma$

       $value = t_i [\alpha_g]$

       $parent(\alpha_g, GenValue, value)$

       $t_i [\alpha_g] = GenValue$

   end for

   Finally, the level vector has to be adapted:

   $levelV [\alpha_g] = levelV [\alpha_g] + 1$

5. Match tuples

   The set of matched tuples is determined for each tuple as described in section 4.3. Tuples, that fulfill the k-anonymity constraint are excluded from further search. *sumCardinalities* sums up the cardinality values of *matchedTuples*.

   for all $t_i \in \Gamma$

       $matchedTuples = matchedSet(t_i, T_{Agg})$

       $counter = sumCardinalities(matchedTuples)$

       $if(counter \geq k)$

           $\Gamma = \Gamma \setminus t_i$

   end for

       If no violating tuple is left, $(\Gamma = \emptyset)$, a suitable generalisation has been found.

   $if(\Gamma = \emptyset)$

       The set of necessary generalisation steps are applied to every record of the data set to be released

5   Prototype Implementation

The anonymisation algorithm has been implemented in SWI Prolog. Both hierarchy description and data description models are mapped to prolog facts. In order to fill the metadata models the data set to be released has to be analyzed accurately. Attribute values with dentical semantics may be coded in multiple ways due to spelling messings or synonyms. We had to screen all value occurrences and recode them to standardized values adequately. Moreover, defining hierarchies suitable for medical studies and weighted generalisation steps turned out to be a challenging task. Our example data set consists of 8,124 patients with carcinoma extracted from the tissue sample database of the Institute of Pathology, Medical University of Graz. For simplicity, a small subset of four attributes was chosen for anonymisation: tumour staging T, staging N, staging M and age of patients. 925 distinct value combinations were identified, whereas nearly 50 % of all patients have unique value combinations for those attributes. We used categorical hierarchies for the staging attributes and an interval-based hierarchy for the patient age. The prototype allows to check whether the k-anonymity constraint holds on a certain data set and it generates generalisation transformations for each record violating that constraint. Priorities and generalisation limits may be specified and included in the anonymisation process. Search for alternative generalisations and evaluation of acceptable solutions will be implemented in the next steps.

6   Conclusion

We have presented an anonymisation algorithm that takes different weights for attribute generalisations. On the one hand, penalties are assigned to generalisation steps allowing to quantify each transformation and measure the overall information loss. On the other hand, priorities can be used to reflect changing requirements of data quality. Important attributes may be protected from extensive generalisations while non-relevant attributes are transformed to more general values. Moreover, generalisation limits can be declared for each attribute separately to guarantee that the anonymised data meet medical study criteria. We will focus on the comparisons of alternative generalisation solutions, the modelling of alternative hierarchies and dynamic generalisations of numerical attributes in our future work.

References

1. A biobank for the advancement of medicine. *http://www.bioresource-med.com*.
2. Benjamin C. M. Fung, Ke Wang, and Philip S. Yu. Top-down specialization for information and privacy preservation. In *ICDE*, pages 205–216, 2005.
3. Genomeresearch in Austria. *http://www.gen-au.at/english/content.jsp*.
4. LatanyaSweeney. Computational disclosure control for medical microdata, 1997.
5. Kristen LeFevre, David J. DeWitt, and Raghu Ramakrishnan. Incognito: Efficient full-domain k-anonymity. In *SIGMOD Conference*, pages 49–60, 2005.
6. Kristen LeFevre, David J. DeWitt, and Raghu Ramakrishnan. Multidimensional k-anonymity. In *Technical Report 1521, University of Wisconsin, 2005.*, 2005.
7. L. Sweeney P. Samarati. Protecting privacy when disclosing information: k-anonymity and its enforcement through generalization and suppression. *Proceedings of the IEEE Symposium on Research in Security and Privacy*, 1998.
8. P. Samarati. Protecting respondents' identities in microdata release. *IEEE Transactions on Knowledge and Data Engineering*, 13(6):1010–1027, 2001.
9. Latanya Sweeney. Achieving k-anonymity privacy protection using generalization and suppression. *Int. J. Uncertain. Fuzziness Knowl.-Based Syst.*, 10(5):571–588, 2002.
10. Ke Wang, Philip S. Yu, and Sourav Chakraborty. Bottom-up generalization: A data mining solution to privacy protection. In *ICDM*, pages 249–256, 2004.

Achieving k-Anonymity by Clustering in Attribute Hierarchical Structures

Jiuyong Li[1], Raymond Chi-Wing Wong[2], Ada Wai-Chee Fu[2], and Jian Pei[3]

[1] Department of Mathematics and Computing, The University of Southern Queensland,
Australia
[2] Department of Computer Science and Engineering, The Chinese University of Hong Kong
[3] School of Computing Science, Simon Fraser University, Canada
jiuyong@usq.edu.au, cwwong, adafu@cse.cuhk.edu.hk, jpei@cs.sfu.ca

Abstract. Individual privacy will be at risk if a published data set is not properly de-identified. k-anonymity is a major technique to de-identify a data set. A more general view of k-anonymity is clustering with a constraint of the minimum number of objects in every cluster. Most existing approaches to achieving k-anonymity by clustering are for numerical (or ordinal) attributes. In this paper, we study achieving k-anonymity by clustering in attribute hierarchical structures. We define generalisation distances between tuples to characterise distortions by generalisations and discuss the properties of the distances. We conclude that the generalisation distance is a metric distance. We propose an efficient clustering-based algorithm for k-anonymisation. We experimentally show that the proposed method is more scalable and causes significantly less distortions than an optimal global recoding k-anonymity method.

1 Introduction

A vast amount of operational data and information has been stored at different vendors and organizations. Most of the stored data is useful only when the data is shared and analysed with other related data. However, this kind of data normally contains some personal details and sensitive information. The data can only be allowed to be released when the private information is protected.

More and more powerful data mining tools require a large amount of data from various sources to produce promising results. On the other hand, these powerful data mining tools may be maliciously used to uncover personal-related sensitive information in data. Therefore, privacy preservation becomes a fundamental issue in data mining.

Cryptographic technique is a choice since it can hide data from unauthorised users. However, cryptographic methods may restrict data access and exchange too much. Furthermore, cryptographic privacy-preserving methods [15,22,24] usually tailor some specific data mining tasks, and therefore lose generality.

Random perturbation can provide certain privacy protection [5,4,18], but they are suitable for data of numerical attributes. When data contains categorical values, the methods are not quite effective.

Data generalisation is applicable to both categorical and numerical data, and k-anonymity provides a practical model for privacy protection [21,20,19]. Since the

A Min Tjoa and J. Trujillo (Eds.): DaWaK 2006, LNCS 4081, pp. 405–416, 2006.

k-anonymity model is simple and practical, it has been extensively studied in recent years [14,6,23,10,13]. A more general view of k-anonymisation is clustering with a constraint of the minimum number of objects in every cluster [3]. A number of methods approach identity protection by clustering [4,1]. However, these methods are applicable to numerical attributes only. A recent work [9] extends a clustering-based method [8] to ordinal attributes, but it does not deal with attributes in hierarchical structures. Other works [2,17] dealing with categorical attributes do not consider attribute hierarchies. In this paper, we focus our effort on achieving k-anonymity in hierarchical attribute structures. We define some general metrics in attribute hierarchies for measuring the quality of k-anonymous tables, and map them to generalisation distances which can be minimised in the process of k-anonymisation. This greatly facilitates achieving k-anonymity by local recoding via clustering. To the best of our knowledge, this work is the first work to do such mapping. We also present an efficient algorithm for this purpose, and demonstrate that our method causes less distortions than an optimal k-anonymity algorithm.

2   Preliminary Definitions

The objective of k-anonymisation is to make every tuple of privacy-related attributes in a published table identical to at least $(k - 1)$ other tuples. As a result, no privacy-related information can be easily inferred.

For example, young people with stress and obesity are potentially identifiable by their unique combinations of gender, age and postcode attributes in Table 1a.

To preserve their privacy, we may generalise their gender and postcode attribute values such that each tuple in attribute set {Gender, Age, Postcode} has two occurrences. The view after the generalisation is listed in Table 1b.

Table 1. (a) Left: a raw table. (b) Middle: a 2-anonymous view by local recoding. (c) Right: a 2-anonymity view by global recoding.

Gender	Age	Pcode	Problem	Gender	Age	Pcode	Problem	Gender	Age	Pcode	Problem
male	middle	4350	stress	male	middle	4350	stress	*	middle	435*	stress
male	middle	4350	obesity	male	middle	4350	obesity	*	middle	435*	obesity
male	young	**4351**	stress	*	young	**435***	stress	*	young	435*	stress
female	young	**4352**	obesity	*	young	**435***	obesity	*	young	435*	obesity
female	old	4353	stress	female	old	4353	stress	*	old	435*	stress
female	old	4353	obesity	female	old	4353	obesity	*	old	435*	obesity

In this paper, we adopt a simplified postcode scheme, where its hierarchy {4201, 420*, 42**, 4***, *} corresponds to {suburb, city, region, state, unknown}, respectively.

Definition 1 (Quasi-identifier Attribute Set). *A quasi-identifier attribute set is a set of attributes in a table that potentially reveal private information, possibly by joining with other tables.*

For example, attribute set {Gender, Age, Postcode} in Table 1a is a quasi-identifier. Table 1a potentially reveals private information of patients (e.g. young patients with stress and obesity). If the table is joined with other tables, it may reveal more information of patients' disease history. Normally, a quasi-identifier attribute set is understood by domain experts.

Definition 2 (equivalence class). *An equivalence class of a table with respect to an attribute set is the set of all tuples in the table containing identical values for the attribute set.*

For example, tuples 1 and 2 in Table 1a form an equivalence class with respect to attribute set {Gender, Age, Postcode}. Their corresponding values are identical.

Definition 3 (k-anonymity Property). *A table is k-anonymous with respect to a quasi-identifier if the size of every equivalence class with respect to the attribute set is k or more.*

k-anonymity requires that every occurrence within an attribute set has the frequency at least k. For example, Table 1a does not satisfy 2-anonymity property since tuples {male, young, 4351} and {female, young, 4352} occur once.

Definition 4 (k-anonymisation). *A view of a table is said to be a k-anonymisation of the table if the view modifies the table such that the view satisfies the k-anonymity property with respect to the quasi-identifier.*

For example, Table 1b is a 2-anonymous view of Table 1a since the size of all equivalence classes with respect to the quasi-identifier is 2.

A table may have more than one k-anonymous views, but some are better than others. For example, we may have another 2-anonymous view of Table 1a as in Table 1c. Table 1c loses more details than Table 1b. Another objective for k-anonymisation is to minimise distortions. We will give a definition of distortion later. Initially, we consider it as the number of cells being modified.

There are two ways to achieve k-anonymity, namely *global recoding* and *local recoding*. Another name for global recoding is *domain generalisation*. The generalisation happens at the domain level. When an attribute value is generalised, every occurrence of the value is replaced by the new generalised value. Most working models are global recoding models, such as [20,14,6,19,12,23,10] [1]. A global recoding method may *over-generalise* a table. An example of global recoding is given in Table 1c.

A local-recoding method generalises attribute values at cell level. A generalised attribute value co-exists with the original value. A local recoding method does not over-generalise a table and hence may minimise the distortion of an anonymous view. Sweeney studied a local recoding model, but did not present a working local recoding algorithm [21,20]. Sweeney's MinGen algorithm is impractical and DataFly is a global recoding algorithm. Gagan Aggarwal et al. [2] and Adam Meyerson et al. [17] analysed

---

[1] [13] also considers global-recoding. However, the definition is different from our work and most previous work. Suppose there are three dimensions (A, B, C). In their global-recoding model, for each possible value (a, b, c) (where $a \in A, b \in B$ and $c \in C$), all tuples with this value in the data set should be generalised to the same value. However, this formulation is actually a local-recoding in our work and most previous work.

a simplified local recoding model that does not involve hierarchical attributes. Both papers conclude that optimal k-anonymisation is NP-hard. μ- and τ-Argus methods [11], are two working local recoding methods, but μ-Argus does not guarantee k anonymity as discovered in [20]. τ-Argus works efficiently only on limited number of attributes. More recent work of local recoding k-anonymisation was reported in [13] by LeFevre et al. The method deals with numerical values, and does not involve attribute domain hierarchies. An example of local recoding is given in Table 1b.

A global-recoding method causes too much distortions to a table. It is preferable to use a local-recoding method. However, optimal local-recoding is NP-hard [2,17] [2]. Therefore, good heuristic methods are required to achieve k-anonymisation by local recoding.

The objectives of k-anonymisation by local recoding is listed as follows.

- to modify a table to satisfy the k-anonymity property, and
- to minimise the distortion of the view from its original table.

3   Measuring the Quality of k-anonymisation

In this section, we discuss metrics for measuring the quality of generalisation.

A general criterion should be the distortion of a table. A simple measurement of distortion is the *modification rate*. For a k-anonymous view V of table T, the *modification rate* is the fraction of cells being modified within the quasi-identifier attribute set. For example, the modification rate from Table 1a to Table 1b is 22.2% and the modification rate from Table 1a to Table 1c is 66.7%.

This criterion does not consider hierarchical structures. For example, the distortion caused by the generalisation of birth date from D/M/Y to M/Y is significantly different from the distortion caused by the generalisation of gender from M/F to *. The former still keeps most information of Birth Date but the latter loses all information for Gender. The modification rate is too simple to reflect such differences.

We calculate distortions of two tables based on distortions of their corresponding tuple pairs. We first define a metric measuring the distance between different levels in an attribute hierarchy.

Definition 5 (Weighted Hierarchical Distance). *Let h be the height of a domain hierarchy, and let levels $1, 2, \ldots, h-1, h$ be the domain levels from the most general to most specific, respectively. Let the weight between domain level j and $j - 1$ be predefined, denoted by $w_{j,j-1}$, where $2 \leq j \leq h$. When a cell is generalised from level p to level q, where $p > q$. The weighted hierarchical distance of this generalisation is defined as*

$$\text{WHD}(p, q) = \frac{\sum_{j=q+1}^{p} w_{j,j-1}}{\sum_{j=2}^{h} w_{j,j-1}}$$

---

[2] To the best of our knowledge, the global local-recoding K-anonymity problem defined in this paper has not been shown to be NP-hard in the literature. As the definition of the global recoding in [13] is different from ours, the result of the NP-hardness shown in [13] can be regarded for the local-recoding problem in our work.

The right part of Figure 1a shows the numbering methods of hierarchical levels and the left part of Figure 1a shows weights between hierarchical levels. Level 1 is always the most general level of a hierarchy and contains one value.

We can define weight $w_{j,j-1}$ to enforce a priority in generalisation. In the following, we discuss two simple but typical schemes.

1. Uniform Weight: $w_{j,j-1} = 1$, where $2 \leq j \leq h$

This is the simplest scheme where all weights are equal to 1. In this scheme, WHD is the number of steps a cell being generalised over all possible generalisation steps, e.g. $h - 1$. For example, let birth date hierarchy be {D/M/Y, M/Y, Y, 10Y, C/Y/M/O, *}, where 10Y stands for 10-year interval and C/Y/M/O for child, young, middle age and old age. WHD from D/M/Y to Y is $\text{WHD}(6,4) = (1+1)/5 = 0.4$. In gender hierarchy, {M/F, *}, WHD from M/F to * is $\text{WHD}(2,1) = 1/1 = 1$. This means that the distortion caused by the generalisation of five cells from D/M/Y to Y is equivalent to the distortion caused by the generalisation of two cells from M/F to *.

As this scheme is quite simple, this does not capture that the generalisations at different levels yield different distortions. It is expected that the generalisation near to the root should distort the data more compared with the generalisation far from the root. We take the address for illustration. Suppose the address contains three components - street no, street name and postcode. For example, the address is "20, Smith Street, Pcode 4351". Let us consider two generalisations - the generalisation G_1 from "20, Smith Street, Pcode 4351" to "Smith Street, Pcode 4351" and the generalisation G_2 from "Pcode 4351" to "Pcode 435*". It is obvious that G_1 (i.e. the removal of the street no) corresponds to a smaller distortion while G_2 (i.e. the removal of the suburb) corresponds to a larger distortion, because the area coverage by the suburb, of course, is larger than the area coverage by a housing (denoted by the street no). This example motivates us to propose another scheme.

2. Height Weight: $w_{j,j-1} = 1/(j-1)^{\beta}$ where $2 \leq j \leq h$ and β is a real number ≥ 1 provided by a user.

For a fixed β, the intuition of this scheme is that the generalisation near to the top should give greater distortion compared with the generalisation far from the top. Thus, we formulate the height weight scheme, where the weight near to the top is larger and the weight far from the top is smaller. For example, consider a hierarchy: {D/M/Y, M/Y, Y, 10Y, C/Y/M/O, *} for birth date. Let $\beta = 1$. WHD from D/M/Y to M/Y is $\text{WHD}(6,5) = (1/5)/(1/5 + 1/4 + 1/3 + 1/2 + 1) = 0.087$. In gender hierarchy {M/F, *}, WHD from M/F to * is $\text{WHD}(2,1) = 1/1 = 1$. The distortion caused by the generalisation of one cell from M/F to * in gender attribute is more than the distortion caused by the generalisation of 11 cells from D/M/Y to M/Y in birth date attribute.

In some cases, users prefer that the weight near to the leaf node should be equal to a smaller value (compared with the case when $\beta = 1$). Then, in this model, we allow this requirement. In order to satisfy this kind of requirement, we simply set the β value with a larger value (e.g. 2) such that the weight near to the leaf node is smaller.

There are other possible other schemes for various applications.

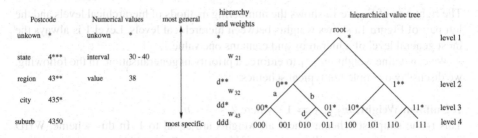

Fig. 1. (a) Left: Two examples of domain hierarchies - one for categorical values and one for numerical values. (b) Right: Depiction of weights between domain levels and a simplified hierarchical value tree.

In the following, we define distortions caused by the generalisation of *tuples* and *tables*.

Definition 6 (Distortions of Generalisation of Tuples). *Let* $t = \{v_1, v_2, \ldots, v_m\}$ *be a tuple and* $t' = \{v'_1, v'_2, \ldots, v'_m\}$ *be a generalised tuple of* t. *Let* $\text{level}(v_j)$ *be the domain level of* v_j *in an attribute hierarchy. The distortion of this generalisation is defined as*

$$\text{Distortion}(t, t') = \sum_{j=1}^{m} \text{WHD}(\text{level}(v_j), \text{level}(v'_j))$$

For example, let the weights of WHD be defined by the uniform weight, attribute Gender be in hierarchy of $\{M/F, * \}$ and attribute Postcode be in hierarchy of $\{dddd, ddd*, dd**, d***, * \}$. Let t_3 be tuple 3 in Table 1a and t'_3 be tuple 3 in Table 1b. For attribute Gender, WHD $= 1$. For attribute Age, WHD $= 0$. For attribute Postcode, WHD $= 1/4 = 0.25$. Therefore, Distortion$(t_3, t'_3) = 1.25$.

Definition 7 (Distortions of Generalisation of Tables). *Let view* D' *be generalised from table* D, t_i *be the* i-*th tuple in* D *and* t'_i *be the* i-*th tuple in* D'. *The distortion of this generalisation is defined as*

$$\text{Distortion}(D, D') = \sum_{i=1}^{|D|} \text{Distortion}(t_i, t'_i)$$

where $|D|$ *is the number of tuples in* D.

From Table 1a and 1b, WHD$(t_1, t'_1) = $ WHD$(t_2, t'_2) = $ WHD$(t_5, t'_5) = $ WHD(t_6, t'_6) $= 0$ and WHD$(t_3, t'_3) = $ WHD$(t_4, t'_4) = 1.25$. The distortion between the two tables is Distortion$(D, D') = 1.25 + 1.25 = 2.5$.

4   Generalisation Distances

In this section, we map distortions to distances and discuss the properties of the mapped distances.

4.1 Distances Between Tuples and Equivalence Classes

An objective of k-anonymisation is to minimise the overall distortions between a generalised table and the original table. We first consider how to minimise distortions when generalising two tuples into an equivalence class.

Definition 8 (Closest Common Generalisation). *All allowable values of an attribute form a hierarchical value tree. Each value is represented as a node in the tree, and a node has a number of child nodes corresponding to its more specific values. Let t_1 and t_2 be two tuples. t_{12} is the closest common generalisation of t_1 and t_2 for all i. The value of the closest common generalisation t_{12} is*

$$
v_{12}^i = \begin{cases} v_1^i & \text{if } v_1^i = v_2^i \\ \text{the value of the closest common ancestor} & \text{otherwise} \end{cases}
$$

where, v_1^i, v_2^i, and v_{12}^i are the values of the i-th attribute in tuples t_1, t_2 and t_{12}.

For example, Figure 1b shows a simplified hierarchical value tree with 4 domain levels and $2^{(l-1)}$ values for each domain level l. Node 0** is the closest common ancestor of nodes 001 and 010 in the hierarchical value tree. Consider another example. Let $t_1 = \{male, young, 4351\}$ and $t_2 = \{female, young, 4352\}$. $t_{12} = \{*, young, 435*\}$.

Now, we define the distance between two tuples.

Definition 9 (Distance between Two Tuples). *Let t_1 and t_2 be two tuples and t_{12} be their closest common generalisation. The distance between the two tuples is defined as*

$$
\text{Dist}(t_1, t_2) = \text{Distortion}(t_1, t_{12}) + \text{Distortion}(t_2, t_{12})
$$

For example, let the weights of WHD be defined by the uniform weights, attribute Gender be in hierarchy of $\{M/F, *\}$ and attribute Postcode be in hierarchy of $\{dddd, ddd*, dd**, d***, *\}$. $t_1 = \{male, young, 4351\}$ and $t_2 = \{female, young, 4352\}$. $t_{12} = \{*, young, 435*\}$. $\text{Dist}(t_1, t_2) = \text{Distortion}(t_1, t_{12}) + \text{Distortion}(t_2, t_{12}) = 1.25 + 1.25 = 2.5$. We discuss some properties of tuple distance in the following.

Lemma 1. *Basic properties of tuple distances*
(1) $\text{Dist}(t_1, t_1) = 0$ (i.e. a distance between two identical tuples is zero)
(2) $\text{Dist}(t_1, t_2) = \text{Dist}(t_2, t_1)$ (i.e. the tuple distance is symmetric), and
(3) $\text{Dist}(t_1, t_3) \leq \text{Dist}(t_1, t_2) + \text{Dist}(t_2, t_3)$ (i.e. the tuple distance satisfies triangle inequality)

Proof. The first two properties obviously follow Definition 9b. We prove property 3 here.

We first consider a single attribute. To make notions simple, we omit the superscript for the attribute. Let v_1 be the value of tuple t_1 for the attribute, v_{13} be the value of the generalised tuple t_{13} for the attribute from tuple t_1 and tuple t_3, and so forth.

Within a hierarchical value tree, $\text{Dist}(t_1, t_3)$ is represented as the shortest path linking nodes v_1 and v_3 and $\text{Dist}(t_1, t_2) + \text{Dist}(t_2, t_3)$ is represented as the path linking v_1

and v_3 via v_2. Therefore, $\text{Dist}(t_1, t_3) \leq \text{Dist}(t_1, t_2) + \text{Dist}(t_2, t_3)$. The two distances are equal only when v_2 is located within the shortest path between v_1 and v_3.

The overall distance is the sum of distances of all individual attributes. The above proof is true for all attributes. Therefore, the property 3 is proved.

An example of Property 3 can be found in the hierarchial value tree of Figure 1b. The distance between 00* and 011 is $(a + b + c)$, the distance between 00* and 010 is $(a+b+d)$, and the distance between 010 and 011 is $(c+d)$. Therefore, $\text{Dist}(00*, 011) < \text{Dist}(00*, 010) + \text{Dist}(010, 011)$. In a special case, $\text{Dist}(00*, 011) = \text{Dist}(00*, 01*) + \text{Dist}(01*, 011)$.

Now, we discuss distance between two groups of tuples.

Definition 10 (Distance between Two equivalence classes). *Let C_1 be an equivalence class containing n_1 identical tuples t_1 and C_2 be an equivalence class containing n_2 identical tuples t_2. t_{12} is the closest common generalisation of t_1 and t_2. The distance between two equivalence classes is defined as follows.*
$$\text{Dist}(C_1, C_2) = n_1 \times \text{Distortion}(t_1, t_{12}) + n_2 \times \text{Distortion}(t_2, t_{12})$$

Note that t_{12} is the tuple that t_1 and t_2 will be generalised if two equivalence classes C_1 and C_2 are merged into one equivalence class. The distance is equivalent to the distortions of the generalisation and therefore the choice of merger should be those equivalence classes with the smallest distances.

5   Algorithm

In this section, we present an algorithm to implement k-anonymisation by local recoding.

The basic idea for the algorithm is finding an arbitrary equivalence class of size smaller than k and merging it with the closest equivalent classes to form a larger equivalent class with the smallest distortion. This process repeats recursively until each equivalent class contains at least k tuples.

We first discuss how to handle the situation that a small equivalent class (e.g. the class containing one tuple) merges to a large equivalent class (e.g. the class containing a hundred of tuples). Should we generalise the whole large equivalent class in order to absorb the small equivalent class? We should not. A better solution is to allocate a small number of tuples. For example, k-1 tuples from the large equivalent class are allocated to merge with the small equivalent class. As a result, information in most tuples of the larger equivalent class is preserved. the set of the tuples allocated in this way is called a *stub* and the set of the remaining tuples is called a *trunk*.

Definition 11 (Stub and Trunk of Equivalent Class). *Suppose a small equivalent class E_1 and a large equivalent class E_2 are to be generalised for k-anonymity. If $|E_1| < k$ and $|E_1| + |E_2| \geq 2k$, E_2 is split into two parts, a stub and a trunk. The stub contains $(k - |E_1|)$ tuples, and the trunk contains $(|E_1| + |E_2| - k)$ tuples.*

After this split, both the generalised equivalent class of E_1 with the stub and the remaining trunk of E_2 satisfy k-anonymity property. The detailed information in the trunk is preserved.

After this definition, we calculate the distance between two equivalent classes E_1 and E_2, where $|E_1| < k$, as follows.

- if $(|E_1| + |E_2| < 2k)$, calculate normal as in Definition 10.
- if $(|E_1| + |E_2| \geq 2k)$, calculate the distance between E_1 and the stub of E_2.

The pseudo code of the proposed algorithm is presented in Algorithm 1.

Algorithm 1. K-Anonymisation by Clustering in Attribute hierarchies (KACA)

1: form equivalence classes from the data set
2: **while** there exists an equivalence class of size $< k$ **do**
3:     randomly choose an equivalence class C of size $< k$
4:     evaluate the pairwise distance between C and all other equivalence classes
5:     find the equivalence class C' with the smallest distance to C
6:     generalise the equivalence classes C and C'
7: **end while**

Line 1 forms equivalent classes. Sorting data in a certain order will speed up the process. One tuple is also called an equivalent class. Normally, the number of equivalent classes is significantly less than the number of tuples in the data set.

The generalisation process continues in lines 2-6 when there is one or more equivalence classes whose size is smaller than k.

In each iteration, we randomly find an equivalence class C of size smaller than k in line 3. Then, we calculate the pairwise distances between C and all other equivalence classes in line 4. Line 5 finds the equivalence class C' with the smallest distance. Line 6 generalises the equivalence classes C and C'.

The above process terminates when there is no equivalent class whose size is smaller than k. The sizes of all equivalent classes are greater than or equal to k, and hence k-anonymity is achieved.

All tuples are sorted and only $O(n)$ passes is needed to find all equivalent classes. The complexity of this step is $O(n\log n)$. Let $|E|$ be the number of equivalent classes in line 2. Each iteration requires to choose an arbitrary equivalence class, which takes $O(1)$ time, evaluate the pairwise distance, which takes $O(|E|)$ time, find the equivalence class with the smallest distance, which takes $O(|E|)$ time, and finally generalise the equivalence class, which takes $O(1)$ time. Thus, the runtime of an iteration is $O(|E|)$. As there are $O(|E|)$ iterations, the overall runtime is $O(n\log n + |E|^2)$.

The above algorithm is easy to extend to handle outlier tuples, which are far away from all other tuples, by setting a minimum distance threshold in line 6 to avoid large distortions caused by generalising two distant equivalent classes. Outlier tuples are suppressed instead of generalised. We did not do this in this algorithm since in the next section we compare an optimal algorithm that does not suppress tuples.

6   Empirical Study

A Pentium IV 2.2GHz PC with 1GM RAM was used to conduct our experiments. The algorithm was implemented in C/C++. In our experiments, we adopted the publicly available data set, Adult Database, from the UCIrvine Machine Learning Repository [7]. This

Table 2. Description of Adult Data Set

	Attribute	Distinct Values	Generalisations	Height
1	Age	74	5-, 10-, 20-year ranges	4
2	Work Class	7	Taxonomy Tree	3
3	Education	16	Taxonomy Tree	4
4	Martial Status	7	Taxonomy Tree	3
5	Occupation	14	Taxonomy Tree	2
6	Race	5	Taxonomy Tree	2
7	Sex	2	Suppression	1
8	Native Country	41	Taxonomy Tree	3
9	Salary Class	2	Suppression	1

data set (5.5MB) was also adopted in [14,16,23,10]. We also used a configuration similar to [14,16]. We eliminated the records with unknown values. The resulting data set contains 45,222 tuples. Nine attributes were chosen as the quasi-identifier, as shown in Table 2.

We evaluated the proposed algorithm in terms of two measurements: execution time and distortion ratio. Let T be the original data set and T' be the data set generalised by an algorithm. Let T'' be the fully generalised data set, where all attributes of all tuples are generalised to the root of the hierarchy. Distortion ratio of a generalised data set T' is equal to the distortion of T' divided by the distortion of T''.

We conducted the experiments ten times and took the average execution time. We compared our algorithm KACA proposed with the best-known global recoding based algorithm Incognito [14].

We conducted the experiments with two types of distortion measures discussed in Section 3 - uniform weight and height weight. Figure 2 shows the results with uniform weight measurement.

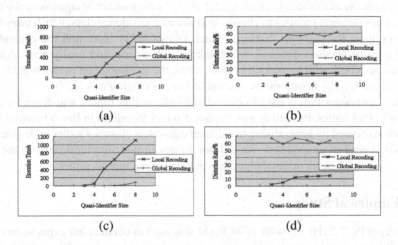

Fig. 2. Execution Time and Distortion Ratio Versus Quasi-identifier Size (Uniform Weight) ($k = 2$ for (a) and (b) and $k = 10$ for (c) and (d))

Figure 2 shows that the execution time of both algorithms increases with the quasi-identifier size. On average, the execution time of the KACA algorithm is larger than that of the Incognito algorithm.

The distortion ratio increases with the quasi-identifer size. This is because it is less likely that two tuples in the original data set are equal to each other when the quasi-identifier size is greater. Thus, a larger distortion is needed. The distortion ratio of the KACA algorithm is 5.57 times lower than that of the Incognito algorithm on average. This is because, as we discussed before, the global recoding algorithm (Incognito algorithm) over-generalises the data set a lot while the KACA algorithm generalises the data set less extent for k-anonymity. When k increases, the distortion ratio of all algorithms increases. As we require more tuples to be identical for larger k, more distortions will be generated for larger k.

We have also conducted the experiments with height weight measurement. For the sake of space, we do not show the results as the results with height weight measurement are similar to Figure 2.

7   Conclusions

In this paper, we study how to achieve k-anonymity by clustering in attribute hierarchies. We define two general metrics of the generalised data sets to measure the quality of k-anonymisation. We define generalisation distances between tuples to characterise distortions of generalisations and discuss the properties of the distances. We conclude that the generalisation distance satisfies properties of metric distances. We propose an efficient algorithm to achieve k-anonymity by clustering in attribute hierarchical structures. We experimentally show that the proposed method causes significantly less distortions than an optimal global recoding k-anonymity method. The distortion ratio of our proposed algorithm is 5.57 times smaller on average.

Acknowledgement

This research was supported by the Innovation and Technology Fund (ITF) in the HKSAR [ITS/069/03] and the RGC Earmarked Research Grant of HKSAR CUHK 4120/05E. This research has also been partially supported by ARC Grant DP0559090, NSERC Grant 312194-05, and NSF Grant IIS-0308001.

References

1. C. C. Aggarwal. On k-anonymity and the curse of dimensionality. In *VLDB '05: Proceedings of the 31st international conference on Very large data bases*, pages 901–909. VLDB Endowment, 2005.
2. G. Aggarwal, T. Feder, K. Kenthapadi, R. Motwani, R. Panigrahy, D. Thomas, and A. Zhu. Anonymizing tables. In *ICDT05: Tenth International Conference on Database Theory*, pages 246–258, 2005.
3. G. Aggarwal, T. Feder, K. Kenthapadi, A. Zhu, R. Panigrahy, and D. Thomas. Achieving anonymity via clustering in a metric space. In *PODS '06: Proceedings of the twentieth ACM SIGMOD-SIGACT-SIGART symposium on Principles of database systems*, 2006.

4. D. Agrawal and C. C. Aggarwal. On the design and quantification of privacy preserving data mining algorithms. In *PODS '01: Proceedings of the twentieth ACM SIGMOD-SIGACT-SIGART symposium on Principles of database systems*, pages 247–255, New York, NY, USA, 2001. ACM Press.

5. R. Agrawal and R. Srikant. Privacy-preserving data mining. In *Proc. of the ACM SIGMOD Conference on Management of Data*, pages 439–450. ACM Press, May 2000.

6. R. Bayardo and R. Agrawal. Data privacy through optimal k-anonymization. In *ICDE05: The 21st International Conference on Data Engineering*, pages 217–228, 2005.

7. E. K. C. Blake and C. J. Merz. UCI repository of machine learning databases, http://www.ics.uci.edu/~mlearn/MLRepository.html, 1998.

8. J. Domingo-Ferrer and J. M. Mateo-Sanz. Practical data-oriented microaggregation for statistical disclosure control. *IEEE Transactions on Knowledge and Data Engineering*, 14(1):189–201, 2002.

9. J. Domingo-Ferrer and V. Torra. Ordinal, continuous and heterogeneous k-anonymity through microaggregation. *Data Mining and Knowledge Discovery*, 11(2):195–212, 2005.

10. B. C. M. Fung, K. Wang, and P. S. Yu. Top-down specialization for information and privacy preservation. In *ICDE05: The 21st International Conference on Data Engineering*, pages 205–216, 2005.

11. A. Hundepool and L. Willenborg. μ-and τ- argus: software for statistical disclosure control. In *Third international seminar on statsitcal confidentiality*, Bled, 1996.

12. V. S. Iyengar. Transforming data to satisfy privacy constraints. In *KDD '02: Proceedings of the eighth ACM SIGKDD international conference on Knowledge discovery and data mining*, pages 279–288, 2002.

13. K. LeFevre, D. DeWitt, , and R. Ramakrishnan. Multidimensional k-anonymity. In *M. Technical Report 1521, University of Wisconsin*, 2005.

14. K. LeFevre, D. J. DeWitt, and R. Ramakrishnan. Incognito: Efficient full-domain k-anonymity. In *SIGMOD '05: Proceedings of the 2005 ACM SIGMOD international conference on Management of data*, pages 49–60, 2005.

15. Y. Lindell and B. Pinkas. Privacy preserving data mining. *Journal of Cryptology*, 15(3):177–206, 2002.

16. A. Machanavajjhala, J. Gehrke, and D. Kifer. *l*-diversity: privacy beyond *k*-anonymity. In *To appear in the 22st International Conference on Data Engineering (ICDE06)*, 2006.

17. A. Meyerson and R. Williams. On the complexity of optimal k-anonymity. In *PODS04: Proceedings of the twenty fourth ACM SIGMOD-SIGACT-SIGART symposium on Principles of database systems*, pages 223–228, 2004.

18. S. Rizvi and J. Haritsa. Maintaining data privacy in association rule mining. In *Proceedings of the 28th Conference on Very Large Data Base (VLDB02)*, pages 682–693. VLDB Endowment, 2002.

19. P. Samarati. Protecting respondents' identities in microdata release. *IEEE Transactions on Knowledge and Data Engineering*, 13(6):1010–1027, 2001.

20. L. Sweeney. Achieving k-anonymity privacy protection using generalization and suppression. *International journal on uncertainty, Fuzziness and knowldege based systems*, 10(5):571 – 588, 2002.

21. L. Sweeney. k-anonymity: a model for protecting privacy. *International journal on uncertainty, Fuzziness and knowldege based systems*, 10(5):557 – 570, 2002.

22. J. Vaidya and C. Clifton. Privacy-preserving k-means clustering over vertically partitioned data. In *The Ninth ACM SIGKDD International Conference on Knowledge Discovery and Data Mining*, pages 24–27, Washington, DC, 2003. ACM Press.

23. K. Wang, P. S. Yu, and S. Chakraborty. Bottom-up generalization: A data mining solution to privacy protection. In *ICDM04: The fourth IEEE International Conference on Data Mining*, pages 249–256, 2004.

24. R. Wright and Z. Yang. Privacy-preserving bayesian network structure computation on distributed heterogeneous data. In *KDD '04: Proceedings of the tenth ACM SIGKDD international conference on Knowledge discovery and data mining*, pages 713–718, New York, NY, USA, 2004. ACM Press.

Calculation of Density-Based Clustering Parameters Supported with Distributed Processing

Marcin Gorawski and Rafal Malczok

Silesian University of Technology,
Institute of Computer Science,
Akademicka 16,
44-100 Gliwice, Poland
{Marcin.Gorawski, Rafal.Malczok}@polsl.pl

Abstract. In today's world of data-mining applications there is a strong need for processing spatial data. Spatial objects clustering is often a crucial operation in applications such as traffic-tracking systems or telemetry-oriented systems. Our current research is focused on providing an efficient caching structure for a telemetric data warehouse. We perform spatial objects clustering for every level of the structure. For this purpose we employ a density-based clustering algorithm. However efficient and scalable, the algorithm requires an user-defined parameter *Eps*. As we cannot get the *Eps* from user for every level of the structure we propose a heuristic approach for calculating the *Eps* parameter. Automatic *Eps* Calculation (AEC) algorithm analyzes pairs of points defining two quantities: distance between the points and density of the stripe between the points. In this paper we describe in detail the algorithm operation and interpretation of the results. The AEC algorithm was implemented in both centralized and distributed version. Included test results compare the two versions and verify the AEC algorithm correctness against various datasets.

1 Introduction

In today's world of computer science and computer applications there is a strong need for processing spatial data. There are on-line services providing very precise and high-quality maps created from satellite images [2]. Another example is traffic tracking in big cities, which results are later used to support decisions of building new bypasses, highways and introducing other rationalizations. More very interesting details can be found in [1].

One very important branch of spatial systems is telemetry. We are working on a telemetric system of integrated meter readings. The system consist of utility meters, collecting nodes and telemetric servers. The meters are located in blocks of flats, housing developments etc. They meter water, natural gas and energy usage and send the readings to the collecting nodes via radio. The collecting nodes

A Min Tjoa and J. Trujillo (Eds.): DaWaK 2006, LNCS 4081, pp. 417–426, 2006.

collect the readings and send them to the telemetric servers through the Ethernet network. Apart from meter readings, the data warehouse database stores information about meters' geographical location, and their attributes (e.g. meter type, installation date etc).

The most typical use for the described data warehouse is to investigate the consumption of the utilities. Our current research is focused on providing fast and accurate answers to spatial aggregate queries. We are in the process of designing and implementing a hierarchical caching structure dedicated for telemetry-specific data. We named the structure a Clustered Hybrid aR-Tree (CHR-Tree) because we intend to use clustering to create the structure nodes, and, like in the aR-Tree [5], the structure nodes store aggregates.

We already have a solution to a problem of storing and processing the aggregates in the CHR-Tree nodes [4]. Currently we are trying to construct the structure of the CHR-Tree. To create the intermediate level nodes we employ density-based clustering algorithm. We decided to use the DBRS algorithm [6]. Although efficient and scalable, the algorithm requires an user-defined parameter Eps. Eps is a parameter defining a half of the range query square side. The side length is used by the clustering algorithm to evaluate range queries when searching for neighboring points. As we cannot get the Eps parameter from the user for every level of the structure, we propose a heuristic approach for calculating the Eps parameter. We named the algorithm an Automatic Eps Calculation (AEC) algorithm. The algorithm is not limited to the telemetry-specific data and can be applied to any set of two-dimensional points. In the following sections we provide an extensive description of the AEC algorithm and its operation and implementation versions. We present also tests results proving that the AEC algorithm is applicable to sets of two-dimensional points of a wide variety and cardinality.

2   AEC Algorithm

As mentioned above, to apply the DBRS algorithm in our research we must be able to define the Eps parameter for proper clustering process. To the best of our knowledge, there is no automatic method for calculating or even estimating the Eps parameter for the density-based clustering. Authors of the DBScan algorithm proposed in [3] a simple heuristics to determine the Eps and $MinPts$ parameters. However, the heuristics cannot be considered automatic as it requires user interaction. In this section we present an Automatic Eps Calculation (AEC) algorithm which, basing on the points distribution characteristics, is able to calculate the Eps parameter value. The sets of points analyzed by the algorithm may be large, hence the amount of processed data must be limited. A random sampling approach alllows obtaining good results in acceptable time.

2.1   Algorithm Coefficients

A dataset containing all points is marked P. The AEC algorithm creates two sets of points. The first set N contains points randomly chosen from the set P.

A function creating the N set takes one optional parameter r, that defines the region from which the points are being picked. When the r parameter is present during the N set generation, we mark the set with an appropriate subscript: N_r. The second set H also contains points randomly picked from the P set. The function creating the set, next to the r optional parameter, whose meaning is identical as for the N set, takes another parameter defining the point that is skipped during random points drawing. The H sets are created for points from the N set. The notation H_{r,n_i} means that the H set was created for the point $n_i \in N$; the point n_i was skipped during random points drawing and the points in H are located in a region r.

The cardinalities of N and H sets are the AEC algorithm parameters. Thanks to the parameterization of those values we can easily control the algorithm precision and operation time. The cardinality of the N set is defined as the percent of the whole P set. The cardinality of the H set is defined directly by the number of points creating the set.

The AEC algorithm coefficients are calculated using the N and H sets. The algorithm picks random points from the set P creating the set N. In the next step, for each point $n_i \in N$ the algorithm creates set H_{n_i}.

Distance Between Points. The first AEC algorithm coefficient is a distance between two points. The distance analysis is based on calculating the Euclidean distances between the point n_i and all the points from the related H_{n_i} set. The distances are calculated for all points in the N set and all related H sets.

Points In Stripe and Stripe Density To evaluate the *Eps* parameter the AEC algorithm requires the knowledge about the neighborhood of the analyzed points; actually about the points in the region between the investigated points p_i and p_j. We decided to introduce a coefficient PIS (Points In Stripe). The value of $PIS(p_i, p_j)$ is the number of points located in a *stripe* connecting the points p_i and p_j. To evaluate the PIS coefficient value for a pair of points we use one spatial query and four straight lines equations. Having the p_i and p_j points coordinates we can easily calculate the parameters a and b of the straight line L equation $y = ax + b$. The line L contains the points p_i and p_j. In the next step we calculate equations of the lines perpendicular to L in points p_i and p_j, respectively L_{p_i} and L_{p_j} (we do not include the equations because of the complicated notation and straightforward calculations). The final step is to calculate two lines parallel to L, the first above line $L - L_a$ and the second below line $L - L_b$. The distance between the parallel lines and the L line (the difference in the b line equation coefficient) is defined as a fraction of the distance between points p_i and p_j. The fraction is the AEC algorithm parameter named *stripeWidth*; $stripeWidth \in (0,1)$. The lines create a *stripe* between the points, and the *stripe* encompasses some number of points (fig. 1).

Having the lines equations we can easily calculate, whether an arbitrary point from the set P is located inside the stripe between points p_i and p_j or not. In order to reduce the number of points being analyzed we evaluate a rectangle encompassing the whole stripe. The rectangle vertexes coordinates are set by calculating the coordinates of the points where the stripe-constructing lines (L_a, L_b, L_{p_i} and L_{p_j}) cross, and then choosing the extreme crossing points coordinates. Using the stripe-encompassing rectangle we execute the range query, to choose the points which can possibly be located within the stripe between p_i and p_j. In the next step, only the points chosen by the range query are examined whether they are located within the stripe.

Basing on the distance between points: $dist(p_i, p_j)$ and the number of points in a stripe between points $PIS(p_i, p_j)$ we calculate another coefficient which is a density of the stripe between p_i and p_j: $dens(p_i, p_j) = \frac{PIS(p_i,p_j)}{dist(p_i,p_j)^2 \cdot stripeWidth}$.

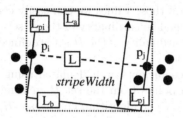

Fig. 1. Stripe between p_i and p_j points containing two points

Equipped with the distance and stripe density coefficients we are able to ascertain whether two points are relatively close to each other, and whether they are located in dense neighborhood. Our approach is not to search for a distance between points in clusters or for the thinnest cluster diameter, but rather for a minimal distance between clusters. The distance, or at least a value based on the distance, can be used as the *Eps* parameter in the density-based clustering algorithm. Using a minimal distance between clusters as the *Eps* parameter should result in grouping all the points whose distances to their closest neighbors are shorter than the minimal distance between clusters (they are in one cluster) and not grouping points when the distance between them is greater than the minimal distance between clusters.

2.2   Algorithm Operation

The AEC algorithm applies an iterative approach. In every iteration the algorithm tries to minimize the possible minimal distance between clusters. In the first step the algorithm sets the initial average distance between clusters $dist_{init}$ and related initial density $dens_{init}$. The values must be set in a way that they reduce the number of iterations to minimum, but on the other hand does not narrow down the set of possible solutions. After many experiments we decided to use an average distance between randomly selected points, and average density related to the distance. The calculation of the initial values uses the N and H sets.

The iterative section of the algorithm performs the following steps:

1. If the current iteration is the first iteration, assume that the current minimum distance between clusters $dist_{cur} = dist_{init}$, and the respective current density is $dens_{cur} = dens_{init}$.
2. Create a new N set, in a way described in subsection 2.1.
3. For every point $n_i \in N$ create a rectangle r_{n_i}, which vertexes coordinates are given by the following equation:
   $r_{n_i}(left, top, right, bottom) = r_{n_i}(n_i.x - dist_{cur}, n_i.y + dist_{cur}, n_i.x + dist_{cur}, n_i.y - dist_{cur})$.
4. For every point $n_i \in N$ create a set $H_{r_{n_i}, n_i}$ skipping the point n_i.
5. Evaluate an average density of the r_{n_i} rectangle.
6. For every point n_i, and points from the related H_{n_i} set calculate a set of quantities: distance, PIS and density of the stripe between points.
7. From all the results choose the shortest distance, for which the $PIS > 0$ and the density is less than the average density of the r_{n_i}. If there is no such result, do not return anything.
8. Compare the result obtained for the point n_i with the current values of $dist_{cur}$ and $dens_{cur}$. If $dist_i < dist_{cur}$ and $dens_i <= dens_{cur}$ then update the current values of minimal distance and minimal density between clusters: $dist_{cur} := dist_i$ and $dens_{cur} := dens_i$. If only the first part of the condition holds $(dist_i < dist_{cur})$, then check a *suspected region* defined by using the coordinates of points for which the $dist_i$ was calculated. Details of this operation are described below. The operation of checking a *suspected region* can possibly return a pair of results: the distance $dist_s$ and related density $dens_s$. The returned pair is compared with the iteration results and if $dist_s < dist_{cur}$ and $dens_s <= dens_{cur}$ then the results of the iteration are updated: $dist_{cur} := dist_s$ and $dens_{cur} := dens_s$.
9. Check the iteration breaking condition. The iterations can be broken in two cases: (1) the number of performed iterations is greater than the declared number of iterations (which is another AEC algorithm parameter), and (2) if the result returned by consecutive iterations was repeated a fixed number of times. Breaking the iteration caused by the second condition is more desirable, because we can expect that the algorithm found a minimal distance between clusters that cannot be replaced by any other distance.

Suspected Regions Analysis. The case of a *suspected region* is considered for points p_i, p_j when only the distance condition $(dist(p_i, p_j) < dist_{cur}))$ holds, the density condition $(dens(p_i, p_j) <= dens_{cur}))$ does not. Our experiments show that there are two possible scenarios resulting in examining the *suspected region*:

1. the points p_i, p_j are located close to each other inside a cluster. Then the distance is short, but the density of the stripe between the points is high.
2. the points p_i, p_j are located in separate clusters but they are not border points (according to the definition presented in [6]). The density of the stripe between the points is increased by the presence of the border points of both clusters.

Of considerable interest is the second case. The AEC algorithm does not analyze distances with the zero PIS coefficient. There are many cases when clusters' shapes make it difficult to randomly pick two points so that one of them is a border point of the first cluster and the second is located near the border of the second cluster. The analysis of *suspected region* is performed as follows:

1. define the *suspected region*. The rectangle r_s for the *suspected region* has its center directly between the points p_i and p_j. In the next step calculate the density $dens_{r_s}$ of the r_s.
2. create a set of points N_{r_s}.
3. for each point $n_i \in N_{r_s}$ create a set H_{n_i, r_s}, then calculate distances and densities of the stripe between points n_i and the related points $h_j \in H_{n_i, r_s}$. As the result choose the minimal distance with the minimal density.

In the event the calculated result density is less than the average density of the r_s region, the *suspected region* analysis results are compared with the results of the analysis in the iterative section of the AEC algorithm. For a pair of points located inside a cluster the *suspected region* analysis does not influence the results because the density condition is not satisfied (the density is high inside a cluster). But for the points located in two different clusters the analysis often gives important results.

The amount of points checked during *suspected regions* analysis depends on the number of points in the r_s rectangle. If the number is less than the N set cardinality, then all the points are checked. But if the number is greater, the cardinality of the N_{r_s} set equals the cardinality of the N set created in the iterative section of the algorithm. The situation is identical for the H sets.

Clustering with AEC-calculated *Eps* Parameter. Application of the calculated *Eps* parameter to density-based clustering results in creating clusters which number and cardinalities depend on the points distribution characteristics. If the density of all clusters is similar (the distances between neighboring points in all clusters are always less than the distances between border points of the closest clusters), then the result of the AEC algorithm is the distance between a pair of closest clusters. Having the estimated distance between the closest clusters we can define the *Eps* parameter for the density-based clustering as 85% – 90% of the obtained distance. Decreasing the value of the distance we prevent merging of the closest clusters during clustering process.

If the points are grouped in clusters of significantly different density then the AEC algorithm outcome depends on the density of the sparse clusters. If the distance between dense clusters is lower than the distance between neighboring points in the most sparse cluster, then the AEC algorithm outcome is the distance between the dense clusters. Performing the clustering results in creating the dense clusters and, in sparse clusters, merging points located close to each other. But if distances between neighboring points inside all kinds of clusters (both dense and sparse) are less than the minimal distance between border points of two closest clusters, then the AEC algorithm outcome is the minimal distance between clusters. Performing the clustering results in proper creating both dense and sparse clusters.

2.3   Implementation

The process of calculating the *Eps* parameter by means of the AEC algorithm is time-intensive. In order to improve the efficiency we used distributed processing. The architecture of the distributed implementation is based on the client-server standard. Every server stores the set of all points P and every server performs the same operations but for different subsets of points. Each server is assigned a set of points from which it creates the N sets. The sets are disjoint for all servers. Thus we minimize the possibility that some servers examine the same pair of points. The H sets are created from the whole P set, without limitations. We implemented two different distributed versions of the AEC algorithm.

1. The first version named *at once* (AO) assumes, that the client and servers do not communicate during the process of *Eps* evaluation. The servers calculate the minimum distance between clusters with the lowest density and return the results to the client which selects the best result (the shortest distance with the lowest related density). Disadvantage of this approach is that the servers calculations are less precise because they use N sets which cardinalities are only $\frac{1}{K}$ cardinality of the sets used in the centralized version (where K is the number of servers).

2. The second version named iterative (IT) assumes that the client requests the servers to perform the i iteration of the whole process. The servers return results of the i iteration to the client. The client selects the best result from all the answers. In the next step, the client transfers the chosen result to all the servers. The servers use the result as the initial distance and initial density for the next $i + 1$ iteration. The number of performed iterations and the number of repeated consecutive results are controlled by the client. Operation of the servers is *synchronized* by setting the initial distance and initial density. In this approach client and servers communicate more often, but the obtained results are more precise.

3   Test Results

In this section we present tests results obtained for eight various sets of points. The sets were marked from A to H; they vary with cardinality, points distribution and clusters shapes (fig. 2). The A set contains about 650 points grouped in 10 dense clusters; density of all clusters is very similar. The next set, B, contains about 200 points grouped in three relatively sparse clusters; density of all clusters is similar. The C set contains only about 120 points grouped in eight small clusters. In the D set 400 points are grouped in three dense clusters, one less dense, and one sparse cluster. The E and F sets contain over 400 points. The G and H sets contain respectively 1000 and 1500 points. In all four sets, clusters have similar density but significantly differ in shapes. Small clusters located inside the big ones were intended to disrupt the AEC algorithm when calculating

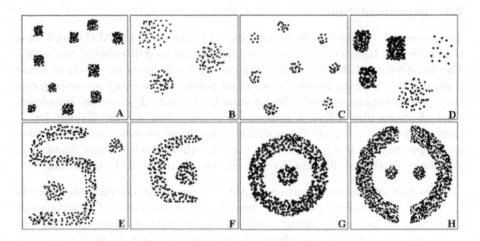

Fig. 2. Sets of points used for testing

the *PIS* coefficient. For each dataset we performed a set of experiments with the following parameters:

- the cardinality of the N set was 5, 15, 25 and 35% of the input dataset cardinality,
- the cardinality of the H set was 5, 15, 25 and 35 points for each value of the N set cardinality,
- the number of iterations was set to 10, 20 and 30 for each combination of N and H sets cardinality.

As can be easily calculated, a single test set contained $4 \times 4 \times 3 = 48$ tests. In our tests the iterations were broken if the result of the consecutive iterations was repeated more than 5 times. The iteration breaking was always caused by the number of repeated consecutive results. Thus we can treat the tests for identical cardinality of N and H sets as three repeated tests, which is useful in the presence of the random factor. We performed the tests for a centralized version of the algorithm, and for two distributed versions AO and IT.

The AEC algorithm is written in Java. All the experiments were run on machines equipped with Pentium IV 2.8 GHz and 512 MB RAM. The software environment was Windows XP Professional, Java Sun 1.5 and Oracle 10g. The distributed environment consisted of four machines connected with Ethernet 100Mbit network. The communication was based on Java RMI.

The main purpose of the experiments was to verify the AEC algorithm correctness and efficiency against various datasets. The AEC algorithm was run with a given set of parameters. The calculated *Eps* parameter was passed to the DBRS algorithm, which was returning the number of created clusters. If the number of clusters declared for a given dataset equaled the number of clusters found by the DBRS, we marked the experiment as success. If the number of clusters was not equal, we marked the experiment as failure.

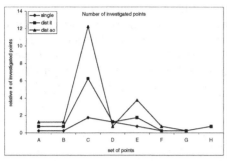 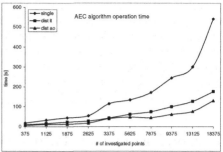

Fig. 3. Relative number of points checked **Fig. 4.** AEC algorithm operation times as for correct *Eps* calculation   function of investigated points number

The graph in figure 3 illustrates the relative number of investigated points for various set of points. The number of investigated points calculated as $|N| \cdot |H|$ was related to the cardinality of the set P, hence we can compare the results for sets of different cardinality on a single plot. In figure 4 we present a graph comparing AEC algorithm operation times for the three implementation versions. The x axis shows the number of investigated points. The y axis shows AEC algorithm operation times in seconds. We considered only the cases when the algorithm gave the correct results. As expected, the centralized version execution consumes much more time when compared to the distributed versions. For small cardinalities of investigated points sets (less than 3000) the differences in operation times are not significant. But for greater cardinalities the distributed versions operate much more efficiently. For cardinalities exceeding 10000 points we observe nearly linear speed-up.

Summarizing the tests results we notice that for all tested sets of points the AEC algorithm gives proper results. There are more and less *difficult* sets of points but the algorithm is able to correctly analyze all of them. The most difficult to analyze are sets of points with a big number of small clusters. The algorithm operation is not disturbed by the differences in densities and/or shapes of the clusters. Also the presence of small clusters inside big ones does not negatively affect the algorithm operation. The accuracy of the AEC algorithm is determined by the algorithm parameters. The bigger the N and H sets cardinalities (the more pairs of points the algorithm investigates) and the more iterations performed, the more accurate the results. However, every investigated pair of points has its influence on the algorithm operation time. The parameters should be set according to the tested dataset. If the dataset characteristics are not known in advance (as with the presented test scenario) the obtained results show that investigating 25% of a dataset and setting the maximal number of iterations to 10 always gives accurate results.

The centralized version of the AEC algorithm gives the most accurate results. For all tested sets of points the centralized version always required the smallest

N and H sets. This version also needed the smallest number of iterations for obtaining the correct results. The AO distributed version operates most efficiently (is able to examine the biggest number of pairs of points in the shortest time), but on the other hand, the AO version always requires the biggest N and H sets, and the biggest number of iterations. Therefore, the best choice is the iterative distributed version (IT). It is faster than the centralized version and gives better results than the distributed AO version.

4   Conclusions and Future Work

This paper presents an empirical approach to a problem of automatic calculation of Eps parameter applicable in density-based clustering algorithms such as DBRS and DBScan. In our approach the AEC algorithm, working iteratively, chooses randomly a fixed number of sets of points and calculates three coefficients: distance between the points, number of points located in a stripe between the points and density of the stripe. Then the algorithm chooses the best possible result, which is the minimal distance between clusters. The calculated result has an influence on the sets of points created in the next iteration.

We implemented the AEC algorithm in one centralized and two distributed versions. We presented test results for a collection of eight different sets of points. With appropriately high number of examined points the algorithm was able to calculate the proper Eps parameter for all tested sets of points. Our future work includes further improving the AEC algorithm efficiency. We want to eliminate the most time-intensive part of the algorithm which is calculating the value of the PIS coefficient. We are currently searching for conditions allowing us to skip the PIS coefficient calculation.

References

1. Barclay T., Slutz D.R., Gray J.: TerraServer: A Spatial Data Warehouse, Proc. ACM SIGMOD 2000, pp: 307-318, June 2000
2. http://maps.google.com
3. Ester M., Kriegel H.-P., Sander J., Wimmer M.: A Density-Based Algorithm for Discovering Clusters in Large Spatial Databases with Noise. In proc. of 2nd International Conference on Knowledge Discovery and Data Mining, 1996
4. Gorawski, M., Malczok, R.: On Efficient Storing and Processing of Long Aggregate Lists. DaWaK, Copenhagen, Denmark 2005.
5. Papadias D., Kalnis P., Zhang J., Tao Y.: Effcient OLAP Operations in Spatial Data Warehouses. Spinger Verlag, LNCS 2001
6. Wang X., Hamilton H.J.: DBRS: A Density-Based Spatial Clustering Method with Random Sampling. In proceedings of the 7th PAKDD, Seoul, Korea, 2003

Cluster-Based Sampling Approaches to Imbalanced Data Distributions

Show-Jane Yen and Yue-Shi Lee

Department of Computer Science and Information Engineering, Ming Chuan University
5 The-Ming Rd., Gwei Shan District, Taoyuan County 333, Taiwan
{sjyen, leeys}@mcu.edu.tw

Abstract. For classification problem, the training data will significantly influence the classification accuracy. When the data set is highly unbalanced, classification algorithms tend to degenerate by assigning all cases to the most common outcome. Hence, it is important to select the suitable training data for classification in the imbalanced class distribution problem. In this paper, we propose cluster-based under-sampling approaches for selecting the representative data as training data to improve the classification accuracy in the imbalanced class distribution environment. The basic classification algorithm of neural network model is considered. The experimental results show that our cluster-based under-sampling approaches outperform the other under-sampling techniques in the previous studies.

1 Introduction

The classification techniques usually assume that the training samples are uniformly-distributed between different classes. A classifier performs well when the classification technique is applied to a dataset evenly distributed among different classes. However, many datasets in real applications involve imbalanced class distribution problem [5, 7]. The imbalanced class distribution problem occurs while there are much more samples in one class than the other class in a training dataset. In an imbalanced dataset, the *majority class* has a large percent of all the samples, while the samples in *minority class* just occupy a small part of all the samples. In this case, a classifier usually tends to predict that samples have the majority class and completely ignore the minority class.

One simple method of under-sampling is to select a subset of MA randomly and then combine them with MI as a training set, which is called *random under-sampling approach*. Several advanced researches are proposed to make the selective samples more representative. The under-sampling approach based on distance [7] uses distinct modes: the nearest, the farthest, the average nearest, and the average farthest distances between MI and MA, as four standards to select the representative samples from MA. For every minority class sample in the dataset, the first method "nearest" calculates the distances between all majority class samples and the minority class samples, and selects k majority class samples which have the smallest distances to the minority

A Min Tjoa and J. Trujillo (Eds.): DaWaK 2006, LNCS 4081, pp. 427–436, 2006.

class sample. If there are n minority class samples in the dataset, the "nearest" approach would finally select $k \times n$ majority class samples ($k \geq 1$). However, some samples within the selected majority class samples might duplicate.

Similar to the "nearest" approach, the "farthest" approach selects the majority class samples which have the farthest distances to each minority class samples. For every majority class samples in the dataset, the third method "average nearest" calculates the average distance between one majority class sample and all minority class samples. This approach selects the majority class samples which have the smallest average distances. The last method "average farthest" is similar to the "average nearest" approach; it selects the majority class samples which have the farthest average distances with all the minority class samples. The above under-sampling approaches based on distance in [7] spend a lot of time selecting the majority class samples in the large dataset, and they are not efficient in real applications.

In 2003, J. Zhang and I. Mani [6] presented the compared results within four informed under-sampling approaches and random under-sampling approach. The first method "NearMiss-1" selects the majority class samples which are close to some minority class samples. In this method, majority class samples are selected while their average distances to three closest minority class samples are the smallest. The second method "NearMiss-2" selects the majority class samples while their average distances to three farthest minority class samples are the smallest. The third method "NearMiss-3" take out a given number of the closest majority class samples for each minority class sample. Finally, the fourth method "Most distant" selects the majority class samples whose average distances to the three closest minority class samples are the largest. The final experimental results in [6] showed that the NearMiss-2 approach and random under-sampling approach perform the best.

In this paper, we study the effects of under-sampling [1, 3, 6] on the backpropagation neural network technique and propose some new under-sampling approaches based on clustering, such that the influence of imbalanced class distribution can be decreased and the accuracy of predicting the minority class can be increased.

2   Our Approaches

In this section, we present our approach SBC (under-Sampling Based on Clustering) which focuses on the under-sampling approach and uses clustering techniques to solve the imbalanced class distribution problem. Our approach first clusters all the training samples into some clusters. The main idea is that there are different clusters in a dataset, and each cluster seems to have distinct characteristics. If a cluster has more majority class samples and less minority class samples, it will behave like the majority class samples. On the opposite, if a cluster has more minority class samples and less majority class samples, it doesn't hold the characteristics of the majority class samples and behaves more like the minority class samples. Therefore, our approach SBC selects a suitable number of majority class samples from each cluster by considering the ratio of the number of majority class samples to the number of minority class samples in the cluster.

2.1 Under-Sampling Based on Clustering

Assume that the number of samples in the class-imbalanced dataset is N, which includes majority class samples (MA) and minority class samples (MI). The size of the dataset is the number of the samples in this dataset. The size of MA is represented as $Size_{MA}$, and $Size_{MI}$ is the number of samples in MI. In the class-imbalanced dataset, $Size_{MA}$ is far larger than $Size_{MI}$. For our under-sampling method SBC, we first cluster all samples in the dataset into K clusters. The number of majority class samples and the number of minority class samples in the ith cluster ($1 \leq i \leq K$) are $Size_{MA}^i$ and $Size_{MI}^i$, respectively. Therefore, the ratio of the number of majority class samples to the number of minority class samples in the ith cluster is $Size_{MA}^i / Size_{MI}^i$. If the ratio of $Size_{MA}$ to $Size_{MI}$ in the training dataset is set to be $m{:}1$, the number of selected majority class samples in the ith cluster is shown in expression (1):

$$SSize_{MA}^i = (m \times SizeMI) \times \frac{Size_{MA}^i / Size_{MI}^i}{\sum\limits_{i=1}^{K} Size_{MA}^i / Size_{MI}^i} \tag{1}$$

In expression (1), $m \times SizeMI$ is the total number of selected majority class samples that we suppose to have in the final training dataset. $\sum\limits_{i=1}^{K} Size_{MA}^i / Size_{MI}^i$ is the total ratio of the number of majority class samples to the number of minority class samples in all clusters. Expression (1) determines that more majority class samples would be selected in the cluster which behaves more like the majority class samples. In other words, $SSize_{MA}^i$ is larger while the ith cluster has more majority class samples and less minority class samples. After determining the number of majority class samples which are selected in the ith cluster, $1 \leq i \leq K$, by using expression (1), we randomly choose majority class samples in the ith cluster. The total number of selected majority class samples is $m \times Size_{MI}$ after merging all the selected majority class samples in each cluster. At last, we combine the whole minority class samples with the selected majority class samples to construct a new training dataset. Table 1 shows the steps for our under-sampling approach.

For example, assume that an imbalanced class distribution dataset has totally 1100 samples. The size of MA is 1000 and the size of MI is 100. In this example, we cluster this dataset into three clusters. Table 2 shows the number of majority class samples $Size_{MA}^i$, the number of minority class samples $Size_{MI}^i$, and the ratio of $Size_{MA}^i$ to $Size_{MI}^i$ for the ith cluster.

Assume that the ratio of $Size_{MA}$ to $Size_{MI}$ in the training data is set to be 1:1, in other words, there are 100 selected majority class samples and the whole 100 minority class samples in this training dataset. The number of selected majority class samples in each cluster can be calculated by expression (1). Table 3 shows the number of selected

Table 1. The structure of the under-sampling based on clustering approach *SBC*

Step1.	Determine the ratio of $Size_{MA}$ to $Size_{MI}$ in the training dataset.
Step2.	Cluster all the samples in the dataset into some clusters.
Step3.	Determine the number of selected majority class samples in each cluster by using expression (1), and then randomly select the majority class samples in each cluster.
Step4.	Combine the selected majority class samples and all the minority class samples to obtain the training dataset.

Table 2. Cluster descriptions

Cluster ID	Number of majority class samples	Number of minority class samples	$Size_{MA}^i / Size_{MI}^i$
1	500	10	500/10=50
2	300	50	300/50=6
3	200	40	200/40=5

Table 3. The number of selected majority class samples in each cluster

Cluster ID	The number of selected majority class samples
1	$1 \times 100 \times 50 / (50+6+5) = 82$
2	$1 \times 100 \times 6 / (50+6+5) = 10$
3	$1 \times 100 \times 5 / (50+6+5) = 8$

majority class samples in each cluster. We finally select the majority samples ran domly from each cluster and combine them with the minority samples to form the new dataset.

2.2 Under-Sampling Based on Clustering and Distances

In *SBC* method, all the samples are clustered into several clusters and the number of selected majority class samples is determined by expression (1). Finally, the majority class samples are randomly selected from each cluster. In this section, we propose other two under-sampling methods, which are based on *SBC* approach. The difference between the two proposed under-sampling methods and *SBC* method is the way to select the majority class samples from each cluster. For the two proposed methods, the majority class samples are selected according to the distances between the majority class samples and the minority class samples in each cluster. Hence, the distances between samples will be computed.

For a continuous attribute, the values of all samples for this attribute need to be normalized in order to avoid the effect of different scales for different attributes. For example, suppose *A* is a continuous attribute. In order to normalize the values of attribute *A* for all the samples, we first find the maximum value Max_A and the minimum value Min_A of *A* for all samples. To lie an attribute value a_i in between 0 to 1, a_i is normalized to $\frac{a_i - Min_A}{Max_A - Min_A}$. For a categorical or discrete attribute, the distance between two attribute values x_1 and x_2 is 1 (i.e. x_1-x_2=1) while x_1 is not equal to x_2, and the distance is 0 (i.e. x_1-x_2=0) while they are the same.

Assume that there are N attributes in a dataset and V_i^X represents the value of attribute A_i in sample X, for $1 \leq i \leq N$. The Euclidean distance between two samples X and Y is shown in expression (2).

$$\text{distance}(X,Y) = \sqrt{\sum_{i=1}^{N}(V_i^X - V_i^Y)^2} \qquad (2)$$

The two approaches we proposed in this section first cluster all samples into K ($K \geq$ 1) clusters as well, and determine the number of selected majority class samples for each cluster by expression (1). For each cluster, the representative majority class samples are selected in different ways. The first method *SBCMD* (Sampling Based on Clustering with *Most Distant*) selects the majority class samples whose average distances to M closest minority class samples in the ith cluster are the farthest. The second method, which is called *SBCMF* (Sampling Based on Clustering with Most Far), selects the majority class samples whose average distances to all minority class samples in the cluster are the farthest.

3 Experimental Results

For our experiments, we use three criteria to evaluate the classification accuracy for minority class: the precision rate P, the recall rate R, and the F-measure for minority class. Generally, for a classifier, if the precision rate is high, then the recall rate will be low, that is, the two criteria are trade-off. We cannot use one of the two criteria to evaluate the performance of a classifier. Hence, the precision rate and recall rate are combined to form another criterion F-measure, which is shown in expression (3).

$$\text{MI's F-measure} = \frac{2 \times P \times R}{P + R} \qquad (3)$$

In the following, we expression (3) to evaluate the performance of our approaches *SBC*, *SBCMD*, and *SBCMF* by comparing our methods with the other methods *AT*, *RT*, and *NearMiss-2* on synthetic datasets. The method *AT* uses all samples to train the classifiers and does not select samples. *RT* is the most common-used random under-sampling approach and it selects the majority class samples randomly. The last method *NearMiss-2* is proposed by J. Zhang and I. Mani [6], which has been discussed in section 1. The two methods *RT* and *NearMiss-2* have the better performance than the other proposed methods in [6]. In the following experiments, the classifiers are constructed by using the artificial neural network technique in *IBM Intelligent Miner for Data V8.1*.

For each generated synthetic dataset, the number of samples is set to 10000, the number of numerical attributes and categorical attributes are set to 5, respectively. The dataset DSi means that the dataset potentially can be separated into i clusters, and our methods also cluster the dataset DSi into i clusters. Figure 1 shows the

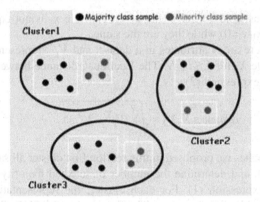

Fig. 1. The distribution of samples in a dataset

distribution of samples in a dataset which has three clusters inside. Moreover, in order to make the synthetic datasets more like real datasets, the noisy data are necessary.

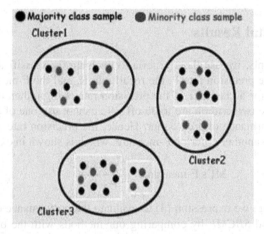

Fig. 2. Example for disordered samples

The synthetic datasets have two kinds of noisy data: disordered samples and exceptional samples. The disordered samples mean that some majority class samples (or minority class samples) lie to the area of minority class samples (or majority class samples). The disordered samples are illustrated with Figure 2. As for exceptional samples, they distribute irregularly in a dataset and outside the clusters. The samples outside the clusters in Figure 3 are exceptional samples. A dataset DSi with j% exceptional samples and k% disordered samples is represented as DSiEjDk. If there is no disordered sample in the synthetic dataset, the dataset is represented as DSiEjDN.

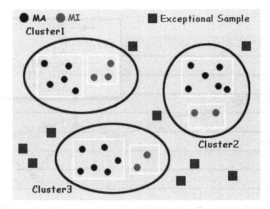

Fig. 3. Example for exceptional samples

Figure 4 shows the experimental results in the datasets in which the ratios of the number of majority class samples to the number of minority class samples are 2:1, 4:1, 9:1, 18:1, 36:1, and 72:1, respectively. For each specific ratio, we generate several synthetic datasets DSiE10D20 in which i is from 2 to 16. Hence, the average MI's F-measures are computed from all the datasets for each specific ratio. In Figure 4, we can see that the average MI's F-measure for *SBC* is higher than the other methods in most cases.

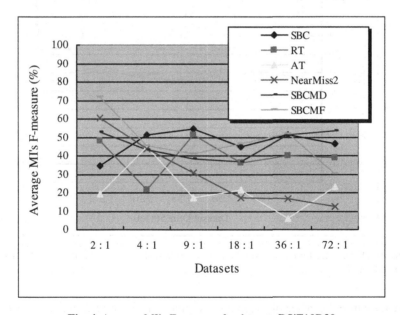

Fig. 4. Average MI's F-measure for datasets DSiE10D20

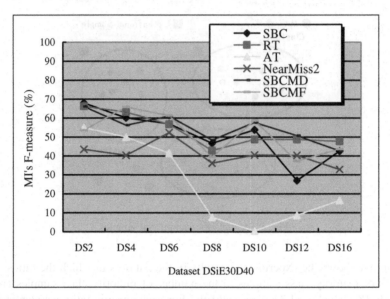

Fig. 5. MI's F-measure for each method on the datasets with 30% exceptional samples and 40% disordered samples

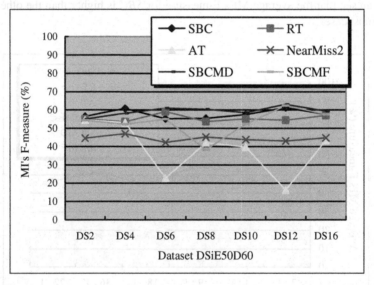

Fig. 6. MI's F-measure for each method on the datasets with 50% exceptional samples and 60% disordered samples

We raise the percentage of exceptional samples and disordered samples to 30% and 40%, respectively. And then we continue to raise the percentage of exceptional samples and disordered samples to 50% and 60%, respectively. Figure 5 and Figure 6 show the experimental results in DSiE30D40 and DSiE50D60, respectively, in which i is from 2 to 16. The experimental results show that *SBCMD* is the most stable method and has high MI's F-measure in each synthetic dataset. *RT* is also a stable method in the experiments, but the performance for *SBCMD* is better than *RT* in most cases. Although the MI's F-measure for *SBCMF* is higher than the other methods in some cases, the performance for *SBCMF* is not stable. Hence, the performance for *SBCMD* is the best in most of the cases when the datasets contain more exceptional samples and disordered samples, and *SBC* is stable and performs well in any case.

The average execution time for each method is shown in Figure 7. The execution time includes the time for executing the under-sampling method and the time for training the classifiers. According to the results in Figure 7, both *SBC* and *RT* are most efficient among all the methods, and *NearMiss-2* spends too much time for selecting the majority class samples.

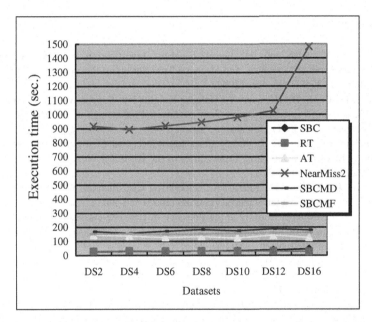

Fig. 7. Average execution time for each method

4 Conclusion

In a classification task, the effect of imbalanced class distribution problem is often ignored. Many studies [2, 4] focused on improving the classification accuracy but did not consider the imbalanced class distribution problem. Hence, the classifiers which are constructed by these studies lose the ability to correctly predict the correct decision class for the minority class samples in the datasets which the number of majority class samples are much greater than the number of minority class samples. Many real applications, like rarely-seen disease investigation, credit card fraud detection, and internet intrusion detection always involve the imbalanced class distribution problem. It is hard to make right predictions on the customers or patients who that we are interested in.

In this study, we propose cluster-based under-sampling approaches to solve the imbalanced class distribution problem by using backpropagation neural network. The other two under-sampling methods, Random selection and *NearMiss-2*, are used to be compared with our approaches in our performance studies. In the experiments, our approach *SBC* has better prediction accuracy and stability than other methods. *SBC* not only has high classification accuracy on predicting the minority class samples but also has fast execution time. *SBCMD* has better prediction accuracy and stability when the datasets contain more exceptional samples and disordered samples. However, *SBCMF* does not have stable performances in our experiments. The two methods take more time than *SBC* on selecting the majority class samples as well.

References

1. Chawla, N. V.: C4.5 and Imbalanced Datasets: Investigating the Effect of Sampling Method, Probabilistic Estimate, and Decision Tree Structure. Proceedings of the ICML'03 Workshop on Class Imbalances (2003).
2. Caragea, D., Cook, D., Honavar, V.: Gaining Insights into Support Vector Machine Pattern Classifiers Using Projection-Based Tour Methods. Proceedings of the KDD Conference, San Francisco, CA (2001) 251-256.
3. Drummond, C., Holte, R. C.: C4.5, Class Imbalance, and Cost Sensitivity: Why Under-Sampling Beats Over-Sampling. Proceedings of the ICML'03 Workshop on Learning from Imbalanced Datasets (2003).
4. del-Hoyo, R., Buldain, D., Marco, A.: Supervised Classification with Associative SOM. Lecture Notes in Computer Science, Vol.2686 (2003) 334–341.
5. Japkowicz, N.: Concept-learning in the Presence of Between-class and Within-class Imbalances. Proceedings of the Fourteenth Conference of the Canadian Society for Computational Studies of Intelligence (2001) 67–77.
6. Zhang, J., Mani, I.: kNN Approach to Unbalanced Data Distributions: A Case Study Involving Information Extraction. Proceedings of the ICML'2003 Workshop on Learning from Imbalanced Datasets (2003).
7. Chyi, Y.M.: Classification Analysis Techniques for Skewed Class Distribution Problems, Master Thesis, Department of Information Management, National Sun Yat-Sen University (2003).

Efficient Mining of Large Maximal Bicliques

Guimei Liu, Kelvin Sim, and Jinyan Li

Institute for Infocomm Research, 21 Heng Mui Keng Terrace, Singapore 119613
{visgmliu, shsim, jinyan}@i2r.a-star.edu.sg

Abstract. Many real world applications rely on the discovery of maximal biclique subgraphs (complete bipartite subgraphs). However, existing algorithms for enumerating maximal bicliques are not very efficient in practice. In this paper, we propose an efficient algorithm to mine large maximal biclique subgraphs from undirected graphs. Our algorithm uses a divide-and-conquer approach. It effectively uses the size constraints on both vertex sets to prune unpromising bicliques and to reduce the search space iteratively during the mining process. The time complexity of the proposed algorithm is $O(nd \cdot N)$, where n is the number of vertices, d is the maximal degree of the vertices and N is the number of maximal bicliques. Our performance study shows that the proposed algorithm outperforms previous work significantly.

1 Introduction

Graphs can be used to model a wide range of real world applications. In this paper, we study the problem of mining maximal complete bipartite subgraphs (not necessarily induced subgraphs) from undirected graphs. Complete bipartites are also called bicliques. A biclique has two disjoint sets of vertices, and there is an edge between two vertices if and only if the two vertices are in different vertex sets. A biclique is maximal if the biclique is not a proper subgraph of another biclique. Maximal bicliques have been used to solve the edge covering problem [7], and they have many other arising applications.

Web community discovery. Websites that are part of the same community frequently do not reference one another for many reasons [11]. Linkage between these related pages can nevertheless be established by a different phenomenon: related pages are frequently visited together. Related pages and the Web users visiting these pages form a biclique or a dense bipartite. Web communities can be discovered by first enumerating maximal bicliques from Web log data as community cores, and then find the rest of the community members using community cores.

Topological structure discovery from protein-protein interaction networks. In the last several years, high-throughput interaction detection approaches have led to the discovery of thousands of interactions between proteins. Some hidden topological structures discovered from protein-protein interaction networks, such as cliques and bicliques, consist of biologically relevant functional groups [6].

A Min Tjoa and J. Trujillo (Eds.): DaWaK 2006, LNCS 4081, pp. 437–448, 2006.

Maximal concatenated phylogenetic dataset discovery. A phylogenetic tree is a tree showing the evolutionary interrelationships among various species or other entities that are believed to have a common ancestor. To improve the accuracy of tree reconstruction, phylogeneticists are extracting increasingly large multigene data sets from sequence databases [18]. Determining whether a database contains at least k genes sampled from at least m species is to determine whether there are k genes and m species forming a biclique. Complete phylogenetic datasets can be discovered by enumerating all the maximal bicliques satisfying the size constraints.

In real world problems, such as the applications described above, those bicliques with a very small vertex set are usually of no interest. It is therefore desirable to mine only large interesting bicliques. A biclique is large if the size of its both vertex sets is no less than a predefined threshold. Mining maximal bicliques has been studied previously. Alexe et al. [2] use consensus algorithms to enumerate all maximal bicliques, which may generate many uninteresting small bicliques. Li et al. [12] have proved that there is a correspondence between maximal bicliques and frequent closed itemsets. On one hand, a closed itemset and the set of transactions containing the closed itemset form a biclique. On the other hand, the adjacency matrix of a graph can be viewed as a transaction database, and a biclique corresponds to a pair of frequent closed itemsets in the transaction database. Li et al. suggest to use frequent closed itemset mining techniques [23,22,13,20] to mine maximal bicliques. However, the large maximal biclique mining problem has size constraints on both vertex sets, while the frequent itemset mining problem put size constraint on only one side—the transaction set. Traditional frequent itemset mining algorithms also use only the size constraint on transaction set to prune the search space. As a result, using frequent closed itemset mining algorithms to mine maximal bicliques also generates many small bicliques. Another problem with the frequent itemset mining approach is that each maximal biclique is generated twice in undirected graphs. This paper introduces the problem of mining large maximal biclique subgraphs and proposes an efficient algorithm to solve the problem. Our algorithm takes a divide-and-conquer approach, and it effectively uses the size constraints on both sides to iteratively prune the search space. Non-maximal bicliques as well as duplicate bicliques are pruned efficiently during the mining process.

The rest of the paper is organized as follows. Section 2 formulates the problem, our algorithm is described in Section 3. Section 4 reports experiment results. Related work is reviewed in Section 5. Section 6 concludes the paper.

2   Definitions and Properties

In this section, we formulate the problem of mining large maximal bicliques. An *undirected graph* G is defined as a pair (V, E), where V is a set of vertices, and E is a set of edges between the vertices. Two vertices are *adjacent* if there is an edge between them. The *adjacency list* of a vertex v in $G = (V, E)$, denoted as $\Gamma(v, G)$, is defined as the set of vertices adjacent to v, that is,

$\Gamma(v, G) = \{u | \{u, v\} \in E\}$. The adjacency list of a set of vertices X in $G = (V, E)$ is defined as $\Gamma(X, G) = \{u | u \in V \text{ and } \forall v \in X, \{u, v\} \in E\} = \{u | u \in V \text{ and } X \subseteq \Gamma(u)\}$. We denote $\Gamma(X, G)$ as $\Gamma(X)$ if G is clear from the context. The adjacency lists of vertex sets have the anti-monotone property.

Proposition 1. *Let V_1 and V_2 be two sets of vertices in $G = (V, E)$ and $V_1 \subseteq V_2$. We have $\Gamma(V_2) \subseteq \Gamma(V_1)$.*

Given a graph $G = (V, E)$, graph $G' = (V', E')$ is a *subgraph* of G if $V' \subseteq V$, $E' \subseteq E$ and $\forall \{u, v\} \in E'$, $u, v \in V'$. If $V' \subset V$ or $E' \subset E$, then we say G' is a proper subgraph of G. A graph $G = (V, E)$ is a *bipartite* if its vertex set V can be partitioned into two disjoint nonempty sets V_1 and V_2 such that every edge in E connects a vertex in V_1 and a vertex in V_2, that is, no edge in E connects either two vertices in V_1 or two vertices in V_2. Bipartite G is also denoted as $G = (V_1, V_2, E)$.

Definition 1 (Biclique). *A bipartite $G = (V_1, V_2, E)$ is called a biclique if for each $v_1 \in V_1$ and $v_2 \in V_2$, there is an edge between v_1 and v_2, that is, $E = \{\{u, v\} | u \in V_1, v \in V_2\}$.*

The edge set E of a biclique $G = (V_1, V_2, E)$ can be completely determined by the two vertex sets V_1 and V_2, so we omit the edge set and denote a biclique G simply as $G = (V_1, V_2)$. Let $G = (V, E)$ be an undirect graph, V_1 and V_2 be two subsets of V. If V_1, V_2 and all the edges between V_1 and V_2 form a biclique subgraph of G, we say that V_1 and V_2 form a biclique subgraph of G. According to the definition, for any subset V_1 of V, V_1 and $\Gamma(V_1, G)$ form a biclique subgraph of G.

Proposition 2. *Let $G' = (V_1, V_2, E')$ be a biclique subgraph of $G = (V, E)$. We have $V_1 \subseteq \Gamma(V_2, G)$ and $V_2 \subseteq \Gamma(V_1, G)$.*

If $G = (V_1, V_2, E)$ is a biclique, then any induced subgraph $G' = (V_1', V_2', E')$ of G such that $V_1' \neq \phi$, $V_2' \neq \phi$, $V_1' \subseteq V_1$ and $V_2' \subseteq V_2$ is also a biclique. The bicliques induced from a biclique G provides no more information than G, so we focus on mining maximal bicliques in this paper.

Definition 2 (Maximal biclique). *Let G' be a biclique subgraph of graph G. If there does not exist any other biclique subgraph G'' of G such that G' is a proper subgraph of G'', then G' is a maximal biclique of G.*

Proposition 3. *Let V_1 and V_2 be two sets of vertices in graph $G = (V, E)$ and $E' = \{\{u, v\} | u \in V_1, v \in V_2 \text{ and } \{u, v\} \in E\}$. Graph $G' = (V_1, V_2, E')$ is a maximal biclique subgraph of G if and only if $\Gamma(V_1, G) = V_2$ and $\Gamma(V_2, G) = V_1$.*

The proof of this proposition can be found at [12].

Corollary 1. *Let V_1 be a set of vertices in $G = (V, E)$. $G' = (V_1, \Gamma(V_1, G))$ is a maximal biclique subgraph of G if and only if $\Gamma(\Gamma(V_1, G), G) = V_1$.*

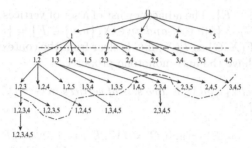

Fig. 1. The search space

A maximal biclique G' is called a **large maximal biclique** if the size of its both vertex sets is no less than a predefined threshold ms. The task of mining large maximal biclique subgraphs is to enumerate all the large maximal biclique subgraphs with respect to ms from a given graph.

Given a graph $G = (V, E)$, any subset of V can form a biclique with another subset of V. Therefore, the search space of the large maximal biclique subgraph mining problem is the power set of V. Figure 1 shows the search space of a graph with five vertices $\{1, 2, 3, 4, 5\}$. We are interested in only those large maximal bicliques. A vertex set is not of interest if itself is too small or its adjacency list is too small. Therefore, in Figure 1, only those vertex sets between the two borders (indicated by dotted lines) are of interest. The vertex sets above the two borders are uninteresting because themselves are too small, and the vertex sets below the two borders are uninteresting because their adjacency lists are too small. We use the following proposition and Proposition 1 to prune uninteresting bicliques.

Proposition 4. *If a vertex set* $|V_1| < ms$, *then* $\forall V' \subset V_1$, *we have* $|V'| < ms$.

Proposition 4 implies that if a vertex set is smaller than the minimum size threshold, then there is no need to consider the subsets of the vertex set. This proposition can be used to prune the uninteresting vertex sets above the two borders. Proposition 1 implies that if the adjacency list of a vertex set is smaller than the minimum size threshold, then there is no need to consider the supersets of the vertex set because their adjacency lists are also smaller than the minimum size threshold. This proposition can be used to prune those uninteresting vertex sets below the two borders.

The maximal biclique mining problem is related to the frequent closed itemset mining problem [24,12]. A graph G can be mapped to a transaction database [1], denoted as $D(G)$, by treating *each vertex* as an item and the *adjacency list* of each vertex as a transaction. Table 1 shows a mapping example. In the frequent itemset mining problem, the concept of frequent closed itemsets is proposed to remove redundant itemsets [16]. An itemset X is *closed* if there does not exist another itemset Y such that Y is a superset of X and $T(Y) = T(X)$, where $T(X)$ denotes the set of transactions containing X, that is, $T(X) = \{t | t \in D(G), X \subseteq t\}$. This definition is equivalent to Definition 2 because $T(X) = \{t | t \in D(G),$

Table 1. A graph G is mapped into a transaction database $D(G)$

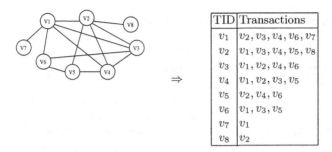

TID	Transactions
v_1	v_2, v_3, v_4, v_6, v_7
v_2	v_1, v_3, v_4, v_5, v_8
v_3	v_1, v_2, v_4, v_6
v_4	v_1, v_2, v_3, v_5
v_5	v_2, v_4, v_6
v_6	v_1, v_3, v_5
v_7	v_1
v_8	v_2

$X \subseteq t\}$ defined on the transaction database is equivalent to $\Gamma(X) = \{u | u \in G, X \subseteq \Gamma(u)\}$ defined on the graph.

Li et al. [12] has proved that there is a correspondence between maximal bicliques and closed itemsets, that is, a maximal biclique in G corresponds to a pair of closed itemsets in $D(G)$. Based on this observation, mining large maximal bicliques with respect to ms from a graph G is equivalent to mining frequent closed itemsets with respect to ms from $D(G)$, and the size of the frequent itemsets should be no less than ms. However, using existing frequent closed itemset mining algorithms [23,22,13,20] to mine large maximal bicliques has several drawbacks. First, the large maximal biclique mining problem has size constraints on both vertex sets, but existing closed itemset mining algorithms only use the size constraint on transaction sets to prune the search space, which not only generate many uninteresting small maximal bicliques but also waste mining cost. Secondly, a maximal biclique corresponds to a pair of closed itemsets, so each maximal biclique is generated twice using frequent closed itemset mining algorithms. Finally, frequent itemset mining algorithms produce only itemsets, so a post-processing step is necessary to obtain the corresponding transaction set for each frequent closed itemset. The post-processing step can be costly when both the number of closed itemsets and the transaction database are very large. Algorithms that adopt the vertical mining approach can be modified to produce both itemsets and transaction sets during the mining process, but they still have the first two drawbacks. In the next section, we present an algorithm which mine maximal bicliques directly.

3   New Algorithm for Mining Large Maximal Bicliques

Given a graph $G = (V, E)$, the search space of the large maximal biclique mining problem is the power set of V. The search space can be represented by a set enumeration tree as shown in Figure 1. The root of the tree represents the empty set. Each node at level k represents a vertex set containing k vertices. The subtree rooted at vertex set X is called the sub search space tree of X. In a search space tree, the vertices are sorted into some order. For every vertex set X in the tree, only vertices after the last vertex of X can appear in the sub search space tree of X. This set of vertices are called *tail vertices* of X, denoted as $tail(X)$. For example, in the search space tree shown in Figure 1, vertices are sorted into lexicographic order, so vertex 4 is in $tail(\{1,3\})$, but vertex 2 is not a tail vertex of $\{1,3\}$ because vertex 2 is before vertex 3.

In a search space tree, the search space of every internal vertex set is partitioned into several disjoint sub search spaces by the child nodes of the vertex set. We explore the search space tree in depth-first order to recursively partition the whole search space into small sub search spaces. At each node, we generate the adjacency list of the corresponding vertex set X. Based on Proposition 1, if the size of the adjacency list is less than the predefined size threshold ms, the search on that branch should be terminated to avoid mining those vertex sets whose adjacency lists are smaller than ms. If the adjacency list of a vertex set is no less than ms, we call the vertex set as *frequent*. For each frequent vertex set X, we identify those vertices v from $tail(X)$ such that $|\Gamma(X \cup \{v\})| \geq ms$, and the child nodes of X representing these vertices should be explored further. The mining is performed on these child nodes recursively.

The vertex sets that themselves are too small are pruned based on Proposition 4. The vertex sets appearing in the sub search space of a vertex set X are subsets of $X \cup tail(X)$. Based on Proposition 4, if $|X| + |tail(X)|$ is less than ms, then there is no need to search in the subtree rooted at X because all the vertex sets in that subtree contain less than ms vertices. Similarly, if there are less than $ms - |V|$ vertices $v \in Tail(X)$ such that $\Gamma(X \cup \{v\}) \geq ms$, then there is no need to search in the subtree rooted at X either.

Algorithm 1 shows the pseudo-codes of the mining algorithm. When the algorithm is first called on a graph $G = (V, E)$, X is set to the empty set, and $\Gamma(X)$ and $tail(X)$ are set to V. For a vertex set X, we first remove those vertices v from $tail(X)$ such that the adjacency list of $X \cup \{v\}$ is less that ms (line 1-3). Then we check whether $|X| + |tail(X)|$ is less than ms. If it is true, then the search should be terminated based on Proposition 4 (line 4-5). If $|X| + |tail(X)|$ is no less than ms, then the algorithm is recursively called for each $v \in tail(X)$ (line 7-14). Before we search in the sub search space tree of $X \cup v$, we check whether $|X \cup \{v\}| + |tail(X \cup \{v\})|$ is no less than ms. Only if $|X \cup \{v\}| + |tail(X \cup \{v\})|$ is no less than ms, the search in the sub search space tree of $X \cup v$ should continue (line 9).

We sort the vertices in $tail(X)$ into ascending order of $|\Gamma(X \cup \{v\})|$ (line 6), that is, for any two vertices $u, v \in tail(X)$, if $|\Gamma(X \cup \{u\})| > |\Gamma(X \cup \{v\})|$, then u is after v in the order. The ascending ordering method has been adopted in many frequent itemset mining algorithms and has been proved to be very effective for pruning the search space. The rationale behind this ordering method is to let the vertex set with a smaller adjacency list have a larger number of tail vertices and the vertex set with a larger adjacency list have a smaller number of tail vertices so that the vertex sets in the sub search space tree of the vertex set with a smaller adjacency list are likely to be pruned because of their small adjacency lists, and the vertex sets in the sub search space tree of the vertex set with a larger adjacency list are likely to be pruned because of their small tail vertex sets.

Algorithm 1. MineLMBC Algorithm

Input:
    X is a vertex set
    $\Gamma(X)$ is the adjacency list of X
    $tail(X)$ is the tail vertices of X
    ms is the minimum size threshold;
Description:
1: **for all** vertex $v \in tail(X)$ **do**
2:    **if** $|\Gamma(X \cup \{v\})| < ms$ **then**
3:        $tail(X) = tail(X) - \{v\}$
4: **if** $|X| + |tail(X)| < ms$ **then**
5:    return ;
6: Sort vertices in $tail(X)$ into ascending order of $|\Gamma(X \cup \{v\})|$;
7: **for all** vertex $v \in tail(X)$ **do**
8:    $tail(X) = tail(X) - \{v\}$;
9:    **if** $|X \cup \{v\}| + |tail(X)| \geq ms$ **then**
10:       $Y = \Gamma(\Gamma(X \cup \{v\}))$;
11:       **if** $((Y - (X \cup \{v\})) \subseteq tail(X))$ **then**
12:          **if** $|Y| \geq ms$ **then**
13:            Output $(Y, \Gamma(X \cup \{v\}))$ as a large maximal biclique;
14:          MineLMBC($Y, \Gamma(X \cup \{v\})$), $tail(X) - Y, ms$);

One optimization can be made to Algorithm 1 is to prune the adjacency list of a vertex set based on Proposition 4. Let v be a vertex in $\Gamma(X)$. If v is adjacent to less than $ms - |X|$ vertices in $tail(X)$, then v cannot be adjacent to any superset Y of X such that $|Y| \geq ms$. Hence vertex v can be removed from $\Gamma(X)$. By pruning the adjacency list, those vertex sets with a small adjacency list can be identified and pruned earlier.

Pruning non-maximal bicliques. Non-maximal bicliques are identified and pruned during the mining process. Let X be a vertex set in the search space tree. Based on Corollary 1, biclique $G' = (X, \Gamma(X))$ is maximal if and only if $\Gamma(\Gamma(X)) = X$ is true. If G' is not a maximal biclique, that is, $\Gamma(\Gamma(X)) \neq X$, then $\Gamma(\Gamma(X))$ must be a proper superset of X based on Proposition 2. We can prune the sub search space of X based on the following proposition.

Proposition 5. *Let X be a vertex set. For any maximal biclique $G' = (V_1, V_2)$ such that $X \subseteq V_1$, we have $\Gamma(\Gamma(X)) \subseteq V_1$.*

Proof. Biclique G' is maximal, so we have $V_2 = \Gamma(V_1)$. Vertex set X is a subset of V_1, so we have $V_2 = \Gamma(V_1) \subseteq \Gamma(X)$ based on Proposition 1, and hence based on Proposition 1 again, we have $\Gamma(\Gamma(X)) \subseteq \Gamma(V_2) = V_1$.

The above proposition indicates that if a maximal biclique has a vertex set containing X, then the vertex set must also contain $\Gamma(\Gamma(X))$. If biclique $G' = (X, \Gamma(X))$ is not maximal, there are two cases. One case is that $\Gamma(\Gamma(X)) - X$ is a subset of $tail(X)$. For this case, the maximal bicliques that have a vertex set containing X are in the sub search space of X. Since any maximal biclique that have a vertex set containing X must also contain $\Gamma(\Gamma(X))$, we use $\Gamma(\Gamma(X))$ to replace X and remove vertices in $\Gamma(\Gamma(X)) - X$ from $tail(X)$ to prune those non-maximal bicliques that have a vertex set containing X but not containing $\Gamma(\Gamma(X))$. The other case is that there exists a vertex $v \in (\Gamma(\Gamma(X)) - X)$ such that v is not in $tail(X)$. For this case, none of the bicliques discovered from the sub search space tree of X can be maximal because these bicliques have a vertex set containing X but this vertex set does not contain v. To avoid mining non-maximal bicliques, we check whether $\Gamma(\Gamma(X)) = X$ is true before searching in the sub search space tree of X. If it is not true and there exists a vertex $v \in \Gamma(\Gamma(X))$ such that v is not in $tail(X)$, then we skip the sub search space tree of X (line 11).

Pruning duplicate bicliques. A biclique has two disjoint vertex sets. Our search strategy is based on vertex set searching. Therefore, every maximal biclique is generated twice in Algorithm 1. It is desirable to avoid generating duplicate bicliques to save mining cost. We prune duplicate bicliques based on the following observation, which is inspired by the pruning technique for mining maximal bicliques [5,19]. Given a vertex v in a graph $G = (V, E)$, the adjacency list of any subset of $\Gamma(v)$ must contain v because v is adjacent to all the vertices in $\Gamma(v)$. If we have generated all the vertex sets containing v and their adjacency lists, then there is no need to generate any subset of $\Gamma(v)$. To maximize the number of vertex sets being pruned, we pick the vertex with the largest adjacency list and prune all the subsets of its adjacency list.

We use the graph shown in Table 1 to illustrate the pruning of duplicate bicliques. We set ms to 2. There are 6 vertices whose adjacency list is no less than 2. We sort the 6 vertices in ascending order of their adjacency list size, and we get $\{v_6, v_5, v_4, v_3, v_2, v_1\}$. Vertex v_1 has the largest adjacency list. We adjust the ordering by putting those vertices adjacent to v_1 to the end of the ordering, and we get $\{v_5, v_1, v_6, v_4, v_3, v_2\}$. All the vertex sets discovered from the sub search space tree of v_6, v_4, v_3 and v_2 must be subsets of $\Gamma(v_1) = \{v_2, v_3, v_4, v_6, v_7\}$, thus their adjacency lists must contain v_1. All the vertex sets containing v_1 have already been discovered from the sub search space tree of v_5 and v_1. Therefore, there is no need to search in the sub search space tree of v_6, v_4, v_3 and v_2.

Using the above method, many duplicate bicliques can be pruned especially when there is a vertex in the graph with a very high degree. However, we cannot guarantee that all of the duplicate bicliques can be pruned using the above method. The remaining duplicate bicliques can be identified by comparing a vertex set with its adjacency list. The adjacency list of a vertex set is also a vertex set in the search space tree. If the adjacency list of a vertex set is before the vertex set in the search space tree in depth-first order, it means that the biclique has been generated from the adjacency list before and the biclique generated from the vertex set itself is a duplicate.

When mining maximal bicliques from bipartite graphs, duplicate maximal bicliques can be completely avoided. Let $G = (V_1, V_2, E)$ be a bipartite graph. Since there is no edge between two vertices in V_1 or two vertices in V_2, the two vertex sets of a biclique discovered from G cannot both be subsets of V_1 or subsets of V_2. Therefore, it is sufficient to use only one vertex set of bipartite graph G to form the search space. We pick the smaller vertex set to form the search space. The adjacency lists of the vertex sets generated during the mining process must be from the other vertex set of G, and they are never searched. Hence duplicate bicliques can be avoided.

The correctness of Algorithm 1 is guaranteed by Propositions 1, 3, 4 and 5.

Theorem 1. *Given a graph G and a minimum size thres-hold ms, Algorithm 1 generates all the large maximal biclique subgraphs with respect to ms from G, and only the large maximal biclique subgraphs of G are generated.*

For a complexity analysis on the time and space of Algorithm 1, we use the following notations: n is the total number of vertices, d the maximal degree of the vertices, m the number of edges and N the number of maximal bicliques.

In algorithm 1, before we search in the sub search space tree of a vertex set X, we first check whether $\Gamma(\Gamma(X)) \subseteq (X \cup tail(X))$ is true. If it is not true, then there is no need to explore the sub search space tree of X because no biclique in the sub search space tree of X is maximal. Hence Algorithm 1 is called only for each maximal biclique. The cost for generating $\Gamma(\Gamma(X))$ is bounded by d^2. When exploring the sub search space tree of a vertex set X, we first find all those vertices $v \in tail(X)$ such that $|\Gamma(X \cup \{v\})| \geq ms$ (line 1-3). The cost of this step is bounded by $|tail(X)| \cdot |\Gamma(X)| \leq nd$. The cost for sorting the vertices in $tail(V)$ is bounded by $|tail(X)| \cdot log(|tail(X)|) \leq n \cdot logn$. Therefore, the worst-case time complexity of Algorithm 1 is $O(nd \cdot N)$.

During the mining process, we keep the whole graph in the memory. The space overhead for storing the graph is $O(m)$. When exploring the search space in depth-first order, we need to keep the adjacency lists of the vertex sets on the path this is currently being visited. The maximal depth of the path is bounded by d and the maximal size of the adjacency list of a vertex set is also bounded by d. Hence the space complexity of Algorithm 1 is $O(m + d^2)$.

4 A Performance Study

We conducted a set of experiments to demonstrate the efficiency and flexibility of our algorithm. Our experiments were conducted on a PC with an Intel Pentium IV 3.6GHz processor and 2GB of main memory. The operating system is Fedora Core 4. Our algorithm was implemented using C++ and complied using g++.

We compared our algorithm with two other algorithms. The first algorithm is MICA [2], which uses consensus algorithms to generate maximal bicliques. The MICA algorithm is available at `http://genome.cs.iastate.edu/supertree/download/biclique/README.html`. The second algorithm is the current fastest closed pattern mining algorithm—LCM, which shows the best performance in a comparative study of frequent itemset mining implementations [3]. We used the latest version of LCM—LCM3 [21] in our experiments, which is kindly provided by Takeaki Uno. Table 2 shows some information of three graphs used in our experiments. All of them are obtained from the Second DIMACS Challenge benchmarks [1]. Here, the edge density of a graph is the number of edges of the graph divided by the total possible number of edges of the graph.

We observed that most graphs in the Second DIMACS Challenge benchmarks are very dense and all the algorithms takes a long time to finish. Here we report results on three graphs shown in Table 2, on which at least one of the algorithms

---

[1] `ftp://dimacs.rutgers.edu/pub/challenge/graph/benchmarks/clique/`

Table 2. Three dense graphs

Graph	#vertices n	#Edges	edge density
johnson8-4-4	70	1855	0.768
keller4	171	9435	0.649
c-fat200-2	200	3235	0.163

can terminate within one hour. For sparse graphs in the benchmarks, such as johnson8-2-4, c-fat200-1, c-fat500-1 and p_hat300-1, all the algorithms can terminate within several seconds, so we do not show the results on these sparse graphs due to the limit of space.

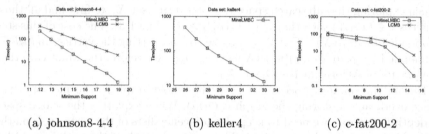

(a) johnson8-4-4   (b) keller4   (c) c-fat200-2

Fig. 2. Running time (The running time of MICA exceeds one hour on all the datasets, so it is not shown in the figures.)

Figure 2 shows the running time (y-axis) of the three algorithms with respect to the minimum size threshold (x-axis). The MICA algorithm cannot complete the mining task in any of the three datasets within one hour. LCM is unable to complete the task for keller4 because keller4 has a high edge density of 0.649 and a large number vertices of 171. Only our algorithm (denoted mineLMBC in the figure) is able to enumerate the large maximal bicliques from all the three graphs within one hour. The similar performance of MineLMBC and LCM3 in graph c-fat200-2 may be attributed to the fact that c-fat200-2 has a much lower edge density than the other two graphs.

5   Related Work

Enumerating all maximal bicliques from graphs is a NP-complete problem [2]. Some related problems have been studied. The maximal vertex biclique problem is to decide whether or not a bipartite graph contains a biclique such that $|V_1| + |V_2| \geq k$, and it can be solved in polynomial time [10]. If the constraint is that $|V_1| = |V_2| = k$ (this is called the balanced biclique problem) or $|V_1| \cdot |V_2| = k$ (this is called the maximal edge biclique problem), then the problem is NP-complete [10,17]. Geerts et al. [9] developed an approximate algorithm to find tilings—a collection of tiles from transaction databases, where a tile is a region in the database consisting solely of ones. Besson et al. [4] proposed an algorithm D-Miner to compute constrained concepts, i.e., closed sets and associated transaction sets. Mishra et al. [15] propose a new formulation of the conceptual clustering problem where the goal is to explicitly output a collection of simple and meaningful conjunctions of attributes that define the clusters. Connections between this conceptual clustering problem and the maximum edge biclique problem are made. Randomized algorithms are given that discover a collection of approximate conjunctive cluster descriptions in sublinear time.

Several algorithms have been proposed to mine maximal bicliques. Makino et al. [14] propose three algorithms to mine bicliques from bipartite graphs. The first algorithm runs with $O(M(n) \cdot N)$ time complexity and $O(n^2)$ space, the second one runs with $O(d^3 \cdot N)$ time complexity and $O(n+m)$ space, and the last one runs with $O(d^2 \cdot N)$ time complexity and $O(n+m+d \cdot N)$ space, where n is the number of vertices, $M(n)$ is the time needed to multiply two $n \times n$ matrices, m is the number of edges, d is the maximal degree of vertices and N is the number of maximal bicliques. Eppstein [8] proves that all maximal bipartite cliques can be enumerated in time $O(a^3 \cdot 2^{2a} \cdot (n+m))$, where a is the minimum number of forests into which the edges of the graph can be partitioned and it can easily be around 10 to 20 in practice. Alexe et al. [2] use consensus algorithms to mine maximal bicliques. Their algorithms need to keep all the maximal bicliques in memory, so the space complexity of their algorithm is $O(N)$, and the time complexity of their algorithm is $O(n^3 \cdot N)$. Our algorithm has better complexities than the above algorithms. Furthermore, the algorithms proposed by Makino et al. are limited to bipartite graphs. Our algorithm can be applied to any undirected graphs.

6   Conclusion

In this paper, we have presented an efficient algorithm for mining large maximal biclique subgraphs from undirected graphs. The proposed algorithm explores the search space in depth-first order. It effectively utilizes size constraints on both vertex sets to prune the search space. Our performance study shows that the proposed algorithm outperforms previous algorithms significantly.

References

1. R. Agrawal, T. Imielinski, and A. N. Swami. Mining association rules between sets of items in large databases. In *Proc of the 1993 ACM SIGMOD Conference*, pages 207–216, 1993.
2. G. Alexe, S. Alexe, Y. Crama, S. Foldes, P. L. Hammer, and B. Simeone. Consensus algorithms for the generation of all maximal bicliques. *Discrete Applied Mathematics*, 145(1):11–21, 2004.
3. R. J. Bayardo, B. Goethals, and M. J. Zaki, editors. *Proc. of the IEEE ICDM Workshop on Frequent Itemset Mining Implementations*, volume 126 of *CEUR Workshop Proceedings*. CEUR-WS.org, 2004.
4. J. Besson, C. Robardet, and J.-F. Boulicaut. Constraint-based mining of formal concepts in transactional data. In *Proc. of the 8th PAKDD Conference*, pages 615–624, 2004.

5. C. Bron and J. Kerbosch. Algorithm 457: finding all cliques of an undirected graph. *Communications of the ACM*, 16(9):575–577, 1973.
6. D. Bu, Y. Zhao, L. Cai, H. Xue, X. Zhu, H. Lu, J. Zhang, S. Sun, L. Ling, N. Zhang, G. Li, and R. Chen. Topological structure analysis of the protein protein interaction network in budding yeast. *Nucleic Acids Research*, 31(9):2443–2450, 2003.
7. F. Chung. On the coverings of graphs. *Discrete Applied Mathematics*, 30(2):89–93, 1980.
8. D. Eppstein. Arboricity and bipartite subgraph listing algorithms. *Information Processing Letters*, 51(4), 1994.
9. B. G. Floris Geerts and T. Mielikáínen. Tiling databases. In *Proc. of the 7th International Conference on Discovery Science*, pages 278–289, 2004.
10. M. Garey and D. Johnson. *Computers and Intractability: A guide to the theory of NP-completeness*. Freeman, San Francisco, 1979.
11. R. Kumar, P. Raghavan, S. Rajagopalan, and A. Tomkins. Trawling the web for emerging cyber-communities. In *Proceeding of the 8th international conference on World Wide Web*, pages 1481–1493, 1999.
12. J. Li, H. Li, D. Soh, and L. Wong. A correspondence between maximal complete bipartite subgraphs and closed patterns. In *Proc. of the 9th PKDD Conference*, pages 146–156, 2005.
13. G. Liu, H. Lu, W. Lou, and J. X. Yu. On computing, storing and querying frequent patterns. In *Proc. of the 9th ACM SIGKDD Conference*, pages 607–612, 2003.
14. K. Makino and T. Uno. New algorithms for enumerating all maximal cliques. In *Proc. of the 9th Scandinavian Workshop on Algorithm Theory*, pages 260–272, 2004.
15. N. Mishra, D. Ron, and R. Swaminathan. A new conceptual clustering framework. *Machine Learning*, 56(1-3), 2004.
16. N. Pasquier, Y. Bastide, R. Taouil, and L. Lakhal. Discovering frequent closed itemsets for association rules. In *Proc. of the 7th ICDT Conference*, pages 398–416, 1999.
17. R. Peeters. The maximum edge biclique problem is np-complete. Research Memorandum 789, Tilburg University, Faculty of Economics and Business Administration, 2000.
18. M. J. Sanderson, A. C. Driskell, R. H. Ree, O. Eulenstein, and S. Langley. Obtaining maximal concatenated phylogenetic data sets from large sequence databases. *Molecular Biology and Evolution*, 20(7):1036–1042, 2003.
19. E. Tomita, A. Tanaka, and H. Takahashi. The worst-case time complexity for generating all maximal cliques. In *International Computing and Combinatorics Conference (COCOON 2004)*, pages 161–170, 2004.
20. T. Uno, M. Kiyomi, and H. Arimura. Lcm ver. 2: Efficient mining algorithms for frequent/closed/maximal itemsets. In *Proc. of the ICDM 2004 Workshop on Frequent Itemset Mining Implementations*, 2004.
21. T. Uno, M. Kiyomi, and H. Arimura. Lcm ver. 3: Collaboration of array, bitmap and prefix tree for frequent itemset mining. In *Proc. of the ACM SIGKDD Open Source Data Mining Workshop on Frequent Pattern Mining Implementations*, 2005.
22. J. Wang, J. Pei, and J. Han. Closet+: Searching for the best strategies for mining frequent closed itemsets. In *Proc. of the 9th ACM SIGKDD Conference*, pages 236–245, 2003.
23. M. J. Zaki and C.-J. Hsiao. Charm: An efficient algorithm for closed itemset mining. In *Proc. of SIAM International Conference on Data Mining*, pages 398–416, 2002.
24. M. J. Zaki and M. Ogihara. Theoretical foundations of association rules. In *Proc. of the 3rd SIGMOD Workshop on Research Issues in Data Mining and Knowledge Discovery*, 1998.

Automatic Image Annotation by Mining the Web

Zhiguo Gong, Qian Liu, and Jingbai Zhang

Faculty of Science and Technology
University of Macau
P.O. Box 3001 Macao, PRC
{zggong, ma46620, ma46597}@umac.mo

Abstract. Automatic image annotation has been becoming an attractive research subject. Most current image annotation methods are based on training techniques. The major weaknesses of such solutions include limited annotation vocabulary and labor-intensive involvement. However, Web images possess a lot of texts, and rich annotation of samples is provided. Therefore, this report provides a novel image annotation method by mining the Web that term-image correlation is obtained from the Web not by learning. Without question, there are many noises in that relation, and some cleaning works are necessary. In the system, entropy weighting and image clustering technique are employed. Our experiment results show that our solution can achieve a satisfactory performance.

1 Introduction

With the huge amount of Web images, it is a strong need to automatically extract term-image correlation by mining the Web. And the relation can be used to annotate images or to perform image semantic explanation. In most current researches, image annotation refers to the process of automatically labeling the image contents with a predefined set of concepts representing the semantic content of images, and that method can be called the traditional image annotation. Generally, the process of tackling that traditional image annotation has several steps:

- preprocess image, including segmentation and visual content extraction.
- label sample images.
- classification problem, including clustering units, training visual feature classifier or semantic content classifier.

For the traditional image annotation, in the first step, the main optional work is to segment images into regions. Actually, the accuracy of segmentation is still an open problem. Thus, some recent systems utilize regions as sub-units and others use the whole image as a unit. And another important component is extraction of visual features. The conventional approaches of visual content-based image retrieval can be employed. The visual features of images, such as color,

A Min Tjoa and J. Trujillo (Eds.): DaWaK 2006, LNCS 4081, pp. 449–458, 2006.

texture and shape, can be extracted. Labeling images is the second step which is tedious and needs much human involvement. In this step, the predefined word set, which is used to label images manually, confines the application scope of the traditional image annotation. The third steps is the core of the annotation work, which is to construct the correlation between the terms and visual features. The current approaches have provided several models to learn that correlation, including LDA model[1], cross-media relevance model[2], 2D HMM[3], translation model[4], co-occurrence model[5] and continuous-space relevance model[6]. Their common point is to correlate the evidence about the probability of the units of images and the annotated keywords. Finally, that evidence is used to annotate unlabeled images.

As we all know, the key point in the traditional image annotation is how to learn the relationship between the semantic concepts and visual features of images. As a matter of the fact, with the explosive increase of Web information, Web images are becoming one of the most indispensable information representation types on the Web. More importantly, those Web images have two types of inherent contents attached: visual contents and semantic content. Therefore, there is a rich resource about term-image correlations and it is possible and advantageous to utilize that resource to annotate unlabeled images. And this report describes an novel approach to automatically annotate unlabeled images based on those Web image resource. That approach is called Web-based image annotation which contains two stages. The first stage is content extraction of Web images, including semantic content extraction and visual feature extraction. In the second stage, the key work is data cleaning instead of learning. Some techniques in data clustering and traditional document retrieval are employed for this purpose.

The reminder of the report is organized as follows. Sect. 2 introduces some related works. Sect. 3 shows detail discussion on semantic content extraction and visual feature extraction techniques of the Web images. Sect. 4 describes our solution on term-image correlation enhancement or noise cleaning from the aspect of both the semantic and visual feature. In Sect. 5 our evaluations are presented. And Sect. 6 gives the conclusion.

2   Related Work

Image annotation is to give the meaning of images based on existed evidence of images and the keywords. Its basic idea is to give the possible keywords of unlabeled images based on the similarity between visual features of unlabeled images and those of annotated images with keywords. That similarity can be measured by color, shape and texture. The earliest attempt at transformation of "image-to-word" was Mori et al.[5], who used co-occurrence model to annotate images based on trained clusters with predicted keywords after clustering the fix-sized regions which images are divided into. And then, different models of image annotation came forth. Barnard and Forsyth[7] considered visual features and the semantic of images are different language contexts and utilized translation model to give keywords to regions which was similar to the language translation. Blei and Jordan[1] proposed the Latent Dirichlet Allocation (LDA) model to handle the words and images, which generated the mixture of latent factors for words and units of images. Li and Wang[3] proposed two-dimensional multiresolution hidden Markov (2D HMM) model to associate concepts to images. Jeon et al.[2] propounded cross-media relevance model, which considered image annotation as the cross-lingual retrieval problem. Chang et al.[8] used the Bayes Point Machine to associate the images with the keywords at image level. All those methods are based the traditional supervised learning principle. To achieve better performance, the training set is large enough, and then causes plenty of manual work.

To overcome the problem of the large training set, Feng and Chua[9] provided bootstrapping method, which was to start from a small set of labeled training samples, and to successively annotate the larger set of unlabeled images by co-training. They demonstrated that the method reached a relative better performance to the traditional supervised learning method. To overcome the problems that the performance is influenced by clustering and the mutual independence of the events of observing region, Rui et al.[10] proposed clustering with pair-wise constrained and formulated Semi-Naïve Bayesian model to annotate images. To deal with the problem of the keyword sparseness, Cheng and Chien[11] provided three levels to annotate images, including image level, keyword level and concept level.

As a summary of the past works, two main weaknesses exist, including (1) limited scope of annotation vocabulary and (2) labor-intensive expert involvement. Those weaknesses seriously confine the application areas of the traditional image annotation. Meanwhile, Web images provide many rich sample images with large amount of dynamic and abundant terms. Therefore, it is both possible and valuable to annotate images based on the Web image resource.

3   Automatic Image Annotation

Image annotation is based on the assumption that images with the same kind in semantic content are similar in visual features. And in the traditional image annotation, the basic works include extracting visual features of units of images or the whole images and labeling the sample images. After that, the key work is to construct the term-image correlation before annotating unlabeled images. And the correlation between the terms and visual features is obtained during the process of learning. That correlation can be represented into the following pseudometric.

$$\text{Metric}_{\text{ImageTerm}} = \begin{pmatrix} ttf_{i_1t_1} & ttf_{i_1t_2} & \cdots & ttf_{i_1t_N} \\ ttf_{i_2t_1} & ttf_{i_2t_2} & \cdots & ttf_{i_2t_N} \\ \vdots & \vdots & \ddots & \vdots \\ ttf_{i_Mt_1} & ttf_{i_Mt_2} & \cdots & ttf_{i_Mt_N} \end{pmatrix} \tag{1}$$

In metric 1, there are N keywords and M visual features of images. And each row presents the information of visual features of an unit of images or an image and each column is a word. Thus, each element in the metric $ttf_{i_jt_k}$ represents the association between term t_k and image i_j. The metric is the basis of image annotation.

In Web-based image annotation, the relationships between terms and visual features is also represented with that metric, but the metric is obtained not by learning from the labeled samples but from Web image mining. Therefore, the metric is built while the process of the content extraction from Web images on semantic level and visual feature level. While the Web has a huge and comprehensive source of sample images, there are many noises. Therefore, it is necessary to clean the noises before annotating unlabeled images. The architecture of our image annotation system is shown in Fig. 1.

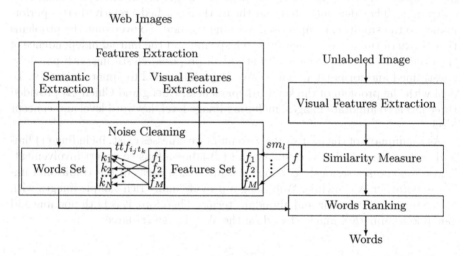

Fig. 1. The Architecture of the System

In Fig. 1, sm_l, which can be calculated by Euclidean distance between visual features, is the similarity between unlabeled images and annotated images, $ttf_{i_jt_k}$, M and N are the same as those in metric. It can be seen from Fig. 1 that sm_l is how much similarity between unlabeled images and the annotated images and $ttf_{i_jt_k}$ is the association between keywords and the annotated images, what is important is how to determine the association between keywords and unlabeled images based on that information. Out of question, the association can be obtained by the product of sm_l and $ttf_{i_jt_k}$. Therefore, in the process of keywords ranking, the formula 2 is used to calculate the association of the keyword t_k to images i_n:

$$ttf_{i_nt_k} = \sum_{l=1}^{M} \frac{sm_l}{\sum_{j=1}^{M} sm_j} * ttf_{i_lt_k}. \qquad (2)$$

Therefore, there are two basic components necessary in Web-based image annotation: one is semantic content extraction for $ttf_{i_j t_k}$ and the other is visual feature extraction for sm_l.

3.1 Semantic Content Extraction

In most works of the traditional image annotation, the sample images are usually labeled by human beings, which involves extensive work and may produce many problems, such as keyword sparseness comparing with the rich semantic terms used in the real world. Meanwhile, huge and comprehensive images associated with texts are available on the Web and those valuable images can just overcome the limitations caused by the traditional methods. Furthermore, the dynamic Web can well support the evolution of the annotation vocabulary.

Before extracting the semantic of Web images, the text sources must be determined. Based on the relationship of the embedded images and the Web pages, there are several text sources with potential semantic relevant to the Web images: images title, images alt, images caption, pages title[12,13,10] and other surrounding text[12,10]. Some another sources, such as HTML meta data, maybe provide some information in some cases, but generally, they often cause the confusion. At length, we choose five parts, image's title(STT), image's alt(STA), image's caption(STC), page's title(STP) and nearest surrounding text(STS) for the semantic sources.

When extracting the semantic, term oriented representation model[12] is utilized. The basic idea is to consider each word independently and the terms have different weights which are based on the relevance of different text sources to Web images. A variable of TFIDF model[12] can describe the association of term t_k to image i_j as follows:

$$ntf(t_k)|_{ST_l} = \frac{tf(t_k)|_{ST_l}}{|ST_l|} \tag{3}$$

In (3), $tf(t_k)|_{ST_l}$ is the frequency of term t in the text block type ST_l, where the text block type may be STT, STA, STC, STP or STS. $|ST_l|$ is the size of text block type ST_l. Thus, the total term association to image i_j is calculated as:

$$ttf(t_k)|_{i_j} = \sum_{k=1}^{L} w_l * ntf(t_k)|_{ST_l} \tag{4}$$

In (4), L is the total number of the text block type, and w_l is the weight factor of ST_l, which is defined according to how much this semantic word contributes to the image i_j. Without loss of generality, after normalizing w_l, $\sum_{k=1}^{L} w_l = 1$.

3.2 Visual Content Extraction

To annotate unlabeled images, there are two key issues: one is the association of keywords to annotated images which is $ttf_{i_j t_k}$ in the metric 1, and the other is the similarity between visual features of unlabeled images and annotated images. Currently, the available visual features include color, texture and shape. Those features can be based on whole images or based on the units of images. But the technologies to segment images into regions is still open problem. Therefore, the global color feature and global texture feature are utilized.

For color feature, HSL color space is selected because it is tractable and perceptually uniform and easy and possible to transform from popular RGB color space to HSL color space. There are several forms of color feature, including color histogram, color coherence vector[14], color correlogram, color moments and color set[15]. And in Web-based image annotation, the form of color feature is quantized color histogram. In HSL, hue is quantized into 18 levels, and lightness and saturation are quantized into 3 levels respectively. Thus, there are 162(18*3*3) color in HSL color space. In addition, grey color is quantized into 4 levels. At length, the color histogram is 166-dimension.

For texture feature, Daubechies wavelet transform is chosen because of its better performance in the time and frequency domain. Each image is decomposed into four frequencies at each level, diagonal coefficients(HH), vertical coefficients(HL), approximation coefficients(LL), horizontal coefficients(LH). For those frequencies, except HH, each frequency is decomposed again because HH is unstable. And for each frequency at each level, the mean and variance are used as the components of texture feature vector, which can be described as follow:

$$\overrightarrow{fvt} = \{\frac{\mu_{11}}{\delta_{\mu_{11}}} \frac{\sigma_{11}}{\delta_{\sigma_{11}}} \frac{\mu_{12}}{\delta_{\mu_{12}}} \frac{\sigma_{12}}{\delta_{\sigma_{12}}} \cdots \frac{\mu_{ij}}{\delta_{\mu_{ij}}} \frac{\sigma_{ij}}{\delta_{\sigma_{ij}}} \cdots \frac{\mu_{NM}}{\delta_{\mu_{NM}}} \frac{\sigma_{NM}}{\delta_{\sigma_{NM}}}\} \qquad (5)$$

In (5), N is the level of the transform and M is the number of frequency of each level and here, M is four denoting the number of one approximation frequency and three detail frequencies. μ_{ij} and σ_{ij} is respectively the mean and variance of the frequency j in level i. And $\delta_{\sigma_{ij}}$ and $\delta_{\mu_{ij}}$ are standard deviations of σ_{ij} and μ_{ij} respectively in the entire database. For each unit of images, 4-level wavelet transform is performed. Therefore, texture feature vector is 320(4*(1+3+9+27)*2)-dimension. And the distance between those visual features can be measured by Euclidean distance.

Up to now, the metric is obtained from Web pages. Metric 1 is dynamic, efficient and automatically expanded with the increase of Web pages. Inevitably, there are some noises. Therefore, the metric must be cleaned in order to raise the annotation performance.

4 Methods for Cleaning

As we know, in Web pages, many associated words of Web images are irrelevant to the semantic of the images. Those words may produce many noises in the metric 1 and there is a strong need to clean those noises in order to raise the performance. In our approach, we employ three techniques available for noise cleaning, including word weighting with respect to inter-image dissimilarity, non-semantic term removing and image clustering.

From the metric 1, it is obvious that the relationship between visual features and words is similar to that between text documents and words. And further, for Web pages, some words are often used but they are noises, such as term 'image'. Therefore, some methods of document term weighting, such as inter-image weight strategy, can be used to recalculate the association between images and terms in order to clean effectively the noises. Typical weight strategies include boolean weighting, word frequency, $tf \times idf$ weighting, tfc weighting, ltc weighting and entropy weighting. Entropy weighting produces a better performance [16]. And the formula of entropy weighting is calculated as:

$$ttfw_{i_j t_k} = log(ttf_{i_j t_k} + 1) + \left(1 + \frac{1}{log(N)} \sum_{l=1}^{N} \left[\frac{ttf_{i_l t_k}}{n_k} log\left(\frac{ttf_{i_l t_k}}{n_k}\right)\right]\right) \quad (6)$$

where $ttfw_{i_j t_k}$ is the item of metric 1, N the number of images and n_i is the sum of the association of word i to all images. Through that method, some noises, such as 'image' can be assigned with lower association.

From the aspect of linguistics, it is notable that image annotation is based on the meaningful terms. However, the associated text of Web images often contains many less meaningful terms which are called non-semantic terms, such as the size description, identifier, and created time of the images. Those terms have little helps for image annotation. In our system, that associated text is the form of number term, which can account for more than 12% of the words extracted. Therefore, in our system, those non-semantic terms are removed to raise the annotation performance.

The above techniques are used to reduce the adverse affections caused by the noise terms and the improvement of the performance can be found from Table 2. Further, visual features of Web images also include many noises. As we know from metric 1, each word is associated with a list of Web images. As a matter of the fact, large percent of the images in the list are irrelevant to the concepts. That is, we can naturally suppose that Web images associated to a word can be classified into two clusters, one for relevant images and the other for irrelevant images. Further, the relevant images actually construct a dense set, while the irrelevant class tends to be a spare set. And more importantly, in those two clusters, inversely and generally, the dense set is considered as more close to the word with smaller mean and variance, and it is called relevant image set, and the spare set is considered as irrelevant image set. In other words, the relevant set of images have similar visual features, and irrelevant set is hard to converge to some points, and the mean and variance of distances of the relevant images are smaller than those of irrelevant image set. However, in relevant image set, although those images have the same semantic with most probability, the relevant degrees are different greatly. Therefore, it is necessary to enhance that relevance. It is opposite for irrelevant image set. And we know, $ttf_{i_j t_k}$ is inverse to the mean and variance of the distance in the sets and this relation can be used to recalculate $ttf_{i_j t_k}$ in order to cleanse. Supposed that clustering method can be utilized to obtain the two sets and m is the mean of the distance for each set and v is its variance, $ttf_{i_j t_k}$ can be recalculated again by the formula:

$tffc_{i_j t_k} = \frac{tff_{i_j t_k}}{log(m \times v)^{\alpha}}$, where α is the coefficient and denotes how much m and v affect $ttf_{i_j t_k}$. And then the effect of those irrelevant images is scaled down and that of those relevant images is enhanced in the process of annotating unlabeled images. Now, the performance of clustering is shown in Table 1. In Table 1,

Table 1. Clustering Performance

topic	Precision	Recall	F1
umac	0.37766	0.747368	0.501767
dv	0.506849	0.536232	0.521127
camera	0.298734	0.751592	0.427536
printer	0.151515	0.882353	0.258621
calculator	0.188889	0.607143	0.288136
game	0.34728	0.734513	0.471591
scanner	0.226667	0.894737	0.361702
Average	0.287891375	0.74892675	0.415906217

the performance of some topic is very low, which is due to that the number of those topic is not enough, such as topic 'scanner' with only 18 images in database. From Table 1, the association of most images with same sematic has been enhanced as expected, although the precision is not very high.

5   Performance Evaluation

To evaluate the performance, the prototype system is implemented based on the architecture described in Fig. 1. In our experiments, more than 12000 Web images from 50000 Web pages are gathered after noise images, such as icons, banners, logos and any image with size less than 5k, removed. And there are more than 50000 keywords. In our experiments, the performance is evaluated by Mean Reciprocal Rank (MRR) method in (7),

$$MRR = \frac{1}{N} \sum_{k=1}^{N} \frac{1}{n_k} \qquad (7)$$

where N is the number of testing images used and n_k is the position of the first correct word in the image annotation. About the performance evaluation, Cheng and Chien[11] used a method about the relation of the position and the precision and the recall at that position. However, that method is not suitable for our experiments due to the reasons: (1) The prototype system has abundant words while in [11] there is word sparseness. Abundant words produce great effect on the precision and the recall. For example, an image, which is about a notebook, can be annotated with word 'notebook' or 'laptop' and so on by different Web developer and those words are unexpected. Therefore, when evaluating annotation, more relevant words are added to the testing image, higher the precision is but lower the recall is. It is opposite for the precision and the recall when the relevant words is less. But that inverse action does not in [11]; and (2) The unlabeled image can be considered as single content, if not, it is possible to segment an image into several images, because multi-content images can lead to low precision based on visual features. Therefore, it is little valuable to give another relevant semantic word to an image when the first correct word has been added to the image. That is, the first correct word is more important. Therefore, MRR approach is suitable to make the performance evaluation.

100 test images are used to evaluate the performance of Web image annotation. And Table 2 is the annotation performance. In Table 2, baseline value is to

Table 2. Annotation Performance

	Baseline	Word Cleaning	Clustering Cleaning
MRR	0.129422	0.292236	0.349141

use the original data in metric 1 to make the annotation. Its MRR is 0.129422. It is not satisfactory because of there are so many noises. Therefore, some obvious noises are removed, such as number terms. And then, the entropy weighting is used to recalculate $ttf_{i_j t_k}$. That process is called word cleaning and better performance is obtained with MRR 0.292236. And then, clustering cleaning is performed. And it uses the similarity between the images to cluster the images associated to some term into two sets and degrades the effect of the noises based on the relation that $ttf_{i_j t_k}$ is inversely related to the mean and the variance of the similarity within the same set. Finally, the performance is further improved and acceptable with MRR 0.349141.

6 Conclusion

Image annotation is an attractive research area. There is a lot of contribution made and many famous models have been produced, such as LDA model, cross-media relevance model, 2D HMM, translation model, co-occurrence model and continuous-space relevance model. Those models are all based on training data, with limited word vocabulary and extensive manual works. To overcome those problems in the traditional works, in this report, we proposes automatic image annotation techniques based on Web image resource. However, there are many noises from both the semantic aspect and visual feature aspect. Therefore, some document processing method and image clustering technique are used to clean the noises from both aspects. With such techniques, the performance of our annotation system can provide a satisfied result.

References

1. David M. Blei and Michael I. Jordan. Modeling annotated data. In *SIGIR* [17], pages 127–134.
2. Jiwoon Jeon, Victor Lavrenko, and R. Manmatha. Automatic image annotation and retrieval using cross-media relevance models. In *SIGIR* [17], pages 119–126.

3. James Z. Wang and Jia Li. Learning-based linguistic indexing of pictures with 2-d mhmms. In *MULTIMEDIA '02: Proceedings of the tenth ACM international conference on Multimedia*, pages 436–445, New York, NY, USA, 2002. ACM Press.

4. Kobus Barnard, Pinar Duygulu, David A. Forsyth, Nando de Freitas, David M. Blei, and Michael I. Jordan. Matching words and pictures. *Journal of Machine Learning Research*, 3:1107–1135, 2003.

5. Y. Mori, H. Takahashi, and R. Oka. Image-to-word transformation based on dividing and vector quantizing images with words, 1999.

6. Victor Lavrenko, R. Manmatha, and Jiwoon Jeon. A model for learning the semantics of pictures. In Sebastian Thrun, Lawrence K. Saul, and Bernhard Schölkopf, editors, *NIPS*. MIT Press, 2003.

7. Kobus Barnard and David A. Forsyth. Learning the semantics of words and pictures. In *ICCV*, pages 408–415, 2001.

8. Edward Y. Chang, Kingshy Goh, Gerard Sychay, and Gang Wu. Cbsa: content-based soft annotation for multimodal image retrieval using bayes point machines. *IEEE Trans. Circuits Syst. Video Techn.*, 13(1):26–38, 2003.

9. HuaMin Feng and Tat-Seng Chua. A bootstrapping approach to annotating large image collection. In Nicu Sebe, Michael S. Lew, and Chabane Djeraba, editors, *Multimedia Information Retrieval*, pages 55–62. ACM, 2003.

10. Rui Shi, Wanjun Jin, and Tat-Seng Chua. A novel approach to auto image annotation based on pairwise constrained clustering and semi-naïve bayesian model. In Yi-Ping Phoebe Chen, editor, *MMM*, pages 322–327. IEEE Computer Society, 2005.

11. Pu-Jen Cheng and Lee-Feng Chien. Effective image annotation for searches using multilevel semantics. *Int. J. on Digital Libraries*, 4(4):258–271, 2004.

12. Zhiguo Gong, Leong Hou U, and Chan Wa Cheang. An implementation of web image search engines. In *ICADL*, pages 355–367, 2004.

13. Heng Tao Shen, Beng Chin Ooi, and Kian-Lee Tan. Giving meanings to www images. In *MULTIMEDIA '00: Proceedings of the eighth ACM international conference on Multimedia*, pages 39–47, New York, NY, USA, 2000. ACM Press.

14. Greg Pass, Ramin Zabih, and Justin Miller. Comparing images using color coherence vectors. In *ACM Multimedia*, pages 65–73, 1996.

15. John R. Smith and Shih-Fu Chang. Visualseek: A fully automated content-based image query system. In *ACM Multimedia*, pages 87–98, 1996.

16. Susan T. Dumais. Improving the retrieval of information from external sources. In *Behavior Research Methods, Instruments, and Computers 23(2)*, pages 229–236, 1991.

17. *SIGIR 2003: Proceedings of the 26th Annual International ACM SIGIR Conference on Research and Development in Information Retrieval, July 28 - August 1, 2003, Toronto, Canada*. ACM, 2003.

Privacy Preserving Spatio-temporal Clustering on Horizontally Partitioned Data*

Ali İnan and Yücel Saygın

Sabancı University, Faculty of Engineering and Natural Sciences,
34956, Istanbul, Turkey
inanali@su.sabanciuniv.edu
ysaygin@sabanciuniv.edu

Abstract. Time-stamped location information is regarded as spatio-temporal data and, by its nature, such data is highly sensitive from the perspective of privacy. In this paper, we propose a privacy preserving spatio-temporal clustering method for horizontally partitioned data which, to the best of our knowledge, was not done before. Our methods are based on building the dissimilarity matrix through a series of secure multi-party trajectory comparisons managed by a third party. Our trajectory comparison protocol complies with most trajectory comparison functions and complexity analysis of our methods shows that our protocol does not introduce extra overhead when constructing dissimilarity matrix, compared to the centralized approach.

1 Introduction

Advances in wireless communication technologies resulted in a rapid increase in usage of mobile devices. PDAs, mobile phones and various other devices equipped with GPS technology are now a part of our daily life. One direct consequence of this change is that, using such devices, locations of individuals can be tracked by wireless service providers. Individuals sometimes voluntarily pay for being tracked by means of Location Based Services (LBS) such as vehicle telematics that offer vehicle tracking and satellite navigation. Tracking is also enforced by law in some countries, as in the case of the Enhanced-911 mandate, passed by U.S. Federal Communications Commission in 1996. The mandate requires that any cellular phone calling 911, the U.S. nationwide emergency service number, be located within at least 50 to 100 meters.

Time-stamped location information is regarded as spatio-temporal data due to its time and space dimensions and, by its nature, is highly vulnerable to misuse. In fact, privacy issues related to collection, use and distribution of individuals' location information is the main obstacle against extensive deployment of LBSs. Suppressing identifiers from the data does not suffice since trajectories can easily be re-bound to individuals using publicly available information such as home and work addresses. Therefore new privacy preserving knowledge discovery methods, designed specifically

---

* This work was funded by the Information Society Technologies programme of the European Commission, Future and Emerging Technologies under IST-014915 GeoPKDD project.

A Min Tjoa and J. Trujillo (Eds.): DaWaK 2006, LNCS 4081, pp. 459–468, 2006.

to handle spatio-temporal data, are required. Existing privacy preserving data mining techniques are not suitable for this purpose since time-stamped location observations of an object are not plain, independent attributes of this object.

In this work, we propose a privacy preserving clustering technique for horizontally partitioned spatio-temporal data where each horizontal partition contains trajectories of distinct moving objects collected by a separate site. Consider the following scenario where the proposed techniques are applicable: In order to solve traffic congestion, traffic control offices want to cluster trajectories of users. However, the required spatio-temporal data is not readily available but can be collected from GSM operators. GSM operators are not eager to share their data due to privacy concerns. The solution is running a privacy preserving spatio-temporal clustering algorithm for horizontally partitioned data.

Our method is based on constructing the dissimilarity matrix of object trajectories in a privacy preserving manner which can then be input to any hierarchical clustering algorithm. Main contributions are introduction of a protocol for secure multi-party computation of trajectory distances and its application to privacy preserving clustering of spatio-temporal data. We also provide complexity and privacy analysis of the proposed method.

In Section 2, we provide related work in the area and then formally define the problem in Section 3. Classification of trajectory comparison functions is provided in Section 4. Communication and computation phases of our method are explained in Sections 5 and 6 respectively. We provide complexity and privacy analysis in Section 7 and finally conclude in Section 8.

2 Related Work

Privacy preserving data mining has become a popular research area in the past 5 years. The aim of privacy preserving data mining is ensuring individual privacy while maintaining the efficacy of data mining techniques. Agrawal and Srikant initiated research on privacy preserving data mining with their seminal paper on constructing classification models while preserving privacy [7]. Saygin et al. propose methods for hiding sensitive association rules before releasing the data [14]. Privacy preserving data mining methods can be classified under two headings: data sanitization and secure multi-party computation. Data sanitization approaches sacrifice accuracy for increased privacy, while secure multi-party computation approaches try to achieve both accuracy and privacy at the expense of high communication and computation costs.

Researchers developed methods for privacy preserving clustering. Most of these methods are based on sanitizing the input and they address only centralized data. Merugu and Ghosh propose methods for constructing data mining models from the input data. These models are not considered private information. The overall clustering schema is constructed by merging these models coming from vertically or horizontally distributed data sources [9]. Oliveira and Zaiane propose methods for preserving privacy by reducing the dimensionality of the data [5]. Their method is not applicable to horizontally partitioned data and moreover, results in loss of accuracy. Vaidya and Clifton propose a secure multi-party computation protocol for k-means clustering on vertically partitioned data [10]. Jha et al. [8] propose a privacy preserving, distributed k-means protocol on horizontally partitioned data through secure multi-party computation of cluster means. Inan et al. propose another privacy preserving clustering algorithm over horizontally partitioned data that can handle numeric, categorical and alphanumeric data [6].

Privacy of spatio-temporal data is of utmost importance for individuals since such data is highly vulnerable to misuse. In this work, we focus on spatio-temporal data and propose a secure multi-party comparison protocol that is applicable to most trajectory comparison functions. Previous work on ensuring individual privacy for spatio-temporal data is limited to sanitization approaches and access control mechanisms. Gruteser and Hoh propose confusing paths to garble trajectories of individuals [11]. Beresord and Stajano introduce "mix zones", in which identification of users is blocked and pseudonyms of incoming user trajectories are mixed up while leaving these mixed zones [12]. A detailed discussion on privacy mechanisms through access control and anonymization can be found in [13]. To the best of our knowledge, this work is the first to introduce a secure multi-party solution to privacy problems in spatio-temporal data without any loss of accuracy.

3   Problem Formulation

Spatio-temporal knowledge discovery deals with time-stamped location observations of moving objects. In some applications spatial component may interpreted in a different way. For example, in stock market analysis, trajectory of a stock is the one-dimensional vector of price fluctuations in time. In weather forecasting, observations are two dimensional measurements of atmospheric pressure and temperature at weather stations. In this paper, we primarily focus on moving objects and assume that location information is two dimensional as in the case of GPS, neglecting the altitude.

Trajectory T of a moving object X is a set of location observations in the form O = (t, d) where t represents the time dimension and d represents the two dimensional location information. Number of observations for this trajectory is denoted as $length(X)$ and i^{th} element of T_X is denoted by $T_X(i)$. Figure 1 depicts these notions for the sample one dimensional spatio-temporal data provided in Table 1.

Table 1. Spatio-temporal data for trajectories X and Y

X	Time				
	1	4	7	10	16
Location	2,3	4,5	6,7	3	2
Y	Time				
	2	4	6	8	
Location	4,3	3,6	7	3	

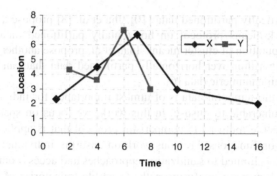

Fig. 1. Trajectories X and Y. $length(X) = 5$ and $length(Y) = 4$

Suppose that there are K data holders, such that $K \geq 2$, which track locations of with unique object id's. The number of objects in data holder k's database is denoted as $size_K$. Data holders want to cluster the trajectories of moving objects without publishing sensitive location information so that clustering results will be public to each data holder at the end of the protocol. There is a distinct third party, denoted as TP, who serves as a means of computation power and storage space. TP's role in the protocol is: (1) managing the communication between data holders, (2) privately constructing the global dissimilarity matrix, (3) clustering the trajectories using the dissimilarity matrix, and (4) publishing the results to the data holders.

Involved parties, including the third party, are assumed to be semi-honest which means that they follow the protocol as they are expected to, but may store any information that is available in order to infer private data in the future. Semi-trusted behavior is also called honest-but-curious behavior. Another assumption is that, all parties are non-colluding, i.e. they do not share private information with each other.

4 Trajectory Comparison Functions

Clustering is the process of grouping similar objects together. In order to measure the similarity between object trajectories, robust comparison functions are needed. However, trajectory comparison is not an easy task since spatio-temporal data is usually collected through sensors and therefore is subject to diverse sources of noise. Under ideal circumstances, object trajectories would be of the same length and time-stamps of their corresponding elements would be equal. The distance between two trajectories satisfying these conditions could be computed using Euclidean distance, simply by summing the distance over all elements with equal time-stamps. In real world, on the other hand, non-overlapping observation intervals, time shifts and different sampling rates are common. Although various trajectory comparison functions have been proposed to cope with these difficulties, this topic is still an ongoing research area.

Most trajectory comparison functions stem from four basic algorithms: (1) Euclidean distance, (2) Longest Common Subsequence (LCSS), (3) Dynamic Time Warping

(DTW), and (4) Edit distance. We classify these algorithms into two groups with respect to penalties added per pair-wise element comparisons: real penalty functions and quantized penalty functions. Real penalty functions measure the distance in terms of the Euclidean distance between observations while quantized penalty functions increment the distance by values 0 or 1 at each step depending on spatial proximity of the compared observations. In the following subsections we explain crucial trajectory comparison functions briefly and provide the reasoning behind this classification. For a detailed discussion on characteristics of these algorithms, please refer to [1].

Significance of our privacy preserving trajectory comparison protocol is due to the fact that it is applicable to all comparison functions explained below. Furthermore, the protocol does not trade accuracy against privacy unlike previous work.

4.1 Comparison Functions with Real Penalty

Euclidean distance, Edit distance with Real Penalty (ERP) and DTW are the comparison functions with real penalty. Euclidean distance is a naïve method based on comparing the corresponding observations of trajectories with the same length. The algorithm terminates in $O(n)$ time, returning the sum of real penalties. Euclidean distance function is sensitive to time shifts and noise but the output is a metric value.

ERP [4] measures the minimum cost of transforming the compared trajectory to the source trajectory using insertion, deletion and replacement operations. Cost of each operation is calculated using real spatial distance values. Cost of replacing observation i with observation j is $dist(i, j)$, where $dist$ is the Euclidean distance. However in case of insertion (or deletion), added cost is the distance between the inserted (or deleted) observation and the constant observation value g, defined by the user. ERP compares all pairs of elements in the trajectories, returning a metric value in $O(n^2)$ time. The algorithm is resistant to time shifts but not to noise.

DTW was initially proposed for approximate sequence matching in speech recognition but is generalized to similarity search in time series by authors of [3]. The algorithm is very similar to Edit distance but instead of insertions and deletions, stutters are used. The ith stutter on x dimension, denoted as $stutter_i(x)$, repeats the ith element and shifts following elements to the right. Computation cost is $O(n^2)$ as expected and resultant distance value is non-metric. Allowing repetitions strengthens the algorithm against time shifts but does not help with noise.

4.2 Comparison Functions with Quantized Penalty

Trajectory comparison functions with quantized penalty are LCSS [2] and Edit distance on Real Sequence (EDR) [1]. Both algorithms try to match all pairs of elements in the compared trajectories and therefore have a computation cost of $O(n^2)$. A pair of observations is considered a match if they are close to each other in space by less then a threshold, ε. LCSS returns the length of the longest matched sequence of observations while EDR returns the minimum number of insertion, deletion or replacement operations required to transform one trajectory to the other. Although these algorithms are resistant to time shifts and noise, distance values are not metric.

5 Communication Phase

As explained before, the protocol for privacy preserving comparison of trajectories consists of two phases: communication phase and computation phase. In the communication phase, data holders exchange data among themselves and the third party (TP), who will carry out the computation phase and publish the clustering results.

Prior to the communication phase we assume that every involved party, including the third party, has already generated pair-wise keys. These keys are used as seeds to pseudo-random number generators which disguise the exchanged messages. Diffie-Hellman key exchange protocol is perfectly suitable for key generation [15].

Dissimilarity matrix is an object by object structure. In case of spatio-temporal data, an entry $D[i][j]$ of the dissimilarity matrix D is the distance between trajectories of objects i and j calculated using any comparison function. In Section 6, we show that our privacy preserving comparison protocol is suitable for all comparison functions explained in Section 4. If trajectories of both i and j are held by the same site, this site can calculate their distance locally and send it to the third party. However, if trajectories of i and j are at separate sites, these sites should run the protocol explained below. Assuming K data holders, $C(K,2)$ runs are required, one for each pair of data holders.

Suppose that two data holders, DH_A and DH_B, with $size(A)$ and $size(B)$ trajectories respectively, want to compare their data. Assume that the protocol starts with DH_A. For each trajectory T in DH_A's database, two pseudo-random number generators are initialized, rng_{AB} and rng_{AT}. The seed for rng_{AB} is the key shared with DH_B and the seed for rng_{AT} is the key shared with TP. Then, for each dimension of spatial component of T's elements (i.e. x and y), DH_A disguises its input as follows: if the pseudo-random number generated by rng_{AB} is odd, DH_A negates its input and increments it by the pseudo-random number generated by rng_{AT}. Finally, DH_A sends the disguised values to DH_B.

```
Begin
   For j=0 to size(DH_A)
      Initialize rng_AB with the key K_AB
      Initialize rng_AT with the key K_AT
      For m=0 to length(DH_A[j])
         DH_A[j][m].x =rng_AT + DH_A[j][m].x * -1^rng_AB%2
         DH_A[j][m].y =rng_AT + DH_A[j][m].y * -1^rng_AB%2
   Send DH_A to DH_B
End
```

Fig. 2. Pseudo code of trajectory comparison protocol at site DH_A

Upon receiving data from DH_A, DH_B initializes a matrix M of size $size(B){\times}size(A)$, which will be DH_B's output. For each trajectory T in its database, DH_B initializes a pseudo-random number generator rng_{AB} with the key shared with DH_A and negates its inputs in a similar fashion. This time negation is done when the generated number is even. DH_B then starts filling values into M. An entry $M[i][j][m][n]$ of M is DH_A's j^{th} trajectory's n^{th} observation compared to DH_B's i^{th} trajectories m^{th} observation. DH_B simply adds its input to the input received from DH_A. At the end, M is sent to TP by DH_B.

```
Begin
  For i=0 to size(DH_B)
    For j=0 to size(DH_A)
      For n=0 to length(DH_B[i])
        Initialize rng_AB with the key K_AB
        For m=0 to length(DH_A[j])
          M[i][j][n][m].x +=DH_B[i][n].x * -1^(rng_AB +1)%2
          M[i][j][n][m].y +=DH_B[i][n].y * -1^(rng_AB+1)%2
  Send M to TP
End
```

Fig. 3. Pseudo code of trajectory comparison protocol at site DH_B

TP subtracts the random numbers added by DH_A using a pseudo-random number generator, rng_{AT}, initialized with the key shared with DH_A. Now, absolute value of any entry $M[i][j][m][n]$ is $| DH_A[j][n] - DH_B[i][m] |$. These values are all that is needed by any comparison function to compute the distance between trajectories i and j.

Pseudo codes for the roles described above are given in Figures 2, 3 and 4. Discussion on the necessity of each pseudo-random number generator used in the protocol is provided in Section 7.

```
Begin
  For i=0 to size(DH_B)
    For j=0 to size(DH_A)
      For n=0 to length(DH_B[i])
        Initialize rng_AT with the key K_AT
        For m=0 to length(DH_A[j])
          M[i][j][n][m].x = |M[i][j][n][m].x - rng_AT|
          M[i][j][n][m].y = |M[i][j][n][m].y - rng_AT|
End
```

Fig. 4. Pseudo code of trajectory comparison protocol at site TP

6 Computation/Aggregation Phase

The third party can compute pair-wise trajectory distances for data holder sites A and B, once the comparison matrix M is built through the protocol in Section 5. If the comparison function measures distances using real penalty, then $M[i][j][m][n]$ is the cost for A's j^{th} trajectory's n^{th} observation with respect to B's i^{th} trajectory's m^{th} observation. Otherwise, if a quantized penalty comparison function is to be employed, TP simply checks whether $M[i][j][m][n] < \varepsilon$ to match these two observations.

What remains is performing comparisons of the form $M[i][j]$, where both i and j are trajectories of the same data holder site. In such cases, another privacy preserving protocol is not required to compute these values, since conveying local dissimilarity matrices to TP does not leak any private information, proven in [5].

In order to build the dissimilarity matrix, TP must ensure that every data holder site has sent its local dissimilarity matrix and run the pair-wise comparison protocol with every other data holder. Figure 5 is the pseudo-code for constructing local dissimilarity matrices where *distance* denotes the comparison function.

```
Begin
  For m=0 to size(DH)
    For n=0 to m
      D[m][n]= distance(DH[m], DH[n])
End
```

Fig. 5. Pseudo code for local dissimilarity matrix construction

After gathering comparison results for all pairs of trajectories, *TP* normalizes the values in the dissimilarity matrix. These normalized distances are the only required input for most clustering algorithms, such as k-medoids, hierarchical and density based clustering algorithms. Another key observation here is that using our protocol, *TP* may use any clustering algorithm depending on requirements of the data holders.

At the end of the clustering process, the third party sends the clustering results to the data holders. The results are in the form of lists of objects identifiers, since publishing the dissimilarity matrix itself would cause private information leakage. The third party can also publish clustering quality parameters, if requested by the data holders.

7 Complexity and Privacy Analysis

In this section, we analyze the communication and computation costs of the pair-wise comparison protocol and local dissimilarity matrix construction. An analysis of the privacy offered by the protocol follows.

Every data holder has to send its local dissimilarity matrix to the third party. Computation cost of constructing the matrix is $O(n^2 * distance)$ where n is the number of trajectories and *distance* denotes the complexity of the comparison function. For Euclidean, the cost becomes $O(n^2*p)$ and for the other comparison functions it is $O(n^2*p^2)$ where p is the maximum number of observations in a trajectory.

The initiator of the comparison protocol, DH_A in Section 5, has a computation cost of $O(n*p)$. The follower, DH_B, on the other hand makes $O(n*m*p^2)$ computations where m is the number of trajectories at site DH_B. Communication costs are parallel to computation costs since every party sends the result of the computation without any further operation.

There is an apparent imbalance in the computation and communication costs of the follower and initiator parties. *TP* can easily solve this problem by arranging the sequence that pair-wise comparison protocols are carried out such that every party will be the initiator at least $\lfloor (K-1)/2 \rfloor$ times in a setting of *K* data holders.

Sharing dissimilarity matrices does not leak any private information according to [5], as long as the private data is kept secret. The proof of the theorem relies on the fact that given the distance between two data points, there are infinitely many pairs of points that are equally distant. Since we assume that involved parties do not collude with each other and honestly follow the protocol, *TP* can not collude with a data holder site to infer private information of another data holder. Therefore sharing local dissimilarity matrices does not harm privacy unless the comparison protocol introduces inference channels that may leak private information.

In the comparison protocol, the message sent by the initiator is a matrix containing values of the form $(n + r)$ or $(-n + r)$ where n is initiator's input and r is a random number. In either case, these values are completely random to the follower. On the other hand, follower sends TP a matrix of values of the form $(n - m + r)$ or $(m - n + r)$. Although TP knows r, $(n - m)$ or $(m - n)$ does not help inferring either n or m, since there are infinitely many pairs (m, n) whose distance is $| m - n |$.

Purpose of the pseudo-random number generator shared between the initiator and the follower is preventing TP from inferring whose input is larger. Suppose that always the follower subtracts its input from the initiator's input. If $m > n$, $(n + r - m - r)$ $= (n - m)$ would be negative, pointing out that follower's input is greater. Shared pseudo-random number generator garbles the negation sequence and prevents such inferences.

One possible attack against our comparison protocol could be statistical analysis. Notice that observations of every trajectory in initiator's database with the same index is disguised using the same random number. This is due to the fact that the pseudo-random number generator is re-initialized at each step. Given enough statistics on the data and assuming that the databases are large enough to contain many repetitions of spatial values, such an attack is realizable. But considering that the domain of spatial values is very large and such statistics is not publicly available, we regard these types of attacks as very unlikely to succeed.

8 Conclusion

In this paper, we proposed a protocol for privacy preserving comparison of trajectories and its application to clustering of horizontally partitioned spatio-temporal data. The main advantage of our protocol is its applicability to most trajectory comparison functions and different clustering methods such as hierarchical clustering. The data holder sites can decide the clustering algorithm of their choice and receive clustering quality parameters together with the results. Only a small share of existing privacy preserving clustering algorithms can handle horizontally partitioned data and these algorithms do not specifically address spatio-temporal attributes.

We also provided complexity and privacy analysis of our protocol and observed that communication and computation costs are parallel to the computation costs for clustering local data. Privacy analysis shows that an attack using statistics of spatial components is possible but very unlikely to succeed. A proof-of-concept implementation of the clustering algorithm in C# language is available at [17]. We used real spatio-temporal datasets from the R-Tree Portal [16] for debugging and verifying the software.

References

1. Chen, L., Özsu, M. T., Oria V.: Robust and Fast Similarity Search for Moving Object Trajectories. In: Proc. of the 2005 ACM SIGMOD. (2005) 491-502
2. Vlachos, M., Kollios, G., Gunopulos, D.: Discovering Similar Multidimensional Trajectories. In: Proc. of the 18th ICDE. (2002) 673-684

3. Yi, B-K., Jagadish, H. V., Faloutsos, C.: Efficient Retrieval of Similar Time Sequences Under Time Warping. In: Proc. of the 14th ICDE. (1998) 201-208
4. Chen, L., Ng, R.: On the Marriage of Edit Distance and Lp-Norms. In: Proc. of the 2004 VLDB. (2004) 792-803
5. Oliveira, S.R.M., Zaiane, O.R.: Privacy Preserving Clustering by Object Similarity-Based Representation. In: Proc. of the 2004 ICDM Workshop on Privacy and Security Aspects of Data Mining. (2004) 40-46
6. Inan, A., Saygin, Y., Savas, E., Hintoglu, A.A., Levi, A.: Privacy Preserving Clustering on Horizontally Partitioned Data. In: Proc. of the 22nd ICDE Workshop on Privacy Data Management. (2006)
7. Agrawal, R., Srikant, R.: Privacy Preserving Data Mining. In: Proc. of the 2000 ACM SIGMOD. (2000) 439-450
8. Jha, S., Kruger, L., Mc Daniel, P.: Privacy Preserving Clustering. In: Proc. of the 10th European Symposium on Research in Computer Security. (2005) 397-417
9. Merugu, S., Ghosh, J.: Privacy Preserving Distributed Clustering using Generative Models. In: Proc. of the 3rd ICDM. (2003) 211-218
10. Vaidya, J., Clifton, C.: Privacy Preserving K-Means Clustering over Vertically Partitioned Data. In: Proc. of the 9th ACM SIGKDD. (2003) 206-215
11. Hoh, B., Gruteser, M.: Protecting Location Privacy through Path Confusion. In: Proc. of the 2005 SecureComm. (2005)
12. Beresford, A.R., Stajano, F.: Mix Zones: User Privacy in Location-Aware Services. In: Proc. of PerCom Workshops. (2004) 127-131
13. Beresford, A.R.: Location Privacy in Ubiquitous Computing. Ph.D. Dissertation, University of Cambridge. (2004)
14. Saygin, Y., Verykios, V.S., Clifton, C.: Using Unknowns to Prevent Discovery of Association Rules. In: SIGMOD Record 30(4). (2001) 45-54
15. Diffie, W., Hellman, M.E.: New Directions in Cryptography. In: IEEE Transactions on Information Theory. (1976) IT-200, 644-654
16. The R-Tree Portal. <http://isl.cs.unipi.gr/db/projects/rtreeportal/trajectories.html>. (March 28, 2006)
17. "ppSTClusteringOnHP.zip" [3510K].
    <http://students.sabanciuniv.edu/~inanali/ppSTClusteringOnHP.zip>. (March 28, 2006)

Discovering Semantic Sibling Associations from Web Documents with XTREEM-SP

Marko Brunzel and Myra Spiliopoulou

Otto-von-Guericke-University Magdeburg
forename.name@iti.cs.uni-magdeburg.de

Abstract. The semi-automatic extraction of semantics for ontology enhancement or semantic-based information retrieval encompasses several open challenges. There are many findings on the identification of vertical relations among concepts, but much less on indirect, horizontal relations among concepts that share a common, a priori unknown parent, such as Co-Hyponyms and Co-Meronyms. We propose the method XTREEM-SP (Xhtml TREE Mining for Sibling Pairs) for the discovery of such binary "sibling"-relations between concepts of a given vocabulary. While conventional methods process an appropriately prepared corpus, XTREEM-SP operates upon an arbitrarily heterogeneous Web Document Collection on a given topic and returns sibling relations between concepts associated to it. XTREEM-SP is independent of domain and language and does not rely on linguistic preprocessing nor on background knowledge beyond the ontology it is asked to enhance. We present our evaluation results with two gold standard ontologies and show that XTREEM-SP performs well, while being computationally inexpensive.

1 Introduction

The discovery of semantic relations among terms is a crucial task in many applications on text retrieval and understanding. Ontologies, the backbone of the Semantic Web, rely on making semantic relations explicit. There are many methods for the discovery of vertical hierarchical relations. There is less work on the discovery of concepts that stand in a horizontal relation to each other and are the children of a common, not a priori known and possibly not interesting parent concept; "Co-Hyponym relations" and "Co-Meronym relations" are two types of such horizontal relationships. In this paper, we propose a method that identifies such *sibling relations*. In ontology engineering, there are different approaches for the discovery of semantic relations. Most of them [FN99, MS00, and BCM05] use unstructured plain text as input; semi-structured text is converted to plain text. There are also approaches that exploit resources like dictionaries, glossaries or database schemata [K99], but are limited to the rare case when such resources are available. Our method rather uses semi-structured content as input, exploiting the XHTML document structure.

The core of our method is XTREEM, a mechanism that performs Xhtml TREE Mining. In [BS06b], we have proposed XTREEM-SG that discovers groups of sibling concepts; an earlier version appeared in [BS06a]. In this paper, we extend the XTREEM core to find sibling pairs characterized by association strength, whereby the concepts come from a given vocabulary. XTREEM-SP does not use linguistic

A Min Tjoa and J. Trujillo (Eds.): DaWaK 2006, LNCS 4081, pp. 469–480, 2006.
© Springer-Verlag Berlin Heidelberg 2006

resources, nor a prepared corpus; it uses publicly available Web Documents. We show that XTREEM-SP finds pairs of concepts in Co-Hyponymy or Co-Meronymy relation with higher accuracy than conventional approaches.

In the next section, we discuss related work. In section 3, we present XTREEM-SP. Section 4 is devoted to experiments and evaluation using two gold standard ontologies from the domain of tourism. The last section concludes our study.

2   Related Work

The idea of using structural similarities [ZLC03, B04], including path structures, of XHTML/XML Documents is used for several goals, such as clustering documents on structural similarities [DCWS04, TG06, and CMK06]. In contrast we use the Path information to infer siblings. The constitution of the paths is not used itself; no comparison with paths from other documents is performed with XTREEM-SP.

The broad domain of research is *ontology learning*: A comprehensive overview on this subject has appeared recently in [BCM05]. Those approaches are focusing on ontology learning from text. There are also approaches performing *Ontology Learning from structure* [K99]: However, these methods use existing database schemas or other conceptualizations as input and are therefore limited to cases where such schemas are available, which is usually not the case. Closer related are studies also discovering semantics on the Web [FS02, AHM00].

Hearst patterns [H92] are used to find relations among terms in text collections. Also Co-Hyponym relations can be found with this approach. But the disadvantage is that such patterns are rare, the coverage is low, even on big document collections. Cimiano et al also discover (Co-)Hyponym relations by finding and analyzing examples of Hearst patterns on the WWW [CS04, CS05]. In [P05] instances of WordNet concepts are found within big Web Document Collections with a rule based mechanism ignoring the Mark-Up. The document structure is taken into account for the establishment of a knowledge base of extracted entities from the WWW in [ECD04].

The Acquisition of Co-Hyponym semantics from text with association measures is performed by [HLQ01], but there the document structure is not used. Kruschwitz [K01a, K01b] uses *Mark-Up* sections of Web Documents to learn a *domain model*. Similarly to our approach, Kruschwitz exploits the Mark-Up for the representation of similar concepts inside Web Documents. However, as opposed to our approach, the tree structure of (X)HTML documents is not incorporated. [ST04] uses also different tags of HTML documents for acquiring Hyponymy relations. They only use list *itemizations*. There is no mentioning of using the tree structure of (X)HTML documents in general, where contributions also from other tags than item elements can be expected.

3   Finding Sibling Groups with XTREEM-SP

XTREEM-SP is based on mark-up conventions that can be found in almost all Web Documents: Different authors use different nested tags to structure pieces of information in Web Documents, but tend to adhere to similar structures. XTREEM-SP exploits this observation to find terms appearing within the same syntactic structure of an XHTML (or HTML) document. Pairs of such terms are potentially correlated, so XTREEM-SP applies statistical to identify strongly associated pairs. Hence, XTREEM-SP can find pairs of correlated terms, even if they are not co-located inside the same narrow context window. This can be seen in the headings example of Table1: Both text spans "WordNet" and "Germanet" appear within the same syntactic structure, i.e. the sequence of HTML tags leading to them. Hence, XTREEM-SP uses such syntactic structures to infer semantic relatedness.

Table 1. Semantically related terms, located in different paragraphs or separated by other terms

Headings, located in different paragraphs	Highlighted keywords, separated by normal text

...
`<h2>WordNet</h2>`
`<p>Was developed`
`...</p>`
`<h2>Germanet</h2>`
`<p>Analogous ...</p>`
...
	... `<p>` ... there are different important standards for building the `<strong>Semantic Web</strong>`. ... is `<strong>RDF</strong>`. ... `<strong>RDFS </strong>` adds ... whereas `<strong>OWL </strong>` is ... `</p>` ...

The XTREEM-SP procedure, which aims to organize a given vocabulary of terms into Co-Hyponym groups, entails Pre-processing (Group-By-Path, the core of the XTREEM-SP approach) and Processing (Association Strength Calculation), which are shown in the following data–flow diagram (Fig. 1) and described in section 3.2.

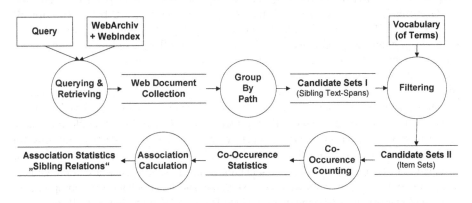

Fig. 1. Data-Flow Diagram of the XTREEM-SP procedure

We now introduce our algorithm XTREEM-SP that takes as input a collection of documents, observing each document as collection of Text-Span sets. On the elements of those sets a Co-Occurrence statistic is created. Upon this statistic association strength on term pairs is calculated. so that the terms with a strong association stand in sibling (Co-Hyponym, Co-Meronym) relationship to each other.

Step 1 – Querying & Retrieving: The XTREEM procedure operates on a *Web Document Collection*. Such a Web Document Collection is obtained by querying a *Archive+Index Facility* on a *query Q* with a Web Document Collection $W=\{d_1,...,d_s\}$ as result, for which Q is satisfied. Q constitutes the domain of interest whereupon semantics should be discovered. It should therefore encircle the Documents which are supposed to entail domain relevant content, e.g. "tourism*".

The Web Document Collection should be big enough to contain manifold occurrences of the desired concepts. The Web Document Collection is not supposed to be a small manually handcrafted document collection; bigger amounts of web content which have an appropriate coverage of the domain are more desirable. Here, recall is more important than precision. To obtain such a comprehensive Web Document Collection, alternatively a *focused web crawl* can be performed; when a vocabulary is given, this vocabulary can also be used to obtain Web Document references via the web services of internet search engines.

Step 2 - Group-By-Path: The Group-By-Path operation, described in detail in [BS06b] represents the core of the overall XTREEM-SP method. We consider Web Documents to find sibling relations among terms. We group Text-Spans that have the same Tag Path as its predecessor. The Group-By-Path approach performs a transition of a Web Document from a tree, to a collection of Pairs(Tag-Path, Text-Span) to a collection of Text-Span sets. For each $d_i \in W$ with i=1,...,s the Group-By-Path algorithm is applied. As result we obtain the collection of Text-Span sets $H'=(b_1,...b_u)$.

Step 3 - Filtering: The aim of the procedure described in this publication is to infer semantically motivated sibling Pairs. Let $V=\{v_1,...,v_p\}$ be the vocabulary of terms given as input. For the following steps we only consider all Text-Spans $e \in b$ which are contained in V. $H''=(b_1,...,b_u)$ so that for all $e \in b$ it is also true $e \in V$.

Step 4 – Co-Occurrence Counting: In this step a Co-Occurrence statistic is created. Co-Occurrence is obtained from all pair wise occurrences of $e_1 \in b_i \cap e_2 \in b_i$ for all $b_i \in H''$ with i=1,...,u. Such pairs are only obtained from b_i with cardinality > 1 since only sets containing at least two elements are able to reflect a sibling relation among their elements. For all Combinations of $v_1 \in V \cap v_2 \in V$ with $v_1 \neq v_2$ a count is associated reflecting how often a combination occurred in H''.

Step 5 – Association Calculation: From the counts on term pairs obtained in Step 4, the strength of the association between the pair components can be inferred in many ways. From simply using the raw Co-Occurrence frequency, through the many association measures from statistics (such as χ^2-Association [MS00]) to information theoretic measures (such as Mutual Information). For a comprehensive overview on association measures see [E04]. χ^2-Association is the association measure of our choice, since in the experiments it showed the best results and its application is appropriate on sufficiently large data sets as the ones obtained from big Web Document Collections.

4   Experiments and Evaluation

As evaluation reference we use two gold standard ontologies (GSO). The GSO's contain sibling relations besides other content. They also provide the closed vocabulary whereupon sibling relations are automatically derived by the XTREEM-SP procedure.

In Experiment 1 we will contrast the results obtained with XTREEM-SP (Group-By-Path) on sibling semantics against the results obtained on the traditional Bag-Of-Words vector space model and a further alternative method based on Mark-Up. In experiment 2 we will contrast the influence an Association Measure has compared to the solely usage of Co-Occurrence frequency. In experiment 3 we will investigate the influence of the input query which constitutes the Web Document Collection processed. In Experiment 4 we will vary the required minimum support of terms within the Web Document Collection to be processed.

4.1 Description of Experimental Influences

Evaluation Reference: The Evaluation is performed on two gold standard ontologies, from the tourism domain. The concepts of these ontologies are also terms, thus in the following the expressions "concepts" and "terms" are used interchangeably.

Sibling relations can be obtained from the GSO's for all Sub-Concepts where the corresponding Super-Concept has more than one Sub-Concept; if there are at least two child Concepts of a Parent Concept. As a result, there is a number of Concept Pairs which stand in a sibling relation, whereas other Concept Pairs are not conceptualized as standing in sibling relation. We only use the direct Super-Concept Sub-Concept relation to derive sibling relations.

The *"Tourism GSO"*[1] contains 293 concepts grouped into 45 sibling sets resulting in 1176 concept pairs standing in sibling relation; the *"Getess annotation GSO"*[2] contains 693 concepts grouped into 90 sibling sets resulting in 4926 concept pairs standing in sibling relation.

There are three Inputs to the XTREEM-SP procedure described in the following:

Input(1) : Archive+Index Facility: We have performed a topic focused web crawl on "tourism" related documents. The overall size of the document collection is about 9.5 million Web Documents. The Web Documents have been converted to XHTML. With an n-gram based language recognizer non-English documents have been filtered out. The Documents are indexed, so that for a given query a Web Document Collection can be retrieved.

Input(2) : Queries: For our experiments we consider four document collections which result from querying the Archive+Index Facility. The constitution is given by all those documents adhering to Query1 - "touris*", Query2 - "accommodation" and by the whole topic focused Web Document Collection reflected by Query3 – "*". Additionally we give the results for Query4 – "accomodation". Query4 was foremost misspelling on Query2, but since this variant is present in millions of Web Documents we will present theses results. Those variations are object of Experiment 3.

Input(3) : Vocabulary: The GSO's described before, are lexical ontologies. Each concept is represented by a term. These terms constitute the vocabulary whereupon sibling relations are calculated.

The overall XTREEM-SP procedure is constituted of preprocessing and processing:

Procedure (1) : Preprocessing method: For the evaluation of the Group-By-Path sub procedure we will contrast our Group-By-Path (GBP) method with the traditional

---

1 http://www.aifb.uni-karlsruhe.de/WBS/pci/TourismGoldStandard.isa
2 http://www.aifb.uni-karlsruhe.de/WBS/pci/getess_tourism_annotation.daml

Bag-Of-Words (BOW) vector space model The BOW is the widespread established method on processing of textual data, while The variation of these influences is object Experiment 1.

Procedure (2) : Processing – Association Strength Derivation: From the raw sibling sets obtained by the Pre-processing, the Co-Occurrence frequency of Term Pairs is counted. This frequency can be used as indicator of association strength. We will refer to this method by "frequency". With the χ^2-Association Measure, more statistical stable values of association strength can be calculated. The variation of these influences is object of Experiment 1 and Experiment 2.

In our experiments we found that some of the terms of the vocabulary are never or very rarely found on rather big Web Document Collections. E.g. one reference contains the errors "Kindergarden" instead of the correct English "Kindergarten". To eliminate the influence of errors in the reference, we also vary the *required minimum feature support*. The support is given by the frequency of the features (terms) in the overall text of the Web Document Collection. We used minimum support thresholds from 0 (all features are used, nothing is pruned) to 100000 (0, 1, 10, 100, 1000, 10000, 100000). When the support is varied, only those features of the Vectorization and of the reference fulfilling these criteria are incorporated into the evaluation. The variation of these influences is object Experiment 4.

4.2 Evaluation Criteria

From the gold standard ontologies we extract all Concept Pairs which stand in a sibling relation to each other. This is in the following also referred to as "Reference".

Object of the evaluation is a ranked list of automatic obtained Concepts Pairs, whereas the ranking is given according to the Association Strength of the Concept Pair. For each automatic obtained Concept Pair can be determined if this relation is also supported by the Reference which gives a positive count. If a Concept Pair is not supported be the Reference a negative count is assumed. With this, for each position in the ranked list, recall and precision can be calculated. The recall is the number of already seen true Sibling Pairs (#positive) to the number of Sibling Pairs given by the Reference (#overall). The precision is the number of true Sibling Pairs (#positive) to the number of seen automatic generated Pairs (#positive + #negative).

$$recall = \frac{\# positive}{\# overall} \qquad precision = \frac{\# positive}{\# positive + \# negative}$$

For a ranked list of associated Term Pairs a recall precision chart line can be obtained by a series of measurements on recall precision values.

4.3 Experiments

In the following we will show the results obtained from the experiments. Table 2 shows the number of documents which adhere to a certain query. This corresponds to the size of the Web Document Collection which is processed by the subsequent following processing steps. Table 2 also shows the number of candidate sibling sets obtained after performing the Pre-processing on different Queries for the two vocabularies. Only terms which are present in the input vocabulary are observed in the subsequent. Table 2 also shows the number of observed pairs derived from these sets.

Table 2. Experimental Data Numbers

Query Name	Query Phrase	Number of Documents	Number of Candidate Sets II obtained with GBP		Number of Sibling Pairs (from Candidate Sets II)	
			GSO1	GSO2	GSO1	GSO2
Query1	"touris*"	1,468,279	222,037	318,009	1,600,440	3,804,214
Query2	"accommodation"	1,612,108	293,225	373,802	2,092,432	3,885,532
Query3	"*"	9,437,703	924,045	1,326,843	5,763,596	14,071,016
Query4	"accomodation"	471,540	78,289	98,886	686,108	1,198,224

Experiment 1: Group-By-Path in comparison to alternatives Methods
In this experiment we will contrast the quality of results on sibling relations obtained with the Bag-Of-Words (BOW) vector space model, on a usage of Mark-Up without Path Information as described in [K01a] against our new Group-By-Path method. Query1 was chosen as the query constituting the Web Document Collection. The comparison was performed for two methods on association strength (frequency, χ^2) and for both references (GSO1,GSO2).

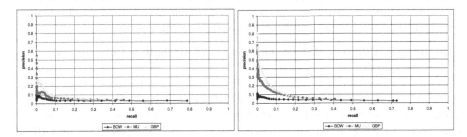

Fig. 2. and 3. Pre-processing - BOW vs. MU vs. GBP (Frequency,Query1) for GSO1 and GSO2

The diagrams which result on the usage of "frequency", Fig. 2 and Fig. 3, show that GBP performs best for both GSO's. MU performs better than BOW. The overall measured results are relatively low. On the top ranked association Pairs, GBP (and MU) shields a high precision which then rapidly declines. For higher recall values the chart lines converge. Since a recall above 40 percent is only obtained on BOW, we can conclude that some sibling relations never occur up on Marked-Up Web Document Structure. This does not necessarily mean that GBP is weak; since the ontologies do not directly encode sibling relations, there may exist Concepts which tend not to occur together. E.G. "ski school" and "surf school" may be sub-concepts of "sport school" but are rather unlikely to be discovered from content. The evaluation criteria can not prevent from such cases.

Fig. 4 and Fig. 5 show the results by using the association strength calculated by the χ^2-Association Measure. In contrast to the usage of "frequency", the results of MU are nearly the same as for GBP. An explanation for this is that the χ^2-Association Measure here performs well on diminishing sporadic occurrences which can happen on MU in comparison to GBP. BOW performs again worst. All the experiments

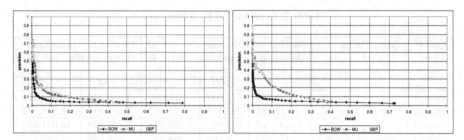

Fig. 4. and 5. Pre-processing - BOW vs. MU vs. GBP (χ^2,Query1) for GSO1 and GSO2

within this publication are performed on a closed vocabulary. The choice of Pairs observed in the documents is therefore drastically limited in comparison when using an open vocabulary. When using an open vocabulary the alignment of association generated with GBP towards sibling semantics, in comparison to MU, becomes more visible than measured on the limit vocabulary.

Conclusion: Our experiments on automatically obtaining sibling relations showed that our Group-by-Path method, the core of the XTREEM-SP procedure, shows the best results. Though it was not claimed that the Bag-Of-Words model is strong on capturing sibling semantics, we can confirm our hypothesis that the results obtained with XTREEM-SP (based on GBP) are motivated by sibling semantics.

Experiment 2: Different Methods on Association Strength in Comparison

In this Experiment we will focus on how variations on the method association strength is obtained influences the results. Specifically we will use the Co-Occurrence frequency and the χ^2-Association Measure [MS00]. In Experiment 1 for the different association strength methods this was done in series; in contrast Fig. 6 shows the chart lines on GBP of Fig. 2 and Fig. 4 together. Fig. 7 shows the chart lines on GBP of Fig. 3 and Fig. 5 together.

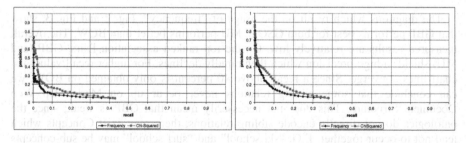

Fig. 6. and 7. Association Strength - Frequency vs. χ^2 (GBP,Query1) for GSO1 and GSO2

Fig. 6 and Fig. 7 show that on both vocabularies/references the usage of χ^2 - Association strength shielded the best results.

We also used Mutual Information and Poison Sterling Association Measure as well as cosines distance; the results are comparable to χ^2-Association or worse but better than just frequency. The literature on the quality of these association measures mentions that different association measures perform sometimes better, sometimes worse than other with no clear conclusions. In the experiments of this publication χ^2-Association Measure gave the best results compared to the solely frequency support.

Experiment 3: Varying the Topic Focus

XTREEM-SP relies on constituting a Web Document Collection by a query. A query therefore represents the focus of the data analyzed. Here we will investigate how variations on the query influence the obtained results on sibling semantics. The different Queries are shown in Table 2.

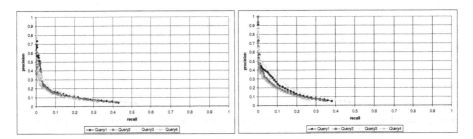

Fig. 8. and 9. Results on different Web Document Collection constituting Queries (GBP, χ^2) for GSO1 and GSO2

As Fig. 8 shows, the results of all for Queries are closely together for GSO1. For GSO2 the results vary more than for GSO1. For both GSO's, Query3 – "*" which depicts the full topic focused Web Document Crawl shielded the best results. A explanation for this is that with the single phrase queries (Query1,Query2 and Query4) always a too focused Web Document Collection is processed. The Reference contains terms – and relations which are not present on Web Documents adhering to a certain "focused" query. This means that for practical settings a combined query (E.G. "touris* OR accommodation OR holidays OR 'sport event' … ") may be the better choice. On the other hand a ontology engineer will rather focus on a fraction of the conceptualization to be obtained or improved at one moment and therefore focused Queries are appropriate.

Experiment 4: Variations on the required support

In the last experiment we will investigate the influence of the term frequency in the Web Document Collection on the obtained results. As a side effect of an increased required support, "misconceptualization", present in the reference ontologies, is outweighed. With increasing required support more and more relations are not relevant, which is reflected by eliminating these Pairs from the reference. Table 3 shows the decreasing number of relations by increased required term support. We used the support of terms, not of the Co-Occurrence of term Pairs which would be an alternative approach. As Fig. 10 and Fig. 11 show, for increased required support, better results regarding recall and precision are obtained. This means that recall and precision on sibling relations of high frequent terms are found better than on low frequent ones.

478   M. Brunzel and M. Spiliopoulou

Table 3. Decreasing number of reference sibling relations on increased required support

Required support		0	1	10	100	1000	10000	100000
Number of reference sibling relations	GSO1	1176	1120	1033	844	637	404	161
	GSO2	4926	4553	4073	3439	2653	1006	582

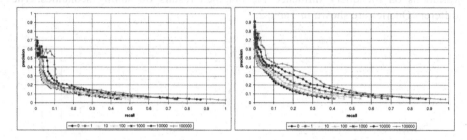

Fig. 10. and 11. Variations on the Required Support (Query1,GBP, χ^2) for GSO1 and GSO 2

5 Conclusions and Future Work

We have presented XTREEM-SP, a method that discovers binary horizontal semantic relations among concepts by exploiting the structural conventions of Web Documents XTREEM-SP processes Web Documents collected from the WWW and thus eliminates the need for a well-prepared document corpus. Furthermore, it does not rely on linguistic pre-processing or NLP resources. So, XTREEM-SP is much less demanding of human resources. Our experiments with two golden standard ontologies and with several parameter variations show that XTREEM-SP delivers good results, i.e. semantically meaningful sibling pairs.

Our method is only a first step on the exploitation of the structural conventions in Web Documents for the discovery of semantic relations. In our future work we want to investigate the impact of individual Mark-Up element tags like <p>, <li>, and <dt> on the results. Discovering the corresponding Super-Concept for the Sub-Concepts standing in sibling relation is a further desirable extension.

References

[AHM00] E. Agirre, O. Ansa, E. Hovy, and D. Martinez. Enriching very large ontologies using the WWW, Proc. of the Workshop on Ontology Construction ECAI-2000

[B04] D. Buttler. A short survey of document structure similarity algorithms. In Proc. of the *International Conference on Internet Computing*, June 2004.

[BCM05] P. Buitelaar, P. Cimiano, Bernardo Magnini, Ontology Learning from Text: Methods, Evaluation and Applications, Frontiers in Artificial Intelligence and Applications Series Volume 123, IOS Press, Amsterdam, 2005

[BS06a]   M. Brunzel, M. Spiliopoulou. Discovering Multi Terms and Co-Hyponymy from XHTML Documents with XTREEM. In Proc. of *PAKDD Workshop on Knowledge Discovery from XML Documents (KDXD 2006)*, LNCS 3915, Singapore, April 2006

[BS06b]   M. Brunzel, M. Spiliopoulou. Discovering Semantic Sibling Groups from Web Documents with XTREEM-SG. In Proc. of *EKAW* 2006 (accepted for publication), Podebrady, Czech Republic, October 2006

[CMK06]   I. Choi, B. Moon, H-J- Kim. A Clustering Method based on Path Similarities of XML Data. Data & Knowledge Engineering, vol. no. pp.0-0, Feb. 2006

[CS04]   P. Cimiano and S. Staab. Learning by googling. *SIGKDD Explorations*, 6(2):24-34, December 2004.

[CS05]   P. Cimiano, S. Staab. Learning concept hierarchies from text with a guided hierarchical clustering algorithm. *Workshop on Learning and Extending Lexical Ontologies at ICML 2005*, Bonn 2005.

[DCWS04]   T. Dalamagas, T. Cheng, K. J. Winkel, T. Sellis, Clustering XML documents using structural summaries, in Proc. of the *EDBT Workshop on Clustering Information over the Web (ClustWeb04)*, Heraklion, Greece, 2004

[E04]   Stefan Evert, The Statistics of Word Cooccurrences: Word Pairs and Collocations. PhD dissertation, University of Stuttgart. 2004

[ECD04]   O. Etzioni, M. Cafarella, D. Downey, S. Kok, A.-M. Popescu, T. Shaked, S. Soderland, D. S. Weld, A. Yates. Web-Scale Information Extraction in KnowItAll. Proc. of the *13th International WWW Conference*, New York, 2004

[FN99]   D. Faure, C. Nedellec. Knowledge acquisition of predicate argument structures from technical texts using machine learning: the system ASIUM, In Proc. of *EKAW 1999*

[FS02]   A. Faatz, R. Steinmetz, Ontology Enrichment with Texts from the WWW, Proc. of the *First International Workshop on Semantic Web Mining, ECML 2002*, Helsinki 2002

[H92]   M. Hearst, Automatic acquisition of hyponyms from large text corpora. In Proc. of the *14th International Conference on Computational Linguistics*, 1992

[HLQ01]   G.Heyer; M. Läuter, U. Quasthoff, Th. Wittig, Ch. Wolff. Learning Relations using Collocations. In Proc. *IJCAI Workshop on Ontology Learning, Seattle/WA*, 2001

[K01a]   U. Kruschwitz, A Rapidly Acquired Domain Model Derived from Mark-Up Structure. In Proc. of the *ESSLLI'01 Workshop on Semantic Knowledge Acquisition and Categorization*, Helsinki, 2001.

[K01b]   U. Kruschwitz. Exploiting Structure for Intelligent Web Search. Proc. of the *34th Hawaii International Conference on System Sciences (HICSS)*, Maui Hawaii 2001, IEEE

[K99]   V. Kashyap. Design and creation of ontologies for environmental information retrieval. Proc. of the *12th Workshop on Knowledge Acquisition, Modeling and Management*. Alberta, Canada. 1999.

[MS99]   C. Manning, H. Schütze. Foundations of Statistical Natural Language Processing. MIT Press. Cambridge, MA: May 1999.

[MS00]   A. Maedche and S. Staab. Discovering conceptual relations from text. In Proc. of *ECAI 2000*

[P05]   M. Pasca. Finding Instance Names and Alternative Glosses on the Web: WordNet Reloaded. In: *CICLing-2005*, LNCS 3406, 2005.

[ST04]   K. Shinzato and K. Torisawa. Acquiring hyponymy relations from Web Documents. In Proc. of the 2004 *Human Language Technology Conference (HLT-NAACL-04)*, Boston, Massachusetts, 2004.

[TG06]   A. Tagarelli, S. Greco. Toward Semantic XML Clustering. *6th SIAM International Conference on Data Mining (SDM '06)*. Bethesda, Maryland, USA, April 20-22, 2006

[ZLC03]   Z. Zhang, R. Li, S. Cao, and Y. Zhu. Similarity metric for XML documents. In Proc. of the *Workshop on Knowledge and Experience Management*, October 2003.

Difference Detection Between Two Contrast Sets*

Hui-jing Huang[1], Yongsong Qin[2], Xiaofeng Zhu[2], Jilian Zhang[2],
and Shichao Zhang[3,**]

[1] Bureau of Personnel and Education, Chinese Academy of Sciences, Beijing, China
[2] Deparment of math and Computer Science, Guangxi Normal University, China
[3] Faculty of Information Technology, UTS, PO Box 123, Broadway NSW 2007, Australia
hjhuang@cashq.ac.cn, ysqin@mailbox.gxnu.edu.cn,
xfzhu_dm@163.com, zhangjilian@yeah.net, zhangsc@it.uts.edu.au

Abstract. Mining group differences is useful in many applications, such as medical research, social network analysis and link discovery. The differences between groups can be measured from either statistical or data mining perspective. In this paper, we propose an empirical likelihood (EL) based strategy of building confidence intervals for the mean and distribution differences between two contrasting groups. In our approach we take into account the structure (semi-parametric) of groups, and experimentally evaluate the proposed approach using both simulated and real-world data. The results demonstrate that our approach is effective in building confidence intervals for group differences such as mean and distribution function.

1 Introduction

In intelligent data analysis, identifying the mean and distribution differences between two groups is useful in predicting the properties of a group using one another. In medical research, it is interesting to compare the mean value of prolonging patient's life between a group using a new product (medicine) and a group with another product; In research of children's growth, the height below/over the standard are important, since the median height (near the standard) is associated with normal growth status, it may be meaningful with children's growth to compare two groups on the basis of both below the standard or over the standard of height. In this paper we are interested in constructing confidence intervals for mean and distribution differences between two data groups.

Work in [2, 3, 4, 17] focus on mining contrast sets: conjunctions of attributes and values that differ meaningfully in their distribution across groups. This allows us to answer queries of the form, "How are History and Computer Science students different?" or "What has changed from 1993 through 1998?"

Another kind of related work is change mining in [7, 12, 16]. In the change mining problem, there are an old classifier, representing some previous knowledge about

---

* This work is partially supported by Australian large ARC grants (DP0449535 and DP0559536), a China NSF major research Program (60496327), a China NSF grant (60463003), a National Basic Research Program of China (2004CB318103), and a National Science Foundation of China (60033020).
** Correspondence author.

A Min Tjoa and J. Trujillo (Eds.): DaWaK 2006, LNCS 4081, pp. 481–490, 2006.

classification, and a new data set that has a changed class distribution. The goal of change mining is to find the changes of classification characteristics in the new data set. Change mining has been applied to identifying customer buying behavior [6], association rules [1], items over continuous append-only and dynamic data streams [18], and predicting source code changes [10].

The work of [8] uses the bootstrap approach to measure the uncertainty in link discovery (LD), while most current LD algorithms do not characterize the probabilistic properties of the hypothesis derived from the sample of data. The authors adopt the bootstrap resampling to estimate group membership and their associated confidence intervals, because it makes no assumptions about the underlying sampling distribution and is ideal for estimating statistical parameters.

Different from the above work, our approach takes into account the structure of a group: parametric, semi-parametric, or nonparametric; the imputation method when contrasting groups are with missing data; and confidence intervals for the mean and distribution differences between two groups. Use F and G to denote the distribution functions of groups x and y, respectively. We construct confidence intervals for the mean and distribution differences between contrasting groups x and y using an empirical likelihood (EL) model.

The rest of this paper is organized as follows. Section 2 presents the semi-parametric model, data structure and imputation method. In Section 3, the empirical likelihood ratio statistic and the empirical likelihood (EL) based confidence intervals (CIs) for the mean and distribution function differences are constructed. In Section 4, we give the experimental results both on the simulation data and a real medical dataset. Conclusion and future work are given in Section 5.

2 Semi-parametric Model, Data Structure and Imputation Method

We use $F(x)$ and $G_{\theta_0}(y)$ to denote the distribution functions of groups x and y, respectively, where G is known, F and θ_0 are unknown. This is regarded as Semi-parametric model. We are interested in constructing confidence intervals for some differences of x and y such as the differences of the means and the distribution functions of two groups. In general, either F or G is unknown, or both. So nonparametric methods are developed to address this situation. In the case of complete observations, related work can be found in [9].

For any difference, denoted by Δ, the following information is available:

$$E \omega \ (\ x \ , \theta_0 \ , \Delta \ ) = 0 \tag{1}$$

Where ω is a function in a known form. Some examples that fit (2.1) are given in the following.

Difference of means: Denote $\mu_1 = E(x), \mu_2 = E(y) = \mu(\theta_0)$ and $\Delta = \mu_2 - \mu_1$, Let

$$\omega(x, \theta_0, \Delta) = x - \mu(\theta_0) + \Delta \tag{2}$$

Difference of distribution functions: For fixed x_0, denote $p_1 = F(x_0)$, $p_2 = G_{\theta_0}(x_0) = p(\theta_0)$ and $\Delta = p_2 - p_1$. Let

$$\omega(x, \theta_0, \Delta) = I(x \le x_0) - p(\theta_0) + \Delta \qquad (3)$$

Where $I(.)$ is the indicator function. Note that we can assume that F follows exponential or normal distribution in order to construct the model (denote as exponential and normal distribution model respectively).

We use a simple method to represent the data. Consider the following simple random samples of data associated with groups x and y, we denoted them as (x, δ_x) and y respectively,

$$(x_i, \delta_{x_i}), i = 1, \cdots, m; \quad y_j, j = 1, \cdots, n.$$

Where

$$\delta_{x_i} = \begin{cases} 0, & if \ x_i \ is \ missing \\ 1, & otherwise, \end{cases} \qquad (4)$$

We assume that x and y are missing completely at random (MCAR) [11], i.e. $P(\delta_x = 1 | x) = P_1$ (constant) throughout this paper. We also assume that (x, δ_x) and y are independent. Next, an example from real life application is given below in order to illustrate the goal of this paper.

In the medical analysis of a kind of disease, the breast cancer for example, some data are obtained from the patients (see Table 1).

Table 1. Breast Cancer data

Patient ID	Radius	Smoothness	Perimeter	Diagnosis
1	13.5	0.09779	78.04	benign
2	21.16	0.1109	94.74	malignant
3	12.5	0.0806	62.11	benign
4	14.64	0.01078	97.83	benign
...	...	...	...	...

There are two problems that we concerned most. One, what is the difference of the benign and malignant patients with regard to a specified feature? The other is, how reliable the difference is, when we calculated it from the sample data of the benign and malignant patients?

One can compute the difference of a specified feature of two groups by using simple statistical methods or other more sophisticated data mining techniques [2, 3, 4, 17]. While for the second problem, we use the empirical likelihood (EL) method to construct the confidence intervals, under a significance level α, for the difference Δ of two groups with missing data.

A common method for handling incomplete data is to impute a value for each missing value and then apply standard statistical methods to the complete data as if they were true observations. Commonly used imputation methods include deterministic imputation and random imputation [15]. We refer to the reader to [11] for examples and excellent account of parametric statistical inferences with missing data.

Let $r_x = \sum_{i=1}^{m} \delta_{x_i}, m_x = m - r_x$. Denote the sets of respondents and nonrespondents with respect to x as S_{rx} and S_{ry}, respectively. We use random hot deck imputation method to impute the missing values. We do not use the deterministic imputation as it is improper in making inference for distribution functions [15]. Let x_i^* be the imputed values for the missing data with respect to x. Random hot deck imputation selects a simple random sample of size m_x with replacement from s_{rx}, and then uses the associated x-values as donors, that is, $x_i^* = x_j$ for some $j \in s_{rx}$. Let $x_{I,i} = \delta_{x_i} x_i + (1 - \delta_{x_i}) x_i^*$ represent the 'complete' data after imputation, where $i=1,\cdots,m, j=1,\cdots,n,$.

We will investigate the asymptotic properties of the empirical likelihood ratio statistic for Δ based on $x_{I,i}, i=1,\cdots,m; y_{I,j}, j=1,\cdots,n$. The results are used to construct asymptotic confidence intervals for Δ .

3   Building CI for Δ Based on Empirical Likelihood

At first, the empirical likelihood ratio statistic is constructed. It is interesting to notice that the empirical likelihood ratio statistic under imputation is asymptotically distributed as a weighted chi-square variable χ_1^2 [13, 14], which is used to construct the EL based confidence interval for Δ . The reason for this deviation from the standard χ_1^2 is that the complete data after imputation are dependent.

Let t_α satisfy $P(\chi_1^2 \le t_\alpha) = 1 - \alpha$, we can construct an EL based confidence interval on Δ with coverage probability $1-\alpha$, that is $\{\Delta : -2\omega \log(R(\Delta, \theta_{m,n})) \le t_\alpha\}$, where ω is the weight [13, 14].

This result can directly apply to test the hypotheses on Δ . For instance, if the hypothesis is $H_0: \Delta = \Delta_0, H_1: \Delta \neq \Delta_0$, we first construct the confidence interval on Δ . Then check if Δ_0 is in the interval. If Δ_0 is in the interval, we accept the hypothesis H_0 and reject H_1 ; otherwise, H_0 should be rejected and H_1 is accepted.

We also want to notice that the result can apply to the data without missing values. In complete data situation, we can see that the asymptotic distribution of the EL statistic is found to be a standard χ_1^2 distribution. The EL based confidence interval for Δ in complete data case is thus constructed as $\{\Delta : -2\log(R(\Delta, \theta_{m,n})) \le t_\alpha\}$.

4 Experiments

Extensive experiments were conducted on a DELL Workstation PWS650 with 2G main memory and 2.6GHz CPU, the operating system is WINDOWS 2000.

4.1 Simulations Models

We conducted a simulation study on the finite sample performance of EL based confidence intervals on the mean difference $\Delta_1 = E(y) - E(x)$, and the distribution function difference $\Delta_2 = G_{\theta_0}(x_0) - F(x_0)$ for fixed x_0. For the purpose of simulating the real world data distributions as closely as possible, we generated two groups of $x_i s$ and $y_i s$ from the exponential distributions ($\exp(1)$ and $\exp(2)$) and the normal distributions ($N(2,2)$ and $N(3,2)$) respectively, because these two data distributions are the most popular and common distributions in real world applications. And then the exponential and normal distribution models are running on these different distributed datasets. The following two cases of response probabilities were used under the MCAR assumption (in which the response rates is denoted as P): Case 1: $P_1 = 0.6$;   Case 2: $P_1 = 0.9$. The response rates in Case 2 were higher than those in case 1, which were chosen to compare the performance of EL confidence intervals under different response rates.

Sample sizes were chosen as (m, n) = (100, 100), and (m, n) = (200, 150) for the purpose to compare the performance of EL confidence intervals under different sample sizes. For each of the cases of different response rates and sample sizes, we generated 1,000 random samples of incomplete data $\left\{ (x_i, \delta_{x_i}), i=1, \cdots, m; \ y_j, j=1, \cdots, n \right\}$. For nominal confidence level $1 - \alpha = 0.95$, using the simulated samples, we evaluated the coverage probability (CP), the average left endpoint (LE), the average right endpoint (RE) and the average length of the interval (AL) of the empirical likelihood based (EL) intervals.

Tables 2-9 present the performance of proposed method for finding CIs of the mean difference and distribution function with different models on different distributed datasets. More detailed experimental settings can be seen in the table titles.

Table 2. CIs of the mean difference for the exponential distribution model (with exponential distributed data, true difference $x_0 = 1$)

Case	(m,n)	CP(%)	LE	RE	AL
1	(100,100)	100	0.374348	1.664007	1.289659
1	(200,150)	99.69	0.381603	1.552474	1.170871
2	(100,100)	99.78	0.498466	1.548741	1.050275
2	(200,150)	98.77	0.518341	1.454267	0.935926

Table 3. CIs of the mean difference for the normal distribution model   (with exponential distributed data, true difference Δ_1 =1)

Case	(m,n)	CP(%)	LE	RE	AL
1	(100,100)	96.78	0.259185	1.233423	0.974238
1	(200,150)	92.46	0.401004	1.204256	0.803252
2	(100,100)	88.15	0.556322	1.168804	0.612482
2	(200,150)	88.82	0.572257	1.176884	0.604627

Table 4. CIs of the distribution function difference for the exponential distribution model (with exponential distributed data, fixed x_0 =2, true difference Δ_2 =-0.2325)

Case	(m,n)	CP(%)	LE	RE	AL
1	(100,100)	90.98	-0.259507	-0.10194	0.158
1	(200,150)	89.50	-0.253168	-0.126162	0.127
2	(100,100)	85.64	-0.224214	-0.134105	0.091
2	(200,150)	82.86	-0.227793	-0.158197	0.079

Table 5. CIs of the distribution function difference for the normal distribution model (with exponential distributed data, fixed x_0 =2, true difference Δ_2 =-0.1915)

Case	(m,n)	CP(%)	LE	RE	AL
1	(100,100)	92.21	-0.415641	-0.193948	0.222
1	(200,150)	87.62	-0.403683	-0.218695	0.185
2	(100,100)	83.50	-0.401349	-0.266323	0.135
2	(200,150)	84.62	-0.399944	-0.264595	0.135

Table 6. CIs of the mean difference for the exponential distribution model (with normal distributed data, true difference Δ_1 =1)

Case	(m,n)	CP(%)	LE	RE	AL
1	(100,100)	100	0.304478	2.04389	1.739411
1	(200,150)	99.67	0.28442	1.98484	1.70043
2	(100,100)	100	0.42359	1.8026	1.379
2	(200,150)	98.68	0.38113	1.7308	0.979761

Table 7. CIs of the mean difference for the normal distribution model (with normal distributed data, true difference Δ_1 =1)

Case	(m,n)	CP(%)	LE	RE	AL
1	(100,100)	98.76	0.362515	1.561752	1.199237
1	(200,150)	99.01	0.453377	1.408632	0.955255
2	(100,100)	98.37	0.475443	1.373007	0.897564
2	(200,150)	94.12	0.599176	1.306111	0.706935

Table 8. CIs of the distribution function difference for the exponential distribution model (with normal distributed data, fixed x_0 =2, true difference Δ_2 =-0.2325)

Case	(m,n)	CP(%)	LE	RE	AL
1	(100,100)	93.64	-0.216152	0.139717	0.355869
1	(200,150)	90.52	-0.175146	0.13745	0.312596
2	(100,100)	88.10	-0.162031	0.111836	0.273867
2	(200,150)	87.58	-0.130788	0.104844	0.261068

Table 9. CIs on the distribution function difference for the normal distribution model (fixed x_0 =2, true difference Δ_2 =-0.1915)

Case	(m,n)	CP(%)	LE	RE	AL
1	(100,100)	91.42	-0.419944	-0.202104	0.2178
1	(200,150)	90.48	-0.39838	-0.228987	0.169
2	(100,100)	88.75	-0.377728	-0.238151	0.13958
2	(200,150)	89.68	-0.379188	-0.270484	0.10870

Tables 2-9 reveal the following results:

For every response rate and sample size, the coverage probabilities (CPs) of all EL-based confidence intervals for mean are close to the theoretical confidence level 95%. In almost all situations, the lengths of CIs also become smaller as the sample size increases. The same trends occur when considering different response rates. While the ALs for distribution function difference fluctuate slightly with respect to different sample size and response rates.

Another interesting phenomenon is that the CIs built by using normal distribution model for mean difference are shorter than those by exponential distribution model, without much loss of coverage accuracy. That is to say, we can use the normal distribution model to construct CIs in real applications when we have no prior knowledge about the distribution of the data.

We can see from above results that the length of CIs will be shorter when the amount of sample data increases, because the information that is useful for building the CIs also increases. So under the same significance level α , the shorter CIs will give the same confidence of the difference. Note that higher response rate means that there are more data available when building CIs than those under lower response rate.

4.2 Experiments on UCI Dataset

We also conducted extensive experiments on real world dataset, due to the fact that the real world data do not fit the ideal statistical distributions exactly. What's more, there may be noises in real world data, which will distort the distribution of the real world data.

We used the medical dataset, Wisconsin Diagnostic Breast Cancer (WDBC), which is downloaded from [5]. It contains 569 instances in total and 32 features for each instance. Each instance, represented a patient, has been classified as benign and malignant according to these features. The WDBC dataset contains 357 benign instances and 212 malignant instances. For interesting of space, we only report the experimental results of attribute 4 and 27. We give some statistical information of these two features in Table 10, more detailed information about these features can be seen in [19]. In order to verify the effectiveness of our method, we randomly divide WDBC into two parts. One (contains 2/3 instances, denoted as BS) is used to construct the CI, the other (contains 1/3 instances, denoted as VS) is used to verify the coverage probability (CP) of the CI. We then divide the BS into two groups, that is, the Benign and Malignant groups. Let the values of attribute A from Benign group be the group x, and those from Malignant be group y. Then CI is built based on group x and y using the techniques described in Section 3. In the verification process of CP, we divide the VS into two groups (Benign and Malignant) and compute the difference $\hat{\Delta}$ of them with respect to attribute A. Thus we can easily see whether $\hat{\Delta}$ falls into the range of the constructed CI.

Table 10. Statistics for attribute 4 and 27 of Wisconsin Diagnostic breast Cancer

	Mean		Distribution function	
	A4	A27	A4 ($x_0=15$)	A27 ($x_0=0.1$)
Malignant	21.6	0.1448	0.0189	0.0094
Benign	17.91	0.1249	0.2437	0.1092
Difference Δ	3.69	0.0198	-0.2248	-0.0998

(A4: Mean texture, A27: Worst smoothness)

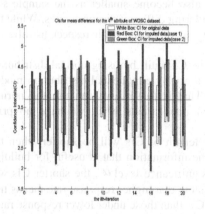

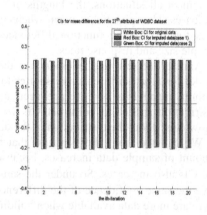

Fig. 2. CIs for attribute 4   **Fig. 3.** CIs for attribute 27

Figures 2, 3, and 4 compare the CIs for mean on the complete and imputed dataset WDBC under different missing rates. We give the experimental results of CIs for mean difference of attribute 4 and 27 in Figures 2 and 3. In Figure 2, we can see that the length of CIs built from imputed data (case-1) is much larger than those built from original data (without missing). While the length of CIs built from imputed data (case-2) is very close to the original data's CIs. This means that with a lower missing rate, the length of CIs are shorter. The same phenomenon can be seen in CIs of DF for attribute 4 (see Figure 4). As for attribute 27, the lengths of CIs built from case-1, case-2 and the

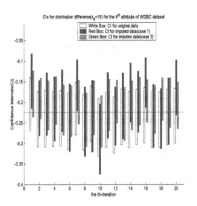

Fig. 4. CIs for distribution function of attribute 4

original data are very close, which almost give the same coverage probabilities. However, we don't present the CIs of DF for attribute 27, due to lack of space.

The average left, right endpoint (LE, RE), length and CP are listed in table 11. An interesting observation is that the value of CP is decreesing from 70% to 60% when the response rate P (note that missing rate=1-P) is increasing from (0.6, 0.7) to (1, 1). Note that the original data has the response rate (P1=1, P2=1). On the other hand, the average length AL is also decreasing when the response rate is increasing, that is, the AL is longer when the groups contain more missing data, which are imputed by random imputation. By combining these two facts, we know that the length of CIs will be shorter when using lower missing rate data, but the CP will be lower. On the contrary, the length of CIs will be longer when using higher missing rate data, resulting in a higher CP.

For group with small range of values, attribute 27 for example, the LE, RE, AL and CP of CIs are comparatively stable under different response rates.

Table 11. Average intervals, ALs and CP for mean

	LE	RE	AL	Average	CP (%)
A.4 (Original)	2.789261	4.198938	1.409677		60
Case 1(0.6, 1)	2.560288	4.617375	2.057087	4.124679	75
Case 2(0.9, 1)	2.781663	4.362656	1.580993		65
A.27 (Original)	-0.19973	0.237031	0.436765		100
Case 1(0.6, 1)	-0.19981	0.237	0.43681	0.022297	100
Case 2(0.9, 1)	-0.19961	0.237172	0.436782		100

5   Conclusions

In this paper we have proposed a new method based on empirical likelihood (EL) for identifying confidence intervals for the mean and distribution differences between two contrasting groups. The mean and distribution differences between two contrasting groups assist in predicting the properties of a group using one another. To extend the applied range, our method takes into account the situation of two contrasting groups, one group is known well, and the other is unknown (for example, having no information about the form of distribution and parameters). In comparing of the differences of two contrasting groups with missing data, we have shown that the EL-based confidence intervals works well in making inference for various differences between the two groups, especially for the mean and distribution function differences. We have also shown that this result can directly be used to test the hypotheses on the differences, and that the result can apply to the complete data settings.

References

1. Au, W., Chan, K. (2005), Mining changes in association rules: a fuzzy approach. Fuzzy Sets and Systems, 149(1): 87-104.
2. Bay, S., and Pazzani, M. (1999), Detecting Change in Categorical Data: Mining Contrast Sets. KDD'99, pp. 302-306.
3. Bay, S., and Pazzani, M. (2000), Characterizing Model Erros and Differences. ICML'00, pp. 49-56.
4. Bay, S., and Pazzani, M. (2001), Detecting Group Differences: Mining Contrast Sets. Data Mining and Knowledge Discovery, 5(3): 213-246.
5. Blake, C., and Merz,C. (1998). UCI Repository of machine learning database. http://www.ics.uci.edu/~mlearn/
6. Cho, Y.B., Cho, Y.H., & Kim, S. (2005), Mining changes in customer buying behavior for collaborative recommendations. Expert Systems with Applications, 28(2): 359-369.
7. Cong, G., and Liu, B. (2002). Speed-up Iterative Frequent Itemset Mining with Constraint Changes. ICDM'02, pp 107-114.
8. Adibi, J. Cohen, P., and Morrison, C. (2004), Measuring Confidence Intervals in Link Discovery: A Bootstrap Approach. KDD'04.
9. Hall, P., and Martin, M. (1988), On the bootstrap and two-sample problems. Austral. J. Statist, 30A, pp 179-192.
10. Li, H.F., Lee, S.Y., and Shan, M.K., (2005). Online Mining Changes of Items over Continuous Append-only and Dynamic Data Streams. The Journal of Universal Computer Science, 11(8): 1411-1425 (2005).
11. Little, R. and Rubin, D. (2002), Statistical analysis with missing data. 2nd edition. John Wiley & Sons, New York.
12. Liu, B., Hsu, W., Han, H. and Xia, Y. (2000), Mining Changes for Real-Life Applications. DaWaK'00, pp337-346.
13. Qin, J., (1994). Semi-empirical likelihood ratio confidence intervals for the difference of two sample mean. Ann. Inst. Statist. Math. 46, 117-126.
14. Qin, J. and lawless, J. (1994), Empirical likelihood and general estimating equations. Ann. Statists. 22, 300-325.
15. Rao, J. (1996). On variance estimation with imputed survey data. J. Amer. Statist. Assoc., 91: 499-520.
16. Wang, K., Zhou, S., Fu, A., and Yu, X. (2003). Mining Changes of Classification by Correspondence Tracing. SIAMDM'03, 2003.
17. Webb, G., Butler, S., and Newlands, D. (2003), On detecting differences between groups. KDD'03, pp. 256-265.
18. Ying, A., Murphy, G., Raymond, T., and Mark, C. (2004), Predicting Source Code Changes by Mining Change History. IEEE Trans. Software Eng., 30(9): 574-586.
19. W.N. Street, W.H. Wolberg and O.L. Mangasarian1993. Nuclear feature extraction for breast tumour diagnosis. IS&T/SPIE 1993 volume 1905, pages 861-870, San Jose, CA, 1993.

EGEA : A New Hybrid Approach Towards Extracting Reduced Generic Association Rule Set (Application to AML Blood Cancer Therapy)

M.A. Esseghir, G. Gasmi, S. Ben Yahia, and Y. Slimani

Département des Sciences de l'Informatique
Faculté des Sciences de Tunis
Campus Universitaire, 1060 Tunis, Tunisie
mohamedemir@gawab.com

Abstract. To avoid obtaining an unmanageable highly sized association rule sets– compounded with their low precision– that often make the perusal of knowledge ineffective, the extraction and exploitation of compact and informative generic basis of association rules is a becoming a must. Moreover, they provide a powerful verification technique for hampering gene mis-annotating or badly clustering in the Unigene library. However, extracted generic basis is still oversized and their exploitation is impractical. Thus, providing critical nuggets of extra-valued knowledge is a compellingly addressable issue. To tackle such a drawback, we propose in this paper a novel approach, called EGEA (Evolutionary Gene Extraction Approach). Such approach aims to considerably reduce the quantity of knowledge, extracted from a gene expression dataset, presented to an expert. Thus, we use a genetic algorithm to select the more predictive set of genes related to patient situations. Once, the relevant attributes (genes) have been selected, they serve as an input for a second approach stage, i.e., extracting generic association rules from this reduced set of genes. The notably decrease of the generic association rule cardinality, extracted from the selected gene set, permits to improve the quality of knowledge exploitation. Carried out experiments on a benchmark dataset pointed out that among this set, there are genes which are previously unknown prognosis-associated genes. This may serve as molecular targets for new therapeutic strategies to repress the relapse of pediatric acute myeloid leukemia (AML).

Keywords: Generic association rules, Genetic Algorithms, Neural networks, Frequent Closed itemset algorithms, Bioinformatics.

1   Introduction

High-throughput sequencing and functional genomic technologies provided to the scientific community a human genome sequence and have enabled large-scale genotyping and gene expression profiling of human populations [1]. Biological databases contain heterogeneous information such as annotated genomic

A Min Tjoa and J. Trujillo (Eds.): DaWaK 2006, LNCS 4081, pp. 491–502, 2006.

sequence information, results of microarray experiments, molecular structures and properties of proteins, etc. In addition, an increasing number of databases from the medical domain, containing medical records and valuable information on diseases and phenotypes, become available. Data Mining techniques and/or tools, aiming to go further beyond the top of the Iceberg, delve and efficiently discover valuable, non-obvious information from large microarray databases (*e.g.*, information about diseases and their relation to sub-cellular processes). Microarrays provide a prolific, "exciting" and challenging contexts for the application of data mining techniques. For recent overviews, please refer to recently edited books respectively by Wang *et al.* [1] and Chen [2].

In this respect, extracting generic basis of association rules seems to be an efficient approach for providing extra-added value knowledge for biologists. In this case, we expect that a biologist may not only discover synexpression groups but may also identify correlations between a group of genes and a particular cell type. However, the unmanageably large association rule sets, even though generic association rule set size is known to be compact, compounded with their low precision often make the perusal of knowledge ineffective, their exploitation time-consuming, and frustrating for the user.

In this paper, and aiming to tackle this highly important topic, we propose a novel approach towards reducing "shrewdly" and informatively the amount of knowledge to be presented to a user, we propose an hybrid approach showing the potential benefits from the synergy of genetic algorithms and association rule extraction. Thus, we used a genetic algorithm to select the more predictive set of genes related to the patient situation. Then, we extract generic association rules from this reduced set of genes. The notably decrease of the generic association rules, extracted from the selected genes, permits to ameliorate the quality of knowledge exploitation.

Experiments were carried out on a dataset of the AFFIMETRIX GENECHIP Human Genome U95Av2 oligonucleotide microarray (Affymetrix, Santa Clara, CA) that contains 12 566 probe sets. This dataset contains Analysis of mononuclear cells from 54 chemotherapy treated patients less than 15 years of age with acute myeloid leukemia (AML). Mononuclear cells taken from peripheral blood or bone marrow. Treatment results describing patient situation associated with *complete remission* and *relapse* with resistant disease are also reported. After the chemotherapy treatment, most patients with Acute Myeloid Leukemia (AML) enter complete remission. However, some of them enter relapse with a resistant disease. Obtained results showed that Also, among this set, there are genes which are previously unknown prognosis-associated genes. This may serve as molecular targets for new therapeutic strategies to repress the relapse of pediatric AML.

The remainder of the paper is organized as follows. Section 2 details the proposed hybrid approach. The genetic algorithm applied for the selection of most predictive attributes is described. Section 3 presents the obtained results from the carried out experiments on the benchmark dataset. Section 4 concludes this paper and points out future perspectives.

2   Dimensionality Reduction: Selection of a Predictor Set of Genes

Applying classical association rule extraction framework to dense microarrays leads to an unmanageably highly sized association rule sets– compounded with their low precision– that often make the perusal of knowledge ineffective, their exploitation time-consuming, and frustrating for the user. Even though extracting and exploiting compact and informative generic basis of association rules can be an advisable remedy, a glance to their size can be nightmarish to the user (c.f, reported statistics in Experiments section). Another avenue to tackle the high dimensionality problem in gene expression datasets, is to assess and select one of the more discriminatory set of genes to the target. In fact, *feature selection* refers to the problem of selecting the more predictive and valuable attributes, in terms classification and class separability, correlated with a given output. Numerous studies have focused on the selection of relevant features, by discarding misleading and noisy ones [3]. Such studies, involving different techniques can be viewed under two families: *wrappers* and *filters*. Wrappers evaluate attributes by using accuracy estimates provided by the actual target learning algorithm. Alternatively, filters use general characteristics of the data to evaluate attributes and operate independently of any learning algorithm [4]. Indeed, an exhaustive search within the large set of feature combination is very consuming in term of computational time, since the search space of possible combination increases exponentially with the number of genes. An exhaustive search of all possible combinations of attributes is impractical, especially when the evaluation procedure for the generated solutions involves a learning algorithm. In this respect, the use of AI global search techniques, such as genetic algorithms (GA) seems to be very promising, since they have proven to be valuable in the exploration of large and/or complex problem spaces [5]. GA attempt to apply evolutionary techniques to the field of the problem solving notably in combinatorial optimization [6,7]. In fact, GA may be used to select the more predictive set of genes related to the target class (patient situation). Our genetic algorithm evolves a set of feasible solutions evaluated with an artificial neural network as a wrapper. Subsets of variables are assessed within the evaluation procedure according to their generalization accuracy in classification.

Believing that combining classifiers and boosting methods can lead to improvements in performance, in this paper, we propose, a new hybrid model whose the driving idea is the go towards assessing potential benefits form a synergy of two data mining techniques, namely feature selection by Artificial neural networks and GA and association rule extraction.

Figure 1 graphically sketches the model and shows that it is composed of two steps. On, the first stage selects the best set of inputs having a predictive relationship with the target class. Whereas, the second step consists in the generation of a compact set of generic association rules using the selected genes. It is noteworthy that the whole process, i.e., sequentially applying feature selection and rule extraction, is performed in an iterative process. From an iteration to another one, and acting towards a more reduced and guided search space, the

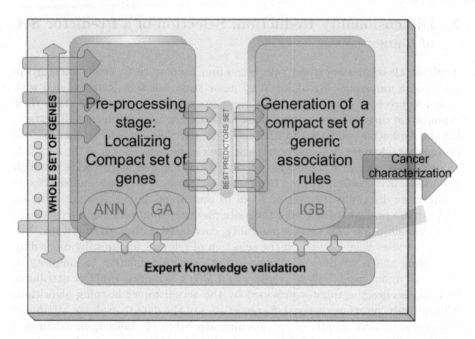

Fig. 1. The proposed hybrid model

system can be fed by biological apriori knowledge or given by experts or pointed out by generic association rules.

2.1   Preprocessing Stage: Dimensionality Reduction

In this section we look to the problem of building a representative set of relevant features. In fact Data reduction techniques was successfully applied in in numerous gene expression data analysis using as well wrapper as filters [8,9,10]. Narayanan *et al.* [11] have applied different data mining techniques, mainly based on neural network classifiers, to mine knowledge enfolded in microarrays data using also neural networks as a wrapper to tackle the high dimensional data.

Believing that feature selection methods, to use as well in the definition of a compact pattern representation as in mining knowledge with robust and interpretable methods, depends mainly both on wrapper accuracy -quality of the evaluation procedure- and on the search procedure applied. We decide to opt for a stochastic global search procedure to explore the search space of feasible subsets of relevant non-redundant features: *Genetic algorithms*. In addition, the wrapper consists of an artificial neural networks trained with the *backpropagation* learning algorithm [12]. The genetic algorithm, presented here, will be applied to select a subset of genes involved in the prediction of patient situation: *complete remission* or *relapse*. Each set of candidate solutions are evolved through a fixed number of generations. The pseudo-code for localizing compact predictive set of genes is provided by *Algorithm 1*. GA process is roughly summarized in what follows:

– *Representation*: Each generation consists of a set of candidate solutions represented using a binary encoding. Any possible solution to the problem is encoded as binary string of 12625 genes, where the code 1 means that the gene is selected to build an ANN and 0 when it is discarded (*c.f.*, Figure 2).

Fig. 2. Chromosome representation

– *Initialization*: An initial set of solutions is randomly generated. For each individual a number of genes are randomly selected by setting the corresponding bits equal to 1. Once the initial set is generated, the evaluation process starts. A fitness value is assigned to each chromosome. The first generation of solutions is derived by applying a tournament selection to the evaluated set.
– *Evaluation*: Two steps are required to evaluate each chromosome. First a neural network, with the selected genes in the chromosome as input, is built and partially trained. Next, the trained network is evaluated using the test set. The test set presents to the network a new data which is not trained with it. The chromosome evaluation assesses the predictive generalization ability of the neural network and consequently of the set of involved genes . Our fitness involves two evaluation criteria: the proportion of incorrectly classified instances and the mean square error on the test set.

$$fitness = (ICI + TMSE)/2 \qquad (1)$$

Where ICI and $TMSE$ denotes respectively the proportion of incorrectly classified instances in the data set and the mean square error found on the test set.

2.2 Generic Association Rule Extraction

An association rule $R : X \Rightarrow Y - X$ is a relation between two frequent itemsets $X \subset Y$. X and $(Y - X)$ are called, respectively, premise and conclusion of the rule R. An association rule is valid whenever its strength metric, confidence$(R) = \frac{support(Y)}{support(X)}$, is greater than or equal to the minimal threshold of confidence *minconf*.

However, in practice, the number of valid association rules is very high. Indeed, this number was estimated to be equal to $2^{2 \times l}$, where l is the length of the longest frequent itemset [13].

Consequently, the user can not interpret and exploit efficiently a such amount of knowledge. To palliate this problem, a solution consists in extracting a **reduced** subset of association rules, called *generic basis*. On the demand of the user, we have to be able to derive all the remaining association rules (*i.e..*, generic basis extraction should be done **without information loss**). For this reason, generic basis extraction have to fulfill the following requirements: [14]

Algorithm 1. Feature selection: Localizing compact set of genes

---

Input:
S: set of genes
N_i: initial population size
N: population size
t: tournament size
p_{mut}: mutation probability
p_{cross}: Crossover probability
it: number of training iterations
Maxgen: number of generations
h: number of hidden nodes
η: learning rate
m: momentum value
Output: S1: Best subset of gene predictors

```
1  Begin
2     Population P_0, P,P_tmp
3     P_0=P=P_tmp= ∅;
4     P_0=GenerateInitialPopulation(N_i)
5     Evaluate (P_0, η, m, h, it)
6     P=Select(P_0, N, t) //Applying a tournament to select N chromosomes from
       P_0
7     i=0
8     While i < Maxgen do
9        P_tmp=Select (P, N, t)
10       Crossover(P_tmp, p_cross)
11       Mutate(P_tmp, p_mut)
12       Evaluate(P_tmp, η, m, h, it)
13       Replace(P_tmp, P) //replacing solutions from P by newest ones from P_tmp
          using reverse tournament
14       i=i+1
15    S1=P.bestChromosome().extractGenes() // extracting selected chromosome
       genes
16    Return(S1)
17 End
```

- **"Derivability"**: An inference mechanism should be provided (*e.g.*, an axiomatic system). The axiomatic system has to be valid (*i.e.*, should forbid derivation of non valid rules) and complete (*i.e.*, should enable derivation of all valid rules).
- **"Informativeness"**: The generic basis of association rules allows to retrieve exactly the support and confidence of the derived (redundant) association rules.

To extract a reliable number of association rules, we use the $\mathcal{IGB}$ (Informative Generic Basis) basis [14]. This choice is justified by:

1. **Conveying maximum of useful knowledge:** Association rules of the $\mathcal{IGB}$ basis convey the maximum of useful knowledge. Indeed, $\mathcal{IGB}$ is defined as follows:

Definition 1. *Let $\mathcal{FCI}_{\mathcal{K}}$ be the set of frequent closed itemsets* [1] *extracted from an extraction context $\mathcal{K}$. For each entry f in $\mathcal{FCI}_{\mathcal{K}}$, let MG_f be the set of its minimal generators* [2]. *The $\mathcal{IGB}$ generic basis is given by: $\mathcal{IGB} = \{R : g_s \Rightarrow (f\text{-}g_s) \mid f \in \mathcal{FCI}_{\mathcal{K}} \wedge f \neq \emptyset \wedge g_s \in MG_{f_1}, f_1 \in \mathcal{FCI}_{\mathcal{K}} \wedge f_1 \subseteq f \wedge confidence(R) \geq minconf \wedge \nexists g \mathbin{/} g \subset g_s \wedge confidence(g \Rightarrow f\text{-}g) \geq minconf\}$.*

Thus, a generic association rule of $\mathcal{IGB}$ is based on the extraction of frequent closed itemsets from whose we generate minimal generic association rules, i.e., with minimal premise part and maximal conclusion part. It was shown that this type of association rules conveys the maximum of useful knowledge [15];

2. **Information lossless:** It was pointed out that the $\mathcal{IGB}$ basis is extracted without information loss [14];

3. **Compactness:** In [14] and by comparing obtained set cardinalities, we showed that $\mathcal{IGB}$ is by far more compact than the following:
   - The Non-Redundant association Rules $\mathcal{NRR}$ basis, defined by Zaki et al. [16,17];
   - The Generic Basis of Exact rules and the Transitive reduction of Generic Basis of Approximative rules ($\mathcal{GBE}$, $\mathcal{TGBA}$), defined by Bastide et al. [18].

Algorithm 2. Evaluate procedure

Input:
P: population
h: number of hidden nodes
it: number of training iterations
η: learning rate
m: momentum value
Output: P: Population evaluated

```
1 Begin
2     Foreach Chromosome ch ∈ P do
3         I=extractGeneIndexes(ch)
4         TestSet=GenerateTestSet(I)
5         TrainSet=GenerateTrainSet(I)
6         N=new Network(I, h, 1) // building an ANN with the I selected genes
7         N.train(Trainset, it, η, m) //Training N for it epochs with Trainset
8         Eval(N, TestSet, TMSE , ICI) //Evaluating ANN generalization ability
9         ch.fitness=(TMSE + ICI)/2 // computing ch fitness value
10    Return(P)
11 End
```

---

[1] A closed frequent itemset is a the largest set of items sharing the same transactions (objects).

[2] A minimal generator is the smallest set of items sharing the same transactions (objects).

3   Experiments

3.1   Feature Selection Settings

Modeling tools based on a ANN can not be trained or assessed by a raw dataset. In our case, fortunately all the variable values have a numerical representation, and thus data have to be normalized. ANN algorithms require data to range within the unit interval. The chosen method for data normalization is the *linear transform scaling* [19]:

$$\nu_n = \frac{\nu_i - min\{\nu_1..\nu_n\}}{max\{\nu_1..\nu_n\} - min\{\nu_1..\nu_n\}} \tag{2}$$

Where ν_n and ν_i respectively represent the normalized and the actual values. This expression takes values and maps them them into corresponding values in the unit interval $[0, 1]$. The main advantage of the linear scaling is that it introduces no distortion to the variable distributions.

During carried out experiments, we have tested different values for each parameter. Table 1 summarizes neural network and genetic algorithm parameters, that permitted to obtain the best results.

Table 1. GA and ANN parameter settings

GA parameters		ANN parameters	
Parameter	Value	Parameter	Value
Number of generations	200	Number of iterations	250
Crossover probability(p_{cross})	80%	learning rate (η)	0.25
Mutation probability (p_{mut})	20%	Number of hidden nodes	10
Initial population size	30	Weights initialization range	$[-0.1..0.1]$
population size	20	Architecture	Feed forward fully-connected

Table 2. The 45 selected genes

Code	Probe set ID	average level	Code	Probe set ID	average level	Code	Probe set ID	average level
1	31469-s-at	43.54	2	32004-s-at	390.79	3	33647-s-at	432.65
4	34589-f-at	190.60	5	34600-s-at	411.39	6	36399-at	65.98
7	36411-s-at	538.70	8	32352-at	987.98	9	33495-at	70.75
10	33981-at	15.60	11	34037-at	13.90	12	34495-r-at	614.79
13	36770-at	11.76	14	37159-at	54.96	15	37483-at	146.19
16	39672-at	881.20	17	31853-at	111.69	18	31891-at	213.32
19	32672-at	42.20	20	33237-at	242.10	21	33334-at	110.69
22	34189-at	129.69	23	34664-at	91.65	24	36044-at	220.39
25	36927-at	17.32	26	39783-at	354.10	27	40449-at	22.81
29	40451-at	170.80	30	40485-at	201.10	31	40870-g-at	254.10
32	33344-at	40.20	33	34825-at	200.89	34	35775-at	14.90
35	37383-f-at	16806.40	36	39118-at	983.20	37	39494-at	432.87
38	39848-at	114.40	39	39922-at	57.70	40	40532-at	84.50
41	40958-at	132.45	42	32583-at	951.20	43	33144-at	53.87
44	942-at	65.21	45	323-at	98.43			

Starting with the previously defined parameters, we obtained a highly compact set genes whose size is by far lower than the initial number of genes, *i.e.*, more than twelve thousands. Table 2 sketches the 45 genes retained from among more than twelve thousands. Even though, more compact gene sets were obtained, the retained gene set achieves high generalization performance on test set: around 93% of accuracy.

3.2 Generic Association Rule Extraction

Table 3 illustrates cardinalities of the different generic basis extracted from the discretized "54×12 566" matrix for an absolute *minsup* value equal to 1 patient. Indeed, extraction context matrix has been translated into a boolean context by considering that a gene is over-expressed in a patient whenever his expression value level is greater than or equal to its expression level average at the different patients for the same gene.

Table 3. Extraction of generic association rules from the initial context

$minconf$	$\mathcal{IGB}$	$(\mathcal{GBE}, \mathcal{TGBA})$	$\frac{\mathcal{IGB}}{(\mathcal{GBE}, \mathcal{TGBA})}$
0.05	1058829	6511866	0.162
0.3	5887121	6420922	0.916
0.5	5920969	6381928	0.927
0.7	6348233	6374305	0.995
1	999848	999848	999848

Table 3 shows important profits in terms of compactness of the $\mathcal{IGB}$ basis. Indeed, the third column of Table 3 shows that the ratio between the cardinality of $\mathcal{IGB}$ and that of $(\mathcal{GBE}, \mathcal{TGBA})$ ranges between 0.162 and 1.

Table 3 points out that the unmanageably highly sized association rule sets makes the perusal of knowledge ineffective. To palliate such drawback, we applied a feature selection process we retrieved only 45 "interesting" genes. From the selected genes, we constructed a binary $\mathcal{K}'$ context composed of 47 columns (45 genes, complete remission and relapse) and 54 rows (patients). Table 4 illustrates the cardinalities of the different generic basis. From Table 3 and Table 4, we can

Table 4. Extraction of generic association rules from filred context

$minconf$	$\mathcal{IGB}$	$(\mathcal{GBE}, \mathcal{TGBA})$	$\mathcal{NRR}$	$\frac{\mathcal{IGB}}{(\mathcal{GBE}, \mathcal{TGBA})}$	$\frac{\mathcal{IGB}}{\mathcal{NRR}}$
0.05	852	3683	1974	0.231	0.431
0.3	3063	3432	1803	0.892	1.698
0.5	2398	2928	1422	0.818	1.686
0.7	1187	1336	605	0.888	1.961
1	850	850	24	1	35.416

conclude that the number of the generic association rules considerably decreased and this may permit to ameliorate the quality of the knowledge exploitation.

From the extracted generic rules of $\mathcal{IGB}$, we selected those whose conclusion part at least contains *complete remission / relapse*. Indeed thanks to the "Augmentation" axiom defined in [14], it is possible to straightforwardly derive "classification rules", i.e., rules whose the conclusion part refers to the class attribute. For example, from the post- feature selection process extracted generic rules– whose a sample is sketched by Figure 3– one may remark the following rule "22/129.69, 33/200.89 $\Rightarrow$ 26/354.10, Complete Remission". From such rule, we can derive the following classification rule: "22/129.69, 33/200.89,26/354.10 $\Rightarrow$ Complete Remission". This may permit to easily identify prognosis-associated genes. In order to facilitate the interpretation of the generic rules, we colored the patient situation (the green color corresponds to the complete remission, whereas the red one corresponds to the relapse). Also, it is important to mention that under an explicit request from experts, we decorated genes within the extracted rules by statistical information. This information represents the average of minimal expression level for each gene. Such information was considered of paramount importance by biologists since they were interested in checking the presence or absence of a given gene in conjunction with a significant signature appearance level.

22/129.69 26/354.10 ===>	Complete Remission	Support : 6	Confiance : 1.000000			
22/129.69 33/200.89 ===>	26/354.10	Complete Remission	Support : 5	Confiance : 1.000000		
2/390.79 7/538.70 ===>	27/624.79	Complete Remission	Support : 5	Confiance : 1.000000		
2/390.79 26/354.10 ===>	Complete Remission	Support : 5	Confiance : 1.000000			
28/170.80 35/16806.440/84.50 ===>	Relapse	Support : 4	Confiance : 1.000000			
28/170.80 33/200.89 40/84.50 ===>	Relapse	Support : 4	Confiance : 1.000000			
26/354.10 27/624.79 30/201.10 ===>	Complete Remission	Support : 4	Confiance : 1.000000			
24/220.39 33/200.89 40/84.50 ===>	Relapse	Support : 4	Confiance : 1.000000			
19/42.20 24/220.39 33/200.89 ===>	26/354.10	Relapse	Support : 4	Confiance : 1.000000		
22/129.69 30/201.10 ===> 4/190.60	26/354.10	33/200.89	Complete Remission	Support : 4	Confiance : 1.000000	
4/190.60 30/201.10 33/200.89 ===>	22/129.69	26/354.10	Complete Remission	Support : 4	Confiance : 1.000000	
4/190.60 26/354.10 30/201.10 ===>	22/129.69	33/200.89	Complete Remission	Support : 4	Confiance : 1.000000	
4/190.60 22/129.69 26/354.10 ===>	30/201.10	33/200.89	Complete Remission	Support : 4	Confiance : 1.000000	
4/190.60 22/129.69 33/200.89 ===>	26/354.10	30/201.10	Complete Remission	Support : 4	Confiance : 1.000000	
19/42.20 22/129.69 ===> 26/354.10	Complete Remission	Support : 4	Confiance : 1.000000			
19/42.20 21/110.69 28/170.80 ===>	26/354.10	Relapse	Support : 4	Confiance : 1.000000		
17/111.69 21/110.69 31/254.10 ===>	Relapse	Support : 4	Confiance : 1.000000			
16/881.20 24/220.39 ===> 40/84.50	Relapse	Support : 4	Confiance : 1.000000			
16/881.20 40/84.50 ===> 24/220.39	Relapse	Support : 4	Confiance : 1.000000			
7/538.70 28/170.80 33/200.89 ===>	Relapse	Support : 4	Confiance : 1.000000			
2/390.79 26/354.10 27/624.79 ===>	7/538.70	Complete Remission	Support : 4	Confiance : 1.000000		
2/390.79 7/538.70 26/354.10 ===>	27/624.79	Complete Remission	Support : 4	Confiance : 1.000000		
2/390.79 4/190.60 5/411.39 28/170.80 ===>	Relapse	Support : 4	Confiance : 1.000000			
24/220.39 39/57.70 ===>	33/200.89	Relapse	Support : 3	Confiance : 1.000000		
28/170.80 38/114.40 ===>	27/624.79	Relapse	Support : 3	Confiance : 1.000000		
26/354.10 34/14.90 ===>	28/170.80	Relapse	Support : 3	Confiance : 1.000000		
31/254.10 42/951.20 ===> 21/110.69	26/354.10	33/200.89	Complete Remission	Support : 3	Confiance : 1.000000	
26/354.10 33/200.89 42/951.20 ===>	21/110.69	31/254.10	Complete Remission	Support : 3	Confiance : 1.000000	
21/110.69 42/951.20 ===>	26/354.10	31/254.10	33/200.89	Complete Remission	Support : 3	Confiance : 1.000000
31/254.10 40/84.50 ===>	17/111.69	Relapse	Support : 3	Confiance : 1.000000		
4/190.60 28/170.80 39/57.70 ===>	Complete Remission	Support : 3	Confiance : 1.000000			

Fig. 3. The extracted rules

4   Conclusion

Under some number of hypothesis, generic association rules can constitute a gene annotation framework based on a strong correlation clustering. However, and even though they are compact, their high size can hamper their exploitation by experts.

In this paper, we proposed a novel approach towards filtering the most "predictive" compact set of genes. This approach, firstly uses genetic algorithms to filter out significant set of genes. Second, using this compact, we extracted reasonably sized generic association rules. Carried out experiments on a benchmark dataset showed the potential benefits of such approach. Indeed from more twelve thousands genes (possibly from which we may extract millions of generic rules and one imagine the number of all extractable association rules), we selected only 45 gene. From such reduced set of gene, it was possible to straightforwardly extract classification rules by means of associated derivation axioms.

References

1. Wang, J., M.J.Zaki, Toivonen, H., Shasha, D.: Data Mining in Bioinformatics. Advanced Information and Knowledge Processing. Springer (2005)
2. Chen, Y.: Bioinformatics Technologies. Advanced Information and Knowledge Processing. Springer (2005)
3. Kohavi, R., John, G.H.: Wrappers for feature subset selection. Artificial Intelligence **97** (1997) 273–324
4. Hall, M.A., Holmes, G.: Benchmarking attribute selection techniques for discrete class data mining. IEEE Transactions on Knowledge and Data Eengineering **15** (2003)
5. Cornujols, A., Miclet, L., Kodratoff, Y., Mitchell, T.: Apprentissage artificiel : concepts et algorithmes. Eyrolles (2002)
6. Goldberg, D.E.: Genetic algorithms in search, optimization and machine learning. Addison Wesley (1989)
7. Trabelsi, A., Esseghir, M.A.: New evolutionary bankruptcy forecasting model based on genetic algorithms and neural networks. 17th IEEE International Conference on Tools with Artificial Intelligence (ICTAI'05) (2005) 241–245
8. Liu, H., Li, J., Wong, L.: A comparative study on feature selection and classification methods using gene expression profiles and proteomic patterns. Genome Informatics **13** (2002) 51–60
9. Shang, C., Shen, Q.: Aiding classification of gene expression data with feature selection: A comparative study. International Journal of Computational Intelligence Reasearch **1** (2005) 68–76
10. Esseghir, M.A., Yahia, S.B., Abdelhak, S.: Localizing compact set of genes involved in cancer diseases using an evolutionary conectionist approach. In: European Conferences on Machine Learning and European Conferences on Principles and Practice of Knowledge Discovery in Databases. ECML/PKDD Discovery Challenge. (2005)
11. A. Narayanan, A. Cheung, J.G.E.K.C.V.: Artificial neural networks for reducing the dimensionality of gene expression data. Bioinformatics Using Computational Intelligence Paradigms. Springer Verlag **176** (2005) 191–211
12. Rumelhart, D.E., Hinton, G.E., Williams, R.J.: Learning internal representations by error propagation. In: Parallel Distributed Processing: Explorations in the Microstructure of Cognition. MIT Press, Cambridge (1986)
13. Zaki, M.J.: Mining non-redundant association rules. Data Mining Knowledge Discovery **9** (2004) 223–248

14. Gasmi, G., BenYahia, S., Nguifo, E.M., Slimani, Y.: $\mathcal{IGB}$: A new informative generic base of association rules. In: Proceedings of the Intl. Ninth Pacific-Asia Conference on Knowledge Data Discovery (PAKDD'05), LNAI 3518, Hanoi, Vietnam, Springler-Verlag (2005) 81–90
15. Kryszkiewicz, M.: Representative association rules and minimum condition maximum consequence association rules. In: Proceedings of Second European Symposium on Principles of Data Mining and Knowledge Discovery (PKDD), 1998, LNCS, volume 1510, Springer-Verlag, Nantes, France. (1998) 361–369
16. Zaki, M.: Mining Non-Redundant Association Rules. Data Mining and Knowledge Discovery (2004) 223–248
17. Zaki, M.J.: Generating non-redundant association rules. In: Proceedings of the 6th ACM-SIGKDD International Conference on Knowledge Discovery and Data Mining, Boston, Massachusetts, USA. (2000) 34–43
18. Bastide, Y., Pasquier, N., Taouil, R., Lakhal, L., Stumme, G.: Mining minimal non-redundant association rules using frequent closed itemsets. In: Proceedings of the International Conference DOOD'2000, LNAI, volume 1861, Springer-Verlag, London, UK. (2000) 972–986
19. Pyle, D.: Data Preparation for Data Mining. (1999)

AISS: An Index for Non-timestamped Set Subsequence Queries

Witold Andrzejewski and Tadeusz Morzy

Institute of Computing Science
Poznan University of Technology
Piotrowo 2, 60-965 Poznan, Poland
{wandrzejewski, tmorzy}@cs.put.poznan.pl

Abstract. In many recent applications of database management systems data may be stored in user defined complex data types (such as sequences). However, efficient querying of such data is not supported by commercially available database management systems and therefore efficient indexing schemes for complex data types need to be developed. In this paper we focus primarily on the indexing of non-timestamped sequences of sets of categorical data, specifically indexing for set subsequence queries. We address both: logical structure and implementation issues of such indexes. Our main contributions are threefold. First, we specify the logical structure of the index and we propose algorithms for set subsequence query execution, which utilize the index structure. Second, we provide the proposition for the implementation of such index, which uses means available in all of the "of the shelf" database management systems. Finally, we experimentally evaluate the performance of the index.

1 Introduction

Many of todays commercially available database management systems allow users to define complex datatypes, such as sets, sequences or strings. One of the most important complex datatypes is the sequence. Sequences are very convienient in modelling such objects as protein sequences, DNA chains (sequences of atomic values of a small alphabet), time series (composed of real values), and Web server logs (composed of events). Purchases made by customers in stores are also sequential. Here, sequences are composed of sets of products bought by the customer, which are ordered by the date of purchase. The problem of indexing and querying sequences has recently received a lot of attention [7,12].

Although modern database management systems provide users with the means to create sequences, they do not support efficient querying of this data type. To illustrate the problem, let us consider the following example. We are given the database of four sequences of sets (for example database of sequences of purchases) shown on Table 1 and the sequence $\mathcal{Q} = \langle \{2\}, \{1\} \rangle$. The problem is to find all sequences from the database such that they contain the sequence $\mathcal{Q}$. By sequence containment we mean that the sequence $\mathcal{Q}$ is contained within

A Min Tjoa and J. Trujillo (Eds.): DaWaK 2006, LNCS 4081, pp. 503–512, 2006.

Table 1. Running example database

Id	Sequence
1	$S^1 = \langle \{1, 2\}, \{1, 2\}, \{1, 6\} \rangle$
2	$S^2 = \langle \{2, 7\}, \{1, 3\}, \{1, 5\} \rangle$
3	$S^3 = \langle \{2, 8\}, \{1, 3\}, \{1, 4\} \rangle$
4	$S^4 = \langle \{1, 3\}, \{3, 9\}, \{1, 6\} \rangle$

the sequence S IFF it may be obtained by removing of some of the items from the sequence S. Here, sequence Q is contained within sequences S^1, S^2 and S^3, but not in S^4. Such queries are very common in many database application domains, such as: market basket sequence mining, web log mining and mining results analysis. As can be easily seen the problem is difficult. If there is no indexing structure for the database, then, in order to answer the query, we need to read all sequences from database one by one, and for each such sequence check whether it contains the given sequence Q. Unfortunately, for large databases, brute force solution may be very costly.

Concluding, there is evidently a need to research efficient, possibly general, indexing schemes for sequences. Several indexing schemes for sequences have been proposed so far. Most of them were designed either for time series [1,4] or sequences of atomic values [14,9]. Almost nothing has been done with regard to indexing sequences of sets. According to out knowledge, the only index for sequences of sets developed so far was proposed by us in [3]. However, this index was designed for sequences of timestamped sets and its main task was to support a very special case of set subsequence queries, where sets were also timestamped.

The original contribution of this paper is the proposal of a new indexing scheme capable of efficient retrieval of sequences of non-timestamped sets. Moreover, the index also supports retrieval of multisets. We present the physical structure of the index and we develop algorithms for query processing. We also present algorithms for incremental set/sequence insertion, deletion and update in the index. The index has a very simple structure and may be easily implemented over existing database management systems.

The rest of the paper is organized as follows. Section 2 contains an overview of the related work. In Section 3 we introduce basic definitions used throughout the paper. We present our index in Section 4. Experimental evaluation of the index is presented in Section 5. Finally, the paper concludes in Section 6 with a summary and a future work agenda.

2   Related Work

Most of research on indexing of sequential data is focused on three distinct types of sequences: time series, strings, and web logs.

Indexes proposed for time series support searching for similar or exact subsequences by exploiting the fact, that the elements of the indexed sequences are numbers. This is reflected both in index structure and in similarity metrics.

Popular similarity metrics include Minkowski distance [16], compression-based metrics [6], and dynamic time warping metrics [13]. Often, a technique for reduction of the dimensionality of the problem is employed [1].

String indexes usually support searching for subsequences based on identity or similarity to a given query sequence. Most common distance measure for similarity queries is the Levenshtein distance [8], and index structures are built on suffix tree [15] or suffix array [10].

Indexing of web logs is often based on indexing of sequences of timestamped categorical data. Among the proposed solutions, one may mention: SEQ family of indexes which use transformation of the original problem into the well-researched problem of indexing of sets [11], ISO-Depth index [14] which is based on a trie structure and SEQ-Join index [9] which uses a set of relational tables and a set of B$^+$-tree indexes.

Recently, works on sequences of categorical data were extended to sequences of sets. The Generalized ISO-Depth Index proposed in [3] supports timestamped set subsequence queries and timestamped set subsequence similarity queries. Construction of the index involves storing all of the sequences in a trie structure and numbering the nodes in depth first search order. Final index is obtained from such trie structure.

3   Basic Definitions and Problem Formulation

Let $I = \{i_1, i_2, \ldots, i_n\}$ denote the set of *items*. A non-empty set of items is called an *itemset*. We define a *sequence* as an ordered list of itemsets and denote it: $S = \langle s_1, s_2, \ldots, s_n \rangle$, where s_i, $i \in \langle 1, n \rangle$ are itemsets. Each itemset in the sequence is called an *element* of a sequence. Each element s_i of a sequence S is denoted as $\{x_1, x_2, \ldots, x_n\}$, where x_i, $i \in \langle 1, n \rangle$ are items. Given the item i and a sequence S we say that the item i is *contained* within the sequence S, denoted $i \vdash S$, if there exists any element in the sequence such that it contains the given item. Given a sequence S and an item i, we define $n(i, S)$ as a number of elements in a sequence S containing the item i. Given sequences S and T, the sequence T is a *subsequence* of S, denoted $T \sqsubseteq S$, if the sequence T may be obtained from sequence S by removal of some of items from the elements and removal of any empty elements which may appear. Conversely, we say that the sequence S *contains* the sequence T and that S is a *supersequence* of T.

In order to present the structure of the proposed index, additional notions and definitions are needed. A *multiset* is an itemset where items may appear more then once. We denote multisets as $S_M = \{(x_1 : n_1), (x_2 : n_2), \ldots, (x_m : n_m)\}$, where x_i, $i \in \langle 1, m \rangle$ are items, and n_i are *counters* which denote how many times the items x_i appear in the multiset. We omit such items, that their counters are equal to zero (i.e. they do not appear in the multiset). Given the S_M and T_M multisets, the T_M multiset is a *subset* of the multiset S_M, denoted $T_M \subseteq S_M$ if the multiset T_M may be obtained from multiset S_M by removal of some of the items.

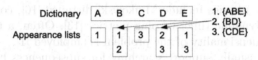

Fig. 1. Basic Inverted File Index structure

We define a *database*, denoted $\mathcal{DB}$, as a set of either sequences or multisets, called *database entries*. Each database entry in the database has a unique *identifier*. Without the loss of generality we assume those identifiers to be consecutive, positive integers. A database sequence identified by the number i is denoted $\mathcal{S}^i$, whereas a database multiset is denoted S_M^i. Given the *query sequence* $\mathcal{Q}$, the *set subsequence query* retrieves a set of identifiers of all sequences from the database, such that they contain the query sequence, i.e. $\{i : \mathcal{S}^i \in \mathcal{DB} \wedge \mathcal{Q} \sqsubseteq \mathcal{S}^i\}$. Given the *query multiset* Q_M, the *subset query* retrieves a set of identifiers of all multisets from the database such, that the multiset Q_M is their subset, i.e. $\{i : S_M^i \in \mathcal{DB} \wedge Q_M \subseteq S_M^i\}$.

4 The AISS Index

Now, we will proceed to the presentation of our index for sequences of non-timestamped sets. The idea of the index is based on the well known Inverted File Index [5]. The new structure allows to search for supersequences of sequences of sets and supersets of multisets.

The general idea for the index is as follows. We transform sequences from database to multisets by discarding data about which items belong to which itemsets and about the order of the itemsets. Next, we store these multisets in the structure based on the idea of the Inverted File Index. To perform a query, we transform the query sequence to a multiset, and retrieve all the supersets of such multiset from the index. Because we discard some of the data, additional verification phase is needed to prune false positives.

Basic Inverted File structure, which is used for indexing itemsets, is composed of two parts: *dictionary* and *appearance lists*. The dictionary is the list of all the items that appear at least once in the database. Each item has an appearance list associated with it. Given the item i, the appearance list associated with item i lists identifiers of all the sets from database, that contain that item. Structure of the basic Inverted File Index is shown on Figure 1.

In order to be able to store multisets in the above presented structure we propose a straightforward modification. We alter appearance lists, so that they store counters which show how many times the item appears in the set as well as identifiers. Notice, that such modification allows us to store full information about multisets. In order to be able to store sequences of sets in such index, we use a *sequence to multiset transformation* which is introduced by the Definition 1.

Algorithm 1. AISS index creation.

1. Build a dictionary by scanning a database and retrieving all distinct items stored in the database.
2. For each of the sequences $\mathcal{S}^j \in \mathcal{DB}$ or for each of the multisets $S_M^j \in \mathcal{DB}$ perform the following steps:
   (a) if $\mathcal{DB}$ is a database of sequences, perform the following transformation: $S_M^j = T(\mathcal{S}^j)$.
   (b) For each of the pairs $(x_i : n_i) \in S_M^j$ create an entry (j, n_i) in the appearance list associated with the item x_i.

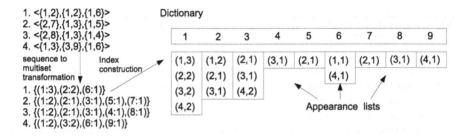

Fig. 2. AISS Index for exemplary database

Definition 1. *Sequence to multiset transformation.*

Sequence is transformed to a multiset by creating a multiset, that contains all the items from the sequence. Formally,

$$T(\mathcal{S}) = \{(x_i : n_i) : x_i \vdash \mathcal{S} \wedge n_i = n(x_i, \mathcal{S})\} \tag{1}$$

Example 1. We want to transform the sequence $\mathcal{S}^1 = \langle \{1, 2\}, \{1, 2\}, \{1, 6\} \rangle$ from the running example database to a multiset. In this sequence, item 1 occurs three times, item 2 occurs two times, and item 6 occurs one time. Therefore the multiset should contain three items 1, two items 2 and a single item 6.

$$S_M^1 = T(\mathcal{S}^1) = T(\langle \{1, 2\}, \{1, 2\}, \{1, 6\} \rangle) = \{(1 : 3), (2 : 2), (6 : 1)\}$$

The steps for AISS index creation, which utilizes a sequence to multiset transformation, are shown by algorithm 1. It is easy to notice that both steps of the algorithm 1 can be performed during a single database scan. The process of building the AISS index for the running example database is presented on Figure 2.

Basic steps for procesing subset queries are given by algorithm 2. It is easy to notice, that the basic algorithm would run faster, if the items in the query multiset were ordered by their frequency of appearance in the database. Therefore, before executing the query, we should calculate, for each item of the multiset, how many multisets in the database contain this item. This of course needs to be done only once, and can be easily updated incrementally after database updates.

Algorithm 2. Subset query algorithm utilizing the AISS index.

Parameter: query multiset $Q_M = \{(x_1 : n_1), (x_2 : n_2), \ldots, (x_l : n_l)\}$

- For each entry (j_1, m_1) from the appearance list of item x_1, if $n_1 < m_1$, do:
    1. $level \leftarrow 2$
    2. While $level <= l$ do:
        (a) Find entry (j_{level}, m_{level}) on appearance list for item x_{level}, such that $j_{level} = j_1$. If such entry does not exist, break the while loop.
        (b) If $(n_{level} < m_{level})$ then $level \leftarrow level + 1$ else break the while loop.
    3. If $level = l + 1$ then the set j_1 contains the query set.

Algorithm 3. Incremental updating of the AISS Index.

---

1. For each such item, that it appears both in the new and old version of the multiset, correct the counters on the respective appearance lists.
2. For each such item, that it appears only in the new version of the multiset, create appropriate entry on the respective appearance lists, creating an appearance list if necessary. Increase frequency counters of such items by one.
3. For each such item, that it appears only in the old version of the multiset, delete appropriate entry from the respective appearance lists, deleting appearance lists if they become empty. Decrease frequency counters of such items by one.

After that we need to execute the steps of the algorithm 2 starting with the least frequent items.

In order to perform set subsequence queries, two steps need to be added. First, before we start processing the query, we must transform the query sequence to a multiset using a sequence to multiset transformation. Because such transformation loses information about the order of items in the sequence, a verification phase needs to be added, to prune the false positives. In order for verification phase to work efficiently, we must make an assumption that each of the sequences in the database is placed at a single location on disk and may be easily accessed by rowid. During the verification phase, we access all of the sequences that were returned from index and check whether they fulfill the query conditions or not.

Algorithms for incremental updates are also very simple. Due to the lack of space we will present only the algorithm for updates. Algorithms for insertions and deletions may be easily derived from it. In order to update index after modification of the multiset, perform the steps shown by algorithm 3. For databases of sequences of sets update algorithms are almost the same. The only difference is the necessity of transformation of the updated sequence (both old and new version) to the multiset before proceeding.

The performance of the index depends mainly on its physical implementation. In this paper we propose a way of implementing the AISS index, which uses functionality offered by any commercially available database management system. Both, the dictionary and appearance lists may be represented by a B^+-tree or a

Table 2. Synthetic data and experiment parameters

Parameter	Exp.1	Exp.2	Exp.3
size of the domain [items]	150000	150000	150000
item distribution	zipfian and uniform		
minimal set size [items]	1	1	5 – 95
maximal set size [items]	30	30	15 – 105
minimal set number [sets]	1	5 – 95	5
maximal set number [sets]	10	15 – 105	15
number of sequences	10000 – 100000	10000	10000
page/node size [bytes]	4096B	4096B	4096B

B*-tree structure. These structures allow very fast mapping of key values to some values associated with them. Let us consider the following key-value pair. Let the key be a pair $(item, id)$, where $item$ is some item from the dictionary and id is the multisets unique identifier, and let the $value$ be a number of appearances of the $item$ in the multiset identified by the id. If we assume lexicographic order imposed on key pairs, then the groups of consecutive entries in leaves of the B^+-tree will form appearance lists. To read an appearance list of the item x_i we just need to locate the first leaf entry, which corresponds to the item x_i, and read consecutive entries, until we find the first entry for the next appearance list. If we need to locate an entry corresponding to the multiset j on the appearance list of the item x_i, we can easily locate it, because the (x_i, j) forms a key. Notice, that such implementation has other advantages: very easy insertion, deletion and modification of entries, as well as "automatic" removal, or insertion of appearance lists (each list only exists, if there is at least one entry from it stored in the tree).

An additional structure, which maps multiset/sequence id to rowid, is needed to locate multisets or sequences on disk. This is especially important for sequences, for which there is additional phase of verification. Such mapping could be easily performed by the second B^+-tree. Frequency counters for items should be stored in memory when database is up, and therefore they do not any need special structures to store.

5   Performance Tests

We have performed three experiments testing the impact of the number of sequences of sets in the database, average number of sets in the sequence, average size of sets in the sequence and average length of the query sequence on the index performance. Performance of index was measured as an average time of query execution, including the time of verification phase. Due to lack of competitors, we compare query processing times when using index only to the brute force solution of scanning the whole database. Table 2 summarizes the parameters in experiments.

The first experiment tested the impact of the number of sequences stored in database on the index performance. Figure 3 presents the performance of the

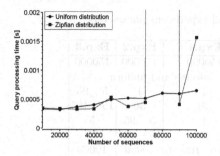
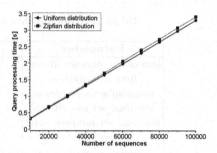

Fig. 3. Average size of sets   **Fig. 4.** Average size of sets (no index)

AISS index for zipfian and uniform distributions. Figure 4 presents the same experiments without the index. Analysing Figure 3 one may notice few things. First, query execution time for databases with uniform distribution grows linearly with respect to the number of sequences. Second, for databases with zipfian distribution of items, the trend of growth is also linear, however the query processing times are not "stable". This is caused by random generation of queries. When a short query with frequent items is generated, there is a large set of possible results which need to be verified, and therefore query processing times grow considerably. For example, the peak obtained during querying database of 80000 sequences appeared during processing of a query sequence that contained only a single item. Partial solution to this problem may be based on an observation that when the query sequence contains only a single item, no verification is necessary, as the results obtained from index will be accurate. Queries for databases with uniform distribution of items are more "stable" because there are no such items, that appear in a very large number of sequences, which could be the cause of a long verification phase. When we compare query processing times to those presented on Figure 4 we may notice, that they are three orders of magnitude smaller.

The second experiment tested the impact of the average number of sets in the sequence on the index performance. Figure 5 presents the performance of the AISS index for zipfian and uniform distributions. Figure 6 presents the same experiments without the index. Once again, when analysing Figure 5 one may notice linear dependency of query processing time on average number of elements in the sequence. One may also notice divergence of query processing times for zipfian and uniform distributions. Better performance of the AISS index for zipfian distribution is caused by the optimization described in Section 4, in which we start processing the query with the least frequent item of the query multiset. Once again, when we compare query processing times to those presented on Figure 6 we may notice, that they are three orders of magnitude smaller.

The third experiment tested the impact of the average sizes of sets in the sequences on the index performance. Figure 7 presents the performance of the AISS index for zipfian and uniform distributions. Figure 8 presents the same experiments without the index. Once again we may notice linear dependency of

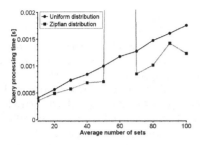

Fig. 5. Average number of sets

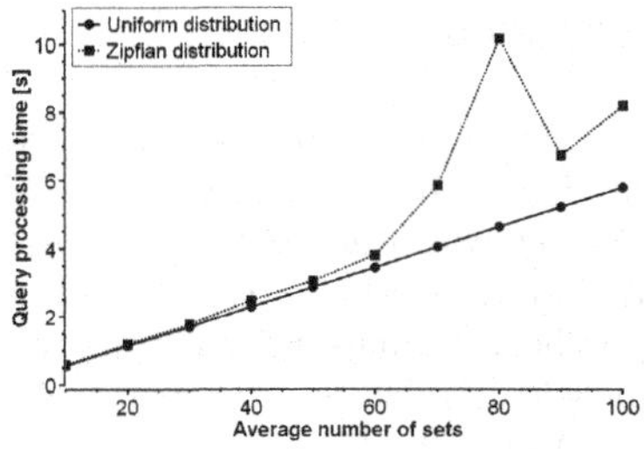

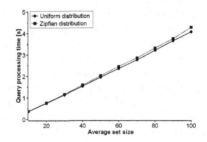

Fig. 6. Average number of sets (no index)

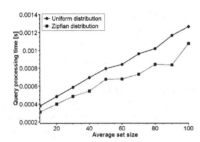

Fig. 7. Average size of sets

Fig. 8. Average size of sets (no index)

query processing time on average size of sets in the sequence and three orders of magnitude improvent over full scan of database.

During the experiments, the verification phase took from 5% to 50% of the query processing time with the exception of the observed peaks, when it took about 95% of the query processing time.

Let us notice, that theoretically we could create other solutions for indexing sequences of sets based on other solutions for indexing sets. However, as we have experimentally shown in [2] Inverted File Index outperforms all other solutions in subset queries and therefore we know in advance, that other solutions, will not be as good as the one presented in this paper.

6 Conclusions

To the best of authors' knowledge, the AISS index presented in this paper is the only index for sequences of sets supporting set subsequence queries without timestamps. We have presented both: logical and physical structure as well as algorithms for set subsequence query execution and incremental updates. Experiments show that the ratio of speed-up for set subsequence queries is three to four orders of magnitude when compared to brute-force approach.

In the future we plan to perform additional extensive experiments to determine weak points of our index. We also plan to design a new index, which is able to answer set subsequence queries without verification and apply such index to improve speed of sequential pattern mining algorithms.

References

1. R. Agrawal, C. Faloutsos, and A. N. Swami. Efficient similarity search in sequence databases. In *Proceedings of the 4th International Conference on Foundations of Data Organization and Algorithms*, pages 69–84. Springer-Verlag, 1993.
2. W. Andrzejewski, Z. Królikowski, and M. Morzy. Performance evaluation of hierarchical bitmap index supporting processing of queries on setvalued attributes (polish). *Archiwum Informatyki Teoretycznej i Stosowanej*, 17(4):273–288, 2005.
3. W. Andrzejewski, T. Morzy, and M. Morzy. Indexing of sequences of sets for efficient exact and similar subsequence matching. In *Proceedings of the 20th International Symposium on Computer and Information Sciences*, pages 864–873. Springer-Verlag, 2005.
4. C. Faloutsos, M. Ranganathan, and Y. Manolopoulos. Fast subsequence matching in time-series databases. In *Proceedings of the 1994 ACM SIGMOD international conference on Management of data*, pages 419–429. ACM Press, 1994.
5. S. Helmer and G. Moerkotte. A study of four index structures for set-valued attributes of low cardinality, 1999.
6. E. Keogh, S. Lonardi, and C. A. Ratanamahatana. Towards parameter-free data mining. In *KDD '04: Proceedings of the 2004 ACM SIGKDD international conference on Knowledge discovery and data mining*, pages 206–215. ACM Press, 2004.
7. A. Lerner and D. Shasha. Aquery: Query language for ordered data, optimization techniques, and experiments. In *VLDB*, pages 345–356, 2003.
8. V. I. Levenshtein. Binary codes capable of correcting deletions, insertions and reversals. *Doklady Akademia Nauk SSSR*, 163(4):845–848, 1965.
9. N. Mamoulis and M. L. Yiu. Non-contiguous sequence pattern queries. In *Proceedings of the 9th International Conference on Extending Database Technology*, 2004.
10. U. Manber and G. Myers. Suffix arrays: a new method for on-line string searches. In *Proceedings of the first annual ACM-SIAM symposium on Discrete algorithms*, pages 319–327. Society for Industrial and Applied Mathematics, 1990.
11. A. Nanopoulos, Y. Manolopoulos, M. Zakrzewicz, and T. Morzy. Indexing web access-logs for pattern queries. In *WIDM '02: Proceedings of the 4th international workshop on Web information and data management*, pages 63–68. ACM Press, 2002.
12. R. Sadri, C. Zaniolo, A. M. Zarkesh, and J. Adibi. Optimization of sequence queries in database systems. In *Symposium on Principles of Database Systems*, 2001.
13. M. Vlachos, M. Hadjieleftheriou, D. Gunopulos, and E. Keogh. Indexing multidimensional time-series with support for multiple distance measures. In *ACM KDD*, 2003.
14. H. Wang, C.-S. Perng, W. Fan, S. Park, and P. S. Yu. Indexing weighted-sequences in large databases. In *Proceedings of International Conference on Data Engineering*, 2003.
15. P. Weiner. Linear pattern matching algorithms. In *Proceedings 14th IEEE Annual Symposium on Switching and Automata Theory*, pages 1–11, 1973.
16. B.-K. Yi and C. Faloutsos. Fast time sequence indexing for arbitrary lp norms. In *Proceedings of the 26th International Conference on Very Large Data Bases*, pages 385–394. Morgan Kaufmann Publishers Inc., 2000.

A Method for Feature Selection on Microarray Data Using Support Vector Machine

Xiao Bing Huang and Jian Tang

Memorial University of Newfoundland,
Computer Science Department,
St. John's, NL, A1B3X5, Canada

Abstract. The data collected from a typical *microarray* experiment usually consists of tens of samples and thousands of genes (i.e., features). Usually only a small subset of features is relevant and non-redundant to differentiate the samples. Identifying an optimal subset of relevant genes is crucial for accurate classification of samples. In this paper, we propose a method for relevant gene subset selection for microarray gene expression data. Our method is based on gap tolerant classifier, a variation of support vector machine, and uses a hill-climbing search strategy. Unlike most other hill-climbing approaches, where classification accuracies are used as a criterion for feature selection, the proposed method uses a mixture of accuracy and SVM margin to select features. Our experimental results show that this strategy is effective both in selecting relevant and in eliminating redundant features.

1   Introduction

In a typical microarray data set, only tens of samples are available altogether for training and testing while each sample has thousands of genes as the features. Usually only a small subset of features is relevant and non-redundant to differentiate the samples. Searching for the optimal feature subset, i.e., Feature Subset Selection (FSS), is crucial for the accuracy of classifications of the samples. In theory, the goal of FSS is to select a minimum sized set of features that produce the same or close classification accuracy as the full feature set[1].

The algorithms that tackle the FSS problem can be generally classified into two main categories, *filter* and *wrapper* [7][10]. Filter methods [1][8][9] filter out irrelevant features before the learning occurs and use general characteristics of the training set to select features. The main weakness of filter approaches is that it pays little attention to redundance avoidance. Wrappers algorithms [10] utilize as a black box a learning algorithm, which runs on the training data and the accuracy of the resulting classifier is used as a metric for scoring. It employs a search strategy to obtain the optimal subset. Besides being computationally more expansive, the performance of wrapper approaches depends on such factors as the classifiers used, the validation methods, etc. Recently, some algorithms were developed that combine the merits of both approaches [5][11][20][15]. Among them

---

[1] In practices, since irrelevant features introduce noises to samples, well selected feature subset will produce higher classification accuracy than a full feature set.

A Min Tjoa and J. Trujillo (Eds.): DaWaK 2006, LNCS 4081, pp. 513–523, 2006.

the most relevant to ours is in [5], where a *Recursive Feature Elimination* (RFE) algorithm is proposed. It is based on SVM. Starting from the full set of genes, RFE calculates the score for each gene, an indicator of its discriminative power. It then eliminates the gene with the worst score. The process then repeats itself for the subset of the genes. The merit of RFE is that with a single training on the current training set, the scores for all the genes are calculated, and hence is less expensive than a general wrapper algorithm. On the other hand, redundant genes normally receive bad scores, improving the weakness of a filter algorithm. However, the use of the backward feature elimination strategy still incurs considerable cost. In fact, to speed up the process, RFE has to resort to 'chunk at a time' elimination strategy. This, however, will adversely affect its effectiveness.

In this paper, we propose a method for feature selection for microarray gene expression data. Our method is based on gap tolerant classifier, a variant of support vector machine, and uses a forward hill-climbing search strategy. Unlike most other hill-climbing approaches, where classification accuracies are used as a criterion for feature selection, our method uses a mixture of accuracy and SVM margin to select features. Our experimental results show that this strategy is effective both in selecting relevant and in eliminating redundant features.

The rest of the paper is organized as follows. Section 2 reviews some basic concepts about support vector machine and related gap tolerant classifiers. Section 3 introduces our feature selection method. Section 4 presents the experimental results. Section 5 concludes the paper by summarizing the main results.

2   Concepts

2.1   Support Vector Machine (SVM)

We explain the idea only for the basic case. (For general case, refer to [19].) Given the training data points $\{x_i, y_i\}, i = 1, \ldots, N, x_i \in \mathcal{R}^d, y_i = \{-1, 1\}$, suppose there exists some hyperplane in R^d which separates the positive from the negative samples (See Figure 1). Let this hyperplane be defined by the function $x^T \beta + \beta_0 = 0$, where β is normal to the hyperplane. Thus $\frac{|\beta_0|}{\|\beta\|}$ is the perpendicular distance from the hyperplane to the origin. In addition, let the training points satisfy the following constraints[2]

$$x_i^T \beta + \beta_0 \geq +1 \; for \; y_i = +1 \tag{1}$$

$$x_i^T \beta + \beta_0 \leq -1 \; for \; y_i = -1. \tag{2}$$

The two constraints can be combined into one set of inequalities:

$$y_i(x_i^T \beta + \beta_0) - 1 \geq 0 \; \forall i. \tag{3}$$

Now consider the points for which the equality in Equation 1 holds. These points lie on the hyperplane $H_1 : x_i^T \beta + \beta_0 = 1$ with normal β and perpendicular

---

[2] Note that for separable case, this is always possible.

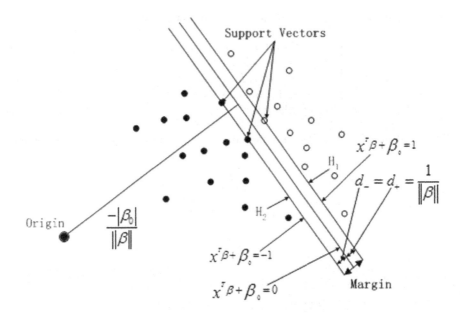

Fig. 1. The Linear Separating Hyperplane with Three Support Vectors

distance from the origin $\frac{|1-\beta_0|}{\|\beta\|}$. Similarly, the points for which the equality in Equation 2 holds lie on the hyperplane $H_2 : x_i^T\beta + \beta_0 = -1$, with normal β, and perpendicular distance from the origin $\frac{|-1-\beta_0|}{\|\beta\|}$. Let d_+ and d_- be the distances from the separating hyperplane to H_1 and H_2, respectively. Thus $d_+ = d_- = \frac{1}{\|\beta\|}$, and $d_+ + d_- = \frac{2}{\|\beta\|}$. (This value is called the "margin" of the separating hyperplane [18].) Note that H_1 and H_2 are parallel and no training points fall between them. The SVM training process searches for the separating hyperplane with the largest margin. This can be formulated by the following optimization problem:

$$\min_{\beta,\beta_0} \|\beta\|^2 \quad \text{subject to} \quad y_i(x_i^T\beta + \beta_0) \geq 1, i = 1,\ldots,N \tag{4}$$

Those training data points for which the equalities in Equation 4 hold are called *support vectors*. This is illustrated in Figure 1. Let β and β_0 be the solution to the above optimization problem. The SVM classifies an arbitrary point x according to the following rule:

$$class(x) = sign(x^T\beta + \beta_0) \text{if } |x^T\beta + \beta_0| \geq \lambda \tag{5}$$

where $\lambda \geq 0$ is a pre-determined small value.

2.2 Gap Tolerant Classifier (GTC)

A GTC consists of a sphere S, called a decision domain, and two parallel decision planes L_p and L_n that intersect with S [2], as shown in Figure 2. For any point

x, the classification of a GTC abides by the following rules:

$$
class(x) = \begin{cases}
+ & \text{If } dist(x, L_n) = dist(x, L_p) + dist(L_n, L_p) \\
  & \text{and } x \text{ belongs to } S \\
- & \text{If } dist(x, L_p) = dist(x, L_n) + dist(L_n, L_p) \\
  & \text{and } x \text{ belongs to } S \\
\text{reject} & \text{otherwise}
\end{cases} \tag{6}
$$

The condition for the plus rule indicates that L_n and the points in plus-class

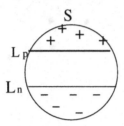

Fig. 2. A Gap Tolerant Classifier

are on the opposite sides of plane L_p, and the condition for the minus rule is symmetric. The rejection rule signifies that the classifier cannot make a decision when a point either falls between the two planes or is outside of the decision domain. A GTC is rarely used as is in reality for classifications. Its significance lies on its easy-to-analyze feature, and its similarity to SVM.

2.3   Error Rate and VC-Dimension for GTC

Define the error rate of a classifier as the probability that it incorrectly classifies a random point. Since it depends on the underlying data distribution that is unknown, the error rate can only be estimated. Many work has been done in this direction. One of the most influential results is in [19][2], where the authors introduce a probabilistic upper bound independently of the underlying distribution. Let C be a set of classifiers. With probability $1 - \alpha$, the error rate for *any* classifier $c \in C$ is

$$
R(c) \leq R_{emp}(c) + \sqrt{\frac{h(ln(2\ell/h) + 1) - ln(\alpha/4)}{\ell}} \tag{7}
$$

where $R_{emp}(c)$ is the testing error of c, ℓ is the size of the testing set, and h is the *VC-dimension* of class C. (Roughly, the VC-dimension of a set of classifiers measures the generalization ability of the classifiers in that set: the higher the VC-dimension, the lower its generalization ability. For more detail, see [19].) In reality, accurate VC-dimensions are unavailable for most classes of classifiers. We have to resort to upper bounds for their estimation. Well established upper bounds include those for the class of GTCs [19][2]. Let C be a set of GTCs with maximum diameter of D for the spheres, and minimum decision margin of M. Then the following is true:

$$h \leq min\{\lceil D^2/M^2 \rceil, d\} + 1 \qquad (8)$$

3 Relevant Subset Selection Using Minimum Upper Bound (RSSMUB)

3.1 Motivation

Let R be the set of genes already selected so far. Theoretically, we wish to add to R a gene, q, only if $R \cup \{q\}$ minimizes the error rate among all the remaining genes. In addition, this error rate should be smaller than that introduced by R. The question is, in the context of microarray data, is it feasible to approximate such an idea using the upper bounds in expressions 7 and 8? The answer is positive. The next subsection gives the justification.

3.2 Using GTC to Simulate SVM on Microarray Data Sets

Any microarray data needs to be preprocessed to eliminate noises passed down from the preceding hybridization phase. One of the often used measures is to set up a threshold on all the expression values. If a value is larger than the threshold in absolute value, then it will be considered non-informative, and either discarded or circumvented by replacing it with a smaller value. Let H be the threshold for the microarray in the experiment, where d genes have been selected. Let B be the training set drawn from the (unknown) data distribution, and T be the SVM trained on B. For simplicity, assume the training classes are separable. Let P_1 and P_2 be the parallel planes where the support vectors reside. Thus no training points fall between P_1 and P_2. Let S be a sphere centering at the origin with a radius of $\sqrt{d}H$ in the d-dimensional space. Consider a random point $q = < f_1, \cdots, f_d >$. If q is valid, we must have $|f_i| \leq H$ for all i, implying $\|q\| = \sqrt{\Sigma_{i=1}^d f_i^2} \leq \sqrt{d}H$. Thus $q \in S$. On the other hand, if B is selected truly at random, we can expect it to be a good approximation of the underlying data distribution. Thus the likelihood that any data point will fall between P_1 and P_2 is negligible. This means T can be viewed as a GTC. Let $D = 2\sqrt{d}H$ and $M = dist(P_1, P_2)$. Let C be the set of all GTCs in the d-dimensional space with maximum diameter of D for the sphere and minimum margin of M. Thus $T \in C$. We say C is formed from T. From Section 2.3, the VC-dimension h for C has the upper bound given in 8. Thus, the error rate for T can be estimated using the upper bound in 7, with h being substituted by the upper bound in 8.

3.3 Selection Criteria

Again, let R be the set of genes that have already been selected. Suppose we are considering gene q for possible selection next. We could require the upper bound on the generalization error for $R \cup \{q\}$ to be lower than that for R as a condition for selecting q. To enforce more stringent scrutiny over irrelevant/redundant genes, we use the following alternative: each term in the upper bound for $R \cup \{q\}$ must be lower than the corresponding term in the upper bound for R. (Note the upper bound contains two terms, as shown in 7.) More precisely, let T_R and $T_{R \cup \{q\}}$ be the SVMs trained respectively for R and $R \cup \{q\}$, C_R and $C_{R \cup \{q\}}$ be the classes of GTCs formed respectively from T_R and $T_{R \cup \{q\}}$, and h_R and $h_{R \cup \{q\}}$ be the VC-dimensions respectively for C_R and $C_{R \cup \{q\}}$. We select q only if both of the folowing conditions hold true:

$$R_{emp}(T_{R \cup \{q\}}) < R_{emp}(T_R) \tag{9}$$

$$\sqrt{\frac{h_{R \cup \{q\}}(ln(2\ell/h_{R \cup \{q\}}) + 1) - ln(\alpha/4)}{\ell}} < \sqrt{\frac{h_R(ln(2\ell/h_R) + 1) - ln(\alpha/4)}{\ell}} \tag{10}$$

Note that (10) is implied by $h_{R \cup \{q\}} < h_R$. Using (8), we can get the upper bounds for $h_{R \cup \{q\}}$ and h_R, the VC-dimensions for $C_{R \cup \{q\}}$ and C_R. We then use these upper bounds in places of $h_{R \cup \{q\}}$ and h_R in the last inequality. More specifically, let D_R and M_R be the maximum diameter for the spheres and minimum margin, respectively, for C_R. Let $D_{R \cup \{q\}}$ and $M_{R \cup \{q\}}$ be the maximum diameter for the spheres and minimum margin, respectively, for $C_{R \cup \{q\}}$. Thus, we require

$$min\{\lceil D^2_{R \cup \{q\}}/M^2_{R \cup \{q\}} \rceil, |R| + 1\} + 1 < min\{\lceil D^2_R/M^2_R \rceil, |R|\} + 1 \tag{11}$$

Inequality 11 implies

$$min\{\lceil D^2_{R \cup \{q\}}/M^2_{R \cup \{q\}} \rceil, |R| + 1\} = \lceil D^2_{R \cup \{q\}}/M^2_{R \cup \{q\}} \rceil \tag{12}$$

Since $min\{\lceil D^2_R/M^2_R \rceil, |R|\} \leq \lceil D^2_R/M^2_R \rceil$, we have

$$\lceil D^2_{R \cup \{q\}}/M^2_{R \cup \{q\}} \rceil < \lceil D^2_R/M^2_R \rceil \tag{13}$$

implying

$$D^2_{R \cup \{q\}}/M^2_{R \cup \{q\}} < D^2_R/M^2_R \tag{14}$$

On the other hand, we have shown that in a d-dimensional space, the diameter of the sphere for a GTC for a microarray is $2\sqrt{d}H$ where H is the threshold. (Refer to Section 3.2.) Substituting $2\sqrt{|R|}H$ and $2\sqrt{|R| + 1}H$ for D_R and $D_{R \cup \{q\}}$, respectively, in (14) and rearranging the result, we have

$$M_{R \cup \{q\}}/\sqrt{|R| + 1} > M_R/\sqrt{|R|} \tag{15}$$

In our algorithm, (15) will be used in place of (10) as a criterion to select genes.

3.4 The Hill-Climbing Method

The algorithm uses a working set of genes, initially empty, that expands one gene per iteration. The following notations are used in the algorithm: S_1 and S_2 are the sample points in class 1 and class 2, respectively; G denotes the entire set of genes; R is the working set; $error\_rate(S_1, S_2, B)$ is the error rate for the SVM trained on $S_1 \cup S_2$ using feature set B[3]; $Margin(S_1, S_2, B)$ is the margin of the separating hyperplane between S_1 and S_2 for the aforementioned SVM,

Algorithm 1–**RSSMUB**

---

1. $mg_1 \leftarrow 0$ //maximum margin in the last iteration
2. $er_1 \leftarrow \infty$ //minimum error rate in the last iteration
3. $R \leftarrow \Phi$
4. *while* $R \neq G$ *do*
5. $er_2 \leftarrow \min\{error\_rate(S_1, S_2, \{q\} \cup R) : q \in G - R\}$
6. $mg_2 \leftarrow \max\{margin(S_1, S_2, \{q\} \cup R) : q \in G - R$ &
                         $error\_rate(S_1, S_2, \{q\} \cup R) = err\}$
7.   *if* $er_2 > er_1$ *or* $\frac{mg_2}{\sqrt{|R|+1}} \leq \frac{mg_1}{\sqrt{|R|}}$ *return* R
8. $p \leftarrow q$ *such that* $q \in \{G - R\}$ & $margin(S_1, S_2, \{q\} \cup R) = mg_2$ &
                         $error\_rate(S_1, S_2, \{q\} \cup R) = er_2$
9. $R \leftarrow R \cup \{p\}$
10. $er_1 \leftarrow er_2$
11. $mg_1 \leftarrow mg_2$
12. *end while*

The outer loop from lines 4 to 12 expands the working set, R, one gene per iteration. Line 5 returns the minimum error rate of the SVMs trained on $S_1 \cup S_2$ for all the working set expansions. In line 6, the maximum margin for the genes that generate the minimum error rate is retrieved. This margin then participates in line 7 in a comparison expression with the maximum margin generated in the last iteration. The other comparison expression in line 7 involves the error rates of the current and the last iteration. These implement the criteria in (9) and (15) in the previous section.

4   Experimental Results

We have done experiments on a number of data sets. Due to the space limitation, we present results only on one of them, the Leukemia data set [4][4]. (For the results on other data sets, refer to http://www.cs.mun.ca/ xbhuang/.)We compare our method with RFE in[5]. The reason we choose RFE for comparison is because (1) both methods are based on SVM, and (2) the authors of RFE have already shown that their method out perform other well established methods [5].

---

[3] In this paper, this error rate is generated from cross-validation on the training set.
[4] The implementation was written with Java 1.5 on a Linux 2.4.26 kernel and tested on a computer with a X86-64 AMD architecture CPU.

4.1 Description of the Data Set

The Leukemia data set contains two types of cancer data, *Acute Lymphocytic Leukemia* (ALL) and *Acute Myelogenous Leukemia* (AML). It is formed by two subsets, the training set and the test set. The training set consists of 38 samples (27 ALL and 11 AML) from bone marrow specimens. The test set has 34 samples (20 ALL and 14 AML), prepared under different experimental conditions, and includes 24 bone marrow and 10 blood sample specimens. All samples have 7129 genes. The preprocessing procedure has normalized the original data by setting the minimum threshold to 20 and the maximum to 16000. We also standardized the data set as suggested in [4], namely, from each gene expression value, we subtracted its mean and divided the result by its standard deviation.

4.2 Results of Comparisons

We train the SVM for feature selection using the training set, as described by Algorithm 1. When we run the algorithm, twenty four genes are selected. Among them we select some subsets to run classifiers on the test set. Three main results are observed: 1. The classification accuracy; 2. The size of the gene subset; 3. The information provided by the generated subset. We use two classifiers, SVM and C4.5, to classify the observations in the testing set. The reason we use C4.5 is because we would like to see how a widely used non-SVM based classifier adapts its performance to the genes selected by the two methods. The results are shown in Table 1.

Table 1. Comparisons of Classification Results

# of genes	selection methods	SVM classifier	C4.5
1	RSSMUB	65%	65%
	RFE	59%	59%
2	RSSMUB	82%	79%
	RFE	56%	59%
4	RSSMUB	71%	71%
	RFE	65%	76%
8	RSSMUB	74%	71%
	RFE	59%	56%
16	RSSMUB	71%	79%
	RFE	76%	82%
full set of genes		82%	91%

The left most column lists the numbers of genes selected by each method. We start from 1, and, except for the last row, the numbers are a power of 2. This is because the RFE eliminates the gene set on the boundary of power of two. The reason that we use the gene sets only with sizes up to 16 is because not only we prefer a gene set with high relevancy, but also we would like it to have very low redundancy. Thus, both accuracy and size need to be considered for the qualities of the set of the genes selected. From the table, it can be seen that with only the top two genes selected by RSSMUB, the SVM classifier can attain the same

Table 2. Annotations of top 8 genes selected by RSSMUB

gene name	annotation explanation	source
LEPR Leptin Receptor	A polymorphism in LEPR, Gln223Arg, might influence susceptibility to obesity in survivors of childhood ALL	[13]
C-myb	Highly expressed in ALL recognized based on mutual information and the P-metric value	[6]
Liver mRNA for interferon-gamma inducing factor	Maintaining graft-versus-leukemia effect after allogeneic bone marrow transplantation (BMT)	[12]
GB DEF: Homeodomain protein HoxA9 mRNA	Hoxa9 collaborates with other genes to produce highly aggressive acute leukemic disease	[17]
ELL2	Homologous to the product of the human ELL gene, a frequent target for translocations in AML	[14]
ADH4 for class II alcohol dehydrogenase	no annotation has been found	
Leukotriene C4 synthase (LTC4S) gene	Elevated leukotriene C4 synthase activity observed in peripheral blood granulocyte suspensions from patients with chronic myeloid leukemia	[16]
PTMA: Prothymosin alpha	loss of PTMA in induced human myeloid leukemia (HL-60) cells is a differentiation-related event	[3]

accuracy as the full set of genes, while it needs sixteen genes selected by the RFE to attain the highest accuracy, which is still 6% lower than that for the full gene set. We also note that for the top four out of five gene sets, the RSSMUB leads the RFE in accuracies when the SVM is used. On the other hand, when the decision tree classifier is used, the RSSMUB leads RFE in accuracies for the three out of five gene sets.

The above result shows that for both SVM and C4.5, the accuracies on the full data set are higher than that on any selected subset of genes by both RSSMUB and RFE. Although this matches the theory (i.e., the full data set provides the most information), this is unusual from practical point of view. We attribute this result to the fact that due to the preprocessing step, by both the original producer and our experiment, the Leukemia data set has been cleaned a great deal. Thus the irrelevant features most likely exhibits only moderate noisy behavior, which are largely neutralized by those strong relevant features. We also observe that the overall accuracy is not very high. This is because the data used for training and testing are not exactly from the same tissues, and therefore represent somewhat different distributions. This will necessarily affect the accuracies in the testing.

It is also interesting to examine our selected features from a biological point of view. We have taken the top 8 genes selected by RSSMUB. We found that seven of them have been annotated by the biological literatures as being related to the Leuhemia one way or another. The results are shown in Table 2.

5   Conclusions

We propose a new approach for feature selection for microarray expression data. Our method is based on the observation that when SVM is applied to a microarray data set, it can be viewed as a gap tolerant classifier. This allows us to build our feature selection method on a well established statistical upper bound on the generalization error. We use a forward search strategy to select genes that decrease the upper bound. The experimental results show that, compared with the similar work, our method can eliminate more irrelevant as well as redundant genes while at the same time attain high accuracy.

References

1. H. Almuallim and T.G. Dietterich. Learning with many irrelevant features. In *Proceedings of the Ninth National Conference on Artificial Intelligence*, volume 2, pages 547–552, 1991.
2. C. J. C. Burges. A tutorial on support vector machines for pattern recognition. *Data Mining and Knowledge Discovery*, 2(2):121–167, 1998.
3. M. Dosil, L. Alvarez-Fernandez, and J. Gomez-Marquez. Differentiation-linked expression of prothymosin alpha gene in human myeloid leukemic cells. *Experimental Cell Research*, 204(1):94–101, 1993.
4. T.R. Golub, D.K. Slonim, P. Tamayo, C. Huard, M. Gaasenbeek, J.P. Mesirov, H. Coller, M. Loh, J.R. Downing, M.A. Caligiuri, C.D. Bloomfield, and E.S. Lander. Molecular classification of cancer: Class discovery and class prediction by gene expression monitoring. *Science*, 286(5439):531–537, 1999.
5. I. Guyon, J. Weston, S. Barnhill, and V. Vapnik. Gene selection for cancer classification using support vector machines. *Machine Learning*, 46(1-3):389–422, 2002.
6. Kyu-Baek Huang, Dong-Yeon Cho, Sang-Wook Park, Sung-Dong Kim, and Byoung-Tak Zhang. Applying machine learning techniques to analysis of gene expression data: cancer diagnosis. *Methods of Microaray Data Analysis*, 2001.
7. G.H. John, R. Kohavi, and K. Pfleger. Irrelevant features and the subset selection problem. In *Proceedings of the Eleventh International Conference on Machine Learning*, pages 121–129, 1994.
8. K. Kira and L. Rendell. The feature selection problem: Traditional methods and a new algorithm. In *Tenth National Conference on Artificial Intelligence*, pages 129–134, 1992.
9. K. Kira and L. Rendell. A practical approach to feature selection. In *Nineth International Conference on Machine Learning*, 1992.
10. R. Kohavi and G.H. John. Wrappers for feature subset selection. *Journal of Artificial Intelligence Research*, 97(1-2):273–324, 1997.
11. K.Z. Mao. Feature subset selection for support vector machines through discriminative function pruning analysis. *IEEE Transactions on Systems, Man and Cybernetics, Part B*, 34(1):60–67, 2004.
12. P. Reddy, T. Teshima, G. Hildebrandt, U. Duffner, Y. Maeda, K. Cooke, and J. Ferrara. Interleukin 18 preserves a perforin-dependent graft-versus-leukemia effect after allogeneic bone marrow transplantation. *Blood*, 100(9):3429–3431, 2002.
13. J. Ross, K. Oeffinger, S. Davies, A. Mertens, E. Langer, W. Kiffmeyer, C. Sklar, M. Stovall, Y. Yasui, and L. Robison. Genetic variation in the leptin receptor gene and obesity in survivors of childhood acute lymphoblastic leukemia: a report from the childhood cander survivor study. *Journal of clinical Ontology*, 22(17):3558–3562, 2004.
14. A. Shilatifard, D. Duandagger, D. Haque, C. Florence, E. Schubach, J. Conaway, and R. Conaway. Ell2, a new member of an ell family of rna polymerase ii elongation factors. *Proceedings of Natural Academic Science*, 94:3639–3643, 1997.

15. V. Sindhwani, S. Rakshit, D. Deodhare, D. Erdogmus, J.C. Principe, and P. Niyogi. Feature selection in mlps and svms based on maximum output information. *IEEE Transactions on Neural Networks*, 15(4):937– 948, 2004.

16. M. Sjolinder, L. Stenke, B. Glaser, S. Widell, J. Doucet, P. Jakobsson, , and J. Lindgren. Aberrant expression of active leukotriene c4 synthase in cd16+ neutrophils from patients with chronic myeloid leukemia. *Blood*, 95(4):1456–1464, 2000.

17. U. Thorsteinsdottir, J. Krosl, E. Kroon, A. Haman, T. Hoang, , and G. Sauvageau. The oncoprotein e2a-pbx1a collaborates with hoxa9 to acutely transform primary bone marrow cells. *Molecular Cell Biology*, 19(9):6355–6366, 1999.

18. V. Vapnik. *The Nature of Statistical Learning Theory*. Springer-Verlag,New York, 1995.

19. V. Vapnik. *Statistical Learning Theory*. John Wiley and Sons, New York, 1998.

20. D.F. Wang, P.P.K. Chan, D.S. Yeung, and E.C.C. Tsang. Feature subset selection for support vector machines through sensitivity analysis. In *Proceedings of the Third International Conference on Machine Learning and Cybernetics*, volume 7, pages 4257–4262, 2004.

Providing Persistence for Sensor Data Streams by Remote WAL

Hideyuki Kawashima, Michita Imai, and Yuichiro Anzai

Information and Computer Science, Keio University
3-14-1 Hiyoshi, Kohoku-ku, Yokohama, JAPAN

Abstract. Rapidly changing environments such as robots, sensor networks, or medical services are emerging. To deal with them, DBMS should persist sensor data streams instantaneously. To achieve the purpose, data persisting process must be accelerated. Though write ahead logging (WAL) acceleration is essential for the purpose, only a few researches are conducted.

To accelerate data persisting process, this paper proposes **remote WAL with asynchronous checkpointing** technique. Furthermore this paper designs and implements it. To evaluate the technique, this paper conducts experiments on an object relational DBMS called KRAFT.

The result of experiments shows that remote WAL overwhelms performance disk based WAL. As for throughput evaluation, best policy shows about 12 times better performance compared with disk based WAL. As for logging time, the policy shows lower than 1000 micro seconds which is the period of motor data acquisition on conventional robots.

1 Introduction

In the fields of sensor networks (SN) [1] or data stream management systems (DSMS) [2], immediate data persisting process is not considered at all. However, if it is realized, the application domains of data warehouse can be expanded to real-time or ubiquitous computing fields such as robots [3].

To realize the vision, a new type of database management system (DBMS) should be designed for managing sensor data streams. The DBMS should be able to (C1) manage massive data, (C2) providing persistence for data certainly, (C3) manage variable length tuple, and **(C4) providing persistence for data instantaneously**. Most of conventional DBMS satisfy (C1), (C2), and (C3). However, only (C4) is not satisfied yet. Consequently, we set the purpose of this paper as realizing a technique which accelerates reliable data persisting processing on DBMS. To efficiently avoid data loss at system crash, DBMS makes log records, writes them onto persistent storage, and then updates durable storage [4]. In this paper, the process to write log records onto persistent storage is denoted as "persisting process".

To accelerate persisting process, differential logging [5] and remote logging [6,7] are proposed. [5] is for main memory database system (MMDB). Since it prepares a log file for each page, log files are divided and persisting process is accelerated. [6] is also for MMDB. It uses two remote memories as persistent storage with 2 phase commit protocol. Since remote memory is faster than than local disk, it accelerates persisting

A Min Tjoa and J. Trujillo (Eds.): DaWaK 2006, LNCS 4081, pp. 524–533, 2006.

process. [7] also uses remote memories, and the application domain is focused on sensor data. Inherently sensor data has continuous nature and thus it is considered that a few data loss can be recovered by interpolation. Based on the concept, the paper proposes imprecise remote logging.

Unfortunately, these techniques do not satisfy the above four conditions. Since differential logging [5] is for MMDB and thus the number of log files are limited. Therefore the technique is difficult to apply for our purpose. Since neighbor-WAL [6] does not describe how to deal with remote memory overflow, this technique is difficult to apply for our purpose. Since imprecise-WAL [7] is unreliable, this technique is difficult to apply for our purpose.

To achieve the purpose, this paper proposes **remote WAL with two level asynchronous checkpointing** technique, and realizes it on an object relational database system KRAFT [8].

This paper is organized as follows. Section 2 summaries related work. Section 3 formulates problems and describes basic architecture of object relational DBMS called KRAFT for the preparation of the proposition. Section 4 presents the two level asynchronous checkpointing technique. Section 5 describes experiments to evaluate the proposition. Section 6 discusses with this work. Finally Section 7 describes conclusions and future work.

2 Related Work

Differential Logging. P*TIME [5] adopts "differential logging" technique to accelerate WAL for MMDB. Differential logging adopts transient logging method and it reduces the amount of log records compared with ARIES [9] method since transient logging requires bit-level XOR difference of before image and after image while ARIES method requires both of them. Although the differential logging technique shows great performance, the maximum size of data which P*TIME can deal with is restricted to the size of physical memory. Since the size of sensor data increases monotonically as time goes, it is obvious that sensor data devours physical memories soon. Therefore differential logging technique is not proper for frequently sensor data insertion environment unfortunately.

Neighbor-WAL. Neighbor-WAL [6] uses two remote computer's memories (remote memories) as a persistent storage instead of a disk. The transfer of log records is executed on two phase commit protocol. Since the response time of remote memories is faster than a local disk, neighbor-WAL achieves faster performance compared with traditional disk based WAL. The weak point of neighbor-WAL is memory overflow. Since log records are stored on remote memories, the memories often overflow. Although this is the most important problem, no approach is described in [6].

Imprecise WAL. To accelerate sensor data insertion, imprecise WAL method is proposed in [7] as a modification of neighbor-WAL. This technique accelerates neighbor-WAL by reducing network traffic cost. On the imprecise WAL, DBMS does not receive any ACK of log record transfer from remote log servers. Although some log records might be lost, the authors of [7] consider that they can be interpolated since they are

Table 1. Comparison of Related Work

Study	Massive Data Management (C1)	Precise Persistence (C2)	Variable Length Tuple (C3)	Fast Data Insertion (C4)
Differential Logging [5]	Never	Good	Good	Good
Neighbor-WAL [6]	Never	Good	Good	Good
Imprecise WAL [7]	Good	Never	Never	Good
Conventional DBMS	Good	Good	Good	Bad
DSMS [2]	Never	Never	Good	Never
Ideal	Good	Good	Good	Good

gradually changing sensor data. To achieve performance, the imprecise WAL method loses certain persistence for each data. Since the target of this paper is providing persistence for all of sensor data to realize predictor applications, the technique is not proper for our purpose.

The summary of related work is shown in Table 1. We present the technique from the rest of this paper, and conducts the performance on our prototype DBMS called KRAFT.

3   Preparation

This Section prepares for our proposition in Section 4. The first subsection formulates problems to achieve our purpose, and the second subsection describes basic architecture the database system KRAFT in which we will built our proposition.

3.1   Problem Formulation

The purpose of this paper is realizing a technique which accelerates reliable data persisting processing on DBMS. In other words, a technique to solve (C4) should be proposed, and furthermore it should be realized on DBMS.

To evaluate the contribution of our proposition to (C4), we measure throughput of transactions, logging time of for a transaction, and blocking time to deal with remote memory overflow on KRAFT. Thus, we formulate the problems of this paper as follows.

(P1) : Maximizing Throughput on DBMS

(P2) : Minimizing Logging Time on DBMS

3.2   Basic Architecture of KRAFT

The proposition of this paper is based on an object relational database system KRAFT which we have developed. To clarify the novelty of the proposition, we describe basic architecture of KRAFT here. The implementation was done by programming language C on FreeBSD 5.3 Release. The number of lines is over 15000.

Overview. KRAFT is a database system that supports a variety of sensor data, and provides the following features: (1) freshness for sensor data without losing persistence, (2) abstract data type for sensor data, and (3) efficient periodic monitoring.

Data Model. KRAFT provides object relational data model as shown in Figure 1. Each tuple is constituted of RELATION part and SENSOR part and the format is dynamically set by CREATE TABLE command. The types which a tuple can have are INT (fixed length 4 byte), TEXT (variable length, however, the size should be lower than DBMS buffer pool size), and SENSOR which is constructed by the set of sensor data objects. A sensor object has four attributes: arrival time(16 byte), generate time (16 byte), sensor data (8 byte), and meta data (64 byte).

Software Architecture. Fig.2 shows basic software architecture of KRAFT. Since KRAFT conducts remote logging for persisting process, it is constituted of **DBMS Server** and **Log Server**. Although KRAFT has many modules, only **RecoveryManager**, **LogReceiver**, **CheckPointer**, **BufferManager** relate to the proposition of this paper.

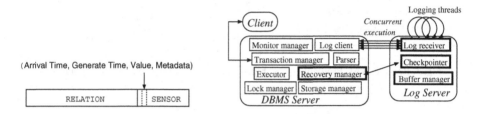

Fig. 1. Data Model of KRAFT   **Fig. 2.** KRAFT Architecture

Transaction Model and Operations. KRAFT supports INSERT, DELETE, and APPEND operations. INSERT and DELETE are used to manipulate tuples, while APPEND operation is used for inserting new sensor data objects to SENSOR area.

KRAFT recognizes **one operation as one transaction**. In other words, each operation is executed transactionally. Therefore, all of data on buffer pools are assured to be finished the persisting process.

Buffer Pool. Buffer pool is managed by storage manager on DBMS Server. If all of page are used, one page is selected as a victim. And the victim page is written to disk (durable storage), and it is initialized for next requirement. Buffer pool is constituted of N-th buffer pages. To optimize disk I/O, the size of each buffer page is set to the multiplies of PAGESIZE variable which is dependent on hardware.

Basic Remote WAL Protocol. KRAFT conducts remote WAL for the persisting process. The basic protocol of KRAFT's remote logging protocol is shown in the Fig.3. This figure omits error handling because of space limitation.

4   Approach to Problems

4.1   Two Level Asynchronous Checkpointing

To solve the problems which Section 3.1 described, blocking time should be decreased. To decrease the blocking time, this paper proposes the **two level asynchronous checkpointing** technique. The overview of the technique is shown in Fig.4.

When a **Logger** detects the end of k-th **LogPage**, it immediately switches to $k+1$-th **LogPage**. The switching time is the blocking time which have to be decreased. As Fig.4 shows, the technique is constituted of four threads, **Redoer**, **Logger**, **LogWriter**, and **LogTransfer**. And, Fig.4 shows asynchronous **buffer transfer** (log server's memory → log server's disk) and asynchronous **file transfer** (remote disk → DBMS storage area).

```
1: if (Send Log to LogSrv1 == timeout) {
2:     Recover using LogSrv2; }
3: if (Send Log to LogSrv2 == timeout) {
4:     Recover using LogSrv1; }
5: if (ACK from LogSrv1 == timeout) {
6:     Recover using LogSrv2; }
7: if (ACK from LogSrv2 == timeout) {
8:     Recover using LogSrv1; }
```

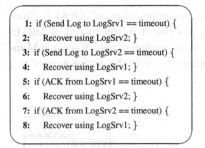

Fig. 3. Remote WAL Protocol   **Fig. 4.** Two Level Asynchronous Checkpointing

```
1:  Set Current LogPage C = 0; (Initialization);
2:  while (TRUE) {
3:      Recv log record L;
4:      Lock entire LogArea & Lock C;
5:      if (C is full) {
6:          Unlock C & Switch C &Lock C; }
7:      Unlock entire LogArea;
8:      Write L's size to C's header;
9:      Write L onto C;
10:     Unlock C; }
```

```
1:  Dirty LogPage D = 0; (Initialization)
2:  while (TRUE) {
3:      if (C > D) {
4:          Get Ti (Current Time);
5:          Make a log file of which name is Ti;
6:          Transfer D to Ti;
7:          Switch D; }
8:      sleep(TIME_LW); }
```

Fig. 5. Logger Algorithm   **Fig. 6.** LogWriter Algorithm

```
1:  while (TRUE) {
2:      while (log file Ti exists) {
3:          Compress Ti & send it to DBMS Srv;
4:          Recv ACK from DBMS Srv;
5:          Delete Ti;}
6:      sleep(TIME_LT);}
```

```
1:  while (TRUE) {
2:      Receive the size of Ti;
3:      Allocate space to extract Ti;
4:      Recv Ti & Extract Ti;
5:      ptr = header of the first log record;
6:      while (ptr != NULL) {
7:          REDO using a log indicated by ptr;
8:          ptr = ptr->next; }
9:      Release allocated space;}
```

Fig. 7. LogTransfer Algorithm   **Fig. 8.** Redoer Algorithm

4.2 Algorithm Descriptions

This subsection presents the description of algorithms to realize Redoer, Logger, Log-Writer, and LogTransfer.

The algorithm of Logger is shown in Fig.5 Each log record has header area in which the size of log record is stored. Without the headers, it is impossible to reorganize log record from LogPage.

The algorithm of LogWriter is shown in Fig.6. LogWriter chases the current page C, but it never passes C. If LogWriter works slow, Logger soon finishes up all of log pages and waits for LogWriter, and it incurs blocking phenomenon. To avoid it, TIME_LW (Fig.6) should be slow enough.

Fig.7 shows LogTransfer algorithm. As long as log files T_i exists, LogTransfer compresses T_i and transfers it to Redoer. The compression reduces the amount of necessary network resource. In our experiment, the compression enhanced the performance of our system.

Fig.8 shows Redoer algorithm. Redoer receives compressed T_i, extracts it, conducts REDO processing by calculating the address of each log record. If the address is not written by storage manager, Redoer discards the log records because the access must make old the state of the page, which is never permitted.

5 Evaluation

5.1 Experimental Environment

Hardware and System Parameters

Hardware. The specification of a machine for DBMS server and clients is Pentium 4 (3 GHz) CPU, 4GB RAM, and FreeBSD 5.3-Release OS.And, the specification of machines for log servers are Pentium4 (2.4 GHz) CPU, 1GB RAM, and FreeBSD 5.3-Release OS. For network, 100 Mbps Ethernet interfaces and Gigabit Switching Hub FXG-08TE were used for the experiment.

System Parameters. Both TIME_LW (Fig.6) and TIME_LT (Fig.7) were adjusted as 1 micro second. The number of DBMS buffer pools was 32. FIFO was applied for page replacement algorithm. The number of log buffer pages on each log server was 128, and each size was 16 KB. To improve network response time, TCP_NODELAY option was set not to use Nagle algorithm on TCP/IP. For each experiment, all of clients are generated on a DBMS Server machine. The number of log servers is 2 for each experiment.

Comparison Methods. "DWAL (GC)" shows disk-based "Willing To Wait" policy group commit implementation on KRAFT.

"RWAL (Simple)" shows RWAL without group commit. In other words, all of log transfers are executed isolately. In this case, the number of Logger threads on each log server is the same as the number of DBMS clients which means the number of sensor data streams in this experiment. In this case, the size of log record is smaller than 1 KB.

"RWAL (GC)" shows RWAL-based "Willing To Wait" policy group commit implementation on KRAFT. The number of Logger threads on each log server is one since log transfers are integrated for group commit. The size of WAL buffer on DBMS Server is 16 KB.

"PostgreSQL" shows PostgreSQL-7.3.6 which implements "Willing To Wait" policy group commit.

Experiment Descriptions. We conduct three experiments. They are "throughput", "logging time" and "log insertion time on log server". As for "throughput", each client generages 1000 operations. Clients are concurrently executed. Total execution time is measured and then throughput is calculated. "Logging time" is the time for one WAL execution. This is measured at the internal of DBMS Server. "Log insertion time on a log server" is the time for LogPage modification on a log server. If memory overflow incurs blocking, this values would show high.

5.2 Results

Throughput. Fig.9 shows average of throughput. It shows that RWAL overwhelms DWAL. "RWAL (Simple)" shows 12 times better performance compared with "DWAL (GC)" in the maximum case (4 concurrency). However, "DWAL (GC)" shows worse performance than "PostgreSQL". Though we do not clarity the precise reason, the difference of buffer management algorithm (FIFO vs. clock) or "Willing To Wait" optimization might be related.

Fig.10 shows standard deviation of throughput. Though "RWAL (Simple)" shows unstable behavior, the reason is not clarified.

Logging Time. Fig.11 shows the average of logging time. "RWAL (Simple)" shows lower than 1000 micro seconds while concurrency is low, but the performance degrades in accordance with concurrency obtaining 4000 micro seconds at 500 concurrency. However, in all of concurrency, "RWAL (Simple)" shows better performance than "RWAL (GC)".

Fig.12 shows standard deviation of logging time. Though "RWAL (Simple)" shows unstable behavior, the reason is not clarified.

Log Insertion Time on a Log Server. Fig.13 shows average of one log record insertion time on a log server. In the worst case, "RWAL (Simple)" shows 7 micro seconds while "RWAL (GC)" shows 25 micro seconds. From the results, it is considered that blocking did not occur on log servers. the difference of 7 micro seconds and 25 micro seconds would be related to the size of insertion size. For "RWAL (Simple)", only one log record is written while sets of log records are written for "RWAL (GC)".

Fig.14 shows standard deviation time of one log record insertion time on each log server. All of values are smaller than 18 micro seconds, which are enoughly small.

Summary. As for performance "RWAL (Simple)" policy showed the best performance in all of experiments. Since the policy overwhelms disk based WAL as for throughput, it satisfies **(P1) Maximing Throughput on DBMS**. In addition, since the policy also showed better performance than "RWAL (GC)", it most appropriately satisfies **(P2) Minimizing Logging Time on DBMS**. The reason why logging time was minimized, was because of non-blocking on log servers, which was clarified in the experiments with log insertion times.

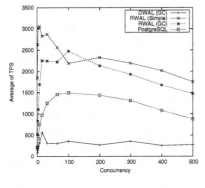

Fig. 9. Average of Throughput

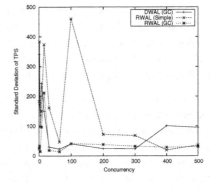

Fig. 10. Standard Deviation of Throughput

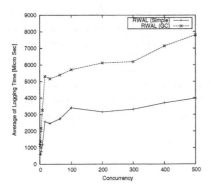

Fig. 11. Average of Logging Time

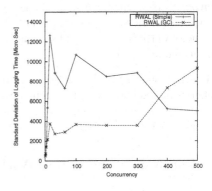

Fig. 12. Standard Deviation of Logging Time

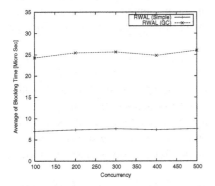

Fig. 13. Average of Log Insert Time

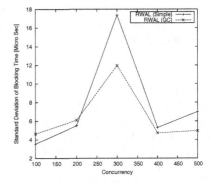

Fig. 14. Standard Deviation of Log Insert Time

6   Discussion

Persistence Strongness of Log Records by Remote WAL. If failure occurs on a host
which log server runs, all of log records stored in the log server are lost. To cope with
such a situation, our protocol shown in Fig.3 requires database server sending a log

record to two log servers. Therefore, our remote WAL protocol does not lose log records unless both of hosts failures at the same time, and we think the probability of the phenomenon would not be high. We think this philosophy is the same as the ClustRa [6] which is accepted for industry community. Therefore we consider remote WAL provide enough strongness of persistence for log records.

Preciousness of Sensor Data Stream. Currently sensor data streams are not considered to be enough to precious to persist in the field of sensor network community or data stream community. However we consider it will be precious in this decade, because (1) sensory/image communication is easier to understand compared with text based communication, (2) the price of disk is rapidly decreasing, and (3) real-time applications which use sensor data are emerging. Therefore we predict that data warehouses would store fine-grained sensor data streams in the near future.

Having N disks. Having N disks on the DBMS server, the performance of DWAL may be increased. However, the ratio would be low since (1) conventional group commit technology [10] is highly established and (2) the management of multiple group commit buffers requires cost.

SAN. By using SAN, the performance of DWAL would improve dramatically since batteries are equipped on disk cache device and thus no need to write some data on harddrive to persist the data. However, this paper focuses on low-end devices and thus expensive SAN is out of range.

7   Conclusions and Future Work

The purpose of this paper was to propose a technique which accelerates reliable data persisting processing on DBMS. To achieve the purpose, this paper proposed the **two level asynchronous checkpointing** technique, and implemented the proposition on an actual DBMS. And, this paper tackled the following three problems. (1) Maximizing throughput. (2) Minimizing logging time.

The result of experiments showed that remote WAL provided better performance than disk based WAL. As for throughput evaluation, the "RWAL (Simple)" policy showed about 12 times better performance compared with disk based WAL in the maximum case. As for logging time, the policy showed lower than 1000 micro seconds which is the period of motor data acquisition for conventionally used robots. Furthermore it also showed stable performance on log insertion time on log server. Therefore we consider the "RWAL (Simple)" policy most appropriately solves problems formulated in Section 3.1.

Therefore the proposition in this paper satisfies (C4) in Table 1. Furthermore, KRAFT already satisfies (C1), (C2), and (C3). Therefore new KRAFT reinforced by this paper satisfies all of four conditions in Table 1. Hence we conclude that our work achieved the purpose of this paper.

For further improvement, non volatile memories such as ram-disks should be used. Even if non volatile memories are used, the two level check pointing technique we proposed in this paper should be used because the available size of non volatile memories is still limited.

References

1. Madden, S. R., Franklin, M. J., Hellerstein, J. M. and Hong, W.: The Design of an Acquisitional Query Processor for Sensor Networks, *Proceedings of the 2003 ACM SIGMOD International Conference on Management of Data*, pp. 491–502 (2003).
2. Babcock, B., Babu, S., Datar, M., Motwani, R. and Widom, J.: Models and Issues in Data Stream Systems, *ACM Symposium on Principles of Database Systems* (2002).
3. Imai, M. and Narumi, M.: Generating common quality of sense by directed interaction, *Proceedings of the 12th IEEE International Workshop on Robot and Human Interactive Communication(RO-MAN 2003)*, pp. 199–204 (2003).
4. Gray, J. and Reuter, A.: *Transaction Processing: Concepts and Techniques*, Morgan Kaufmann Publishers (1993).
5. Cha, S. K. and Song, C.: P*TIME: Highly Scalable OLTP DBMS for Managing Update-Intensive Stream Workload, *Proceedings of 30th International Conference on Very Large Data Bases*, pp. 1033–1044 (2004).
6. Hvasshovd, S.-O., Torbjørnsen, Ø., Bratsberg, S. E. and Holager, P.: The ClustRa Telecom Database: High Availability, High Throughput, and Real-Time Response, *Proceedings of the 21th International Conference on Very Large Data Bases*, pp. 469–477 (1995).
7. Kawashima, H., Toyama, M., Imai, M. and Anzai, Y.: Providing Persistence for Sensor Streams with Light Neighbor WAL, *Proceedings of Pacific Rim International Symposium on Dependable Computing(PRDC2002)*, pp. 257–264 (2002).
8. Kawashima, H., Imai, M. and Anzai, Y.: Improving Freshness of Sensor Data on KRAFT Sensor Database System, *International Workshop on Multimedia Information Systems*, pp. 1–8 (2004).
9. Mohan, C.: Repeating History Beyond ARIES, *Proceedings of 25th International Conference on Very Large Data Bases*, pp. 1–17 (1999).
10. Spiro, P. M., Joshi, A. M. and Rengarajan, T. K.: Designing an Optimized Transaction Commit Protocol, *Digital Technical Journal*, Vol. 3, No. 1, pp. 1–16 (1991).

Support Vector Machine Approach for Fast Classification

Keivan Kianmehr[1] and Reda Alhajj[1,2]

[1] Department of Computer Science, University of Calgary, Calgary, Alberta, Canada
{kiamehr, alhajj}@cpsc.ucalgary.ca
[2] Department of Computer Science, Global University, Beirut, Lebanon

Abstract. In this study, we propose a new technique to integrate support vector machine and association rule mining in order to implement a fast and efficient classification algorithm that overcomes the drawbacks of machine learning and association rule-based classification algorithms. The reported test results demonstrate the applicability, efficiency and effectiveness of the proposed approach.

Keywords: classification, association rules, support vector machines, classification rules, data mining, machine learning.

1 Introduction

Classification is supervised categorization of a given set of items into classes. It is beneficial for several applications, such as preventing theft and saving lives, medical diagnosis, increasing revenue and market analysis, better decision making, predicting customer behavior, signaling potentially fraudulent transactions, etc. A wide variety of research has considered the use of popular machine learning techniques, such as Neural Network, Decision Trees, Baysian Network and Support Vector Machine, in the classification task to automate the discovery of classification rules and to build a classifier model based on the extracted rules. The accuracy and efficiency of the model is usually evaluated by a combination of statistical techniques and domain experts.

Despite showing outstanding performance in many real applications, machine learning classification techniques are not able to discover all interesting and understandable rules. Also, the discovered rules may not be of the domain expert's interest. In fact, machine learning techniques work based on mathematical and statistical algorithms. So, rules generated by these algorithms are domain independent and difficult to be investigated by domain experts. For example, there might be some rules which may play an important role in understanding the classification task, but not discovered by machine learning techniques.

To overcome the understandability problem of the classification task, association rule-based classification techniques have been recently proposed and have received a great consideration. Association rule mining is the process of discovering all association rules having support and confidence greater than a predetermined threshold. In association rule-based classification, the focus is on a

A Min Tjoa and J. Trujillo (Eds.): DaWaK 2006, LNCS 4081, pp. 534–543, 2006.
© Springer-Verlag Berlin Heidelberg 2006

subset of association rules, the consequent of each is class attribute. This set of rules is known as class association rules [4].

The main steps in building a classifier based on association rules are: 1) Rule Generator: generates from the training set the set of association rules in the form $(attributes \Rightarrow class - label)$; 2) Rule Pruning: pruning the set of generated association rules to find the best set of rules that cover the training set, and 3) Classifier Builder: building the best classifier that can predict the class of a new unseen object.

The related literature indicates that association rule-based classification techniques have better and more accurate results than machine learning classification algorithms. However, they suffer from efficiency issues. First, the rule generator algorithm generates a large number of rules, and it is difficult to store the rules, retrieve the related rules, prune and sort the rules [5]. Second, it is challenging to find the best subset of rules to build the most robust and accurate classifier.

As a result of the above analysis, the main motivation of the research efforts described in this paper is to overcome the drawbacks of machine learning and association rule-based classification algorithms. By considering the advantages of both techniques, we try to integrate both trends into a novel, fast and accurate classification technique that solves their weaknesses. We propose a new classification algorithm based on association rule mining combined with Support Vector Machine (SVM). The task involves using an available method for generating class-based rules. Our proposed approach then extracts the strong rules with the most uneven class distribution for each class, i.e., rules that are more often valid for one class than the other class. The validity of these rules for each data sample is then used to build a binary feature vector as an input to the SVM classification algorithm. Finally, the SVM algorithm builds the classifier using the binary feature vector, which represents the coverage distribution of the rules (covered/not covered) by each data sample of the training set. The conducted experiments and comparative study demonstrate the applicability, efficiency and effectiveness of the proposed approach.

The rest of the paper is organized as follows. Section 2 describes the association rule-based classification problem. Section 3 presents a review of association rule-based classifier techniques and highlights our contribution to this problem. Section 4 explains our approach to build an association rule-based classifier in detail. Section 5 provides detailed explanation on the selected evaluation model, the conducted experiments and the achieved results. Section 6 is summary and conclusions.

2 Association Rule-Based Classification: Problem Description

The association rule-based classification problem may be described as follows: Given a transactional dataset D consisting of transactions $T = \{t_1, t_2, \ldots, t_n\}$, a set of items $I = \{i_1, i_2, \ldots, i_k\}$ consisting of all items in D, which is also the range of possible values for the transactions, a set of class labels $C = \{c_1, c_2, \ldots, c_n\}$, support and confidence thresholds; the objective is to generate the set of strong class-association rules in the form ($attributes \Rightarrow class - label$), and to build the best classifier that can predict the class of a new unseen object under the constraints: The transactional data set D is a normalized dataset to positive integer values, the domain of the class label is $\{0, 1\}$, and class-based association rules are in the form ($attributes \Rightarrow class - label$).

In this study, we assume that the input to the classifier is a uniform dataset consisting of integer values of the attributes and a class label. However, in general datasets contain continuous and/or categorical data. In order to normalize all the values to integers, we map all categorical values to consecutive positive integers. For continuous values, we first discretize them into intervals, and then map the intervals to the consecutive positive integers.

The above formulation highlights an important aspect of rule-based classification, namely building a classifier based on class-based association rules. A class-based association rule takes the form $I' \rightarrow c$, where $I' \subseteq I$ and $c \in C$. The problem of generating strong class-based association rules from a set of transactions D is to find the class-based association rules such that their support and confidence are greater than the user-defined thresholds.

3 Related Work and Our Contribution

As described in the literature, association rule-based classification includes two major techniques: ordered rule based classifier techniques and unordered rule based classifier techniques. Alternative approaches have been also proposed to combine different techniques to improve the classification task. In the rest of this section, we will briefly describe several well-known association rule-based classification algorithms.

3.1 Classification Based on Single Class Association Rules

A subset of strong rules, called candidate set, is sorted in descending order of rules' accuracy (a rule is accurate if both its confidence and support are above the pre-determined thresholds). When classifying a new unseen data object, the first rule in the sorted candidate set that matches the object makes the prediction. The candidate set also contains a default class at the end. The class label of uncovered training data objects by the last rule in the candidate set which has the majority is identified as the default class. When there is no rule to cover the new coming data object, it will be classified to the default class. CBA [4] and C4.5 [10] are two techniques that work based on single class association rules.

The CBA approach sorts the rules in descending order of rules' confidence and support. If there are rules with the same confidence and support, the rule generated earlier will be selected as a classifier rule. This sorting task guarantees that the most accurate rules will be selected for the classifier. After ordering the rules, the data set is scanned for each rule to find those data samples covered by the selected rule. If the selected rule can classify at least one data sample correctly, it will be a candidate for the classifier. After scanning all the class association rules and selecting the candidate rules for the classifier, a default class is also added to the classifier. After building the candidate rules set, the total number of errors made by candidate rules and the default class is determined; and rules that decrease the accuracy of classification are ignored. The remaining rules and the default class will form the final classifier. The obvious problem with this approach is over-fitting. After a data sample is covered by a highly accurate rule, all other rules that cover the data sample may be discarded if they do not cover any other data sample.

The C4.5 rule-based approach is derived from C4.5 decision tree [10]. The rules are generated and C4.5 decision tree is trained first. Then, every path from the root to a leaf is extracted as an initial rule by considering all the test conditions appearing in the path as the conjunction between rule antecedents and the class label. Afterward, each initial rule is induced by removing antecedents that do not improve the discriminating process of a specific class from other classes. This task is performed by a pessimistic estimate of the accuracy of the rule. After the rules induction process, they are grouped into rule sets corresponding to the classes, respectively. All rule sets are pruned with the minimum description length principle technique [11] so that rules which have no effect on the accuracy of a rule set are removed. Then, the rule sets are sorted according to the ascending order of their false positive error rates. Finally, a default class is also added to the set for dealing with data objects that don't have any matching rule in the set of generated rules. The default class is the one that contains the most training data objects not covered by any rule. Rule set generated by C4.5 is too small to cover the possible missing values in a new unseen dataset.

3.2   Classification Based on Multiple Class Association Rules

The candidate set of strong rules is not sorted and most matching rules may participate in the classification process. Simply if the new data object is covered by all candidate rules, it will be assigned to the class label of candidate rules; otherwise the majority vote of candidate rules will specify the class label of the new object. CPAR [14] employs this technique to classify new data objects. Another method is to divide candidate rules into groups according to class labels and then to compute the actual effect obtained from the multiple rules for all groups. The group with the highest efficiency will identify the class of the new object; CMAR [5] employs this method.

CMAR determines the class label by a set of rules instead of relying on a single rule for classification. To assign a class to a new given sample, CMAR selects a subset of highly related rules with high confidence, and analyzes the correlation among those rules. After selecting a set of rules for classification, if the rules are not consistent in class labels, CMAR divides the rules into groups according to class labels and compares the effects of the groups based on their strengths. If the rules are highly correlated in a group and have high support value, the group should have strong effect. A strength measurement technique called X^2 has been developed to compare the strength of the groups. It specifies how strong the rule is under both conditional support and class distribution. There are many possible ways to measure X^2 value. However, the weighted X^2 measure [6] is the best among a good set of candidate measure formulas that can be applied. The main drawback of CMAR approach is that it is time consuming to extract classifier rules, group the rules and compare their X^2 measures when the dataset is large.

CPAR applies the idea of FOIL [12] in rule generation and integrates the features of associative classification in predictive rule analysis. FOIL is a greedy algorithm that learns rules to distinguish between positive and negative samples. In CPAR, FOIL is modified to propose PRM [14] (Predictive Rule Mining), which achieves higher accuracy and efficiency in rule mining. Since the number of rules generated by FOIL is very small, it does not achieve high accuracy as PRM. In PRM, the weight of the rule is decreased by a factor if it correctly classifies an example. By using this weighting strategy instead of removing the rules, PRM generates more rules and a positive example might be covered several times. Although has higher efficiency than associative classification, PRM has lower accuracy. CPAR combines the advantages of both FOIL and PMR to generate a smaller set of high quality predictive rules. It also generates the rules by considering the set of previously generated rules to avoid redundancy. CPAR predicts the class label of an example by using the best set of rules covering the example.

4   The Proposed Association Rule-Based Classifier

In the different subsections of this section, we describe the steps of the proposed approach.

4.1   Discretization and Normalization of a Data Set

The problem in class-based association rule mining arises mainly when the data sets used for classification contain continuous values for some attributes, discrete attributes and categorical attributes. Actually, mining association rules in such data sets is still a major research problem. The general method used to deal with this kind of data sets is Discretization and Normalization.

Discretization is the process of mapping the range of possible values associated with a continuous attribute into a number of intervals each identified by a unique integer label; and converting all the values associated with this attribute to the corresponding integer labels. Continuous data attributes take values that are real numbers within some range defined by minimum and maximum limits. Normalization is also the process of mapping values associated with categorical attributes to unique integer labels. Categorical data attributes take values selected from an available list of values. There are several algorithms already described in the literature for data set discretization.

4.2   Class-Based Rule Generator

We have implemented a class-based rule generator algorithm which is based on the Apriori algorithm [1]. Apriori is adapted to find all class-based association rules that satisfy the minimum support and minimum confidence constraints. The algorithm generates all the frequent rule-items by making multiple passes over the data. In the first pass, it counts the support of each individual rule-item and determines whether it is frequent.

In each subsequent pass, it starts with the seed set of rule-items found to be frequent in the previous pass. It uses this seed set to generate new possibly frequent rule-items, called candidate rule-items. The actual supports for these candidate rule-items are calculated during the pass over the data. At the end of the pass, it determines which of the candidate rule-items are actually frequent. From this set of frequent rule-items, it produces the class-based association rules. As a result of this process, we have a set of all class-based rules. So, we are ready to implement the next step, which is extracting strong rules with the most uneven class distribution for each class.

4.3   Separating and Sorting Rules

In this study, we consider the binary classification problem. We assume one of the class labels as the positive class and the other one as the negative class. Therefore, we can identify the extracted rules as the positive classifier rules and negative classifier rules. A rule having a positive label on the right hand side (consequent) is called a positive classifier rule and a rule having a negative label on its consequent is called negative classifier rule. In order to build a monotonous feature vector based on discrimination ability of the positive and negative rules, we separate positive and negative rules into two different subsets and call them the subset of positive classifier rules and the subset of negative classifier rules, respectively. The ordering of the rules inside each subset is important because we prefer to select the most discriminate positive and negative rules from each rule subset. We would like to order the rules inside a subset such that they conform to the order imposed by rules strengths.

In order to perform the ordering inside each subset, we specify the strengths of the rules according to their confidence and support values. Rules with greater confidence values are stronger than the rules with smaller confidence values. For all the rules that have the same confidence, the rule with higher value of support is considered as the strongest rule. If there are more than one rule with the same confidence and support values, we sort them randomly. The results of the sorting of the subsets are two classes: one containing ordered positive classifier rules and the other one containing ordered negative classifier rules.

4.4   Building the Binary Feature Vector

The SVM classification algorithm accepts feature vectors as input to generate a classifier model. In a feature vector, features are usually representatives of the attributes of a data item. In other words, a feature vector consists of values that represent the key properties of the data item to be classified. Our SVM classification method runs on binary feature vectors. A data object represented by a binary feature vector takes the form $x = (a_1, \ldots, a_n)$ and $a_i = 1$ or 0, $\forall i \in \{1 \ldots n\}$.

Our approach is to build a new binary feature vector for each data item in the original training set by utilizing rules. This way each data item in the original training set is represented as a binary feature vector. This new binary feature vector is different from the traditional feature vector that captures the key attributes of a data item. In order to build a binary feature vector for each data item, first we select a predefined percentage (which can be considered as a threshold) of strong positive classifier rules from the positive rules subset and the same percentage of strong negative classifier rules from the negative rules subset. Since the rules in each subset are sorted based on their strength, we pick up the rules starting from the beginning of each subset until we have enough number of rules that satisfy the threshold value. A feature in the vector is a predicate indicating whether each selected rule (positive and negative) is covered by the data item in the original dataset. So the number of features in the feature vector is equal to the number of rules that have been selected from the two subsets of positive and negative rules. If a rule is covered by a data item, the value of the feature representing that rule in the feature vector is assigned the value 1; otherwise it is assigned the value 0. The binary feature vector is a popular representation in many learning methodologies (e.g., Rule learning like k-DNF and CNF, decision tree); it is used in a wide range of applications (e.g., automatic diagnosis [8], classifying Web pages and emails [15], and mining graphs [16]).

5   Experimental Results

In this section, we report the test results of the experiments conducted, using Pima, a well-known datasets downloaded from UCI ML Repository [9]. We conducted an extensive performance study to evaluate the accuracy of our proposed technique. Our target is to demonstrate the effectiveness of the classification method proposed in this paper. We also compare the proposed method with other existing approaches. The selected dataset has two class labels; thus the binary classification is applicable.

For our experiments, we used Personal Computer with Intel P4 2.4GHZ CPU and 1GB memory. Our main performance metric is classification accuracy. An increase in the classification accuracy is an indicator of how accurate the proposed model is. A 10-fold cross validation is used to estimate the accuracy of the proposed classification technique. First, the datasets are discretized and normalized using the Entropy method described in [3]. The code is taken from MLC++ machine learning library [7]. The SVM technique used in our classification method is implemented using a Matlab interface of LIBSVM [2] in Matlab 7; LIBSVM is a library for SVM classification and regression.

In the first experiment, we evaluated the accuracy of the proposed model by varying the number of rules participating in the construction process of the feature vectors. Then, we compared the result of using binary feature vector with the case where we used the original dataset as the input feature vectors to the SVM algorithm. We also compared the classifiers produced by our algorithm against those produced by C4.5, CBA, CMAR and CPAR.

Table 1. Experimental Results on Pima Dataset

Dataset	Rules(%)	SVM (Binary FV)		SVM (Original FV)	
		Linear	Non-Linear	Linear	Non-Linear
Pima	10	78.26	77.73	74.87	73.31
	20	78.26	76.30		
	30	77.47	75.00		
	40	83.07	80.99		
	50	94.14	93.10		
	60	98.83	98.31		
	70	99.22	99.22		
	80	99.87	100.00		
	90	100.00	100.00		
	100	100.00	100.00		

Table 1 reports experimental results on the *Pima* dataset. It demonstrates that the accuracy of the proposed model is better than the accuracy of SVM (using the original dataset as the input feature vectors) in all cases as we increase the number of rules from 10% to 100% by steps of 10. Table 1 also demonstrates that the classification accuracy decreases (still it is better than the standard SVM) when we increase the percentage of the selected rules from 10% to 20% and from 20% to 30%. Also, it is worth noting that starting at 40% of the class-based rules, the classification accuracy of the proposed model on the *Pima* dataset is getting higher. By adding more extracted class-based rules to our model, we can improve the classification accuracy. When we select 90% of the rules to build the binary feature vectors, both Linear and Non-Linear SVM using binary feature vectors give 100% classification accuracy.

Figures 1 compares the accuracy of the proposed model with C4.5, CBA, CMAR and CPAR. Actually, these approaches are independent from the percentage value of the selected rules. This is the reason that the accuracy of these approaches is displayed as straight lines in the chart; there are constant values of accuracy for all cut-offs along the X-axis. We added these straight lines to the chart for the purpose of the comparison. As it can be seen from the chart reported in Figure 1, the proposed model performs better than all the mentioned approaches.

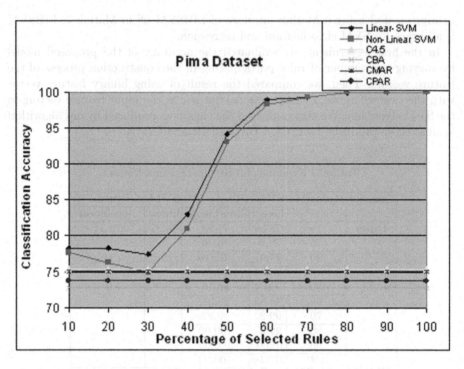

Fig. 1. Comparing the accuracy of the proposed approach with other existing approaches

6   Summary and Conclusions

In this paper, we proposed a new classification algorithm which integrates SVM and association rule mining. Consequently, we achieved a major goal, which is satisfied by having the proposed approach powerful enough to overcome the drawbacks and weaknesses of both machine learning and association rule-based classification techniques. In our classification framework, the focus is on a subset of association rules such that the consequent of each rule is class attribute (class-based rules). The class-based rules are used as the base for building new set of binary feature vectors. The binary feature vectors are then used as inputs to the SVM algorithm, which in turn builds a classifier model using the binary feature vectors. Our expectation from this approach is to increase the classification accuracy. The proposed method has been evaluated through performance experiments on aa well-known dataset. The class-based rules obtained from mining the dataset have been used to build the feature vectors. The performance of our method has been compared with four well-known existing approaches. From the conducted experiments, it has been observed that a considerable increase in classification accuracy can be obtained when the binary feature vectors built based on class-based rules are used in the learning process of the SVM classifier.

References

1. R. Agrawal and R. Srikant, "Fast algorithms for mining association rules", *Proc. of the International Conference on Very Large Databases, 1994.*
2. C.C. Chang and C.J. Lin, "LIBSVM: A Library for Support Vector Machines", 2001. URL: http://www.csie.ntu.edu.tw/ cjlin/libsvm.
3. U. M. Fayyad and K.B. Irani, "Multi-interval Discretization of Continuous-Valued Attributes for Classification Learning", *Proc. of International Joint Conference on Artificial Intelligence,* pp.1022-1027, 1993.
4. B. Liu, W. Hsu and Y. Ma, "Integrating Classification and Association Rule Mining", *Proc. of ACM International Conference on Knowledge Discovery and Data Mining, 1998.*
5. W. Li, J. Han and J. Pei, "CMAR: Accurate and Efficient Classification Based on Multiple Class-Association Rules", *Proc. of IEEE International Conference on Data Mining, 2001.*
6. W. Li, "Classification Based on Multiple Association Rules", *M.Sc. Thesis,* Simon Fraser University, April 2001.
7. R. Kohavi, G. John, R. Long, D. Manley and K. Pfleger, "MLC++: A Machine Learning Library in C++", *Proc. of IEEE International Conference on Tools for Artificial Intelligence,* pp.740-743, 1994.
8. L. A. Kurgan, K.J. Cios, R. Tadeusiewicz, M. Ogiela, and L. S. Goodenday, "Knowledge Discovery Approach to Automated Cardiac Spect Diagnosis", *Artificial Intelligence in Medicine,* Vol.23, No.2, pp.149169, 2001.
9. C.J, Merz and P. Murphy, UCI repository of machine learning database, [http://www.cs.uci.edu/ mlearn/MLRepository.html], 1996.
10. J.R. Quinlan, *C4.5: Programs for Machine Learning,* San Mateo, CA:Morgan Kaufmann, 1993.
11. J.R. Quinlan and R.L. Rivest, "Inferring Decision Trees Using the Minimum Description Length Principle", *Inform. Comput.,* Vol.80, No.3, pp.227248, 1989.
12. J.R. Quinlan and R.M. Cameron-Jones, "FOIL: A midterm report", *Proc. of the Europian Conference on Machine Learning,* pp. -20, Vienna, Austria, 1993.
13. G. Wahba, "Spline Models for Observational Data", *Proc. of SIAM. CBMS-NSF Regional Conference Series in Applied Mathematics,* v.59, 1990.
14. X. Yin and J. Han, "CPAR: Classification based on predictive association rules", *Proc. of SIAM International Conference on Data Mining, 2003.*
15. H. Yu, K. C. Chang, and J. Han, "Heterogeneous Learner for Web Page Classification", *Proc. of IEEE International Conference on Data Mining, 2002.*
16. X. Yan and J. Han, "Closegraph: Mining Closed Frequent Graph Patterns", *Proc. of ACM International Conference on Knowledge Discovery and Data Mining, 2003.*

Document Representations for Classification of Short Web-Page Descriptions*

Miloš Radovanović and Mirjana Ivanović

University of Novi Sad
Faculty of Science, Department of Mathematics and Informatics
Trg D. Obradovića 4, 21000 Novi Sad
Serbia and Montenegro
{radacha, mira}@im.ns.ac.yu

Abstract. Motivated by applying Text Categorization to sorting Web search results, this paper describes an extensive experimental study of the impact of bag-of-words document representations on the performance of five major classifiers – Naïve Bayes, SVM, Voted Perceptron, kNN and C4.5. The texts represent short Web-page descriptions from the dmoz Open Directory Web-page ontology. Different transformations of input data: stemming, normalization, logtf and idf, together with dimensionality reduction, are found to have a statistically significant improving or degrading effect on classification performance measured by classical metrics – accuracy, precision, recall, F_1 and F_2. The emphasis of the study is not on determining the best document representation which corresponds to each classifier, but rather on describing the effects of every individual transformation on classification, together with their mutual relationships.

1 Introduction

Text Categorization (TC – also known as *Text Classification* or *Topic Spotting*) is the task of automatically sorting a set of documents into *categories* (or *classes*, or *topics*) from a predefined set [1]. Applications of TC include text filtering (e.g. protection from spam e-mail), word sense disambiguation, and categorization of Web pages.

The initial motivation for this paper lies in the development a meta-search engine which uses TC to enhance the presentation of search results [2]. From the context of this system, we intended answer the three questions posed in [3]: (1) what representation to use in documents, (2) how to deal with the high number of features, and (3) which learning algorithm to use. This paper focuses on question one and its interaction with question three, trying (but not completely succeeding) to avoid question two.

Although the majority of works in TC employ the bag-of-words approach to document representation [4], studies of the impact of its variations on classification started appearing relatively recently. Leopold and Kindermann [5] experimented with the Support Vector Machine (SVM) classifier with different kernels, term frequency transforms

---

* This work was supported by project *Abstract Methods and Applications in Computer Science* (no. 144017A), of the Serbian Ministry of Science and Environmental Protection.

A Min Tjoa and J. Trujillo (Eds.): DaWaK 2006, LNCS 4081, pp. 544–553, 2006.

and lemmatization of German. They found that lemmatization usually degraded classification performance, and had the additional downside of great computational complexity, making SVMs capable of avoiding it altogether. Similar results were reported for neural networks on French [6]. Another study on the impact of document representation on one-class SVM [7] showed that, with a careful choice of representation, classification performance can reach 95% of the performance of SVM trained on both positive and negative examples. Kibriya et al. [8] compared the performance of SVM and a variant of the Naïve Bayes classifier, emphasizing the importance of term frequency and inverse document frequency transforms for Naïve Bayes.

This paper presents an extensive experimental study of bag-of-words document representations, and their impact on the performance on five classifiers commonly used in TC. An unorthodox evaluation methodology is used to measure and compare the effects of different transformations of input data on each classifier, and to determine their mutual relationships with regards to classification performance.

The next section outlines the experimental setup – how datasets were collected, which document representations were considered, and which classifiers. Section 3 presents the results – the representations that were found best, and the effects of and relationships between different transformations: stemming, normalization, logtf and idf. The final section concludes, and gives guidelines for future work.

2   The Experimental Setup

The WEKA Machine Learning environment [9] was used to perform all experiments described in this paper. The classical measures – accuracy, precision, recall, F_1 and F_2 [1] – were chosen to evaluate the performance of classifiers on many variants of the bag-of-words representation of documents (i.e. short Web-page descriptions) from the dmoz Open Directory.

Datasets. A total of eleven datasets were extracted from the dmoz ontology, one for each top-level category chosen for the meta-search system, namely *Arts, Business, Computers, Games, Health, Home, Recreation, Science, Shopping, Society* and *Sports*. The examples are either positive – taken from the corresponding category, or negative – distributed over all other categories, making this a binary classification problem.

When constructing the datasets and choosing the number of examples (around 700), care was taken to keep the number of features below 5000, for two reasons. The first reason was to give all classifiers an equal chance, because some of them are known not to be able to handle more than a couple of thousand features, and to do this without using some explicit form of feature selection (basically, to avoid question two from the Introduction). The second reason was the feasibility of running the experiments with the C4.5 classifier, due to its long training time. However, results from Section 3 (regarding the idf transform) prompted us to utilize the simple dimensionality reduction (DR) method based on term frequencies (TFDR), eliminating features representing the least frequent terms, at the same time keeping the number of features at around 1000. Therefore, two bundles of datasets were generated, one with and one without TFDR.

Document representations. Let W be the *dictionary* – the set of all terms (words) that occur at least once in a set of documents D. The bag-of-words representation of document d_j is a vector of weights $w_j = (w_{1j}, \ldots, w_{|W|j})$. For the simplest binary representation where $w_{ij} \in \{0, 1\}$, let the suffix 01 be added to the names of the datasets, so, for instance, Arts-01 denotes the binary representation of the *Arts* dataset. Similarly, the suffix tf will be used when w_{ij} represent the frequency of the ith term in the jth document. *Normalization* (norm) can be employed to scale the frequencies to values between 0 and 1, accounting for differences in document lengths. The logtf transform may be applied to term frequencies, replacing the weights with $\log(1 + w_{ij})$. The *inverse document frequency* (idf) transform is expressed as: $\log(|D|/\text{docfreq}(D, i))$, where $\text{docfreq}(D, i)$ is the number of documents from D the ith term occurs in. It can be used by itself, or be multiplied with term frequency to yield the tfidf representation.

All these transformations, along with stemming (m), add up to 20 different variations of document representations, summarized in Table 1. This accounts for a total of $11 \cdot 20 \cdot 2 = 440$ different datasets for the experiments.

Table 1. Document representations

Not stemmed		Stemmed	
Not normalized	Normalized	Not normalized	Normalized
01		m-01	
idf		m-idf	
tf	norm-tf	m-tf	m-norm-tf
logtf	norm-logtf	m-logtf	m-norm-logtf
tfidf	norm-tfidf	m-tfidf	m-norm-tfidf
logtfidf	norm-logtfidf	m-logtfidf	m-norm-logtfidf

Classifiers. Five classifiers implemented in WEKA are used in this study: ComplementNaiveBayes (CNB), SMO, VotedPerceptron (VP), IBk, and J48.

CNB [10,8] is a variant of the classic Naïve Bayes algorithm optimized for applications on text. SMO is an implementation of Platt's Sequential Minimal Optimization algorithm for training SVMs [11]. VP was first introduced by Freund and Schapire [12], and shown to be a simple, yet effective classifier for high-dimensional data. IBk implements the classical k-Nearest Neighbor algorithm [13], and J48 is based on revision 8 of the C4.5 decision tree learner [14].

All classifiers were run using their default parameters, with the exception of SMO, where the option not to normalize training data was chosen. IBk performed rather erratically during initial testing, with performance varying greatly with different datasets, choices of k and distance weighing, so in the end we kept $k = 1$ as it proved most stable. Only later we realized this was because of IBk's use of the Euclidian distance measure, which tends to deform with high numbers of features. For IBk we will report only results without TFDR, since TFDR completely broke its performance.

3   Results

A separate WEKA experiment was run for every classifier with the 20 document representation datasets, for each of the 11 major categories. Results of all evaluation measures were averaged over five runs of 4-fold cross-validation. Measures were compared between *datasets* using the corrected resampled t-test implemented in WEKA, at $p = 0.05$, and the number of statistically significant wins and losses of each document representation added up for every classifier over the 11 categories.

For the sake of future experiments and the implementation of the meta-search system, best representations for each classifier were chosen, based on wins–losses values summed-up over all datasets. The declared best representations were not winners for all 11 categories, but showed best performance overall. Table 2 shows the best document representations for each classifier, along with their wins–losses values, before and after TFDR. Binary representations were practically never among the best, for all datasets.

Table 2. Wins–losses values of best document representations for each classifier, on datasets without (left columns) and with TFDR

	CNB		SMO		VP		IBk		J48	
	m-norm-tf		m-norm-logtf		m-logtf		m-norm-logtf		m-logtf	
Accuracy	41	1	1	37	15	2	119		40	40
Precision	45	1	20	6	29	12	11		−6	−5
Recall	4	1	−4	68	0	0	67		56	57
F_1	28	1	0	47	7	0	120		59	52
F_2	9	0	−3	71	0	0	78		63	57
Total	127	4	14	229	51	14	395		212	201

To illustrate the impact of document representations on classification, Table 3 summarizes the performance of classifiers on the best representations, and the improvements over the worst ones, on the *Home* dataset, without TFDR. Note that the emphasis of this paper is not on fine-tuning the classifiers using document representations, as much as it is on determining the impacts and relationships between different transforms (stemming, normalization, logtf, idf) and TFDR, with regards to each classifier. This is the prevailing subject of the remainder of this section.

Table 3. Performance of classification (in %) using the best document representations on the *Home* dataset *without* TFDR, together with improvements over the worst representations (statistically significant ones are in **boldface**)

	CNB	SMO	VP	IBk	J48
Accuracy	82.56 (**5.26**)	83.19 (1.67)	78.38 (**5.12**)	74.93 (**21.96**)	71.77 (**3.64**)
Precision	81.24 (**8.66**)	85.67 (**3.86**)	80.45 (**7.85**)	71.32 (**14.32**)	90.24 (1.60)
Recall	83.91 (1.81)	78.93 (3.80)	74.06 (0.96)	81.66 (**45.20**)	47.59 (**10.59**)
F_1	82.48 (**3.64**)	82.07 (2.17)	77.02 (**4.23**)	76.07 (**33.90**)	62.12 (**9.09**)
F_2	83.31 (2.19)	80.14 (3.30)	75.20 (2.16)	79.31 (**39.72**)	52.48 (**10.41**)

Effects of stemming. The effects of stemming on classification performance were measured by adding-up the wins–losses values for stemmed and nonstemmed datasets, and examining their difference, depicted graphically in Fig. 1. It can be seen that stemming improves almost all evaluation measures, both before and after TFDR. After TFDR, the effect of stemming is generally not as strong, which is understandable because its impact as a dimensionality reduction method is reduced. CNB is then practically unaffected, only SMO exhibits an increased tendency towards being improved. Overall, J48 is especially sensitive to stemming, which can be explained by its merging of words into more discriminative features, suiting the algorithm's feature selection method when constructing the decision tree.

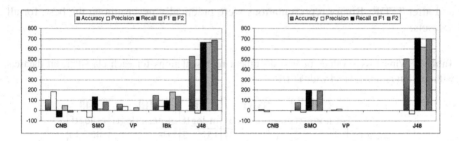

Fig. 1. The effects of *stemming* before (left) and after TFDR

To investigate the relationships between stemming and other transformations, a chart was generated for each transformation, measuring the effect of stemming on representations with and without the transformation applied. Figure 2 shows the effect of stemming on non-normalized and normalized data, without TFDR. It can be noted that normalized representations are affected by stemming more strongly (for the better). The same holds with TFDR applied. The logtf transform exhibited no influence on the impact of stemming, regardless of TFDR.

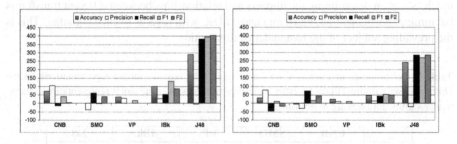

Fig. 2. The effects of *stemming* on non-normalized (left) and normalized datasets, *without* TFDR

The above analysis confirms the common view of stemming as a method for improving classification performance for English. However, this may not be the case for other languages, for instance German [5] and French [6].

Effects of normalization. The chart in Fig. 3 shows that normalization tends to improve classification performance in a majority of cases. Without TFDR, VP was virtually unaffected, CNB and SMO were improved on all counts but recall (and consequently F_2), while the biggest improvement was on IBk, which was anticipated since normalization assisted the comparison of document vectors. J48 was the only classifier whose performance worsened with normalization. Apparently, J48 found it tougher to find appropriate numeric intervals within the normalized weights, for branching the decision tree. After TFDR, CNB joined VP in its insensitivity, while SMO witnessed a big boost in performance when data was normalized.

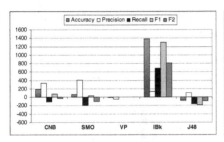 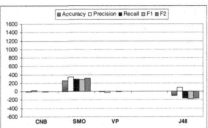

Fig. 3. The effects of *normalization* before (left) and after TFDR

No significant interaction between normalization and stemming was revealed, only that stemmed J48 was more strongly worsened by normalization. It seems that normalization misleads J48 from the discriminative features introduced by stemming.

Normalization and the logtf transform exhibited no notable relationship, while with idf transformed data, normalization had stronger influence on classification. After dimensionality reduction, this tendency was especially noticeable with the improvement of the precision of SMO (Fig. 4). This can be explained by the fact that idf severely worsens the performance of SMO after TFDR, and normalization compensated somewhat for this. This compensating effect of one transform on the performance degrading influences of another was found to be quite common in the experiments.

It is important to emphasize that the datasets used in the experiments consist of short documents, thus normalization does not have as strong an impact as it would have if the differences in document lengths were more drastic. Therefore, the conclusions above may not hold for the general case, for which a more comprehensive study is needed.

Effects of the logtf transform. As can be seen in Fig. 5, the logtf transform causes mostly mild improvements of classification performance. After TFDR, improvements are greater on SMO, while the impact on other classifiers is weaker.

Figure 6 shows that logtf has a much better impact on CNB when idf is also applied, without TFDR. This is similar to the compensating effect of normalization on idf with the SMO classifier. Relations change quite dramatically when TFDR is applied (both charts resemble Fig. 6 right), but the effect of logtf on SMO is again compensating. The improvements on CNB in both cases are especially significant, meaning that logtf and idf work together on improving classification.

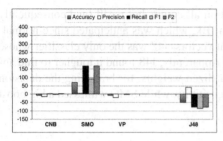
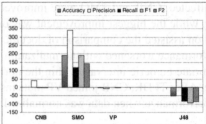

Fig. 4. The effects of *normalization* on datasets without (left) and with the idf transform applied to tf, *with* TFDR

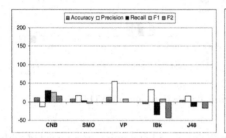
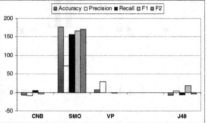

Fig. 5. The effects of the logtf transform before (left) and after TFDR

Before TFDR, the interaction of logtf and norm varied across classifiers: logtf improved CNB and IBk on normalized data, while others were improved without normalization. After TFDR, logtf had a weaker positive effect on normalized data, especially for CNB and SMO, which were already improved by norm (charts not shown).

Understandably, the logtf transform has a stronger positive impact on nonstemmed data, regardless of dimensionality reduction, with the exception of VP which exhibited no variations. This is in line with the witnessed improvements that stemming introduces on its own, and the already noted compensation phenomenon.

Effects of the idf transform. Applying the idf transform turned out to have the richest repertoire of effects, from significant improvement to severe degradation of classification performance. Figure 7 (left) illustrates how idf drags down the performance of all classifiers except SMO, without TFDR. For this reason we introduced TFDR in the first place, being aware that our data had many features which were present in only a few documents. We expected idf to improve classification, or at least degrade it to a lesser extent. That did happen, as Fig. 7 (right) shows, for all classifiers *except* SMO, whose performance drastically degraded! The simple idf document representation rose from being one of the worst, to one of the best representations, for all classifiers but SMO.

No significant correlation was detected by applying idf on stemmed and nonstemmed data. However, plenty of different effects were noticeable with regards to normalization. Without TFDR (Fig. 8), a stronger worsening effect on non-normalized data was exhibited with CNB, VP and IBk, while for SMO normalization dampened idf's

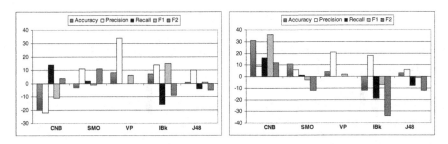

Fig. 6. The effects of the logtf transform on datasets without (left) and with the idf transform applied to tf, *without* TFDR

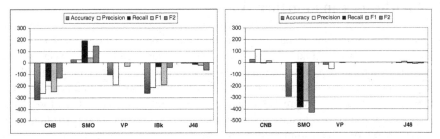

Fig. 7. The effects of idf applied to tf before (left) and after TFDR

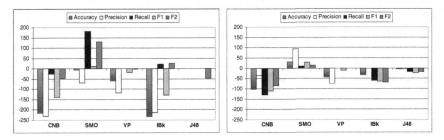

Fig. 8. The effects of idf applied to tf on non-normalized (left) and normalized datasets, *without* TFDR

improvement of recall, but overturned the degradation of accuracy and precision. With TFDR, the picture is quite different (Fig. 9): normalization improved the effects on CNB and VP, with SMO witnessing a partial improvement on precision, while J48 remained virtually intact. The impact of idf on (non-)logtfed datasets showed no big differences.

The above analysis shows the need to be careful when including the idf transform in the representation of documents. Removing infrequent features is an important prerequisite to its application, since idf assigns them often unrealistic importance, but that may not be enough, as was proved by the severe degradation of SMO's performance.

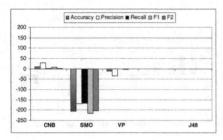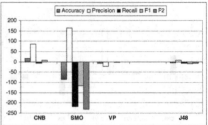

Fig. 9. The effects of idf applied to tf on non-normalized (left) and normalized datasets, *with* TFDR

4   Conclusions and Further Work

By using transformations in bag-of-words document representations there is, essentially, no new information added to a dataset which is not already there (except for the transition from 01 to tf representations). The general-purpose classification algorithms, however, are unable to derive such information without assistance, which is understandable because they are not aware of the nature of data being processed. Therefore, it can be expected of transforms to have a significant effect on classification performance, as was demonstrated at the beginning of Section 3.

Besides determining a best representation for each classifier, the experiments revealed the individual effects of transforms on different measures of classification performance, and some of their relationships. Stemming generally improved classification, partly because of its role as a dimensionality reduction method. It had an exceptionally strong improving impact on J48, which can be explained by its merging of words into more discriminative features, suiting the algorithm's feature selection method when constructing the decision tree. Normalization enhanced CNB, SMO and especially IBk, leaving VP practically unaffected and worsening J48. Although dmoz data consists of short documents, normalization did have a significant impact, but no definite conclusions may be drawn for the general case. The logtf transform had mostly a mild improving impact, except on SMO after TFDR, which exhibited stronger improvement. SMO is known to work well with small numeric values, which explains its sensitivity to normalization and logtf. The situation with idf was trickier, with the effects depending strongly on dimensionality reduction for CNB and SMO, but in opposite directions: CNB was degraded by idf before, and improved after TFDR; for SMO it was vice versa.

The most common form of relationship between transforms that was noticed were the compensating effects of one transform on the performance degrading impact of another (e.g. norm and logtf on idf). The logtf and idf transforms seemed to work together on improving CNB after TFDR. The impact of idf on normalization was most complex, with great variation in the effects on different evaluation measures. Note that the method for determining relations between transforms appeared not to be commutative, e.g. the effects of normalization on idfed data and of idf on normalized data were not the same.

The comments above refer to the general case of performance measuring. Some transforms (e.g. idf) may improve one measure, at the same time degrading another.

Often, the preferred evaluation measure, chosen with the application of the classifier in mind, will need to be monitored when applying the results presented in this paper.

The main difficulty with comprehensive TC experiments is sheer size. Roughly speaking, factors such as datasets, document representations, dimensionality reduction methods, reduction rates, classifiers, and evaluation measures, all have their counts multiplied, leading to a combinatorial explosion which is hard to handle. We tackled this problem by excluding detailed experimentation with DR, and using dmoz as the only source of data. Therefore, no definite truths, but only pointers can be derived from the described experience. A more comprehensive experiment, featuring other common corpora (Reuters, OHSUMED, 20Newsgorups etc.), and more dimensionality reduction methods, is called for to shed more light on the relationships of all above mentioned factors. In the next phase, however, we plan to conduct experiments with DR methods on dmoz data, with the document representations that were determined best for each classifier, before applying the winning combination to categorization of search results.

References

1. Sebastiani, F.: Text categorization. In Zanasi, A., ed.: Text Mining and its Applications. WIT Press, Southampton, UK (2005)
2. Radovanović, M., Ivanović, M.: CatS: A classification-powered meta-search engine. In: Advances in Web Intelligence and Data Mining. Studies in Computational Intelligence 23, Springer-Verlag (2006)
3. Mladenić, D.: Text-learning and related intelligent agents. IEEE Intelligent Systems, Special Issue on Applications of Intelligent Information Retrieval **14**(4) (1999) 44–54
4. Gabrilovich, E., Markovitch, S.: Text categorization with many redundant features: Using aggressive feature selection to make SVMs competitive with C4.5. In: Proceedings of ICML04, 21st International Conference on Machine Learning, Baniff, Canada (2004)
5. Leopold, E., Kindermann, J.: Text categorization with Support Vector Machines. How to represent texts in input space? Machine Learning **46** (2002) 423–444
6. Stricker, M., Vichot, F., Dreyfus, G., Wolinski, F.: Vers la conception automatique de filtres d'informations efficaces. In: Proceedings of RFIA2000, Reconnaissance des Formes et Intelligence Artificielle. (2000) 129–137
7. Wu, X., Srihari, R., Zheng, Z.: Document representation for one-class SVM. In: Proceedings of ECML04, 15th European Conference on Machine Learning. LNAI 3201, Pisa, Italy (2004)
8. Kibriya, A.M., Frank, E., Pfahringer, B., Holmes, G.: Multinomial naive bayes for text categorization revisited. In: Proceedings of AI2004, 17th Australian Joint Conference on Artificial Intelligence. LNAI 3339, Cairns, Australia (2004) 488–499
9. Witten, I.H., Frank, E.: Data Mining: Practical Machine Learning Tools and Techniques. 2nd edn. Morgan Kaufmann Publishers (2005)
10. Rennie, J.D.M., Shih, L., Teevan, J., Karger, D.R.: Tackling the poor assumptions of naive Bayes text classifiers. In: Proceedings of ICML03, 20th International Conference on Machine Learning. (2003)
11. Platt, J.: Fast training of Support Vector Machines using Sequential Minimal Optimization. In: Advances in Kernel Methods – Support Vector Learning. MIT Press (1999)
12. Freund, Y., Schapire, R.E.: Large margin classification using the perceptron algorithm. Machine Learning **37**(3) (1999) 277–296
13. Aha, D., Kibler, D., Albert, M.K.: Instance-based learning algorithms. Machine Learning **6**(1) (1991) 37–66
14. Quinlan, R.: C4.5: Programs for Machine Learning. Morgan Kaufmann Publishers (1993)

GARC: A New Associative Classification Approach

I. Bouzouita, S. Elloumi, and S. Ben Yahia

Faculty of Sciences of Tunis,
Computer Science Department, 1060 Tunis, Tunisia
{samir.elloumi, sadok.benyahia}@fst.rnu.tn

Abstract. Many studies in data mining have proposed a new classification approach called *associative classification*. According to several reports associative classification achieves higher classification accuracy than do traditional classification approaches. However, the associative classification suffers from a major drawback: it is based on the use of a very large number of classification rules; and consequently takes efforts to select the best ones in order to construct the classifier. To overcome such drawback, we propose a new associative classification method called GARC that exploits a generic basis of association rules in order to reduce the number of association rules without jeopardizing the classification accuracy. Moreover, GARC proposes a new selection criterion called *score*, allowing to ameliorate the selection of the best rules during classification. Carried out experiments on 12 benchmark data sets indicate that GARC is highly competitive in terms of accuracy in comparison with popular associative classification methods.

Keywords: Associative Classification, Generic Basis, Classification Rules, Generic association rules, Classifier.

1 Introduction

In the last decade, a new approach called *associative classification* (AC) was proposed to integrate association rule mining and classification in order to handle large databases. Given a training data set, the task of an associative classification algorithm is to discover the classification rules which satisfy the user specified constraints denoted respectively by minimum support (*minsup*) and minimum confidence (*minconf*) thresholds. The classifier is built by choosing a subset of the generated classification rules that could be of use to classify new objects or instances. Many studies have shown that AC often achieves better accuracy than do traditional classification techniques [1,2]. In fact, it could discover interesting rules omitted by well known approaches such as C4.5 [3]. However, the main drawback of this approach is that the number of generated associative classification rules could be large and takes efforts to retrieve, prune, sort and select high quality rules among them. To overcome this problem, we propose a new approach called GARC which uses generic bases of association rules. The

A Min Tjoa and J. Trujillo (Eds.): DaWaK 2006, LNCS 4081, pp. 554–565, 2006.

main originality of GARC is that it extracts the generic classification rules directly from a generic basis of association rules, in order to retain a small set of rules with higher quality and lower redundancy in comparison with current AC approaches. Moreover, a new score is defined by the GARC approach to find an effective rule selection during the class label prediction of a new instance, in the sake of reducing the error rate. This tackled issue is quite challenging, since the goal is to use generic rules while maintaining a high classifier accuracy.

The remainder of the paper is organized as follows. Section 2 briefly reports basic concepts of associative classification and scrutinizes related pioneering works. Generic bases of association rules are surveyed in section 3. Section 4 presents our proposed approach, where details about classification rules discovery, building classifier and prediction of test instances are discussed. Experimental results and comparisons are given in section 5. Finally, section 6 concludes this paper and points out future perspectives.

2 Associative Classification

An association rule is a relation between itemsets having the following form: $R : X \Rightarrow Y - X$, where X and Y are frequent itemsets for a minimal support *minsup*, and $X \subset Y$. Itemsets X and $(Y-X)$ are called, respectively, *premise* and *conclusion* of the rule R. An association rule is valid whenever its strength metric, confidence$(R) = \frac{support(Y)}{support(X)}$, is greater than or equal to the minimal threshold of confidence *minconf.*

An associative classification rule (ACR) is a special case of an association rule. In fact, an ACR conclusion part is reduced to a single item referring a class attribute. For example, in an ACR such as $X \Rightarrow c_i$, c_i must be a class attribute.

2.1 Basic Notions

Let us define the classification problem in an association rule task. Let D be the training set with n attributes (columns) $A_1, .., A_n$ and $|D|$ rows. Let C be the list of class attributes.

Definition 1. *An object or instance in D can be described as a combination of attribute names and values a_i and an attribute class denoted by c_i [4].*

Definition 2. *An item is described as an attribute name and a value a_i [4].*

Definition 3. *An itemset can be described as a set of items contained in an object.*

A classifier is a set of rules of the form $A_1, A_2, ..., A_n \Rightarrow c_i$ where A_i is an attribute and c_i is a class attribute. The classifier should be able to predict, as accurately as possible, the class of an unseen object belonging to the test data set. In fact, it should maximise the equality between the predicted class and the hidden actual class.

The AC achieves higher classification accuracy than do traditional classification approaches [1,2]. The classification model is a set of rules easily understandable by humans and that can be edited [1,2].

2.2   Related Work

One of the first algorithms to use association rule approach for classification was CBA [4]. CBA, firstly, generates all the association rules with certain support and confidence thresholds as candidate rules by implementing the Apriori algorithm [5]. Then, it selects a small set from them by evaluating all the generated rules against the training data set. When predicting the class attribute for an example, the highest confidence rule, whose the body is satisfied by the example, is chosen for prediction.

CMAR [6] generates rules in a similar way as CBA with the exception that CMAR introduces a CR-tree structure to handle the set of generated rules and uses a set of them to make a prediction using a weighted χ^2 metric [6]. The latter metric evaluates the correlation between the rules.

ARC-AC and ARC-BC have been introduced in [7,8] in the aim of text categorization. They generate rules similar to the Apriori algorithm and rank them in the same way as do CBA rules ranking method. ARC-AC and ARC-BC calculate the average confidence of each set of rules grouped by class attribute in the conclusion part and select the class attribute of the group with the highest confidence average.

The CPAR [2] algorithm adopts FOIL [9] strategy in generating rules from data sets. It seeks for the best rule itemset that brings the highest gain value among the available ones in data set. Once the itemset is identified, the examples satisfying it will be deleted until all the examples of the data set are covered. The searching process for the best rule itemset is a time consuming process, since the gain for every possible item needs to be calculated in order to determine the best item gain. During rule generation step, CPAR derives not only the best itemset but all close similar ones. It has been claimed that CPAR improves the classification accuracy whenever compared to popular associative methods like CBA and CMAR [2].

A new AC approach called Harmony was proposed in [10]. Harmony uses an instance-centric rule generation to discover the highest confidence discovering rules. Then, Harmony groups the set of rules into k groups according to their rule conclusions, where k is the total number of distinct class attributes in the training set. Within the same group of rules, Harmony sorts the rules in the same order as do CBA. To classify a new test instance, Harmony computes a score for each group of rules and assign the class attribute with the highest score or a set of class attributes if the underlying classification is a multi-class problem. It has been claimed that Harmony improves the efficiency of the rule generation process and the classification accuracy if compared to CPAR [2].

The main problem with AC approaches is that they generate an overwhelming number of rules during the learning stage. In order to overcome this drawback, our proposed approach tries to gouge this fact by the use of generic bases of association rules in the classification framework. In the following, we begin by recall some key notions about the Formal Concept Analysis (FCA), a mathematical tool necessary for the derivation of generic bases of association rules.

3 Generic Bases of Association Rules

The problem of the relevance and usefulness of extracted association rules is of primary importance. Indeed, in most real life databases, thousands and even millions of highly confident rules are generated among which many are redundant. In the following, we are interested in the lossless information reduction of association rules, which is based on the extraction of a generic subset of all association rules, called *generic basis* from which the remaining (redundant) association rules may be derived. In the following, we will present the generic basis of Bastide *et al.* [11,12] and $\mathcal{IGB}$ [13] after a brief description of FCA mathematical background necessary for the derivation of generic bases of association rules.

3.1 Mathematical Background

Interested reader for key results from the Galois lattice-based paradigm in FCA is referred to [14].

Formal context: A formal context is a triplet $\mathcal{K} = (\mathcal{O}, \mathcal{I}, \mathcal{R})$, where $\mathcal{O}$ represents a finite set of transactions, $\mathcal{I}$ is a finite set of items and $\mathcal{R}$ is a binary (incidence) relation (*i.e.*, $\mathcal{R} \subseteq \mathcal{O} \times \mathcal{I}$). Each couple $(o, i) \in \mathcal{R}$ expresses that the transaction $o \in \mathcal{O}$ contains the item $i \in \mathcal{I}$.

Frequent closed itemset: An itemset $I \subseteq \mathcal{I}$ is said to be *closed* if $\omega(I) = I^{(1)}$ [15]. I is said to be *frequent* if its *relative support*, $\text{Support}(I) = \frac{|\psi(I)|}{|\mathcal{O}|}$, exceeds a user-defined minimum threshold, denoted *minsup*.

Minimal generator [12]**:** An itemset $g \subseteq \mathcal{I}$ is said to be *minimal generator* of a closed itemset f, if and only if $\omega(g) = f$ and does not exist $g_1 \subseteq g$ such that $\omega(g_1) = f$. The set $\mathcal{G}_f$ of the minimal generators of f is: $\mathcal{G}_f = \{g \subseteq \mathcal{I} \mid \omega(g) = f \wedge \nexists\, g_1 \subset g$ such as $\omega(g_1) = f\}$.

3.2 The Generic Basis for Exact Association Rules ($\mathcal{GBE}$) and the Informative Basis for Approximate Association Rules ($\mathcal{GBA}$)

Bastide *et al.* considered the following rule-redundancy definition [12]:

Definition 4. *Let $\mathcal{AR}$ be a set of association rules derived from an extraction context $\mathcal{K}$ and c be a confidence value. A rule R: $X \overset{c}{\Rightarrow} Y \in \mathcal{AR}$ is redundant in comparison with R_1: $X_1 \overset{c}{\Rightarrow} Y_1$ if R fulfills the following constraints:*

1. *$\text{Support}(R) = \text{Support}(R_1)$ and $\text{Confidence}(R) = \text{Confidence}(R_1) = c$;*
2. *$X_1 \subseteq X \wedge Y \subset Y_1$.*

The *generic basis for exact association rules* is defined as follows:

Definition 5. *Let $\mathcal{FCI}_\mathcal{K}$ be the set of frequent closed itemsets extracted from the extraction context $\mathcal{K}$. For each frequent closed itemset $f \in \mathcal{FCI}_\mathcal{K}$, let $\mathcal{G}_f$ be the set of its minimal generators. The generic basis of exact association rules*

---

[1] The closure operator is indicated by ω.

$\mathcal{GBE}$ is given by: $\mathcal{GBE} = \{R: g \Rightarrow (f - g) \mid f \in \mathcal{FCI}_\mathcal{K}$ and $g \in \mathcal{G}_f$ and $g \neq f^{(2)}\}$.

Bastide *et al.* also characterized the informative basis for approximate association rules, defined as follows [12]:

Definition 6. *Let $\mathcal{FCI}_\mathcal{K}$ be the set of frequent closed itemsets extracted from the extraction context $\mathcal{K}$. The $\mathcal{GBA}$ basis is defined as follows [12]:*
$\mathcal{GBA} = \{R \mid R: g \Rightarrow (f_1 - g) \mid f, f_1 \in \mathcal{FCI}_\mathcal{K}$ and $\omega(g) = f$ and $f \preceq f_1$ and $Confidence(R) \geq minconf\}$.

The pair $(\mathcal{GBE}, \mathcal{GBA})$ is informative, sound and lossless [12,16] and rules belonging to this pair are referred as *informative association rules*.

3.3 Informative Generic Basis ($\mathcal{IGB}$)

The $\mathcal{IGB}$ basis is defined as follows:

Definition 7. *Let $\mathcal{FCI}_\mathcal{K}$ be the set of frequent closed itemsets and $\mathcal{G}_f$ be the set of minimal generators of all the frequent itemsets included or equal to a closed frequent itemset f. The $\mathcal{IGB}$ basis is defined as follows [13]:*

$IGB = \{R: g_s \Rightarrow (f_1 - g_s) \mid f, f_1 \in \mathcal{FCI}_\mathcal{K}$ and $(f - g_s) \neq \emptyset$ and $g_s \in \mathcal{G}_f \wedge f_1 \preceq f \wedge confidence(R) \geq minconf \wedge \nexists\, g' \subset g_s$ such that $confidence(g' \Rightarrow f_1\text{-}g') \geq minconf\}$.

$\mathcal{IGB}$ basis [13] presents the following characteristics:

1. **Conveying maximum of useful knowledge**: Association rules of the $\mathcal{IGB}$ basis convey the maximum of useful knowledge. Indeed, a generic association rule of $\mathcal{IGB}$ is based on a frequent closed itemset and has the minimal premise since the latter is represented by one of the smallest frequent minimal generators satisfying *minconf* threshold. It was shown that this type of association rules conveys the maximum of useful knowledge [17];
2. **Information lossless:** It was pointed out that the $\mathcal{IGB}$ basis is extracted without information loss [13];
3. **Compactness:**the $\mathcal{IGB}$ basis is more compact than other informative generic basis [13], *e.g.*, the pair $(\mathcal{GBE}, \mathcal{GBA})$.

4 GARC: A New Associative Classification Approach

In this section, we propose a new AC method GARC[3] that extracts the generic classification rules directly from a generic basis of association rules in order to overcome the drawback of the current AC approaches, i.e., the generation of a large number of associative classification rules. In the following, we will present and explain in details the GARC approach.

---

[2] The condition $g \neq f$ ensures discarding non-informative rules of the form $g \Rightarrow \emptyset$.

[3] The acronym GARC stands for: Generic Association Rules based Classifier.

4.1   Rule Generation

In this step, GARC extracts the generic basis of association rules. Once obtained, generic rules are filtered out to retain only rules whose conclusions include a class attribute. Then, by applying the decomposition axiom, we obtain new rules of the form $A_1, A_2, ..., A_n \Rightarrow c_i$. Even though, the obtained rules are redundant, their generation is mandatory to guarantee a maximal cover of the necessary rules.

The $\mathcal{IGB}$ basis is composed of rules with a small premise which is an advantage for the classification framework when the rules imply the same class. For example, let us consider two rules R_1: A B C D $\Rightarrow$cl1 and R_2: B C $\Rightarrow$cl1. R_1 and R_2 have the same attribute conclusion. R_2 is considered to be more interesting than R_1, since it is needless to satisfy the properties A D to choose the class cl1. Hence, R_2 implies less constraints and can match more objects of a given population than R_1.

Let us consider a new object O_x: B C D. If we have in the classifier just the rule R_1, we cannot classify O_x because the attribute A does not permit the matching. However, the rule R_2, which has a smaller premise than R_1, can classify O_x. This example shows the importance of the generic rules and, especially, the use of the $\mathcal{IGB}$ basis to extract the generic classification rules. In fact, such set of rules is smaller than the number of all the classification rules and their use is benefical for classifying new objects.

4.2   Classifier Builder

Once the generic classification rules obtained, a total order on rules is set as follows. Given two rules R_1 and R_2, R_1 is said to precede R_2, denoted $R_1 > R_2$ if the followed condition is fulfilled:

- $confidence(R_1) > confidence(R_2)$ or
- $confidence(R_1) = confidence(R_2)$ and $support(R_1) > support(R_2)$ or
- $confidence(R_1) = confidence(R_2)$ and $support(R_1) = support(R_2)$ and R_1 is generated before R_2.

The data set coverage is similar to that in CBA. In fact, a data object of the training set is removed after it is covered by a selected generic rule.

The major difference with current AC approaches [4,6,7,8,10] is that we use generic ACR directly deduced from generic bases of association rules to learn the classifier as shown by algorithm 1.

4.3   New Instance Classification

After a set of rules is selected for classification, GARC is ready to classify new objects. Some methods such as those described in [4,7,8,10] are based on the support-confidence order to classify a new object. However, the confidence measure selection could be misleading, since it may identify a rule A $\Rightarrow$ B as an interesting one even though, the occurrence of A does not imply the occurrence of B [18]. In fact, the confidence can be deceiving since it is only an estimate of

---

Data: $\mathcal{D}$: Training data, $\mathcal{GR}$: a set of generic classification rules
Results: $\mathcal{C}$: Classifier
Begin
    $\mathcal{GR}$=sort($\mathcal{GR}$) in a descending order;
    Foreach *rule* $r \in \mathcal{GR}$ **do**
        Foreach *object* $d \in \mathcal{D}$ **do**
            If *d matches r.premise* **then**
                remove d from $\mathcal{D}$ and mark r if it correctly classifies d;
            If *r is marked* **then**
                insert r at the end of $\mathcal{C}$;
                select a default class;

    add the default class at the end of the classifier;
    return Classifier $\mathcal{C}$;
End

Algorithm 1: GARC: *selected generic rules based on database coverage*

the conditional probability of itemset B given an itemset A and does not measure the actual strength of the implication between A and B. Let us consider the example shown in Table 1 which shows the association between an item A and a class attribute B. A and $\overline{A}$ represent respectively the presence and absence of item A, B represents a class attribute and $\overline{B}$ the complement of B. We consider the associative classification A $\Rightarrow$ B. The confidence of this rule is given by *confidence*(A $\Rightarrow$ B)$=\frac{support(AB)}{support(A)} = \frac{201}{250} = 80.4\%$. Hence, this rule has high confidence. Now, let us calculate the correlation between A and B by using the lift metric [18]. $lift$(A $\Rightarrow$ B)$=\frac{support(AB)}{support(A)*support(B)} = \frac{0.201}{0.250*0.900} = 0.893$. The fact that this quantity is less than 1 indicates negative correlation between A and B.

Table 1. Example

	B	$\overline{B}$	Total
A	201	49	250
$\overline{A}$	699	51	750
Total	900	100	1000

To avoid the lacuna of using only confidence metric, we define a new lift based score formula as follows:

$$Score = \frac{1}{|Premise|}*lift^{\frac{|Premise|}{numberofitems}} = \frac{1}{|Premise|}*\left(\frac{support(Rule)}{support(Premise)*support(Conclusion)}\right)^{\frac{|Premise|}{numberofitems}}$$

The introduced score includes the lift metric. In fact, the lift finds interesting relationships between A and B. It computes the correlation between the occurrence of A and B by measuring the real strength of the implication between them which is interesting for the classification framework. Moreover, the lift is divided by the cardinality of the rule premise part in order to give a preference to rules with small premises. Thus, GARC collects the subset of rules matching the new object attributes from the classifier. Trivially, if all the rules matching it have the same class, GARC just assigns that class to the new object. If the rules do not imply the same class attribute, the score firing is computed for each rule. The rule with the highest score value is selected to classify the new object.

5   Experiments

We have conducted experiments to evaluate the accuracy of our proposed approach GARC, developed in C++, and compared it to the well known classifiers CBA, ID3, C4.5 and Harmony. Experiments were conducted using 12 data sets taken from UCI Machine Learning Repository[4]. The chosen data sets were discretized using the LUCS-KDD [5] software.

The features of these data sets are summarized in Table 2. All the experiments were performed on a 2.4 GHz Pentium IV PC under Redhat Linux 7.2.

Table 2. Data set description

Data set	# attributes	# transactions	# classes
Monks1	6	124	2
Monks2	6	169	2
Monks3	6	122	2
Spect	23	80	2
Pima	38	768	2
TicTacToe	29	958	2
Zoo	42	101	7
Iris	19	150	3
Wine	68	178	3
Glass	48	214	7
Flare	39	1389	9
Pageblocks	46	5473	5

Classification accuracy can be used to evaluate the performance of classification methods. It is the percentage of correctly classified examples in the test set and can be measured by splitting the data sets into a training set and a test set.

During experiments, we have used available test sets for data sets Monks1, Monks2 and Monks3 and we applied the 10 cross-validation for the rest of data sets, in which a data set is divided into 10 subsets; each subset is in turn used as testing data while the remaining data is used as the training data set; then the average accuracy across all 10 trials is reported.

The parameters are set as the following. In the rule generation algorithm, *minsup* is set to 10% and *minconf* to 80%. In order to extract generic association

---

[4] *Available at* http://www.ics.uci.edu/~mlearn/MLRepository.html

[5] *Available at* http://www.csc.liv.ac.uk/~frans/KDD/Software/LUCS-KDD-DN/ lucs-kdd DN.html

rules, we used the PRINCE algorithm [19] to generate both the pair $(\mathcal{GBE}, \mathcal{GBA})$ and $\mathcal{IGB}$ bases.

To evaluate C4.5 and ID3, we used the WEKA[6] software and the Harmony prototype was kindly provided by its authors. We have implemented the CBA algorithm in C++ under Linux.

In the following, we will compare the effectiveness of the use of generic bases of the pair $(\mathcal{GBE}, \mathcal{GBA})$ and $\mathcal{IGB}$ for the classification framework. For this, we conducted experiments with reference to accuracy in order to compare the classifiers GARC$_B$ and GARC$_I$ issued respectively from the generic bases of the pair $(\mathcal{GBE}, \mathcal{GBA})$ and $\mathcal{IGB}$ without using the score firing.

Moreover, to show the impact of the score firing on the quality of the produced classifiers, we report the accuracy results of GARCS$_B$ and GARC deduced respectively from the generic bases of the pair $(\mathcal{GBE}, \mathcal{GBA})$ and $\mathcal{IGB}$ using the score firing.

5.1   The Score Firing Impact

Table 3 represents a comparison between the classifiers deduced from the generic bases of the pair $(\mathcal{GBE}, \mathcal{GBA})$ and $\mathcal{IGB}$ when using or not the score firing.

Table 3. Accuracy comparison of GARC$_B$, GARC$_I$, GARCS$_B$ and GARC algorithms for $minsup$=10% and $minconf$=80%

Data set	Without using the score		Using the score	
	GARC$_B$	GARC$_I$	GARCS$_B$	GARC
Monks1	92.0	92.0	92.0	92.0
Monks2	56.0	56.0	56.0	56.0
Monks3	96.3	96.3	96.3	96.3
Spect	67.0	68.9	67.0	68.9
Pima	73.0	73.0	73.0	73.0
TicTacToe	65.0	67.4	65.0	65.0
Zoo	89.0	89.0	89.0	90.0
Iris	95.0	94.7	95.6	95.4
Wine	89.2	89.4	90.0	89.8
Glass	58.0	59.3	58.0	64.0
Flare	85.0	85.0	85.0	85.0
Pageblocks	92.0	89.8	92.0	89.8
Average accuracy	79.7	80.0	79.9	**80.4**

Table 3 points out that the use of the score firing increases the accuracy performance for the classifiers deduced from the pair $(\mathcal{GBE}, \mathcal{GBA})$. In fact, GARCS$_B$ has a better average accuracy than GARC$_B$. Moreover, for the classifiers deduced from $\mathcal{IGB}$, the use of the score firing ameliorates the accuracy for four data sets. In fact, GARC outperforms GARC$_I$ on Zoo, Iris, Wine and Glass data sets.

---

[6] *Available at* http://www.cs.waikato.ac.nz/ml/Weka

Thus, the best average accuracy, highlighted in bold print, is given by GARC. Furthermore, as shown in Table 4, the number of rules generated by GARC is less than that generated by the approaches deduced from the pair $(\mathcal{GBE}, \mathcal{GBA})$, *i.e.*, GARC$_B$ and GARCS$_B$. In the following, we put the focus on comparing GARC accuracy versus that of the well known classifiers ID3, C4.5, CBA and Harmony.

Table 4. Number of associative classification rules for *minsup*=10% and *minconf*=80%

Data set	# generic ACR deduced from $\mathcal{IGB}$	# generic ACR deduced from $(\mathcal{GBE}, \mathcal{GBA})$
Monks1	12	12
Monks2	4	4
Monks3	20	20
Pima	20	20
TicTacToe	15	15
Zoo	832	1071
Iris	22	24
Wine	329	471
Glass	31	36
Flare	237	561
Pageblocks	128	128

5.2 Generic Classification Rules Impact

Table 5 represents the accuracy of the classification systems generated by ID3, C4.5, CBA, Harmony and GARC on the twelve benchmark data sets. The best accuracy values obtained for each of data sets is highlighted in bold print. Table 5 shows that GARC outperforms the traditional classification approaches, *i.e.*, ID3 and C4.5 on six data sets and the associative classification approaches on nine data sets.

Table 5. Accuracy comparison of ID3, C4.5, CBA, Harmony and GARC algorithms

Data set	ID3	C4.5	CBA	Harmony	GARC
Monks1	77.0	75.0	**92.0**	83.0	**92.0**
Monks2	64.0	**65.0**	56.0	48.0	56.0
Monks3	94.0	**97.0**	96.3	82.0	96.3
Spect	65.0	64.0	67.0	-	**68.9**
Pima	71.3	72.9	**73.0**	**73.0**	**73.0**
TicTacToe	83.5	**85.6**	63.1	81.0	65.0
Zoo	**98.0**	92.0	82.2	90.0	90.0
Iris	94.0	94.0	**95.3**	94.7	95.4
Wine	84.8	87.0	89.5	63.0	89.8
Glass	64.0	69.1	52.0	**81.5**	64.0
Flare	80.1	84.7	**85.0**	83.0	**85.0**
Pageblocks	92.3	**92.4**	89.0	91.0	89.8

Statistics depicted by Table 5 confirm the fruitful impact of the use of the generic rules. The main reason for this is that GARC classifier contains generic rules with small premises. In fact, this kind of rule allows to classify more objects than those with large premises.

6   Conclusion

In this paper, we introduced a new classification approach called GARC that aims to prune the set of classification rules without jeopardizing the accuracy and even ameliorates the predictive power. To this end, GARC uses generic bases of association rules to drastically reduce the number of associative classification rules. Moreover, it proposes a new score to ameliorate the rules selection for unseen objects. Carried out experiments outlined that GARC is highly competitive in terms of accuracy in comparison with popular classification methods. In the near future, we will investigate new metrics for the rule selection and we will apply GARC approach to a wide range of applications like text categorization and biological applications.

Acknowledgements. We are deeply grateful to Frans Coenen at the university of Liverpool for providing us the discretized UCI data sets and addressing our questions. We also thank Jianyong Wang for providing us the Harmony executable code.

References

1. Zaiane, O., Antonie, M.: On pruning and tuning rules for associative classifiers. In: Ninth International Conference on Knowledge Based Intelligence Information And Engineering Systems (KES'05), Melbourne, Australia (2005) 966–973
2. Xiaoxin Yin, J.H.: CPAR: Classification based on Predictive Association Rules. In: Proceedings of the SDM, San Francisco, CA (2003) 369–376
3. Quinlan, J.R.: C4.5 : Programs for Machine Learning. (1993)
4. Liu, B., Hsu, W., Ma, Y.: Integrating classification and association rule mining. In: Knowledge Discovery and Data Mining. (1998) 80–86
5. Agrawal, R., Srikant, R.: Fast algorithms for mining association rules. In Bocca, J.B., Jarke, M., Zaniolo, C., eds.: Proceedings of the 20th Intl. Conference on Very Large Databases, Santiago, Chile. (1994) 478–499
6. Li, W., Han, J., Pei, J.: CMAR: Accurate and efficient classification based on multiple class-association rules. In: Proceedings of IEEE International Conference on Data Mining (ICDM'01), San Jose, CA, IEEE Computer Society (2001) 369–376
7. Antonie, M., Zaiane, O.: Text Document Categorization by Term Association. In: Proc. of the IEEE International Conference on Data Mining (ICDM'2002), Maebashi City, Japan (2002) 19–26
8. Antonie, M., Zaiane, O.: Classifying Text Documents by Associating Terms with Text Categories . In: Proc. of the Thirteenth Austral-Asian Database Conference (ADC'02), Melbourne, Australia (2002)
9. Quinlan, J., Cameron-Jones, R.: FOIL: A midterm report. In: Proceedings of European Conference on Machine Learning, Vienna, Austria. (1993) 3–20

GARC: A New Associative Classification Approach 565

10. Wang, J., Karypis, G.: HARMONY: Efficiently mining the best rules for classification. In: Proceedings of the International Conference of Data Mining (SDM'05). (2005)

11. Bastide, Y.: Data mining : algorithmes par niveau, techniques d'implantation et applications. Phd thesis, Ecole Doctorale Sciences pour l'Ingénieur de Clermont-Ferrand, Université Blaise Pascal, France (2000)

12. Bastide, Y., Pasquier, N., Taouil, R., Lakhal, L., Stumme, G.: Mining minimal non-redundant association rules using frequent closed itemsets. In: Proceedings of the International Conference DOOD'2000, LNAI, volume 1861, Springer-Verlag, London, UK. (2000) 972–986

13. Gasmi, G., BenYahia, S., Nguifo, E.M., Slimani, Y.: $\mathcal{IGB}$: A new informative generic base of association rules. In: Proceedings of the Intl. Ninth Pacific-Asia Conference on Knowledge Data Discovery (PAKDD'05), LNAI 3518, Hanoi, Vietnam, Springler-Verlag (2005) 81–90

14. Ganter, B., Wille, R.: Formal Concept Analysis. Springer-Verlag (1999)

15. Pasquier, N., Bastide, Y., Taouil, R., Lakhal, L.: Efficient Mining of Association Rules Using Closed Itemset Lattices. Journal of Information Systems **24** (1999) 25–46

16. Kryszkiewicz, M.: Concise representations of association rules. In: Proceedings of Exploratory Workshop on Pattern Detection and Discovery in Data Mining (ESF), 2002, LNAI, volume 2447, Springer-Verlag, London, UK. (2002) 92–109

17. Kryszkiewicz, M.: Representative association rules and minimum condition maximum consequence association rules. In: Proceedings of the Second European Symposium on Principles of Data Mining and Knowledge Discovery (PKDD), 1998, LNCS, volume 1510, Springer-Verlag, Nantes, France. (1998) 361–369

18. Han, J., Kamber., M.: Data Mining : Concepts and Techniques. Morgan Kaufmann. (2001)

19. Hamrouni, T., BenYahia, S., Slimani, Y.: PRINCE : An algorithm for generating rule bases without closure computations. In Tjoa, A.M., Trujillo, J., eds.: Proceedings of 7th International Conference on Data Warehousing and Knowledge Discovery (DaWaK 2005), Springer-Verlag, LNCS 3589, Copenhagen, Denmark. (2005) 346–355

Conceptual Modeling for Classification Mining in Data Warehouses

Jose Zubcoff[1] and Juan Trujillo[2]

[1] Departamento de Ciencias del Mar y Biología Aplicada.
Universidad de Alicante. Spain
Jose.Zubcoff@ua.es
[2] Departamento de Lenguajes y Sistemas Informáticos.
Universidad de Alicante. Spain
jtrujillo@dlsi.ua.es

Abstract. Classification is a data mining (DM) technique that generates classes allowing to predict and describe the behavior of a variable based on the characteristics of a dataset. Frequently, DM analysts need to classify large amounts of data using many attributes. Thus, data warehouses (DW) can play an important role in the DM process, because they can easily manage huge quantities of data. There are two approaches used to model mining techniques: the Common Warehouse Model (CWM) and the Predictive Model Markup Language (PMML), both focused on metadata interchanging and sharing, respectively. These standards do not take advantage of the underlying semantic rich multidimensional (MD) model which could save development time and cost. In this paper, we present a conceptual model for Classification and a UML profile that allows the design of Classification on MD models. Our goal is to facilitate the design of these mining models in a DW context by employing an expressive conceptual model that can be used on top of a MD model. Finally, using the designed profile, we implement a case study in a standard database system and show the results.

Keywords: Data warehouses, conceptual modeling, multidimensional modeling, data mining, UML extension, classification, decision trees.

1 Introduction

Classification is one of the most commonly applied data mining techniques due to its usability and simplicity. It consists of input data analysis, distinguishing between the corresponding classes on the basis of data features, and of rules deduced in order to classify each new observation into one of the existing classes. The rules can take the form of a tree (called Decision Tree), able to classify and describe the data (Fig.1).

Data mining techniques are used to extract patterns from large amounts of input data such as files, databases or DWs. Among the advantages of using DW lies the fact that they contain subject-oriented data, prepared for analysis, integrated from several sources, cleansed from different input errors. Furthermore, in DW data is aggregated and may contain hierarchies describing the data at different levels of detail. It is

A Min Tjoa and J. Trujillo (Eds.): DaWaK 2006, LNCS 4081, pp. 566–575, 2006.

widely accepted that the development of DW is based on MD modeling, as these models easily represent the main DW concepts. Therefore, this extra information provided by the MD models can be used in decision making.

There are two approaches to representing data mining models, the CWM [12] and the PMML [13]. The former focuses on metadata interchange, while the latter aims at sharing data between DM applications. However, these approaches do not take advantage of the previously designed structure to reduce time and cost. On the other hand, the MD can provide additional semantics for DM models. For example, a dimension hierarchy allows users to analyze the data at different abstraction levels.

The present work proposes a conceptual model for the Classification mining technique. A conceptual model represents the semantics of a given domain without any concern for logical aspects or platform specific issues. Therefore, this conceptual model will provide support for the analysis process in order to obtain rich models able to aid in the Classification process. Users can thus focus on their main objective: discovering knowledge by using Classification.

We also propose a definition of the semantics and primitives to design Classification processes on DW, in a well-known visual modeling language. We employ the Unified Modeling Language (UML) [11] that allows us to extend its meta-model and semantics to a specific domain. In order to adapt it to this particular domain we use the "lightweight" method of extending the UML with a Profile. This is a mechanism for adapting an existing meta-model to a particular domain without changing the UML meta-model, by using domain specific constructs. This lightweight extension is also employed in our previous work: the Profile to design MD models [1] and the Profile for designing Association Rules (AR) mining models on MD models [5]. The latter uses attributes from the MD model of the data warehouse to represent AR.

The present paper is structured as follows: Section 2 illustrates the conceptual model for Classification. Section 3 proposes the new UML profile for Classification Mining based on MD modeling. Section 4 presents a case study. Section 5 sketches some further implementation issues. Section 6 presents related efforts that have dealt with Data Mining, Data Warehouses and modeling. Finally, Section 7 comprises the main conclusions and introduces immediate and future work.

2   A Conceptual Model for Classification

In this section, we outline our approach to Classification Mining. We propose a conceptual model for this technique, based on UML 2.0 [11]. The goal of Classification is to sequentially partition the data to maximize the differences among the values of the dependent variable, the predicted one [4]. From the root node, grow the branches (that correspond to certain data features) that try to maximize the differences between them. The process of classification starts again at every node.

Classification can be used as a diagnostic tool, for example in hospital emergencies, when heart attack patients are admitted in a hospital, several tests are performed to obtain physiological measures such as heart rate, blood pressure, and so on. Personal information is also gathered, such as the patient's age and medical history. The patients' data is subsequently evaluated to see if they will survive the heart attack for a specific number of days, for instance 30 days. It can be useful in developing specific treatments for heart attack patients, to identify for example high-risk patients (those who are not likely to survive at least 30 days). One Classification Tree that Breiman et al. [3] developed to address this problem was a simple, three-question decision tree. This Classification Tree can be described with the statement: "If the patient's minimum systolic blood pressure over the initial 24 hour period is greater than 91, then if the patient's age is over 62 years, then if the patient displays sinus tachycardia, then and only then the patient is predicted not to survive for at least 30 days." In Figure 1, we show all the nodes derived from the previous analysis that helps decision-makers to analyze the risk level of a patient.

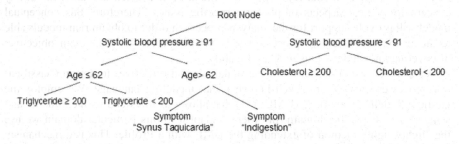

Fig. 1. Decision Tree for coronary disease risk based on risk factors

In order to perform a Classification, we must select which attributes of the input data will predict the others. Classification uses each Input attribute as a split candidate (regressor) to predict the Predict attribute. The case constitutes the entity under study that relates all dimensions and the fact included. Case, Input and Predict are attributes of the CMModel class and clearly define the model structure (Fig. 2).

There are several parameters that control the tree growth, shape and other characteristics, thus helping to provide users more accurate trees. *MinSupp* specifies that a node should never be split if it contains fewer rows than a specified value. *MinConf* is the minimum confidence a node must fulfill. *MaxTreeLevels* is the maximum number of levels in the tree that the user wants to obtain. This is a threshold parameter of feature selection. When the number of predictable attributes is greater than this parameter value, selecting the most significant attributes is required. The same selection is involved for a number of selected input attributes greater than *MaxInputAttributes*. *Algorithm* is the function used to classify the data. *SplitMethod* specifies if the nodes split into two (binary) or more branches. *HomogeneityMetrics* indicate the homogeneity criteria to split nodes (the most common criteria are Entropy and Gini Index). The *TrainingSize* establishes the maximum size of the training data. The *Filter* parameter specifies the exclusions of the itemset. Users can provide additional constraints on the input data in order to improve the generated tree. Useless branches of the tree are pruned using these settings (attributes of the CMSettings class).

We can derive rules from a decision tree. In the case of a decision tree, a conjunction of split conditions encountered on the path from the root to each node becomes the left part (antecedent or *Body*) of the rule and the classifier distribution becomes the right part (consequent or rule *Head*). Each rule has its own *Support* and *Confidence* values. These attributes belong to the CMResults class (shown in Fig. 2).

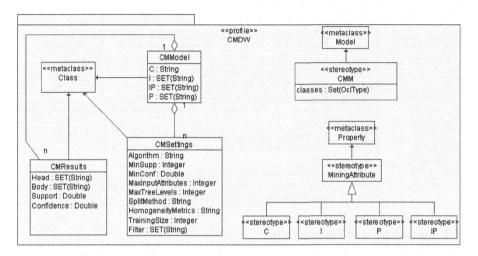

Fig. 2. Profile for Classification

3 UML Profile for Classification

Based on the previously described conceptual model for Classification, this section defines the profile that uses this schema. We start by describing the profile and the prerequisite extensions, we then propose the new stereotypes and tagged values, as well as the well-formedness rules, and, finally, the profile comments.

3.1 Description

The present UML extension defines a set of tagged values, stereotypes, and constraints, which enable us to create Classification models with constraints shared with MD models. We outline our approach to DW conceptual modeling [1] in the subsection on prerequisites extension. Well-formedness rules are defined through a set of domain constraints. Our extension uses Object Constraint Language (OCL) [10] for expressing well-formedness rules of the new defined elements, thereby avoiding an arbitrary use of this extension.

3.2 Prerequisite Extensions

This UML profile (Fig.2) reuses stereotypes that were previously defined in [1]. In order to facilitate the understanding of the profile presented in the present paper we resume the main characteristic in the Table 1.

Table 1. Stereotypes from the UML profile for conceptual MD modeling [1]

Name	Base Class	Description
Fact	Class	Classes of this stereotype represent facts in a MD model
DegeneratedFact	Class	Classes of this stereotype represent degenerated facts in a MD model
Dimension	Class	Classes of this stereotype represent dimensions in a MD model
Base	Class	Represent dimension hierarchy levels in a MD model
OID	Property	OID attributes of Facts, Dimension or Base classes in a MD model
Fact-Attributes	Property	Represent attributes of Fact classes in a MD model
Degenerated Dimension	Property	Attributes of this stereotype represent degenerated dimensions in a MD model
Descriptor	Property	Descriptor attributes of Dimension or Base classes in a MD model
Dimension-Attribute	Property	Attributes of Dimension or Base classes in a MD model
Rolls-upTo	Association	Represent associations between Base classes
Completeness	Association	Represent the completeness of an association between a Dimension class and a Base class or between two Base classes

3.3 Stereotypes and Tagged Values

This section presents the defined stereotypes. Fig.2 sketches the profile containing the new stereotypes and their attributes. Table 2 shows the detailed description, the name, the base class, the constraints and the icon that represents each new stereotype. For the sake of simplicity, in this paper we present only the definition for the *CMModel* stereotype (the OCL constraints are therefore omitted in the following table).

Table 2. Stereotypes defined in the Profile

Name	CMModel	Icon	CMModel
Base Class	Class		
Description	Contains the Classification model that define the structure of the model		
Constraints	- An CMModel can only contain C, I, IP and P attributes. - An CMModel can only be associated to CMS or CMR classes. - An CMModel must contain at least one C - An CMModel must contain at least one I or IP - An CMModel must contain at least one IP or P		

A *CMModel* Class must contain at least one *Case*. The *Case* stereotype can be any discrete attribute from a *Fact* class or from a *Dimension* class (continuous values must be previously categorized). We must select at least one *Input* and at least one *Predict* or *InputAndPredict* attribute for each *CMModel* class. This means that we can design Classification mining models with more than one *Input* and *Predict* attributes. The *CMSettings* class contains nine attributes that helps users to tune the accuracy of the mining model. Finally, the *CMResults* class stereotype contains the patterns in rule form using the *Head, Body, Support* and *Confidence* attributes. Table 3 illustrates the defined tagged values.

Table 3. Tagged values defined in the Profile

Name	Type	Default Value	Description
Classes	Set(OCLType)	None	Classes that are involved in a rule
MinSupp	Integer	10	Is the minimum number that must contain a node to split.
MaxInputAttributes	Integer	255	It specifies the maximum number of input attributes.
MinConf	Double	0.01	It specifies the minimum confidence of one node.
MaxTreeLevels	Integer	20	It specifies the maximum number of levels in the tree
SplitMethod	String	Binary	It specifies the splitting method
HomogeneityMetrics	String	Gini	It indicates the homogeneity criteria to split nodes
TrainingSize	Integer	0	Is the maximum size of the training data
Algorithm	String	DT	It specifies the function used to obtain the result
Filter	Set(String)	None	It specifies the exclusions of the itemset
Head	Set(String)	None	It specifies the head of the rule
Body	Set(String)	None	It specifies the body of the rule
Support	Double	None	It specifies the support of the rule
Confidence	Double	None	It specifies the confidence of the rule

3.4 Well-Formedness Rules

We specify the well-formedness rules of the profile, used to determine whether a model is semantically consistent with itself, in both natural language and OCL constraints. These rules are presented in Table 4.

Table 4. Well-Formedness constraints

- Correct type of the case stereotype:
The case (C) must be defined for an OID attribute of a Fact or Dimension class of the model
context Model **inv** self.classes-> forÄll(a I a.attributes ->forÄll(c I c.C) -> notEmpty() implies self.attribute.oclIsTypeOf(OID))
- Categorization of continuous values of an Input and Predict tagged value of attribute
Input (I) and Predict (P) or (IP) must be Type of Integer or must be discrete
context Model **inv** self.classes-> forÄll(a I a.attributes ->forÄll(p I p.P) -> notEmpty() implies self.attribute.oclType(Integer)) or self.attribute.oclType(Set(String))) self.classes-> forÄll(a I a.attributes ->forÄll(p I p.I) -> notEmpty() implies self.attribute.oclType(Integer)) or self.attribute.oclType(Set(String))) self.classes-> forÄll(a I a.attributes ->forÄll(p I p.IP) -> notEmpty() implies self.attribute.oclType(Integer)) or self.attribute.oclType(Set(String)))

3.5 Comments

Along with the previous constraints, the users can define specific OCL constraints. If the *Input* or *Predict* values depend on the value of an instance attribute, this can be captured by an OCL expression. Aside from the restrictions imposed by the tagged values definitions, we do not impose any other restriction on the content of these notes in order to give the designer higher flexibility.

4   A Case Study

The main objective of our proposal is to facilitate the design of Classification models in a MD framework by taking advantage of this structured data and by using a visual modeling language. We show the use of the profile described in this paper with an example that analyzes the characteristics of Marine Areas to obtain a classification of "Relative Abundance" by Marine Area type (Protected or not), Catch Per Unit Effort (CPUE), Posidonia and Rock cover percentages, total marine area and maximum depth. This classification will serve to describe the current state of the studied Marine Areas and to serve as "diagnosis" tool for the behavior of other Marine Areas. Due to the diversity and the large amount of data we use a DW as a repository. We select the granularity of the fact, the dimensions, and the attributes to be analyzed. The design process of the DW gives users a suitable knowledge of the domain and structures. The benefit is to use it to obtain knowledge to support the decision-making. For the sake of simplicity, we will use a reduced version of the DW (Fig.3). This contains only one fact (*Observation*), and three dimensions (*Species*, *Time* and *MarineArea*). This DW stores historical observation data for different marine areas, at different times, for different species, and coming from diverse sources.

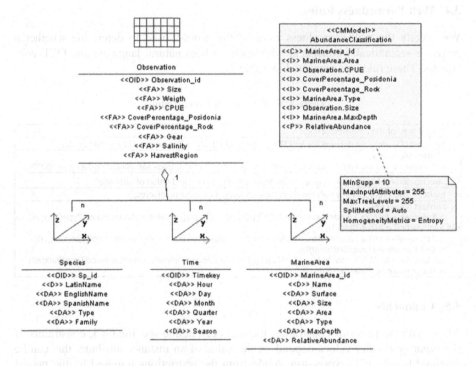

Fig. 3. Example of a Classification model

Therefore, in order to discover classes in this MD model we follow three steps: first to select the case we want to analyze, second to select *Input* and *Predict* attributes, third to adjust the parameters that control the final decision tree. In this example, we will classify the *RelativeAbundance* attribute, based on the values observed for the other previously mentioned attributes. Thus, we set *RelativeAbundance* as *Predict*, while the *CPUE, CoverPercentage_Posidonia, CoverPercentage_Rock, MarineArea.Type, Size* and *MaxDepth* attributes are set as *Input*, meaning that they will be used to classify the *Predict* attribute. The result of this mining process will give us a diagnosis tool for the status of a Marine Area on the basis of the previously enumerated variables. The situation is captured by Fig.3. The designed mining model is self-descriptive. Users can design models based on their domain knowledge. No constraints are imposed on the number of models users can design.

5 Implementation

The model described above was implemented in SQL Server 2005 that allows the implementation of mining techniques on data stored in DW. Based on the case study (Fig. 3), we have defined the Classification model, using *RelativeAbundance* as *Predict_only*, *Observation_id* as the nested table key, and *CPUE, Size, Cover-Percentage_Posidonia,   CoverPercentage_Rock,   MarineArea.Type,   Area, MaxDepth* as *Input*. The code below shows the instruction that creates the mining model.

```
CREATE MINING MODEL AbundanceClassification{
MarineArea_Id long key,
MarineArea_Type text discrete,
MaxDepth long discretized,
Area long discretized,
RelativeAbundance long discrete predict_only,
Observation Table (
Observation_id long key,
CPUE long continuous,
CoverPercentage_Posidonia long continuous,
CoverPercentage_Rock long continuous)
} USING Microsoft_Decision_Trees(MINIMUM_SUPPORT = 15)
```

After applying this mining model to the DW, we obtain a decision tree that indicates the main attributes to analyze, their categories and their probabilities. The derived decision tree could therefore be used not only to describe the behavior of the studied Marine Areas, but also to predict the state of other not yet studied marine areas, by observing only the characteristics that lead to the diagnosis of the respective area, with their corresponding probability values.

The results shown in Fig. 4 suggest that the most important characteristic to be observed in Protected Marine Areas is the Cover Percentage of Posidonia. If it is greater than 60%, then the next variable to be observed is Size (the categorized species sizes). Otherwise, the next indicator is the CPUE. The final decision tree is very helpful for the evaluation of marine areas, and also gives decision-makers a classification of the most important indicators to be observed in diagnosing marine areas.

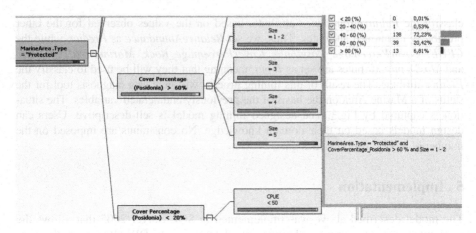

Fig. 4. Results obtained from Classification

6   Related Work

The rapid growth of data mining techniques and algorithms is partially due to multidisciplinary contributions (machine learning, statistic and database communities). From the first investigations on Classification [3, 4], there are some proposals integrating the mining process into databases or DW using SQL queries [2, 6]. However, they use DW just as a data repository, not employing the important information underneath. In [8, 9] the authors proposed SQL-like primitives for databases. This represents an important advance in building a relationship between Data Mining and databases. A Pattern Base Management is proposed by [7] who manages data with a database management system, not integrated in a DW framework.

There are two main proposals to model Data Mining learning models: the Common Warehouse Model (CWM) [12] and the Predictive Model Markup Language (PMML) [13]. The former addresses metadata definition for the business intelligence field, mainly focusing on metadata interchange. On the other hand, the latter is an XML-based language that provides a platform for sharing learning models among different vendor's applications, by describing all properties, structures and instances of the models. Still, using PMML does not improve modeling, its main goal is to be a standard that allows interchanging information, structures and algorithm properties among applications. These efforts do not take advantage of the information given by the underlying MD model, thus, this information is missing.

Therefore, we claim that there is still a gap between the use of mining techniques on DW and the multi-dimensional modeling process. The existing approaches to model data mining do not take advantage of the semantic rich MD model.

7   Conclusions and Future Work

The main purpose of this work is to provide an expressive Conceptual Model that facilitates the design and implementation of Classification using DW. We have defined a

UML 2.0 Profile that allows users to represent Classification on top of multidimensional objects with several advantages such as a structured model underneath, and the use of historical, cleansed and integrated data from the DW. We have applied our Profile to a case study to demonstrate the usability and, finally, we have also shown how the resulted model is implemented on a commercial data base management server with data mining facilities such as Microsoft SQL Server 2005. Consequently, all the classifications we defined in the multidimensional modeling at conceptual level are directly implemented in the final DW. Our next goal is to apply transformations in our model to obtain platform specific models in order to align this proposal with the Model Driven Architecture (MDA). We are also working on extending UML to represent other data mining techniques.

References

[1] S. Luján-Mora, J. Trujillo and I. Song. *A UML profile for multidimensional modeling in data warehouses.* Data & Knowledge Engineering (DKE) (in press). May 2006

[2] Günzel, H., Albrecht, J., and Lehner, W. *Data Mining in a Multidimensional Environment.* In: Proceedings of ADBIS'99. pages 191-204. 1999. Springer-Verlag.

[3] L. Breiman, J. H. Friedman, R. A. Olshen, and C. J. Stone. *Classification and regression trees.* Chapman & Hall. Wadsworth, Inc. 1984.

[4] J. R. Quinlan. *Induction of decision trees.* Machine Learning, 1:81–106, 1986.

[5] J.Zubcoff and J. Trujillo. *Extending the UML for Designing Association Rule Mining Models for Data Warehouses.* In Proc. DaWaK 2005: 11-21.

[6] X. Shang, K. Sattler. *Processing Sequential Patterns in Relational Databases.* In Proc. DaWaK 2005: 438-447.

[7] S. Rizzi. *UML-Based Conceptual Modeling of Pattern-Bases.* In Proc. 1st Int. Workshop on "Pattern Representation and Management (PaRMa'04), Crete, Greece, March 2004.

[8] T. Imielinski, A. Virmani. *MSQL: A Query Language for Database Mining.* Data Mining and Knowledge Discovery, 3. 1999: 373-408

[9] J. Han, J. Fu, W. Wang, K. Koperski, O. Zaiane. *DMQL: A Data Mining Query Language for Relational Databases.* In DMKD'96, Montreal, Canada, 1996.

[10] J. Warmer and A. Kleppe. *The Object Constraint Language Second Edition. Getting Your Models Ready for MDA.* 2003: Addison Wesley.

[11] OMG, Object Management Group. *UML Infrastructure Specification, v2.0.* Internet: www.omg.org/cgi-bin/doc?ptc/2004-10-14. October 2004.

[12] OMG: *CWM Common Warehouse Metamodel Specification.* www.omg.org.

[13] DMG, Data Mining Group. *PMML Specification, v3.0.* www.dmg.org/pmml-v3-0.html

Author Index

Lecture Notes in Computer Science

For information about Vols. 1–4037

please contact your bookseller or Springer

Vol. 4088: Z.-Z. Shi, R. Sadananda (Eds.), Agent Computing and Multi-Agent Systems. XVII, 827 pages. 2006. (Sublibrary LNAI).

Vol. 4085: J. Misra, T. Nipkow, E. Sekerinski (Eds.), FM 2006: Formal Methods. XV, 620 pages. 2006.

Vol. 4082: K. Bauknecht, B. Pröll, H. Werthner (Eds.), E-Commerce and Web Technologies. XIII, 243 pages. 2006.

Vol. 4081: A M. Tjoa, J. Trujillo (Eds.), Data Warehousing and Knowledge Discovery. XVII, 578 pages. 2006.

Vol. 4079: S. Etalle, M. Truszczyński (Eds.), Logic Programming. XIV, 474 pages. 2006.

Vol. 4077: M.-S. Kim, K. Shimada (Eds.), Geometric Modeling and Processing - GMP 2006. XVI, 696 pages. 2006.

Vol. 4076: F. Hess, S. Pauli, M. Pohst (Eds.), Algorithmic Number Theory. X, 599 pages. 2006.

Vol. 4075: U. Leser, F. Naumann, B. Eckman (Eds.), Data Integration in the Life Sciences. XI, 298 pages. 2006. (Sublibrary LNBI).

Vol. 4074: M. Burmester, A. Yasinsac (Eds.), Secure Mobile Ad-hoc Networks and Sensors. X, 193 pages. 2006.

Vol. 4073: A. Butz, B. Fisher, A. Krüger, P. Olivier (Eds.), Smart Graphics. XI, 263 pages. 2006.

Vol. 4072: M. Harders, G. Székely (Eds.), Biomedical Simulation. XI, 216 pages. 2006.

Vol. 4071: H. Sundaram, M. Naphade, J.R. Smith, Y. Rui (Eds.), Image and Video Retrieval. XII, 547 pages. 2006.

Vol. 4070: C. Priami, X. Hu, Y. Pan, T.Y. Lin (Eds.), Transactions on Computational Systems Biology V. IX, 129 pages. 2006. (Sublibrary LNBI).

Vol. 4069: F.J. Perales, R.B. Fisher (Eds.), Articulated Motion and Deformable Objects. XV, 526 pages. 2006.

Vol. 4068: H. Schärfe, P. Hitzler, P. Øhrstrøm (Eds.), Conceptual Structures: Inspiration and Application. XI, 455 pages. 2006. (Sublibrary LNAI).

Vol. 4067: D. Thomas (Ed.), ECOOP 2006 – Object-Oriented Programming. XIV, 527 pages. 2006.

Vol. 4066: A. Rensink, J. Warmer (Eds.), Model Driven Architecture – Foundations and Applications. XII, 392 pages. 2006.

Vol. 4065: P. Perner (Ed.), Advances in Data Mining. XI, 592 pages. 2006. (Sublibrary LNAI).

Vol. 4064: R. Büschkes, P. Laskov (Eds.), Detection of Intrusions and Malware & Vulnerability Assessment. X, 195 pages. 2006.

Vol. 4063: I. Gorton, G.T. Heineman, I. Crnkovic, H.W. Schmidt, J.A. Stafford, C.A. Szyperski, K. Wallnau (Eds.), Component-Based Software Engineering. XI, 394 pages. 2006.

Vol. 4062: G. Wang, J.F. Peters, A. Skowron, Y. Yao (Eds.), Rough Sets and Knowledge Technology. XX, 810 pages. 2006. (Sublibrary LNAI).

Vol. 4061: K. Miesenberger, J. Klaus, W. Zagler, A. Karshmer (Eds.), Computers Helping People with Special Needs. XXIX, 1356 pages. 2006.

Vol. 4060: K. Futatsugi, J.-P. Jouannaud, J. Meseguer (Eds.), Algebra, Meaning, and Computation. XXXVIII, 643 pages. 2006.

Vol. 4059: L. Arge, R. Freivalds (Eds.), Algorithm Theory – SWAT 2006. XII, 436 pages. 2006.

Vol. 4058: L.M. Batten, R. Safavi-Naini (Eds.), Information Security and Privacy. XII, 446 pages. 2006.

Vol. 4057: J.P.W. Pluim, B. Likar, F.A. Gerritsen (Eds.), Biomedical Image Registration. XII, 324 pages. 2006.

Vol. 4056: P. Flocchini, L. Gąsieniec (Eds.), Structural Information and Communication Complexity. X, 357 pages. 2006.

Vol. 4055: J. Lee, J. Shim, S.-g. Lee, C. Bussler, S. Shim (Eds.), Data Engineering Issues in E-Commerce and Services. IX, 290 pages. 2006.

Vol. 4054: A. Horváth, M. Telek (Eds.), Formal Methods and Stochastic Models for Performance Evaluation. VIII, 239 pages. 2006.

Vol. 4053: M. Ikeda, K.D. Ashley, T.-W. Chan (Eds.), Intelligent Tutoring Systems. XXVI, 821 pages. 2006.

Vol. 4052: M. Bugliesi, B. Preneel, V. Sassone, I. Wegener (Eds.), Automata, Languages and Programming, Part II. XXIV, 603 pages. 2006.

Vol. 4051: M. Bugliesi, B. Preneel, V. Sassone, I. Wegener (Eds.), Automata, Languages and Programming, Part I. XXIII, 729 pages. 2006.

Vol. 4049: S. Parsons, N. Maudet, P. Moraitis, I. Rahwan (Eds.), Argumentation in Multi-Agent Systems. XIV, 313 pages. 2006. (Sublibrary LNAI).

Vol. 4048: L. Goble, J.-J.C.. Meyer (Eds.), Deontic Logic and Artificial Normative Systems. X, 273 pages. 2006. (Sublibrary LNAI).

Vol. 4047: M. Robshaw (Ed.), Fast Software Encryption. XI, 434 pages. 2006.

Vol. 4046: S.M. Astley, M. Brady, C. Rose, R. Zwiggelaar (Eds.), Digital Mammography. XVI, 654 pages. 2006.

Vol. 4045: D. Barker-Plummer, R. Cox, N. Swoboda (Eds.), Diagrammatic Representation and Inference. XII, 301 pages. 2006. (Sublibrary LNAI).

Vol. 4044: P. Abrahamsson, M. Marchesi, G. Succi (Eds.), Extreme Programming and Agile Processes in Software Engineering. XII, 230 pages. 2006.

Vol. 4043: A.S. Atzeni, A. Lioy (Eds.), Public Key Infrastructure. XI, 261 pages. 2006.

Vol. 4042: D. Bell, J. Hong (Eds.), Flexible and Efficient Information Handling. XVI, 296 pages. 2006.

Vol. 4041: S.-W. Cheng, C.K. Poon (Eds.), Algorithmic Aspects in Information and Management. XI, 395 pages. 2006.

Vol. 4040: R. Reulke, U. Eckardt, B. Flach, U. Knauer, K. Polthier (Eds.), Combinatorial Image Analysis. XII, 482 pages. 2006.

Vol. 4039: M. Morisio (Ed.), Reuse of Off-the-Shelf Components. XIII, 444 pages. 2006.

Vol. 4038: P. Ciancarini, H. Wiklicky (Eds.), Coordination Models and Languages. VIII, 299 pages. 2006.